UNITED STATES CONSTITUTIONAL AND LEGAL HISTORY

A TWENTY VOLUME SERIES REPRODUCING OVER 450 OF THE MOST IMPORTANT ARTICLES ON THE TOPIC

Edited with Introductions by
KERMIT L. HALL

A GARLAND SERIES

CONTENTS OF THE SERIES

FEDERALISM: A NATION OF STATES

MAJOR HISTORICAL INTERPRETATIONS

Edited with an Introduction by
KERMIT L. HALL

GARLAND PUBLISHING, INC.
NEW YORK • LONDON   1987

Library of Congress Cataloging-in-Publication Data

Federalism: a nation of states.

(United States constitutional and legal history ; v. 3)
Bibliography: p.
1. Federal government—United States—History.
I. Hall, Kermit. II. Series.
KF4600.A75F43   1987   342.73'042   86-31929
ISBN 0-8240-0131-1   347.30242

The volumes in this series have been printed on acid-free,
250-year-life paper.

Printed in the United States of America.

ACKNOWLEDGMENTS

Samuel Beer, "The Modernization of American Federalism," *Publius* 3 (Fall 1973): 49–95. Reprinted by permission of *Publius: The Journal of Federalism.*

Michael Les Benedict, "Preserving Federalism: Reconstruction and the Waite Court," *Supreme Court Review* (1978): 39–79. Reprinted by permission of the University of Chicago Press.

Arthur Bestor, "The American Civil War as a Constitutional Crisis," *American Historical Review* 69 (January 1964): 327–352. Reprinted by permission of the American Historical Association.

Arthur C. Cole, "The South and the Right of Secession in the Early Fifties," *Mississippi Valley Historical Review* 1 (December 1914): 376–399.

Edward S. Corwin, "The Passing of Dual Federalism," *Virginia Law Review* 36 (1950): 1–24. Reprinted by permission of Fred B. Rothman & Company.

David P. Currie, "Federalism and the Admiralty: 'The Devil's Own Mess,'" *Supreme Court Review* (1960): 158–221. Reprinted by permission of the University of Chicago Press.

Martin Diamond, "*The Federalist* on Federalism: 'Neither a National Nor a Federal Constitution, But a Composition of Both.'" Reprinted by permission of the Yale Law Journal Company and Fred B. Rothman & Company, from *The Yale Law Journal,* Vol.86, pp.1273–1285.

Allison Dunham, "Congress, the States and Commerce," *Journal of Public Law* 8 (Spring 1959): 47–65. Reprinted by permission of the *Emory Law Journal* (formerly *Journal of Public Law*) of the Emory University School of Law.

Daniel J. Elazar, "Civil War and the Preservation of American Federalism," *Publius* 1 (1971): 39–58. Reprinted by permission of *Publius: The Journal of Federalism.*

Daniel J. Elazar, "Federal-State Collaboration in the Nineteenth-Century United States." Reprinted with permission from *Political Science Quarterly* (79) (June 1964): 248–281.

v

William Graebner, "Federalism in the Progressive Era: A Structural
    Interpretation of Reform," *Journal of American History* 64
    (September 1977): 331–357. Reprinted by permission of the
    Journal of American History.
William T. Hutchinson, "Unite to Divide; Divide to Unite: The
    Shaping of American Federalism," *Mississippi Valley
    Historical Review* 46 (June 1959): 3–18. Reprinted by
    permission of the *Journal of American History*, (formerly the
    Mississippi Valley Historical Review).
Herbert A. Johnson, "Toward a Reappraisal of the 'Federal'
    Government." This article originally appeared in the *American
    Journal of Legal History*, Vol. 8, 1964, pages 314–325.
Andrew C. McLaughlin, "The Background of American
    Federalism," *American Political Science Review* 12 (May
    1918): 215–240. Reprinted by permission of the *American
    Political Science Review*.
Peter Onuf, "Toward Federalism: Virginia, Congress, and the
    Western Lands," *William and Mary Quarterly* 34 (July 1977):
    353–374. Reprinted by permission of the *William and Mary
    Quarterly*.
John C. Ranney, "The Bases of American Federalism," *William and
    Mary Quarterly* 3 (January 1946): 1–35. Reprinted by
    permission of the *William and Mary Quarterly*.
John R. Schmidhauser, "'States' Rights' and the Origin of the
    Supreme Court's Power as Arbiter in Federal-State Relations,"
    Wayne Law Review 4 (Spring 1958): 101–114. Reprinted by
    permission of the *Wayne Law Review*.
David L. Smiley, "Revolutionary Origins of the South's
    Constitutional Defenses," *North Carolina Historical Review* 44
    (July 1967): 256–269. Reprinted by permission of the *North
    Carolina Historical Review*.
Kenneth M. Stampp, "The Concept of a Perpetual Union," *Journal
    of American History* 65 (June 1978): 5–33. Reprinted by
    permission of the *Journal of American History*.
M.J.C. Vile, "Federalism and Labor Regulation in the United States
    and Australia." Reprinted with permission from *Political
    Science Quarterly* (71) (June 1956): 223–241.
Jean Yarbrough, "Federalism in the Foundation and Preservation of
    the American Republic," *Publius* 6 (Summer 1976): 43–60.
    Reprinted by permission of *Publius: The Journal of
    Federalism*.

CONTENTS

INTRODUCTION

Few constitutional concepts have proven more important and more intractable than that of federalism. For example, when asked in 1973 to define federalism, Governor of Georgia and future President Jimmy Carter replied: "I don't know the exact definition of federalism. To me, it's the interrelationship between or among different elements of government."[1] Exactly what Carter meant remains elusive, but his trouble specifying the meaning of federalism is doubtless typical of most Americans, even those in high office.

Our difficulty in coming to terms with federalism stems from the actions of the Philadelphia Convention in 1787. The Federalist delegates to the convention wanted to find a way of accommodating existing state governments while enhancing the authority of the new central government. They succeeded in doing so, but only after they divided the indivisible. Sir William Blackstone, the foremost authority on English law in the eighteenth century, had written that it was "a solecism in politics for two coordinate sovereignties to exist together."[2] What emerged from the Philadelphia Convention was "a system hitherto unknown"—a plan for "a perfect confederation of independent states."[3]

Federalism is a system of government under which there exists simultaneously a federal or central government and several state governments. A federal system contrasts with a unitary government. The "original understanding" of federalism reached by the framers in 1787, according to the historian Harry Scheiber, rested on a "compound principle"—it was both structural and operational[4] It engrafted a system of national government onto existing states by giving the states direct and equal representation in the Senate and by leaving with the states the major responsibility to control the process of elections and the establishment of citizenship. The Constitution granted the national government, mostly in Article I (the legislative), only enumerated powers, but with the proviso that Congress retained authority "to make all laws necessary and proper for carrying [them] into execution."[5] The new government could,

ix

for example, levy taxes, raise armies, and regulate commerce among the states and with foreign nations. Those powers not specifically enumerated remained with the states.

Federalism cut the other way as well. Fear of a "democratic despotism" through state legislative authority persuaded the delegates to place certain prohibitions on the states, such as restricting their authority to coin money and interfere with private contracts. Such prohibitions, according to James Wilson, were necessary because in the states the people did not delegate enumerated powers but rather "invested their representatives with every right and authority which they did not in explicit terms reserve."[6]

These were modest limitations. The states retained the power to provide for the morals, health, safety, and welfare of their citizens. These police powers, as they came to be known, enabled each state to act directly on persons without fear of interference by the national government. They have constituted over the generations the single most important source of authority for the state governments, and these powers have extended into areas as diverse as mandatory education and maximum hour legislation for workers.

The framers refrained from putting a bill of rights in the Constitution on the logical grounds that the document established a government of limited, enumerated powers. As Hamilton observed, there was no point declaring "that things shall not be done which there is no power to do."[7] Antifederalists did win a victory of sorts when they obtained pledges from several state conventions that their ratification depended upon Congress subsequently amending the Constitution to include a bill of rights. The first Congress, followed by ratification of three-fourths of the states, added ten amendments. The first eight affirmed basic rights; the ninth provided that the people retained rights not otherwise enumerated; and the tenth granted the state those "powers" (not rights) not given to the national government or denied to the states by the Constitution. This bill of rights applied only against the national government. The framers simply did not envision the federal government serving as an umpire over the conduct of the states in matters of individual liberty. That modern conception only emerged after adoption of the Fourteenth Amendment in 1868 and the revolution in federal-state relations that flowed from it.

Since 1868 the balance of authority in the federal system has shifted away from the states and toward the national government. The system remains federal, but the central government has moved into areas that once were exclusively the domain of the states. In matters of economic regulation and promotion, for example, the national government has taken an increasingly greater role, especially since the Great Depression. In civil liberties and civil rights there has been change as well. The Supreme Court has nationalized many of the provisions of the Bill of Rights through holdings that incorporate them under the Fourteenth Amendment as protections against state action. The civil rights revolution of the 1960s, for example, would not have been possible without the power of the national government to break through entrenched local interests unwilling to accept black Americans as equals.

Americans during the past two-hundred years have debated incessantly the issue of federalism, and perhaps no other concept, save judicial review, has stirred more controversy. Much of this controversy has to do with states' rights. An important strain in American constitutional thought has held that the states, and not the people are the basic units of sovereign authority. That notion began with the Antifederalists' efforts to block ratification of the Constitution and continued through the Virginia and Kentucky Resolutions of the late 1790s, the Nullification Crisis of the early 1830s, the Secession Crisis of 1861, and the Massive Resistance Movement of the late 1950s.

The essays in this volume treat federalism from several perspectives. Some of the essays concentrate on the origins of federalism during the American Revolution; other essays examine the evolution of federalism as a theory of government. Some detail the great crisis of the Union produced by the secession movement; and others probe the distinctive constitutional structures that federalism mandated. The essays give special attention to the interaction of public and private rights in our federal system and the protean quality of federalism in shaping economic and social decision making. Readers interested in the distributive economic and social consequences of federalism will find the work of Harry Scheiber, some of which is listed in the Additional Reading section, of value. Also, issues of federalism are addressed elsewhere in this collection, especially in Volume 12, *Civil Rights in American History,* Volume 15, *Civil Liberties in American History,* and Volume 16, *The law of Business and Commerce.*

As intractable as the concept of federalism may be, these materials leave no doubt that it has been of central importance in our constitutional and legal history. These essays also reveal, as Harry Scheiber has argued, that in the last analysis the settlement of conflicts between the states and Congress has been left historically as much to "an informal political process" as to decisions by the Supreme Court.[8]

Kermit L. Hall

Notes

1. As quoted in Tony Freyer, "A Nation of States," in Herman Belz, ed., *This Constitution* , (forthcoming 1987).
2. As quoted in Forrest McDonald, *Novus Ordo Seclorum: The Intellectual Origins of the Constitution* (1985), p. 277.
3. Harry N. Scheiber, "Federalism and the Constitution: The Original Understanding, " in Lawrence M. Freidman and Harry N. Scheiber eds., *American Law and the Constitutional Order: Historical Perspectives* (1978), pp. 88.
4. Ibid
5. U.S. Constitution, Article I, sec.18.
6. McDonald, *Novus Ordo Seclorum* , p. 270
7. Ibid., p. 269.
8. As quoted in Scheiber, "Federalism and the Constitution," p. 89.

ADDITIONAL READING

Martin Diamond, "What the Framers Meant by Federalism, " in Robert A. Goldwin, ed., *A Nation of States: Essays on the American Federal System* (1963), pp. 24–41
Daniel Elazar, *The American Partnership* (1962).
Arthur Selwyn Miller, *The Modern Corporate State: Private Governments and the American Constitution* (1976)
Harry N. Scheiber, "American Federalism and the Diffusion of Power: Historical and Contemporary Perspectives," *University of Toledo Law Review* 9 (1978): 619–680.
Harry N. Scheiber, "Federalism and the American Economic Order, 1789–1910," *Law and Society Review* 10 (1975): 57–118.
Harry N. Scheiber, "Federalism and the Constitution: The Original Understanding, " in Lawrence M. Freidman and Harry N. Scheiber eds., *American Law and the Constitutional Order* (1978), pp. 85–98.

The Modernization Of American Federalism

Samuel H. Beer

Contents

1

50 Samuel H. Beer

The purpose of this essay is to present a theoretical model of the development of intergovernmental relations in a modernizing society. This model will, I trust, shed some light on the broad causes of centralization and decentralization in modern political systems. It is sufficiently general to be relevant to any advanced country and to be used in comparative study. In this essay, however, it will be applied only to the United States. My object will be to outline a scheme for describing and explaining what has happened and especially what is happening to intergovernmental relations in the American political system. The main task is to understand that general, but not exclusive, trend toward centralization that has characterized the history of Federal-state relations.

I have used the term "intergovernmental relations" rather than "federalism" because of the ambiguity of the more familiar term. Like any important term in political science federalism has been used in different ways. At least three meanings are relevant to the present discussion. Sometimes federalism is simply a convenient way of indicating our two (or three) tier pattern of intergovernmental relations. This usage refers merely to an observed division of power and activity without any implication as to the grounds or causes of that division.

A second meaning of federalism refers to the juristic device of giving exceptional legal protection to the powers of governments of territorial subdivisions of a polity. Such protections may be more or less elaborate, varying in topics covered and in the effectiveness of their provisions. As Riker has observed, such federal devices can be classified along an axis ranging from strong to weak protection.[1] On the basis of this definition the home rule provision of a state constitution can be said to establish a mild, but real, intrastate federalism. Such juristic devices are intended to have an effect upon federalism in the first sense, i.e. upon intergovernmental relations. They are expected to influence the actions and decisions of chief executives, legislatures and courts and in this manner to help maintain some prescribed division of power between levels of government, if necessary against the influence of other forces, personal, political, economic, etc.

[1] William H. Riker, "Federalism," in Fred Greenstein (ed.), The Handbook of Political Science (to be published).

No serious student is likely to say that these devices have never had any influence. After all, when we celebrate the virtues of the Constitution in comparison with the Articles of Confederation we mean that the provisions of the Constitution did make a great differ-ence in the way the Republic was governed. On the other hand, the effect of these provisons upon the history of American intergovern-mental relations—in particular their effect upon decisions of the Supreme Court relating to the division of power between Federal and state governments—is highly problematical. Some argue that the Court has had little independent influence upon the changing distri-bution of power between states and Federal government, which has been determined by other forces, such as economic development or the non-centralized character of the American party system. Others contend that the Court's influence has been great, although they may differ over whether the Court has maintained the original meaning of the Constitution or has imposed its own changing views of what constitutes the proper division of power.

3

In a third meaning, federalism refers to certain attitudes deeply embedded in the political culture of a country. These attitudes sup-port the belief that the governments of the territorial subdivisions of the system—in the American case, the states—have authority that is not derivative from, but independent of, the nation. The implica-tion is that the states have rights and powers that the nation cannot touch because they are derived not from the national will, but from the will of each state as a political community. Such attitudes, as expressed in the rhetoric of state sovereignty, were powerful in the generations before the Civil War and helped legitimize and incite secession. For many years they continued to affect speech and action under the banner of "states rights." Today, I should say, they have dwindled to insignificance as a behavioral influence.

Both as a juristic device and as an element of political culture, federalism has influenced the pattern of intergovernmental relations. The model presented in this essay, however, does not depend upon either of these influences in developing its scheme of explanation. It is, as I have already suggested, as applicable to a country that is unitary in legal structure and political attitudes as it is to the United States. The more successful the model as an explanation of the devel-opment of American intergovernmental relations, therefore, the less is left to be explained by federalism in the constitutional or cultural sense. While this essay can be only suggestive, its sense is that we should look not to federalism, but to modernization as the principal source of the changing division of power between levels of govern-ment.

This conclusion bears directly upon the complex of questions raised in the first of the Issue Topics. Perhaps the essential hypothesis suggested by those questions is the following: that the "ground rules" defining the distribution of federal power have been recently and radically changed by decisions of the Court, Congress and the President, with the result that a system of rules which for some long period of time had limited federal power now permits great and, indeed, excessive centralization. Taking "ground rules" to mean the juristic protections of federalism, the implication of the analysis in this essay is that the major grounds of centralization and decentralization are to be found not in such "ground rules" but rather in the forces of economic and political development.

Moreover, this analysis finds that it would be quite false to suppose that the federal division of power has some single classic form that was maintained for most of our history, only recently to be radically altered by the Supreme Court and other agencies of the federal government. On the contrary, when the American experience is examined in the light of the model presented here, it appears that there has been continual development in the relations of federal and state governments. The balance of power and activity has often shifted in the past, sometimes toward the states, but on the whole toward the federal center. In the United States, as in other modernizing societies, the general historical record has spelled centralization. While in recent years a new phase of this centralizing process has set in—which I call technocratic federalism—the main reasons for this change are not to be found in the personal, partisan or ideological preferences of office-holders, but in the new forces produced by an advanced modernity.

The function of the model presented here is analytic, not normative. It seeks to throw light on causes, rather than to present a rationale for justification or criticism. Above all, I do not want to produce one more useless blueprint of what the relations of the federal and state governments "ought" to be. This neither means that I am free of value preferences nor that I have no interest in defining a more effective role for the states. I will not, however, try to define that role by deduction from some normative model of American federalism. On the contrary, I do not think federalism is a national value. As a juristic device, it is instrumental and subordinate to national values, such as democracy, liberty, and equality. As an element of American political culture, it is a remnant of the tragic ambivalence in our sense of national identity that helped disrupt the Union. My analysis, therefore, poses the rude question: what use are the states? This question, I believe, should orient radical and unsparing inquiry, free of any presumption that federalism stands for a national value or that the states ought for such a reason to be preserved. Examined by this cold, pragmatic light, without any tinge of nostalgia or rhetoric, the states will, I believe, prove to have great promise as instruments in the further building of a national democracy. The essay will therefore conclude its discussion of intergovernmental relations with a consideration of the emerging functions of the states.

These functions show the states to have great promise as agencies in the further development of the American nation. This is my ultimate concern: the course and causes of national development. The theme of this essay, centralization and decentralization, derives from that concern, which inevitably directs attention to the roles of the state and federal governments in the development—or decline—of the nation. The question is not merely about the past. Nation-building did not end with the ratification of the Constitution, or the era of good feelings, or the surrender at Appomattox, or the admission of the 50th state. It has continued, and still continues, making advances, suffering reverses; chancy, indeterminate, and devoid of certainties; often morally ambiguous, yet providing for many millions a concrete, human community with which they identify, for which they make great exertions and in which they find fulfillment. I will conclude with some of the larger questions raised by the Issue Topics relating to the role of government in American society today and the prospects for the future of our national democracy.

5

I

A MODEL OF THE DEVELOPMENT OF INTERGOVERNMENTAL RELATIONS IN THE MODERNIZING POLITY

The image is familiar. In the beginning a segmented society consisting of a number of communities, small, undeveloped and similar, related to one another by few and insubstantial ties. Gradually these segments are drawn together by trade and industry; government and political activity; education and communications. Increasing interdependence introduces outside influences into the original communities, at once disrupting their solidarity and binding the resulting fragments into ever larger systems. These systems themselves are increasingly differentiated, interdependent and centralized.

This broad formula of development has been used by many students of social and political change from the evolutionary sociologists of the 19th century to the students of developing nations today. It can be used to analyze the transition from a traditional to a modern society or the growth of government and nation in a modern society. The United States fits the latter description. From our

earliest beginnings, and certainly from the Revolution, our orientation toward economic, political and most other spheres of behavior
has been strongly modern. Our traditions themselves have been the
traditions of modernity, supporting a flexible, calculating, secular
outlook, open to expansive aspirations and anticipating growing
power and abundance.

These attitudes of instrumental, technological rationalism and of
expansive democratic aspiration make intelligible the central mechanism of the process of modernization. That mechanism is the interaction between *differentiation* and *scale* from which issue those ever
larger and more complex networks of *interdependence* constituting
the background conditions for the continual trend of modern society
toward greater *centralization*. Basically similar processes take place in
the polity and other subsystems of modern society, but economic
development provides the most familiar illustration of the mechanism and its results. The operation of the model can be briefly summarized.

(1) Differentiation and increase in scale vary independently as
they respond, respectively, to the advance of science and technology
and to the democratization of wants. For instance, while science and
technology have driven forward the productive power of the modern
economy through new stages of specialization, the growth in scale
constituted by the expansion of demand has also at times led the
way in economic advance. (2) Differentiation and increase in scale
interact, mutually reinforcing one another. Growth of demand promotes a division of labor, mechanical or technological or both. Similarly, an advance in productivity leading to further division of labor
stimulates a search for, and possibly the creation of, new markets to
absorb the additional product. (3) The result of this twofold process
of greater differentiation and wider scale is an increase in interdependence. Division of labor by itself does not increase productivity.
That arises from such changes as the greater skill of the workman or
the new technology expressed in the new specialized tasks and
machines. For the social structure the important consequence of
division of labor is that the members of the system—whether individuals or collectivities—now are involved in a greater number of differentiated relationships. The volume and variety of transactions in the
system has risen. Thus, for instance, economic modernization joins
together increasingly differentiated and less self-sufficient parts of
the growing economy in more and more complex networks of exchange.

The terms used in this analysis of development may be explained
graphically. Figures 1 and 2 contrast a segmented and a developed
economy.

FIGURE I

FIGURE 2
(relations of only
A and B shown)

Segmented Economy

Developed Economy

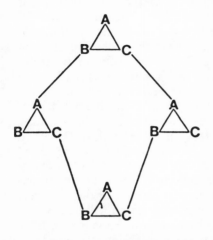

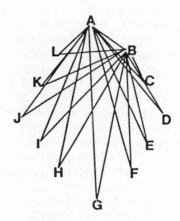

7

Index of specialization	3	12
Index of scale	16	66
Index of interdependence	2 or 3	11
Index of output	12	48

Figure 1 represents a segmented society with a very simple division of labor, consisting of three occupations (or members) A, B and C, as indicated by the index of specialization. The society contains four local communities, each identical in number of members and their occupations, and linked by simple ties of exchange. The lines show exchange relations. The scale of the economy is indicated by the total number of interrelations, 16. The interdependence of the members is slight, each having only two or, at the most, three connections with other members. Given the primitive level of specialization, productivity is low. Supposing the productivity of each member to be equal, it can be represented by 1,making the index of total output 12. Figure 2 presents the contrast of a developed economy. In constructing this figure, it was supposed that the division of labor had increased to the point of there being 12 occupations. The local communities have been dissolved in a single system. Supposing that each individual unit stands in an exchange relation with all other units, the index of scale would have risen to 66 and the index of interdependence to 11. Supposing also that productivity has increased fourfold, the index of output would be 48.

The primary thrust of the model is to show how, given a society oriented by the values of modernity, large, complex networks of interdependent action tend to grow up. This idea throws some light upon the questions raised in Issue Topic 2. One hypothesis implied by those questions is that various subsystems of American society, apart from the political system itself, show increasing "nationwide unification" and "standardization" and that these developments in some unspecified ways tend to promote governmental centralization. The relevance of the present analysis to this hypothesis is twofold. In the first place, the model presented here confirms the impression that a modern society such as the United States will indeed display such tendencies toward "nationwide unification," demonstrating that these tendencies are not transitory or superficial, but proceed from the basic processes of modernization and are, accordingly, hard to restrict or control. Moreover, by accounting for the tendency toward ever greater interdependence, the model explains the principal background condition for governmental centralization. This sets the theme for the bulk of the following pages which will be devoted to examining the specific ways in which interdependence leads to centralization.

Regarding the rise of standardization, however, the model offers no unambiguous implication. Its image of increasing specialization, on the contrary, spells ever greater diversity. And indeed many of the early observers of the effect on society of the division of labor saw in it a force that threatened, in the words of Auguste Comte, to "snuff out the spirit of togetherness." The need for standardization can readily be shown—for instance, the need for a common system of law throughout an area of expanding trade and for more intangible identities in evaluation and outlook among the members of a growing network of political, social and economic interaction. In this regard the model clearly does imply a certain standardization among the members of the society, since it is presupposed that they will share a modernist orientation. Few, if any, other societies have satisfied that requirement of the model more adequately than America at the time it won its independence. In other words, with our consensus on modernity, we started out with what was in crucial respects a highly standardized outlook. How much we retain of that outlook today is a complex question. At any rate, it is obviously false to say that the 210 million Americans of the present time are more standardized than the four millions who established the Republic.

The Politics of Centralization

The model of modernization shows how large, complex networks of interdependent action arise. Such networks are a principal background condition for governmental centralization. They are not, however, a sufficient explanation of it. To be sure, greater interdependence and complexity require a greater measure of coordination. But coordination can be and often is provided by what Lindblom calls "partisan mutual adjustment" as illustrated by the free market.[2] To understand why and when interdependence leads to centralization (in Lindblom's phrase, "centrally directed decision-making") one must turn to politics. It is politics—the formation of coalitions to influence the action of government—that provides the intervening link between interdependence and centralization. Such political action itself, however, is shaped by the structural features of the growing networks of interdependence.

Modernization consists not merely in the quantitative change of growing interdependence. It also embraces qualitative changes as the structure of these large networks develops new features. I detect four phases of modernization in each of which certain structural features tend to produce a certain kind of political coalition, viz., the pork-barrel coalition, the spillover coalition, the class coalition and the technocratic coalition. In the history of any actual polity, coalitions of all four types can be found in pure and in mixed form at almost any period of time. Yet the model implies, and history tends to support the implication, that they occur in a certain succession, each coming to prominence at a certain phase of modernization. (See Table 1.) Moreover, the succession seems to be cumulative, so that as a society develops, its politics becomes differentiated into the four types. Certainly, all four can be abundantly illustrated from the politics of present-day America.

TABLE 1

Phases in the Development of American Federalism

Politics	Policy	Intergovernmental relations	Federalism	Period
Porkbarrel	Distributive	Decentralizing	States rights	Jacksonian
Spillover	Regulatory	Centralizing	Dual	Republican
Class	Redistributive	Centralizing	Cooperative	New Deal
Technocratic	Instrumental	Centralizing	Technocratic	Postwar

Each type of coalition pursues a distinctive type of policy, the four classifications being distributive, regulatory, redistributive and

[2] Charles E. Lindblom, *The Intelligence of Democracy: Decision Making through Mutual Adjustment* (New York: MacMillan, 1965).

technocratic.[3] Each type of policy not only shapes government action in a certain phase; it also tends to produce the structural changes
that characterize the succeeding phase of development. The long-run
tendency of each type of policy is to lead to the next stage of
modernization. Thus, for instance, the regulatory phase of policy
seems to have promoted a kind and degree of economic development
leading to the class politics that produced the welfare state, which in
turn involved that vast expansion of the public sector that has been a
main ground for the present tendencies toward technocracy.

In the following pages, as each type of politics is analyzed against
the background of the model of modernization, its predicted effect
upon intergovernmental relations will be compared with the history
of American federalism. My object will be to see if the theoretical
implications of the model help us identify and characterize different
periods in American federal development and especially whether
they help identify and explain the observable tendencies to centralization or decentralization at various times.

II

PORKBARREL COALITIONS

The porkbarrel coalition is familiar to anyone with a passing
acquaintance with American politics of any period. In pure form, it
is one of the most ancient and common forms of political action—
simply one set of people with nothing in common getting together to
get something for themselves, respectively, at the expense of some
other people. Its powerful relevance to intergovernmental relations,
however, was first suggested to me by a brilliant article by Philip
Monypenny in the *National Tax Journal* for March, 1960.[4] This
article, frequently cited by students of the grant in aid system, is also
a rich example of the deflationary approach to government rhetoric.

Monypenny takes up a number of the common justifications of
grants-in-aid to the states and shows—to his own satisfaction—that
none hold water. The grants are not equalizing, do not function to
maintain a minimum level of essential services, do not express a
national concern, do not stimulate state and local activity in a field
of national interest, do not put the greater fiscal strength of the
federal government at the service of the weaker state and local units,
and so on. He then goes on to offer his own highly political hypothe-

[3] The first three terms I have adapted from Lowi. See Theodore Lowi, "American
Business, Public Policy, Case Studies and Political Theory," *World Politics*, Vol. XVI, No. 4
(July, 1964).

[4] Philip Monypenny, "Federal Grants-in-Aid to State Governments: a Political Analysis," *National Tax Journal*, Vol. 13, No. 1 (March, 1960).

sis. This is that each program is the product of a specific coalition consisting of members with very different objects, who therefore could not agree on an all-federal program and so concerted their pressure to get money from the federal government with such vague requirements that each member of the coalition could use it pretty much as he liked within his own jurisdiction.

The structure of the segmented society tends to produce pork-barrel coalitions. Its member units have internal coherence and the capacity to decide how to pursue their respective self-interests and utilize their respective gains. But in relation to one another they have relatively few common interests, values or sentiments. Stress needs to be kept on the term "relatively." The porkbarrel coalition may well characterize the politics of a country in its early stages of development when local or regional groups combine to seek advantages at the expense of other parts of the country. Yet as Monypenny's example reminds us, the "raid on the Treasury" can also occur at stages of high development. The members of the coalition he conceives to have been the author of these grants-in-aid programs are members of a segmented system in relation to the relevant fields of policy, although in other spheres they may share strong ties with one another and the rest of the country.

11

While the term porkbarrel has the connotation of being exploitative, the actual outcomes of such politics may be constructive for the society as a whole. In the economic development of a country, for instance, it is common for various sections to swap advantages through action by the central government, e.g., subsidies for your rivers and harbors in exchange for protection of my industries. With regard to each section some interest requires action that transcends the capacities of the lesser jurisdictions. By log-rolling with similarly situated sections, each is able to get from the central government the action it needs.

Behavior of this sort utilizes in government the kind of decision-making that economists have analyzed in their study of the market and that Lindblom has studied under the more general heading of "partisan mutual adjustment." In the polity, as in the economy, such behavior can coordinate interdependent activities without involving any intention to coordinate, or a conscious policy or plan to achieve some particular pattern of coordinated social action. Uncoordinated government decision-making may unintentionally promote national development, just as the higgling of buyers and sellers in the free marketplace may promote the growth of the wealth of the nation. In politics as in economics, we can sometimes observe the working of an "invisible hand." Whether the outcome is good or bad for the country, however, the action is quite different from the action of a coalition whose members aim at the same outcome.

Distributive Policy

The structure of the situation from which the porkbarrel coalition emerges implies a kind of political purpose. The members have no common interest; in positive terms this is to say their purpose consists in a collection of particular interests or goals. The policy emerging from such politics is, in Lowi's terms, "disaggregable"; that is, it consists not of a common program in which all the various parts are required if the desired outcome is to be achieved, but in a series of discrete programs or benefits which do not significantly affect one another.[5] To this sort of policy Lowi has given the name "distributive," a term taken from the land distribution policies of the Jacksonian period.

While distributive policy might consist in a series of specific programs of action by the central government, the diversity of interests among the members of the coalition will impel them to try to find the least differentiated substance for distribution. Unimproved land is suitable. The ideal, of course, is money, which simplifies the calculation of advantages and shares and can be readily converted by each recipient into a form of action suitable to his discrete purposes.

When one looks at intergovernmental relations the same logic applies. With regard to grant programs, for instance, log-rolling among groups might under some conceivable circumstances produce a set of categorical programs, each of which was desired by only one of the groups. But much more likely is simply a straightforward distribution of money without strings or categorical requirements; in short, unconditional revenue sharing. This inference throws light on one kind of coalition that would make it possible for a revenue-sharing proposal to get through Congress. The coalition would consist in a set of member groups which are connected with the governments of lesser jurisdictions and which are seeking resources to carry out programs that are diverse and non-uniform within the nation. Moreover, the members would be marginally more interested in using these resources for such distributive purposes than for nationally uniform and centrally directed programs. Such a measure has passed on at least one occasion, viz., the distribution among the states of the federal surplus in 1837. Indeed, the connection between that measure and current proposals for revenue sharing was emphasized by Professor William Anderson a few years ago when he denounced one of the then current proposals. Comparing that proposal to the distribution of 1837, he said: "One who has read some American his-

12

[5] See Lowi's discussion of distributive policy in the article cited in footnote 3 above.

tory can look upon it as nothing more than another old-fashioned raid on the Treasury."[6]

Are there any clear implications with regard to the centralizing or decentralizing effects of porkbarrel politics? Obviously it is centralizing in that it makes use of the central government. Indeed, in its crude exploitative form, the porkbarrel coalition constitutes what some of the more excited enemies of centralization regard as the typical form of central government action: one group despoiling another. In its milder versions, when blessed with serendipity, logrolling can have not only centralizing, but also nation-building effects. On the other hand, porkbarrel politics also may set in motion powerful decentralizing tendencies which threaten disintegration. Porkbarrel politics reflects the diversity of interests of a segmented system and nourishes these diverse interests by adding to the resources devoted to promoting them. We may value the porkbarrel as supplementing and counterbalancing the centralist tendencies of other types of politics when it operates as one among several differentiated types of politics of a developed polity. As the exclusive or dominant form, however, its logic is not only to reflect segmentation, but also to heighten it cumulatively. As the dominant form, porkbarrel politics would seem to be centrifugal to the point of secession.

13

States Rights Federalism

The preceding theoretical analysis throws light on the reasons for one of the gravest failures of the American system of government, the outbreak of the Civil War. When I call this a failure, I mean to reject the notion that armed conflict was inevitable. Certainly, the slavery issue could not be put off; and one way or another the country was bound not only to put a stop to the extension of slavery, but also to set it on the way to ultimate extinction. What I wish to stress is that the problem was not only the necessity of a national solution for the issue of slavery, but also the low capacity of the American system to give national solutions to any major problem. This had not always been the case, as the founding and first decades of the Republic had shown. The decline in capacity for conscious national policy-making had taken place during the generation before 1860.

There is something very puzzling about this loss of political capacity in the light both of theory and of comparative history. The Jacksonian era was a time of rapid economic development and expanding democracy. In other Western countries in the 19th and 20th

---

[6] William Anderson, "The Myths of Tax Sharing." *Public Administration Review*, Vol. XXVIII, No. 1 (January/February, 1968), p. 10.

centuries, both sorts of change, the economic and the political, have usually strengthened rather than weakened the central authority. Likewise, thinking broadly in terms of the model of modernization presented earlier in these pages, one would expect that these developments would increase that volume and variety of transactions that constitute a major background condition for centralization.

On closer analysis, however, the model also suggests that the two lines of development came into conflict. On the one hand, economic growth continued to expand and multiply interests seeking national action, and the early Whig proposals for central action reflected these pressures. On the other hand, however, the democratic thrust, extending the vote and increasing participation, shifted influence away from business elites aware of the nationalizing trends and toward farmers and working men whose economic position made them less directly implicated in the nationalizing economy.

14

The structure of the political parties—first the Democrats then ultimately the Whigs—showed the consequences: not only democratization, but also pronounced decentralization as American parties became, for the first time, coalitions of state and local machines. Under this "second party system," as Richard P. McCormick has shown, each party consisted of a collection of factions from various states without unifying national perspectives or interests.[7] Curiously—but logically—this embodiment of the porkbarrel principle enabled the parties to flourish in most states throughout the nation. If they had reflected the real conflicts of interest, which were sectional, this superficial appearance of being national parties would not have been possible.

Distribution of the Surplus in 1837

The disintegration that had been brought on by political modernization working at cross purposes with economic modernization afflicted especially the political parties and the class of political leaders. One can illustrate the point from a look at the distribution of the Treasury surplus in 1837. As policy, this measure was indubitably "distributive." As shown both by the debates in Congress and the manner in which the states used the money, there was no national program being served. In one place or another just about every function then performed by state and local government benefitted from the distribution. The ultimate in distributive politics was achieved in Maine, where the money was split up and given out to individuals, the amount per capita coming to about $3.00. Such was the fate of

[7] Richard P. McCormick, *The Second American Party System: Party Formation in the Jacksonian Era* (Chapel Hill: University of North Carolina Press, 1966).

national resources that John Quincy Adams had hoped would be spent on internal improvements, a national university, scientific expeditions, a stronger Navy, etc.

But the most interesting aspect of the whole operation was its political foundation, i.e., the coalition that produced it. Since the money went to the states, one might expect to find some grouping of those states with more to gain against those with less. Such was not the case. On the contrary, the vote in the House, for instance, was almost a straight party vote. Moreover, the party favoring the distribution was the Whigs. One can make sense of this in the light of the fact·that the banks in which the money would be kept by the states was a matter of great political importance to the parties. The question of the Democratic "pet banks" showed how important this could be. At the time of the vote in the House, however, most state governments were in the hands of the Whigs. It is a fair inference that the prospect of Whig banks getting this windfall did much to stimulate the porkbarrel coalition under the guise of a party majority that voted the distribution.

15

It was as a polity habituated to porkbarrel politics that the nation confronted the eruption of the slavery issue in the 1850's. We no longer had a political class with the perspective and skills produced by a conscious, national, decision-making approach. Lincoln, needless to say, recognized the level of strategy called for. But by then it was too late for a peaceful solution.

To put the matter starkly: it was not so much the slavery issue that disintegrated the nation; but the disintegrated condition of the nation, especially its political class, that made it impossible to cope with the slavery issue. In terms of the model, the explanation might be phrased as premature democratization in the context of the sequential nationalization of classes.

III

SPILLOVER COALITIONS

The notion of spillover has been used by economists concerned with finding a rationale for federal grants-in-aid to state or local governments. They point out that, when only a part of the benefits of a program carried on by a state government are realized within the state, there will be a tendency for that government to evaluate and fund the program only in terms of its benefits to the home state. If the interstate benefits were considered, however, it might make good economic sense for the larger society to invest in a much bigger program than the state feels justified in supporting. In technical lan-

guage, if the marginal national benefits exceed marginal benefits to
the state, the expenditure by the state will tend to be sub-optimal. In
such a situation, there is a case for the federal government making a
grant to the state government which will bring total funding of the
program up to the point where marginal cost to all governments will
equal marginal national benefit. George Break, for instance, develops
this idea in his theory of "optimizing grants," that is, federal grants
to optimize total expenditures on programs with significant spillovers.[8]

In the present discussion, I am not interested in this normative use
of the concept of spillovers, but in its use as a tool of analysis to
describe and explain how people and governments act in certain
typical situations produced by a modernizing society. We already
have a good deal of empirical confirmation of the kind of behavior
presupposed by the normative use of the concept—for instance,
studies measuring spillovers of benefits from one jurisdiction into
others and showing underfunding where such benefits are substantial.[9] I propose taking the further step of proposing that during the
development of an economy, as the flow of interlocal and interstate
benefits and costs increases, coalitions tend to form in the national
political arena seeking action by the central government. Such coalitions, it seems to me, constitute a very large part of the typical
interest group activity of American politics.

The idea of the spillover coalition is a crucially important hypothesis in the study of the centralizing tendencies of modernization
because it explains one of the principal ways in which the structure
of complex interdependence is linked with political pressure for conscious central control. The hypothesis that spillovers will tend to
produce such political pressure is valid only insofar as the actors in
the society, whether individuals or groups or governments, weigh
alternatives and calculate consequences in a rationalistic way—i.e.,
are "utility maximizing." A general prevalence of such attitudes is
included in the model by its presupposition of a modernist orientation.

The Theory of Externalities

It will be useful to turn briefly to the theory from which the
hypothesis is derived. One reason is to link the hypothesis with classical economic analysis and so clarify its meaning and perhaps

---

[8] George F. Break, *Intergovernmental Fiscal Relations in the United States* (Washington, D.C.: Brookings, 1967), Ch. II, "Functional Grants-in-Aid."

[9] See Burton A. Weisbrod, *External Benefits of Public Education: an economic analysis*
(Princeton, N.J.: Princeton University Press, 1964) and Robert F. Adams, "On the variation
in the consumption of public services." *Review of Economics and Statistics* Vol. 47, No. 4,
pp. 400-405.

strengthen its credibility. A more important reason is to develop the concept of centralization itself. The centralization with which this essay has to do concerns intergovernmental relations. But as the theory underlying the spillover hypothesis will show, similar situations and a similar logic produce that primary centralization consisting in the movement of control from the private to the public sector—a question raised in items 3, 4 and 8 of the Issue Topics.

The basis of the analysis is the doctrine of external costs and benefits derived from Alfred Marshall's concept of external economies and diseconomies and developed by Pigou, Robertson, Baumol and others. "Spillover" is simply an adaptation of the technical term "externality." An externality is a consequence of the activity of an individual or firm which is incidental (or "external") to its main activity but which is indivisible from that main activity and which affects the utility of another individual or firm favorably (benefit) or unfavorably (cost). For instance, a firm while producing automobiles also produces smoke—a typical external cost. Another firm conducts a training program for its employees which raises their educational level, thus incidentally making them better neighbors and more attractive prospects for other employers. The result of an externality—for instance, a benefit—is that marginal private net product falls short of marginal social net product. The training program, for instance, produces returns to the community at large which would justify much larger expenditure on it, but since the firm will pay only for the gain to itself, the further expenditure will not be forthcoming.

There is, in short, a failure of the market. In the case of the firm producing external benefits, fewer resources are devoted to its activity than social utility would justify since the benefit it gives the community involves no compensation to the firm. In the case of the firm producing external costs, more resources are devoted to it than social utility would justify, since the drain it imposes on the community is not reckoned into the cost of its product. The nub of the problem is not that the externalities are incidental or unintended by-products, but that technically they are *indivisible* from the main activity of the firm. The firm cannot sell the benefits of its training program to the neighbors or prospective employers of its workers, since it cannot withhold these benefits from the beneficiaries in case they do not care to pay. Similarly with regard to external costs, the people bearing them—for instance, the people suffering from smoke pollution—cannot bar the use of the air around their dwellings to the flow of smoke. In Musgrave's terms, the "exclusion principle," an essential of the operation of the free market, does not hold. Externalities cannot be "separately packaged." [10]

[10] Richard A. Musgrave, *The Theory of Public Finance: a Study in Public Economy* (New York: McGraw-Hill, 1959), pp. 9, 86.

Welfare economists argue that in each case there are grounds for government intervention. In the case of the benefits, there is reason for the government to subsidize the firm producing them, or itself to carry on the beneficial activity, for instance, in public schools. In the case of costs, the government might take such action as fining the firm and using the money for an anti-pollution program, or compelling the firm itself to install smoke-control apparatus. Such government action, it is crucially important to emphasize, does not alter the operation of the free market, rather it *perfects* it. Government intervenes to get the result that the free and rational action of individuals and firms would produce, if it were not for the technical fact of the indivisibility of external costs and benefits. This point must be emphasized because it defines the type of public policy associated with spillover coalitions. Such government action does not seek to alter the property relations of the free economy. It does not try to change the allocation of resources as dictated by the free economy or the distribution of income and wealth. It involves no change in social values. It is not redistributive. It merely regulates the economy in such a way as to eliminate the imperfections resulting from externalities. Such policy I call "regulatory" and find typical of the coalitions that are brought into existence by externalities.

Economic externalities not only justify government intervention; in a rational modern democracy, they also produce political action. They are the structural basis of spillover coalitions which typically consist of such prospective beneficiaries of government intervention. Such intervention may be called centralization, since it substitutes, with regard to some specific field of decision, conscious government control for the patisan mutual adjustment of the free (to be sure, imperfectly free) market. Decision-making with respect to the allocation of resources in this specific field is moved from the free market to government. Such increase in the public relative to the private sector may be called *primary centralization*.

Similar structures and a similar logic, however, also may explain the movement of decision-making from lower to higher jurisdictions—a type of centralization that I will call *secondary centralization*. In an early segmented phase of a society's development, the externalities of its economic activities—for instance, sanitary conditions—may be dealt with quite adequately by lesser jurisdictions such as town or city governments. As the economy develops, however, benefits and costs of activity in each locality spill over into a wider area. People in all or most jurisdictions suffer (or benefit) from these impacts, but it does not make sense for any single jurisdiction to take action by itself since, in the face of conditions created by activity throughout the area, its lone action can accomplish little. In such a case, therefore, there is every reason for persons and groups affected to turn to the jurisdiction with authority over the whole area. The field of regulation that was formerly handled by the lesser jurisdiction, now is shared by or taken over by the higher jurisdiction. The same logic that initially led to government intervention or primary centralization has now led to secondary centralization. Thus, towns first assumed the responsibility for public health problems which, as the economy developed, later led to the establishment of state boards of health and ultimately to intervention by the federal government.

According to the logic of spillovers, while the emergence of economic externalities in the early stages of modernization leads to intervention by local governments, the increasing flow of interlocal and interstate costs (or benefits) will tend to produce secondary centralization in higher jurisdictions. The seats of basic innovation would be the lesser jurisdictions, since it is they that first confront the emerging problems and opportunities of a modernizing society. While the central government would be gathering more power and responsibility to itself, it could be expected to model its policies on the precedents already provided by states and cities. Moreover, the process of secondary centralization would be gradual since it would be controlled by the incremental growth of the economy and by the piecemeal efforts of single-purpose interest groups. Finally, one might argue also that in a federal system during the period for which the spillover coalition is the dominant form producing secondary centralization, the term *dual federalism* is appropriate. Although the logic of the nationalization of externalities would be continually adding to federal power, there would remain functions which, though diminishing in number, would still have effects confined largely within state boundaries. With regard to these functions, states would still be "laboratories of experimentation."

19

Internalities and Decentralization

In developing the theory of externalities, economists often find it convenient to write as if externalities affect all members of the community equally and in the same sense. Once the exposition of basic theory is taken care of, however, any presumption of a unanimous community or harmony of interests must be critically examined. In contrast to porkbarrel coalitions, the members of a spillover coalition do have a common interest. While they are no less moved by self-interest, the goal they seek is not diverse but identical for all, for example, an anti-pollution program. This community of interest among the members, however, may involve sharp conflict with other groups in the society. Conflicts so rooted are the typical substance of pressure politics. In the history of American federalism, this type of political force has been responsible for large shifts in responsibility from lower to higher governments.

The fact that conflict may arise from the differential impact of externalities suggests a possible grounds for decentralization. Taking note of such conflicts, Mancur Olson observes that where a government program will benefit only a subset of the population of a jurisdiction (thus constituting what he calls an "internality"), it will probably be resisted by the remainder of the population. [11] In such cases, he argues, it would promote a better allocation of resources to let the prospective beneficiaries have a separate government empowered to finance and carry out the program. In general, his argument is that there should be a separate jurisdiction for every public good with a unique boundary, so that those who benefit will also be those who pay.

This normative proposal suggests an explanation of a prominent feature of American local government, the proliferation of special districts. Among political scientists, the special district has a bad name. Yet there obviously is a great deal to be said for it, so long as it conforms to Olson's criteria. In trying to estimate the incidence of such decentralization in the course of modernization, one can see how it might be likely during a middle phase when the interlocal flow of social costs and benefits had breached local boundaries, but had not reached the stage of interdependence of the present day. At present, however, it is virtually impossible to identify government programs that would not have impacts beyond the boundaries of such small jurisdictions as those Olson proposes. His own examples of what might be devolved—a civilian police review board, a course in Afro-American history—show that he is thinking of symbolic rather than economic functions.

Spillover Politics and Dual Federalism

The spillover model, it seems to me, fits quite well with many of the main features and developments of American federalism during the great Republican period that stretched from the Civil War to the New Deal. In contrast with the conflicts of the periods preceding and succeeding it, this period was one of substantial consensus on the basic forms of the economic system. Even the Progressives did not

[11] Mancur Olson, Jr., "The Principle of 'Fiscal Equivalence': The Division of Responsibilities among Different Levels of Government," *American Economic Review*, Vol. 59, No. 2 (May, 1969).

seek to change the system, but merely make it more faithful to itself. Politics did not seek to alter, but to perfect the free economy. This period was accordingly a classic era of interest group politics. In this time appropriately Arthur Bentley wrote his classic on politics, *The Process of Government* (1906), in which the whole of decision-making was resolved into the balancing of groups. One can trace the action of spillover coalitions gradually bringing about secondary centralization both within states and within the nation. The movement of control from state to federal jurisdiction marked many fields of regulation, such as railroads, quarantine, pure food and drug legislation, and water pollution control.

The states were still vigorous innovators and, in much of the regulatory legislation, provided the precedents for national action. In contrast with the Jacksonian period of "states rights federalism," when the states were the principal instruments of social choice while the federal government languished and declined, both state and federal governments were active. While the logic of the nationalization of externalities was continually adding to federal authority, there remained functions which, though diminishing in number, still had effects confined largely within state boundaries. For this period, therefore, the term commonly applied to it is appropriate: dual federalism.

21

IV

CLASS COALITIONS

Spillover coalitions continue to flourish, as do porkbarrel coalitions. But there is a kind of policy which has its roots in the electorate but which cannot be reduced to either the porkbarrel or spillover bases. It is a coalition which seeks not simply to perfect the free market, but in major ways to supersede it. Lowi refers to such a policy orientation as "redistributive." What I am thinking of is at least redistributive. Under the impulsion of such policy, federal grants to a state, for instance, seek not merely to help the state to overcome the hindrances that spillovers put in the way of its fulfilling its priorities, but rather to change these priorities to accord with a national policy. The more common phrase, Welfare State, gets the connotation better than redistribution.

Among the conventional tools of social science, the concept of class best suggests the structural basis for such coalitions. Classes are based on the division of labor and their components consist of the occupational groupings of the modern economy. As many studies have shown, occupation is the governing clue to class identity and far more determining than associated traits of income, education or style

of life. In a modernizing economy as specialization proceeds, these
subgroups become more variegated and numerous. Typically, among
the working class, they provide the membership of a trade union
movement differentiated on the basis of craft, industry and other
traits. As the economy grows to a national scale, the forces of competition produce standardization; the workers on a job become, so to
speak, interchangeable, as do managers, products and supplies. This
process creates, on a nationwide basis, sets of people who have similar functions (jobs), similar characteristics (capacities, training) and
similar interests.

A class, however, is not only an interest group like the members of
a spillover coalition. The sub-groups of a class are given an overarch-
ing common interest by a very special circumstance common to all.
This is their power position in the economic organizational unit.
Accepting Dahrendorf's definition, I should agree that a class is a
collectivity sharing interests that arise from the authority structure
of the imperatively coordinated association. [12] Classes and class conflict have their foundation in the differentiation of power within not
only the industrial firm—as in Dahrendorf's account—but also all
modern organizations. This definition is in conformity with the fact
that class conflict occurs in socialist as well as capitalist economies.
Private ownership has been one way in which the differentiation of
power has been expressed. But the need for managers charged with
the coordinating function and given authority to carry it out also
persists in economies with collective ownership. Managerialism, not
capitalism, is the root of that relative deprivation of power that
makes the manual and non-supervisory occupations into the working
class.

Classes appear as soon as organization appears in industry, commerce and other forms of economic activity. In the early phases of
modernization, they may be confined to the localized markets of a
segmented society and the incidence of class conflict may extend
only to local politics. In Jacksonian politics, while the organized
workingmen of Philadelphia and New York City were active in those
places they did not try to join together in a larger movement. A set
of people with common economic interests linked by a similar deprivation (or possession) of organizational authority does not constitute
a class. They must also be impelled to concerted action by their
implication in the same economy. When their interests are affected
similarly by the same cause, then we may expect class action in the
corresponding political arena.

[12] Ralf Dahrendorf, *Class and Class Conflict in Industrial Society* (Stanford University
Press, 1959) p. 238.

This implication in the larger economy may occur at different times for different classes. One would not be surprised to find the managerial class responding to nationalizing influences first, only to be opposed by the parochial goals of manual workers already conscious of their class interests, but more distantly affected by the larger economy than the business elites. If, as in Jacksonian politics, political power was distributed in favor of the lower classes, the economically based parochialism of the majority would result in the paradox of decentralizing politics in a time of rapid economic modernization. The question needs investigation. The hypothesis of the sequential nationalization of economic strata could prove helpful in explaining political conflicts in modernizing societies.

The New Deal and Class Politics

While class politics appeared in local and state arenas in the United States in earlier times, it did not become a major, indeed the dominant, form of national politics until the New Deal. The period of its greatest influence, the twenty years from the election of Roosevelt to that of Eisenhower, was marked at the beginning and the end by the works of two perceptive observers. In 1933 Arthur Holcombe in his *New Party Politics* perceived the change from "the old rustic sectional politics" to the new urban "class politics," while in 1951 Samuel Lubell in *The Future of American Politics* (which was actually about the recent past) reported on "the underlying class consciousness which permeates American politics today." [13] In 1952 the voting preferences of lower-income groups in the United States (outside the South) favored the Democrats as heavily and in almost exactly the same proportion as similar strata supported the Labour Party in Britain, a country in which class plays a larger role in determining voter preferences than in any other country.

I quote these authorities and cite these data because class politics may seem rather un-American. The objection is not frivolous. In the first place, it is quite true that, with regard to rhetoric, American politics cannot match the exploitation of class in countries with substantial socialist movements. This reflects a lack of class themes in our political culture, a lack that undoubtedly has substantial behavioral consequences in making it much more difficult to rally and maintain class-based political organizations. In the second place, and this is an even more serious point, the Roosevelt coalition was by no means confined to the working class. Arthur Schlesinger, Jr. suggests

23

---

[13] Arthur N. Holcombe, *The New Party Politics* (New York: Norton, 1933) p. 11. Samuel Lubell, *The Future of American Politics*, 2nd edn. (New York: Harper-Row, 1956) p. 228.

how miscellaneous it was in summing up its components: the South; the city machines; labor; the newer immigrants; Negroes; women, and intellectuals. [14] Reporting on attitudes in the mid-1950s, *The American Voter* found that the "Democrats were still thought to help groups primarily of lower status: the common people, working people, the laboring man, Negroes, farmers, and (in 1956 only) the small businessman. The Republicans, on the other hand, were thought to help those of higher status: big businessmen, the upper class, the well-to-do." [15]

In the United States, as in other countries, a class coalition had to become something more in order to win national power. Yet following Holcombe and Lubell, I would emphasize the dominating influence of class on the action and accomplishments of the Roosevelt Coalition. Moreover, once that coalition had been formed, it endured as a powerful force in American politics. Even in the late 1960's, although Everett Ladd, Jr. found other and different cleavages dividing American voters, he also reported the old "liberal" vs. "conservative" cleavage dating back to "an era of class politics" when "business and labor were at opposite poles." [16] Likewise, in his analysis of Congressional legislation, Lowi has identified redistributive coalitions which are highly structured, stable and class based in contrast with the haphazard and transient coalitions of regulatory politics. [17] Class politics, in short, while in decline from its position of a generation ago, has joined porkbarrel and spillover coalitions as a persisting model of national political action.

My effort in the preceding paragraphs has been to establish that class coalitions are distinctive modes of political action and cannot be reduced to one of the other basic types. Class coalitions also have characteristic policy aims. Given their basis in the structure of the advanced modern economy, these aims (in the case of working class coalitions) center on redressing relative deprivations in power and the material fruits of power. This dual theme provides an organizing thread for what appears at first sight to be the great jumble of measures introduced by the New Deal. The problems to which it addressed itself had been forcing themselves on people's consciousness ever since the "social problem" came to the fore early in

[14] Arthur M. Schlesinger, Jr., *The Politics of Upheaval* (Boston: Houghton Mifflin, 1960) Chapter 23, "The Roosevelt Coalition."

[15] Angus Campbell *et al.*, *The American Voter.* Abridged edn. (New York: John Wiley, 1964) p. 19.

[16] Everett Carll Ladd, Jr., *Ideology in America: Change and Response in a City, A Suburb and a Small Town* (New York: Norton, 1972) pp. 174-175.

[17] Theodore Lowi, "Decision Making vs. Policy Making: Towards an Antidote for Technocracy," *Public Administration Review*, Vol. XXX, No. 3 (May/June, 1970).

the 20th century. The problems were, on the one hand, a great concentration of economic power; and, on the other, serious inequities in the distribution of material well-being. While the New Deal often digressed in various other directions, it was along the axes of these two problem areas that its lasting programs clustered.

With regard to the concentration of economic power, the old remedy of regulation was sometimes used, and the still older approach of trust-busting was not entirely neglected. The distinctive approach of the New Deal, however, was the creation of what later came to be called "countervailing power." Leading examples are the Wagner Act, the AAA and the TVA. Similarly, with regard to the problem of material deprivation, there were new approaches centering on a wide use of the taxing and spending powers. The programs sometimes directly provided services, as in the case of social insurance or public housing, which involved a degree of redistribution of income. Among the more important were the Social Security Act and the Wage-Hour Act, not to mention the vast emergency work relief measure programs.

One can summarize the main thrust of the New Deal as an effort, on the one hand, to create a new balance of economic power and, on the other, to establish a minimum level of economic security. This was a sharp and major departure from the approach of the previous period, even in its Progressive phase. And a new terminology was appropriately introduced into American politics. For the first time the term "liberal" came to be used widely to describe coalitions and policies, shortly to be joined by "conservative" as a label for the opposition. As Hofstadter remarks, the demands of a large and powerful labor movement, coupled with the interests of the unemployed, gave the later New Deal a "social-democratic" tinge that had never before been present in American reform movements. Because of this change in political base, he continues, American reformism which in the past had been mainly concerned with reforms of an entrepreneurial sort and only marginally with social legislation was now fated to take responsibility on a large scale for legislation concerned with social security, unemployment, wages and hours and housing. [18]

Cooperative Federalism

Class action on a national basis was a major force making the New Deal a highly centralizing regime. In many respects, New Deal action constituted primary centralization, bringing into the sphere of

[18] Richard Hofstadter, *The Age of Reform: From Bryan to F.D.R.* (New York: Random House, 1955) p. 308.

government regulation areas of activity that had previously been left
to the operation of the free market. Yet it must be stressed that
many of the basic measures of the New Deal were modelled on social
legislation undertaken in some of the states. Assistance for older
people and for "deserving mothers"—the beginning of the present
massive OAA and AFDC programs—not to mention much labor legislation, had already been launched in some states and Roosevelt used
people with backgrounds in this state experience in designing and
administering the new reforms.

One cannot, of course, deny the very great innovation represented
by the transfer of these few and usually quite small-scale initiatives
into the vast, growing and nationally uniform programs of the New
Deal. While the states played an accustomed role in providing precedents and models for central action, they also acquired what was in
substance a radically new function in the American system of government. From the earliest times, states had been induced to carry out
national policy by means of federal grants. The innovation of New
Deal days was that this practice was so greatly increased that it
amounted virtually to a new phase of federalism. Appropriately a
new term, "cooperative federalism," was invented to characterize
this new phase. The term was coined by Jane Perry Clark in her
pioneering book of 1938.[19] She fully recognized that this relationship involved a major new step in federal centralization. In her analysis, the reason was a growing interdependence which vastly heightened the "need for a minimum of uniform national policy."[20] That
broad aim was implemented in various fields of policy, especially
through a great growth in the use of the grants-in-aid from the federal to state governments. This was "cooperation" which established
a division of labor vesting direction and policy-making in the federal
government, leaving to the states the administrative responsibility for
carrying out national policy. This use of the states as instruments of
national policy reminds one of the same development that had been
going on in central-local relations in Britain because of similar industrial and social conditions and with a similar wide use of grants-in-
aid.

V

TECHNOCRATIC POLITICS

In the study of politics, the closer one gets to the present time, the
harder it gets to sort out the important from the unimportant and

[19] Jane Perry Clark, *The Rise of a New Federalism: Federal State Cooperation in the United States* (New York: Russell, 1938).
[20] *Ibid.*, p. 7.

the influential from the trivial. If, however, one looks broadly at politics in the United States and the West during the past generation and asks what major new forces have appeared bearing on the question of centralization and decentralization, one answer would clearly be technocracy. This trend consists primarily in the great and growing power in government of technically and professionally trained persons. People with such qualifications have long been a distinctive component of the modern state, constituting its bureaucratic core. But various recent developments have immensely heightened their specialized capacities and influence.

The most prominent is that acute phase of the scientific revolution which set in during the past two or three decades. One result has been that increasingly scientific advance is directly embodied in public policy. For instance, discoveries in medical science, very likely based on research financed by the National Institutes of Health, are often directly embodied in federal programs. This new direct relationship is significant. Science has always affected political development, but for most of modern times the relation has been indirect. Typically, scientific and technological advances have led to economic development and so to those problems and opportunities that gave rise to centralizing coalitions.

27

The political importance of this new direct relation of science to public policy arises from the fact that it shifts the initiative in government from the economic and social environment of government to government itself. The old pressure group model that found the origin of laws and programs in demands arising outside government does not hold of technocratic politics. In technocratic policy-making the pressures and proposals arise *within* government and its associated circles of professionals and technically trained cadres. In a democratic country, of course, the electorate must be informed and its consent won, but in recent times it tends less and less to be the source of policy initiatives.

This shift in initiative from society to government—a new type of primary centralization—springs in part from the growing complexity of the knowledge which is used in identifying and solving contemporary problems and which accordingly, involves an ever-greater dependence on experts in policy-making. But the new centralizing trend also has another and independent foundation. Government itself—the public sector—has become such a large proportion of the total society that it generates within itself powerful forces leading to further government action. Centralization, in short, breeds further centralization. The following paragraphs will be concerned with this important mode of expansion of the public sector.

Governmental Spillovers (engrenage)

In the analysis of this new process of primary centralization, the concept of spillover is once again useful. Students of regional integration have used the idea to show how arrangements for regional government, such as those for the various types of common markets that have been set up in recent years, may expand their authority into new areas of activity.[21] In their analysis the term spillover means the "functional linkage of tasks" (*engrenage*), but the logic is much the same as that of the economic externality, except, of course, that the principal source of these spillovers is public rather than private action.

The original model of modernization showed how the interaction of specialization and scale lead to the growth of larger and more complex networks of interdependent activity. Up to the present point in the analysis, the model has been illustrated mainly by reference to economic development, surely the major field of its operation in American history. Basically the same processes, however, take place in the development of government. On the one hand, increases in scale take the form of expanding democratic demands and, on the other, specialization in the bureaucratic element of government reflects the advance of government's technical power. As democratic demands are met by a wider use of bureaucratic power, new networks of interdependence are created. The process is like that of the growing economy, except, of course, that the coordinating agency of these transactions is not the market, but the conscious imperative control of the polity. The welfare state with its massive social programs coordinating the activities of millions of people—taxpayers, bureaucrats and beneficiaries—is a major current illustration of such a network of interdependence created and maintained by government.

Within these vast networks of governmental activity, externalities arise, much as they do within the economy. In some instances these unintended costs (or benefits) affect the utilities of various groups in the private sector, leading the groups to make demands for government action to correct (or extend) the externality. In the case of external costs these demands could result in abolition of the government program (primary decentralization). It seems more likely, however, that, as in the case of its action toward externalities in the private sector, government is more likely to add a program modifying the burdensome effects, while maintaining the main activity. In other words, just as a government does not shut down the polluter, but arranges for anti-pollution programs, so it does not shut down an

[21] See J. S. Nye, "Comparing Common Markets: a Revised Neo-Functionalist Model," in Leon N. Lindberg and Stuart A. Scheingold (eds.), *Regional Integration: Theory and Research* (Cambridge, Mass.: Harvard University Press, 1971).

educational or correctional program with anti-social side-effects, but adds some new program which it hopes will prevent or offset these effects.

A second type of governmental spillover leading to centralization occurs when the externality affects a private group by way of another program directed to this group. In this instance, one agency interferes with the success of another and the affected interest groups in the society join with the interested bureaucratic elements to seek remedial action. Again, while such pressures theoretically could lead to a measure of primary decentralization, in actual fact they seem more likely to lead to further government activity. Finally, there is the case in which the externalities of government programs do not have their centralizing effects indirectly, through a response in the private sector, but directly within the public sector. Spillovers of this sort typically constitute the substance of coordination problems. The resulting conflicts are instances of pure bureaucratic politics and may very well be solved by further government action to reconcile the demands of the agencies in conflict. Thus, conflicts within the vast organization of government are settled by further expansion of the activities of the organization.

29

Primary centralization resulting from pure bureaucratic politics highlights a leading characteristic of *technocratic policy*. This is that it is concerned with means rather than ends. The complexity of the problems dealt with necessitates that the means adopted to solve them will be complicated, round-about, and probably dependent upon the activity of several agencies. In such a situation, it is only too easy for a program manager to lose track of the ultimate desired outcome and to devote his main energies essentially to maintaining and improving the programs that are his direct responsibility. Needless to say, as such instrumentalities are developed they may profoundly affect the ends they are intended to serve. An extreme case arises in modern defense policy. There the technicians developing weapons systems are nominally merely providing better instruments whose purposes are to be determined by civilian authority. In fact, large shifts in weapons systems, as from bombers to missiles, has a profoundly limiting and transforming effect upon the kinds of defense and foreign policy that these instrumentalities may be used to serve.

The Professional-Bureaucratic Complex

In identifying the structures of technocratic politics, the military-industrial complex often serves as a leading example. Similar conditions, however, have produced similar structures in other fields of policy. To refer to these structures in general, I use the term professional-bureaucratic complex. Typically, they have four basic elements. As the ultimate source of innovation, perhaps the most important element is the research elite of the various specialized fields. Some may be employed by government, but usually they are in universities or research institutes and if they have a government connection it is as part-time consultants and members of advisory committees and task forces or full-time employees at a high level for a short period. This research elite has close connections with the professional sectors of the federal bureaucracy to which it feeds ideas and from which it gets ideas for applied research. In each field, these federal bureaucrats have close contacts with the appropriate professionals at state and local levels of government, these vertically related bodies of officialdom constituting the second element in a professional-bureaucratic complex.

30 As in earlier models of political influence, there are groups in the private sector that benefit from the programs managed by the bureaucracy (or who represent those who benefit from them). Insofar as initiative in the programs has shifted from the private sector to government, these clientele groups typically arise *after* the program is established and are shaped in membership and basic aims by the corresponding features of the program. Specialized programs in public health, for instance, promote the organization and maintenance of correspondingly specialized associations among beneficiaries or their representatives. A fourth element is Congressional, consisting of members of the House and Senate who champion the interests of the clientele groups in the time-honored manner. Moreover, and this is a more recent development especially linked to the provision of staff to subcommittees and Congressional offices, these politicians often acquire a degree of expertise that enables them to cooperate critically with government professionals and outside groups, to make contributions to policy-making and, especially, as programs emerge and develop, to help mobilize consent to them among the general public and potential beneficiary groups.

In the domestic field, the technocratic coalition, consisting of these four elements, usually extends down through all three levels of government, the central core of professionals, collaborating closely and often resisting attempts of executive offices at any level to control and coordinate their activities. The National Institutes of Public Health with their powerful constituencies and extensions into state and local government are a kind of Pentagon of government medical activity. A similar coalition in the highway complex extends from the Bureau of Public Roads through the various state highway departments and constitutes a phalanx that presidents and governors have found it very difficult to control. As Deil Wright has recently written: "Policy control in this area [highways] usually rests less with governors than with alliances of highway engineers at all levels plus construction contractors and cement and equipment manufacturers." [22] The governmental worlds of welfare, education and housing, and urban development could also provide illustration.

Technocracy and Centralization

Technocratic coalitions can be agents of primary decentralization. This would be the case where one professional-bureaucratic complex was able to force the abandonment or reduction of programs in another complex that were the source of external costs to the first complex. More likely, as I have said, would be new government programs to correct the damage done by such externalities or to neutralize them. For example, the provision of new housing for people dislocated by highways rather than abandonment of the highway program itself. In short, *engrenage* among these professional bureaucratic complexes extending through three levels of government would seem to be a principal mechanism in the increasing activity of the federal government. Government programs create problems which are dealt with by the addition of further government programs.

But there is a more deep-seated reason why scientific knowledge should tend to produce centralization in higher jurisdictions and why persons trained in scientific disciplines should seek wider arenas for the application of their technique. By its nature scientific knowledge is general: that is, it has validity free of reference to any particular time or place. The knowledge that the professional and scientist bring to public policy is theoretical. It can be applied to similar problems whenever and wherever they arise. The very mental equipment of such a person therefore leads him to turn to that government which can deal with all such problems on the widest possible scale. As John Stuart Mill once remarked: "... centralization is based on general ideas; that is, the desire for power to attend in a uniform and general way, to the present and future needs of society." [23] Scientific rationalism (like rationalism of any sort) has this strong tendency toward uniformity and centralization. In any age, under any regime, the best is the enemy of diversity.

Technocratic Federalism

The growing professionalization of government has created a new type of centralizing coalition and a new stage in the development of

31

---

[22] Deil S. Wright, "Governors, Grants and the Intergovernmental System," in Thad Beyle and J. Oliver Williams (eds.), *The American Governor in Behavioral Perspective* (New York: Harper-Row, 1972), p. 188.

[23] Quoted by Angus Maude in *Encounter*, Vol. XXVI, No. 2 (February, 1966), p. 62.

American intergovernmental relations that may be called professionalized or technocratic federalism. Under it the relation of federal and state governments is continuous with the cooperative federalism of the previous generation insofar as the federal government, often through a categorical grant program, continues to use the states as instruments of national policy. A significant difference arises from the quite different manner in which the knowledge now being applied in policy-making has originated. As we have seen earlier, many of the New Deal programs originated from "experimentation" by states and cities. Such *ad hoc* empiricism is a method of seeking knowledge quite different from the theory-oriented research that often underlies the design of new programs today—such as, for instance, the testing by the Ford Foundation of the Ohlin-Cloward theory of juvenile delinquency in New York City before it was offered as the basis for a nationwide program in the war on poverty. Logically, it would seem possible that state and local governments could enlist this sort of resource as a basis for innovations in their jurisdictions. Some states have experimented with creating R&D facilities. Overwhelmingly, however, the research elite and its associated professionals, responding to their rationalist values and to the opportunities of governmental *engrenage*, seek a role in the federal arena. A few years ago, Victor Jones, listing the forty or so new federal programs in the area of the "urban crisis," remarked that no state had made a comparable response and some had not responded at all. [24] In 1969, when the Committee on State-Urban Relations of the Council of State Governments discussed state-local issue areas, with two small exceptions every issue area mentioned was the result of some federal program. [25] The characteristics of technocratic politics do much to explain this near monopoly of innovation by the central government.

32

VI

FUNCTIONS OF THE STATE UNDER

TECHNOCRATIC FEDERALISM

In the various stages of evolution of American federalism, the states have performed different functions in the polity as a whole: from the days when John Adams could call Massachusetts a "com-

[24] Victor Jones, "State and Metropolitan Reorganization." A paper presented at the 72nd National Conference on Government, sponsored by National Municipal League, Boston, November 14, 1966.

[25] Council of State Governments, *Second Annual Report of the Committee on State-Local Relations* (Lexington, Kentucky, 1969).

monwealth," "one moral whole"; through the Jacksonian era, when the states, as the vigorous centers of a mercantilistic democracy, became increasingly the main instruments of social choice; into the long Republican period of nation-building that saw the states as innovators leading and instructing the slow assumption of central responsibility by the federal government; followed by the New Deal when Washington became unmistakably the main agency of social choice. These phases are not merely successive; they are also in a degree cumulative. The centralizing, and occasionally decentralizing, coalitions that dominated the respective stages of this evolution persist into the present day and can be traced in the political and legislative history of national policy.

Similarly, the states continue to perform roles assumed in those earlier periods. In their present functioning in the American system, one can still discern traces of the "commonwealth," the mercantilistic polity, the laboratory of experimentation and the vehicle of "bread and butter" liberalism. For the student of intergovernmental relations, however, the principal question is what functions the states are tending to assume under the impact of the new phase of technocratic federalism. What are the tendencies created by the pressures and opportunities of this new style of politics and policy?

33

The system has not yet taken a stable form, so one must talk about pressures, opportunities and tendencies. Although this looseness of language heightens the temptation to set forth yet one more futile blueprint of what state governments "ought" to do, I shall restrain my impulse to prescribe and try to stick to the probabilities. The emerging new functions of the states, it seems to me, come under two headings: (1) planning and control, and (2) mobilizing consent, the activities under both headings being such as are appropriate to an "intermediate level of decision-making," as some have termed them.

Planning and Control

So much that is bogus has been written on the topic of planning that one must blush to mention the word. Yet it is the best term available to indicate the direction of certain new pressures and opportunities that have arisen at the level of state government. These were recently impressed on me—I will be anecdotal for the sake of concreteness—while working as chairman of a faculty group writing a book on the poverty problem in Massachusetts. [26]

To no one's surprise we discovered that the anti-poverty effort in Massachusetts was very largely federal in inspiration and financing. Total anti-poverty expenditure by all governments was well over one

[26] Samuel H. Beer and Richard Barringer (eds.), *The State and the Poor* (Cambridge, Mass.: Harvard University Press, 1970).

billion dollars, of which 62% had been raised by the federal government and 37% by the state. Washington was the principal center of innovation for the anti-poverty programs and the authors of the book did not hesitate to call on federal leadership for further action. They recognized that such government functions as maintaining economic equilibrium, promoting economic growth, managing the labor market, and redistributing wealth among classes and regions would remain functions of the central government. The function of planning and control that the state was acquiring was not that of an autonomous polity, but rather that of an intermediate decision-making body within a larger political system. Its task was coordination, planning and control with regard to national policies and programs.

This new role was highlighted by an unexpected trend—the declining role of local governments. Even as a channel of anti-poverty expenditure, the state dominated the local governments, the state accounting for 53% of all anti-poverty expenditure, while the local governments accounted for only 14%. The loss of function of the local governments was even more strikingly displayed when one looked at the source of the funds for anti-poverty expenditures. While the federal government raised 62% and the state 37%, local governments in Massachusetts raised less than 1% of total anti-poverty expenditure. In the light of these figures, it is not idle to speculate that, apart from educational expenditures, which themselves quite possibly will be shifted to the state in the near future, the cities and towns will soon bear the financial burden of only a few traditional functions, such as maintaining the physical fabric of streets, public buildings, etc., and preserving law and order, while state and federal governments raise the money for and control the design of the basic policy for other local government activity.

Generally, across the country secondary centralization within the states is marked as states take over functions previously performed by local governments. State government tax effort measured by the amount of taxes per $100 in personal income in a state reflects this shifting of the balance of activity away from local governments and toward state governments. Between 1965 and 1970, state tax effort rose from 5.4% to 6.5%, while local government tax effort remained constant at 5.2%.[27] Although local governments had been raising more and more revenue and increasing property tax rates and/or assessments to do so, in actual fact they were taking no larger a share of the income of the average taxpayer than five years earlier. It may be a reflection of the citizens' estimate of the relative value of state

[27] See below, Table 4.

to local services that there is so much complaint today about the rising local tax burden, although the state tax burden has actually risen more sharply.

The assumption of greater responsibilities by the states is obvious. Whether the states can develop the capacity to handle these responsibilities effectively is less clear. At times it must seem that state government is a principal example of how blind and unguided *engrenage* is leading to a constant expansion of the public sector.

In recent years, to be sure, many states have acted to improve their capacities for conscious central decision-making. Constitutional reform and government modernization have had considerable successes. More particularly, the technocratic potential of state administration has been strengthened and refined in many instances. Between 1965 and 1970 the amounts spent by state governments on "financial administration" and "general control" rose from $948 million to $1.720 billion, although without changing as a percentage of total direct state expenditure. Much of this increase is owing to federal incentives, especially 701 money made available for state planning purposes. At the federal level the proliferation of categorical grant programs in the 1960's was accompanied by an effort to strengthen the planning and control functions of the states, which responded with what have been called "the panaceas of the 1960's—PPBS, planning, coordination, the computer, data banks, issue analysis and systems analysis."[28] Office of Management and Budget Circular A95 gave the governor the important power of review over state plans that were required as a condition of receiving federal formula grants. Armed with this power, the governor's office in some states has mobilized the new resources of information and program development in an attempt to give shape and direction to the multitudinous initiatives of the departments. Against the background of the federal role in initiating and financing such a large part of state activities, as well as in providing the state executive with these tools of planning and control, it is not inappropriate to speak of the governors as the chief "federal systems officers."[29]

Many pressures point toward tighter and more effective planning and control. In our study of anti-poverty programs in Massachusetts, we found that direct expenditures for this purpose by the state government in 1968 amount to over $600 million in a total state expenditure (including trust funds) of about two billion dollars. These anti-poverty expenditures were made by departments across the whole spectrum of state government, involving health, education,

35

---

[28] Beyle and Williams, *op. cit.*, p. 187.
[29] Wright, *loc. cit.*, p. 187.

welfare, manpower, housing, food assistance, and so on. External costs and benefits among these separate departmental and agency efforts were multitudinous and substantial. Potentially, these spill-overs from government programs constituted opportunities and pressures that might well make acceptable to departments a comprehensive system to direct and control anti-poverty activities. Accordingly, one of our recommendations was that the state adopt a comprehensive anti-poverty program. The main element would be an anti-poverty budget, cutting across departmental lines to pick out those items constituting the anti-poverty effort. This budget would not supplement the ordinary budget, but would be used as a control on the allocation of resources within the anti-poverty effort and between it and other objects of public policy. To establish such a central coordinating activity would be to work with, not against, the grain of actual developments.

36

Massachusetts has not adopted an anti-poverty budget. Since 1969, however, it has been engaged in a wide-ranging effort to reorganize and modernize the departmental structure of state government. The aim is to create an administrative and budgeting system that will give managers more effective control over the outputs of individual programs and of state government as a whole. Some 213 separate agencies, boards and commissions have been combined into ten massive secretariats which, on the whole, people of exceptional talent have been found to head. But staffing of the offices of the new secretaries has been inadequate, and crucial questions of coordination and control have yet to be decided. Elsewhere in the country, similar responses to pressures for better planning and control and similar doubts regarding the outcome abound. Allen Schick's recent book on budget innovation in the states bears precisely on this point. He found that, while half the states reported that they had made a start in setting up a PPB system, actually in only one or two had such a system been effectively geared into decision-making. Although generally the states had set up new procedures for costing out work and activities, projecting future spendings, and presenting program comparisons, the basic structure of budgeting did not seem to have changed much nor did the quality of budget choice seem to have greatly improved.[30] Shick does not expect that the states will adopt the whole recipe for PPBS, but he does look forward to the adoption of its essential tools, especially analysis to provide evaluation of ongoing programs and to present the probable results and costs of alternative programs.

[30] Allen Schick, *Budget Innovation in the States* (Washington, D.C.:Brookings, 1971) p. 192.

The planning and control functions of the states have a special character arising from the fact that the states are intermediate in a three-tier system of government. On the one hand, the states are instruments of national policy. With their new technocratic equipment they perform functions of planning, coordination and control in regard to essentially national programs. On the other hand, looking toward the local governments, the state can perform the critical function of adjusting local jurisdictions and boundaries to correspond with program needs. Major examples would be the creation of metropolitan and regional arrangements within the state. Since states have done so little in this regard, one must speak of what could be, rather than what is. It is possible that, with appropriate federal incentives, they may become more active. Even in Massachusetts, which has recently become one of the most "liberal" states in the nation—between 1965 and 1970 the state tax effort rose from 4.3% to 6.1%—the political capacity to seize these opportunities of technocratic federalism have not appeared.

37

Mobilization of Consent

Insofar as states perform successfully as intermediate decision-making bodies in a national polity, one reason is that they are not mere regional administrative agencies, but rather political systems, each of which is endowed with a full panoply of elections, parties, pressure groups, legislators and executives, as well as functionally organized bureaucracies. When one looks at the failure of recent experiments with regard to administrative regions in England, one appreciates the importance of this highly political aspect. It would seem that, in an advanced modern polity, the administration of these massive and complex programs cannot be confined to its bureaucratic core, but must be embedded in a context of politics which will educate the clientele, win their cooperation and endow them with some real power of influencing outputs.

I call this function the mobilization of consent. The need for it is closely connected with the increasingly technical nature of government action. The burdens imposed on citizens are large, growing and often very hard to understand. Even when a program is aimed at conferring benefits there are problems of understanding how to qualify, how to conform to requirements, and what is the bearing on your own long-run interest. Indeed, it is a major problem simply to know what program is available to you as an individual, or institution or government entitled to grants-in-aid.

A few years ago the then Lieutenant-Governor of Georgia, George T. Smith, put his finger on this function when talking to a meeting of HEW regional officials in Atlanta. Stressing the importance to Georgia of federal aid, he reported the lack of education and communication with the citizenry and their confusion regarding certain programs (such as food stamps) and proposed that steps be taken to educate state legislators in federal programs so that they, in turn, could explain these matters to the voters. "People at home," he said, "will listen to state legislators." Congressman John Brademas has described how he, as a national legislator has performed the same function in response to the fact that many local leaders, as well as potential beneficiaries, do not understand much of the relevant federal legislation. "These activities of explaining, justifying, interpreting, interceding," he said, "all help normally, to build acceptance for government policy, an essential process in democratic government." [31]

From my knowledge of state legislators, I doubt that many of them live up to Lt.-Gov. Smith's expectations. The means by which citizens usually learn about state-administered federal programs is the relevant functional state bureaucracy. Indeed, state administration of a federally initiated program often leads to the creation of an organization of beneficiaries, or to the strengthening and adaptation of an existing organization. This is a natural part of the development of a professional-bureaucratic complex. Winning the consent and cooperation of affected private groups, however, cannot be a one-way transaction. The importance of the political context is that it gives the clientele as voters a means of influencing the administration of the program.

Over the course of years, a program which was once new and poorly understood and perhaps distrusted by clienteles and even state bureaucrats themselves, develops a solid base of support. Standards which initially were imposed by central government become generally accepted. The history of the Partnership for Health Act of 1966 illustrates the resulting nationalization of standards. This act consolidated fifteen categorical grants, most of which had been established for some years. The consolidation gave the states greater flexibility in allocating money, state and federal, among these programs (such as tuberculosis, venereal disease and cancer control). Moreover, such relaxation of the categorical requirements could now be risked, because the programs had come to be fully accepted in the states. As the House committee said when reporting out the bill, there was no longer a need for federal stimulation of these services since the states had shown that they now accepted them as a "continuing responsibility." [32]

[31] The Hon. John Brademas, "The Emerging Role of the American Congress." A paper presented at the Conference on the Future of the Legislative Power, Princeton University, April 14-17, 1966.

[32] House Report 2266; 89th Congress, 2nd Session; p. 46.

Gunnar Myrdal has put this central point in a larger context when he observed that the Welfare State, many of whose principles in the beginning were highly controversial, comes to be generally accepted in a polity, creating what he called a welfare culture. [33] In a country as large and complex as the United States, an intermediate tier, such as the states, thanks to their political systems, can perform an important function in this process of constantly building and adjusting consensus.

Finally, it should be noted that the highly political function of mobilizing consent is intimately related to the functions of planning and control. I came across a vivid illustration of this connection recently while interviewing some people in state government in Austin, Texas. The executive branch in Texas is notoriously one of the most fragmented in the country; the constitutional powers of the governor leave him with little beyond his veto as a means of getting action from some 130 agencies. In recent years, the governor's office has been greatly strengthened by the addition of a large corps of highly capable and technically trained—and usually young—people. With the aid of federal money a vigorous little technocracy has been fitted onto the archaic structure of Texas government. They are bubbling with plans, but the problem remains of how to get the agencies to go along, whether in administration or in relations with the legislature. A young technocrat in the Texas Industrial Commission, the agency charged with economic development, described the procedure. Many of their contacts are, of course, with local businessmen, especially the Chambers of Commerce. But, instead of merely asking local chambers what they want, the TIC takes down to them its computerized proposals for developing the area. Once they have won consent to these proposals from local businessmen, they then have a base from which pressure can be applied to legislators and, by means of legislators, to agencies of state government. By this roundabout process, agencies that would otherwise pay no attention to the governor's plans may be brought to see merit in them. The mobilization of consent is an essential stage in the process of planning and control.

39

VII
THE PROBLEM OF THE PUBLIC SECTOR

The preceding discussion of the character of American government in these days of technocratic federalism prepares the way for an examination of some of the large questions posed in Issue Topics 3, 4

---

[33] Gunnar Myrdal, *Beyond the Welfare State: Economic Planning and Its International Implications* (New Haven: Yale University Press, 1960) p. 2.

88   Samuel H. Beer

TABLE 2

Growth of Public Sector, U.S., 1960-1970

$ billion

Year	GNP	Expenditure (all gov'ts)	As % GNP	Defense Expenditure	Defense As % GNP	Non-defense As % GNP
1960	$503.7	$153.1	30.4	$45.9	9.1	21.3
1970	$976.8	$333.8	34.2	$76.8	7.9	26.3

Sources: *Statistical Abstract* (1970); *Government Finances 1969-70*; *Setting National Priorities: The 1973 Budget* (Brookings Institution, Washington, D.C., 1972), pp. 11, 43.

and 8. The question common to all three Issue Topics on which I particularly wish to focus attention concerns the allocation of responsibilities and resources between the private and public sectors.

In recent years, the movement of the line between the two sectors shows a steady and fairly rapid advance of primary centralization. Indeed, in the United States as a whole, the public sector grows more rapidly than the gross national product. According to Table 2, during the 1960's expenditure by all governments, federal, state and local, rose from 30% of national product to 34%. A substantial part of this growth of public expenditure derived from defense budgets and especially from the additional burdens of the Viet Nam War, which in 1970 added some $14.4 billion to federal expenditure—about 1.5% of GNP. But, even apart from military expenditures, the public sector would have been proportionally larger in 1970 than in 1960. In the decade as a whole, civilian spending at all levels of government rose by about 25%. In contrast, defense budgets took a smaller proportion of national product in 1970 than in 1960. Indeed, during the postwar period, defense spending reached its peak as a percentage of national product in 1953—13.6%—after which it declined fairly steadily in comparison with national product and civilian expenditures. Looking only at federal expenditures, a recent Brookings study similarly shows the sharp relative rise of social programs between 1963 and 1973. [34]

It is sometimes said that the public sector—meaning particularly its civilian programs—has been "starved." Answers to this question tend to be less than wholly objective. It is at least clear that during the sixties a significant reordering of priorities took place aimed at nourishing our social needs, and according to the Brookings study, the momentum of this reordering continues in the early seventies.

[34] Charles Schultze *et al.*, *Setting National Priorities: The 1973 Budget* (Washington, D.C.: Brookings, 1972), Table 1.3 p. 11.

In spite of the peculiarities of our situation, it is important to note that the growth of the public sector in the United States parallels a similar growth in other Western countries. In Britain, for instance, there was also a surge in social spending around the middle sixties. Comparative figures for 1969 show taxation in the United States to be of the same order of magnitude as in other advanced countries. (See Table 3.) Similarly, I would suggest, the principal causes of this trend are to be found in those long-run forces of modernization which have been the main topic of this essay and which have powerfully affected Europe as well as America. War—whether cold war or hot war—is a powerful centralizer. But so, also, is the technocratic, welfare state. Even in an era of détente and declining defense budgets, we could expect continued expansion of the public sector.

This comparison also confirms the view that federalism has no direct bearing on the size of the public sector. Taxes take just about the same proposition of the national product in the German Federal Republic as in unitary France and Britain. Indeed, the case of Yugoslavia makes it clear that federalism is entirely compatible with socialism.

TABLE 3

Taxes as percent of GNP (1969)
(all levels of government)

U.S.	U.K.	France	Germany
32	39	38	38

Source: *Setting National Priorities: The 1973 Budget* Washington, D.C.: (Brookings, 1972), p. 427.

Turning to the United States, one sees support for the same general point. Some have argued that, as compared with the federal government, the states are more conservative and specifically less-inclined to tax and spend. Paul Appleby typified this judgment in his remark that when you say the states should do something you mean it should not be done. The states do show relatively lower capacities for innovation, as one would expect in a time when problems are becoming ever more nationalized. But it is emphatically not the case that, quantitatively, the states have failed to keep up with the federal government in taxing and spending. Table 4 shows that in the last half of the 1960's the states, not the federal government, led the way in increasing the tax burden. If they have not been notable innovators, the states have nonetheless continued and increased their massive efforts to finance the traditional programs of the American welfare state. In sum, the way a political system divides power between levels of government seems to have little to do with how it will divide resources and responsibilities between the public and private sectors. It is modernization, not unitary government, that correlates with growth of the public sector.

The growing size and complexity of the public sector raises in an acute form the question of "delivery of services" posed in Issue Topic 5. This terminology suggests a rather humdrum problem of public administration. Nothing could be further from the truth. The failures that give emphasis to this question have been responsible not only for great waste, but also for much human distress. They illustrate the tendencies of programs of the technocratic, welfare state not merely to miss their targets, but to produce side-effects that aggravate the problems with which they are supposed to cope. Medicaid, while providing medical services for many older poor people, has also helped price such services out of the range of others hardly better off. The immense funds of Title I of the Elementary and Secondary Education Act of 1965 have commonly been disbursed simply as additional funds for local school boards instead of reaching the disadvantaged children they were intended to benefit. Salaries have eaten up inordinately large portions of the money appropriated for anti-poverty and model cities programs. Manpower training has probably not increased the number of persons employed. Speculators have profited handsomely from recent housing acts.

This question of "delivery of services" is one aspect of the larger problem of planning and control. However men may disagree on the allocation of resources between public and private spheres, they must agree that, ideally, this allocation should reflect a conscious social choice which is embodied in the actual performance of government. The problem is twofold: the long-run aspect is that the addition, deletion and revision of programs should result from analysis comparing various options, not simply from blind and uncensored *engrenage*; the short-run aspect is that the services should be performed as planned, subject to periodic readjustment in the light of outcomes. As we have seen in the earlier discussion, forces inherent in technocratic federalism run counter to these conditions. The most important is the tendency of means to escape control by a comprehensive view of the ends they are to serve. No less serious is the difficulty of setting up effective systems of evaluation and review without which any grand scheme of overall coordination is itself inoperative. This is not a problem created by ideology. Whether a government is conservative, liberal or radical, it will be confronted with the task of trying to establish effective direction and control over a gigantic public sector.

TABLE 4

Comparative Tax Effort

(Taxes per $100 of personal income)

	1965	1970
Federal Government	19.1	19.8
State Governments	5.4	6.5
Local Governments	5.2	5.2
All Governments	29.6	31.3

Sources: *Governmental Finances, 1964-5, 1969-70*; and *State Government Finances in 1965, 1970*. U.S. Department of Commerce, Bureau of the Census.

43

Once again, it puts the problem in perspective and helps guard against parochial explanations and remedies if we see that the problem of planning and control confronts and often confounds the governments of other advanced countries. There is irony here. For modernity, with its rationalist orientation and scientific skills has endowed the contemporary state with unprecedented power over man and nature. At the same time, however, these instrumentalities continually threaten to break loose from the purposes of public policy and to follow their own chaotic and unintended course. In the days of laissez-faire, men rightly feared the unregulated economy as the source of coercive social forces. Today, the polity, including the very instrumentalities designed to modify and control the economic and social environment, has joined and in some countries superseded the economy as the machine that threatens to master man. Bureaucratization matches industrialization as the source of blind development and unintended social costs. In this respect, the American polity merely shares the fortune of all highly developed modern societies.

The problem of planning and control is severe and the need for new tools—for analysis, evaluation, reorganization—is as great as even students of administration say it is. The trouble is that these themes have little political appeal. In the political marketplace they cannot compete with demands for greater equality, redistribution of income, and new and larger social programs. As a consequence, attempts to strengthen planning and control lack any political thrust that would come from having the support of a large and broad-based coalition. This central problem of the technocratic, welfare state awaits a political solution.

VIII

THE POLITICS OF NATIONAL DEMOCRACY

Even more political are the questions raised by Issue Topics 6, 7 and 9. They relate to a problem of control, meaning not administrative control, however, but the direction and control of government by the democratic electorate. A principal hypothesis implied is that, at the present time, the American people do not exercise adequate control over their government and that this control can and should be made more effective. Without hiding my own preferences, I will look at this question analytically, saying what seems more and what less feasible.

One structural change proposed as a means of raising the efficacy of political participation by citizens—and their feelings of efficacy—is "community control." (See Issue Topic 6.) Proposals of this sort have taken many forms, but, in general, the idea is to decentralize city government to areas in which residents are unified by some strong common interest, ethnic identity or other element of cohesion. The small size of these units would make it possible for people to take a more efficacious part in governing them, while their social basis would reduce conflict and make agreement easier to achieve.

The idea is appealing both as a means of enhancing democracy and of reducing conflict. But, as we observed when discussing Mancur Olson's theory of internalities, it is hard in this day of increasing interdependence to identify functions of government whose impact is so limited geographically as to justify their control being entrusted to small jurisdictions. With regard to jurisdictional structure, the problem of the typical metropolitan area today is that it already contains too many more or less independent governments—hence, the familiar complaint of "Balkanization." The model cities programs do illustrate how a degree of local participation can be linked with the administration of some urban programs. But the very low turnout for these elections and the modest powers of the bodies so elected warn that this scheme is hardly likely to be an important means of meeting the problem of citizen efficacy.

In general, within the states as within the nation, the movement of basic decision-making power is away from the smaller and toward the larger jurisdiction. This trend does not exclude far-reaching measures

44

of administrative decentralization. It is compatible with relaxation of central control where national policies have established strong political and bureaucratic support in state and local systems. It is compatible with revenue-sharing and consolidation of categorical grants. What it does make highly unlikely is any attempt to increase substantially the power and autonomy of the narrower jurisdiction whether neighborhood, city or state, in relation to the more inclusive jurisdiction. Community control, home rule and states rights are doctrines with a restricted future. Decentralization is not likely to be the means by which the problems of responsiveness and efficacy are met.

Indeed, simple arithmetic may seem to cast a shadow on any proposed solution to this problem. How can any modern polity be responsive to the individual voter and in such a way that he sees its responsiveness and so feels the efficacy of his participation? In the company of 75 million other people voting for president, how could any rational man presume that his participation makes a difference (unless, of course, he is one of the leaders who controls or influences large numbers of votes)? This problem, needless to say, darkens the prospects of democracy not only on a nationwide scale but also on a statewide or citywide scale, where constituencies still number in millions or hundreds of thousands. The problem of efficacy would seem insoluble except under a regime of governmental localism that would be totally inadequate to the major problems confronting its participants today.

45

Political science and political experience do have answers to the problem. The classic answer is the political party. By his identification with a body that actually does command enough votes to make a difference in electoral and policy outcomes, the individual can achieve a sense of efficacy. Individuals cannot win elections, but parties can; and one of their functions has been to mediate between individuals and their government, endowing them with a sense of power and self-government. No doubt such feelings include their fair proportion of illusion. On the other hand, a party with a broad material and ideal base may elicit, represent and promote important interests of its members that would otherwise be overlooked in the clash of narrow occupational, ethnic and regional divisions. As we have seen in the historical sections of this essay, American parties have often embraced those coalitions that have produced the political thrust for the next stage in national development. Our political parties, based on these evolving coalitions, have in crucial respects, served as instruments of national democracy.

The record of the past is encouraging, but its contrast with the current state of American parties and American politics is a measure of the present difficulty of the problem of efficacy and responsive-

ness. In recent years, our parties have entered a state of decline
which may or may not be only a stage of transition. Ticket-splitting,
electoral volatility, sharply rising numbers of independents and
declining sentiments of identification with either of the main
parties—these indices of party decomposition are abundantly in evidence. Closely associated with this development are two other major
changes: a steep rise in political disaffection and a striking fragmentation of political sentiment and political effort.

The first constitutes a large and sudden shift in public attitudes.
Only ten years ago in a comparative study of political cultures,
Almond and Verba rendered a buoyant, not to say rapturous report
on the United States. Together with the British, we were outstanding
in our possession of a set of attitudes "supportive of a stable democratic process"—"the civic culture." [35] Indeed, in expressions of
pride in our governmental and political institutions we excelled even
the British—by a score of 85 to 46. Not long after these conclusions
were published, opinion began rapidly to change, plunging to depths
of disapproval in the late sixties. At the present time, for many
Americans, sentiments of hostility and distrust strongly color their
attitudes toward government at all levels. This widespread discontent
impedes the success of programs and so leads to further withdrawal
of consent and cooperation. Its effect is particularly important
where, as in many of the new programs, government is attempting to
change behavior and motivation, for, in the case of these programs,
the atmosphere within which the program is carried out is as important to its success as the material constituents of the programs themselves.

In analyzing our present discontents, commentators sometimes
express fear of "polarization." The image called up by this word,
suggesting as it does the confrontation of two massive forces, hardly
describes our present political environment. During and after the
New Deal, as we have seen, our political alignment did tend toward a
dualism with a fairly clear class basis. This dualism, still strongly
marked as late as 1960, was splintered in the late sixties. Today, blue
collar workers can no longer be taken for granted by Democrats and
rich professionals are no longer automatically Republicans. Even
among the strongly disaffected, conflicts of interest and symbolic
tensions are many and sharp. The voice of the people incoherently
calls for protection of the environment, full employment, civil rights,
freedom of association, reward according to merit, local autonomy,
metropolitan planning, price stability and the rights of labor. Such

---

[35] Gabriel A. Almond and Sidney Verba, *The Civic Culture: Political Attitudes and
Democracy in Five Nations* (Princeton, N.J., Princeton University Press, 1963) p. vii.

fragmentation must make the reformer (and perhaps even the conservative who believes in party government) wish for the return of
that degree of polarization that characterized the era of the Roosevelt coalition.

Again, it helps to see that these troubles afflict not only the
United States. Like other major characteristics of our present society
and polity, they proceed less from peculiarities of the American
system and its history than from forces inherent in modernization.
One of the oldest criticisms of modernity is that, by constantly
pressing the division of labor and raising the mobility of populations,
it reduces social cohesion and tends to atomize the polity. At the
same time, "the acids of modernity"—Walter Lippmann's phrase—eat
away at the structures of authority and consent based on religion,
nationality and ancient communal life. [36] A mood of what some have
called "alienation" or "political cynicism" afflicts not merely the
United States but all Western countries.   47

To understand the causes of our troubles and to see that other
countries share them does not tell us whether or how they will be
remedied. Most comment on the future shape of our politics takes
one well beyond the boundaries of political science and into the
murky realms of prophecy and partisanship. I will say only that I
find that our present discontents, incoherent and negative as they
may be, could be converted into the moral basis of a new plane of
national development. One major feature of the present mood is
both paradoxical and indicative: this is its almost obsessive fixation
upon the nation. To be sure, the nation is usually mentioned only to
be blamed and held wanting, not to say corrosively aspersed. Yet this
very criticism represents an underlying identification with the nation
and a new and higher expectation of what it should do and could be.
I discern here a heightening of national consciousness, now in its
fragmented and negative phase, that may produce a new positive
phase of strength and integration. In such curious ways does American democracy work to make the nation more of a nation.

[36] Walter Lippman, *A Preface to Morals* (New York: Macmillan, 1929) Ch. IV, "The
Acids of Modernity."

MICHAEL LES BENEDICT

PRESERVING FEDERALISM:
RECONSTRUCTION AND
THE WAITE COURT

48

I. NATIONAL SOVEREIGNTY, STATE RIGHTS, AND STATE SOVEREIGNTY

It has become a commonplace of American history that the Chase and Waite Courts subverted Congress's post–Civil War Reconstruction legislation. A typical reading is that the Court engaged in a "judicial counterrevolution," a "judicially-directed perversion of what the abolitionists tried to write into the Constitution," the most "striking instance in American constitutional history of outright judicial disregard for congressional intent."[1] Historians and legal scholars, in recognition that the postwar constitutional amendments were designed to write an antislavery theory of American rights into the Constitution, have damned the Court, essentially for two reasons. First, because the Court was so restrictive in its construction of the Fourteenth Amendment's Privileges and Immunities Clause. Second, because the Court gutted Republican efforts to make the national government the guarantor of citizens' rights. The vehicle for this subversion, it is charged, was the doctrine of "State

---

Michael Les Benedict is Associate Professor of History, Ohio State University.

[1] Gressman, *The Unhappy History of Civil Rights Legislation*, 50 MICH. L. REV. 1323, 1339 (1952); PRITCHETT, THE AMERICAN CONSTITUTION 712 (2d ed. 1968).

action."[2] While this criticism has flourished since the 1930s, John Mabry Matthews and Charles Warren had earlier described the same judicial misbehavior, except that, on the whole, Matthews and Warren approved of it.[3]

No feat of revisionism can turn the Waite Court of the 1870s and 1880s into a firm and unflinching defender of black peoples' rights. But the fact is that the modern criticism distorts our constitutional history. It fails to distinguish the position of the Waite Court from its successors, accepting, for instance, the reactionary decisions of the Fuller Court in civil rights cases as logical extensions of Waite Court doctrines, which they were not. Moreover, the modern criticism proceeds from the assumptions of a constitutional theory of nationalism that is indigenous to our age, presumes that Reconstruction legislation proceeded upon the same theory, and judges the Supreme Court's nationalism against that standard. Historians of Reconstruction, however, are beginning to realize that Civil War–era Republicans adhered to a concept of nationalism far less expansive than what has since emerged. They fought for the Union they had known and loved, a Union in which the authority of the national government was balanced against the rights of the States. And they fought for freedom. After victory they wanted to make the rights inherent in that freedom secure, but they wanted to secure them within the old federal framework. As southern whites contested every inch of freedom's advance, it became ever more apparent that the Republicans' commitments both to federalism and

49

---

[2] BETH, THE DEVELOPMENT OF THE AMERICAN CONSTITUTION, 1877–1917 191–99 (1971); BLAUSTEIN & ZANGRADO, CIVIL RIGHTS AND THE NEGRO: A DOCUMENTARY HISTORY 246–69 (1968); 2 BOUDIN, GOVERNMENT BY JUDICIARY 94–150 (1932); FRANKLIN, FROM SLAVERY TO FREEDOM 331–32 (3d ed. 1967); HARRIS, THE QUEST FOR EQUALITY 58, 82–91 (1960); KELLY & HARBISON, THE AMERICAN CONSTITUTION 462–65 (5th ed. 1976); KLUGER, SIMPLE JUSTICE 62–65 (1976); LOGAN, THE BETRAYAL OF THE NEGRO 105–24 (1965); MAGRATH, MORRISON R. WAITE 130–49 (1963); MILLER, THE PETITIONERS 85–164 (1966); MITCHELL & MITCHELL, THE BIOGRAPHY OF THE CONSTITUTION 304–10 (2d ed. 1975); RODELL, NINE MEN 165–67 (1955); Boudin, Truth and Fiction about the Fourteenth Amendment, 16 N.Y.U. L. REV. 19 (1938); Note, Section 1983 and Federalism, 90 HARV. L. REV. 1133 (1977); Gaffnev, History and Legal Interpretation—Early Distortion of the Fourteenth Amendment by the Gilded Age Court, 25 CATH. U. L. REV. 207, 236–47 (1972); Graham, Our "Declaratory" Fourteenth Amendment, in GRAHAM, EVERYMAN'S CONSTITUTION 295 (1968); Kinoy, The Constitutional Right of Negro Freedom, 21 RUTGERS L. REV. 387 (1967); Woodson, Fifty Years of Negro Citizenship as Qualified by the United States Supreme Court, 6 J. NEGRO HIST. 1 (1921).

[3] MATTHEWS, LEGISLATIVE AND JUDICIAL HISTORY OF THE FIFTEENTH AMENDMENT 97–126 (1909); 2 WARREN, THE SUPREME COURT IN UNITED STATES HISTORY 533–48, 600–18 (rev. ed. 1926).

to security of rights were in conflict, and they were forced to make
an agonizing choice between them. The Supreme Court under Chase
and Waite was faced with the same dilemma. Responding to it, the
Justices did not bow to racism, betray nationalism, and revive discredited theories of federalism. They made the same effort as did
the Republicans to preserve the balance of the old federal system,
to protect the States' rights which had been an implicit element of
nationalism as it had been understood for fifty years, and at the same
time to recognize in Congress enough power to protect civil rights.
In the process they reached surprisingly liberal conclusions about
congressional power under the postwar Amendments, given the
dominant ideas of federalism which provided the context in which
they operated.

50

The essential difference between modern constitutional nationalism and that prevalent at the time of the Civil War was the latter's
acceptance of the notion that there was a reserved area of State
jurisdiction beyond the competence of national authority. Modern
constitutional doctrine reflects the Supreme Court's conclusions in
United States v. Darby—the deathblow to "dual federalism"—that
the jurisdiction of the State governments is defined by that of the
national, that the Tenth Amendment "states but a truism that all is
retained which has not been surrendered."[4]

The focus of our attention has shifted dramatically from where
it was when Americans went to war in 1861. The earlier era was
State centered. In practical terms this was reflected in the small
effect of national government on Americans' daily lives. From birth
to death the only federal officials most Americans were likely to
see in peacetime were their postmaster and a pension agent. Both
were local men appointed for political services rendered in their own
communities.[5] In political terms it was reflected in the continued
domination from the 1830s to the eve of war of a political party
founded upon a narrow conception of national power. And in legal-
constitutional terms it was reflected in the acceptance, even among
those who favored energetic national government, of the principles
of what Edward S. Corwin identified as "dual federalism."

The basic doctrine of dual federalism—what we identify today as

---

[4] 312 U.S. 100, 124 (1941). See Corwin, *The Passing of Dual Federalism*, 36 VA. L.
REV. 1 (1950); Note, *supra* note 2, 90 HARV. L. REV. at 1156–90.

[5] HYMAN, A MORE PERFECT UNION 7–14 (1973); PALUDAN, A COVENANT WITH
DEATH 11–20 (1975).

"States' rights"—was, in Corwin's words, that "the coexistence of the states and their power is of itself a limitation upon the national power."[6] As originally fashioned by Andrew Jackson, other Democratic statesmen and politicians, and the Taney Court from principles articulated by Jefferson and Madison, it proceeded upon the assumption that the States had been sovereign before the ratification of the Constitution; that the Union was an indissoluble compact in which some sovereign jurisdiction was taken from the States and delegated to the national government; that the States retained sovereign jurisdiction in other areas and were therefore the equals of the national government in the federal system; that each of these governments had a complete, independent structure with which to exercise its powers and could not require the other to administer its laws; that the powers of each government were completely distinct and independent with each supreme in its own sphere; that the Tenth Amendment confirmed this structure and guaranteed that national powers would not be interpreted in such a way as to subvert the reserved sovereign jurisdiction of the States; and that the Supreme Court was the umpire of the federal system with the duty to protect the sovereignty of each government from encroachment by the other.[7] (Corwin did not coin the phrase "dual federalism" until the 1930s. Earlier he referred to a "moderate states rights" doctrine, to distinguish it from Calhounite "state sovereignty.")[8] Those who advocated broad expansion of the national role from the Progressive to the New Deal eras—especially Corwin himself—argued that this doctrine of dual federalism had subverted the nationalistic principles expounded by the Marshall Court. But in reality, most Americans had accepted dual federalism as implicit in those principles.

For most pre–Civil War nationalists, the crucial determinant of the constitutionality of national legislation was its purpose. Early nationalists like Marshall and Hamilton were determined to prevent

51

---

[6] Corwin, *The Power of Congress to Prohibit Commerce*, 18 Corn. L. Q. 477, 482 (1933).

[7] See Corwin, The Commerce Power versus States Rights (1936); Corwin, National Supremacy: The Treaty Power v. State Power (1913); Corwin, note 4 *supra*; Corwin, note 6 *supra*.

[8] For a good statement of dual federalist principles, see Schroth, Dual Federalism in Constitutional Law 376–80 (1941) (unpublished Ph.D. dissertation, Princeton University). Schroth, like his mentor Corwin, frequently confuses "dual federalism" with "state sovereignty."

an exaggerated commitment to State jurisdiction from inhibiting the national government from exercising its authority effectively. They stressed the sovereign authority of the national government to fulfill the purposes for which it was created. While they did not articulate the limits upon national jurisdiction very clearly, those limits were plainly there. "Let the end be legitimate, let it be within the scope of the constituton, and all means which are appropriate, which are plainly adapted to that end . . . are constitutional,"[9] wrote Marshall in his most celebrated enunciation of nationalist constitutional theory. This is something quite different from the modern gloss which has sustained a national police power and which might be stated, "Let the means be legitimate, let them be within the scope of the constitution, and all ends which are achieved by those means are constitutional." Although Marshall condoned the framing of legislation to carry out mandated objectives in such a way as to promote more general goals, it is plain that the constitutionality of such legislation depended "on their being the natural, direct, and appropriate means, or the known and usual means, for the execution of the given power."[10] Over and over again in his opinions and his extrajudicial defenses of them, Marshall defined the powers of the national government in terms of their purpose, deducing their constitutionality from the postulate that "in America, the powers of sovereignty are divided between the government of the Union, and those of the states. They are each sovereign with respect to the objects committed to it, and neither sovereign with respect to the objects committed to the other."[11] Although Marshall and his colleagues stressed the national sovereignty aspect of these principles to sustain national legislation against attacks based on State sovereignty, he left no doubt that the sword could cut both ways. In *McCulloch v. Maryland*, Marshall stated plainly: "Should congress under the pretext of executing its powers, pass laws for the accomplishment of objects, not entrusted to the government, it would become the painful duty of this tribunal . . . to say that such an act was not the law of the land."[12] Legal scholars have recognized re-

52

---

[9] McCulloch v. Maryland, 4 Wheat. 316, 421 (1819).
[10] GUNTHER, ED., JOHN MARSHALL'S DEFENSE OF McCULLOCH v. MARYLAND 186 (1969).
[11] 4 Wheat. at 410.
[12] *Id.* at 423.

cently that the divergence between the Marshall and Taney Courts on matters of federalism has been exaggerated, but they have emphasized primarily the Court's continued commitment to national supremacy.[13] The foregoing suggests that the Taney Court's concern for the integrity of State jurisdiction was also implicit in the decisions of its predecessor. Although it is unclear whether Marshall would have accepted all the doctrines of dual federalism, and it is certain that Story rejected most of them, most Americans did not recognize in them any fundamental inconsistency with nationalist principles.[14] Even while disagreeing vigorously with strict constructionists over where the line between national and State jurisdiction lay, a nationalist like Edward Everett agreed that there was "a wise and happy partition of powers between the national and state governments, in virtue of which the national government is relieved from all odium of administration."[15] Webster too admitted the necessity for keeping "the general government and the State government each in its proper sphere."[16] It was that consideration which

53

---

[13] BAXTER, THE STEAMSHIP MONOPOLY: GIBBONS V. OGDEN, 1824 117–18 (1972); FRANKFURTER, THE COMMERCE CLAUSE UNDER MARSHALL, TANEY AND WAITE 46–73 (1937); Garvey, *The Constitutional Revolution of 1837 and the Myth of Marshall's Monolith*, 18 W. POL. Q. 27 (1965); KELLY & HARBISON, note 2 *supra*, at 282, 331; SCHMIDHAUSER, SUPREME COURT AS FINAL ARBITER IN FEDERAL-STATE RELATIONS, 1789–1937 50–79 (1958); SCHWARTZ, FROM CONFEDERATION TO NATION 7, 26–28, 33–37 (1973).

[14] Marshall surely would have disagreed with the Taney Court *dicta* in various Commerce Clause cases that inspection laws, immigration regulations, and the like were, by definition, exercises of police power and, therefore, not subject to congressional commerce regulation. See Gibbons v. Ogden, 9 Wheat. 1 (1824), and Willson v. Blackbird Marsh Creek Co. 2 Pet. 245 (1829), and compare New York v. Miln, 11 Pet. 102 (1837); BALDWIN, A GENERAL VIEW OF THE ORIGIN AND NATURE OF THE CONSTITUTION AND GOVERNMENT OF THE UNITED STATES 181–97 (1837); *The License Cases*, 5 How. 504 (1847); *The Passenger Cases*, 7 How. 283 (1845); and Groves v. Slaughter, 15 Pet. 449 (1841).
Marshall did take a distinctly dual federalist view of Congress's taxing power, when he announced that "Congress is not empowered to tax for those purposes which are in the exclusive province of the states." *Gibbons*, 19 Wheat. at 199; GUNTHER, note 8 *supra*, at 100.
Story was consistent in his rejection of dual federalism. STORY, COMMENTARIES ON THE CONSTITUTION OF THE UNITED STATES §§ 1063–66, §§ 1254–1322, §§ 955–89, §§ 1072–89 (1833). But see Prigg v. Pennsylvania, 16 Pet. 539 (1842). Story believed that "new men and new opinions have succeeded" the nationalistic ones that he and Marshall shared, and he contemplated resigning his place on the Taney Court. 2 STORY, ED., LIFE AND LETTERS OF JOSEPH STORY 527–29 (1851).
Gerald Gunther has indicated that there were limits to Marshall's nationalism, GUNTHER, note 10 *supra*, at 19–21. William H. Hatcher noted, but could not explain, a weakening in the Marshall Court's nationalism in its later years. Hatcher, *John Marshall and States' Rights*, 3 S.Q. 207 (1965).

[15] Quoted in PALUDAN, note 5 *supra*, at 14–15.

[16] WEBSTER, THE GREAT SPEECHES AND ORATIONS OF DANIEL WEBSTER 272 (Whipple ed. 1889).

led him to urge adherence to a strict conceptual differentiation between national regulations of interstate commerce and state police powers affecting commerce, such as inspection and quarantine laws; toll-road, ferry, and bridge regulations; and restrictions on black immigration. "If all these be regulations of commerce," he warned, "does it not admit the power of Congress . . . upon all these minor objects of legislation, . . . acknowledg[ing] the right of Congress over a vast scope of internal legislation, which no one has heretofore supposed to be within its powers" and subjecting "all State legislation over such subjects . . . to the superior power of Congress, a consequence which no one would admit for a moment."[17] Thus, on the eve of Civil War, even the Republican party, the political heir to the nationalist sentiments of the Federalists and Whigs, acknowledged the obligation to preserve "the rights of the States . . . inviolate . . . , and especially the right of each State to order and control its own domestic institutions . . . exclusively, 'rights' essential to that balance of power on which the perfection and endurance of our political fabric depends."[18]

54

It was not the doctrine of dual federalism, or "State rights," that threatened to disrupt the Union in 1861, but rather that of "State sovereignty." While this theory of federalism involved many principles similar to those expressed by dual federalists with the strictest notions of national power, permitting legal and especially political cooperation of adherents of the two theories within the Democratic party, it differed on the crucial question of where authority lay to define constitutional powers. Even the most extreme dual federalist acknowledged the Supreme Court as the ultimate arbiter of the federal system. State sovereignty exponents, convinced that sovereignty was indivisible and therefore that the Union was merely a league of sovereign states, insisted that the people of the individual

[17] Like most Americans in an age of inactive government, Webster did not recognize the inconsistency between such statements and his Storyesque argument in defense of the protective tariff that there could be no inquiry into the motive with which Congress levied duties and imposts once the power was conceded. He may have been blinded to the implications of such an argument because he, like Story, believed protection of domestic industry to be within the acknowledged scope of foreign commerce power and not an indirect benefit of that power. See *id.* at 321.

[18] The phrasing comes from resolutions two and four of the Republican national platform of 1860. PORTER & JOHNSON, NATIONAL PARTY PLATFORMS, 1840–1956 32 (1956). For similar descriptions of pre–Civil War legal theory in regard to federalism, see BENNETT, AMERICAN THEORIES OF FEDERALISM 168–69 (1964); Note, *supra* note 2, 90 HARV. L. REV. at 1138–41.

States had the ultimate right to define the boundaries of the federalism.[19] Moreover, by the 1850s southern adherents of State sovereignty were challenging other fundamental tenets of dual federalism, insisting that as an agent of sovereign states the national government was obligated to use its power to promote the interests of all of them and never to oppose the interests of any of them. Thus, they challenged the cherished notion of their closest allies that the national and State spheres were distinct and independent.[20] When applied to the national government's power to govern United States territories, the conflict disrupted the Democratic party. When State sovereignty doctrines were expressed in the form of nullification and secession, the fundamental differences with even the most anti-national-power dual federalists became apparent, as northern Democrats rallied to the flag. In terms of constitutional theory, the Civil War was fought between the concepts of State sovereignty and what we would now identify as State rights.

55

Historians have accurately perceived in the legislation of the Civil War years an application of constitutional nationalism much more similar to our own than what had gone before—a "Blueprint for Modern America," as one termed it.[21] Even as they fought to maintain national supremacy, northerners divided on whether the very existence of sovereign States imposed some limitation upon the jurisdiction of the national government. Under the pressure of war, Republicans seemed to repudiate the idea, justifying confiscation, emancipation, construction and operation of railroads and telegraphs, and supervision and care of large populations as "necessary and proper" uses of the war power. At the same time they took a modern view of the taxing and spending power, repudiating dual federalist limitations upon it, and reconfirmed interpretations of national authority over interstate and foreign commerce that justified protective tariffs and national support for internal improvements. Traditionalists, mostly Democrats but also conservative ex-

---

[19] BAUER, COMMENTARIES ON THE CONSTRUCTION, 1790–1860 (1952); BENNETT, note 18 supra, at 108–59; 4 BEVERIDGE, THE LIFE OF JOHN MARSHALL 309–96 (1919); CARPENTER, THE SOUTH AS A CONSCIOUS MINORITY, 1789–1861 (1930); HAINES, THE AMERICAN DOCTRINE OF JUDICIAL SUPREMACY 285–344 (1959); MUDGE, THE SOCIAL PHILOSOPHY OF JOHN TAYLOR OF CAROLINE 60–76, 133–44 (1939); SPAIN, The Political Thought of John C. Calhoun (1968); Note, Judge Spencer Roane of Virginia: Champion of States' Rights—Foe of John Marshall, 66 HARV. L. REV. 1242 (1953).

[20] Bestor, State Sovereignty and Slavery: A Reinterpretation of Proslavery Constitutional Doctrine, 1846–1860, 54 J. ILL. H. SOC'Y 1 (1961).

[21] CURRY, BLUEPRINT FOR MODERN AMERICA (1968).

Whigs and Republicans, responded with a barrage of denunciation in the press, Congress, political oratory, legal arguments and court opinions, and treatises on constitutional law.[22]

Even as they set precedents for modern nationalism, however, Republicans could not shake off their commitment to older notions of federalism. Republican reliance upon a broad interpretation of national war powers to sustain their legislation enabled them to isolate the peacetime restrictions from wartime experience. When the war ended Republican leaders urged: "During the prevalence of the war we drew to ourselves here as the Federal Government authority which had been considered doubtful by all and denied by many of the statesmen of this country. That time . . . has ceased and ought to cease. Let us go back to the original condition of things, and allow the States to take care of themselves."[23]

56

This commitment to State rights within the federal system seriously compromised Republican efforts to establish full freedom and equality for the newly freed slaves. Historians now recognize that every Reconstruction-era effort to protect the rights of citizens was tempered by the fundamental conviction that federalism required that the day-to-day protection of the citizen had to remain the duty of the States.[24] Direct national control of the South and early super-

---

[22] See HYMAN, note 5 *supra* at 156–70, 207–62; RANDALL, CONSTITUTIONAL PROBLEMS UNDER LINCOLN (1951); PALUDAN, note 5 *supra* at 109–69; BURGESS, THE CIVIL WAR AND THE CONSTITUTION, 1859–1865 (1901); SILBEY, A RESPECTABLE MINORITY 62–88 (1977). Democrats invited the cooperation of all opponents of Republican policies during the war and after, often denominating themselves Conservatives, announcing "that the aim and object of the Democratic party is to preserve the Federal Union and the rights of the States unimpaired." PORTER & JOHNSON, note 18 *supra*. at 34; SILBEY, *supra*. at 138 and *passim*.

[23] CONG. GLOBE, 39th Cong., 1st Sess., 2446 (1866). These remarks were made by James W. Grimes, one of the most important Republican Senators and a member of the Joint Committee on Reconstruction, which framed the Fourteenth Amendment, in the course of opposing a bill that would have established a national quarantine during the cholera epidemic of 1866—a clear exercise of a national "police" power under the authority of the Commerce Clause. The bill failed, with Republicans dividing and Democrats almost unanimously opposed. See Benedict, *Contagion and the Constitution: Quarantine Agitation from 1859 to 1866*, 25 J. H. MED. & ALLIED SCI. 177 (1970). See also the similar remarks of Fessenden, the chairman of the Joint Committee on Reconstruction, CONG. GLOBE, 39th Cong., 1st Sess., 27–28 (1866); PALUDAN, note 5 *supra*, at 28–48; Benedict, *Preserving the Constitution: The Conservative Basis of Radical Reconstruction*, 61 J. AM. H. 65 (1974) [hereinafter *Preserving the Constitution*.]

[24] BELZ, A NEW BIRTH OF FREEDOM 113–37, 157–82 (1976); *Preserving the Constitution;* HYMAN, note 5 *supra*, at 282–306, 414–542; KELLER, AFFAIRS OF STATE 37–73 (1977); Kelly, *Comment on H. M. Hyman's Paper*, in HYMAN, NEW FRONTIERS OF THE AMERICAN RECONSTRUCTION 40 (1966); PALUDAN, note 5 *supra*; Note, note 2 *supra*, 90 HARV. L. REV. at 1141–47.

vision of the transition from slave to free labor were considered
temporary and justified on grounds expressly contrived to avoid
setting precedents dangerous to the future balance of federalism.[25]
As to the permanent protections for Americans' rights, despite arguments to the contrary by those modern legal scholars who write in
the tradition of a new nationalism, all the evidence of the congressional discussions, the ratification debates, and the public controversy indicates that Republicans intended the States to retain primary jurisdiction over citizen's rights. They attempted to write into
the Constitution an obligation that antislavery theorists already believed incumbent on the States: the requirement that they protect
all citizens equally in fundamental human rights. They did not intend the national government to replace the States in fulfilling that
obligation. Throughout the early years of Reconstruction, the focus
of Republican concern was active State discrimination against blacks
in basic rights. Republicans stressed over and over again that if the
States simply performed their constitutional obligations to protect
citizens equally in basic rights, the Reconstruction legislation and
Amendments would work no substantial change in the federal
system.[26]

57

---

[25] *Preserving the Constitution.*

[26] See, *e.g.,* CONG. GLOBE, 39th Cong., 1st Sess., 1785 (1866) (Sen. Stewart); *id.*
at 476, 600 (Sen. Trumbull); Letter from Ohio Governor Jacob D. Cox to Andrew
Johnson (March 22, 1866); Schurz, *The Logical Results of the War,* in 1 SPEECHES,
CORRESPONDENCE, AND POLITICAL PAPERS OF CARL SCHURZ 377 (F. Bancroft, ed. 1913).
For a clear indication of how State-centered Republicans understood the Fourteenth
Amendment to be, see Fairman, *Does the Fourteenth Amendment Incorporate the Bill of
Rights? The Original Understanding,* 2 STAN. L. REV. 5, especially 41–134 (1949). The
evidence is all the more persuasive because Fairman was dealing with a different question—the scode of rights protected, not which government was to do the protecting. See
also *Preserving the Constitution, passim.*
     An excellent insight into the framers' early interpretation of the national govern-
ment's power to enforce the provisions of the Fourteenth Amendment is revealed by
Representative John A. Bingham, explaining the meaning of the original version, worded
to give Congress direct, positive power to make laws necessary and proper to protect
the civil rights. Insisting that State officials were obligated to protect the rights enumerated in the Bill of Rights, he argued: "The question is, simply, whether you will give
by this amendment to the people of the United States the power, by legislative enactment, to punish officials of States for violations of the oaths enjoined upon them by their
Constitution? That is the question, and the whole question. The adoption of the
proposed amendment will take from the States no rights that belong to the States. They
elect their Legislatures; they enact their laws for the punishment of crimes against life,
liberty, and property; but in the event of the adoption of this amendment, if they conspire
together to enact laws refusing equal protection to life, liberty, or property, the Congress
is thereby vested with powers to hold them to answer before the bar of the national courts
for the violation of their oaths and of the rights of their fellow-men." CONG. GLOBE, 39th

Since Americans believed that the main purpose of government was to protect citizens against wrongs perpetrated by others, Republicans believed that by banning State discrimination they were guaranteeing positive protection to freed slaves. "The presumption was that these States would be obedient to the Constitution and the laws," James G. Blaine remembered.[27] "But for this presumption, legislation would be but idle play, and a government of laws would degenerate at once into a government of force. In enacting the Reconstruction laws, Congress proceeded upon the basis of faith in Republican government."[28] Had southerners only fulfilled this naive expectation, the sanguine prophecy made by Ohio's conservative Republican Governor Jacob Dolson Cox might have come true: "If the Southern people will . . . do right themselves, by legislation of their own which shall break down distinctions between classes . . . , the law itself would become of little practical moment . . . and a very short time would make it a practically dead letter."[29]

58

Cong., 1st Sess. 1090 (1866). The wording of the proposed amendment at this time was: "That Congress shall have power to make all laws which shall be necessary and proper to secure to the citizens of each State all the privileges and immunities of citizens in the several States, and to all persons in the several States equal protection in the rights of life, liberty, and property." *Id.* at 1033–34. Thus, with an amendment apparently worded to give Congress the broadest possible range of powers, its author intended it to operate upon State laws and State officials, not to authorize Congress to establish a general criminal code.

[27] 2 BLAINE, TWENTY YEARS OF CONGRESS 466 (1886).

[28] *Ibid.* The Lockean conviction that "the great and chief end of . . . men uniting into commonwealths and putting themselves under government, is the preservation of their property," by which is meant the individual's "life, liberty and estate," was an axiom of American constitutional thought, enshrined in the Declaration of Independence's avowal that all men were endowed "with certain unalienable Rights" and "[t]hat to secure these rights Governments are instituted among men." See LOCKE, TWO TREATISES ON GOVERNMENT 163–84 (Cook ed. 1947). See also THE FEDERALIST 35 (Rossiter ed. 1961); WILSON, THE WORKS OF JAMES WILSON 171–72 (McCloskey ed. 1967); CHIPMAN, PRINCIPLES OF GOVERNMENT 55–56 (1833); 1 LIEBER, MANUAL OF POLITICAL ETHICS 156–57 (Woolsey ed. 1890) (Joseph Story called this work "the fullest and most correct development of the theory of what constitutes the States that I have ever seen." *Id.* at 3.), 1 LEGGETT, A COLLECTION OF THE POLITICAL WRITINGS OF WILLIAM LEGGETT 162 (Sedgwick ed. 1840); MULFORD, THE NATION: THE FOUNDATIONS OF CIVIL ORDER AND POLITICAL LIFE IN THE UNITED STATES 285–88 (1870); RAWLE, A VIEW OF THE CONSTITUTION OF THE UNITED STATES OF AMERICA 89, 92 (2d ed. 1829); WEDGEWOOD, THE GOVERNMENT AND LAWS OF THE UNITED STATES 66–68 (1867); YOUNG, THE CITIZEN'S MANUAL OF GOVERNMENT AND LAW 17–21 (rev. ed. 1858). Justice Bushrod Washington had placed "protection by the government" at the very head of the list of citizens' privileges and immunities in his celebrated opinion in Corfield v. Coryell, 6 Fed. Cas. 546, 551 (# 3,230) (C.C.E.D. Pa. 1823).

[29] Letter from Jacob D. Cox to Andrew Johnson (March 22, 1866).

It was not until the Ku Klux Klan violence of 1868 through 1872 that Republicans began to recognize that superficially equal laws did not guarantee full protection of rights. As early as 1870 they began to pass laws making it a crime punishable in national courts for individuals to infringe upon citizens' right to vote whether or not they acted under State authority,[30] despite the fact that the Fifteenth Amendment was worded as a prohibition upon States just as the Fourteenth Amendment was.

By 1871, when they passed the so-called Ku Klux Klan Act, Republicans had developed a carefully reasoned constitutional argument that State failure to protect rights guaranteed by the Fourteenth and Fifteenth Amendments amounted to such State action as justified congressional intervention. And that intervention could take the form of positive congressional enactments to punish individual wrongdoers.[31] Even this interpretation, however, stressing as it did the States' primary jurisdiction over crimes, put a tremendous strain upon Republicans. It seemed to encroach upon the heart of State jurisdiction. Key leaders, like Lyman Trumbull, the author of most of the Reconstruction legislation of the 1860s, abandoned the party over the issue. Even as he pressed for direct national punishment of ordinary crimes where States failed to act, John A. Bingham, the chief author of the Fourteenth Amendment, exclaimed, "God forbid . . . that by so legislating we would strike down the rights of the State . . . . I believe our dual system of government essential to our national existence."[32] No one who reads the debates over the Ku Klux Klan Act can fail to be impressed with the effort Republicans made to reconcile their desire to afford protection to citizens in the South with the contours of the federal system they wanted to preserve, one with "a clear and well defined line between the powers of the General Government and the powers of the States."[33]

59

[30] Enforcement Act of 1870, 16 Stat. 140 (1870).

[31] Avins, *The Ku Klux Klan Act of 1871: Some Reflected Light on State Action and the Fourteenth Amendment*, 11 ST. LOUIS U.L.J. 331 (1967); HARRIS, note 2 *supra*, at 41–53. An excellent summary of the development of the arguments may be found in the reader's guide section of AVINS, THE RECONSTRUCTION AMENDMENTS' DEBATES: THE LEGISLATIVE AND CONTEMPORARY DEBATES IN CONGRESS ON THE 13TH, 14TH, AND 15TH AMENDMENTS xx–xxiv (1967).

[32] CONG. GLOBE, 42d Cong., 1st Sess., app. 84 (1871).

[33] Representative Charles Williard, *id.* at app. 187; Lionel A. Sheldon, *id.* at 368–69; Jesse H. Moore, *id.* at app. 112; John B. Hawley, *id.* at 382; Garfield, *id.* at app. 150–53;

The suspension of the privilege of the writ of *habeas corpus* in South Carolina in 1872, the direct interference of the national government to settle disputed elections results in the South in 1872–73 and 1874–75, and especially the 1875 purge of Democrats from contested seats in the Louisiana State legislature at the point of federal bayonets made it ever more difficult to reconcile protection of rights in the South with the federal system Americans wanted to preserve. An old abolitionist expressed the simple but tragic truth when he wrote as Republicans gave up the struggle: "We never contemplated when we took the freed blacks under the protection of the North that the work was to be for an unlimited time. We hoped that if for a few years we lent them a helping hand, self interest, if not a sense of right, would prompt the Southern whites to do their duty by them."[34]

60

Americans' desire to preserve the old balance of federalism was reflected in the post–Civil War writings of legal scholars and political philosophers. Before the war, exaggerated notions of State rights enervated the national government and finally almost destroyed it, the respected jurist Isaac F. Redfield wrote in 1867: "The great danger now will be that things will rush in the opposite direction, and the central authority from being limited and straitened in all its powers and functions, . . . will be in danger of absorbing all the important functions of governmental administration."[35] The most important legal thinker of the post–Civil War era, Michigan Judge Thomas M. Cooley, echoed him: "The proper boundary between national and state powers . . . has been found so satisfactory that we have willingly endured a war in its defence. The cost of that war has been in vain if at its conclusion we propose to treat that boundary as a shadow line which none need regard."[36] The Civil War killed State sovereignty, and the postwar era saw the growing influence of the "organic theory" of American nationalism posited most influentially before the war by Francis

---

Burton H. Cook, *id.* at 485–86; Horatio C. Burchard *id.* at app. 313–15; Note, note 2 *supra,* 90 HARV. L. REV. at 1156.

[34] Letter from Francis Cope to Laura Towne (November 19, 1877), reprinted in ROSE, REHEARSAL FOR RECONSTRUCTION 403–04 (1964).

[35] Redfield, *The Proper Limits between State and National Legislation and Jurisdiction,* 15 AM. L. REG. 193, 197 (1867).

[36] Cooley, *The Legal Aspects of the Louisiana Case,* 1 S.L. REV. (n.s.) 18, 42 (1875).

Lieber. These nationalists asserted that American nationality pre-
dated the Constitution. They argued that the Constitution ema-
nated from an entire people rather than from States or even the
people of the States. But their conclusion also sustained the doctrines of dual federalism. The people of the United States created
both State and national governments. "The two together constitute
the government of the United States," explained Orestes A. Brownson: "The powers of each are equally sovereign . . . . In their respective spheres neither yields to the other. In relation to the matters
within its jurisdiction, each government is independent and supreme
in regard of the other."[37] Another influential nationalist legal scholar
put it more succinctly: "Within their respective spheres, these two
classes of governments are as independent as though they represented different nations."[38] As a recent investigator has observed,
"The nationalist commentators of the post–Civil War era were able   61
to reconcile their uncompromising hostility to the Confederacy . . .
with an ardent advocacy of their own particular version of state
rights. Indeed, it seemed at times that their nationalism consisted
almost solely in their attacks upon the doctrines of nullification and
secession."[39] No wonder, then, that as he left Faneuil Hall after

---

[37] BROWNSON, THE AMERICAN REPUBLIC, ITS CONSTITUTION, TENDENCIES AND
DESTINY 234, 256 (1865).

[38] Pomeroy, *The Force Bill,* 12 THE NATION 268, 269 (1871).

[39] Larsen, *Nationalism and States' Rights in Commentaries on the Constitution after the
Civil War,* 3 AM. J.L. HIST. 360, 366 (1959). For a similar conclusion, see PALUDAN,
note 5 supra, at 219–73; and McCurdy, *Legal Institutions, Constitutional Theory, and the
Tragedy of Reconstruction,* 4 REV. AM. HIST. 203 (1976). Walter H. Bennett concluded
that postwar constitutional theory elevated the United States to the plane of sovereign
equality with the States. BENNETT, note 18 *supra,* at 179–81. For what might be called
"state rights nationalism," see BROWNSON, note 37 *supra;* POMEROY, AN INTRODUCTION
TO THE CONSTITUTIONAL LAW OF THE UNITED STATES (1870), and Pomeroy, *The Supreme Court and Its Theory of Nationality,* 12 THE NATION 445 (1871); HARE, AMERICAN
CONSTITUTIONAL LAW (1889); HURD, THE THEORY OF OUR NATIONAL EXISTENCE, AS
SHOWN BY THE GOVERNMENT OF THE UNITED STATES SINCE 1861 (1881). Cooley was
one of the few nationalist constitutional commentators to adhere to the notion that the
people of the individual states had created the Union, but his acceptance of national
supremacy was as thorough as that of other analysts. COOLEY, A TREATISE ON CONSTITU-
TIONAL LIMITATIONS (2d ed. 1871); Cooley, *The Guarantee of Order and Republican
Government in the United States,* 2 INT'L REV. 57 (1875).

With the works of these legal scholars, compare the analysis of Timothy Farrar, a
Civil War nationalist with ideas more similar to our own. According to Farrar, the
States derived their power not from preexisting sovereignty but from the Constitution.
Since the national government determines whether a subject is under national or state
jurisdiction, it is the United States which is sovereign and not the State government. Like
modern constitutional nationalists, Farrar scouted the notion of implied limitations upon

Charles Sumner delivered his intensely nationalistic lecture, *Are We a Nation?* Sumner's senatorial colleague, Henry Wilson, grumbled, "The States are something still."[40]

II. THE COURT, THE AMENDMENTS, AND FEDERALISM

It was this State-centered nationalism, held in common with different degrees of commitment (especially when compared to the necessity to protect freedmen's rights) by Democrats and Republicans, politicians and jurists, that the Supreme Court articulated in the years following the Civil War. Both the States and the United States held equal places in our scheme of government, each with independent authority within its sphere of jurisdiction—"an indestructible Union, composed of indestructible States," as the Court expressed it in one of its most memorable phrases.[41] And the Constitution imposed just as great a duty to protect and maintain the integrity of the State governments as the national government. "The Supreme Court has thus . . . placed the nation and the States upon the same footing," nationalist constitutional commentator John Norton Pomeroy wrote happily. "As we have in this theory the greatest security for the nation, we have also the greatest security for the several States."[42]

The consequence of such concern for the integrity of State as well as national jurisdiction was the continued adherence to the doctrines of dual federalism. As early as 1864 Republican State courts in Indiana, Wisconsin, and Michigan were applying dual federalist glosses to the doctrines enunciated by Marshall in *McCulloch v. Maryland*, holding unconstitutional provisions of the federal internal revenue code levying stamp taxes upon State court

62

---

national power arising from preexisting State sovereignty. "All state rights and powers must be carved out of what the people of the United States have left after having delegated the powers of the Constitution [to the national government]. . . . They have given no right to anybody, to come in competition with their own supreme law, or any power lawfully exercised under it." Farrar, *State Rights*, 21 NEW ENGLANDER 695, 723 (1862).

[40] 4 PIERCE, MEMOIR AND LETTERS OF CHARLES SUMNER 335 (1893).

[41] Texas v. White, 7 Wall. 700, 725 (1868). For a full appreciation of the state-centeredness of the Supreme Court doctrine expressed in this case, read Lane Cty. v. Oregon, 7 Wall. 71 (1868), decided at the same Term and in conjunction with it.

[42] Pomeroy, note 39 *supra*, at 445. Chase wrote Pomeroy that the opinion reflected many of Pomeroy's ideas. POMEROY, note 39 *supra*, at 521n.

writs, State tax deeds, or surety bonds required of State officers,[43] despite the fact that the Constitution limits the national taxing power only by requiring that taxes be levied directly and for common defense, payment of debts, or the national welfare. With Cooley and future Republican Senator Isaac Christiancy concurring, Michigan Supreme Court Justice James V. Campbell justified such rulings in sweeping dual federalist language: "Our whole system is based upon the principle that local affairs must be administered by state authority. . . . The same supreme power which established the departments of the general government, determined that the local governments should also exist for their own purposes. . . . Each of these several agencies is confined to its own sphere, and all are . . . independent of other agencies, except as thereby made dependent. There is nothing in the constitution which can be made to admit of any interference by Congress with the secure existence of any State authority within its lawful bounds. And any such interference by the indirect means of taxation, is quite as much beyond the bounds of the national legislature, as if the interference were direct and extreme."[44]

63

Cooley endorsed this principle of State immunity from taxation in his *Constitutional Limitations*.[45] Four different United States Attorneys General expressed similar opinions between 1867 and 1871.[46] And the Supreme Court concurred in *Collector v. Day* in 1871[47] and *United States v. R.R. Co.* in 1873.[48] Even while affirming Congress's power to tax State-chartered banks out of existence in one of the most nationalistic decisions of the nineteenth century, the Court agreed that "there are . . . certain virtual limitations [upon the taxing power] arising from the principles of the Constitution itself. . . . It would undoubtedly be an abuse of the power . . . if exercised for

---

[43] Warren v. Paul, 22 Ind. 279 (1864); Jones v. Estate of Keep, 19 Wis. 369 (1865); Sayles v. Davis, 22 Wis. 217 (1867); Fifield v. Close, 15 Mich. 505 (1867); State ex rel. Lakey v. Garton, 32 Ind. 1 (1869).

[44] Fifield v. Close, 15 Mich. at 509.

[45] COOLEY, note 39 *supra*, at 482–83.

[46] The Attorneys General did not hold provisions of the internal revenue laws unconstitutional, but opined that Congress could not have intended to include States and municipalities among taxable corporate bodies because of the principle involved. 12 OP. ATT'Y GEN. 277 (1867); 12 OP. ATT'Y GEN. 376 (1868); 13 OP. ATT'Y GEN. 67 (1869); 13 OP. ATT'Y GEN. 439 (1871).

[47] 11 Wall. 113 (1871).

[48] 17 Wall. 322 (1873).

ends inconsistent with the limited grants of power in the Constitution."[49] Thus the Court rejected Story's views and took the same position that would overturn the Agricultural Adjustment Act some sixty-five years later.[50]

The Justices also displayed a disposition to sustain State police regulations in the 1870s and 1880s. Quick to overturn State interferences with foreign or interstate commerce for the mere purpose of raising revenue and interferences with the free travel of United States citizens,[51] the majority put safety, moral, and health regulations under much milder scrutiny. The Court denied that the "original package rule" of *Brown v. Maryland*[52] meant that the national commerce power superseded State prohibition laws or that national licensing of lottery-ticket or liquor sales to raise money displaced State bans on such sales.[53] It held that States could ban corporations chartered in other States from doing business within their boundaries and that businesses engaged in interstate commerce could be charged more for licenses than those whose business was limited to States or municipalities.[54] The Court sustained broad State taxing authority against charges that State and municipal levies inhibited interstate or foreign commerce.[55] It protected States' power to tax dividends on national bank shares.[56] It followed the precedent of *Willson v. Blackbird Creek Marsh Co.*[57] rather than the *Wheeling*

64

---

[49] Veazie Bank v. Fenno, 8 Wall. 533 (1870). Although the Court held that it could not question the reasonableness of the exercise of legislative power where it is expressly granted, it also relied heavily upon Congress's power to regulate the currency as justification for the tax. The Court was plainly uncomfortable with the implications of the broader argument.

[50] United States v. Butler, 297 U.S. 1 (1936). See also the dual federalist dicta pervading Justice Field's rejection of State court power to enforce writs of habeas corpus on behalf of those claimed to be held by national authority. *Tarble's Case*, 13 Wall. 397, especially at 406–08 (1872).

[51] E.g., Crandall v. Nevada, 6 Wall. 35 (1867); Ward v. Maryland, 12 Wall. 163 (1871); *Case of the State Freight Tax*, 15 Wall. 232 (1873); Henderson v. Mayor of New York, 92 U.S. 259 (1875).

[52] 12 Wheat. 419 (1827).

[53] McGuire v. Commonwealth, 3 Wall. 387 (1866); Pervear v. The Commonwealth, 5 Wall. 475 (1867). See also *The License Tax Cases*, 5 Wall. 462 (1867).

[54] Paul v. Virginia, 8 Wall. 168 (1869); Osborne v. Mobile, 16 Wall. 479 (1873).

[55] Waring v. The Mayor, 8 Wall. 110 (1869); Woodruff v. Parham, 8 Wall. 123 (1869); *Cases of the State Tax on Ry. Gross Receipts*, 15 Wall. 284 (1873).

[56] Van Allen v. Assessors, 3 Wall. 573 (1866); National Bank v. Commonwealth, 9 Wall. 353 (1870).

[57] 2 Pet. 245 (1829).

Bridge case[58] to sustain the State's authority to charter the building of railroad bridges across tidal waters.[59] And, in a forerunner to the *Granger Cases*,[60] the Justices ruled that State requirements that railroads set and post rates once a year, punishing those who levied charges in excess of the stated tariff, were legitimate exercises of the police power rather than commerce regulations.[61]

Constitutional historians recognize that the majority of the Justices adopted a similarly restrained view of the Due Process Clause of the Fourteenth Amendment in the early years of its construction. Despite persistent efforts to set it up as the protector of "vested rights" against legislative infringement, they refused to enforce the Clause as a restraint upon the substance of laws.[62] As late as 1889, Charles A. Kent instructed a college audience, "Many as are the suits in which its jurisdiction rests on the allegation of such a conflict, in perhaps no case has the judgment of the State court been reversed on this ground."[63]

The Supreme Court's construction of the legislation and constitutional amendments of the Reconstruction era must be understood within the context of this State-centered nationalism. For if Republican legislators ultimately came to see that their desire to protect

65

---

[58] Pennsylvania v. Wheeling & Belmont Bridge Co., 13 How. 518 (1851).

[59] Gilman v. Philadelphia, 3 Wall. 713 (1866).

[60] 94 U.S. 113 (1877).

[61] R.R. Co. v. Fuller, 17 Wall. 560 (1873).

[62] The most famous in this line of decisions were the *Granger Cases*, Munn v. Illinois and its sister cases, 94 U.S. 113 (1877). In 1878 a frustrated Justice Miller noted the number of due process cases being filed despite the Court's consistent rebuffs, complaining, "There is here abundant evidence that there exists some strange misconception of the scope of this provision, as found in the Fourteenth Amendment."Davidson v. New Orleans, 96 U.S. 97, 104 (1878). The complaint was repeated by—of all people—Justice Field in Missouri Pac. Ry. v. Humes, 115 U.S. 512, 519–20 (1885). See KELLY & HARBISON, note 2 *supra*, at 468–88, although with hindsight the authors stress how doctrines of "substantive due process" slowly developed rather than how long that development took. See also FAIRMAN, MR. JUSTICE MILLER AND THE SUPREME COURT, 1862–1890 179–206 (1939); MAGRATH, note 2 *supra*, at 173–203.

For the relationship of the doctrine of "vested rights"—the idea that there were strict limitations upon legislative power over property rights—and "substantive due process," see Corwin, *The Doctrine of Due Process of Law Before the Civil War*, 24 HARV. L. REV. 366, 460 (1911); Corwin, *The Basic Doctrine of American Constitutional Law*, 12 *Mich. L. Rev.* 247 (1914).

[63] Kent, *Constitutional Development in the United States, as Influenced by Decisions of the Supreme Court since 1864*, in COOLEY, HITCHCOCK, BIDDLE, KENT, & CHAMBERLAIN, CONSTITUTIONAL HISTORY OF THE UNITED STATES AS SEEN IN THE DEVELOPMENT OF AMERICAN LAW 232 (1889).

rights was at war with their desire to preserve federalism, the Court had to face that dilemma even earlier, and in its starkest aspect, in the *Slaughter-House Cases* of 1873.[64]

The *Slaughter-House Cases* brought into focus the Fourteenth Amendment's potential for revolutionary change in American federalism in a way the black-rights-oriented legislation of Congress simply had not. The doctrines the lawyers for the New Orleans butchers advocated were aimed at more than the Crescent City Live-Stock and Slaughter-House Company's "monopoly" (which was in reality no monopoly at all). Their arguments attacked State legislation regulating the State lottery, municipal gas supply, levee repair, funding of the State debt, "prodigal expenditures and jobs innumerable."[65] The Fourteenth Amendment was designed to protect individuals from State invasion of all citizens' fundamental rights and immunities, broadly construed, they insisted. Assume a narrower purpose and "the State may deny individual rights and liberties, and claim to perform all the offices and duties of society, and under the names of socialism, communism, and other specious pretences, control all the revenues and labor of the State."[66] The argument for broad protection for citizens' privileges and immunities under the Fourteenth Amendment was no effort to secure the rights of black Americans. It was an invitation to the Court to write the "vested rights" doctrine into the Constitution through the Privileges and Immunities Clause in 1873 as they would write it into the Due Process Clause twenty years later. Defendant's counsel saw this clearly: "The result of the argument against the validity of this charter must ... be this: that the 14th amendment does not prohibit State legislatures from passing acts of municipal legislation which abridge the privileges and immunities of citizens, provided such acts appear to be reasonable, but does prohibit the passing of acts which appear to be unreasonable; that it is for this court to determine whether such acts are reasonable or unreasonable."[67]

66

---

[64] 16 Wall. 36 (1873).

[65] Argument for Plaintiff, *Slaughter-House Cases*, 21 L. ED. at 395–99.

[66] Brief for Plaintiff upon Reargument, *Slaughter-House Cases*, 83 U.S. (16 Wall.) 36 (1873), in 6 KURLAND & CASPER (EDS.), LANDMARK BRIEFS AND ARGUMENTS OF THE SUPREME COURT OF THE UNITED STATES: CONSTITUTIONAL LAW 639, 669 (1975) [hereinafter LANDMARK BRIEFS].

[67] Brief for the Defendants, 6 LANDMARK BRIEFS at 587, 601.

Moreover, this proposition was being posited in an era of active congressional civil rights legislation, long before the Supreme Court became the most active protector of rights among the branches of the national government. Although the butchers' lawyers avoided the issue, there was no convincing reason why Congress should not accept the same invitation so temptingly offered the Justices. Even proponents of the broad view worried about such a revolution in the federal system. John Norton Pomeroy tried to demonstrate that the rights secured by the Privileges and Immunities Clause could be enforced only by the judiciary, but he was not very convincing. What was convincing was the terrible consequence he predicted from such an assumption of jurisdiction by Congress: "If the Democratic party should come to power, it is certainly within the range of possibilities that it should endeavor to uphold and sustain the liquor interest by Congressional legislation directed against State prohibitory and license laws. . . . [T]he State laws could be declared void; the States enacting and sustaining them could be described as 'abridging the privileges and immunities of citizens of the United States' . . . " Likewise, Congress could protect privileges and immunities by nullifying Sabbath laws or restrictions against church endowments.[68]

It is in light of the commitment of Americans generally to the idea that the States had a reserved area of jurisdiction that the query in Justice Miller's majority opinion must be read: "Was it the purpose of the fourteenth amendment . . . to transfer the security and protection of all the civil rights [broadly defined] . . . from the States to the Federal Government? . . . [W]as it intended to bring within the power of Congress the entire domain of civil rights heretofore belonging exclusively to the States?"[69] If so, "Congress . . . may pass laws . . . limiting and restricting the exercise of legislative power by the States, in their most ordinary and usual functions," and the Supreme Court would be "constitute[d] a perpetual censor upon all legislation of the States, on the civil rights of their own

67

---

[68] Pomeroy, *Political Precedents,* 12 THE NATION 300, 301 (1871); Pomeroy, *Police Duty,* 12 *id.* at 284–85; Pomeroy, *The Rights of Citizens,* 12 *id.* at 335–36. In his dissenting opinion in *Slaughter-House,* Bradley insisted that the Amendment would virtually be self-executing, but did not echo Pomeroy's strictures against congressional authority. 16 Wall. at 123–24.

[69] 16 Wall. at 77.

citizens, with authority to nullify such as it did not approve as consistent with those rights."[70]

Given such possibilities, it is not surprising that the majority of the Justices sought to avoid what seemed to many the obvious meaning of the Fourteenth Amendment's Privileges and Immunities Clause. And given the doctrines of dual federalism that the Court had already endorsed in *Collector v. Day*, it is not surprising that they found the way out in the notion that Americans held privileges and immunities as citizens of the United States different from those they held as citizens of the individual States.

Constitutional historians have severely criticized the *Slaughter-House* decision for nullifying the plain meaning of the Fourteenth Amendment's Privileges and Immunities Clause as defined by its framers.[71] As early as 1879, a critic wondered what fiery old Thaddeus Stevens's reaction would have been if told that all he had intended to secure through that clause were the rights of ex-slaves to protection on the high seas, to travel freely between States, or to petition the government.[72] There can be no doubt that the point was well made. Whatever Republicans intended "privileges and immunities of citizens of the United States" to mean, it was more than that. But Stevens would have been just as incredulous to learn that he had given Congress or the Supreme Court the power to nullify Louisiana's regulations of slaughterhouses, and that is the nub of the conundrum the Court faced. As the *American Law Review* understood, the problem in construing the Amendment's provisions was to "apply their letter . . . to new states of fact not contemplated by Congress nor the legislatures that made them."[73]

Critics of the *Slaughter-House Cases* argue that the Court majority ignored the well-known intent of the Fourteenth Amendment and that Miller's eloquent articulation of its "one pervading purpose," to secure full liberty to blacks, was merely "a strategic ob-

68

---

[70] *Id.* at 78.

[71] KELLY & HARBISON, note 2 *supra*, at 476; Beth, *The Slaughter-House Cases Revisited*, 23 LA. L. REV. 487 (1963); Graham, *Our "Declaratory" Fourteenth Amendment*, in GRAHAM, EVERYMAN'S CONSTITUTION, note 2 *supra*, at 319–35; MILLER, note 2 *supra*, at 102–69; 4 BOUDIN, note 2 *supra*, at 94–150.

[72] Royall, *The Fourteenth Amendment: The Slaughter-House Cases*, 4 S.L. REV. (n.s.) 558, 576n (1878).

[73] Note, 8 AM. L. REV. 732 (1873).

fuscation of the issues."[74] But it was those who contended for the broad interpretation of privileges and immunities who had to concede they were innovating. "It is possible that those who framed the article were not themselves aware of the far reaching character of its terms," Justice Bradley admitted in his circuit court decision sustaining the butchers.[75] "Yet, if the amendment, as framed and expressed, does in fact bear a broader meaning, and does extend its protecting shield over those who were never thought of when it was conceived and put in form . . . , it must be presumed that the American people, in giving it their imprimatur, understood what they were doing."[76] The butchers' Democratic counsel insisted they were compelled on principle to "assume" a broader meaning for the Amendment than the merely "partisan" one that might be attributed to it.[77] It was the Court majority and the defendant's lawyers, on the other hand, who argued, "So far as can be judged by the public debate upon the subject, it was certainly never intended or contemplated that this Amendment should receive such a construction." "Have Congress and the whole nation been deceived?" they asked. "Have they done what they did not intend to do?"[78]

69

In virtually eliminating the Privileges and Immunities Clause as a source of national power to protect citizens' rights, Miller and the lawyers for the Slaughter-House "monopoly" insisted that they intended no subversion of black men's liberty. As noted, Miller was eloquent upon the "one pervading purpose" of the Amendment to protect black rights, and several of the "monopoly's" lawyers were active radical Republicans.[79] Their conviction that the well-known

---

[74] Beth, note 71 *supra*, at 501.

[75] *Live-Stock Dealers and Butcher's Ass'n v. Crescent City Live-Stock Landing and Slaughter-House Co.*, 15 Fed. Cas. 649, 652 (# 8,408) (C.C.D. La. 1870).

[76] *Ibid.*

[77] Note 66 *supra*, at 657, 668.

[78] Argument for the Defendant, 21 L. Ed. 399, at 401 (1873); Brief for Defendant, Slaughter-House Cases, in 6 LANDMARK BRIEFS at 603–04; Brief for Defendant on Reargument, *id.* at 726–27; 16 Wall. at 67–72.

[79] 16 Wall. at 71. Among defendant's counsel were Thomas J. Durant, a Louisiana radical who had pressed for black suffrage as early as 1864, and Matthew Hale Carpenter, Republican Senator and floor manager of the Civil Rights Act of 1875. Miller himself, a conservative Republican, was impelled to support congressional Reconstruction legislation by southern subversion of freedmen's liberty after the war. FAIRMAN, note 62 *supra*, at 189–93.

purpose of the Amendment "was to secure all citizens and persons the same rights as white citizens and persons"[80] suggests that they placed primary reliance upon its Equal Protection Clause.[81] That ultimately proved to be a weak reed, but there is no reason to believe that a broader definition of the Privileges and Immunities Clause would have provided any stronger support for black rights. The real obstacle to protection for those rights was the Court's insistence that they were protected only against State infringement and not against individual violence. The Privileges and Immunities Clause was subject to the same limitation, and those who sustained a broad view of it made clear that they interpreted it the same way.[82]

70

Moreover, those who advocated a broad interpretation of privileges and immunities intended to leave their definition to the vagaries of the judiciary, just as "due process of law" would be subject to judicial construction decades later. The implications are obvious in the result of *Bradwell v. Illinois,*[83] decided only the next day. In that case three of the four Justices who advocated the broader view of privileges and immunities in Slaughter-House concluded that a regulation barring women from practicing law was a "reasonable" exercise of the State police power. It was consistent with "the divine law of the Creator," which made woman's "paramount destiny and mission . . . to fulfill the noble and benign offices of wife and mother."[84] The same "divine law" could be—and would be—cited to ordain "reasonable" regulations of the privileges and immunities of freedmen.[85]

Just as the almost universal desire of Americans to preserve the basics of the federal system impelled the Justices to avoid the revolutionary potential of the Privileges and Immunities Clause of the

---

[80] Argument for the Defendant, 21 L. Ed. at 402.

[81] See also Miller's discussion of that Clause. 16 Wall. at 81.

[82] *Id.* at 83*ff.*

[83] 16 Wall. 130 (1873).

[84] *Id.* at 141.

[85] In 1880 and 1881 Justices Field and Clifford would deny that the right to sit upon a jury was included even within the broad category of privileges and immunities of citizens of the States. Ex parte Virginia, 100 U.S. 339, 365-66 (1880); Neal v. Delaware, 103 U.S. 370, 406 (1881).

Fourteenth Amendment, it led them to adopt the doctrine of "State action." As early as 1872 they had demonstrated their concern that a broad interpretation of Reconstruction-era legislation might subvert the reserved area of State jurisdiction. In *Blyew v. United States*[86] they had considered the Civil Rights Act's removal provisions, which permitted transfer of cases from State to national courts when they "affected" a person whose rights as defined by the Act were denied. The victim of a crime was not a party legally "affected" in the culprit's prosecution, the Court ruled, nor were witnesses who could not testify in the case because of their color. Once again the Court's opinion reflected the concern for State authority that pervaded its pre-Reconstruction cases: "It will not be thought that Congress intended to give to the District and Circuit Courts jurisdiction over all causes both civil and criminal . . . . And yet if all those who may be called as witnesses in a case, were intended to be described in the class of persons affected by it . . . , there is no cause either civil or criminal of which those courts may not take jurisdiction . . . [because] such an allegation might always be made."[87]

71

In case after case in the 1870s and 1880s the Justices construed the Reconstruction Amendments and legislation in light of these considerations. The practical results in individual cases still shock the researcher—the release of Blyew and his confederate, who butchered an innocent black woman in paranoid expectation of a race war; the freeing of the Colfax rioters, who had massacred defenseless, fleeing blacks.[88] One cannot help but suspect that had the Court been more sensitive to blacks' rights, they would have found the grounds upon which to do justice. But that does not mean that the Justices were motivated by the desire to cement the Union with the blood of the Negro, as some scholars have alleged.[89] It was the duty of the States, not Congress, to punish such outrages, they insisted. To hold otherwise "would be to clothe congress with power to

---

[86] 13 Wall. 581 (1872).

[87] *Id.* at 592.

[88] United States v. Cruikshank, 92 U.S. 542 (1876). United States v. Harris, 106 U.S. 629 (1883), also involved southern white rioters.

[89] MAGRATH, note 2 *supra*, at 136–49; Scott, *Justice Bradley's Evolving Concept of the Fourteenth Amendment from the Slaughter-House Cases to the Civil Rights Cases*, 25 RUTGERS L. REV. 552, 564–69 (1971); Kinoy, note 2 *supra*, at 396–97.

pass laws for the general preservation of social order in every state."[90]

When one assesses the Supreme Court's decisions within the context of the doctrines of dual federalism accepted by most Americans in the nineteenth century, however, what is remarkable is the degree to which the Court sustained national authority to protect rights rather than the degree to which they restricted it. In fact, although the Justices found fault with indictments and ruled Reconstruction legislation unconstitutional for excessive breadth, they made clear that with the exception of a few of the *Civil Rights Cases*,[91] every single prosecution brought before them could have been sustained by an appropriate national law. In the very decisions that released southern defendants as well as in those that affirmed their convictions, the Court rejected nearly all the arguments against national enforcement of rights put forward by its opponents. The Justices adhered to the doctrine of "state action" under the Fourteenth Amendment—the crucial element in the maintenance of the federal system they believed in. They repudiated every other restriction.

In Congress, in political platforms, campaign literature and oratory, and finally in legal briefs, arguments, and opinions, opponents of Reconstruction legislation developed a catalogue of limitations upon national authority to protect civil and political rights that truly would have nullified the constitutional amendments had it been accepted, and caused incalculable embarrassment to modern federal civil rights protection, much of which is still based upon the Reconstruction-era laws.

They insisted that the Thirteenth Amendment itself did no more than abolish the institution of slavery. Legislation authorized by its enforcement provision could reach nothing more than peonage and coolyism. Thus if the Fourteenth Amendment had not been passed, the Civil Rights Act of 1866 would have been unconstitutional.[92] If the Thirteenth Amendment did not give Congress power to pro-

72

---

[90] Bradley in United States v. Cruikshank, 25 Fed. Cas. 707, 710 (# 14,897) (C.C.D. La. 1874).

[91] 109 U.S. 3 (1883).

[92] E.g., CONG. GLOBE, 39th Cong., 1st Sess., 623 (1866) (Rep. Kerr); *id.* at 628 (Rep. Marshall); *id.* at 499 (Sen. Cowan); *id.* at 1156 (Rep. Thornton); *id.* at 476 (Sen. Saulsbury); Bowlin v. Kentucky, 65 Ky. 5 (1867); People v. Brady, 40 Cal. 198 (1870).

tect rights, the Fourteenth and Fifteenth Amendments did little more, according to the conservative argument. Not only were the prohibitions of the Fourteenth and Fifteenth Amendments aimed only at States, they were aimed at States only in their corporate capacities. Thus, they operated directly upon offending State laws, rendering them immediately null and void, but could not authorize criminal or civil action against State officers who carried out those laws. In a federal system in which State and nation were equally sovereign, neither government could impose duties on the officers of the other.[93] And that was even more certainly true if the officer's act was not sanctioned by State law or was in actual contravention of it.[94] Moreover, it was a plain violation of the Constitution to make the same act both a State and a national crime, so no offense against a State law could be prosecuted by the national government merely by giving it another name.[95]

All these positions were grounded in the notion of State independence from national impositions that the Supreme Court itself had recognized in *Collector v. Day* and *United States v. R.R. Co.* But the commitment to maintaining the State's primary jurisdiction over protection of rights against individual infringement, embodied in the State action doctrine, led inexorably to an even more extreme conclusion—that despite provisions directly affirming congressional power to enforce the Amendments by appropriate legislation, Congress had no more power to enforce Fourteenth and Fifteenth Amendment prohibitions than it had to enforce the Constitution's Obligation of Contracts or Ex Post Facto Clauses. In quintessential dual federalist argument against the constitutionality of the 1871 Enforcements Acts, Justice Field's brother, David Dudley Field,

73

---

[93] CONG. GLOBE, 41st Cong., 2d Sess., 3667, appendix, 422 (1870) (Sen. Fowler); *id.* 42d Cong., 1st Sess., app. 231 (1871) (Sen. Blair); *id.* at appendix, 217 (Sen. Thurman formerly chief justice of the Ohio Supreme Court); Brief for Petitioner, Ex parte Virginia, 8 LANDMARK BRIEFS 113–24; Brief for Defendants, United States v. Cruikshank, 7 *id.* at 340; Biddle, *Indictment of Judge Coles,* 6 S.L. REV. (n.s.) 206, 216–20 (1880); Justices Field and Clifford, dissenting in Ex parte Virginia, 100 U.S. at 349–70, and in Fx parte Clarke, 100 U.S. 399, 404-22 (1880). The argument was also made, apparently, by defense counsel in United States v. Given, 25 Fed. Cas. 1329 (# 15,211 C.C.D. Del. 1873). It is implicit in Bowlin v. Kentucky, 65 Ky. 5, 7–14 (1867) (Williams, J. concurring), and State v. Rash, 1 Houston's Crim. Rep. 271 (Del. 1867).

[94] CONG. GLOBE, 41st Cong., 2d Sess., 472–73 (1870) (Sen. Casserly); United States v. Jackson, 26 Fed. Cas. 563 (# 15,459) (C.C.D. Cal. 1874).

[95] CONG. GLOBE, 41st Cong., 2d Sess., 3674 (1870) (Sen. Thurman); *id.,* 42d Cong., 1st Sess., 572 (1871) (Sen. Stockton).

established the underpinnings of such a position: "Congress . . . is judge of the means to be chosen for attaining a desired end, only in this sense, that it must choose *appropriate* means . . . such as are not *expressly or by implication prohibited.* . . . There are many limitations upon the choice of means beyond those which are expressed. They are implied from the nature of the government. . . . The right to declare an act invalid, because incompatible with the Constitution, applies with the same effect where the incompatibility relates to the implied, as where it relates to the express limitations of the Constitution."[96] With every justification Field was able to cite *Collector v. Day* as authority for this argument—"The case itself is the strongest possible example of an implied limitation upon the powers of Congress. Its power to tax is apparently unlimited, and it had passed an act, by the terms of which the salary of a State judge was liable to taxation, but this court pronounced the act unconstitutional, because, in the exercise of an express power, Congress had transgressed the implied limitations."[97] Given the nature of the American federal system, what could Congress do, then, if a State violated the Fourteenth or Fifteenth Amendments? The conclusion Field offered echoed the position Democrats had taken since the introduction of enforcement legislation: "The answer must be, Congress may do nothing whatever, beyond providing judicial remedies in federal courts for parties aggrieved by deprivation of their rights. Beyond this there is no alternative between doing nothing or doing everything, between leaving the States alone or destroying them altogether. Congress cannot do everything, because that would be the annihilation of the States; therefore it can do nothing, beyond providing the judicial remedies here indicated. . . . [A]n act of a State in violation of the prohibitions of the amendments would be a nullity. . . . Congress, being authorized to enforce the prohibitions by appropriate legislation, the natural, the true, and the only constitutional mode of enforcement, is by the judicial remedies to establish and enforce the nullity."[98]

74

---

[96] 7 LANDMARK BRIEFS 430–31. Cooley referred to similar "implied restrictions" upon congressional power, in COOLEY, THE GENERAL PRINCIPLES OF CONSTITUTIONAL LAW IN THE UNITED STATES OF AMERICA 97 (1880).

[97] 7 LANDMARK BRIEFS 432–33.

[98] *Id.* at 441–43. See also Thurman's closely reasoned argument against the constitutionality of the 1871 Enforcement Act. CONG. GLOBE, 42d Cong., 1st Sess., 216, 221–22 (1871), an elaboration of a notion he expressed earlier in opposition to the 1870 En-

Justices Field and Clifford accepted David Dudley Field's argument, going further and finding unconstitutional even the judicial remedy embodied in the 1866 Civil Rights Act's removal provisions. Unconstitutional State laws must be reversed upon appeal to the Supreme Court from State tribunals, they insisted. This "gives to the Federal courts the ultimate decision of Federal questions without infringing upon the dignity and independence of the State courts. By it harmony between them is secured [and] the rights of both Federal and State governments maintained."[99]

The majority of the Justices, however, rejected every one of these arguments. In the process they construed the Amendments in a fashion surprisingly similar to the Court's interpretations of the past twenty years.

First, the Justices never rejected absolutely and without cavil Republican legislators' contentions that Congress might protect rights directly when they were violated by individuals in consequence of State inaction rather than action. Justices Strong and Woods, on the contrary, sustained the Republican position in circuit court decisions shortly after the passage of the 1870 and 1871 Enforcement Acts.[100] In his two seminal Reconstruction-law opinions, the circuit court decision in *United States v. Cruikshank*[101] and the Supreme Court decision in the *Civil Rights Cases*,[102] Justice Bradley spoke, not only in terms of States' primary jurisdiction over private infringement of individual rights, but of the duty of States to protect persons against such infringements and the presumption that they were fulfilling that duty in the absence of allegations to the contrary. Woods expressed a similar presumption when he spoke for the Court in *United States v. Harris*, holding unconstitutional a portion of the 1871 Enforcement Act.[103] In a

75

---

forcement Act. *Id.*, 41st Cong., 2d Sess., 3664 (1870). See Senator Davis's similar argument, *id.* at 3667; *id.* 42d Cong., 1st Sess., appendix, 49 (1871) (Rep. Kerr).

[99] Virginia v. Rives, 100 U.S. 313, 324–28, 338 (1880); Ex parte Virginia, 100 U.S. 339, 349–70 (1880).

[100] United States v. Given, 25 Fed. Cas. 1324 (# 15,210) (C.C.D. Del. 1873); United States v. Hall, 26 Fed. Cas. 79 (# 15,282 C.C.D. Ala. 1871). Woods had not yet been appointed to the Supreme Court when he delivered his opinion. See also the opinion of Judge Bradford in United States v. Given, 25 Fed. Cas. 1328 (# 15,211) (C.C.D. Del. 1873), which put the "state inaction" argument even more forcefully than did Strong.

[101] 25 Fed. Cas. 707, 710, 714 (# 14,897) (C.C.D. La. 1874).

[102] 109 U.S. 3, 14 (1883).

[103] 106 U.S. 629, 639 (1883).

thorough study of the Court's Reconstruction Amendment opinions, Laurent B. Frantz has made about as strong an argument as
possible that such language meant that the Court would have sustained direct congressional protection of civil rights upon demonstration of State dereliction,[104] and he may be right, although there
is much to suggest he is not.

A jurist's conviction that the Fourteenth Amendment restated
the State's positive duty to provide full protection of the laws did
not necessarily mean that he believed Congress could remedy its failure to fulfill it. The nationalist constitutional commentator Pomeroy, who did share this conviction, denied that State dereliction
activated national authority. "If the good and valid laws which legislatures have enacted are not fully administered, there is no legal
remedy to be obtained . . . from Congress . . . ; redress must be
found alone in a change of officers through the ordinary processes
of election and appointment," he insisted.[105] While the Court never
repudiated the notion in words as direct as David Dudley Field's—
"State inaction . . . is no cause for federal action"[106]—neither did it
repeat Woods's dictum from his days as district judge that "denying includes inaction as well as action, . . . the omission to protect,
as well as the omission to pass laws for protection."[107] It would have
been easy to do either.

The Court did, however, reject totally the contention that the
Fourteenth Amendment referred to the action of States only in their
corporate capacities. As early as 1870 federal judges were sustaining
prosecutions of State officers for failures to administer State laws
equally, whether or not the laws were discriminatory on their
face.[108] In circuit court in 1873 Justice Strong upheld the conviction of a tax collector who refused to accept a black man's tender of
taxes required to vote under State law.[109] Seven years later he delivered the Court's opinion that even State judges were liable to con-

76

---

[104] Frantz, *Congressional Power to Enforce the Fourteenth Amendment against Private Acts,*
73 YALE L. J. 1353 (1964).

[105] Pomeroy, *Rights of Citizens,* note 68 supra, at 335.

[106] Note 98 supra, at 437.

[107] United States v. Hall, 26 Fed. Cas. 79, 81 (# 15282) (C.C.D. Ala. 1871).

[108] McKay v. Campbell, 16 Fed. Cas. 157 (# 8,839) (D.C.D. Ore. 1870); United States
v. Petersburg Judges of Election, 27 Fed. Cas. 506 (# 16,036) (C.C.E.D. Va. 1874).

[109] United States v. Given, 25 Fed. Cas. 1324 (# 15,210) (C.C.D. Del. 1873).

viction for carrying out unfairly nonjudicial functions imposed by superficially equal State laws.[110] Moreover, in a cognate case, Strong made clear that even if a State officer deprived a person of a right in direct contravention of State law, such a violation would both make him "liable to punishment at the instance of the State and under the laws of the United States."[111] At the same time the Court upheld congressional laws aimed directly at State officers' interference with voting rights at federal elections.[112]

While we might take such decisions for granted today, within the context of nineteenth-century federalism these were bold rulings indeed. (In fact, from around 1900 until *United States v. Classic* in 1941[113] the federal courts refused to sustain prosecutions or suits against State officers for civil rights violations that apparently violated State as well as national laws.[114]) The laws the Court thus sustained asserted "a power inconsistent with, and destructive of, the independence of the States," Field and Clifford insisted in dissent.[115] "The right to control their own officers, to prescribe the duties they shall perform, without the supervision or interference of any other state authority . . . is essential to that independence."[116]

77

In response Strong and Bradley, speaking for the majority in different cases, went to the verge of repudiating the entire notion of dual sovereignty. In language that the Roosevelt Court would echo sixty years later, Strong rejected the idea of "implied limitations" on congressional authority. "The prohibitions of the Fourteenth Amendment are directed to the States," he answered, "and they are to a degree restrictions of State power. It is these which Congress is empowered to enforce, and to enforce against State action, however put forth. . . . Such enforcement is no invasion of State sovereignty. No law can be, which the people of the United States have, by the Constitution of the United States, empowered Congress to enact."[117]

---

[110] Ex parte Virginia, 100 U.S. 339 (1880).

[111] Virginia v. Rives, 100 U.S. 313, at 321 (1880).

[112] Ex parte Siebold, 100 U.S. 371 (1880); Ex parte Clarke, 100 U.S. 399 (1880).

[113] 313 U.S. 299 (1941).

[114] Note, note 2 *supra*, 90 HARV. L. REV. at 1160–61n, 1167–69.

[115] 100 U.S. at 409.

[116] *Ibid.*

[117] Ex parte Virginia, 100 U.S. 339, 346 (1880).

Such language rebuffed the argument that Congress was limited to providing judicial remedies for State violations of the constitutional amendments. "It seems often overlooked that a National Constitution has been adopted in this country, establishing a real government therein, operating upon persons and territory and things," Bradley observed in rebutting the narrow view of national power.[118] At the same time he attacked the sentiment that lay at the foundation of dual federalism, confronting the "mistaken notions with regard to the relations which subsist between the State and national Governments."[119] The national government "is, or should be, as dear to every American citizen as his State Government is," he insisted.[120] "[I]f we allow ourselves to regard it as a hostile organization, opposed to the proper sovereignty and dignity of the State Governments, we shall continue to be vexed with difficulties as to its jurisdiction and authority. . . . Both are essential to the preservation of our liberties and the perpetuity of our institutions. But, in endeavoring to vindicate the one, we should not allow our zeal to nullify or impair the other."[121] With justification, Field perceived in such reasoning "a new departure."[122] In the less restrained world of journalism, the editor of a newspaper established in 1880 to boost Field's presidential ambitions, exploded, "They are revolution. They are a complete overthrow of our institutions."[123]

Even more enlightening is the reasoning by which the Supreme Court tried to sustain national authority to protect individual rights directly without permitting precedents that might later destroy the established lines between State and national power. The Justices did this through doctrines first propounded by Bradley in his circuit court opinion in *Cruikshank*.[124] In that prosecution the United States district attorney for Louisiana, James Beckwith, sought the convictions of the Grant Parish rioters under section six of the Enforcement Act of 1870, which made it illegal for two or more people to

78

---

[118] Ex parte Siebold, 100 U.S. 371, 393–94 (1880).

[119] *Ibid.*

[120] *Ibid.*

[121] *Ibid.*

[122] Ex parte Clarke, 100 U.S. 399, 414 (1880).

[123] *Richmond Daily Commonwealth*, March 5, 1880.

[124] 25 Fed. Cas. 707 (# 14,897) (C.C.D. La. 1874).

injure or threaten any citizen "with intent to prevent or hinder his
free exercise and enjoyment of any right or privilege granted or
secured to him" by the United States Constitution or laws. The indictment alleged several counts of murder with the intent to deprive
the victims of various rights secured by the Constitution—to bear
arms, to assemble peaceably, to equal protection of the laws, to enjoyment of life and liberty unless deprived of them by due process
of law, to rights secured by the State and national constitutions
because of their color, the right to vote, and all the privileges and
immunities of citizens of the United States.

The defendants' lawyers attacked the constitutionality of the law
itself, insisting it usurped the States' jurisdiction over individual
crimes. Bradley agreed that the Fourteenth Amendment prohibited
State action only and that protection of rights was primarily the
duty of the States. Any other holding "would be to clothe congress
with power to pass laws for the general preservation of social order
in every state."[125] Yet despite these strictures, he upheld the law as
an exercise of congressional power, not under the Fourteenth
Amendment, but under the Thirteenth and Fifteenth.

79

The Thirteenth Amendment, Bradley asserted, involved more
than the mere nullification of the formal institution of slavery. It
implied the vesting of the positive rights of freedom. Therefore it
authorized Congress "to make it a penal offense to conspire to deprive a person of, or hinder him in, the exercise and enjoyment of
the rights and privileges conferred by the 13th amendment and the
laws thus passed in pursuance thereof."[126] So not only was Congress
freed of the "State action" limitation by Bradley's construction, but
the "rights and privileges" protected by the Enforcement Act were
those of citizenship in general, not the limited ones the Supreme
Court perceived incident to United States citizenship in *Slaughter-
House*. Still committed to preserving the basic demarcations of the
federal system, Bradley carefully defined the power he was con-
ceding: Congress could punish directly only those offenses perpetrated to deprive persons of rights because of race, color, or previous condition of servitude, not offenses motivated by ordinary mal-
ice or greed. As an example, he cited the case where a freedman
sought to lease and cultivate a farm but was prevented from doing

125 *Id.* at 710–11.

126 *Id.* at 711.

so on account of his color by whites. "It cannot be doubted that this would be a case within the power of Congress to remedy and redress. It would be a case of interference with that person's exercise of his rights as a citizen because of his race."[127] If, however, the same offense were motivated by other considerations, "without any design to interfere with his rights of citizenship or equality before the laws, as being a person of a different race or color . . . , it would be an ordinary crime, punishable by the state law only."[128] Thus, in 1875, Bradley construed the Thirteenth Amendment in a manner not revived by the Twentieth-Century Supreme Court until it decided *Jones v. Mayer* in 1968.[129]

80

    Bradley went even further, concluding that the "rights and privileges" directly protected by the Enforcement Act included voting rights. Since the Amendment simply states that the citizen's right to vote "shall not be denied or abridged by the United States or any State" on account of race or previous condition, Bradley was interpreting away what seems to be another State action limitation. Despite its unusual formulation, Bradley asserted, the Fifteenth Amendment "confers a right not to be excluded from voting by reason of race, color, or previous condition of servitude."[130] In essence it was "a constitutional extension of the civil rights bill, conferring upon the emancipated slave . . . another specific right" of citizenship.[131] Just as in the case of Thirteenth Amendment rights, "Congress has the power directly to enforce the right and punish individuals for its violation,"[132] no matter what the State does in the premises. "There is no essential incongruity in the coexistence of concurrent laws, state and federal, for the punishment of the same unlawful acts."[133]

    But once again, Bradley carefully defined Congress's jurisdiction. The "right and privilege" protected by the Enforcement Act was the right not to be deprived of the power to vote because of color.

---

[127] *Id.* at 712.

[128] *Ibid.*

[129] 392 U.S. 409 (1968). See Casper, *Jones v. Mayer: Clio, Bemused and Confused Muse,* 1968 SUPREME COURT REVIEW 89.

[130] United States v. Cruikshank, 25 Fed. Cas. 707, 712 (# 14.897) (C.C.D. La. 1874).

[131] *Ibid.*

[132] *Id.* at 713.

[133] *Ibid.*

Congress did not acquire general power to regulate voting from the
Fifteenth Amendment.[134]

Having defined Congress's powers in such a way as to sustain
broad authority to protect rights, Bradley found the individual
counts of the indictment wanting. Some claimed an intent to violate
rights not guaranteed or secured by the Constitution; others were
too vague. But the biggest obstacle was the very ground upon
which Bradley had protected national power. Under his construction, the Colfax rioters must have intended to violate their victims'
rights on account of their color or previous condition of servitude
in order to be convicted. Because Beckwith had failed to allege that
motivation, convictions were reversed on counts that otherwise
would have been sustained. "Perhaps such a design may be inferred
from the allegation that the persons injured were of the African
race . . . . But it ought not to have been left to inference; it should
have been alleged."[135] Throughout his discussion of the individual
counts, Bradley—having conceded so much to Congress—seemed
intent on assuring that the counts of the Colfax rioters' indictment
transgress by not one inch over what he had reserved to the States.[136]

81

The Court endorsed Bradley's expansive view of congressional
authority to enforce the Fifteenth Amendment against individual
infringements of the rights to vote in both *United States v. Reese*[137]
and *United States v. Cruikshank*,[138] agreeing that Congress could
punish private offenses against citizens' voting rights so long as they
were motivated by race or previous condition of servitude. In *Reese*,
the Court ruled unconstitutional two provisions of the 1870 Enforcement Act. One punished State officials who at any election
refused to accept ballots from voters who had been denied the opportunity to meet voting qualifications by others on account of
their race. The other punished anyone who tried to interfere with
any citizen's effort to meet voting qualifications. Although the second provision posited no State action, the Court did not rule it unconstitutional on those grounds. Nor did the Justices accept the
argument that Congress could impose no duties on officers of the

---

[134] *Id.* at 714.

[135] *Id.* at 715.

[136] *Ibid.*

[137] 92 U.S. 214 (1876).

[138] 92 U.S. 542 (1876).

"independent" State sovereignties. Still less did they accept David Dudley Field's argument, made on behalf of Cruikshank, that Congress could do no more than provide judicial remedies. Instead, Waite took the position which Bradley had developed in his *Cruikshank* circuit court opinion. Although the citizen's right to vote does not emanate from the national government and the government therefore has no general power over it, the Amendment "has invested citizens with a new constitutional right which is in the protecting power of Congress. The right is exemption in the exercise of the elective franchise on account of race, color, or previous condition of servitude."[139] The two Enforcement Act provisions were unconstitutional, not because of any State action requirements, but because they did not require the allegation that offenses be motivated by the race or previous condition of the victims. It was true that the indictments themselves alleged the requisite motivation. But that could not cure the defect. The statute covered offenses both within and without congressional jurisdiction. Like Bradley, having conceded Congress direct power in an area at the heart of State jurisdiction, the Court was unwilling to concede one inch more. Reese and his codefendants were released, not because Congress lacked authority to punish them, but because it "ha[d] not as yet provided by 'appropriate legislation' for the punishment of the offense."[140]

In *Cruikshank*,[141] Waite once more followed Bradley's construction of the Fifteenth Amendment, holding invalid the counts of the indictment alleging intent to deprive voting rights for failure to allege racial motivation, rather than for lack of State action. Waite again sustained Congress's power to protect voting rights against racially motivated private assaults two years later, while trying the Ellenton, South Carolina, rioters on circuit.[142] And Justice Woods reaffirmed the Bradley construction in 1883 in *United States v. Harris*,[143] while holding a provision of the 1871 Enforcement Act unconstitutional because it did not require racial motivation for the offense against voting rights that it punished. As in

---

[139] United States v. Reese, 92 U.S. 214, 218 (1876).

[140] *Id.* at 221.

[141] United States v. Cruikshank, 92 U.S. 542 (1876).

[142] United States v. Butler, 25 Fed. Cas. 213 (No. 14,700) (C.C.D.S.C. 1877).

[143] 106 U.S. 629 (1883).

Reese, the fact that such motivation was alleged in the indictment and proved could not rescue the Act itself. Once again, the offenders would have been liable to conviction for the same acts under a properly drawn statute.

The Court went further in sustaining congressional power to protect voting rights. In his *Reese* opinion, Waite expressly limited to local and State elections his argument that States retained general authority over voting, implying broader congressional power over federal elections.[144] As in the Ellenton riot case he tried on circuit in 1878, he ruled that in federal elections Congress had plenary power to protect the rights of all voters against individual interference whether motivated by racial hostility or not.[145] And the entire Court took the same view in the 1880s,[146] sustaining convictions of white voting officials and rioters for precisely the same acts alleged in *Reese* and *Cruikshank*.[147] Thus the Waite Court established Congress's power to protect voting rights against private infringement in State and local elections in any case where the offense was racially motivated, and on any grounds whatever in federal elections.

It is not clear whether the whole Court immediately accepted Bradley's recognition of broad congressional power to enforce the Thirteenth Amendment. Bradley's colleagues certainly did not reject it when his *Cruikshank* opinion came before them a year later.[148] Waite's majority opinion sustaining Bradley's circuit court judgment is unclear on the grounds on which the Justices upheld the constitutionality of the Enforcement Act provisions before them. Waite, however, followed Bradley's analysis of the specific counts closely, and Bradley did not write a separate opinion, suggesting that he saw nothing inconsistent between Waite's views and his own. In *United States v. Harris*,[149] where a lynch mob was accused of killing their victims with intent to deny their right to equal protection of the laws, Justice Woods tested the provisions of the Enforcement Act against Congress's power to protect rights di-

83

---

[144] 92 U.S. at 216, 218.

[145] United States v. Butler, 25 Fed. Cas. 213 (No. 14,700) (C.C.D.S.C. 1877).

[146] Ex parte Siebold, 100 U.S. 371 (1880); Ex parte Clarke, 100 U.S. 399 (1880); Ex parte Yarbrough, 110 U.S. 651 (1884).

[147] United States v. Reese, 92 U.S. 214 (1875); United States v. Cruikshank, 92 U.S. 542 (1876).

[148] United States v. Cruikshank, 92 U.S. 542 (1876).

[149] 106 U.S. 629 (1883).

rectly under the Thirteenth Amendment, but without committing
the whole Court to Bradley's views. "Even if the Amendment is
held to be directed against the action of private individuals," he
wrote, "the law under consideration covers cases both within and
without the provisions of the Amendment" because it does not require racial motivation for the offense. Therefore, under the rule of
construction enunciated in *Reese,* the law fell.[150]

But if the Court did not endorse Bradley's views unequivocally
in *Cruikshank* or *Reese,* it certainly acquiesced in them when he
wrote the opinion striking down the Civil Rights Act of 1875. In
the famous (or perhaps infamous) *Civil Rights Cases,*[151] Bradley
tested the law against both the Fourteenth and the Thirteenth
Amendments. Rejecting arguments that the businesses and institutions covered by the act were quasi-state agencies, he held the law
unwarranted by the Fourteenth Amendment on State action
grounds.[152] But when it came to treating the Thirteenth Amendment, Bradley took advantage of the opportunity to write his expansive views of that Amendment—the heritage of the antislavery
legal argument—squarely into the Court's opinion. "It is true, that
. . . the Thirteenth Amendment may be regarded as nullifying all
State laws which establish or uphold slavery. But it has a reflex
character also, establishing and decreeing universal civil and political freedom throughout the United States; and it is assumed, [by
those upholding the law,] that the power vested in Congress to enforce the article by appropriate legislation, clothes Congress with
power to pass all laws necessary and proper for abolishing all badges
and incidents of slavery in the United States."[153] Bradley conceded

84

---

[150] 106 U.S. at 640–41. Woods added that this particular offense—acting with intent
to deprive persons of equal protection of the laws—could not be punished under Thirteenth Amendment authority in any case, even if the law required racial motivation. Since
only governments can pass laws, he wrote, denial of their protection by individuals could
be accomplished only by violating a law. "[I]f, therefore, we hold that [the law] . . .
is warranted by the Thirteenth Amendment, we should . . . accord to Congress the
power to punish every crime by which the right of any person to life, property, or
reputation is invaded." *Id.* at 643. This is a troubling *dictum,* directly counter to Bradley's
dictum in the circuit court *Cruikshank* opinion, 25 Fed. Cas. at 715, implying that a count
alleging such an offense, if racially motivated, could be sustained if its specifications
were made clear. For example, Bradley's *dictum* would sustain, and Woods's would
condemn, a national antilynching law.

[151] 109 U.S. 3 (1883).

[152] *Id.* at 8–19.

[153] *Id.* at 20.

the truth of the assumption,[154] but then rejected the proposition that denial of equal accommodations and privileges was an incident of slavery.[155]

Bradley's problem was that his own interpretation of the Thirteenth Amendment threatened to justify national punishment of any private invasion of a citizen's rights where race was the motive, to sustain a national criminal code protecting blacks against ordinary crimes against life and property. He apparently felt impelled to draw the line somewhere. In his cruel sentence—"When a man has emerged from slavery, . . . there must be some stage in the progress of his elevation when he takes the rank of a mere citizen, and ceases to be the special favorite of the laws, and when his rights as a . . . man, are to be protected in the ordinary modes by which other men's rights are protected"[156]—Bradley, it would seem, was referring to stages of law, not time. Direct national legislation protecting basic rights inherent in freedom was legitimate; legislation protecting more elevated rights was not. Moreover, Bradley believed that State courts had held the common law to require equal access for all citizens to inns and public conveyances. Any change in that requirement would have to be made by statute. He implied that if such statute caused an unjust discrimination, it would violate the Fourteenth Amendment.[157] And he carefully avoided any suggestion that Congress lacked authority to pass a similar law restricted in its application to interstate conveyances and United States territory and the District of Columbia.[158]

A recent analyst has stated aptly that "both the majority position in the *Civil Rights Cases* and the Harlan dissent . . . were fashioned by Joseph Bradley."[159] Like Bradley, Harlan rejected the *Slaughter-House Cases'* narrow conception of congressional authority under the Fourteenth Amendment to protect rights of citizenship.[160] But

85

---

[154] *Id.* at 20–21, 23.

[155] *Id.* at 23–25.

[156] *Id.* at 25.

[157] *Ibid.*

[158] *Id.* at 19.

[159] Scott, note 89 *supra*, at 564.

[160] Harlan went about it a different way. Instead of rejecting the Court's differentiation between rights of United States citizens and rights of State citizens, Harlan argued that Congress had power to protect rights under the first clause of the Amendment defining citizenship. 109 U.S. at 46–48.

that was a lost cause. Harlan's dissent challenged Bradley most powerfully by accepting Bradley's own views of the Thirteenth Amendment. "The Thirteenth Amendment, it is conceded, did something more than to prohibit slavery as an *institution*, resting upon distinctions of race, and shielded by positive law," Harlan wrote.[161] "My brethren admit that it established and decreed universal *civil freedom*. . . . They admit . . . that there are burdens and disabilities, the necessary incidents of slavery, which constitute its substance and visible form; that Congress, by the [Civil Rights] Act of 1866, passed in view of the Thirteenth Amendment, . . . undertook to remove certain burdens and disabilities . . . and secure to all citizens of every race and color . . . those fundamental rights which are the essence of civil freedom . . . ; that under the 13th Amendment . . . legislation, so far as necessary and proper to eradicate all forms and incidents of slavery and involuntary servitude may be direct and primary, operating upon the acts of individuals, whether sanctioned by state legislation or not."[162] Harlan recognized what most scholars have not; to reverse Bradley's judgment it was not necessary to challenge his construction of the constitutional amendments. It was merely necessary to challenge his definition of the "incidents" of slavery.[163]

In sum, then, the Supreme Court's construction of congressional power under the constitutional amendments hardly subverted Republican intent. Committed, as were nearly all Americans of the time, to maintaining the State's primary jurisdiction over criminal offenses, endorsing the basic concepts of dual federalism, the Court still managed to sustain Congress's power to protect directly citizens' fundamental civil and political rights. That Congress did not take advantage of that opportunity reflected the fact that other issues had become more important to a majority of Americans than protection of civil rights. One should not forget, however, that the first time Republicans regained control over all three branches of

---

[161] *Id.* at 34.

[162] *Id.* at 35–36.

[163] Citing *Reese* and *Cruikshank*, Harlan pointed to the Court's own recognition, based upon the theories Bradley articulated in his circuit court *Cruikshank* opinion, that emancipation had created a national privilege not to be deprived of rights on account of color—that racial discrimination was the most fundamental "incident" of slavery. "If, then, exemption from discrimination in respect of civil rights, is a new constitutional right, . . . why may not the nation . . . protect and enforce that right?" he asked. *Id.* at 50.

the national government after 1874, they attempted to pass a law to protect voting rights according to the guidelines set by the Waite Court. It was draconian enough to be called the Force Act of 1890—the direct heir of the Force Act of 1871.[164]

Nearly all of the Waite Court's assertions of broad congressional power under the Thirteenth and Fifteenth Amendments were *dicta*. It was this that permitted the Fuller Court to ignore them in later years. One need only compare the Court's opinion in *Williams v. Mississippi*[165] with Strong's language in *Strauder* and *Ex parte Virginia* to recognize the magnitude of the change.[166] In *James v. Bowman*,[167] the Fuller Court ignored the Waite Court's *dicta* and held the Fifteenth Amendment subject to the same State action limitations as the Fourteenth. In doing so, the Justices overturned a district court decision to the contrary[168] which had been based squarely upon the *dicta* in *Cruikshank*, *Reese*, and *Harris*. The Court merely announced that the Fifteenth Amendment incorporated the same limitations as the Fourteenth and then cited the Waite Court's Fourteenth Amendment opinions as authority. In *Barney v. City of New York*,[169] it held that offenses of State officers in violation of State law could not constitute State action. And in a series of cases it refused to provide relief to blacks disenfranchised under the new southern constitutions of the 1890s and early 1900s.[170] Once again, one need only compare the Fuller Court's language with that of the Waite Court in *Ex parte Yarbrough* to appreciate the difference in the attitudes of the Justices.

Of course neither black Americans nor radical Republicans felt

87

[164] HIRSHON, FAREWELL TO THE BLOODY SHIRT 200–33 (1962).

[165] 170 U.S. 213 (1898).

[166] In this case the Fuller Court ignored the obvious discrimination in the administration of Mississippi's new voting laws of the 1890s, accepting the State's argument that they purged from the voting rolls persons with certain "characteristics," not persons of a certain race. Thus all-white juries chosen from the purged voting lists did not violate the Constitution.

[167] 190 U.S. 127 (1903).

[168] United States v. Lackey, 99 Fed. 952 (D.C.D. Ky. 1900).

[169] 193 U.S. 430 (1904). It is not clear that the Court intended to preclude national authority in all such circumstances in this property-rights case, but it was so interpreted. See Note, note 2 *supra*, 90 HARV. L. REV. at 1160–61n.

[170] Mills v. Green, 159 U.S. 651 (1895); Giles v. Harris, 189 U.S. 475 (1903); Jones v. Montague, 194 U.S. 147 (1904); Selden v. Montague, 194 U.S. 153 (1904); Giles v. Teasley, 193 U.S. 146 (1904).

much like thanking the Waite Court for sustaining congressional power while they released southern killers and election riggers. Democrats and "liberal" or "Mugwump" Republicans demanding sectional reconciliation at the price of black rights praised Court decisions that protected "State rights" by releasing undoubted criminals upon technicalities of statutory construction. It was in their interests politically to ignore the fact that these decisions were based on technicalities, that beneath the surface most of Congress's power to protect rights remained unimpaired. But when one steps back from the immediate political circumstances of the decisions, when one assesses them in light of contemporary doctrines of federalism rather than our own, one reaches a more balanced conclusion. No one can accuse the Justices of the Waite Court of wearing their hearts upon the sleeves of their robes, but they left a heritage of sanctioned congressional power over civil rights that was ignored by their immediate successors and only recently resurrected, without credit to them, by the new abolitionists of the mid-twentieth century.

The American Civil War as a Constitutional Crisis

ARTHUR BESTOR*

WITHIN the span of a single generation—during the thirty-odd years that began with the annexation of Texas in 1845 and ended with the withdrawal of the last Union troops from the South in 1877—the United States underwent a succession of constitutional crises more severe and menacing than any before or since. From 1845 on, for some fifteen years, a constitutional dispute over the expansion of slavery into the western territories grew increasingly tense until a paralysis of normal constitutional functioning set in. Abruptly, in 1860–1861, this particular constitutional crisis was transformed into another: namely, that of secession. Though the new crisis was intimately linked with the old, its constitutional character was fundamentally different. The question of how the Constitution ought to operate as a piece of working machinery was superseded by the question of whether it might and should be dismantled. A showdown had come, and the four-year convulsion of Civil War ensued. Then, when hostilities ended in 1865, there came not the hoped for dawn of peace, but instead a third great constitutional struggle over Reconstruction, which lasted a dozen years and proved as harsh and divisive as any cold war in history. When the nation finally emerged from three decades of corrosive strife, no observer could miss the profound alterations that its institutions had undergone. Into the prodigious vortex of crisis and war every current of American life had ultimately been drawn.

So all-devouring was the conflict and so momentous its effects, that to characterize it (as I have done) as a series of constitutional crises will seem to many readers an almost irresponsible use of language, a grotesque belittling of the issues. Powerful economic forces, it will be pointed out, were pitted against one another in the struggle. Profound moral perplexities were generated by the existence of slavery, and the attacks upon it had social and psychological repercussions of incredible complexity. The various questions

89

* Mr. Bestor, professor of history at the University of Washington, presented a version of this paper, May 3, 1963, to a joint session of the Mississippi Valley Historical Association and the American Studies Association in Omaha. He has also incorporated a few passages from a paper read, August 28, 1963, to the Pacific Coast Branch of the American Historical Association in San Francisco. Mr. Bestor has examined certain points in the present discussion more fully in a previous article: "State Sovereignty and Slavery: A Reinterpretation of Proslavery Constitutional Doctrine, 1846–1860" (*Journal of the Illinois State Historical Society*, LIV [Summer 1961]).

at issue penetrated into the arena of politics, shattering established parties and making or breaking the public careers of national and local leaders. Ought so massive a conflict to be discussed in terms of so rarified an abstraction as constitutional theory?

To ask such a question, however, is to mistake the character of constitutional crises in general. When or why or how should they arise if not in a context of social, economic, and ideological upheaval? A constitution, after all, is nothing other than the aggregate of laws, traditions, and understandings—in other words, the complex of institutions and procedures—by which a nation brings to political and legal decision the substantive conflicts engendered by changes in all the varied aspects of its societal life. In normal times, to be sure, routine and recurrent questions of public policy are not thought of as constitutional questions. Alternative policies are discussed in terms of their wisdom or desirability. Conflicts are resolved by the ordinary operation of familiar constitutional machinery. A decision is reached that is essentially a political decision, measuring, in some rough way, the political strength of the forces that are backing or opposing some particular program of action, a program that both sides concede to be constitutionally possible, though not necessarily prudent or desirable.

90

When controversies begin to cut deep, however, the constitutional legitimacy of a given course of action is likely to be challenged. Questions of policy give place to questions of power; questions of wisdom to questions of legality. Attention shifts to the Constitution itself, for the fate of each particular policy has come to hinge upon the interpretation given to the fundamental law. In debating these constitutional questions, men are not evading the substantive issues. They are facing them in precisely the manner that the situation now requires. A constitutional dispute has been superadded to the controversies already present.

Should the conflict become so intense as to test the adequacy of existing mechanisms to handle it at all, then it mounts to the level of a constitutional crisis. Indeed the capability of producing a constitutional crisis is an ultimate measure of the intensity of the substantive conflicts themselves. If, in the end, the situation explodes into violence, then the catastrophe is necessarily a constitutional one, for its very essence is the failure and the threatened destruction of the constitutional framework itself.

The secession crisis of 1860–1861 was obviously an event of this kind. It was a constitutional catastrophe in the most direct sense, for it resulted in a civil war that destroyed, albeit temporarily, the fabric of the Union.

There is, however, another sense—subtler, but perhaps more significant—in which the American Civil War may be characterized as a constitutional crisis. To put the matter succinctly, the very form that the conflict finally took was determined by the pre-existing form of the constitutional system. The way the opposing forces were arrayed against each other in war was a consequence of the way the Constitution had operated to array them in peace. Because the Union could be, and frequently had been, viewed as no more than a compact among sovereign states, the dissolution of the compact was a conceivable thing. It was constitutional theorizing, carried on from the very birth of the Republic, which made secession the ultimate recourse of any group that considered its vital interests threatened.

Since the American system was a federal one, secession, when it finally occurred, put the secessionists into immediate possession of fully organized governments, capable of acting as no *ad hoc* insurrectionary regime could possibly have acted. Though sometimes described as a "Rebellion" and sometimes as a "Civil War," the American conflict was, in a strict sense, neither. It was a war between pre-existing political entities. But it was not (to use a third description) a "War between the States," for in war the states did not act severally. Instead, the war was waged between two federations of these states: one the historic Union, the other a Confederacy that, though newly created, was shaped by the same constitutional tradition as its opponent. In short, only the pre-existing structure of the American Constitution can explain the actual configuration even of the war itself.

91

The *configurative* role that constitutional issues played is the point of crucial importance. When discussed in their own terms and for their own sakes, constitutional questions are admittedly theoretical questions. One may indeed say (borrowing a phrase that even academicians perfidiously employ) that they are academic questions. Only by becoming involved with other (and in a sense more "substantive") issues, do they become highly charged. But when they do become so involved, constitutional questions turn out to be momentous ones, for every theoretical premise draws after it a train of practical consequences. Abstract though constitutional issues may be, they exert a powerful shaping effect upon the course that events will in actuality take. They give a particular direction to ′ ᵣces already at work. They impose upon the conflict as a whole a unique, a. ˋ an otherwise inexplicable, pattern or configuration.

To speak of a configuration of forces in his. ⸴ is to rule out, as essentially meaningless, many kinds of questions that are popularly supposed to be both answerable and important. In particular, it rules out as futile any effort to decide which one of the various forces at work in a given historical situation was "*the* most important cause" of the events that followed, or "*the* decisive factor" in bringing them about, or "*the* crucial issue" involved. The reason is simple. The steady operation of a single force, unopposed and un-interrupted, would result in a development so continuous as to be, in the most literal sense, eventless. To produce an event, one force must impinge upon at least one other. The event is the consequence of their interaction. Historical explanation is, of necessity, an explanation of such interactions.

If interaction is the crucial matter, then it is absurd to think of assigning to any factor in history an intrinsic or absolute weight, independent of its context. In the study of history, the context is all-important. Each individual factor derives its significance from the position it occupies in a complex structure of interrelationships. The fundamental historical problem, in short, is not to measure the relative weight of various causal elements, but instead to discover the pattern of their interaction with one another.[1]

A cogent illustration of this particular point is afforded by the contro-versy over slavery, which played so significant a role in the crisis with which this paper deals. Powerful emotions, pro and con, were aroused by the very existence of slavery. Powerful economic interests were involved with the fate of the institution. Nevertheless, differences of opinion, violent though they were, cannot, by themselves, account for the peculiar configuration of events that historically occurred. The forces unleashed by the slavery con-troversy were essentially indeterminate; that is to say, they could lead to any number of different outcomes, ranging from simple legislative emancipa-tion to bloody servile insurrection. In the British West Indies the former occurred; in Haiti, the latter. In the United States, by contrast with both, events took an exceedingly complicated course. The crisis can be said to have commenced with a fifteen-year dispute not over slavery itself, but over its expansion into the territories. It eventuated in a four-year war that was avowedly fought not over the issue of slavery, but over the question of the legal perpetuity of the Union. The slavery controversy, isolated from all other issues, cannot begin to explain why events followed so complex and devious a course. On the other hand, though other factors must be taken into account in explaining the configuration of events, these other factors, isolated from those connected with slavery, cannot explain why tensions mounted so high as to reach the breaking point of war.

[1] A contrary view is advanced by Sidney Hook: "The validity of the historian's findings will ... depend upon his ability to discover a method of roughly measuring the relative strength of the various factors present." (Social Science Research Council, Bulletin 54, *Theory and Prac-tice in Historical Study: A Report of the Committee on Historiography* [New York, 1946], 113.) Hook, writing as a philosopher, insists that his criterion is part of the "pattern of inquiry which makes a historical account scientific." (*Ibid.*, 112.) But, as another philosopher, Ernest Nagel, points out, "the natural sciences do not appear to require the imputation of relative importance to the causal variables that occur in their explanations." On the contrary, "if a phenomenon occurs only when certain conditions are realized, all these conditions are equally essential, and no one of them can intelligibly be regarded as more basic than the others." (Ernest Nagel,

No single factor, whatever its nature, can account for the distinctive form that the mid-nineteenth-century American crisis assumed. Several forces converged, producing a unique configuration. Men were debating a variety of issues simultaneously, and their various arguments intertwined. Each conflict tended to intensify the others, and not only to intensify them but also to alter and deflect them in complicated ways. The crisis was born of interaction.

The nature of these various converging conflicts is abundantly clear. They are spread at length upon the historical record. Documents, to be sure, are not always to be taken at face value; there are occasions when it is legitimate to read between the lines. Nevertheless, the documentary record is the foundation upon which historical knowledge rests. It can be explained, but it cannot be explained away, as many writers on the causes of the Civil War attempt to do. Most current myths, indeed, depend on such wholesale dismissals of evidence. Southern apologetics took form as early as 1868 when Alexander H. Stephens unblinkingly asserted that "this whole subject of Slavery, so-called, . . . was, to the Seceding States, but a drop in the ocean compared with . . . other considerations,"[2] by which he meant considerations of constitutional principle. The dogma of economic determinism can be sustained only by dismissing, as did Charles and Mary Beard in 1927, not merely that part of the record which Stephens rejected but also the part he accepted. Having decided, like Stephens, that "the institution of slavery was not the fundamental issue," the Beards went on to assert that constitutional issues likewise "were minor factors in the grand dispute."[3]

When the historical record is as vast as the one produced by the mid-nineteenth-century American crisis—when arguments were so wearisomely repeated by such multitudes of men—it is sheer fantasy to assume that the issues discussed were not the real issues. The arguments of the period were public ones, addressed to contemporaries and designed to influence their actions. If these had not touched upon genuine issues, they would hardly have been so often reiterated. Had other lines of argument possessed a more compelling force, they would certainly have been employed.

The only tenable assumption, one that would require an overwhelming mass of contrary evidence to rebut, is that men and women knew perfectly well what they were quarreling about. And what do we find? They argued

93

"Some Issues in the Logic of Historical Analysis," *Scientific Monthly*, LXXIV [Mar. 1952], 162–69, esp. 167.)

[2] Alexander H. Stephens, *A Constitutional View of the Late War between the States* (2 vols., Philadelphia, 1868–70), I, 542.

[3] Charles A. and Mary R. Beard, *The Rise of American Civilization* (2 vols., New York, 1927), II, 40, 42.

about economic measures—the tariff, the banking system, and the Homestead Act—for the obvious reason that economic interests of their own were at stake. They argued about slavery because they considered the issues it raised to be vital ones—vital to those who adhered to the ideal of a free society and vital to those who feared to disturb the *status quo*. They argued about the territories because they felt a deep concern for the kind of social order that would grow up there. They argued about the Constitution because they accepted its obligations (whatever they considered them to be) as binding.

These are the data with which the historian must reckon. Four issues were mentioned in the preceding paragraph: the issue of economic policy, the issue of slavery, the issue of the territories, and the issue of constitutional interpretation. At the very least, the historian must take all these into account. Other factors there indubitably were. To trace the interaction of these four, however, will perhaps suffice to reveal the underlying pattern of the crisis and to make clear how one of these factors, the constitutional issue, exerted a configurative effect that cannot possibly be ignored.

Conflicts over economic policy are endemic in modern societies. They formed a recurrent element in nineteenth-century American political conflict. To disregard them would be an even greater folly than to assume that they determined, by themselves, the entire course of events. Between a plantation economy dependent upon the sale of staples to a world market and an economy in which commerce, finance, and manufacturing were rapidly advancing, the points of conflict were numerous, real, and important. At issue were such matters as banks and corporations, tariffs, internal improvements, land grants to railroads, and free homesteads to settlers. In a general way, the line of division on matters of economic policy tended, at mid-century, to coincide with the line of division on the question of slavery. To the extent that it did so (and it did so far less clearly than many economic determinists assume), the economic conflict added its weight to the divisive forces at work in 1860–1861.

More significant, perhaps, was another and different sort of relationship between the persistent economic conflict and the rapidly mounting crisis before the Civil War. To put the matter briefly, the constitutional theories that came to be applied with such disruptive effects to the slavery dispute had been developed, in the first instance, largely in connection with strictly economic issues. Thus the doctrine of strict construction was pitted against the doctrine of loose construction as early as 1791, when Alexander Hamilton originated the proposal for a central bank. And the doctrine of nullification was worked out with ingenious thoroughness in 1832 as a weapon against the protective tariff. Whatever crises these doctrines precipitated proved to be relatively minor ones so long as the doctrines were applied to purely economic issues. Within this realm, compromise always turned out to be possible. The explosive force of irreconcilable constitutional theories became apparent only when the latter were brought to bear upon the dispute over slavery.

Inherent in the slavery controversy itself (the second factor with which we must reckon) were certain elements that made compromise and accommodation vastly more difficult than in the realm of economic policy. To be sure, slavery itself had its economic aspect. It was, among other things, a labor system. The economic life of many regions rested upon it. The economic interests that would be affected by any tampering with the institution were powerful interests, and they made their influence felt.

Nevertheless, it was the noneconomic aspect of slavery that made the issues it engendered so inflammatory. As Ulrich B. Phillips puts it, "Slavery was instituted not merely to provide control of. labor but also as a system of racial adjustment and social order." The word "adjustment" is an obvious euphemism; elsewhere Phillips speaks frankly of "race control." The effort to maintain that control, he maintains, has been "the central theme of Southern history." The factor that has made the South "a land with a unity despite. its diversity," Phillips concludes, is "a common resolve indomitably maintained—that it shall be and remain a white man's country."[4]

It was this indomitable resolve—say rather, this imperious demand—that lay at the heart of the slavery controversy, as it lies at the heart of the struggle over civil rights today. To put the matter bluntly, the demand was that of a master race for a completely free hand to deal as it might choose with its own subject population. The word "sovereignty" was constantly on the lips of southern politicians. The concept they were invoking was one that Blackstone had defined as "supreme, irresistible, absolute, uncontrolled authority."[5] This was the kind of authority that slaveholders exercised over their chattels. What they were insisting on, in the political realm, was that the same species of power should be recognized as belonging to the slaveholding states when dealing with their racial minorities. "State Sovereignty" was, in essence, the slaveowner's authority writ large.

If slavery had been a static system, confined geographically to the areas where the institution was an inheritance from earlier days, then the demand of the slaveholding states for unrestricted, "sovereign" power to deal with

[4] Ulrich B. Phillips, *The Course of the South to Secession*, ed. E. Merton Coulter (New York, 1939), 152.
[5] William Blackstone, *Commentaries on the Laws of England* (4 vols., Oxford, Eng., 1765–69), I, 49.

it was a demand to which the majority of Americans would probably have reconciled themselves for a long time. In 1861, at any rate, even Lincoln and the Republicans were prepared to support an ironclad guarantee that the Constitution would never be amended in such a way as to interfere with the institution within the slaveholding states. An irrepealable amendment to that effect passed both houses of Congress by the necessary two-thirds vote during the week before Lincoln's inauguration.[6] The incoming President announced that he had "no objection" to the pending amendment,[7] and three states (two of them free) actually gave their ratifications in 1861 and 1862.[8] If the problems created by slavery had actually been, as slaveowners so vehemently maintained, of a sort that the slaveholding states were perfectly capable of handling by themselves, then the security offered by this measure might well have been deemed absolute.

As the historical record shows, however, the proposed amendment never came close to meeting the demands of the proslavery forces. These demands, and the crisis they produced, stemmed directly from the fact that slavery was *not* a static and local institution; it was a prodigiously expanding one. By 1860 the census revealed that more than half the slaves in the nation were held in bondage *outside* the boundaries of the thirteen states that had composed the original Union.[9] The expansion of slavery meant that hundreds of thousands of slaves were being carried beyond the territorial jurisdictions of the states under whose laws they had originally been held in servitude. Even to reach another slaveholding state, they presumably entered that stream of "Commerce . . . among the several States," which the Constitution gave Congress a power "to regulate."[10] If they were carried to United States territories that had not yet been made states, their presence there raised questions about the source and validity of the law that kept them in bondage.

Territorial expansion, the third factor in our catalogue, was thus a

---

[6] Joint Resolution to Amend the Constitution, Mar. 2, 1861, 12 US Statutes at Large 251. It passed the House by a vote of 133 to 65 on February 28, 1861, and the Senate by a vote of 24 to 12 on the night of March 3–4, 1861. Technically, the sitting of March 2, 1861, was still in progress in the Senate, hence the date attached to the joint resolution as officially published. (*Congressional Globe*, 36 Cong., 2 sess., 1285, 1403 [Feb. 28, Mar. 2, 1861].)

[7] First inaugural address, Mar. 4, 1861, *The Collected Works of Abraham Lincoln*, ed. Roy P. Basler *et al.* (9 vols., New Brunswick, N. J., 1953–55), IV, 270.

[8] Ohio on May 13, 1861, Maryland on Jan. 10, 1862, Illinois on Feb. 14, 1862. (Herman V. Ames, *The Proposed Amendments to the Constitution of the United States during the First Century of Its History*, Annual Report, American Historical Association, 1896 [2 vols., Washington, D. C., 1897], II, 363.)

[9] Of the 3,953,760 slaves in the United States in 1860, 2,174,996 were held in the 9 states of Kentucky, Tennessee, Florida, Alabama, Mississippi, Missouri, Arkansas, Louisiana, and Texas. (US, Ninth Census [1870], Vol. I, *The Statistics of the Population* [Washington, D. C., 1872], 3–8 [a corrected recompilation of previous census figures].)

[10] US Constitution, Art. I, Sec. 8 [clause 3].

crucial element in the pattern of interaction that produced the crisis. The timing of the latter, indeed, indicates clearly the role that expansion played. Slavery had existed in English-speaking America for two centuries without producing any paralyzing convulsion. The institution had been brought to an end in the original states of the East and North by unspectacular exercises of legislative or judicial authority. Federal ordinances barring slavery from the Old Northwest had operated effectually yet inconspicuously since 1787. At many other points federal authority had dealt with slavery, outlawing the foreign slave trade on the one hand and providing for the return of fugitive slaves on the other. Prior to the 1840's constitutional challenges to its authority in these matters had been few and unimportant. Indeed, the one true crisis of the period, that of 1819–1821 over Missouri, was rooted in expansionism, precisely as the later one was to be. The nation was awaking to the fact that slavery had pushed its way northward and westward into the virgin lands of the Louisiana Purchase. Only when limits were drawn for it across the whole national domain did the crisis subside.

97

Suddenly, in the election of 1844, the question of territorial expansion came to the fore again. Events moved rapidly. Within the space of precisely a decade, between the beginning of 1845 and the end of 1854, four successive annexations added a million and a quarter square miles to the area under undisputed American sovereignty.[11] Expansion itself was explosive; its interaction with the smoldering controversy over slavery made the latter issue explosive also.

The annexation of Texas in 1845, the war with Mexico that followed, and the conquests in the Southwest which that war brought about gave to the campaign against slavery a new and unprecedented urgency. Within living memory the plains along the Gulf of Mexico had been inundated by the westward-moving tide of slavery. Alabama and Mississippi, to say nothing of Arkansas and Missouri, furnished startling proof of how quickly and ineradicably the institution could establish itself throughout great new regions. Particularly telling was the example of Texas. There slavery had been carried by American settlers to nominally free soil beyond the boundaries of the United States; yet in the end the area itself was being incorpo-

---

11 The area of so-called "continental" United States (exclusive of Alaska as well as of Hawaii) is officially put at 3,022,387 square miles. It attained this size in 1854. More than two-fifths of this area, that is, 1,234,381 square miles, is conventionally regarded as having been acquired through the annexation of Texas by joint resolution in 1845, the partition of the Oregon country by agreement with Great Britain in 1846, the cessions from Mexico by the treaty ending the Mexican War in 1848, and the additional territory acquired from the latter country by the Gadsden Purchase of 1853–1854. The conventional reckoning (which disregards all the complex questions created by prior American claims) is given in US Bureau of the Census, *Historical Statistics of the United States, Colonial Times to 1957: A Statistical Abstract Supplement* (Washington, D. C., 1960), 236.

rated in the Union. To guard against any possible repetition of these developments, antislavery forces reacted to the outbreak of the Mexican War by introducing and supporting the Wilmot Proviso. Originally designed to apply simply to territory that might be acquired from Mexico, it was quickly changed into an all-encompassing prohibition: "That there shall be neither slavery nor involuntary servitude in any territory on the continent of America which shall hereafter be acquired by or annexed to the United States . . . in any . . . manner whatever."[12] The steadfast refusal of the Senate to accept the proviso did not kill it, for the prospect of continuing expansion kept the doctrine alive and made it the rallying point of antislavery sentiment until the Civil War.

This prospect of continuing expansion is sometimes forgotten by historians who regard the issue of slavery in the territories as somehow bafflingly unreal. Since 1854, it is true, no contiguous territory has actually been added to the "continental" United States. No one in the later 1850's, however, could know that this was to be the historic fact. There were ample reasons to expect otherwise. A strong faction had worked for the annexation of the whole of Mexico in 1848. Filibustering expeditions in the Caribbean and Central America were sporadic from 1849 to 1860. As if to spell out the implications of these moves, the notorious Ostend Manifesto of 1854 had announced (over the signatures of three American envoys, including a future President) that the United States could not "permit Cuba to be Africanized" (in plainer language, could not allow the slaves in Cuba to become free of white domination and control), and had defiantly proclaimed that if Spain should refuse to sell the island, "then, by every law, human and divine, we shall be justified in wresting it from Spain if we possess the power."[13] This was "higher law" doctrine with a vengeance.

Behind the intransigent refusal of the Republicans in 1860–1861 to accept any sort of compromise on the territorial question lay these all too recent developments. Lincoln's letters during the interval between his election and his inauguration contained pointed allusions to filibustering and to Cuba.[14]

---

[12] This was the form in which the proviso was adopted by the House on February 15, 1847. (*Congressional Globe*, 29 Cong., 2 sess., 424–25 [Feb. 15, 1847].) In its original form, as moved by David Wilmot of Pennsylvania on August 8, 1846, and adopted by the House the same day, it spoke only of "the acquisition of any territory from the Republic of Mexico." (*Ibid.*, 29 Cong., 1 sess., 1217 [Aug. 8, 1846].)

[13] Ostend Manifesto (actually dated at Aix-la-Chapelle), Oct. 18, 1854, *The Ostend Conference, &c.* (*House Executive Documents*, 33 Cong., 2 sess., X, No. 93), 131. Though the Secretary of State, William L. Marcy, was forced by public opinion to repudiate the manifesto, James Buchanan was helped to the presidency in 1857 by the fact that his signature was on it.

[14] *Collected Works of Lincoln*, ed. Basler *et al.*, IV, 154, 155, 172. It should be noted that Stephen A. Douglas, in his third debate with Lincoln, at Jonesboro, Illinois, on September 15, 1858, declared in forthright language that the doctrine of popular sovereignty ought to apply "when we get Cuba" and "when it becomes necessary to acquire any portion of Mexico or

And his most explicit instructions on policy, written on February 1, 1861, to William H. Seward, soon to take office as his Secretary of State, were adamant against any further extension of slavery in any manner:

> I say now, . . . as I have all the while said, that on the territorial question—that is, the question of extending slavery under the national auspices,—I am inflexible. I am for no compromise which *assists* or *permits* the extension of the institution on soil owned by the nation. And any trick by which the nation is to acquire territory, and then allow some local authority to spread slavery over it, is as obnoxious as any other.

The obnoxious "trick" that Lincoln feared was, of course, the acceptance of Stephen A. Douglas' doctrine of popular sovereignty. The supreme importance that Lincoln attached to the territorial issue was underlined by the final paragraph of his letter, wherein he discussed four other issues on which antislavery feeling ran high: the Fugitive Slave Act, the existence of slavery in the national capital, the domestic slave trade, and the slave code that the territorial legislature of New Mexico had enacted in 1859. Concerning these matters, Lincoln wrote Seward:

99

> As to fugitive slaves, District of Columbia, slave trade among the slave states, and whatever springs of necessity from the fact that the institution is amongst us, I care but little, so that what is done be comely, and not altogether outrageous. Nor do I care much about New-Mexico, if further extension were hedged against.[15]

The issues raised by territorial expansion were, however, not merely prospective ones. Expansion was a present fact, and from 1845 onward its problems were immediate ones. Population was moving so rapidly into various parts of the newly acquired West, most spectacularly into California, that the establishment of civil governments within the region could hardly be postponed. Accordingly, within the single decade already delimited (that is, from the beginning of 1845 until the end of 1854), state or territorial forms of government were actually provided for every remaining part of the national domain, except the relatively small enclave known as the Indian Territory (now Oklahoma). The result was an actual doubling of the area of the United States within which organized civil governments existed.[16] This process of political creation occurred not only in the new

---

Canada, or of this continent or the adjoining islands." (*Ibid.*, III, 115.) The word was "when," not "if."

[15] Lincoln to Seward, Feb. 1, 1861, *ibid.*, IV, 183.

[16] At the beginning of 1845 the United States comprised approximately 1,788,000 square miles (exclusive of its claims in the Oregon country). Of this total, 945,000 square miles were within the boundaries of the 26 full-fledged states of the Union; another 329,000 square miles belonged to organized territories; and the remaining 514,000 square miles were without organized civil governments. At the end of 1854 the total area had increased to approximately 3,022,000 square miles, of which 1,542,000 lay within the 31 states that were now members of the Union (Florida, Texas, Iowa, Wisconsin, and California having been admitted during the decade); another 1,410,000 square miles belonged to organized territories; and only 70,000

acquisitions, but it also covered vast areas, previously acquired, that had been left unorganized, notably the northern part of the old Louisiana Purchase. There, in 1854, the new territories of Kansas and Nebraska suddenly appeared on the map. With equal suddenness these new names appeared in the newspapers, connected with ominous events.

The process of territorial organization brought into the very center of the crisis a fourth factor, the last in our original catalogue, namely, the constitutional one. The organization of new territories and the admission of new states were, after all, elements in a constitution-making process. Territorial expansion drastically changed the character of the dispute over slavery by entangling it with the constitutional problem of devising forms of government for the rapidly settling West. Slavery at last became, in the most direct and immediate sense, a constitutional question, and thus a question capable of disrupting the Union. It did so by assuming the form of a question about the power of Congress to legislate for the territories.

This brings us face to face with the central paradox in the pre-Civil War crisis. Slavery was being attacked in places where it did not, in present actuality, exist. The slaves, close to four million of them, were in the states, yet responsible leaders of the antislavery party pledged themselves not to interfere with them there.[17] In the territories, where the prohibition of slavery was being so intransigently demanded and so belligerently resisted, there had never been more than a handful of slaves during the long period of crisis. Consider the bare statistics. The census of 1860, taken just before the final descent into Civil War, showed far fewer than a hundred slaves in all the territories,[18] despite the abrogation of restrictions by the Kansas-Nebraska Act and the Dred Scott decision. Especially revealing was the

---

square miles remained in the unorganized Indian Territory. Boundaries are shown in Charles O. Paullin and John K. Wright, *Atlas of the Historical Geography of the United States* (Washington, D. C., 1932), plates 63A and 63B (for the situation in 1845), plates 63B, 64A, and 64C (for 1854).

[17] In his first inaugural, Lincoln reiterated a statement he had made earlier in his debates with Douglas: "I have no purpose, directly or indirectly, to interfere with the institution of slavery in the States where it exists. I believe I have no lawful right to do so, and I have no inclination to do so." (*Collected Works of Lincoln*, ed. Basler *et al.*, IV, 263.) The statement was originally made in the debate at Ottawa, Illinois, August 21, 1858. (*Ibid.*, III, 16; see also the discussion of the proposed constitutional amendment of Mar. 2, 1861, above, notes 6–8.)

[18] US, Eighth Census (1860), *Preliminary Report on the Eighth Census, 1860* (Washington, D. C., 1862), 131; confirmed in the final report, *Population of the United States in 1860* (Washington, D. C., 1864), 598–99. Slaves were recorded in only three territories: fifteen in Nebraska, twenty-nine in Utah, and two in Kansas; a total of forty-six. Certain unofficial preliminary reports gave slightly higher figures: ten slaves in Nebraska, twenty-nine in Utah, twenty-four in New Mexico, and none in Kansas; a total of sixty-three. (*American Annual Cyclopaedia, 1861* [New York, 1862], 696.) It should be noted that the census figures for 1860 were tabulated in terms of civil divisions as they existed early in 1861. Thus Kansas was listed as a state, though it was not admitted until January 29, 1861, and statistics were presented for the territories of Colorado, Dakota, and Nevada, though these were organized only in February and March 1861.

situation in Kansas. Though blood had been spilled over the introduction of slavery into that territory, there were actually only 627 colored persons, slave or free, within its boundaries on the eve of its admission to statehood (January 29, 1861). The same situation obtained throughout the West. In 1846, at the time the Wilmot Proviso was introduced, the Union had comprised twenty-eight states. By the outbreak of the Civil War, more than two and a third million persons were to be found in the western areas beyond the boundaries of these older twenty-eight states, yet among them were only 7,687 Negroes, free or slave.[19] There was much truth in the wry observation of a contemporary: "The whole controversy over the Territories . . . related to an imaginary negro in an impossible place."[20]

The paradox was undeniable, and many historians treat it as evidence of a growing retreat from reality. Thus James G. Randall writes that the "larger phases of the slavery question . . . seemed to recede as the controversies of the fifties developed." In other words, "while the struggle sharpened it also narrowed." The attention of the country was "diverted from the fundamentals of slavery in its moral, economic, and social aspects," and instead "became concentrated upon the collateral problem as to what Congress should do with respect to slavery in the territories." Hence "it was this narrow phase of the slavery question which became, or seemed, central in the succession of political events which actually produced the Civil War." As Randall sees it, the struggle "centered upon a political issue which lent itself to slogan making rather than to political analysis."[21]

Slogan making, to be sure, is an important adjunct of political propaganda, and slogans can easily blind men to the relatively minor character of the tangible interests actually at stake. Nevertheless, a much more profound force was at work, shaping the crisis in this peculiar way. This configurative force was the constitutional system itself. The indirectness of the attack upon slavery, that is to say, the attack upon it in the territories, where

101

[19] Census figures for the six states admitted from 1846 to 1861, inclusive (Iowa, Wisconsin, California, Minnesota, Oregon, and Kansas), and for the seven organized territories enumerated in the census of 1860 (Colorado, Dakota, Nebraska, Nevada, New Mexico, Utah, and Washington) showed an aggregate of 2,305,096 white persons, 7,641 free persons of color, and 46 slaves; making a total (including also "civilized Indians" and "Asiatics") of 2,382,677 persons. (Eighth Census [1860], *Population*, 598–99.) Ironically enough, the aborigines in the Indian Territory held in slavery almost as many Negroes as were to be found, slave or free, in the entire area just specified. (Eighth Census [1860], *Preliminary Report*, 136.) This special tabulation for the Indian Territory (not incorporated in the regular census tables) showed 65,680 Indians, 1,988 white persons, 404 free colored persons, and 7,369 slaves.

[20] James G. Blaine, *Twenty Years of Congress* (2 vols., Norwich, Conn., 1884), I, 272, quoting an unnamed "representative from the South."

[21] James G. Randall, *The Civil War and Reconstruction* (Boston, 1937), 114–15. In a later work, Randall described the issue of slavery in the territories, when debated by Lincoln and Douglas in 1858, as "a talking point rather than a matter for governmental action, a campaign appeal rather than a guide for legislation." (*Lincoln the President* [4 vols., New York, 1945–55], I, 125.)

it was merely a future possibility, instead of in the states, where the institution existed in force, was the unmistakable consequence of certain structural features of the American Constitution itself.

A centralized national state could have employed a number of different methods of dealing with the question of slavery. Against most of these, the American Constitution interposed a barrier that was both insuperable and respected.[22] By blocking every form of frontal attack, it compelled the adoption of a strategy so indirect as to appear on the surface almost timid and equivocal.[23] In effect, the strategy adopted was a strategy of "containment." Lincoln traced it to the founding fathers themselves. They had, he asserted, put into effect a twofold policy with respect to slavery: "restricting it from the new Territories where it had not gone, and legislating to cut off its source by the abrogation of the slave trade." Taken together, these amounted to "putting the seal of legislation against its spread." The second part of their policy was still in effect, but the first, said Lincoln, had been irresponsibly set aside. To restore it was his avowed object:

> I believe if we could arrest the spread [of slavery] and place it where Washington, and Jefferson, and Madison placed it, it would be in the course of ultimate extinction, and the public mind would, as for eighty years past, believe that it was in the course of ultimate extinction. The crisis would be past.[24]

Whether or not slavery could have been brought to an end in this manner is a totally unanswerable question, but it requires no answer. The historical fact is that the defenders of slavery regarded the policy of containment as so dangerous to their interests that they interpreted it as signifying "that a war must be waged against slavery until it shall cease throughout the United States."[25] On the other hand, the opponents of slavery took an uncompromising stand in favor of this particular policy because it was the only one that the Constitution appeared to leave open. To retreat from it

---

[22] As I have written elsewhere: "The fact that the controversy of 1846–1860 turned on the extension of slavery to the territories (and, to a lesser extent, on the fugitive-slave law) showed that antislavery leaders, far from flouting the Constitution, were showing it a punctilious respect. Had they been disposed, as their opponents alleged, to ride roughshod over constitutional limitations, they would hardly have bothered with the question of the territories or the question of fugitive slaves." (Arthur Bestor, "State Sovereignty and Slavery," *Journal of the Illinois State Historical Society*, LIV [Summer 1961], 127.)

[23] The failure of the Republicans to mount a frontal attack upon slavery in the slaveholding states seemed to the Beards sufficient reason for treating the attack upon slavery as hardly more than a sham battle. Secession, they argued, was the southern planters' "response to the victory of a tariff and homestead party that proposed nothing more dangerous to slavery itself than the mere exclusion of the institution from the territories." (Beard, *Rise of American Civilization*, II, 37, see also 39–40.)

[24] First debate with Douglas, Ottawa, Ill., Aug. 21, 1858, *Collected Works of Lincoln*, ed. Basler *et al.*, III, 18 (italics of the original not reproduced here).

[25] "Declaration of the Immediate Causes which Induce and Justify the Secession of South Carolina from the Federal Union," Dec. 24, 1860, *Journal of the Convention of the People of South Carolina, Held in 1860, 1861 and 1862* (Columbia, S. C., 1862), 465.

would be to accept as inevitable what Lincoln called "the perpetuity and nationalization of slavery."[26]

To understand the shaping effect of the Constitution upon the crisis, one must take seriously not only the ambiguities that contemporaries discovered in it, but also the features that all alike considered settled. The latter point is often neglected. Where constitutional understandings were clear and unambiguous, responsible leaders on both sides accepted without serious question the limitations imposed by the federal system. The most striking illustration has already been given. Antislavery leaders were willing to have written into the Constitution an absolute and perpetual ban upon congressional interference with slavery inside the slaveholding states. They were willing to do so because, as Lincoln said, they considered "such a provision to now be implied constitutional law," which might without objection be "made express, and irrevocable."[27]

Equally firm was the constitutional understanding that Congress had full power to suppress the foreign slave trade. On the eve of secession, to be sure, a few fire-eaters proposed a resumption of the importation of slaves. The true index of southern opinion, however, is the fact the Constitution of the Confederate States outlawed the foreign trade in terms far more explicit than any found in the Constitution of the United States.[28]

Far more surprising, to a modern student, is a third constitutional understanding that somehow held firm throughout the crisis. The Constitution grants Congress an unquestioned power "To regulate Commerce with foreign Nations, and among the several States, and with the Indian Tribes."[29] Employing this power, Congress had outlawed the foreign slave trade in 1808, with the general acquiescence that we have just noted. To anyone familiar with twentieth-century American constitutional law, the commerce clause would seem to furnish an obvious weapon for use against the domestic slave trade as well. Since the 1890's the power of Congress to regulate interstate commerce has been directed successively against lotteries, prostitution, child labor, and innumerable other social evils that are observed to propagate themselves through the channels of interstate commerce.

103

[26] *Collected Works of Lincoln*, ed. Basler *et al.*, III, 18.

[27] First inaugural, Mar. 4, 1861, *ibid.*, IV, 270; see also above, notes 6–8.

[28] In the US Constitution the only reference to the slave trade is in a provision suspending until 1808 the power of Congress to prohibit "the Migration or Importation" of slaves. (Art. I, Sec. 9 [clause 1].) The power itself derives from the commerce clause (Art. I, Sec. 8 [clause 3]), and Congress is not required to use it. By contrast, the Confederate Constitution not only announced that the foreign slave trade "is hereby forbidden," but also went on to *require* its Congress to pass the necessary enforcement laws. (Constitution of the Confederate States, Art. I, Sec. 9 [clause 1]; text in Jefferson Davis, *The Rise and Fall of the Confederate Government* [2 vols., New York, 1881], I, 657.)

[29] US Constitution, Art. I, Sec. 8 [clause 3].

The suppression of the domestic slave trade, moreover, would have struck a far more telling blow at slavery than any that could possibly have been delivered in the territories. Only the unhampered transportation and sale of slaves from the older seaboard regions can account for the creation of the black belt that stretched westward through the new Gulf States. By 1840 there were already as many slaves in Alabama and Mississippi together, as in Virginia. During the twenty years that followed, the number of slaves in the two Gulf States almost doubled, while the number of slaves in Virginia remained almost stationary.[30]

The migration of slaveholding families with the slaves they already possessed can account for only part of this change. The domestic slave trader was a key figure in the process. His operations, moreover, had the indirect effect of pouring money back into older slaveholding states like Virginia, where slavery as an economic system had seemed, in the days of the Revolution, on the verge of bankruptcy. Furthermore, a direct attack upon the domestic slave trade might well have aroused less emotional resentment than the attack actually made upon the migration of slaveholders to the territories, for the slave trader was a universally reprobated figure, the object not only of antislavery invective but even of southern distrust and aversion.

No serious and sustained effort, however, was ever made to employ against the domestic slave trade the power of Congress to regulate interstate commerce. The idea was suggested, to be sure, but it never received significant support from responsible political leaders or from public opinion. No party platform of the entire period, not even the comprehensive, detailed, and defiant one offered by the Liberty party of 1844, contained a clear-cut proposal for using the commerce power to suppress the interstate traffic in slaves. Public opinion seems to have accepted as virtually axiomatic the constitutional principle that Henry Clay (who was, after all, no strict constructionist) phrased as follows in the set of resolutions from which the Compromise of 1850 ultimately grew:

> *Resolved*, That Congress has no power to prohibit or obstruct the trade in slaves between the slaveholding States; but that the admission or exclusion of slaves brought from one into another of them, depends exclusively upon their own particular laws.[31]

[30] In 1840 there were 448,743 slaves in Alabama and Mississippi, as against 448,987 in Virginia. In 1860 there were 871,711 slaves in the two Gulf States, as against only 490,865 in Virginia. During the same twenty years there was a net increase of 365,911 in the white population of the two Gulf States, and a net increase of 306,331 in the white population of Virginia. (US, Ninth Census [1870], I, *Population*, 3–8.)

[31] Last of the eight resolutions introduced in the Senate by Henry Clay, *Congressional Globe*, 31 Cong., 1 sess., 246 (Jan. 29, 1850). According to Clay himself, the resolution proposed no new legislation, but merely asserted "a truth, established by the highest authority of law in this country." He expected, he said, "one universal acquiescence." (*Ibid.*)

Careful students of constitutional history have long been at pains to point out that the broad interpretation that John Marshall gave to the commerce clause in 1824 in the notable case of *Gibbons* v. *Ogden*[32] represented a strengthening of federal power in only one of its two possible dimensions. The decision upheld the power of Congress to sweep aside every obstruction to the free flow of interstate commerce. Not until the end of the nineteenth century, however, did the commerce power begin to be used extensively for the purpose of regulation in the modern sense, that is to say, restrictive regulation. The concept of a "federal police power," derived from the commerce clause, received its first clear-cut endorsement from the Supreme Court in the Lottery Case,[33] decided in 1903. These facts are well known. Few scholars, however, have called attention to the dramatic illustration of the difference between nineteenth- and twentieth-century views of the Constitution that is afforded by the fact that the commerce clause was never seriously invoked in connection with the slavery dispute. This same fact illustrates another point as well: how averse to innovation in constitutional matters the antislavery forces actually were, despite allegations to the contrary by their opponents.

105

Various other constitutional understandings weathered the crisis without particular difficulty, but to catalogue them is needless. The essential point has been made. The clearly stated provisions of the Constitution were accepted as binding. So also were at least two constitutional principles that rested upon no specific written text, but were firmly ingrained in public opinion: the plenary authority of the slaveholding states over the institution within their boundaries and the immunity of the domestic slave trade to federal interference.

In the Constitution as it stood, however, there were certain ambiguities and certain gaps. These pricked out, as on a geological map, the fault line along which earthquakes were likely to occur, should internal stresses build up to the danger point.

Several such points clustered about the fugitive slave clause of the Constitution.[34] Clear enough was the principle that slaves might not secure their freedom by absconding into the free states. Three vital questions, however, were left without a clear answer. In the first place, did responsibility for returning the slaves to their masters rest with the states or the federal government? As early as 1842, the Supreme Court, in a divided opinion, placed responsibility upon the latter.[35] This decision brought to the fore a second

[32] 9 Wheaton 1 (1824).
[33] *Champion* v. *Ames*, 188 US Reports 321 (1903).
[34] US Constitution, Art. IV, Sec. 2 [clause 3].
[35] *Prigg* v. *Pennsylvania*, 16 Peters 539 (1842).

question. How far might the free states go in refusing cooperation and even impeding the process of rendition? The so-called "personal liberty laws" of various northern states probed this particular constitutional question. Even South Carolina, originator of the doctrine of nullification, saw no inconsistency in its wrathful denunciation of these enactments, "which either nullify the Acts of Congress or render useless any attempt to execute them."[36] A third question arose in connection with the measures adopted by Congress to carry out the constitutional provision, notably the revised Fugitive Slave Act of 1850. Were the methods of enforcement prescribed by federal statute consistent with the procedural guarantees and underlying spirit of the Bill of Rights? From the twentieth-century viewpoint, this was perhaps the most profound of all the constitutional issues raised by the slavery dispute. It amounted to a direct confrontation between the philosophy of freedom and the incompatible philosophy of slavery. Important and disturbing though the issues were, the mandate of the fugitive slave clause was sufficiently clear and direct to restrain all but the most extreme leaders from outright repudiation of it.[37]

Of all the ambiguities in the written Constitution, therefore, the most portentous proved in fact to be the ones that lurked in the clause dealing with territory: "The Congress shall have Power to dispose of and make all needful Rules and Regulations respecting the Territory or other Property belonging to the United States."[38] At first glance the provision seems clear enough, but questions were possible about its meaning. Eventually they were raised, and when raised they turned out to have so direct a bearing upon the problem of slavery that they would not down. What did the Constitution mean by mingling both "Territory" and "other Property," and speaking first of the power "to dispose of" such property? Was Congress in reality given a power to govern, or merely a proprietor's right to make regulations for the orderly management of the real estate he expected eventually to sell? If it were a power to govern, did it extend to all the subjects on which a full-fledged state was authorized to legislate? Did it therefore endow Congress with

106

---

[36] South Carolina, "Declaration," Dec. 24, 1860, *Journal of the Convention*, 464.

[37] In 1844, to be sure, the Liberty party solemnly repudiated this specific obligation: "We hereby give it to be distinctly understood, by this nation and the world, that, as abolitionists, . . . we owe it to the Sovereign Ruler of the Universe, as a proof of our allegiance to Him, in all our civil relations and offices, whether as private citizens, or as public functionaries sworn to support the Constitution of the United States, to regard and to treat the [fugitive slave clause] of that instrument . . . as utterly null and void, and consequently as forming no part of the Constitution of the United States, whenever we are called upon, or sworn, to support it." (*National Party Platforms, 1840–1956*, ed. Kirk H. Porter and Donald B. Johnson [Urbana, Ill., 1956], 8.) Lincoln, on the other hand, solemnly reminded the nation in his first inaugural that public officials "swear their support to the whole Constitution—to this provision as much as to any other." (*Collected Works of Lincoln*, ed. Basler *et al.*, IV, 263.)

[38] US Constitution, Art. IV, Sec. 3 [clause 2].

powers that were not federal powers at all but municipal ones, normally reserved to the states? In particular, did it bestow upon Congress, where the territories were concerned, a police power competent to deal with domestic relations and institutions like slavery?

This chain of seemingly trivial questions, it will be observed, led inexorably to the gravest question of the day: the future of slavery in an impetuously expanding nation. On many matters the decisions made by territorial governments might be regarded as unimportant, for the territorial stage was temporary and transitional. With respect to slavery, however, the initial decision was obviously a crucial one. A single article of the Ordinance of 1787 had eventuated in the admission of one free state after another in the Old Northwest. The omission of a comparable article from other territorial enactments had cleared the way for the growth of a black belt of slavery from Alabama through Arkansas. An identical conclusion was drawn by both sides. The power to decide the question of slavery for the territories was the power to determine the future of slavery itself.

107

In whose hands, then, had the Constitution placed the power of decision with respect to slavery in the territories? This was, in the last analysis, the constitutional question that split the Union. To it, three mutually irreconcilable answers were offered.

The first answer was certainly the most straightforward. The territories were part of the "Property belonging to the United States." The Constitution gave Congress power to "make all needful Rules and Regulations" respecting them. Only a definite provision of the Constitution, either limiting this power or specifying exceptions to it, could destroy the comprehensiveness of the grant. No such limitations or exceptions were stated. Therefore, Congress was fully authorized by the Constitution to prohibit slavery in any or all of the territories, or to permit its spread thereto, as that body, in exercise of normal legislative discretion, might decide.

This was the straightforward answer; it was also the traditional answer. The Continental Congress had given that answer in the Ordinance of 1787, and the first Congress under the Constitution had ratified it. For half a century thereafter the precedents accumulated, including the precedent of the Missouri Compromise of 1820. Only in the 1840's were these precedents challenged.

Because this was the traditional answer, it was (by definition, if you like) the conservative answer. When the breaking point was finally reached in 1860–1861 and four identifiable conflicting groups offered four constitutional doctrines, two of them accepted this general answer, but each gave it a peculiar twist.

Among the four political factions of 1860, the least well-organized was the group that can properly be described as the genuine conservatives. Their vehicle in the election of 1860 was the Constitutional Union party, and a rattletrap vehicle it certainly was. In a very real sense, however, they were the heirs of the old Whig party and particularly of the ideas of Henry Clay. Deeply ingrained was the instinct for compromise. They accepted the view just stated, that the power of decision with respect to slavery in a particular territory belonged to Congress. But they insisted that one additional understanding, hallowed by tradition, should likewise be considered constitutionally binding. In actually organizing the earlier territories, Congress had customarily balanced the prohibition of slavery in one area by the erection elsewhere of a territory wherein slaveholding would be permitted. To conservatives, this was more than a precedent; it was a constitutional principle. When, on December 18, 1860, the venerable John J. Crittenden offered to the Senate the resolutions summing up the conservative answer to the crisis, he was not in reality offering a new plan of compromise. He was, in effect, proposing to write into the Constitution itself the understandings that had governed politics in earlier, less crisis-ridden times. The heart of his plan was the re-establishment of the old Missouri Compromise line, dividing free territories from slave.[39] An irrepealable amendment was to change this from a principle of policy into a mandate of constitutional law.

That Congress was empowered to decide the question of slavery for the territories was the view not only of the conservatives, but also of the Republicans. The arguments of the two parties were identical, up to a point; indeed, up to the point just discussed. Though territories in the past had been apportioned between freedom and slavery, the Republicans refused to consider this policy as anything more than a policy, capable of being altered at any time. The Wilmot Proviso of 1846 announced, in effect, that the time had come to abandon the policy. Radical though the proviso may have been in a political sense, it was hardly so in a constitutional sense. The existence of a congressional power is the basic constitutional question. In arguing for the existence of such a power over slavery in the territories, the Republicans took the same ground as the conservatives. In refusing to permit mere precedent to hamper the discretion of Congress in the *use* of that power, they broke with the conservatives. But the distinction they made between power and discretion, that is, between constitutional law and political policy, was neither radical nor unsound.

One innovation did find a place in antislavery, and hence in Republican, constitutional doctrine. Though precedent alone ought not to hamper the

[108]

[39] *Congressional Globe*, 36 Cong., 2 sess., 114 (Dec. 18, 1860).

discretion of Congress, specific provisions of the Constitution could, and in Republican eyes did, limit and control that discretion. With respect to congressional action on slavery in the territories, so the antislavery forces maintained, the due process clause of the Fifth Amendment constituted such an express limitation. "Our Republican fathers," said the first national platform of the new party in 1856, "ordained that no person shall be deprived of life, liberty, or property, without due process of law." To establish slavery in the territories "by positive legislation" would violate this guarantee. Accordingly the Constitution itself operated to "deny the authority of Congress, of a Territorial Legislation [*sic*], of any individual, or association of individuals, to give legal existence to Slavery in any Territory of the United States."[40] The Free Soil platform of 1848 had summed the argument up in an aphorism: "Congress has no more power to make a SLAVE than to make a KING; no more power to institute or establish SLAVERY, than to institute or establish a MONARCHY."[41] As a doctrine of constitutional law, the result was this: the federal government had full authority over the territories, but so far as slavery was concerned, Congress might exercise this authority in only one way, by prohibiting the institution there.

The conservatives and the Republicans took the constitutional system as it stood, a combination of written text and historical precedent, and evolved their variant doctrines therefrom. By contrast, the two other factions of 1860—the northern Democrats under Stephen A. Douglas, and the southern Democrats whose senatorial leader was Jefferson Davis and whose presidential candidate was John C. Breckinridge—appealed primarily to constitutional theories above and beyond the written document and the precedents. If slogans are meaningfully applied, these two factions (each in its own way) were the ones who, in 1860, appealed to a "higher law."

For Douglas, this higher law was the indefeasible right of every community to decide for itself the social institutions it would accept and establish. "Territorial Sovereignty" (a more precise label than "popular sovereignty") meant that this right of decision on slavery belonged to the settlers in a new territory fully as much as to the people of a full-fledged state. At bottom the argument was one from analogy. The Constitution assigned responsibility for national affairs and interstate relations to the federal government; authority over matters of purely local and domestic concern were reserved to the states. So far as this division of power was concerned,

---

[40] *National Party Platforms*, ed. Porter and Johnson, 27. This argument from the due process clause went back at least as far as the Liberty party platform of 1844. (*Ibid.*, 5.) It was reiterated in every national platform of an antislavery party thereafter: in 1848 by the Free Soil party, in 1852 by the Free Democrats, and in 1856 and 1860 by the Republicans. (*Ibid.*, 13, 18, 27, 32.)

[41] *Ibid.*, 13. Repeated in the Free Democratic platform of 1852. (*Ibid.*, 18.)

Douglas argued, a territory stood on the same footing as a state. It might not yet have sufficient population to entitle it to a vote in Congress, but its people were entitled to self-government from the moment they were "organized into political communities." Douglas took his stand on what he regarded as a fundamental principle of American political philosophy: "that the people of every separate political community (dependent colonies, Provinces, and Territories as well as sovereign States) have an inalienable right to govern themselves in respect to their internal polity."[42]

Having thus virtually erased the constitutional distinction between a territory and a state—a distinction that was vital (as we shall see) to the state sovereignty interpretation—Douglas proceeded to deal with the argument that since a territorial government was a creation of Congress, the powers it exercised were delegated ones, which Congress itself was free to limit, to overrule, or even to exercise through direct legislation of its own. He met the argument with an ingenious distinction. "Congress," he wrote, "may institute governments for the Territories," and, having done so, may "invest them with powers which Congress does not possess and can not exercise under the Constitution." He continued: "The powers which Congress may thus *confer* but can not *exercise,* are such as relate to the domestic affairs and internal polity of the Territory."[43] Their source is not to be sought in any provision of the written Constitution, certainly not in the so-called territorial clause,[44] but in the underlying principle of self-government.

Though Douglas insisted that the doctrine of popular sovereignty embodied "the ideas and principles of the fathers of the Revolution," his appeal to history was vitiated by special pleading. In his most elaborate review of the precedents (the article in *Harper's Magazine* from which quotations have already been taken), he passed over in silence the Northwest Ordinance of 1787, with its clear-cut congressional ban on slavery.[45] Douglas chose instead to dwell at length upon the "Jeffersonian Plan of government for the Territories," embodied in the Ordinance of 1784.[46] This plan, it is true, treated the territories as virtually equal with the member states of the Union, and thus supported (as against subsequent enactments) Douglas' plea for the largest measure of local self-government. When, however, Douglas went on

[42] Stephen A. Douglas, "The Dividing Line between Federal and Local Authority: Popular Sovereignty in the Territories," *Harper's Magazine,* XIX (Sept. 1859), 519–37, esp. 526.
[43] *Ibid.,* 520–21.
[44] Douglas insisted that this clause referred "exclusively to property in contradistinction to persons and communities." (*Ibid.,* 528.)
[45] He likewise ignored all subsequent enactments of the same sort, save to register agreement with the dictum of the Supreme Court, announced in the Dred Scott opinion, that the Missouri Compromise had always been unconstitutional. (*Ibid.,* 530.)
[46] *Ibid.,* 525–26.

to imply that the "Jeffersonian Plan" precluded, in principle, any congressional interference with slavery in the territories, he was guilty of outright misrepresentation. Jefferson's original draft (still extant in his own hand) included a forthright prohibition of slavery in all the territories.[47] The Continental Congress, it is true, refused at the time to adopt this particular provision, a fact that Douglas mentioned,[48] but there is no evidence whatever to show that they believed they lacked the power to do so. Three years later, the same body exercised this very power by unanimous vote of the eight states present.[49]

Disingenuousness reached its peak in Douglas' assertion that the Ordinance of 1784 "stood on the statute book unrepealed and irrepealable . . . when, on the 14th day of May, 1787, the Federal Convention assembled at Philadelphia and proceeded to form the Constitution under which we now live."[50] Unrepealed the ordinance still was, and likewise unimplemented, but irrepealable it was not. Sixty days later, on July 13, 1787, Congress repealed it outright and substituted in its place the Northwest Ordinance,[51] which Douglas chose not to discuss.

Despite these lapses, Douglas was, in truth, basing his doctrine upon one undeniably important element in the historic tradition of American political philosophy. In 1860 he was the only thoroughgoing advocate of local self-determination and local autonomy. He could justly maintain that he was upholding this particular aspect of the constitutional tradition not only against the conservatives and the Republicans, but also (and most emphatically) against the southern wing of his own party, which bitterly repudiated the whole notion of local self-government, when it meant that the people of a territory might exclude slavery from their midst.

This brings us to the fourth of the parties that contested the election of 1860, and to the third and last of the answers that were given to the question of where the Constitution placed the power to deal with slavery in the territories.

[47] Report to Congress, Mar. 1, 1784, and revised report, Mar. 22, 1784, *The Papers of Thomas Jefferson*, ed. Julian P. Boyd *et al.* (16 vols., Princeton, N. J., 1950–), VI, 604, 608.
[48] Douglas, "Federal and Local Authority," 526. The antislavery provision came to a vote in the Continental Congress on April 19, 1784, under a rule requiring the favorable vote of the majority of the states for adoption. Six states voted in favor of the provision, only three against it. One state was divided. Another state could not be counted, because a quorum of the delegation was not present, but the single delegate on the floor voted "aye." (*Journals of the Continental Congress*, ed. Worthington C. Ford *et al.* [34 vols., Washington, D. C., 1904–37], XXVI, 247.)
[49] *Ibid.*, XXXII, 343. This was the vote on July 13, 1787, adopting the Ordinance of 1787 with its antislavery article; only one member voted against the ordinance. There is no evidence of opposition to the antislavery article itself, which was added as an amendment in the course of the preceding debate.
[50] Douglas, "Federal and Local Authority," 526.
[51] *Journals of the Continental Congress*, ed. Ford *et al.*, XXXII, 343. As if anticipating

At first glance there would appear to be only two possible answers. Either the power of decision lay with the federal government, to which the territories had been ceded or by which they had been acquired; or else the decision rested with the people of the territories, by virtue of some inherent right of self-government. Neither answer, however, was acceptable to the proslavery forces. By the later 1850's they were committed to a third doctrine, state sovereignty.

The theory of state sovereignty takes on a deceptive appearance of simplicity in most historical accounts. This is because it is usually examined only in the context of the secession crisis. In that situation the corollaries drawn from the theory of state sovereignty were, in fact, exceedingly simple. If the Union was simply a compact among states that retained their ultimate sovereignty, then one or more of them could legally and peacefully withdraw from it, for reasons which they, as sovereigns, might judge sufficient. Often overlooked is the fact that secession itself was responsible for reducing the argument over state sovereignty to such simple terms. The right to secede was only one among many corollaries of the complex and intricate doctrine of the sovereignty of the states. In the winter and spring of 1860–1861, this particular corollary, naked and alone, became the issue on which events turned. Earlier applications of the doctrine became irrelevant. As they dropped from view, they were more or less forgotten. The theory of state sovereignty came to be regarded simply as a theory that had to do with the perpetuity of the Union.

The simplicity of the theory is, however, an illusion. The illusion is a consequence of reading history backward. The proslavery constitutional argument with respect to slavery in the territories cannot possibly be understood if the fifteen years of debate prior to 1860 are regarded simply as a dress rehearsal for secession. When applied to the question of slavery, state sovereignty was a positive doctrine, a doctrine of power, specifically, a doctrine designed to place in the hands of the slaveholding states a power sufficient to uphold slavery and promote its expansion *within* the Union. Secession might be an ultimate recourse, but secession offered no answer whatever to the problems of power that were of vital concern to the slaveholding states so long as they remained in the Union and used the Constitution as a piece of working machinery.

As a theory of how the Constitution should operate, as distinguished from a theory of how it might be dismantled, state sovereignty gave its own distinctive answer to the question of where the authority lay to deal with mat-

---

Douglas' contention that the earlier ordinance was "irrepealable," the Congress that had adopted it not only repealed it, but declared it "null and void."

ters involving slavery in the territories. All such authority, the theory insisted, resided in the sovereign states. But how, one may well ask, was such authority to be exercised? The answer was ingenious. The laws that maintained slavery—which were, of course, the laws of the slaveholding states—must be given extraterritorial or extrajurisdictional effect.[52] In other words, the laws that established a property in slaves were to be respected, and if necessary enforced, by the federal government, acting as agent for its principals, the sovereign states of the Union.

At the very beginning of the controversy, on January 15, 1847, five months after the introduction of the Wilmot Proviso, Robert Barnwell Rhett of South Carolina showed how that measure could be countered, and proslavery demands supported, by an appeal to the *mystique* of the sovereignty of the several states:

> Their sovereignty, unalienated and unimpaired . . . , exists in all its plenitude over our territories; as much so, as within the limits of the States themselves. . . . The only effect, and probably the only object of their reserved sovereignty, is, that it secures to each State the right to enter the territories with her citizens, and settle and occupy them with their property—with whatever is recognised as property by each State. The ingress of the citizen, is the ingress of his sovereign, who is bound to protect him in his settlement.[53]

113

Nine years later the doctrine had become the dominant one in proslavery thinking, and on January 24, 1856, Robert Toombs of Georgia summed it up succinctly: "Congress has no power to limit, restrain, or in any manner to impair slavery: but, on the contrary, it is bound to protect and maintain it in the States where it exists, and wherever its flag floats, and its jurisdiction is paramount."[54] In effect, the laws of slavery were to become an integral part of the laws of the Union, so far as the territories were concerned.

Four irreconcilable constitutional doctrines were presented to the American people in 1860. There was no consensus, and the stage was set for civil war. The issues in which the long controversy culminated were abstruse. They concerned a seemingly minor detail of the constitutional system. The arguments that supported the various positions were intricate and theoretical. But the abstractness of constitutional issues has nothing to do, one way or the other, with the role they may happen to play at a moment of crisis. The sole question is the load that events have laid upon them. Thanks to the structure of the American constitutional system itself, the abstruse issue of slavery in the territories was required to carry the burden of well-nigh all

---

[52] These terms were suggested, and their propriety defended, in my article, "State Sovereignty and Slavery," 128–31, 147.

[53] *Congressional Globe*, 29 Cong., 2 sess., Appendix, 246 (Jan. 15, 1847).

[54] Speech in Boston, reprinted in an appendix to Stephens, *Constitutional View*, I, 625–47, esp. 625.

the emotional drives, well-nigh all the political and economic tensions, and well-nigh all the moral perplexities that resulted from the existence in the United States of an archaic system of labor and an intolerable policy of racial subjection. To change the metaphor, the constitutional question of legislative authority over the territories became, so to speak, the narrow channel through which surged the torrent of ideas and interests and anxieties that flooded down from every drenched hillside upon which the storm cloud of slavery discharged its poisoned rain.

114

THE SOUTH AND THE RIGHT OF SECESSION IN THE EARLY FIFTIES *

The danger of a rupture of the Union and of civil war ten years before the firing of the first gun on Fort Sumter is only beginning to be appreciated by historians. In the troublous days of agitation that preceded the compromise arrangement of 1850, hot-headed and even sober-minded southerners, harassed by the aggressiveness of northern Wilmot-provisoism, began to calculate the value of the Union. This inevitably tended to con- firm their doubts that, in the absence of a guarantee that northern aggressions would find a prompt and proper limit, the South had anything to gain from its continuance. Many came to despair of being able to block the Wilmot proviso by regular legislative methods or by the veto of the president; they therefore considered it bad policy to wait till the dreaded and final blow was struck by Congress before a finger should be raised by way of warning or defense. Under the circumstances active advocates of the application of extreme particularistic doctrines became numerous in various parts of the South.

Sentiment in South Carolina was strongly in favor of a withdrawal from a union which the people felt had proved, in the words of R. Barnwell Rhett, "a splendid failure of the first modern attempt by people of different institutions to live under the same government." That a constitutional right of secession existed was hardly questioned in the state which was proud to be represented in the United States Senate by the man who had led the nullification movement of the early thirties and who had in his last formal speech addressed to that body laid down conditions for the continuance of the South in the Union that were generally regarded as either impossible or impracticable. Calhoun's followers at home doubted whether the Constitution could

* This paper was read at Columbia, South Carolina, before a joint meeting of the American Historical Association and the Mississippi Valley Historical Association in 1913.

be relied on by their section and were sometimes inclined to consider it as an impediment rather than a protection to the rights of the South.[1]   But the South Carolina leaders, realizing that they had long borne the odium of discredited radicalism, saw that some other state would have to lead off, if the issue of coöperative withdrawal from the Union was to be successfully made.

When in the summer of 1849 a state convention was called in Mississippi to assemble at Jackson "to consider the threatening relations between the North and the South," Calhoun outlined the work which he felt such a convention ought to undertake in defense of southern rights.[2]   Accordingly, it issued an address inviting the southern states to participate in a convention at Nashville in June of the following year.   This call gave the hotspurs and fatalists a cause about which to rally and South Carolina promptly endorsed the proposal and made arrangement for taking a prominent part in the deliberations of the convention. Most of the other southern states also provided for representation although the Whigs and some Democrats condemned the convention, because they felt that the strongest supporters of the movement were determined to "press on the consideration of the Nashville Convention the propriety of the treasonable project of disunion."[3]   But the combined force of the introduction of Clay's compromise resolution, the announcement of Webster's seventh of March speech, and even the possibility of an adjustment in Congress as a result of the powerful efforts of an able group of conservative senators from both sections and both parties, did not affect the meeting of the convention nor the participation of any except those who had been lukewarm from the outset.

When the convention met on the third of June the hotspurs

116

[1] See speech of Colonel S. W. Trotti of Barnwell, South Carolina in *South Carolina Telegraph*, May 29, 1850, quoted in *National Intelligencer*, June 5, 1850.

[2] Calhoun to Colonel C. S. Tarpley, June 9, 1849, in *Jackson Southron*, May 24, 1850; also in *National Intelligencer*, June 4, 1850; J. F. Jameson, *Correspondence of John C. Calhoun* (American Historical Association, *Annual Report*, 1889, vol. 2 — Washington, 1900), 1206. It was charged that Daniel Wallace of South Carolina attended as the agent of his state or of Calhoun to influence the deliberations of the convention. Wallace denied this in a letter to the editor of the *Jackson Southron*, June 4, 1850, printed in that paper, June 14, 1850.

[3] *Jackson Southron*, May 31, 1850; see A. C. Cole, *The Whig Party in the South* (Washington, 1913), 157-162, 168-171.

assumed control but were held in check by an active group of
moderates.⁴ A series of resolutions of the Calhoun type were
adopted and an address from the pen of R. Barnwell Rhett of
South Carolina.⁵ The speeches of the supporters of the address,
which contained the "choicest of disunion tenets" and which
met some opposition on account of its radicalism, savored
strongly of disunion. Judge Beverly Tucker, professor of constitutional and common law at William and Mary College, who
had gone there as a delegate with the avowed intention of advocating secession, made a powerful appeal for disunion in case
that California should be admitted as a free state.⁶ Langdon
Cheves appealed to Virginia to take the lead in a movement for
the secession of the southern states.⁷

The convention issued an ultimatum requiring as an alternative to disunion, the extension of the Missouri compromise line
to the Pacific, "an extreme concession on the part of the South,"
and made provision for reassembling six weeks after the ad-
journment of Congress. Meantime, the various features of the
"Omnibus" bill had been enacted into law and labelled collectively with the sacred name of "Compromise." Ratification
meetings, especially in the lower South, had stamped their approval upon the work of the convention,⁸ but upon the success of
the congressional measures many of the moderates, including
practically all the Whigs,⁹ withdrew from the movement. Nevertheless, a small body of the faithful assembled at Nashville in
November; they adopted a set of resolutions which combined an
unqualified condemnation of the compromise measures with a
formal promulgation of the doctrine of the right of secession.

117

⁴ Proceedings in *Nashville Republican Banner*, June 4, 5, 6, 7, 8, 10, 11, 12, 13, 1850.
⁵ *Jackson Southron*, June 28, 1850. On June 21, the same journal stated: "Neither John C. Calhoun, Robt. Y. Hayne, nor Geo. McDuffie, even in the palmiest days of ultra nullification, ever conceived anything to surpass it."
⁶ Tucker to his nephew, March 25, 1850, in *William and Mary Quarterly*, 18:45; speech in *Jackson Southron*, June 28, 1850.
⁷ *Petersburg Intelligencer*, July 27, 1850, quoted in *National Intelligencer*, July 30, 1850.
⁸ *Washington Union*, July 17, 27, 29, etc.
⁹ Judge Sharkey, a Mississippi Whig who had presided over the convention and who now refused to issue the call for the adjourned meeting, was one of these. *National Intelligencer*, September 21, October 19, 1850.

They further suggested the holding of a southern congress with full power to deal with the situation.[10]

The enactment of the adjustment measures of 1850 does not seem to have had as immediate effect upon the situation in the South as has often been believed. The news of their passage was hailed with joy by most Whigs and by a small contingent of Union Democrats, but in many sections of the lower South their combined forces could not claim a majority.   On the other hand, a South Carolina orgaʌ of disunion, anticipating the passage of the compromise measures, had already sounded the call, "To arms!" and answer was made by the Democratic leaders and the Democratic press in all parts of the South. "We are not afraid to meet the raw head and bloody bones disunion, face to face," the central organ of the Democracy of Mississippi had declared on August 16.[11] When the success of the congressional adjustment was announced, the *Vicksburg Sentinel,* asserting that the South had lost all in the controversy, raised the question whether it would submit or resist: "For one we are for resistance; who speaks next?"[12] "We recommend State Secession," announced the *Natchez Free Trader,* "it is a constitutional, peaceful, and safe remedy. . . . Hereafter in arguing this matter we shall term the two parties SECESSIONISTS and SUBMISSIONISTS, for we believe that these are the only issues before the country."[13] "The issue is at last upon us," repeated Colonel J. J. Seibels, the editor of the *Montgomery* (Alabama) *Advertiser* and the colleague of Yancey in advocating the withdrawal of the South from the Union, *"Submission,* or *resistance* are now the only alternatives. . . . We shall not hesitate to choose the latter."[14] "We believe in the right of State secession," declared the *Dallas* (Alabama) *Gazette.* "We believe the late compromise measures will warrant the secession of any slaveholding state from the Union. . . . We believe it the duty of every Southern State, collectively or *alone* to secede from the Union as soon as possible."[15]

118

10 Proceedings in *Nashville Republican Banner,* November 13, 14, 15, 18, 19, 1850; resolutions in *National Intelligencer,* November 26, 1850.

11 *Jackson Mississippian,* August 16, 1850.

12 *Vicksburg Sentinel,* September 28, 1850.

13 *Natchez Free Trader,* September 25, 1850.

14 *Montgomery Advertiser,* quoted in *Washington Republic,* October 7, 1850.

15 *Dallas Gazette,* quoted in *Mobile Advertiser,* June 4, 1851.

The Democratic press of Georgia centered its attention upon the question of the state convention, the call of which the legislature had provided for in the present contingency. The *Savannah Georgian* was in favor of such a convention, and was prepared to advocate resort to secession if such was the will of the people as enunciated through their delegates.[16] The *Griffin Jeffersonian* thought that it was either secession or abolitionism and of course preferred the former.[17] The *Columbus Sentinel* urged that the convention as its first act issue a declaration of independence,[18] while a group of leading organs enthusiastically advised secession as a remedy.[19] In Louisiana and in the upper tier of southern states, too, the compromise found strong opponents among the Democratic journals; even Tennessee had a "crying half-dozen" that argued against submission.[20]

The excitement throughout the South was food for the southern fire-eaters. To the meetings that were held to enable the people to express their views on the issues of the day, Rhett of South Carolina, McDonald of Georgia, Yancey of Alabama, and lesser lights addressed their complaints of northern aggression and their arguments for recourse to secession as the only honorable remedy. There began a rally under the slogan of resistance; the demand for secession and resistance seemed to become nearly as strong as the opposition to the compromise.

Governor Towns of Georgia, whose legislature had provided for the contingency, immediately issued the call for a state convention to deal with the matter of federal relations. The executives of Mississippi and South Carolina, doubting whether the South could honorably continue in the Union after it had been insulted, despoiled, and defrauded by the adjustment, recommended similar action in their states. Governor Seabrook of South Carolina and Governor Quitman of Mississippi corresponded privately regarding the course that should be taken.[21]

119

[16] *Savannah Georgian*, September 20, 1850.

[17] *Griffin Jeffersonian* quoted in *Savannah Republican*, September 23, 1850.

[18] *Columbus Sentinel* quoted in *Savannah Republican*, September 25, 1850. "We frankly tell you that, so far as we are concerned, we despise the Union, and hate the North as we do hell itself." *Columbus Sentinel* quoted in *National Intelligencer*, November 15, 1850.

[19] See list in *Savannah Republican*, October 3, 1850.

[20] *Nashville Republican Banner*, October 23, 1850.

[21] J. F. H. Claiborne, *Life and Correspondence of John A. Quitman* (New York, 1860), 37 *et seq.*

Both felt that there could be no salvation except in secession; the influence of the executive offices in these states was, therefore, exerted in favor of this step.

The situation had become quite serious. Agitation was at its height. Men who in the days when the adjustment measures were still being considered in Congress, felt convinced that there was no real disunion excitement in the South except what was stirred up by demagogical politicians out of selfish motives, now became fearful that the situation in their section was not fully appreciated. "Everything on the surface is calm," a Georgia leader reported, "but public opinion is fast settling down in the belief that we may be benefited and that we cannot be worsted by dissolution." [22] The caldron of disunion bubbled angrily in South Carolina but the Palmetto state still hesitated to take the lead; its voters were divided between the advocates of immediate secession by separate state action and those who favored the united action of the South. The national government was fully alive to the danger of disunion. Webster, in his position as secretary of state, seriously considered writing a letter to one of the federal officers in the South who were giving him information as to the situation, taking occasion "to set forth, fully and explicitly, the duty of the Executive Government of the United States, under the constitution and the laws, in case of a collision between the authority of a State, and that of the United States." "I think a paper may be drawn quite applicable to the present state of things," he wrote to President Fillmore, "and be a good Union paper, to send to Congress with your Annual Message." [23]

The Whigs had kept remarkably clear from this secession movement. Although many of them, including prominent leaders, had been nullifiers or near-nullifiers in the thirties, having been brought up on the state rights doctrines of that period, [24]

[22] John H. Lumpkin to H. Cobb, September 3, 1850. Copy of manuscript letter loaned to the author by U. B. Phillips.

[23] Webster to Fillmore, October 25, 1850, Fillmore Private Correspondence, 11: no. 100, manuscripts in the library of the Buffalo Historical Society.

[24] Hilliard had entered politics as a member of the state rights school in Alabama and always pointed with pride to his training. (W. Garrett, *Reminiscences of Public Men in Alabama* [Atlanta, 1872], 96; see his letter of May 23, 1849, in *Mobile Advertiser*, May 26, 1849.) Judge William L. Sharkey of Mississippi had sympathized with nullification in 1833. (*Jackson Mississippian*, October 17, 1851; *Jackson Flag of the Union*, October 24, 1851.) In Georgia, Berrien, Dawson, Stephens, Toombs,

they had now stood out against the Nashville convention and had all but unanimously come to the support of the compromise measures, anxious for a settlement and for the preservation of the Union. "All who are for resistance and for disunion will be found in the ranks of the democratic party," admitted a Union Democratic leader concerning the situation in Georgia,[25] and the same applied to the other states of the South. "The Whig party of the South, as a mass are more united and *sounder* on the question of the Union than the Democratic party," a Tennessee Democratic member of Congress declared, and Senator Foote repeated this sentiment in Mississippi.[26] Despite the grievances of which the South complained, the Whigs especially, though large slave-owners, doubted the advantages that a southern confederacy would give to the slave institution.

121

The Whigs were loyal to their original position in all the events that followed. In the Georgia convention of 1850, they were largely responsible for the adoption of the "Georgia Platform" which was destined to have such an important influence in determining the result in that and other states, with its staunch support of the Union and its firm guarantees for the rights of the South; in the state legislatures and in the Missis-

and Jenkins had been state right leaders in the thirties. They had not then thought it treason to calculate seriously the value of the Union. See the toasts of Toombs, Jenkins, and Dawson, at a local anti-tariff meeting in 1832, drunk under a seven-striped flag symbolic of a southern confederacy of seven states. (*Niles' Register*, 43:77; pointed to by *Mobile Advertiser*, February 23, 1851, and by *Milledgeville Federal Union*, in 1853, in *Savannah Republican*, August 15, 1853.) Berrien played a leading part in the Georgia anti-tariff convention in November, 1832, which adopted strong state rights resolutions. (*Niles' Register*, 43:220, 230.) Stephens' first political speech, delivered on the fourth of July, 1834, was an exposition of the compact theory and a defense of the right of any of the states to withdraw if the compact should be violated by the others. (R. M. Johnston and W. H. Browne, *Life of Alexander H. Stephens* [Philadelphia, 1878], 88.) In the fall of the same year Dawson presented the minority report on Creek affairs in the legislature embodying the Virginia and Kentucky resolutions. He claimed to be an "undeviating advocate of the Jeffersonian doctrine of State Rights and State Remedies." Speech from the *Milledgeville Times and State Rights Advocate*, November 18, 1834, quoted in S. F. Miller, *Bench and Bar of Georgia* (Philadelphia, 1850), 1:262.

25 John H. Lumpkin to Howell Cobb, July 21, 1850; also letter of July 29. U. B. Phillips, *The Correspondence of Robert Toombs, Alexander H. Stephens, and Howell Cobb* (American Historical Association, *Annual Report*, 1911, vol. 2 — Washington, 1913), 208, 209.

26 *Nashville Republican Banner*, December 19, 1850, August 6, 1851; also *Petersburg Intelligencer*, quoted in *Washington Republic*, October 21, 1851.

sippi convention they took a similar stand. It was largely due to the efforts of Whigs that no resolutions affirming even the constitutional right of secession were at this time inscribed upon the statute books of any of the southern states, excepting South Carolina. When they were in a minority they tried obstructive tactics and allied themselves with the Union Democrats to oppose the advocates of resistance. Indeed, such Union parties were actually formed in Georgia, Alabama, and Mississippi, although they were denounced by the southern rights Democrats as being merely "Whiggery in disguise."[27]

The situation was put to a test in the state and congressional elections of 1851. The southern rights organizations, as a result of the failure of their efforts in the legislatures and in the Georgia convention, gradually moderated their tone and came to deny that they were aiming at disunion. They abandoned the resistance issue for the more hopeful one to be found in the abstract question of the right of secession, which they sought to vindicate against their opponents.[28] Their hope was thus to win back the Union Democrats, who had been coöperating with the Whigs in support of acquiescence in the congressional adjustment. The right of secession became the issue upon which the elections turned in the lower South and in certain of the districts of the other southern states.

Alignment on this question revealed the position of Whig and Democrat as essentially contradictory.[29] Even those Democrats who saw in the existing situation no justification for recourse to secession usually defended the doctrine of secession as a remedy against oppressive conditions. A North Carolina Union Democrat assured his colleagues in the state legislature that it was a right in which he believed but which he did not think proper to assert.[30] A Georgia Union Democrat did not hesitate to assert

---

[27] Cole, *Whig Party in the South*, 181 *et seq.*

[28] On the situation in Mississippi see *Natchez Free Trader*, September 10, 1851; *ibid.*, August 20; *Natchez Courier*, June 24, 1851. Colonel Jefferson Davis drew up the resolution adopted by the state rights convention in June, 1851, asserting the right of secession but declaring it inexpedient under existing circumstances.

[29] The *Richmond Enquirer* of November 28, 1850, declared under the caption, The Right of Secession: "The Editors of the Whig and ourselves have been indoctrinated in such different political schools, that upon no subject is it probable that we shall more strongly dissent, than upon that which heads this article." Cf. *Richmond Whig*, November 29, 1850.

[30] *North State Whig*, January 8, 1851.

the right, though he declared that he had never desired the occasion for its application.[31] Governor Collier of Alabama who was a conservative and opposed to recourse to secession and who had not thought the situation required a special session of the state legislature, avowed that it was a clearly acknowledged right.[32]

"We place secession upon the clearly ascertained and well-defined opinions of our people," declared the *Mississippian*.[33] "It is a constitutional, peaceful, and safe remedy," added the *Natchez Free Trader*.[34] In South Carolina, of course, the right of secession was toasted by the Democrats as "the right of all rights, without which all other State rights are nugatory."[35]

The question of the right of secession was canvassed in June among the members of the Nashville convention, and the Democrats, at least, gave the doctrine an unanimous endorsement.[36] A South Carolina member of Congress, in April, 1850, questioned the Democracy of an Illinois representative who had pledged the generous assistance of his state for the coercion of any state that might attempt to secede.[37] The *Raleigh Standard* admitted that secession was a cardinal principle in the Democratic faith.[38] So also declared a member of the Alabama senate who undertook to prove that the Democrats had always maintained the right of secession.[39] Indeed, when after a year or so, an attempt was made to fall back upon old party lines, the southern rights organization, still holding to the doctrines of peaceable secession and unlimited state sovereignty, claimed that it had al-

123

[31] William Rutherford, Jr., to Howell Cobb, April 16, 1850. Phillips, *Correspondence of Toombs, Stephens, and Cobb*, 190.

[32] Letter to citizens of Alabama, October 22, 1850, in *Mobile Advertiser*, November 3, 4, 1850.

[33] *Jackson Mississippian*, quoted in *Congressional Globe*, 32 Congress, 1 Session, ap., 284.

[34] *Natchez Free Trader*, September 25, 1850. The *Mobile Daily Register* which advocated submission to the compromise measures contended for the abstract right of secession "as a supra-constitutional remedy." *National Intelligencer*, August 17, 1851.

[35] *Flag of the Union* (Jackson), August 8, 1851.

[36] *New York Herald*, Washington letter, quoted in *Baltimore Clipper*, June 26, 1850.

[37] *Congressional Globe*, 31 Congress, 1 Session, ap., 431.

[38] *North State Whig*, August 27, 1851.

[39] *Alabama Journal* (Montgomery), December 12, 1851.

ways been the Democratic party.[40] In the Mississippi state rights Democratic convention of January, 1852, which probably represented nine-tenths of the Democrats in the state, Colonel Jefferson Davis boldly took ground that secession was a Democratic doctrine.[41] As a matter of fact, few Democratic journals were ready to deny it and when driven into a corner, those who hesitated to give an affirmative answer avoided giving an explicit expression of their position.[42]

For some reason, probably because of a belief in its widespread acceptance in the South, the supporters of the doctrine of secession made comparatively little effort at the beginning to submit detailed arguments in favor of their interpretation of federal relations. During the exciting discussions in Congress only one southerner essayed an elaborate exposition of the secession remedy and he was a South Carolinian.[43] But in November, the Nashville convention declared that if the northern states, who were parties to the compact of Union, continued to harass the South, "we have a right, as states, there being no common arbiter, to secede" and then formally resolved, "That the Union of the states is a union of equal and independent sovereignties, and that the powers delegated to the federal government can be resumed by the several states, whenever it may seem to them proper and necessary."[44] State conventions of southern rights associations in Alabama and later in Mississippi also

[40] *Savannah Republican*, November 19, 1851.

[41] *Flag of the Union* (Jackson), January 30, 1852; Mrs. Jefferson Davis, *Memoir of Jefferson Davis* (New York, 1890), 1:471.

[42] *St. Louis Intelligencer*, June 16, 18, 21, 27, 1851.

[43] Speech of Daniel Wallace of South Carolina. After submitting his evidence, he summarized his position: "The sovereign parties to the compact of union, at the moment they formed it, declared, in express terms — to which all the States assented — that they entered into the covenant with the understanding, that a breach of any one article, by any one party, leaves all the other parties at liberty to withdraw from it, and re-assume the powers granted whenever, in their judgment, it became necessary to their safety and happiness, and at the same time affirmed the right and duty to resist arbitrary power and oppression, and that the doctrine of non-resistance is absurd, slavish, and destructive of the good and happiness of mankind." He believed the government to be "a confederated Republic of sovereign and equal States." *Congressional Globe*, 31 Congress, 1 Session, ap., 430.

[44] The resolutions of the two sessions of the Nashville convention and of the Georgia state convention are printed in M. W. Cluskey, *Political Text-Book* (Philadelphia, 1858), 596 *et seq*.

asserted the right in equally clear terms.[45] But even then the southern rights leaders and the "secession" press did not for some time awake to the necessity of developing.their arguments. They were, indeed, busied with the more immediate and greater issue of whether or not the passage of the compromise justified the resistance of the slaveholding states.

Gradually, however, they were aroused by the formidable array of arguments directed by their opponents against the right of secession. These were answered by an exposition of the compact theory and of the sovereign character of the states. The Virginia and Kentucky resolutions and Macon's writings were drawn upon to prove that a state had the right to secede.[46] No important mention, however, seems to have been made of Calhoun and the South Carolina exposition.

125

The states as original sovereign and independent communities, it was asserted, had not surrendered their sovereignty by agreeing to the Articles of Confederation, nor even upon the adoption of the federal Constitution of 1787.[47] A Democrat in the North Carolina legislature declared that there was no allegiance owed by the citizens of any state to the general government, that a state had a right to secede at any time, quietly and without disturbing the compact between the other states.[48] Another Democratic member presented resolutions claiming not only this right but the right to punish such citizens as refused to follow the state in secession.[49] The leading Democratic journal in Louisiana declared that secession could not be treason because it did not consist in levying war against the government or adhering to its enemies.[50] One of the most elaborate newspaper arguments in favor of secession was that of the *Louisiana Statesman* which drew a careful distinction between secession as peaceable and revolution as accomplished by a resort to arms. "Two or more parties, for mutual interest, enter into partnership to endure while it is agreeable and advantageous to the

[45] *National Intelligencer*, February 25, 1851.

[46] *Ibid.*, July 22, 1851; *Mobile Advertiser*, June 24, 1851.

[47] *Nashville American*, March 5, 1851, quoted in *Nashville Republican Banner*, March 8, 1851.

[48] *North State Whig*, January 8, 1851.

[49] *Ibid.*, November 27, 1850.

[50] *Louisiana Courier*, quoted in *Mobile Advertiser*, November 6, 1850.

contracting parties; each surrendering to the other certain individual rights to be used and enjoyed in common, but retaining certain other rights to be enjoyed by themselves individually. The duration of the partnership is not specified. Very well. One of the partners after a while perceives that all the advantages of the concern accrue almost entirely to the others, and that they are even encroaching on the rights and interests he specifically reserved for himself — in a word that the partnership has ceased to be desirable and may be ruinous to him. He gives notice to his partners that he will withdraw from the concern and they have no right to prevent him. He takes his portion of the stock, makes his bow, and peaceably retires. This is Secession; if he should seize a musket, rush into the establishment, etc. . . .   that would be Revolution.''[51]

126

But the secession doctrine was enunciated somewhat more formally in the state constituent conventions that met in Mississippi and South Carolina after Union victories all over the South had demonstrated the futility of any attempt at actual secession. In the report on federal relations fathered and vainly supported by the Democratic state rights element in the Mississippi convention the government was declared to be one of delegated powers, limited by a written constitution which had been ratified by the states separately; the reserved rights remained with the states, ''and it necessarily follows that any State possesses the right to judge of infractions of the Constitution, and whenever an exigency shall arise, which in the opinion of the people of the State is sufficient to justify the step, such State has an unquestionable right to resume the delegated powers and withdraw from the Union.''[52]   Six months later the South Carolina convention adopted with little opposition an ordinance declaring the right of secession: ''That South Carolina in the exercise of her sovereign will, as an independent state, acceded to the Federal Union, known as the United States of America; and that in the exercise of the same sovereign will, it is her right without let, hindrance, or molestation from any power whatsoever, to secede from the said Federal Union; and that for the

[51] The *Richmond Enquirer* gave its endorsement to this interpretation, quoting it November 28, 1850.

[52] *Flag of the Union* (Jackson), November 21, 1851.

sufficiency of the causes which may impel her to such separation, she is responsible aloné, under God, to the tribunal of public opinion among the nations of the earth."[53]

The Whigs throughout the South took issue with the Democrats on this point and were about equally united in their denial of any such right. They held that when conditions became intolerably oppressive and all other remedies had been tried and had failed, there remained recourse, in the last resort, only to the inalienable right of revolution. This was the burden of the official and unofficial utterances of their officeholders,[54] of the letters and speeches of their candidates, of the editorials of the Whig press,[55] and of the resolutions of local and state union conventions besides those which the Mississippi constituent convention and the Tennesseé legislature officially adopted under Whig influence.[56] Whig editors worked out elaborate arguments on federal relations to prove their point, some of which had a smack of the logic which Webster used in his famous reply to Hayne. They boldly rejected the compact idea and denied that the states were any longer sovereign and independent communities. They declared the secession theory founded on unsound state-rights arguments; that whatever the status of the states before 1787, the people in their desire to form "a more perfect

127

[53] The vote on the ordinance was one hundred and thirty-six for and nineteen against. Cluskey, *Political Text-Book,* 554.

[54] William A. Graham of North Carolina, who was Fillmore's secretary of the navy, considered the doctrine of secession to be "utterly inconsistent with and repugnant to the Constitution of the United States; it was fully discussed and in my opinion refuted along with nullification in the winter of 1832-3." (Letter of July 26, 1851 to Mr. Haywood and others, in *New Orleans Bulletin,* August 20, 1851.) Governor Campbell of Tennessee in his inaugural address, October 16, declared it "idle and insane to talk about seceding from or dissolving the Union, in quiet and peace, by consent. This is impossible. Civil War will inevitably follow the one or the other." *Nashville Republican Banner,* October 17, 1851.

[55] Discussed in leading editorials in *Louisville Journal,* October 30, 1850; *Mobile Advertiser,* November 3, 6, 27, 1850; *Jackson Southron,* May 10, 17, 1850; *Savannah Republican,* July 3, 1851; *North State Whig,* January 1, 1851; *Richmond Whig,* November 27, 1850, March 17, 1851; *Natchez Courier,* October 1, 18, 1850, January 31, 1851; *Memphis Eagle,* February 17, October 2, 1851.

[56] *Laws of Tennessee, 1851-1852,* p. 719. The Tennessee Whigs later congratulated themselves that they had remained "unseduced by the insidious doctrine of the right of secession taught by some of their adversaries in their midst during the past year and the year before." Address of Whig state convention of 1852, in *Nashville Republican Banner,* February 11, 1852.

Union'' had then yielded to the general government many essential attributes of sovereignity and annulled them to the states; that the federal government was now sovereign in its sphere in all matters delegated to it; that the Constitution of the United States and the laws in pursuance were supreme outriding and overrunning, when they conflict, the constitutions and laws of the states; and, finally, that there was no basis for even a reserved right of secession because then these provisions in the Constitution would be absurd and useless. They asserted that the Constitution provided a mutually appointed umpire to decide differences as to the powers of the federal government; they referred to the supreme court as a tribunal competent to pass upon every possible infraction of the Constitution, with juris-
128 diction over every possible case in law or equity arising under it.[57] Their conclusion was that secession was nothing short of revolution inasmuch as it would defeat the very purposes for which the Union was formed.[58] A timely letter from Daniel Webster, the ''great expositor'' of the Constitution, in which he denied the right of secession and denounced it as revolution, added substantially nothing to the arguments already offered.[59]

The denials of this doctrine were sometimes most vigorous. ''Of all the vagaries that ever straggled into the brain of a politician,'' said the *Memphis Eagle*, ''the one of peaceable secession of a state from the Union, is the most absurd and least calculated of all to inspire confidence in the intelligence or patriotism of him who shall harbor for a moment the monstrous proposition.''[60] It ''is in our view too preposterous to spend words about. We acknowledge no such right,'' declared the *Tuscaloosa*

[57] *Louisville Journal*, October 30, 1850; *Savannah Republican*, July 3, 1851. The *Jackson Southron* of May 10, 1850, refuted the theory of nullification, closing: ''The people of the United States when they formed our Federal Constitution, provided a tribunal competent to decide upon every infraction of that sacred instrument and gave it jurisdiction in every possible case of a violation of its provisions.''

[58] *Memphis Eagle*, February 17, October 2, 1851; *Richmond Whig*, November 27, 1850; *St. Louis Intelligencer*, December 9, 1850; *Savannah Republican*, August 12, 1851; *Natchez Courier*, October 18, 1850, January 31, 1851; *Jackson Southron*, October 11, 1850; *Mobile Advertiser*, November 27, 1850; *Southern Shield*, quoted in *ibid.*, November 11, 1851.

[59] Daniel Webster to ——————, August 1, 1851. *National Intelligencer*, August 5; *Richmond Whig*, August 7; *Memphis Eagle*, August 16, 1851.

[60] *Memphis Eagle*, April 14, 1851.

Monitor.[61] "The laws of Congress now operate directly on individuals without any reference to State action," said the *Mobile Advertiser.* "This Constitution was adopted by the people of the several States, and is as much their government as are the State governments, and nowhere provides that the people of any one State may withdraw, secede, or dissolve from it at pleasure. . . . Anywhere in the Union we are citizens of the Union . . . but State allegiance changes with a change of location. State allegiance is put off at pleasure like a holiday suit, but nothing short of voluntary expatriation releases a man from the allegiance to the Union."[62] "The Whigs deny that the Union of these States is a mere rope of sand," declared the *Jackson Southron,* "they deny that a party of malcontents may cause a State to secede from the Union and not incur the guilt of treason. They have ever held that the federal government is founded on its adoption by the people and creates direct relations between itself and individuals. No State authority can dissolve the Union."[63] "The people framed it; who but the people can unframe it?" asked the *Natchez Courier.*

    Certain Whig journals considered the practical operation of secession to show that it could not be peaceable. The *Mobile Advertiser* took Alabama as a specific case of a seceding state. Immediately the question would arise, it said, as to the payment of duties to the federal officials. The consignee would refuse and when the collector called upon the government of the United States, the former would call upon the state authorities to assist him in resisting the laws of the Union. The result would be a collision; if the state government called upon its citizens to resist by force of arms, it would amount to "levying war against the government and adhering to its enemies," in other words, treason.[64] "The President of the United States and every executive officer under him," declared the editor of the *North State Whig,* "are *sworn* to execute the laws, and if they are resisted, it is his solemn and sworn duty to quell such resistance, and if necessary in order to do it, to use the army and navy and militia of the Country. *War must follow. War as the result of*

129

---

[61] J. Hodgson, *Cradle of the Confederacy* (Mobile, 1877), 297.
[62] *Mobile Advertiser,* November 3, 1850.
[63] *Jackson Southron,* May 17, 1850.
[64] *Mobile Advertiser,* November 6, 1850.

secession is as fatal as any of the eternal purposes of God.'' [65]
"However disagreeable the duties which such a course would
impose upon the other States and upon the Federal authorities,
it will be their bounden duty to suppress this, as they would any
other forcible resistance to the laws and Constitution,'' was the
opinion of the *St. Louis Intelligencer.* [66]

The danger of admitting the abstract right of secession, even
though secession itself was conceded to be unnecessary at that
time, was pointed out by the Whigs. [67] They felt that such an admission would have the effect of giving countenance and encouragement to the disunionists in South Carolina and might be
made the basis for a continued general disunion agitation, as it
had been in South Carolina. "This doctrine of Secession, in
the case of South Carolina, ceases to be a theory or an abstraction, and presents itself as a fearful reality,'' warned the *Alexandria Gazette.* [68] "The right of secession, as claimed by our
opponents,'' declared the editor of the *Macon Journal and Messenger,* "must be either a useless abstraction or a revolutionary
sentiment leading directly to the destruction of the government.
In its practical operation it is intended to cover the retreat of
Souh Carolina from the Union.'' [69]

The Whigs, however, placed themselves squarely upon the
Georgia platform, pledging themselves, in case of any further
aggression, to resist "even to a disruption of every tie which
binds the state to the Union.'' This was the right of revolution,
the ultimate remedy to which the Whigs pointed. [70] Resolutions
of which Stephens was probably the author, giving expression
to loyal devotion to the Union, closed with the declaration: "We
hold ourselves in duty bound to maintain the government as long
as it maintains us, but when it becomes our open enemy, by some
hostile act, if that time should come, then we should be for *Revolution and Independence.''* [71] Stanly of North Carolina indicated the same remedy when the Democrats demanded a state-

130

[65] *North State Whig,* July 16, 1851.
[66] *St. Louis Intelligencer,* December 9, 1850.
[67] *North State Whig,* July 2, 1851; *Richmond Whig,* August 11, 12, 1851.
[68] *Alexandria Gazette,* quoted in *National Intelligencer,* October 22, 1851.
[69] S. T. Chapman to H. Cobb, Macon, June 11, 1851. Phillips, *Toombs, Stephens, and Cobb Correspondence,* 236.
[70] See Tennessee resolutions of February 28, 1852.
[71] *Savannah Republican,* September 9, 1850.

ment of what the Whigs proposed to do if the fugitive slave law
was repealed.[12]   The Whigs declared that the right of secession
was confounded with this inherent and inalienable right of revolution — "a right nobody disputes and terrible to tyrants
only."[13]   They made it clear, however, that it was not a right
fixed by constitutional provision or regulation, that it was justifiable only in case of extreme oppression, that its exercise meant
rebellion against the authority of the general government and
hence bloody civil war, a remedy which the existing situation
surely did not require.

In order to understand the earnestness of both sides at this
time it is essential that one follow the leading contests where the
doctrine of secession was made the issue in the congressional
elections of 1851.   In Virginia, where the regular Democratic
candidates were believers in the doctrine of secession, interest
was centered in the contest between Botts and Caskie in the
Richmond district.   During the canvass Caskie repeatedly
avowed the right of secession: "I do interpose this great constitutional doctrine of the right of a state to secede, in case of a
fundamental violation of the articles of the federal compact.   I
do interpose that doctrine between the aggressions of the North
and the aggressions of the government of the United States."
He thought this preferable to civil war.   Botts, his Whig opponent, who could not acknowledge the right of a state to secede
and who denounced peaceable secession as a ridiculous, abstract
humbug, declared with his accustomed fire: "I would shoot
down every man who dared to resist the fugitive slave law, *or
any other law of the United States.*"   Asked whether he would
be willing, if South Carolina seceded "to whip her in," he replied: "I am not exactly certain.   Personally, I might be willing to let her go; and if she did secede, I might be disposed to
treat her as a foreign nation, and make it a foreign instead of a
civil war; and by the application of the Monroe doctrine . . .
reduce her to subjection, as being dangerous to our institutions
to permit any foreign government to hold territory contiguous
to our own; reduce her to a territorial condition and hold her as
a territory until she reaches years of discretion, . . . or I

131

---

[12] *Washington Republic*, July 22, 1851.
[13] *Memphis Eagle*, February 17, 1851.

might not be willing to let her go at all.'' He preferred to wait until the time came which required a decision of such questions.[14]

The situation in North Carolina was essentially similar. The Democrats accepted the leadership of candidates who, like Venable, condemned the compromise measures, but, claiming not to be nullifiers, were prepared for acquiescence, content with an assertion of the right of secession on the basis of Jefferson's, Madison's, and Macon's stand in 1798 and 1799,[15] or who, like Colonel Ruffin in Stanly's district, seemed to incline to actual recourse to that remedy.[16] Stanly not only denied the right of secession but even pledged his support to the national government in keeping an unruly state in the Union.[17] Alfred Dockery, the Whig candidate in the third district, met his Democratic opponent on the same ground.

132

In Alabama, the contests in the Mobile and Montgomery districts were of especial importance. In the one Yancey met Hilliard on the hustings in a joint canvass in behalf of the candidates of their respective parties. Yancey lost all sight of abstract questions in his zeal to carry the district for immediate secession.[18] Hilliard, however, left no doubt as to his position on the doctrine of secession. ''The Constitution did not give any State the right to secede,'' he argued, ''but every free people have a natural right to rise and demand redress when the charter of their liberties is invaded. If the just demand be refused, they should overthrow the government. Should a State attempt to resume the powers it had delegated to the Constitution, the Constitution would be violated. . . . Should Alabama be called to assist in the reduction of South Carolina, he,

---

[14] *Richmond Whig*, September 17, 26, October 2, 3, 9, etc. ''Keep it before the people that the Democratic organs have denounced all who opposed the doctrine of secession, as Traitors, Consolidationists, Submissionists, and enemies of the South.'' *Ibid.*, October 20.

[15] *National Intelligencer*, July 22, 1851.

[16] *North State Whig*, June 18, July 2, 1851.

[17] *Raleigh Standard*, July 16, 1851; see Edward Stanly to Fillmore, June 10, 1851, Fillmore Private Correspondence, 23: no. 36, in Buffalo Historical Society.

[18] ''Mr. Yancey, while keeping his belief in the abstract right of a state to resume the powers it had delegated to the Union, does not seem, at any time in his career, to have given much attention to that division of his argument.'' J. W. Du Bose, *Life and Times of William Lowndes Yancey* (Birmingham, 1892), 264. Cf. *National Intelligencer*, October 25, 1860.

for one, would remember he had a double duty to perform — a duty to his State and a duty to the Union." [19]

In the southern part of the state, the contestants went into elaborate arguments over federal relations. Bragg, the Democratic southern rights candidate, stated that the Constitution was a mere power of attorney from the states, the latter being sovereign. As sovereign states, they had a right to judge of all infractions of the Constitution and to adopt the "mode and measure of redress." Under this view, the state had a right to secede — not a constitutional right, for he admitted it was given nowhere in the Constitution — but a right resulting from their sovereignty and from the nature of the compact. In a case of palpable violation of the Constitution, he insisted that a state had the right to secede, and denied any right on the part of the general government to coerce it back into the Union. To this Langdon, a Union Whig, then mayor of Mobile and proprietor of the *Mobile Advertiser*, replied, beginning with an exposition of the nature of the Union under the old confederation. The Constitution, he said, provided that the laws of Congress should operate directly on the people. The people of the states voluntarily gave up to the general government certain powers and rights in regard to which they agreed that it should be supreme, a sovereignty which, he made it plain, was delegated by the people. Accordingly, no state could authorize resistance to a law of Congress without violating the Constitution, as the laws operate directly upon the people; resistance must come from the people, and state authority cannot be recognized by the general government. If any portion of the people of a state should think it proper to organize an "armed resistance," the act is declared by the Constitution to be treason. Should the state government interpose its authority to protect its citizens from the penalty imposed by the Constitution, it would evidently violate one of the most important stipulations which it made in agreeing to the Constitution. Such an act would be revolution. On the same principle a state could not secede from the Union, without an utter disregard of all the stipulations of the Constitution and a violation of the fundamental principle upon which

133

[19] Du Bose, *Life of Yancey*, 264; *Alabama Journal* (Montgomery), August 4, 1851; H. W. Hilliard, *Politics and Pen Pictures* (New York, 1892), 252.

the government is founded.   Whenever the act is attempted, it is necessarily revolution.[80]

Within the ranks of the Constitutional Union party of Georgia there was a marked difference of opinion on this point between the Whigs and Democrats who found reasons strong enough to surmount the obstacles to coöperation in a common cause. When the southern rights men there found it wise to moderate their utterances and finally staked the issue on the right of secession, Howell Cobb, the Union candidate for governor, was interrogated for his opinions.   Cobb had thus far failed to make his position clear even to his Union coworkers. His speeches, failing to draw a sharp line between the acts of private citizens in one combination or another and those of the state "in its sovereign capacity," were ambiguous regarding the right of secession and the doctrine of federal coercion.   Union Whigs naturally interpreted them, as the southern rights Democrats anxious to convict Cobb of apostacy charged, as denying the right of secession and he personally encouraged this belief in his private correspondence.[81]   The Union Democrats, however, claimed that Cobb admitted with them the abstract right of a state to secede and that the federal government had no legal or constitutional authority to coerce a sovereign state.[82]

Stephens, his associate in the Union cause, whom illness prevented from taking an active part in the campaign, suggested some points for him to make in his canvass: "In reference to the calling out of the militia, etc., maintain the right of the President and duty of the President to execute the law against all factious opposition whether in Mass. or S. C. Maintain the power to execute the fugitive slave law at the North and the power to execute the Revenue or any other law against any *lawless* opposition in S. C. Turn the whole force of this upon the *revolutionary* movement in S. C. and urge all good citizens who value law and order and the rights of liberty and property to stand by the supremacy of the law. This is the life and soul of a

134

---

[80] *Mobile Advertiser*, June 24, 1851; *ibid.*, July 17, 19.

[81] S. T. Chapman to Howell Cobb, June 11, 1851, Phillips, *Toombs, Stephens, and Cobb Correspondence*, 236.

[82] E. P. Harden to H. Cobb, July 5, 1851; S. W. Flournoy to H. Cobb, July 18, 1851.   *Columbus Enquirer*, July 15, 1851; *Milledgeville Southern Recorder*, July 22, 1851.

republic. Warn the good people of Georgia to beware of revolution — refer to France — and plant yourself against the fac-
tionists of S. C. upon the constitution of the country. The right
of secession treat as an abstract question. It is but a right to
change the Govt., a right of revolution, and maintain that no just
cause for the exercise of such right exists. And keep the main
point prominent that the only question now is whether we should
go into revolution or not. South Carolina is for it. This is the
point to keep prominent." [83] This advice Cobb seems to have
tried to carry out, but it only made it more difficult for him to
suit his views to both elements of the Union party.

With the pressure of Stephens and the Whigs on the one side
and of the Union Democrats on the other, his attempt to give an
exposition of his views on the right of secession resulted in a
letter which when published covered three columns of the *Milledgeville Recorder.* [84] He stated very positively that there was
no constitutional basis justifying the right of a state to secede
from the Union at its own pleasure, that when this right was
conceded, the existence of the government was placed at the
disposal of each state of the Union. Nevertheless, he provided
no effective remedy for such secession and could only advise a
"kind and indulgent policy" to induce the state to return to the
advantages of the Union, instead of coercion "by the strong arm
of military power." He then went on to admit a state's right
to secede in case of oppression or gross and palpable violation
of her constitutional rights "as derived from the reserved sovereignty of the States." He turned from an admission of the
"right of government to *enforce the laws on recusant parties*"
to defend this point: "I admit the right of a State to secede for
just causes, to be determined by herself. Being a party to the
compact, which the constitution forms, she has a right which all
other parties to a compact possess, to determine for herself
when, where, and how the provisions of that compact have been
violated. It is equally clear that the other parties to the compact possess a corresponding right to judge for themselves and

[83] A. H. Stephens to H. Cobb, June 23, 1851. Phillips, *Toombs, Stephens, and Cobb Correspondence*, 238.
[84] Cobb to J. Rutherford, etc., August 12, 1851. *Milledgeville Southern Recorder*, August 19, 1851; also in *Savannah Republican*, August 22, 1851.

there being no common arbiter to decide between them, each must depend for the justification of their course, upon the justice of their cause, the correctness of their judgment and their power and ability to maintain their decision.''

These arguments were bolstered up with the language of the Virginia and Kentucky resolutions, but he concluded that the right was ''therefore revolutionary in its character, and depends for its maintenance upon the stout hearts and strong arms of a free people.'' He qualified this by stating that citizens of a state thus resuming her sovereign powers would not commit treason in conforming to the requirements of their state governments. ''In my opinion no man commits treason who acts in obedience to the laws and authorities of a regular organized government such as we recognize our State governments to be.'' In the course of these arguments Cobb admitted that he did not differ much from many of those who granted the abstract right of secession. It was clearly a deliberate effort on his part to straddle. It would be hard to maintain his consistency in this line of reasoning; like the swinging of a pendulum he oscillated from undoubted latitudinarian views to distinctly state rights principles, for he had a double constituency to satisfy, Union men from the old Whig and Democratic parties, and he found it necessary to compete with the Southern Rights party for the votes of the moderate state rights advocates.

The victory of the Union party in the lower South in the elections of 1851 does not signify the defeat of the doctrine of secession on this the first occasion which elicited its general assertion throughout the southern states. The Union party, made up largely of the Whigs, won because the Democratic party of the South was divided, but the division was not over the right of secession.[85] The ''Union men'' and the ''Southern Rights men''

[85] Some few Democrats did deny the right of secession. Among the more important were B. F. Perry, one of the proprietors and editors of the *Greenville Patriot* (South Carolina), who as a member of the state convention of April, 1852, voted against the ordinance declaring the right of South Carolina to secede. Another, B. G. Shields of Alabama, who was prominently mentioned, especially among the Whigs, as the Union candidate for governor, was willing to leave the field clear to Governor Collier for reëlection provided that he give satisfactory evidence of his soundness. He demanded to know, first, however, whether, if South Carolina should decide to secede and the general government to prevent it, he would do his duty, if

differed primarily in their attitude toward the Union, that of the former being of unswerving loyalty, while the latter, in calculating the value of the federal arrangement, had come to see little but the disadvantages which the bond of Union imposed upon them. Many Democrats who firmly believed in the right of secession had enlisted in the Union cause, when the hotspurs of the party, carried away by the admission of California as a free state and the abolition of the slave trade in the District of Columbia, had demanded the issue of Union or disunion; the fire-eating propensities of the latter had thus frightened, disgusted, and alienated their more moderate associates to an extent that made them doubt the sincerity of the later denials of disunion proclivities.

For nearly ten years little attention was paid by southerners in general to the abstract question of the right of secession.[86] When again the issue was raised by the success of the ''black'' Republicans and Lincoln in 1860, most old line Whigs in the South, who had survived the chaotic condition of the opposition in the intervening period, again found themselves aligned against the Democrats on the question of secession, both as to its legality and as to its expediency. This time, however, they stood alone and unaided, a humble minority, and so were unsuccessful in their opposition. When, upon the evidence of the intention of the federal administration to attempt coercion, the last states

137

called upon as governor of Alabama to coöperate with the other southern states to maintain the supremacy of the Constitution and laws of the Union. (B. G. Shields to H. W. Collier, May 24, 1851, *Mobile Advertiser*, June 13, 1851.) So also William R. King of Alabama, the Democratic candidate for the vicepresidency in 1852, was not a believer in the abstract right of secession. *Washington Union*, July 13, 1851.

[86] *Philadelphia Enquirer*, July 31, 1857. There was an occasional denial of the right of secession. ''We regard it as undeniable that th 3 doctrine of secession and disunion is every day becoming more unpopular in the South, . . . The States have *a right* to the Union, and *need* the Union to discharge the duties imposed upon it by the Constitution and for which it was created. . . For our part we want a strong Union — made so by the exactions of the States — strong enough to hang everybody who treasonably interferes with the rights of the States. . . *The right of a State to secede from the Union is the right of the slave to run away from his master* — the right of a State to compel the Union to do its duty is the right of the master to govern his slave, and require him to do his duty. We claim to be State-Rights men of the highest tone, and that is our notion of State rights.'' *Lynchburg Virginian*, September 26, 1855, quoted in *Mobile Advertiser*, October 5, 1855. See also *Fayetteville Observer*, quoted in *National Intelligencer*, July 31, 1855.

of the South passed their ordinances of secession, when arms were crossed with the federal government and the new confederacy appealed to its citizens to sustain it in the struggle, the Whigs like true Southerners promptly offered their services to aid in effecting the "revolution." [87]

ARTHUR C. COLE

UNIVERSITY OF ILLINOIS
URBANA-CHAMPAIGN

[87] The term "revolution" was rather widely used by former Whigs in discussing secession. See *National Intelligencer*, September 13, 14, 21, October 4, November 29, December 3, 1860; Hilliard, *Politics and Pen Pictures*, 281, 322.

VIRGINIA LAW REVIEW

VOLUME 36   *February, 1950*   NUMBER 1

THE PASSING OF DUAL FEDERALISM

WITHIN the generation now drawing to a close this nation has been subjected to the impact of a series of events and ideological forces of a very imperative nature. We have fought two world wars, the second of which answered every definition of "total war", and have submitted to the regimentation which these great national efforts entailed. We have passed through an economic crisis which was described by the late President as "a crisis greater than war". We have become the exclusive custodian of technology's crowning gift to civilization, an invention capable of blowing it to smithereens, and we greatly hope to retain that honorable trusteeship throughout an indefinite future. Meantime we have elected ourselves the head and forefront of one of two combinations of nations which together embrace a great part of the Western World and in this capacity are at present involved in a "cold war" with the head of the opposing combination; and as one phase of this curious and baffling struggle we find ourselves driven to combat at obvious risk to certain heretofore cherished constitutional values, the menace of a hidden propaganda which is intended by its agents to work impairment of the national fiber against the time when the "cold war" may eventuate in a "shooting war". Lastly, though by no means least, the most wide-spread and powerfully organized political interest in the country, that of organized labor, has come to accept unreservedly a new and revolutionary conception of the role of government. Formerly we generally thought of government as primarily a policeman, with an amiable penchant for being especially helpful to those who knew how to help themselves. By the ideological revolution just alluded to, which stems from the Great Depression and the New Deal, it becomes the duty of government to guarantee economic security to all as the indispensable foundation of constitutional liberty.

Naturally, the stresses and strains to which the nation has been subjected by these pressures has not left our Constitutional Law un-

139

affected. In general terms, our system has lost resiliency and what was once vaunted as a Constitution of Rights, both State and private, has been replaced by a Constitution of Powers. More specifically, the Federal System has shifted base in the direction of a consolidated national power, while within the National Government itself an increased flow of power in the direction of the President has ensued. In this article I shall deal with the first of these manifestations of an altered constitutional order.

I

The medium by which social forces are brought to bear upon constitutional interpretation, by which such forces are, so to speak, rendered into the idiom of Constitutional Law, is Judicial Review, or more concretely, the Supreme Court of the United States. This of course is a commonplace. The nature, on the other hand, of the materials with which the Court works is often a more recondite matter; and it is definitely so in the present instance.

Thus, for one thing, the Court has not been called upon, in adapting the Federal System to the requirements of Total War and other recent exigencies, to assimilate new amendments to the constitutional structure, as was the case after the Civil War. The period in question witnessed, it is true, the adoption of no fewer than four such amendments, the 18th, 19th, 20th and 21st; and the first of these, the Prohibition Amendment, contemplated a considerable augmentation of national power at the expense of the States—so much so, indeed, that some people argued that it transcended the amending power itself. Although the Supreme Court in due course rejected that contention, the controversy continued for some thirteen or fourteen years, when it was terminated in the same abrupt and drastic manner as that in which it had been precipitated, namely, by constitutional amendment. By repealing outright the 18th Amendment, the 21st Amendment restored the *status quo ante* so far as national power was concerned. Nor is the 19th Amendment establishing woman suffrage, or the 20th, changing the dates when a newly elected President and a newly elected Congress take over, relevant to our present inquiry.

Nor again has judicial translation of the power requirements of national crisis into the vocabulary of Constitutional Law been effected for the most part by affixing new definitions to the phraseology in which the constitutional grants of power to the National Government are couched. One thinks in this connection especially of the "commerce clause". The phrase "commerce among the States" was held by the Court five years ago to embrace the making of insurance contracts across State lines[1], but the ruling in question—negligible in itself so far as our purpose goes—was presently considerably diluted in effect by act of Congress.[2] Such expansion of the commerce power as is of relevance to this inquiry has been a *secondary*, even though important, consequence of other more immediate factors of constitutional interpretation.

Finally, the *structural* features of our Federal System still remain what they have always been, to wit: 1. A written Constitution which is regarded as "law" and "supreme law"; 2. As in all federations, the union of several autonomous political entities or "States" for common purposes; 3. The division of the sum total of legislative powers between a "general government", on the one hand, and the "States", on the other; 4. The direct operation for the most part of each center of government, acting within its assigned sphere, upon all persons and property within its territorial limits; 5. The provision of each center with the complete apparatus, both executive and judicial, for law enforcement; 6. Judicial review, that is, the power and duty of all courts, and ultimately of the Supreme Court of the Union, to disallow all legislative or executive acts of either center of government which in the Court's opinion transgress the Constitution; 7. An elaborate and cumbersome method of constitutional amendment, in which the States have a deciding role.

141

Not only have these features of the American Federal System never been altered by constitutional amendment in any way that requires our attention, none has within recent years been *directly* affected by judicial interpretation of the words of the Constitution in a way that need interest us. So far as the form and actual phraseological content of the Constitutional Document are concerned, Professor Dicey's dictum that federalism implies "a legally immutable Constitution", or one nearly immutable, has been fully realized in the American experience.[3]

---

1. United States v. South-Eastern Underwriters Ass'n, 322 U.S. 533, 64 Sup. Ct. 1162, 88 L. Ed. 1441 (1944).

2. 59 Stat. 33, 34 (1945), 15 U.S.C. §§ 1011-1015 (1946); see Prudential Ins. Co. v. Benjamin, 328 U.S. 408, 66 Sup. Ct. 1142, 90 L. Ed. 1342 (1946).

3. A. V. Dicey, Introduction to the Study of the Law of the Constitution 142 (7th ed. 1903).

In just what fashion then has the shift referred to above of our Federal System toward consolidation registered itself in our Constitutional Law in response to the requirements of war, economic crisis, and a fundamentally altered outlook upon the purpose of government? The solution of the conundrum is to be sought in the changed attitude of the Court toward certain postulates or axioms of constitutional interpretation closely touching the Federal System, and which in their totality comprised what I mean by Dual Federalism. These postulates are the following: 1. The national government is one of enumerated powers only; 2. Also the purposes which it may constitutionally promote are few; 3. Within their respective spheres the two centers of government are "sovereign" and hence "equal"; 4. The relation of the two centers with each other is one of tension rather than collaboration. Here I shall sketch briefly the history of each of these concepts in our Constitutional Law and show how today each has been superseded by a concept favorable to centralization.

II

In settling the apportionment of powers between the central and local governments of a Federal System any one of several principles is conceivably available, two of them being illustrated by the great Anglo-American federations. In the United States, as in the Australian Commonwealth, the principle originally adopted was that the National Government should possess only those powers which were conferred upon it in more or less definite terms by the Constitutional Document, while the remaining powers should, unless otherwise specified, be "reserved" to the States; or in the vocabulary of Constitutional Law, the National Government was a government of "enumerated powers", while the States were governments of "residual powers". On the other hand, in the case of the Dominion of Canada, which was established in the near wake of our Civil War, the reverse principle was followed. For taking counsel from that event, the founders of the Dominion thought to avoid yielding too much to "States Rights". Yet surprisingly enough, when "New Deal" programs were being tested judicially under the two constitutions a decade and a half ago, it was the United States Constitution which proved to be, in the final upshot, the more commodious vehicle of national power, the reason being that the draughtsmen of the British North America Act, besides generally using more precise language than. did the Framers, designated certain of the powers which they assigned the Canadian provinces as "exclusive", with the result of rendering them logically restrictive of the powers of the Dominion—or at least the Judicial Committee of the House of Lords so ruled.[4] As we shall see presently, there was a long period of approximately a hundred years when the foes of national power in this country achieved a comparable result through their interpretation of the Tenth Amendment—one which the Supreme Court has definitely discarded only within recent years.

Today the operation of the "enumerated powers" concept as a canon of constitutional interpretation has been curtailed on all sides. Nor in fact did it ever go altogether unchallenged, even from the first.

Article I, section 8, clause 1 of the Constitution reads:

143

> The Congress shall have power to lay and collect taxes, duties, imposts and excises, to pay the debts and provide for the common defense and general welfare of the United States . . .

What is "the general welfare" for which Congress is thus authorized to "provide", and in what fashion is it authorized to provide it? While adoption of the Constitution was pending some of its opponents made the charge that the phrase "to provide for the general welfare" was a sort of legislative joker which was designed, in conjunction with the "necessary and proper" clause, to vest Congress with power to provide for whatever it might choose to regard as the "general welfare" by any means deemed by it to be "necessary and proper." The suggestion was promptly repudiated by advocates of the Constitution on the following grounds. In the first place, it was pointed out, the phrase stood between two other phrases, both dealing with the taxing power—an awkward syntax on the assumption under consideration. In the second place, the phrase was coordinate with the phrase "to pay the debts", that is, a purpose of money expenditure only. Finally, it was asserted, the suggested reading, by endowing Congress with practically complete legislative power, rendered the succeeding enumeration of more specific powers superfluous, thereby reducing "the Constitution to a single phrase."

---

4. Illuminating in this connection is Professor W. P. M. Kennedy's ESSAYS IN CONSTITUTIONAL LAW 105-22, 153-57 (1934).

In the total this argument sounds impressive, but on closer examination it becomes less so, especially today. For one thing, it is a fact that in certain early printings of the Constitution the "common defense and general welfare" clause appears separately paragraphed, while in others it is set off from the "lay and collect" clause by a semicolon and not, as modern usage would require, by the less awesome comma. To be sure, the semicolon may have been due in the first instance to the splattering of a goose quill that needed trimming, for it is notorious that the fate of nations has often turned on just such minute *points*.

Then as to the third argument—while once deemed an extremely weighty one—it cannot be so regarded in light of the decision in 1926 in the case of *Myers* v. *United States*.[5] The Court held that the opening clause of Article II of the Constitution which says that "the executive power shall be vested in a President of the United States," is not a simple designation of office but a grant of power, which the succeeding clauses of the same article either qualify or to which they lend "appropriate emphasis." Granting the soundness of this position, however, why should not the more specific clauses of Article I be regarded as standing in a like relation to the "general welfare" clause thereof? Nor is this by any means all that may be said in favor of treating the latter clause as a grant of substantive legislative power, as anyone may convince himself who chooses to consult Mr. James Francis Lawson's minute and ingenious examination of the subject.[6]

Despite these considerations, or such of them as he was aware of, the great Chief Justice Marshall in 1819 stamped the "enumerated powers" doctrine with his approval. This was in his opinion in *McCulloch* v. *Maryland*,[7] where, in sustaining the right of the National Government to establish a Bank, he used the following expressions:

> This government is acknowledged by all to be one of enumerated powers. The principle, that it can exercise only the powers granted to it, would seem too apparent to have required to be enforced by all those arguments which its enlightened friends, while it was depending before the people, found it necessary to urge. That principle is now universally admitted.[8]

---

5. 272 U.S. 52, 47 Sup. Ct. 21, 71 L. Ed. 160 (1926).

6. The three preceding paragraphs are drawn largely from CORWIN, TWILIGHT OF THE SUPREME COURT 152-54 (1934).

7. 4 Wheat. 316, 4 L. Ed. 579 (U.S. 1819).

8. *Id.* at 405, 4 L. Ed. at 601.

At the same time, however, Marshall committed himself to certain other positions in that same opinion which in their total effect went far in the judgment of certain of his critics to render the National Government one of "indefinite powers". One of these was the dictum that "the sword and the purse, all external relations, and no inconsiderable portion of the industry of the nation, are entrusted to its government". Another was his characterization of "the power of making war", of "levying taxes", and of "regulating commerce", as "great, substantive and independent" powers. A third was his famous and for the purposes of the case, decisive construction of the "necessary and proper" clause as embracing "all [legislative] means which are appropriate" to carry out "the legitimate ends" of the Constitution.[9]

Approaching the opinion from the angle of his quasi-parental concern for "the balance between the States and the National Government", Madison declared its central vice to be that it treated the powers of the latter as "sovereign powers", a view which must inevitably "convert a limited into an unlimited government" for, he continued "in the great system of political economy, having for its general object the national welfare, everything is related immediately or remotely to every other thing; and, consequently, a power over any one thing, not limited by some obvious and precise affinity, may amount to a power over every other." "The very existence," he consequently urged, "of the local sovereignties" was "a control on the pleas for a constructive amplification of national power."[10]

So also did Marshall's most pertinacious critic, John Taylor of Carolina, pronounce the Chief Justice's doctrines as utterly destructive of the constitutional division of powers between the two centers of government.[11] A third critic was the talented Hugh Swinton Legaré of South Carolina, who in 1828 devoted a review of the first volume of Kent's *Commentaries* to a minute and immensely ingenious analysis of Marshall's most celebrated opinion. "That argument", he asserted, "cannot be sound which necessarily converts a government of enumerated into one of indefinite powers, and a confederacy of republics into a gigantic and consolidated empire". Nor did one have

145

---

9. *Id.* at 421, 4 L. Ed. at 605.

10. 8 WRITINGS OF JAMES MADISON 447-53 (Hunt ed. 1908); 2 LETTERS AND OTHER WRITINGS OF JAMES MADISON 143-47 (Phila. 1867).

11. TAYLOR, CONSTRUCTION CONSTRUED AND CONSTITUTIONS VINDICATED 9-28 *passim*, 77-89 *passim* (1820).

to rely on reasoning alone to be convinced of this; one needed only to compare the Constitution itself as expounded in the *Federalist* with the actual course of national legislation. For thus, he wrote:

> He will find that the government has been fundamentally altered by the progress of opinion—that instead of being any longer one of enumerated powers and a circumscribed sphere, as it was beyond all doubt intended to be, it knows absolutely no bounds but the will of a majority of Congress—that instead of confining itself in time of peace to the diplomatic and commercial relations of the country, it is seeking out employment for itself by interfering in the domestic concerns of society, and threatens in the course of a very few years, to control in the most offensive and despotic manner, all the pursuits, the interests, the opinions and the conduct of men. He will find that this extraordinary revolution has been brought about, in a good degree by the Supreme Court of the United States, which has applied to the Constitution—very innocently, no doubt, and with commanding ability in argument—and thus given authority and currency to, such canons of interpretation, as necessarily lead to these extravagant results. Above all, he will be perfectly satisfied that that high tribunal affords, by its own shewing, no barrier whatever against the usurpations of Congress—and that the rights of the weaker part of this confederacy may, to any extent, be wantonly and tyrannically violated, under colour of law, (the most grievous shape of oppression) by men neither interested in its destiny nor subject to its controul, without any means of redress being left it, except such as are inconsistent with all idea of order and government.[12]

These words purported one hundred and twenty years ago to be history; they read today much more like prophecy.

What is the standing today of the "enumerated powers" doctrine as a postulate of constitutional interpretation? Even so recently as 1939 the doctrine received the endorsement of a standard work on Constitutional Law in these words: "The courts in construing the scope of the grants of power to the several organs of the federal government by the federal Constitution do so on the assumption that the people of the United States intended to confer upon them only such powers as can be derived from the terms of the express grants of power made to them in that Constitution".[13]

---

12. 2 The Southern Review 72-113, No. 1 (1828); 2 Writings of Hugh Swinton Legaré 102, 123-33 (1846).

13. Rottschaefer, Handbook of American Constitutional Law 11 (1939).

In point of fact, the doctrine, when applied to Marshall's three "great, substantive and independent powers", that over external relations, the power to levy taxes and, *subaudi,* the power to expend the proceeds, and the power of commercial relations, had become a very shaky reliance. As to the first of these, indeed, it had been directly repudiated by the Court; and while as to the other two fields, it was still valid in a certain sense, its restrictive potentialities had, for reasons which will soon appear, become practically *nil.*

III

We turn now to the second of the above postulates. The question raised is whether it was the intention of the Framers of the Constitution to apportion not only the powers but also the purposes of government between the two centers, with the result of inhibiting the National Government from attempting on a national scale the same ends as the States attempt on a local scale? In view of the latitudinarian language of the Preamble to the Constitution, an affirmative answer to this question might seem to encounter ineluctable difficulties. For all that, it has at times received countenance from the Court. Even in the pages of the *Federalist* can be discerned the beginnings of a controversy regarding the scope of Congress's taxing power which was still sufficiently vital 150 years later to claim the Court's deliberate attention, although the substance of victory had long since fallen to the pro-nationalist view.[14] In brief the question at issue was this: Was Congress entitled to levy and collect taxes to further objects not falling within its other powers to advance? Very early the question became dichotomized into two questions. First, was Congress entitled to lay and collect tariffs for any but revenue purposes; secondly, was it entitled to expend the proceeds from its taxes for any other purpose than to provision the government in the exercise of its other enumerated powers, or as Henry Clay once put the issue, was the power to spend the *cause* or merely the *consequence* of power?

The tariff aspect of the general question was, for instance, debated by Calhoun, speaking for the States Rights view, and by Story in his *Commentaries* by way of answer to Calhoun.[15] Yet not until 1928 did the Court get around to affix the stamp of its approval on Story's

147

---

14. THE FEDERALIST, Nos. 30, 34, 41.
15. See COMMENTARIES § 1090.

argument, and then it did so only on historical grounds. Said Chief Justice Taft for the unanimous Court:

> It is enough to point out that the second act adopted by the Congress of the United States July 4, 1789 . . . contained the following recital:

> "Sec. 1. Whereas it is necessary for the support of government, for the discharge of the debts of the United States, and the encouragement and protection of manufactures, that duties be laid on goods, wares and merchandises imported:

> "Be it enacted, . . . "

> In this first Congress sat many members of the Constitutional Convention of 1787. This court has repeatedly laid down the principle that a contemporaneous legislative exposition of the Constitution when the founders of our government and framers of our Constitution were actively participating in public affairs, long acquiesced in, fixes the construction to be given its provisions. . . . The enactment and enforcement of a number of customs revenue laws drawn with a motive of maintaining a system of protection since the Revenue Law of 1789 are matters of history.[16]

148

In short, the constitutional case against the tariff went by default; and substantially the same is true also of the restrictive conception of the spending power. The classical statement of the broad theory of the spending power is that by Hamilton, in his Report on Manufactures in 1791. Reciting the "lay and collect taxes" clause of Article I, section 8 he says:

> The phrase is as comprehensive as any that could have been used, because it was not fit that the constitutional authority of the Union to appropriate its revenues should have been restricted within narrower limits than the "general welfare," and because this necessarily embraces a vast variety of particulars which are susceptible neither of specification nor of definition. It is therefore of necessity left to the discretion of the National Legislature to pronounce upon the objects which concern the general welfare, and for which, under that description, an appropriation of money is requisite and proper. And there seems to be no room for a doubt that whatever concerns the general interests of learning, of

---

16. Hampton & Co. v. United States, 276 U.S. 394, 411, 48 Sup. Ct. 348, 353, 72 L. Ed. 624, 631 (1928).

agriculture, of manufactures, and of commerce, are within the sphere of the national councils, *as far as regards an application of money.*[17]

Endorsed contemporaneously by Jefferson, stigmatized by him on further reflection, rebutted by Madison in his veto of the Bonus Bill in 1806, rejected by Monroe in the early years of his Presidency, endorsed by him in his famous message of May 4, 1822, Hamilton's doctrine has since the Civil War pointed an ever-increasing trend in Congressional fiscal policy. Yet even as recently as 1923 we find the Court industriously sidestepping the constitutional question and displaying considerable agility in doing so. I refer to a brace of suits in which Massachusetts and a citizen thereof, a Mrs. Frothingham, sought independently to challenge Congress's right to vote money in aid of expectant mothers. It was no function of a State, the Court instructed Massachusetts, to interpose in behalf of the constitutional rights of its citizens, who, being also citizens of the United States, could rely on getting adequate protection against the National Government from the national courts. Thus, at long last was John C. Calhoun's doctrine of State interposition answered. Turning then to Mrs. Frothingham, the Court informed her that her interest as a taxpayer was much too trivial to entitle her to the interposition of the national courts.[18]

Twelve years later, however, in the *A.A.A.* case, the Court at last came to grips with the constitutional issue, which it decided in line with the Hamiltonian thesis. Said Justice Roberts for the Court:

> Since the foundation of the Nation sharp differences of opinion have persisted as to the true interpretation of the phrase, ["lay and collect taxes to . . . provide for . . . the general welfare"]. Madison asserted it amounted to no more than a reference to the other powers enumerated in the subsequent clauses of the same section; that, as the United States is a government of limited and enumerated powers, the grant of power to tax and spend for the general national welfare must be confined to the enumerated legislative fields committed to the Congress. In this view the phrase is mere tautology, for taxation and appropriation are or may be necessary incidents of the exercise of any of the enumerated legislative powers. Hamilton, on the other

149

---

17. 4 WORKS OF ALEXANDER HAMILTON 151 (Federal ed. 1904).
18. Massachusetts v. Mellon, 262 U.S. 447, 43 Sup. Ct. 597, 67 L. Ed. 1078 (1923).

hand, maintained the clause confers a power separate and distinct from those later enumerated, is not restricted in meaning by the grant of them, and Congress consequently has a substantive power to tax and to appropriate, limited only by the requirement that it shall be exercised to provide for the general welfare of the United States. Each contention has had the support of those whose views are entitled to weight. This court has noticed the question, but has never found it necessary to decide which is the true construction. Mr. Justice Story, in his Commentaries, espouses the Hamiltonian position. We shall not review the writings of public men and commentators or discuss the legislative practice. Study of all these leads us to conclude that the reading advocated by Mr. Justice Story is the correct one. While, therefore, the power to tax is not unlimited, its confines are set in the clause which confers it, and not in those of § 8 which bestow and define the legislative powers of the Congress. It results that the power of Congress to authorize expenditure of public moneys for public purposes is not limited by the direct grants of legislative power found in the Constitution.[19]

150

In short, the Court once more ratified the history that Congressional practice had made.

The theory that the enumerated powers may be validly exercised for certain limited purposes only was first passed upon in relation to the commerce power in 1808 under Jefferson's Embargo Act. The proposition offered the Court—the United States District Court for Massachusetts—was that the power of Congress to regulate foreign commerce was only the power to adopt measures for its protection and advancement, whereas the Embargo destroyed commerce. The Court rejected the argument. Pointing to the clause of Article I, section 9, which interdicted a ban on the slave trade till 1808, the judge remarked: "It was perceived that, under the power of regulating commerce, Congress would be authorized to abridge it in favor of the great principles of humanity and justice."[20]

One hundred and ten years later the same argument was revived and revamped in opposition to the congressional embargo on interstate commerce in child-made goods, and this time it prevailed. The act, said the Court, was not a commercial regulation, but a

---

19. United States v. Butler, 297 U.S. 1, 65, 56 Sup. Ct. 312, 319, 80 L. Ed. 477, 488 (1936).
20. United States v. The William, 28 Fed. Cas. No. 16,700, at 421 (D. Mass. 1808).

usurpation of the reserved power of the States to protect the public health, safety, morals, and general welfare.[21] And when Congress next sought to use its taxing power against firms employing child labor, the Court, adopting the narrow purpose concept of the taxing power *ad hoc*, frustrated that attempt too.[22] We shall now see how this course of reasoning has since toppled to the ground along with other supporting canons of interpretation.

IV

Our third .postulate is addressed particularly to this question: By what rule are collisions between the respective powers of the two centers of government supposed by the Constitution to be determined? In answer two texts of the Constitution itself compete for recognition, Article VI, clause 2, which reads as follows:

> This Constitution, and the laws of the United States which shall be made in pursuance thereof, and all treaties made, or which shall be made, under the authority of the United States, shall be the supreme law of the land; and the judges in every State shall be bound thereby, anything in the Constitution or laws of any State to the contrary notwithstanding.

and the Tenth Amendment, which says:

> The powers not delegated to the United States by the Constitution, nor prohibited by it to the States, are reserved to the States respectively, or to the people.

It was quite plainly the intention of the Federal Convention that national laws, otherwise constitutional except for being in conflict with State laws, should invariably prevail over the latter;[23] or, as Madison later phrased the matter, State power should be "no ingredient of national power".[24] This was also Marshall's theory. Indeed, the principle of "national supremacy" was in his estimation the most fundamental axiom of constitutional interpretation touching the federal relationship, one even more vital to the Union and more unmis-

---

21. Hammer v. Dagenhart, 247 U.S. 251, 38 Sup. Ct. 529, 62 L. Ed. 1101 (1918).
22. Bailey v. Drexel Furniture Co., 259 U.S. 20, 42 Sup. Ct. 449, 66 L. Ed. 817 (1922).
23. See 1 RECORDS OF THE FEDERAL CONVENTION 21-22 (Farrand ed. 1911).
24. 2 ANNALS OF CONGRESS col. 1891 (1790-91). See CORWIN, COMMERCE POWER VERSUS STATES RIGHTS 117-72 (1936).

151

takably ordained by the Constitutional Document itself than the doctrine of "loose construction", loosely so-called by his critics.

"If", said he in *McCulloch* v. *Maryland*, "any one proposition could
command the assent of mankind, one might expect it would be this—
that the government of the Union, though limited in its powers, is
supreme within its sphere of action". Nor did the Tenth Amendment affect the question. In omitting from it the word "expressly",
its authors had—and apparently of deliberate purpose—left the question
whether any particular power belonged to the general government "to
depend on a fair construction of the whole instrument".[25] Counsel for
Maryland, Luther Martin, agreed—the Tenth Amendment was "merely
declaratory".[26]

Yet when, five years later the Court came to decide *Gibbons* v.
Ogden,[27] in which the question was whether a New York created
monopoly was compatible with legislation of Congress regulating the
coasting trade, Marshall was confronted with a very different set of
ideas by counsel for the local interest. "In argument", Marshall
recites, "it had been contended that if a law, passed by a State in the
exercise of its acknowledged sovereignty, comes into conflict with a
law passed by Congress in pursuance of the Constitution, they affect
the subject, and each other, like equal opposing powers." This contention Marshall answered as follows:

> But the framers of our constitution foresaw this state of things,
> and provided for it, by declaring the supremacy not only of itself,
> but of the laws made in pursuance of it. The nullity of any act,
> inconsistent with the constitution is produced by the declaration that
> the constitution is the supreme law. The appropriate application of
> that part of the clause which confers the same supremacy on laws
> and treaties, is to such acts of the State Legislatures as do not trans-
> cend their powers, but, though enacted in the execution of acknowl-
> edged State powers, interfere with, or are contrary to the laws of
> Congress made in pursuance of the constitution, or some treaty made
> under the authority of the United States. In every such case, the
> act of Congress, or the treaty, is supreme; and the law of the State,
> though enacted in the exercise of powers not controverted, must
> yield to it.[28]

25. 4 Wheat. 316, 405, 4 L. Ed. 579, 601 (U.S. 1819).
26. *Id.* at 374, 6 L. Ed. at 593.
27. 9 Wheat. 1, 6 L. Ed. 23 (U.S. 1824).
28. *Id.* at 210, 6 L. Ed. at 73.

152

Whence came the notion of National-State "equality", and what effect did it have on the Court's jurisprudence? The germ of it is to be found in the theory of the Constitution's origin developed in the Virginia and Kentucky Resolutions, that it was a compact of "sovereign" states, rather than an ordinance of "the people of America". The deduction from this premise that the National Government and the States, both being "sovereign", faced each other as "equals" across the line defining their respective jurisdictions, was made by John Taylor of Carolina in his critique of the decision in *McCulloch* v. *Maryland*. But earlier, the Virginia Court of Appeals had contributed to Taylor's system of constitutional interpretation the notion that under the "supremacy" clause itself, the State judiciaries were the constitutionally designated agencies for the application of the principle of supremacy.[29] It followed that the Supreme Court no more than Congress was able to bind the "equal" States, nor could they on the other hand bind Congress or the Court.

153

The notion of National-State equality became in due course a part of the constitutional creed of the Taney Court, but stripped of its anarchic implications and reduced to the proportions of a single thread in a highly complicated fabric of constitutional exegesis. It was early in this period that the concept of the Police Power emerged. This, broadly considered, was simply what Taney termed "the power to govern men and things" defined from the point of view of the duty of the State to "promote the happiness and prosperity of the community"; more narrowly, it was a certain central core of this power, namely the power of the States to "provide for the public health, safety, and good order". Within this latter field at least, the powers reserved to the States by the Tenth Amendment were "sovereign" powers, "complete, unqualified, and exclusive". Yet this did not signify that the States, acting through either their legislatures or their courts, were the final judge of the scope of these "sovereign" powers. This was the function of the Supreme Court of the United States, which for this purpose was regarded by the Constitution as standing outside of and over both the National Government and the States, and vested with authority to apportion impartially to each center its proper powers in accordance with the Constitution's intention. And the primary test whether this intention was fulfilled was whether

---

29. See Hunter v. Martin, 4 Munf. 1, 11 (Va. 1814), *rev'd*, Martin v. Hunter's Lessee, 1 Wheat. 304, 4 L. Ed. 97 (U.S. 1816).

conflict between the two centers was avoided.[30]   In Judge Cooley's
words, "The laws of both [centers] operate within the same territory,
but if in any particular case their provisions are in conflict, one or the
other is void", that is, void apart from the conflict itself.[31]

Thus the principle of national supremacy came to be superseded by
an unlimited discretion in the Supreme Court to designate this or that
State power as comprising an independent limitation on national power.
In only one area was the earlier principle recognized as still operative, and that was the field of interstate commercial regulation.   This
field, indeed, was not properly speaking a part of the "reserved
powers" of the States at all; it belonged to Congress's enumerated
powers.   The States, however, might occupy it as to minor phases of
commerce unless and until Congress chose to do so, in which case
154   Article VI, paragraph 2 came into play and conflicting state legislation was superseded.[32]

While, as we have seen, the Police Power was defined in the first
instance with the end in view of securing to the States a near monopoly
of the right to realize the main *objectives* of government, the concept came later to embrace the further idea that certain *subject-
matters* were also segregated to the States and hence could not be
reached by any valid exercise of national power.   That production,
and hence mining, agriculture, and manufacturing, and the employer-
employee relationship in connection with these were among such
subject-matters was indeed one of the basic postulates of the Court's
system of Constitutional Law in the era of *laissez faire*.[33]   The decisions in both the first *Child Labor* case and the *A.A.A.* case were
largely determined by this axiom; and as late as 1936, Justice Sutherland's opinion in the *Bituminous Coal* case gave it classic expression.[34]
The question before the Court concerned the constitutionality of an
attempt by Congress to govern hours and wages in the soft coal mines
of the country.   Said Justice Sutherland for the Court:

> In addition to what has just been said, the conclusive answer is
> that the evils are all local evils over which the federal government
> has no legislative control.   The relation of employer and employee

---

30. On this system of constitutional interpretation, see especially New York v. Miln,
11 Pet. 102, 9 L. Ed. 648 (U.S. 1837); see also License Cases, 5 How. 504, 527-37, 573-74,
588, 613, 12 L. Ed. 256, 266-71, 287-88, 294, 305 (U.S. 1847) *passim*.

31. COOLEY, PRINCIPLES OF CONSTITUTIONAL LAW 152 (3d ed. 1898).

32. Cooley v. Board of Wardens, 12 How. 299, 13 L. Ed. 996 (U.S. 1851).

33. See CORWIN, COMMERCE POWER VERSUS STATES RIGHTS 175-209 (1936).

34. Carter v. Carter Coal Co., 298 U.S. 238, 56 Sup. Ct. 855, 80 L. Ed. 1160 (1936).

is a local relation. At common law, it is one of the domestic relations. The wages are paid for the doing of local work. Working conditions are obviously local conditions. The employees are not engaged in or about commerce, but exclusively in producing a commodity. And the controversies and evils, which it is the object of the act to regulate and minimize, are local controversies and evils affecting local work undertaken to accomplish that local result. Such effect as they may have upon commerce, however extensive it may be, is secondary and indirect. An increase in the greatness of the effect adds to its importance. It does not alter its character.[35]

This entire system of constitutional interpretation touching the Federal System is today in ruins. It toppled in the *Social Security Act* cases and in *N.L.R.B.* v. *Jones & Laughlin Steel Corporation,* in which the Wagner Labor Act was sustained.[36] This was in 1937 while the "Old Court" was still in power. In 1941 in *United States* v. *Darby,*[37] the "New Court" merely performed a mopping-up operation. The Act of Congress involved was the Fair Labor Standards Act of 1938, which not only bans interstate commerce in goods produced under sub-standard conditions but makes their production a penal offense against the United States if they are "intended" for interstate or foreign commerce. Speaking for the unanimous Court, Chief Justice Stone went straight back to Marshall's opinions in *McCulloch* v. *Maryland* and *Gibbons* v. *Ogden,* extracting from the former his latitudinarian construction of the "necessary and proper" clause and from both cases his uncompromising application of the "supremacy" clause.[38]

Today neither the State Police Power nor the concept of Federal Equilibrium is any "ingredient of national legislative power", whether as respects subject-matter to be governed, or the choice of objectives or of means for its exercise.

V

Lastly, we come to the question whether the two centers of government ought to be regarded as standing in a competitive or co-

155

---

35. *Id.* at 308, 56 Sup. Ct. at 871, 80 L. Ed. at 1187.

36. 301 U.S. 1, 57 Sup. Ct. 615, 81 L. Ed. 893 (1937).

37. 312 U.S. 100, 61 Sup. Ct. 451, 85 L. Ed. 609 (1941).

38. *Ibid.* See also United States v. Carolene Products Co., 304 U.S. 144, 58 Sup. Ct. 778, 82 L. Ed. 1234 (1938); Mulford v. Smith, 307 U.S. 38, 59 Sup. Ct. 648, 83 L. Ed. 1092 (1939).

operative relation to each other. The question first emerged at the executive and judicial levels. In Article VI, paragraph 3 the requirement is laid down that members of the State legislatures, their executive and judicial officers shall take an oath, or make affirmation, to support the Constitution, thus testifying, as Hamilton points out in *Federalist* 27, to the expectation that these functionaries would be "incorporated into the operations of the National Government", in the exercise of its constitutional powers. In much early legislation, furthermore, this expectation was realized. The Judiciary Act of 1789 left the State courts in exclusive possession of some categories of national jurisdiction and shared some others with it. The Act of 1793 entrusted the rendition of fugitive slaves in part to national officials and in part to State officials, and the rendition of fugitives from justice from one State to another exclusively to the State executives. Certain later acts empowered State courts to entertain criminal prosecutions for forging paper of the Bank of the United States and for counterfeiting coin of the United States; while still others conferred on State judges authority to admit aliens to national citizenship and provided penalties in case such judges should utter false certificates of naturalization—provisions which are still on the statute books.[39]

The subsequent rise, however, of the States Rights sentiment presently overcast this point of view with heavy clouds of doubt. From the nationalist angle Marshall stigmatized the efforts of Virginia and those who thought her way to "confederatize the Union"; and asserting in *McCulloch* v. *Maryland* the administrative independence of the National Government, he there laid down a sweeping rule prohibiting the States from taxing even to the slightest extent national instrumentalities on their operations. "The power to tax is the power to destroy", said he; and whatever a State may do at all it may do to the utmost extent.[40]

But when a few years later the Taney Court took over, the shoe was on the other foot. In 1842, the State of Pennsylvania was sustained by the Court, speaking by Marshall's apostle Story, in refusing to permit its magistrates to aid in enforcing the fugitive slave provisions of the Act of 1793. Said Story:

> . . . the national government, in the absence of all positive provisions to the contrary, is bound through its own proper depart-

156

39. For references, see Corwin, Court Over Constitution 135-36 and notes (1938).
40. See 4 Wheat. 316, 427-31, 4 L. Ed. 579, 606-7 (U.S. 1819); Brown v. Maryland, 12 Wheat. 419, 439, 6 L. Ed. 678, 685 (U.S. 1827).

ments, legislative, executive, or judiciary, as the case may require, to carry into effect all the rights and duties imposed upon it by the Constitution.[41]

And in *Kentucky* v. *Dennison*, decided on the eve of the Civil War, the "duty" imposed by this same act on State governors to render up fugitives from justice on the demand of the executives of sister States, was watered down to a judicially unenforcible "moral duty". Said the Chief Justice: " . . . we think it clear, that the Federal Government, under the Constitution, has no power to impose on a State officer, as such, any duty whatever, and compel him to perform it; . . . "[42]

Nor was even this the end, for as late as 1871 the Court laid down the converse of Marshall's doctrine in *McCulloch* v. *Maryland*, holding that, since the States enjoyed equal constitutional status with the National Government, what was sauce for the one was sauce for the other too, and that therefore a national income tax could not be constitutionally applied to State official salaries.[43]

The doctrine of tax exemption was the climactic expression of the competitive theory of Federalism, and is today largely moribund in consequence of the emergence of the *cooperative* conception. According to this conception, the National Government and the States are mutually complementary parts of a *single* governmental mechanism all of whose powers are intended to realize the current purposes of government according to their applicability to the problem in hand. It is thus closely intertwined with the multiple-purpose conception of national power and with recent enlarged theories of the function of government generally. Here we are principally interested in two forms of joint action by the National Government and the States which have developed within recent years, primarily through the *legislative* powers of the two centers.

Thus in the first place the National Government has brought its augmented powers over interstate commerce and communications to the support of local policies of the States in the exercise of their reserved powers. By the doctrine that Congress's power to regulate "commerce among the States" is "exclusive", a State is frequently

157

---

41. Prigg v. Commonwealth of Pennsylvania, 16 Peters 539, 616, 10 L. Ed. 1060, 1089 (U.S. 1842).

42. 24 How. 66, 107, 16 L. Ed. 717, 729 (U.S. 1861).

43. Collector v. Day, 11 Wall. 113, 20 L. Ed. 122 (U.S. 1871).

unable to stop the flow of commerce from sister States even when it threatens to undermine local legislation. In consequence Congress has within recent years come to the assistance of the police powers of the States by making certain crimes against them, like theft, racketeering, kidnapping, crimes also against the National Government whenever the offender extends his activities beyond state boundary lines.[44]

Justifying such legislation, the Court has said:

> Our dual form of government has its perplexities, state and Nation having different spheres of jurisdiction . . . but it must be kept in mind that we are one people; and the powers reserved to the states and those conferred on the nations are adapted to be exercised, whether independently or concurrently, to promote the general welfare, material and moral.[45]

158   It is true that in the *Child Labor* case of 1918 this postulate of constitutional interpretation seemed to have been discarded, but the logic of *United States* v. *Darby*, restores it in full force.

Secondly, the National Government has held out inducements, primarily of a pecuniary kind, to the States—the so-called "grants-in-aid"—to use their reserved powers to support certain objectives of national policy in the field of expenditure. In other words, the greater financial strength of the National Government is joined to the wider coercive powers of the States. Thus since 1911, Congress has voted money to subsidize forest-protection, education in agricultural and industrial subjects and in home economics, vocational rehabilitation and education, the maintenance of nautical schools, experimentation in reforestation and highway construction in the States; in return for which cooperating States have appropriated equal sums for the same purposes, and have brought their further powers to the support thereof along lines laid down by Congress.[46]

The culmination of this type of National-State cooperation to date, however, is reached in The Social Security Act of August 14, 1935. The Act brings the national tax-spending power to the support of such States as desire to cooperate in the maintenance of old-age pensions, unemployment insurance, maternal welfare work, vocational rehabilitation, and public health work, and in financial assistance to impoverished old age, dependent children, and the blind. Such legis-

---

44. For references, see CORWIN, COURT OVER CONSTITUTION 148-50 and notes (1938).
45. Hoke v. United States, 227 U. S. 308, 322, 33 Sup. Ct. 281, 284, 57 L. Ed. 523, 527 (1913).
46. CORWIN, *op. cit. supra* note 44, at 157-63.

lation is, as we have seen, within the national taxing-spending power.
What, however, of the objection that it "coerced" complying States
into "abdicating" their powers?   Speaking to this point in the *Social
Security Act* cases, the Court has said: "The . . . contention confuses
motive with coercion . . . .   To hold that motive or temptation is
equivalent to coercion is to plunge the law in endless difficulties."[47]
And again: "The United States and the state of Alabama are not
alien governments.   They co-exist within the same territory.   Unemployment is their common concern.   Together the two statutes
before us [the Act of Congress and the Alabama Act] embody a
cooperative legislative effort by state and national governments, for
carrying out a public purpose common to both, which neither could
fully achieve without the cooperation of the other.   The Constitution
does not prohibit such cooperation."[48]

It has been argued, to be sure, that the cooperative conception of
the federal relationship, especially as it is realized in the policy of the
"grants-in-aid", tends to break down State initiative and to devitalize
State policies. [Actually, its effect has often been the contrary, and
for the reason pointed out by Justice Cardozo in *Helvering* v. *Davis*,[49]
also decided in 1937; namely, that the States, competing as they do
with one another to attract investors, have not been able to embark
separately upon expensive programs of relief and social insurance.]

The other great objection to Cooperative Federalism is more difficult to meet, if indeed it can be met.   This is, that "Cooperative
Federalism" spells further aggrandizement of national power.   Unquestionably it does, for when two cooperate it is the stronger member of the combination who calls the tunes.   Resting as it does
primarily on the superior fiscal resources of the National Government, Cooperative Federalism has been, to date, a short expression for
a constantly increasing concentration of power at Washington in the
instigation and supervision of local policies.

VI

But the story of American federalism may also be surveyed from
the angle of the diverse interests which the federal "contrivance"—

47. Steward Machine Co. v. Davis, 301 U.S. 548, 589, 57 Sup. Ct. 883, 892, 81 L. Ed.
1279, 1292 (1937).
48. Carmichael v. Southern Coal & Coke Co., 301 U.S. 495, 526, 57 Sup. Ct. 868, 880,
81 L. Ed. 1245, 1262 (1937).
49. 301 U.S. 619, 57 Sup. Ct. 904, 81 L. Ed. 1307 (1937).

to use Dicey's apt word—has served. Federalism's first achievement was to enable the American people to secure the benefits of national union without imperilling their republican institutions. In a passage in his *Spirit of the Laws* which Hamilton quotes in *The Federalist*, Montesquieu had anticipated this possibility in general terms. He said:

> It is very probable that mankind would have been obliged at length to live constantly under the government of a single person, had they not contrived a kind of constitution that has all the internal advantages of a republican, together with the external force of a monarchical government. I mean a Confederate Republic.[50]

In fact, the founders of the American Federal System for the first time in history ranged the power of a potentially great state on the side of institutions which had hitherto been confined to small states. Even the republicanism of Rome had stopped at the Eternal City's walls.

Then in the century following, American federalism served the great enterprise of appropriating the North American continent to western civilization. For one of the greatest lures to the westward movement of population was the possibility which federalism held out to the advancing settlers of establishing their own undictated political institutions, and endowing them with generous powers of government for local use. Federalism thus became the instrument of a new, *a democratic, imperialism*, one extending over an "Empire of liberty," in Jefferson's striking phrase.

Then, about 1890, just as the frontier was disappearing from the map, federalism became, through judicial review, an instrument of the current *laissez faire* conception of the function of government and a force promoting the rise of Big Business. Adopting the theory that the reason why Congress had been given the power to regulate "commerce among the several states" was to prevent the states from doing so, rather than to enable the National Government to pursue social policies of its own through exerting a positive control over commerce, the Court at one time created a realm of no-power, "a twilight zone", "a no-man's land" in which corporate enterprise was free to roam largely unchecked. While the economic unification of the nation was undoubtedly aided by this type of Constitutional Law, the benefit was handsomely paid for in the social detriments which attended it, as became clear when the Great Depression descended on the country.

---

50. THE FEDERALIST, No. 9 at 48 (Lodge ed. 1888).

Finally, by the constitutional revolution which once went by the name of the "New Deal" but now wears the label "Fair Deal", American federalism has been converted into an instrument for the achievement of peace abroad and economic security for "the common man" at home. In the process of remolding the Federal System for these purposes, however, the instrument has been overwhelmed and submerged in the objectives sought, so that today the question faces us whether the constituent States of the System can be saved for any useful purpose, and thereby saved as the vital cells that they have been heretofore of democratic sentiment, impulse, and action.

And it was probably with some such doubt in mind that Justice Frankfurter wrote a few years ago, in an opinion for the Court:

> The interpenetrations of modern society have not wiped out state lines. It is not for us to make inroads upon our federal system either by indifference to its maintenance or excessive regard for the unifying forces of modern technology. Scholastic reasoning may prove that no activity is isolated within the boundaries of a single State, but that cannot justify absorption of legislative power by the United States over every activity.[51]

161

These be brave words. Are they likely to determine the course of future history any more than Madison's similar utterance—130 years ago—has done to date?

Edward S. Corwin

Princeton, N. J.

---

51. Polish National Alliance v. NLRB, 322 U.S. 643, 650, 64 Sup. Ct. 1196, 1200, 86 L. Ed. 1509, 1516 (1944). The following striking contrast between the United States of 1789 and the United States of 1942 is from the pen of Professor William Anderson in *Federalism—Then and Now*, 16 State Government 107-12 (May, 1943):

> *Then* a small area, with a small and sparse population, mainly agricultural and poor. *Now* one of the world's great nations in both area and population, largely urban and highly industrial, with tremendous national wealth.
> *Then* largely a debtor people and an exporter of raw materials. *Now* a great creditor nation and large exporter of manufactured as well as agricultural goods.
> *Then* meager and slow transportation facilities, and even poorer provisions for communication. *Now* an equipment of railroads, steamship lines, highways, trucks and buses, air transport, and communications of all kinds unexcelled by any nation and undreamed of in the past.
> *Then* state citizenship, state and local loyalties, interstate suspicions and tariffs, localized business, and considerable internal disunity. *Now* a nation, with national citizenship, primarily national loyalties, a nationwide free market, and nationally organized business, agriculture, labor, professions, press, and political parties.
> *Then* an upstart and divided people, an international weakling, threatened from north and south, with very poor defense arrangements, and looking out over

the Atlantic at an essentially hostile world. *Now* a great world power, an international leader, with a powerful army and navy, and with strong friends and interests (as well as enemies) across both Atlantic and Pacific.

Then inactive, negative, *laissez-faire* government with very few functions, and with only business leaders favoring a national government, and they desiring only to give it enough vigor to protect commerce, provide a nationwide free home market, and a sound currency and banking system. *Now* active, positive, collectivist government, especially at the national level, rendering many services with the support of powerful labor and agricultural elements, while many business leaders have reversed their position.

Then local law enforcement with state protection of the liberties guaranteed in bills of rights. *Now* increasing national law enforcement and national protection of civil liberties even against state and local action.

Then practically no employees of the national government and very few state and local employees. *Now* a national civil service of normally over a million persons reaching into every county of the country, plus extensive state and local civil services.

Then small public budgets at all levels. *Now* public budgets and expenditures, especially for the national government, that reach astronomical figures.

Then (before 1789) no national taxes at all for decades after 1789, only customs and excise taxes on a very limited scale, with state and local governments relying almost entirely on direct property taxes. *Now* tremendously increased and diversified taxes at both national and state levels, with a national government rising swiftly to a dominating position with respect to all taxes except those directly on property.

Then (before 1788) state grants to the Congress of the United States for defense and debt purposes. *Now* grants-in-aid by the national government to the states in increasing amounts and with steadily tightening national controls over state action.

DAVID P. CURRIE

FEDERALISM AND THE ADMIRALTY:
"THE DEVIL'S OWN MESS"

> *"Always do that, wild ducks do. They shoot to the bottom as deep as they can get, sir—and bite themselves fast in the tangle and seaweed—and all the devil's own mess that grows down there. And they never come up again."*
>
> IBSEN

163

The Oregon Employers' Liability Law requires persons responsible for work involving danger to workmen or to the public to use "every device, care and precaution which it is practicable to use for the protection and safety of life and limb."[1] Since *Erie R.R. v. Tompkins*,[2] it is not surprising that federal courts have enforced this provision as a matter of course by the award of damages for personal injury or death.[3] Indeed, state statutes, as distinguished from state decisional law on "general" matters, were consistently enforced in federal courts even during the era of *Swift v. Tyson*.[4] Yet only last Term, in

---

David P. Currie is a law clerk at the United States Court of Appeals for the Second Circuit.

[1] ORE. REV. STAT. §§ 654.305–35 (1959).

[2] 304 U.S. 64 (1938).

[3] *E.g.*, Smith v. Shevlin-Hixon Co., 157 F. 2d 51 (9th Cir. 1946).

[4] 16 Pet. 1 (1842). For example, the Oregon Employers' Liability Law was enforced by a federal court in Swayne & Hoyt, Inc. v. Barsch, 226 Fed. 581 (9th Cir. 1915).

Hess v. United States,[5] three dissenting justices argued strenuously that the application of the Oregon Employers' Liability Law in a death action in a federal court was unconstitutional.

The explanation, of course, lies in the fact that while in *Erie* the injury occurred on a footpath beside a railroad track, the accident in *Hess* took place in the waters of the Columbia River. *Hess* was an action under the Federal Tort Claims Act,[6] which sought to equate the liability of the United States with that of a private party in like circumstances.[7] Because the injury occurred on navigable waters, a corresponding private action could have been brought within the admiralty jurisdiction of the federal district courts.[8]

There is no doubt that had the injury occurred on land the statute could validly have been applied in a federal court. To the uninitiated it may seem somewhat difficult to understand why the fact that the accident occurred on water should make any difference. The cognoscenti, however, sit back with a shrug and wonder why doubts should be voiced—after all, it was an admiralty case. Everyone knows, or is expected to know, that in a diversity case state law governs, and in an admiralty case, federal law.

The distinction is well known, but it is not analytically self-evident. For nearly a hundred years it was not even true. As an original matter it might well be argued that it is necessary and proper to the effective exercise of jurisdiction in both admiralty and diversity cases that Congress have power to prescribe rules of decision to be applied in federal courts,[9] and that in the absence of congressional action the federal courts may apply and enunciate a body of federal common law as an inherent part of the exercise of judicial power.[10] Indeed, there is

164

[5] 361 U.S. 314 (1960).

[6] 28 U.S.C. § 1346(b).

[7] See 72 HARV. L. REV. 1363, 1364 (1959); Comment, 56 YALE L. J. 534, 542, 553 (1947).

[8] Kermarec v. Compagnie Generale Transatlantique, 358 U.S. 625, 628 (1959). See Atlantic Transport Co. v. Imbrovek, 234 U.S. 52, 61–62 (1914); The Plymouth, 3 Wall. 20 (1866) (dictum); GILMORE & BLACK, THE LAW OF ADMIRALTY 21–22 (1957) (hereinafter GILMORE & BLACK).

[9] See, e.g., Reed, J., concurring, in Erie R.R. v. Tompkins, 304 U.S. 64, 90–92 (1938); B. Currie, *Change of Venue and the Conflict of Laws*, 22 U. CHI. L. REV. 405, 468–69 (1955); Clark, *State Law in the Federal Courts: The Brooding Omnipresence of Erie v. Tompkins*, 55 YALE L. J. 267, 278–79 (1946).

[10] See, e.g., 1 CROSSKEY, POLITICS AND THE CONSTITUTION IN THE HISTORY OF THE UNITED STATES 563–674, especially 609, 657, 663 (1953); 2 id. at 818, 902, 904, 916;

much to be said for a uniform law to govern transactions connected with more than one state. Commercial transactions would be made secure thereby against the vagaries of local laws and obligations given identical effect everywhere; persons would be enabled to plan their conduct and their expenses simply and without the discomfort of necessary reference to the laws of every jurisdiction that might be involved; and problems of choice of law, often not susceptible of satisfactory judicial solution, would be avoided. The imposition of judge-made federal law in all these cases, however, would also result in an incursion into state competence which would be at least politically unattractive and, in the eyes of many, repugnant to basic conceptions of a federal system. Moreover, the imposition of complete uniformity might often create injustice; in many matters local variations of circumstances require diversity of rule. Finally, national uniformity in diversity and admiralty cases would be obtained only at the cost of creating a diversity of duties and of rights within a single jurisdiction according to whether the transaction was entirely local or a matter within federal judicial competence.

165

Mr. Justice Story viewed the grants of diversity and admiralty jurisdiction as complementary and utilized them in an attempt to realize the goal of a uniform law for the federal courts in commercial and maritime matters.[11] It was no accident that the author of *Swift v. Tyson* was also in large part responsible for the expansion of the admiralty power and for the concomitant growth of federal maritime law.[12] In the nineteenth century, under the impetus given by Story, the general maritime law and—where state statutes did not apply—the general commercial law were applied in actions in the federal courts, while state courts exercising concurrent jurisdiction of diver-

---

Cook, *The Federal Courts and the Conflict of Laws*, 36 ILL. L. REV. 493, 520–22 (1942); Broh-Kahn, *Amendment by Decision—More on the Erie Case*, 30 KY. L. J. 3, 18, 28, 36–38 (1941).

[11] See Stevens, *Erie R.R. v. Tompkins and the Uniform General Maritime Law*, 64 HARV. L. REV. 246, 249–50 (1950).

[12] The most notable example is Story's memorable decision on circuit in DeLovio v. Boit, 7 Fed. Cas. 418 (No. 3776) (C.C.D. Mass. 1815), holding an action to recover on a policy of marine insurance within the admiralty jurisdiction, contrary to English precedents. See Note, 37 AM. L. REV. 911, 916 (1903) : "It was said of the late Justice Story, that if a bucket of water were brought into his court with a corn cob floating in it, he would at once extend the admiralty jurisdiction of the United States over it."

sity cases and of maritime cases under the saving clause of the
Judiciary Act[13] were free to apply their own laws.[14]

From these parallel origins the two jurisdictional clauses have developed in opposite directions. For a period of several years, beginning in 1917 and corresponding to the awakening of state legislatures
to the barbarism of nineteenth-century conceptions of liability for industrial accident, the Supreme Court under the leadership of Mr.
Justice McReynolds repeatedly invoked the Admiralty Clause and
its policy of uniformity to strike down enlightened state laws even
when applied in state courts.[15] Since that time, although the uniformity principle has not been employed to achieve the same ruthless destruction of state interests, wherever the need for uniformity is recognized it is held that a principle akin to that of the supremacy clause
requires the application of the federal law in state courts as well as in
admiralty.[16] In diversity, of course, the same desire for a uniform outcome in both state and federal forums led to the opposite result.[17] In
both classes of cases it is now quite clear that in nearly all matters
likely to have a serious impact on the outcome of a case the same law
must be applied in state and federal courts. But, while *Southern Pacific
Co. v. Jensen*[18] and *Chelentis v. Luckenbach S.S. Co.*[19] held unconstitutional a state court's attempt to apply state statutory and common law
in a maritime action, *Erie R.R. v. Tompkins* held the application of

166

---

[13] 1 Stat. 76–77 (1789), as amended, 28 U.S.C. § 1333.

[14] *Maritime law: compare* The Catharine v. Dickinson, 17 How. 170, 177 (1855) (collision suit in admiralty, divided damages awarded because of mutual fault), *with* Belden v.
Chase, 150 U.S. 674, 691 (1893) (state court collision suit, contributory negligence complete bar); see Pitney, J., dissenting, in Southern Pacific Co. v. Jensen, 244 U.S. 205, 226,
237, 241–42, 251, 254 (1917); GILMORE & BLACK 374–76 (1957); Palfrey, *The Common
Law Courts and the Law of the Sea*, 36 HARV. L. REV. 777, 778–79 (1923). *Commercial law:*
see Erie R.R. v. Tompkins, 304 U.S. 64, 71–72, 74 (1938); HOLT, THE CONCURRENT
JURISDICTION OF THE FEDERAL AND STATE COURTS 160–88 (1888).

[15] *E.g.*, Southern Pacific Co. v. Jensen, 244 U.S. 205 (1917); Chelentis v. Luckenbach
S. S. Co., 247 U.S. 372 (1918).

[16] *E.g.*, Garrett v. Moore-McCormack Co., 317 U.S. 239 (1942). The supremacy
clause itself appears not to apply to federal common law. See Hart, *The Relations between
State and Federal Law*, 54 COLUM. L. REV. 489, 500 (1954).

[17] Erie R.R. v. Tompkins, 304 U.S. 64 (1958). Professor Crosskey argues that the
result in diversity should be the same as that in admiralty—that federal decisions should
bind state courts in both classes of cases. 1 CROSSKEY, *op. cit. supra* note 10, at 663. In this
he is clearly *vox clamantis in deserto. Cf.* Hart, *supra* note 16, at 501.

[18] 244 U.S. 205 (1917).

[19] 247 U.S. 372 (1918).

federal common law unconstitutional in a diversity case in a federal court.

Erie, of course, was made easier by the provision of the Judiciary Act that "the laws of the several States" should be "regarded as rules of decision" in "trials at common law" in the federal courts.[20] This provision has long been held to require the application of state statutes, as opposed to decisional law, in diversity actions,[21] but it does not govern suits in admiralty.[22] If two decisions of the Supreme Court are to be taken seriously, however, such a provision would be unconstitutional if it applied to admiralty, or even to cases brought in a federal or state court under the saving clause.[23] *Erie*, by contrast, held not only that the statute should be construed to permit state decisional law to apply in diversity cases, but that otherwise construed it was unconstitutional.[24]

The opposite results in the two classes of cases, therefore, are based on the Constitution rather than on the Rules of Decision Act. The plain fact is that while the grant of jurisdiction to the federal courts in "Cases of admiralty and maritime Jurisdiction" gives the federal courts power to evolve and apply a national substantive law,[25]

167

---

[20] 1 Stat. 92 (1789), as amended, 28 U.S.C. § 1652.

[21] This was questioned in Watson v. Tarpley, 18 How. 517, 521 (1856), but the language in that decision was never followed. Burns Mortgage Co. v. Fried, 292 U.S. 487, 495 (1934).

[22] New England Newspaper Pub. Co. v. United States, 18 F. Supp. 674, 679 (D. Mass. 1937); Stevens, *supra* note 11, at 264 (1950). Occasionally a court has gone astray and applied the Rules of Decision Act, but it has seldom been a court familiar with maritime litigation. See, *e.g.*, In re Taylor, 82 F. Supp. 268 (E.D. Mo. 1949).

[23] Knickerbocker Ice Co. v. Stewart, 253 U.S. 149 (1920); Washington v. W. C. Dawson & Co., 264 U.S. 219 (1924).

[24] 304 U.S. at 77–80. See Bernhardt v. Polygraphic Co., 350 U.S. 198, 202 (1956). While this holding has been termed "a bit of judicial hyperbole which . . . should not be permitted to mislead even the most literal-minded reader," B. Currie, *supra* note 9, at 469–69, it has also been emphasized as crucial in that Mr. Justice Brandeis explicitly stated in *Erie* that in the absence of the constitutional difficulty *Swift v. Tyson* would never have been overruled. Hill, *The Erie Doctrine and the Constitution*, 53 Nw. U. L. Rev. 427, 439 (1958). See also Kurland, *Mr. Justice Frankfurter, the Supreme Court and the Erie Doctrine in Diversity Cases*, 67 Yale L. J. 187, 188–204 (1957).

[25] Such a power is also drawn from the grant of jurisdiction over "Controversies between two or more States." Hinderlider v. LaPlata River & Cherry Creek Ditch Co., 304 U.S. 92, 110 (1938). And it is arguable that the power to apply federal common law in cases in which the United States is a party, Clearfield Trust Co. v. United States, 318 U.S. 363 (1943), is derived from the corresponding jurisdictional grant. Often, however, it

the grant of jurisdiction over "Controversies . . . between Citizens of different States" does not.

If uniformity of law for the purposes of planning interstate operations is important in commerce by water, why is it not equally important in commerce by land? The answer lies, to the extent that there is an answer, in the historical purposes that have been attributed to the two jurisdictional grants. Although in the present day the interests appear largely indistinguishable in both classes of cases, a uniform law was apparently one reason for the establishment of the admiralty jurisdiction in 1789,[26] while the diversity jurisdiction is generally regarded as intended only to insure unbiased protection against the provincialism of state courts in the administration of their own laws in cases involving citizens of other states.[27]

At the time of the adoption of the Constitution a major part of commerce was maritime; uniformity was traditional in maritime matters. There remained, long after the disappearance in England of separate commercial law and courts, a substantial common body of laws of the sea, which is the source of our own general maritime law.[28] This tradition served to minimize any state objections to national power in this field; and because of the innumerable contacts with foreign interests, unequalled in land transactions, the preservation of harmony between our law of the sea and those of other nations was a strong

168

seems to be rather an interstitial effectuation of the policy of a federal statute, D'Oench, Duhme & Co. v. F.D.I.C., 315 U.S. 447, 467–75 (1942) (Jackson, J., concurring), or a power stemming from a federal interest in governmental housekeeping functions which is not dependent upon the presence of the United States as a party. Howard v. Lyons, 360 U.S. 593 (1959). See 73 Harv. L. Rev. 1228, 1230 (1960); Kurland, *The Romero Case and Some Problems of Federal Jurisdiction,* 73 Harv. L. Rev. 817, 827–33 (1960); Note, *Exceptions to Erie v. Tompkins: The Survival of Federal Common Law,* 59 Harv. L. Rev. 966 (1946).

[26] Knickerbocker Ice Co. v. Stewart, 253 U.S. 149, 160 (1920); Wright, *Uniformity in the Maritime Law of the United States,* 73 U. Pa. L. Rev. 123, 132–34 (1925); Note, 50 Nw. U. L. Rev. 677 (1955). Both Randolph, 3 Elliot's Debates 571 (2d ed. 1836), and Madison, 3 *id.* at 532, referred to the need for uniformity of decision. Mr. Justice Pitney's contrary view, which attributed both admiralty and diversity jurisdiction to the desire to avoid local prejudice, was rejected. Southern Pacific Co. v. Jensen, 244 U.S. 205, 227–28, 232–34 (1917) (dissenting opinion).

[27] Erie R.R. v. Tompkins, 304 U.S. 64, 74 (1938); Burgess v. Seligman, 107 U.S. 20, 34 (1882); Hill, *supra* note 24, at 451–52; Warren, *New Light on the History of the Federal Judiciary Act of 1789,* 37 Harv. L. Rev. 49, 83 (1923). Professor Crosskey's view is that uniformity of decision was a purpose of the diversity grant as well. 1 Crosskey, *op. cit. supra* note 10, at 646.

[28] See Gilmore & Black 5, 8, 40–42 (1957); Robinson, Admiralty 1–8 (1939).

desideratum.[29] Further, the earmarks of a maritime transaction are far more evident to the participants than is the fact of diverse citizenship; it may well be less disruptive of local order and state law enforcement to utilize federal law to govern marine insurance than to govern the warranty made in a New York department store's sale of perfume to a resident of New Jersey.

Whether or not there is a satisfactory justification for it, the distinction between admiralty and diversity exists. Yet, although the supremacy of federal common law is an accepted postulate in maritime cases today, the proscription of state law is by no means absolute. In its wisdom the Supreme Court has developed a complex maze of technical differentiations to determine whether state law may validly be applied. In a personal-injury case, federal law applies.[30] If the injured man should die, the law of the state becomes applicable.[31] A longshoreman injured on board a ship has been held not to be entitled to workmen's compensation under state law.[32] A carpenter injured in the same place clearly is.[33] In maritime cases of first impression the Supreme Court has created its own rule to determine the shipowner's liability to the injured guest of a crew member;[34] looked to state law for a rule mitigating the effect of a harmless breach of warranty in a policy of marine insurance;[35] and left the matter of contribution between joint tort-feasors in a personal-injury case to Congress, despite the fact that the Court had previously permitted contribution in collision cases and despite the existence of a made-to-order state statute.[36] An employer of maritime workers may be assessed by the state for contributions to an unemployment insurance fund[37] but not for

169

---

[29] Queen Ins. Co. v. Globe & Rutgers Fire Ins. Co., 263 U.S. 487, 493 (1924).

[30] Kermarec v. Compagnie Generale Transatlantique, 358 U.S. 625 (1959).

[31] Hess v. United States, 361 U.S. 314 (1960); The Tungus v. Skovgaard, 358 U.S. 588 (1959).

[32] Clyde S. S. Co. v. Walker, 244 U.S. 255 (1917). A contrary result was recently reached by a state court applying the doctrine of the "twilight zone." Richard v. Lake Charles Stevedores, Inc., 95 So. 2d 830 (La. App. 1957), cert. denied, 355 U.S. 952 (1958).

[33] Grant Smith-Porter Ship Co. v. Rohde, 257 U.S. 469 (1922).

[34] Kermarec v. Compagnie Generale Transatlantique, 358 U.S. 625 (1959).

[35] Wilburn Boat Co. v. Fireman's Fund Ins. Co., 348 U.S. 310 (1955).

[36] Halcyon Lines v. Haenn Ship Ceiling & Refitting Corp., 342 U.S. 282 (1952).

[37] Standard Dredging Corp. v. Murphy, 319 U.S. 306 (1943).

contributions to a reserve to pay claims for workmen's compensation.[38] A state was allowed to create a maritime lien for supplies furnished a vessel in its home port,[39] but not to enforce it,[40] nor to create a lien for supplies furnished on a contractor's order to a vessel away from home.[41] And while a state may not derogate from a right granted by the federal maritime law by shifting to the personal-injury plaintiff the burden of proof of fraud in the procurement of a release,[42] it was held free to impose its own conceptions of *respondeat superior* in order to deny a state court remedy for a maritime tort claim.[43]

I. THE ADMIRALTY CLAUSE AND CHOICE OF LAW: THE COMPETING INTERESTS OF NATION AND STATE

170

"The Constitution itself," wrote Mr. Justice McReynolds, "adopted and established, as part of the laws of the United States, approved rules of the general maritime law."[44] But it has never been made clear when federal common law will be applied.[45] In earlier days, the "common-law remedy" preserved to suitors by the saving clause was declared by Mr. Justice Holmes to afford recourse not only to the processes of state courts but to the substance of state law as well: if federal jurisdiction carried with it lawmaking powers, so did state jurisdiction.[46] One consequence of this theory was that before 1917 the Court never required the application of federal maritime law in a common-law action. In addition, it was held in *The Hamilton*[47] that a state statute enacted under this authority created an *obligatio* enforceable in a federal admiralty court.

---

[38] Washington v. W. C. Dawson & Co., 264 U.S. 219 (1924).

[39] The Lottawanna, 21 Wall. 558 (1875). The matter is now covered by federal statute. 36 Stat. 604 (1910), as amended, 46 U.S.C. §§ 971–75 (1958).

[40] The Glide, 167 U.S. 606 (1897).

[41] The Roanoke, 189 U.S. 185 (1903).

[42] Garrett v. Moore-McCormack Co., 317 U.S. 239 (1942).

[43] Caldarola v. Eckert, 332 U.S. 155 (1947).

[44] Knickerbocker Ice Co. v. Stewart, 253 U.S. 149, 160 (1920).

[45] Cf. Mishkin, *The Variousness of "Federal Law": Competence and Discretion in the Choice of National and State Rules for Decision*, 105 U. PA. L. REV. 797 (1957); see note 25 supra.

[46] The Hamilton, 207 U.S. 398, 404 (1907).

[47] 207 U.S. 398 (1907).

On the other hand, it was fairly well established even before 1917 that a right given by the general maritime law could not be defeated in an admiralty court by adverse state law. While the admiralty adopted with "alacrity" state statutes giving a right to relief, said Mr. Justice White in 1900, state law was never allowed to defeat a right to relief given by the general maritime law.[48] Thus, while state laws were freely applied in common-law courts prior to 1917, state law was to be applied in admiralty only when it helped the plaintiff and to be rejected when it operated to his detriment. This situation seems to have resulted from a conception of the maritime law as an incomplete system, with numerous gaps which could be filled by state statutes or common law, yet supreme in the admiralty court when it afforded a right of action. "The maritime law is not a *corpus juris*," wrote Mr. Justice Holmes in protesting the annihilation of New York's workmen's compensation statute; "it is a very limited body of customs and ordinances of the sea."[49]

171

One early decision stood out sharply to destroy the symmetry of this simple theory and laid the foundation for the tangle of decisions which now plagues the law: the unanimous decision in *The Roanoke*[50] in 1903. This decision denied that Washington had power to create a maritime lien against an Illinois vessel for supplies furnished on the order of a contractor engaged to repair the ship. If the states were free to create liabilities supplementary to the general law, as Justices White and Holmes had said, this was clearly a bad holding. But in *The Roanoke* the Court made explicit for the first time what had been implicit for years: that even when there is no maritime rule, the Admiralty Clause itself has a pre-emptive, negative effect on state law similar to that of the Commerce Clause.[51] This basis for rejection of state law was thrown baldly into the spotlight by Mr. Justice McReynolds in *Jensen*:[52]

> No [state] . . . legislation is valid if it contravenes the essential purpose expressed by an act of Congress or works material prejudice to the characteristic features of the general maritime law or interferes with the proper harmony and uniformity of that law in its international and interstate relations.

---

[48] Workman v. New York City, 179 U.S. 552, 563 (1900).

[49] Southern Pacific Co. v. Jensen, 244 U.S. 205, 220 (1917) (dissent).

[50] 189 U.S. 185 (1903).

[51] See The Lottawanna, 21 Wall. 558, 575 (1875) (dictum).

[52] 244 U.S. 205, 216 (1917).

Because it did all these things, the New York workmen's compensation statute was rejected in maritime cases.

Jensen was revolutionary in two ways. First, it re-established the nearly forgotten principle of *The Roanoke* and thereby buried forever Mr. Chief Justice White's simple world in which state law could always be applied to afford but never to deny recovery. Second, it overturned a number of precedents in establishing the principle that the same law must be applied in all courts in maritime cases. Uniformity is offended as much by application of state law in a common-law court as by its application in admiralty. It was the first of these propositions that was responsible for much of the complexity and uncertainty in the area today. Mr. Justice McReynolds left some room for state relief; it was too late to do otherwise and carry a majority of the Court. Thus the ever-present question has since been whether a particular state law is so disruptive of uniformity as to fall within the *Jensen* proscription. For its immediate result the decision was widely denounced,[53] but the principles which it espoused have never been abandoned.[54]

172

Attempting to discover a simple magic formula to rationalize the distinctions which had been drawn, some commentators drew on the learning of Mr. Justice Holmes to create the "gap" theory. Where the maritime law provided a rule of decision, whether affording or denying recovery, state law had no place. But there were "gaps" or "voids" in the general law, and in these voids the state law could validly be applied. State wrongful-death statutes were permissible, the Court had once said, because the area of death actions was "untouched" by federal law.[55] Workmen's compensation, it was argued, might interfere in some applications with the seaman's right to maintenance and cure. Similarly, it was argued in 1941 that there was a "positive rule" of the maritime law abating a cause of action on the death of the tort-feasor, and thus that state law was barred under the principle of supremacy. The Court's response was brief and devastat-

---

[53] See, *e.g.*, Hough, *Admiralty Jurisdiction—Of Late Years*, 37 HARV. L. REV. 529 (1924); Dodd, *The New Doctrine of the Supremacy of Admiralty over the Common Law*, 21 COLUM. L. REV. 647 (1921).

[54] The doctrine of uniformity was often applauded even by commentators who deplored the immediate result in *Jensen*. See, *e.g.*, Wright, *supra* note 26.

[55] Western Fuel Co. v. Garcia, 257 U.S. 233, 240 (1921); The Harrisburg, 119 U.S. 199, 213 (1886).

ing: "This is a subtlety which we think does not merit judicial adoption."[56] Mr. Justice Harlan recently contributed further to the entombment of the gap theory: "There is a 'void' only in the sense that there is an absence of a right of action in such cases; admiralty does not lack a rule on the subject."[57]

The gap theory was difficult to apply and artificial at best. It appeared to make the result depend on whether the issue had been previously adjudicated, ignored the policies of the states and of the admiralty, and to a great extent denied the creative powers of admiralty courts. Moreover, it failed to explain the cases. *Jensen* was itself a death case; the availability of maintenance and cure to a seaman injured but alive hardly seems relevant to the remedies of the dependents of a stevedore killed in the course of his employment.[58] Death actions, it was said, are an "untouched" area; yet a death remedy was denied in *Jensen* and numerous subsequent workmen's compensation decisions.[59]

173

"The true inquiry," as Mr. Justice Harlan has said, "thus becomes one involving the nature of the state interest . . . [and] the extent to which such interest intrudes upon federal concerns."[60] This examination of competing interests is the inquiry which must be made in the converse situation of the applicability of federal "procedural" law in diversity cases under *Erie;*[61] it is the inquiry which must be made in Commerce Clause adjudication;[62] and it is the inquiry which modern writers have advocated as proper in the conflict of laws.[63] Indeed, it

---

[56] Just v. Chambers, 312 U.S. 383, 391 (1941).

[57] Hess v. United States, 361 U.S. 314, 330 (1960) (dissent).

[58] See 72 HARV. L. REV. 1363, 1365 (1959).

[59] *E.g.,* Spencer Kellogg & Sons, Inc. v. Hicks, 285 U.S. 502 (1932); London Guar. & Acc. Co. v. Industrial Acc. Comm'n, 279 U.S. 109 (1929); Knickerbocker Ice Co. v. Stewart, 253 U.S. 149 (1920).

[60] Hess v. United States, 361 U.S. 314, 331 (1960) (dissent).

[61] See Byrd v. Blue Ridge Rural Elec. Coop., 356 U.S. 525, 538 (1958).

[62] See text *infra,* at notes 71–78.

[63] Professor Currie bases his analysis explicitly on governmental interests. See, *e.g., The Constitution and the Choice of Law: Governmental Interests and the Judicial Function,* 26 U. CHI. L. REV. 9, 9–14 (1958); *Notes on Methods and Objectives in the Conflict of Laws* [1959] DUKE L. J. 171. Professors Cheatham and Reese declare firmly that "The law of the state with the dominant interest should, normally at least, be applied." *Choice of the Applicable Law,* 52 COLUM. L. REV. 959, 972 (1952). Professor Cavers has deplored the territorial theorists' disregard of the content of conflicting rules of law. *A Critique of the*

must be the proper inquiry in maritime cases if the problem is rightly understood. For the problem arises because of a possible conflict of interests. The maritime nature of an occurrence does not deprive a state of its legitimate concern over matters affecting its residents or the conduct of persons within its borders; but the federal admiralty powers were granted to protect certain federal interests in maritime and commercial affairs. An issue created by such a conflict of interests can be resolved only by reference to those interests and by an attempt to maximize the effectuation of the proper concerns of both state and nation.

The conclusion that the maritime applicability of state laws should be determined by a balancing of state and federal interests is buttressed by the examples to be found in two types of cases in which the Supreme Court has often been confronted with the issue of state and federal maritime powers. These cases involved the maritime jurisdiction of state courts and the validity of state laws regulating maritime commercial operations.

174

Congress has extended admiralty jurisdiction to the inferior federal courts since 1789.[64] Concurrent state court jurisdiction has been preserved, however, in many kinds of maritime cases by the saving clause of the Judiciary Act,[65] which also makes available non-admiralty procedures in a federal court if there is an independent basis for jurisdiction. The remedies open to suitors under the saving clause are quite extensive. They include equitable and statutory remedies as well as those known to the common law in 1789;[66] partition of a vessel or its forfeiture for violation of state law;[67] attachment of a vessel for

Choice of Law Problem, 47 HARV. L. REV. 173, 178 (1933). More recently he has come around substantially to the governmental interest position. See *The Conditional Seller's Remedies and the Choice of Law Process—Some Notes on Shanahan*, 35 N.Y. U. L. REV. 1126, 1139 (1960).

[64] 1 Stat. 76–77 (1789), now 28 U.S.C. § 1333.

[65] 1 Stat. 77 (1789). The section now saves to suitors "all other remedies to which they are otherwise entitled." 28 U.S.C. § 1333. Apparently the revision of language made by the 1948 codification was intended to include those decisions holding that states may grant equitable and statutory relief under the saving clause. See, *e.g.*, cases cited in note 66 *infra*. In any event it is clear that no essential change in meaning was intended. See 28 U.S.C.A. § 1333, Reviser's note; Black, *Admiralty Jurisdiction: Critique and Suggestions*, 50 COLUM. L. REV. 259, 270–72 (1950).

[66] See, *e.g.*, Red Cross Line v. American Fruit Co., 264 U.S. 109 (1924); Steamboat Co. v. Chase, 16 Wall. 522 (1873).

[67] C. J. Hendry Co. v. Moore, 318 U.S. 133 (1943) (forfeiture); Madruga v. Superior Court, 346 U.S. 556 (1954) (partition).

satisfaction of a personal judgment or enforcement of claims arising from non-maritime transactions.[68] Probably all that is not included is power to pass title to a vessel free of maritime liens in an action in rem,[69] and to adjudicate the rights of the owner to limitation of liability.[70] Both in limitation proceedings and in suits in rem, a number of claimants against a vessel are parties to a single litigation, and in such cases the federal interest may be said to be at its peak. To permit the fate of the Queen Mary and of all those who furnished her supplies and services to be adjudicated in a single complex proceeding by the City Court of New York might well seem offensive to the policy underlying the grant of federal jurisdiction in admiralty.

In cases involving state regulatory measures the competing considerations have been more sharply defined. The powers of the states to maintain order, to collect revenue, and to promote health and safety have often come into conflict with the federal interest in free and unimpeded commerce. Clearly, the states must be allowed some room for such action. Freedom of commerce simply does not demand that in the absence of congressional action there shall be neither rules of navigation nor penalties for breaches of the peace. Yet state laws have often clearly placed financial burdens on the shipping industry and in some instances, such as quarantine pending health inspection, have actually obstructed commercial operations. In addition, the variation of laws from state to state has increased the difficulty of planning the cost and conduct of the shipping business.

175

In cases such as these, involving public rather than private rights, the Supreme Court usually spoke of the Commerce Clause and the police power rather than of the admiralty jurisdiction.[71] It was, of course, not a necessary inference from the grant of the commerce power that state laws might be struck down when Congress was

---

[68] Leon v. Galceran, 11 Wall. 185 (1871) (attachment); Taylor v. Carryl, 20 How. 583 (1858) (same); Johnson v. Chicago & Pac. Elevator Co., 119 U.S. 388 (1886) (non-maritime lien); Edwards v. Elliott, 21 Wall. 532 (1874) (same).

[69] The Hine v. Trevor, 4 Wall. 555 (1867); The Moses Taylor, 4 Wall. 411 (1867); The Belfast, 7 Wall. 624 (1869); The Glide, 167 U.S. 606 (1897). See Knapp, Stout & Co. v. McCaffrey, 177 U.S. 638 (1900).

[70] Ex parte Green, 286 U.S. 437 (1932); cf. Petition of Red Star Barge Line, Inc., 160 F. 2d 436, 437–38 (2d Cir. 1947), cert. denied, 331 U.S. 850 (1947). See GILMORE & BLACK 692–95.

[71] See, e.g., Cooley v. Board of Port Wardens, 12 How. 299 (1851).

silent,[72] but perhaps because of fear of a proliferation of petty restraints too numerous and, individually, too minor to merit congressional attention,[73] the familiar dichotomy was drawn between "local"
matters, in which diversity of rule is desirable to meet local exigencies, and "national" matters demanding a uniform rule or none at all
throughout the United States.[74] In devising and applying this doctrine
the Supreme Court undertook to determine the existence of state legislative power by balancing various interests of the states against the
hardships imposed on commerce by the state statutes. In the maritime
cases in which state law was sustained, there was usually an interest
which is popularly recognized as a "strong" one: health or safety,[75]
preservation of public order,[76] or compensation for the use of state
property.[77] The problem resulted from the conflict of state and federal
interests, and it was resolved by a comparison of their relative
strengths.

176

In ascertaining the interest of a state in the maritime application of
its laws, profitable use can be made of enlightened theories of conflict
of laws.[78] The first step should be determination of the policies which
are sought to be furthered by the state law in question. To a certain
extent such policies can be discovered by examination of state court
decisions as well as any legislative materials that may be available.
The second step should be an examination of such connecting factors
as the place where the events giving rise to suit occurred, and the
residence of the parties, in order to decide whether the matter has
such an impact on the economy and affairs of a particular state as to
give it a legitimate concern for the application of its laws. If the connection of the state with the matter in suit is such as to give it a
legitimate concern for the advancement of the policy expressed in the

---

[72] See Brown, *The Open Economy: Justice Frankfurter and the Position of the Judiciary*, 67 YALE L. J. 219, 221–22 (1957); Kurland, *The Supreme Court and the Attrition of State Power*, 10 STAN. L. REV. 274, 285–92 (1958).

[73] See Jackson, J., concurring, in Duckworth v. Arkansas, 314 U.S. 390, 400 (1941).

[74] See FRANKFURTER, THE COMMERCE CLAUSE 56 *et seq.* (1937).

[75] *E.g.*, Kelly v. Washington, 302 U.S. 1 (1937).

[76] *E.g.*, Packet Co. v. Catlettsburg, 105 U.S. 559 (1882).

[77] *E.g.*, *ibid.*; Transportation Co. v. Parkersburg, 107 U.S. 691 (1883); *cf.* Smith v. Maryland, 18 How. 71 (1855).

[78] See note 63 *supra*.

law asserted to be applied, that state has an interest in the outcome of the litigation which is entitled to respect.

From the course of Supreme Court decision at least two kinds of federal interests emerge to be opposed to those of the states in maritime cases. The first is an interest in uniformity stemming from the Admiralty Clause itself, a Commerce Clause type of preference for no rule rather than a multiplicity of rules.[79] In *The Roanoke* the Court stated its reasoning in terms relevant to current theory: "It is almost impossible for [the master] . . . to acquaint himself with the laws of each individual State he may visit, and he has a right to suppose that the general maritime law applies to him and his ship, wherever she may go. . . ."[80]

This policy of uniformity, ignored in cases where jurisdiction is based solely on diversity of citizenship, is the primary justification for a federal common law of the sea. It is the policy which was at the root of Mr. Justice McReynolds' arguments against the power of a state to afford workmen's compensation to supplement the maritime law. It is the policy which Mr. Justice Harlan invoked in his dissent in *Hess v. United States*,[81] to contend for the inapplicability of the Oregon Employers' Liability Act in a case within the admiralty jurisdiction. This policy might have been held to invalidate any state law which placed the rights of a party engaged in maritime commerce in jeopardy of detrimental interstate variation; but the cases have shown that here, as well as in determining pre-emption by the Commerce Clause, uniformity is only one of several considerations.

The gap theorists ignored this policy altogether. Their view that state law was acceptable whenever the federal law had not spoken contradicted even the notion of pre-emption developed in the Commerce Clause cases. And the rejection of state laws in admiralty cases went far beyond those involving commerce on land. The Commerce Clause was never held to prohibit relief under state workmen's compensation law.[82] Indeed, before the extensive federal regulation of

177

---

[79] See Southern Pacific Co. v. Jensen, 244 U.S. 205, 216 (1917).

[80] 189 U.S. 185, 195 (1903).

[81] 361 U.S. 314, 322 (1960).

[82] In New York Cent. R.R. v. White, 243 U.S. 188 (1917), Hawkins v. Bleakly, 243 U.S. 210 (1917), and Mountain Timber Co. v. Washington, 243 U.S. 219 (1917), state workmen's compensation statutes were upheld against varied objections ranging from the Due Process Clause to the guarantee of a republican form of government. Although the

railroad liability, the states were never barred from creating private
rights of action for personal injuries against an interstate carrier.[83]

The second kind of interest, seldom distinguished from the first in
the decisions, is the interest in promoting the policy underlying a particular rule of the federal maritime law. This is pre-emption by rule
rather than by silence.[84] In the days of the gap theory this kind of
policy was ignored whenever the maritime law denied relief. Even in
The Roanoke, although mention was made of "injustice" and the intrusion of new lien priorities,[85] state law was rejected largely because
it would have disrupted uniformity.

When the maritime law affords relief, the existence of a federal
interest is apparent. If a seaman may recover indemnity for an injury caused by the unseaworthiness of a vessel, federal policy is concerned with his welfare.[86] But it is far less clear that the existence of a
federal remedy for injury if it was caused by unseaworthiness, but not
if it was caused by negligence,[87] represented a policy of protecting the
shipowner from the imposition of a supplementary liability. The
question to be put is not whether the admiralty courts have previously
enunciated a rule, but rather whether any federal policy prohibits the
grant of relief. The absence of relief for wrongful death did not represent such a policy. No federal interest required immunity for the shipowner from claims of this nature. Rather, the mere absence of precedent was given as the reason for the Court's refusal to award federal
relief.[88] Presumably the Court was concerned lest it exceed its judicial
function if it attempted to fashion a scheme of beneficiaries and other

178

employer in the first case was a railroad engaged in interstate commerce, the Commerce
Clause was not even discussed by the Court.

[83] See Pitney, J., dissenting, in *Jensen*, 244 U.S. at 243–45.

[84] *Cf.* Chicago v. Atchison, T. & S. F. Ry., 357 U.S. 77 (1958).

[85] 189 U.S. at 195–96. The two policies were intertwined to a certain extent. The statute
was said to create injustice because the master must know a number of different laws and
because no provision was made for notice to him of the unpaid claim. For these two reasons it was held "obnoxious to the general maritime law." *Id.* at 196.

[86] See Pope & Talbot, Inc. v. Hawn, 346 U.S. 406 (1953). State law was not permitted
to defeat recovery in the face of such a rule.

[87] The Osceola, 189 U.S. 158 (1903). The passage of the Jones Act eliminated this
unfortunate decision. 41 Stat. 1007 (1920), 46 U.S.C. § 688 (1958). But before the Act
was passed the absence of a federal duty on the shipowner to observe due care toward the
seaman was held to preclude the granting of relief under state law in Chelentis v. Luckenbach S. S. Co., 247 U.S. 372 (1918).

[88] The Harrisburg, 119 U.S. 199, 213 (1886).

detailed provisions of a system of wrongful death. In such a case the only possible impediment to the application of state law is the federal interest in uniformity of maritime obligation, and the lack of uniformity implicit in the application of state law has consistently been held justified by the strength of the state's interest in compensating the dependents of persons killed by wrongful act.[89]

The broad range of relevant federal interests may be illustrated by reference to early cases involving the power of a state to create maritime liens against a vessel. The saving-to-suitors clause did not permit enforcement of maritime liens in a state court, but more than once the Supreme Court has allowed state-created liens to be enforced in a federal court of admiralty. The existence of a lien, it should be emphasized, must be distinguished from the issue of liability. The maritime law recognized a shipowner's liability for necessaries furnished to a vessel in her home port, but it gave no lien to the creditor. No policy of protecting the shipowner from liability was infringed by applying a state lien law to afford an additional remedy; nor, for the same reason, was he subjected to diversity or inconsistency in the laws governing his conduct. State liens for necessaries were enforced.[90] By contrast, in *The Roanoke* the Court struck down a state law which designated persons engaged to repair a vessel as agents of the vessel for the procurement of supplies, and created a lien in favor of the supplier. This statute established not only a new remedy but a liability unknown to the maritime law. The liability might have been contrary to the policy of the maritime law in regard to contractual and agency relationships. Moreover, even if the silence of the maritime law represented an absence of policy, the application of state law would have subjected the shipowner to a variety of rules governing his conduct and primary liabilities. The costs of his operations would have been increased; he would have been required to investigate the laws of all those states into whose ports he sent his vessels in order to plan his conduct and his outlays of funds for contingencies in dealing with contractors in the various ports.

Again, in *The Chusan*,[91] Mr. Justice Story on circuit refused to ap-

179

---

[89] See text *infra*, at notes 139–74.

[90] Peyroux v. Howard, 7 Pet. 324 (1833).

[91] 5 Fed. Cas. 680 (No. 2717) (C.C.D. Mass. 1843).

ply a New York statute that purported to extinguish supply liens against a vessel when it left the state. In terms of interests, this decision is clearly correct. Federal law created a right in the vessel in favor of those who had serviced the ship in a New York port. Federal policy demanded a right of action in rem. A concept akin to that expressed in the supremacy clause but attributed by implication to Article III has, without exception, prevented state law from defeating or in any way limiting in a suit in admiralty a right granted by federal maritime law.

In neither *The Roanoke* nor *The Chusan*, however, was reliance placed on such policy considerations. The determinative fact in both was that the lien was asserted against a foreign rather than a domestic vessel. Similar language is found in *The Lottawanna*,[92] in which a home-port lien for necessaries was upheld despite recognition of the strong federal interest in uniformity. The distinction between home-port and foreign liens is not without merit. *The Roanoke* denied the state's ability to create supplementary liens on foreign vessels because it would be impracticable for a shipowner or master to ascertain and comply with the laws of all the varying jurisdictions. But to apply the law of the owner's domicile as well as that of the sea imposes a far less substantial burden. The shipowner might reasonably, it seems, be held to know the law of his own state as well as the general maritime law; the problem arises when he is subjected to different laws in every port. In addition to the fact that the hardship is less severe when a lien is created by the home state, any lack of uniformity and difficulty to which an owner is subjected is attributable solely to the legislature of the home state. It is that state which is primarily interested in his welfare. It seems far from improper to hold that he must resort to that body with his plea for relief from liens created against his vessel by its laws. The Admiralty Clause cases in other areas, however, have not accepted a distinction between laws of the shipowner's domicile and those of other states. The owner's domicile is seldom mentioned, and the assumption seems to be that two laws are as intolerable as two dozen; the principle of uniformity, where it is operative, requires a single law.

In *Osaka Shosen Kaisha v. Pacific Export Lumber Co.*,[93] the Court did

[92] 21 Wall. 558, 573–74 (1875).

[93] 260 U.S. 490 (1923).

not consider it necessary to mention whether the lien was created by
a home or foreign state, nor did it cite the home-port lien cases. It
simply disallowed a state lien for nonperformance of a charter party
on the ground that the maritime law is "not subject to material alterations by state enactments."[94] The simple policy of *The Chusan* was
not involved. The state law did not impair a federal right of one of the
parties. Further, since the duties and even the monetary liabilities of
the parties were unaffected, it seems singularly unobservant to assert
that the policy of uniformity has anything to do with the case,
whether the lien is created by the state of domicile or by another. It is
also difficult to maintain that the absence of a lien for breach of a
charter party represents a negative policy, while the absence of a lien
for home-port supplies does not. In denying that a federal lien existed
in *Osaka* the Court voiced a strong policy objection to the creation of
new liens because of their secret nature.[95] Probably this policy motivated the rejection of the state lien. It is possible that the Court perceived a greater state interest with respect to home-port supplies than
with respect to breach of a charter party, but the distinction is hardly
patent. Unless it was intended to overrule the home-port lien cases,
Osaka seems clearly to be out of step with the prevailing view of state
power over maritime liens.

181

The denial of state law in *Osaka* raises some doubt as to whether
state liens should ever be enforced in admiralty. For although the enforcement of a lien for recognized liability has no adverse effect on a
shipowner, it can substantially impair the position of other creditors
of the vessel. The creation of a lien by the state gives the lienor rights
against the vessel superior to those of other maritime claimants and
may therefore impair their practical ability to recover on causes of
action recognized by federal law. To be sure, the federal courts retained power to determine the priority of state-created liens as a
matter of federal law,[96] thus narrowing the possibility that state law
would reduce the fund available to the holder of a federal lien. But
this power to determine priorities does not help the lien-less maritime
claimant, such as a Jones Act seaman,[97] whose claim will be sub-

---

[94] 260 U.S. at 495.   [95] *Id.* at 499.
[96] The J. E. Rumbell, 148 U.S. 1 (1893).
[97] Plamals v. The Pinar Del Rio, 277 U.S. 151 (1928).

ordinated to that of a home-port repairman with whom he would formerly have shared the residuary proceeds of the sale of the vessel. The difficulty was recognized by Mr. Justice Brown in *The Roanoke*[98] when he condemned a state lien statute partly on the ground that "it establishes a new order of priority in payment of liens." The closest the Supreme Court has come to holding the order of distribution of proceeds to be an exclusively federal matter was in *Osaka*. But *Osaka* is hardly authority to support such a policy argument, for it did not purport to examine the proper priority of the claim for breach of a charter party as a matter of federal law.

The enactment of the Federal Lien Act in 1910[99] substantially altered the relationship between state and federal laws with respect to maritime liens. That statute supersedes state liens to the extent that it creates a federal lien, *i.e.*, liens for "repairs, supplies, towage, use of dry dock or marine railway, and other necessaries."[100] Some room is left, however, for the operation of state lien statutes. The Lien Act does not apply at all to tort claims, and state wrongful-death liens are still being enforced.[101] Moreover, lower federal courts have occasionally recognized state-created contract liens that are not covered by the statute, such as a lien for master's wages.[102] Although these state lien claims are seldom litigated, the theoretical problems remain.[103]

In every maritime case in which a state is found to have an interest in the application of its law the courts are called upon to determine

182

---

[98] 189 U.S. 185, 196 (1903).

[99] 36 Stat. 604 (1910), as amended, 46 U.S.C. §§ 971–75 (1958).

[100] This language is used to define both the liens created, 46 U.S.C. § 971, and the state liens which are superseded, 46 U.S.C. § 975.

[101] Vancouver S.S. Co. v. Rice, 288 U.S. 445 (1933); Continental Cas. Co. v. The Benny Skou, 200 F. 2d 246 (4th Cir. 1952), *cert. denied*, 345 U.S. 992 (1953). In the latter case the libel was held barred by the state statute of limitations.

[102] *E.g.*, Burdine v. Walden, 91 F. 2d 321 (5th Cir. 1937). The Lien Act was not mentioned.

[103] See GILMORE & BLACK 539–40, 544–45. The state statutes are described as "either moribund or dead." *Id.* at 545. But no reason is given why the statute should be given pre-emptive effect in areas which it does not purport to cover, especially in view of the limited, careful pre-emptive language of § 975. Gilmore and Black concede the continued vitality of state liens for wrongful death; tort liens are entirely beyond the scope of the federal act. *Ibid.*

whether, in the words of Mr. Justice McReynolds in *Jensen*, the state law would "work material prejudice to the characteristic features of the general maritime law." That is, being responsible for the development of a common law for the governance of maritime matters, the federal courts must determine whether the state rule is contrary to any recognized policy of the maritime law. They must also determine the extent of the conflict that would be produced: the effect on the pocketbooks of those engaged in maritime affairs and the effect on the conduct of those persons in their everyday business transactions. As in the choice between the laws of two or more states, in some cases, on analysis, only one sovereign will be found to have an interest. In such an instance the accommodation of federal and state interests is clearly a false problem;[104] this (if not mere political necessity) explains the facility with which even the McReynolds Court accepted state law as applied to transactions that were only of "local" significance.[105]

"Maritime-but-local" was for twenty years after *Jensen* a flourishing basis for decision.[106] Its application was erratic and uncertain; policies were often ignored. Under that doctrine it was easy for an injured worker to miscalculate whether he should apply for state workmen's compensation or federal compensation, and the consequences of an erroneous choice were grave.[107] As a result, in *Davis v. Department of Labor & Industries*,[108] the Supreme Court rewrote the objectionable language of the Longshoremen's and Harborworkers' Compensation Act to meet the exigencies of the situation.[109]

183

---

[104] B. Currie, *supra* note 63 [1959] DUKE L. J. at 174; B. Currie, *Married Women's Contracts: A Study in Conflict-of-Laws Method*, 25 U. CHI. L. REV. 227, 251 (1958).

[105] *E.g.*, Grant Smith-Porter Ship Co. v. Rohde, 257 U.S. 469 (1922).

[106] See GILMORE & BLACK 347.

[107] Not only did a substantial delay result from an erroneous choice, but often the unfortunate claimant might find himself barred by limitation as a result. *E.g.*, Ayers v. Parker, 15 F. Supp. 447 (D. Md. 1936); Romaniuk v. Locke, 3 F. Supp. 529 (S.D. N.Y. 1932).

[108] 317 U.S. 249 (1942).

[109] In an opinion by Mr. Justice Black, the Court reversed a state's denial of compensation in the drowning of a structural steelworker who had fallen from a barge while dismantling a bridge over navigable waters. The great delays in recovery, the likelihood that relief would be barred by limitation, and the burden on employers were described as contrary to the policy of the federal compensation act. Therefore, in the area in which the Court has been unable to articulate a guiding rule, there is now a "twilight zone" in which, apparently, either state or federal relief is available.

Despite the violence done to the maritime-but-local concept by the friends and foes of workmen's compensation, the doctrine has a sound basis in principle. A uniform law is desirable so that those who are engaged in maritime commerce will not be subjected to varying liabilities in various parts of the country, and so that their obligations will be given the same effect everywhere. Another reason for a single law is protection of the rights of foreigners, for whose treatment in American courts the federal government may be held accountable.[110] But surely Mr. Justice McReynolds was right in deciding that such uniformity is not required in the case of an employee of a lumber mill who fastens logs together in a river, and seeks workmen's compensation for an injury sustained in the course of his employment.[111] Neither the employer (whose business is centered in a stationary mill in a single state) nor the employee (whose employment is similarly localized) can ever be subjected to such varying liabilities in the course of their relationship. The employer can plan his expenses on the basis of the applicability of a single law—that of the state in which his business is conducted—and can take precautionary measures accordingly. Similarly, the employee's rights are not unpredictable. On the contrary, in these circumstances application of the general maritime law would inject an element of fortuity and complexity into the otherwise simple and certain system of state law by making the outcome depend on the question—patently irrelevant to the problem of allocating the burden of industrial accidents— whether the injury occurred on land or on navigable waters. When there is no need for a uniform law because of the local nature of the business engaged in by the parties, the federal courts should not impose any limitation on the application of state law by virtue of some policy of general harmony in maritime affairs.

The real difficulties lie in those cases in which both a federal and a state interest can be found. The process of balancing opposing interests is not the ideal one for the judicial process. It is difficult to demonstrate by legal reasoning that the interest of a state in its wrongful-death legislation is greater than its interest in its rules of contract, or

184

---

[110] See 72 HARV. L. REV. 1363, 1364–65 (1959).

[111] Sultan Ry. & Timber Co. v. Department of Labor & Industries, 277 U.S. 135 (1928).

that uniformity is more important than either.[112] The Court might have discharged its responsibility without dealing in "such imponderables" if it had permitted application of state law whenever a state interest appeared, so long as that law did not derogate from a maritime right. This would have left the protection of unarticulated federal interests to Congress. The Court might have solved the problem, on the other hand, by disallowing state law whenever a federal interest could be discerned. Rather boldly, however, the Court has committed itself to the task of determining the relative merits of the interests involved. In so doing it avoids the Balkanization that would result if the protection of federal interests were left to the inattention of an overburdened Congress. Moreover, the Court's approach represents an admirable effort to give appropriate scope to the policies of the states in cases in which, as in criminal law and quarantine cases, the states would otherwise have been paralyzed by a relatively insignificant desire for uniformity. To draw the lines, however, has proved a formidable task.

185

II. FEDERALLY CREATED RIGHTS—THE EASY CASES

The Chusan[113] was perhaps the first of many decisions holding that state law can never defeat or diminish a right of recovery given by maritime law. Long before the days of Mr. Justice McReynolds, the Court had ruled that state law could not be applied in admiralty to defeat a federal claim on grounds of contributory negligence,[114] to limit recovery for breach of a maritime contract by the enforcement of a liquidated damages clause for less than actual damages,[115] or to avoid the liability of a municipality for the maritime tort of its employees.[116] In early days the state was free to defeat recovery in its

---

[112] With reference to interstate conflict of laws, Professor Currie has argued that the balancing of opposing interests is not a proper judicial function. See, e.g., Currie, supra note 63 [1959] DUKE L. J. at 176–77; cf. Jackson, Full Faith and Credit—The Lawyer's Clause of the Constitution, 45 COLUM. L. REV. 1, 28 (1945): "There are no judicial standards of valuation of such imponderables."

[113] 5 Fed. Cas. 680 (No. 2717) (C.C.D. Mass. 1843) (Story, J.).

[114] Attlee v. Packet Co., 21 Wall. 389, 395–96 (1875).

[115] Watts v. Camors, 115 U.S. 353, 361–62 (1885) (dictum).

[116] Workman v. New York City, 179 U.S. 552 (1900).

own courts on the ground of contributory negligence,[117] but decisions of the Court of the Twenties required nonmaritime courts also to apply the general maritime law. In *Union Fish Co. v. Erickson*[118] a unanimous court denied the state court's power to apply its statute of frauds to defeat recovery in an action for breach of a maritime contract of employment.

The doctrine against derogation of a right afforded by the general maritime law in a common-law court has recently been reaffirmed in two cases commonly cited to establish the continued vitality of the principle of uniformity in maritime affairs. In *Garrett v. Moore-McCormack Co.*[119] the Supreme Court held that a state had no power to place upon a seaman the burden of proving fraud in the inducement of a release of liability. And in *Pope & Talbot, Inc. v. Hawn*[120] the Court held that a state rule of contributory negligence had no effect in a diversity action by a carpenter for personal injuries sustained aboard a ship in navigable waters. "While states may sometimes supplement federal maritime policies," said Mr. Justice Black, "a state may not deprive a person of any substantial admiralty rights."[121] Finally, in *Kermarec v. Compagnie Generale Transatlantique*,[122] a judgment in a diversity case, freeing a shipowner from liability under state law for personal injuries suffered by a visitor, was reversed on the ground that maritime law rejected the state law's distinction between licensee and invitee. A dictum in *Hawn* to the effect that, even if the plaintiff had sought to enforce a "state-created remedy" for his injuries, maritime standards would govern,[123] has been hailed as reaffirming the doctrine of uniformity.[124] But in reality the case stands only for the proposition, never seriously disputed in admiralty courts and established for over forty years without exception even as to state courts,

186

---

[117] Belden v. Chase, 150 U.S. 674 (1893).

[118] 248 U.S. 308 (1919).

[119] 317 U.S. 239 (1942).

[120] 346 U.S. 406 (1953).

[121] *Id.* at 409–10.

[122] 358 U.S. 625 (1959).

[123] 346 U.S. at 409.

[124] See, *e.g.*, Hess v. United States, 361 U.S. 314, 327, 328 n. 9 (1960) (Harlan, J., dissenting).

that state law may not be applied in derogation of a right of recovery afforded by the general maritime law.[125]

It would thus appear that *Caldarola v. Eckert*[126] has been overruled. In that puzzling decision a stevedore injured aboard a ship owned by the United States brought suit in a New York state court against a general agent who was in charge of managing the vessel, alleging a breach of the agent's duty to maintain its equipment in sound condition. The New York Court of Appeals held that under state law the relationship of the agent to the vessel was not such as to make him responsible to third persons for her condition.[127] The Supreme Court affirmed: "Whether New York is the source of the right or merely affords the means for enforcing it, her determination is decisive that there is no remedy in its courts for such a business invitee against one who has no control and possession of premises."[128] No further explanation was offered; the remainder of Mr. Justice Frankfurter's opinion was devoted to an interpretation of the government contract, to determine whether it created such a relationship as would impose a duty on the general agent under New York law. The Court concluded that it did not.

187

This decision raised a great deal of controversy. Many commentators felt it was an abandonment of the rule that a state court cannot derogate from a federal maritime right.[129] But the only two cases cited by the Court were decisions concerning the duty of a state court to entertain a suit based on a federal statute.[130] The alternative in those cases was not an adverse judgment on the merits but simply a dismissal without prejudice, leaving the plaintiff free to pursue his remedies in a federal court. Moreover, Mr. Justice Frankfurter "ex-

---

[125] "One constitutional truism may be got out of the way at once: Such state legislation is clearly invalid where it actually conflicts with the general maritime law. . . ." GILMORE & BLACK 43.

[126] 332 U.S. 155 (1947).

[127] Caldarola v. Moore-McCormack Lines, Inc., 295 N.Y. 463 (1946).

[128] 332 U.S. at 158.

[129] *E.g.*, Dickinson & Andrews, *A Decade of Admiralty in the Supreme Court of the United States*, 36 CALIF. L. REV. 169, 195 (1948): "If Caldarola's problems were not matters to be resolved under the national maritime law, whatever the forum, then that law is indeed a thing of shreds and patches."

[130] Testa v. Katt, 330 U.S. 386 (1947); Douglas v. New York, N.H. & H.R.R., 279 U.S. 377 (1929).

plained away" *Caldarola* a few years later in his concurring opinion in
Pope & Talbot, Inc. v. Hawn.[131] The result, he wrote, depends upon
what the state court purports to do. When a state court undertakes to
enforce a right created by maritime law, it must do so without imposing state-created limitations—citing *Garrett*. On the other hand, if the
state court simply decides not to give a remedy—not to entertain the
action—it is free to dismiss. In fact, Mr. Justice Frankfurter appears
to have been eating crow for an unfortunate decision, since the New
York Court had clearly purported to dispose of the case on its merits.[132] But both *Hawn* and *Kermarec*, decided after *Caldarola*, rejected
state law invoked to defeat maritime recovery. Both decisions appear
entirely applicable to suits in state courts. It seems clear, therefore,
that *Caldarola* is now authority only for permitting a state court to
dismiss without prejudice, leaving the plaintiff free to prosecute his
188   claim in any available federal court.

Where an affirmative federal right of recovery is the embodiment
of a policy judgment as to the relative interests of the parties, the principle of *The Chusan*, as extended by *Erickson* and *Garrett*, is a sound
one. In some matters, however, the equities are rather evenly balanced, and the important desideratum is not so much that *A* win or
that *B* win as that it be clear at the outset which of the parties will
prevail, in order that they may plan their transaction accordingly. In
the content of such a rule of commercial convenience there is perhaps
only a minimal federal interest. For the same reasons a strong state
interest seems correspondingly unlikely; but if it can be shown that
there is a strong policy behind a particular state rule and none behind
the federal, the degree of disuniformity will have to be considered,
and it is possible that the state rule might apply.

Further, there are no such federal limits on rights under the
general maritime law as the familiar statute of frauds and statute of
limitations. Both these restrictions are enunciated ordinarily by legislatures rather than by courts. It is fairly clear that the absence of a
federal common-law limitation-of-actions rule is attributable simply
to a felt judicial inability to delimit a positive standard. Surely it is
improbable that federal policy demands the everlasting survival of a

[131] 346 U.S. at 418–19.

[132] "Plaintiff has no cause of action against these defendants." 295 N.Y. at 467. There
was no indication in the opinion that the judgment was not intended also to bar a subsequent suit in admiralty.

cause of action. Thus, no policy objection should be raised to the application of a state statute of limitations to maritime rights of action, unless the period of the statute is so abbreviated as to amount to an effectual infringement of the policy establishing the right of recovery. Accordingly, it is not surprising that the federal courts have utilized the period prescribed by state statutes of limitation to dismiss maritime cases even in admiralty,[133] modified in some cases by the equitable doctrine of excuse or laches.[134] Despite *Erickson*, it is arguable that the same is true of the statute of frauds. The absence of this provision in the maritime law might represent simply a real or imagined inability to formulate such a rule rather than a policy of enlarged freedom of contract. Even if this is true, of course, the desire for uniformity may still require that no state impose its statute of frauds to defeat recovery on a maritime contract valid elsewhere; but the cases would be taken out of the simple principle of *Garrett* if the statute of frauds were treated in this manner.

189

In probably the majority of cases a substantive policy applicable to the particular transaction underlies the federal rule of liability. In tort the shipowner is required to pay indemnity for injuries to maritime workers caused by the unseaworthy condition of the vessel because of a policy that he, rather than the unfortunate workman, should bear the loss.[135] In contract it is the policy of the maritime law that damages commensurate with the loss shall be awarded for breach of a

[133] *E.g.*, Le Gate v. The Panamolga, 221 F. 2d 689 (2d Cir. 1955); Kane v. Union of Soviet Socialist Republics, 189 F. 2d 303 (3d Cir. 1951).

[134] Czaplicki v. The Hoegh Silvercloud, 351 U.S. 525, 533–34 (1956). To the extent that the doctrine of laches represents a policy of federal law as to the rights of the plaintiff, it is arguable that it should apply in an action in a state court as well. But *Caldarola v. Eckert* permitted a state court to close its doors entirely to a maritime claim. Further, even if a state were required to entertain maritime actions in general, *cf.* Hughes v. Fetter, 341 U.S. 609 (1951), it seems that it should be free to impose a reasonable period of limitation, with or without laches, even when the federal court would allow suit, because of its recognized interest in keeping its own dockets clear for more current business. *Cf.* Wells v. Simonds Abrasive Co., 345 U.S. 514 (1953).

In any court, however, an injured seaman may obtain the benefit of the Jones Act's three-year period of limitation as to his claim for unseaworthiness under general maritime law by joining it with a claim under that statute. If a shorter state statute were applied, the Supreme Court has ruled, the Jones Act claim would itself in effect be limited, since the two claims constitute a single cause of action for res judicata purposes and must therefore be brought in a single action. McAllister v. Magnolia Petroleum Co., 357 U.S. 221 (1958); *cf.* Cox v. Roth, 348 U.S. 207 (1955).

[135] Pope & Talbot, Inc. v. Hawn, 346 U.S. 406 (1953).

charter party.[136] To diminish recovery by imposing the state rule of contributory negligence in the one case or liquidated damages in the other would not only subject the rights of maritime workers and contractors to extreme variation and uncertainty at the hands of the various states but also plainly contradict the federal policy. If the federal maritime law is to be given any effect at all—and the constitutional history as well as the decisions affirm that it should[137]—the principle of *Garrett* and *Hawn* must be accepted.

Further, it is good doctrine that the same law must be applied in every court. If federal law is supreme, it ought to be supreme. One of the most notable failings of *Swift v. Tyson* was that the states were free to apply their own commercial laws in state court actions involving citizens of different states. The existence of two systems of law applicable to the same transaction according to the forum in which suit is brought is undesirable. The planning of conduct would be made difficult if not totally unfeasible. The party with the initiative would be encouraged to shop for a forum whose law is favorable to his cause; in these days of the declaratory judgment this might often result in an undignified race to court or to judgment, with the prize to the swift rather than to the deserving. All this is familiar to those who have observed the destruction of the similar double standard in diversity cases. It is no less relevant here.[138]

190

[136] See Watts v. Camors, 115 U.S. 353 (1885).

[137] "If there is any sense at all in making maritime law a federal subject, then there must be some limit to the power of the states to interfere in the field of its working." GILMORE & BLACK 43–44. "Through a liberal and extremely fortunate interpretation of Article III . . . it has become well established that our governing law in maritime matters in this country is a part of the national law safely insulated from the diverse or parochial tendencies of the local laws of the several states." Dickinson & Andrews, *supra* note 129, at 169. See also Stumberg, *Maritime Cases in Common-Law Courts*, 3 TEX. L. REV. 246, 258 (1925).

[138] The soundness of applying the same law in all maritime cases regardless of forum is widely accepted. The Supreme Court has said: "We are asked to use the *Erie-Tompkins* case to bring about the same kind of unfairness it was designed to end. . . . The substantial rights of an injured person are not to be determined differently whether his case is labelled 'law side' or 'admiralty side.' . . ." Pope & Talbot, Inc. v. Hawn, 346 U.S. 406, 411 (1953). For further support see GILMORE & BLACK 45–46; HART & WECHSLER, THE FEDERAL COURTS AND THE FEDERAL SYSTEM 788–89 (1953); Morrison, *Workmen's Compensation and the Maritime Law*, 38 YALE L. J. 472, 476 (1929): "It is difficult to see why one of two litigants should have the privilege not only of choosing the forum, but of selecting one of two varying sets of rules for the determination of the controversy." The storm of protest which greeted the holding in *Jensen* that state

III. Uniformity and the Gap Theory: Wrongful Death and Workmen's Compensation

Maritime law, like common law, recognized no liability for wrongful death.[139] If a person injured by lack of due care or other tortious act died, his action for damages died with him, and no rights existed in his estate or his dependents to recover either for his pain and suffering and medical expenses prior to death or for their own loss of support. Similarly, an action for a maritime tort was never held to survive the death of the tort-feasor; as in the common law, the cause of action abated.[140] But it was also established as early as 1873[141] that a state court might afford relief under its statute for wrongful death occurring on navigable waters. It was not until some years later that state death statutes were held applicable also in suits in admiralty. In *The Harrisburg*[142] the Court had been asked to apply the wrongful-death statutes of Massachusetts or Pennsylvania, but it refused to decide whether they might be validly applied in a federal admiralty court because the action was barred under either statute by state statutes of limitations. In *The Corsair*[143] the Court again refused to enforce a state death statute in admiralty, this time because the statute gave no lien and the suit had been brought in rem. Dicta indicated that a suit in personam might have been maintained.[144]

191

In the Southern District of New York, in 1893, Judge Addison Brown exhaustively reviewed the authorities in *The City of Norwalk*[145] and decided that a state wrongful-death statute might be enforced in an admiralty court as well as in a state court. He cited cases upholding state power to create maritime liens enforceable in admiralty and numerous cases in which pilotage or wharfage charges or regulations

courts must follow admiralty law seems to have been directed primarily toward the Court's complete failure to deal with contrary precedents. See Morrison, *supra*, at 475–76.

[139] The Harrisburg, 119 U.S. 199 (1886). "It is the duty of the courts to declare the law, not to make it." *Id.* at 214. This decision was contrary to that reached earlier by Mr. Justice Chase on circuit in The Sea Gull, 21 Fed. Cas. 909 (No. 12578) (C.C.D. Md. 1865).

[140] See Just v. Chambers, 312 U.S. 383, 391–92 (1941).

[141] Steamboat Co. v. Chase, 16 Wall. 522 (1873); Sherlock v. Alling, 93 U.S. 99 (1876).

[142] 119 U.S. 199 (1886).

[143] 145 U.S. 335 (1892).

[144] *Id.* at 347.

[145] 55 Fed. 98 (S.D. N.Y. 1893).

of fisheries were upheld against Commerce Clause objections. All
these, he said, must rest either on the police power or on the local
nature of the subject. Similarly, the wrongful-death statutes are exercises of police power: they protect life by imposing "one of the most
effectual of all sanctions," a pecuniary indemnity; they are general,
not directed toward maritime commerce alone; and they are local and
do not interfere with any "needful uniformity" of maritime law or
with any interstate or international interests.

The City of Norwalk was not a surprising decision. Before *The
Roanoke*[146] in 1903, the Supreme Court had never struck down, as
violative of the Admiralty Clause, a state law sought to be applied in
a maritime action unless it purported to diminish a right of recovery
afforded by federal law,[147] to substitute a rule of liquidated damages
for the maritime recovery for breach of contract,[148] or to create state
in rem jurisdiction.[149] Indeed the Court, with very little fanfare and
without acknowledging that there was any question of possible conflict with the Admiralty Clause, had permitted proof of a state
wrongful-death claim in a limitation proceeding.[150] In *The Hamilton*
the Court put the issue to rest without citing *The Roanoke:* any doubts
of state power "cannot be serious."[151]

192

Wrongful-death statutes, like state pilotage statutes which were
applicable even in admiralty,[152] perhaps may be regarded as regulations of conduct designed to protect life and limb; Judge Brown so
regarded them. The Massachusetts Act is penal, measuring damages
"with reference to the degree of [the defendant's] . . . culpability,"[153]
rather than to the amount of the loss. Probably the chief purpose of
such a statute, however, unlike the pilotage regulations earlier upheld, was to afford compensation for injury.[154] It is not likely to affect
conduct in any very significant degree that wrongful acts will be the

---

[146] 189 U.S. 185 (1903).

[147] Workman v. New York City, 179 U.S. 552 (1900).

[148] Watts v. Camors, 115 U.S. 353 (1885).

[149] The Hine v. Trevor, 4 Wall. 555 (1867).

[150] The Albert Dumois, 177 U.S. 240 (1900).

[151] 207 U.S. 398 (1907).

[152] Ex parte McNiel, 13 Wall. 236 (1872).

[153] 7A ANN. LAWS MASS. ch. 229, 2C (1955).

[154] See B. Currie, *supra* note 63, 26 U. CHI. L. REV. at 27 and n. 83.

basis of monetary liability in cases of death as well as personal injury. Thus perhaps the state's interest in its wrongful-death laws is
one different in kind from that justifying laws designed for the preservation of the public order. Still, the interest in providing recovery for
dependents of a person killed by an act which would have given rise to
an action for personal injuries short of death is one clearly deserving
of recognition. The Supreme Court has consistently held that this
interest outweighs any need for uniformity in the maritime law, and
the absence of a maritime rule has been attributed simply to history
and the inability of the Court to create a remedy, rather than to any
federal policy protecting defendants from liability in death cases.[155]

On the other hand, the policy of uniformity was held to outweigh
the state's interest in providing relief for a supplier of goods to a vessel on the order of the contractor. Unlike a remedy for wrongful
death, a remedy for supplies furnished to a vessel has little to do with
the safety or health of persons. Traditionally, the state's power to
protect life and limb has been treated as more extensive and entitled to
more respect than its power over commercial transactions. Injuries to
the person seem to be considered more important to the state's affairs
than injuries to business. On the other side of the coin, although both
wrongful death and the supply lien in *The Roanoke* created new liabilities for the shipowner, only the latter worked any change in the
standard of conduct to which he must conform. The wrongful-death
statutes enforced in the early cases gave relief only in cases of death
caused by an act which was in itself wrongful or tortious; they were
never applied to create a new duty unknown to the maritime law.[156]
The conduct of the shipowner was not affected but only the consequences of conduct already unlawful under maritime law; hence no
disuniformity as to required conduct was produced by the wrongful-
death acts. Not only was the state's interest arguably stronger than
in *The Roanoke*, but the statute also interfered less with the federal
interest. Moreover, it is arguable that uniformity is not so pressing a
policy in injury or death cases as it is in commercial matters. It was
only late in the era of *Swift v. Tyson* that the federal common law was

193

---

[155] *E.g.*, The Tungus v. Skovgaard, 358 U.S. 588 (1959); Levinson v. Deupree, 345
U.S. 648 (1953); The Harrisburg, 119 U.S. 199 (1886).

[156] See Harlan, J., dissenting, in Hess v. United States, 361 U.S. 314, 334 (1960).

held to extend to tort actions, and then over strenuous dissent.[157] The heart of a commercial enterprise is the ability to engage in transactions for profit. It is, therefore, of the utmost importance that the contractual rights of persons engaged in maritime commerce be safeguarded from unwarranted impairment by the diverse laws of the states. Tort liability is foreseeable and readily insurable. "Private concerns have rarely been greatly embarrassed, and in no instance, even where immunity is not recognized, has a municipality been seriously handicapped by tort liability. . . . Tort liability is in fact a very small item in the budget of any well organized enterprise."[158] To the extent that uniformity is less important in tort than in contract, the distinction between *The Hamilton* and *The Roanoke* gains further support.

194

Mr. Justice McReynolds did not attempt in *Jensen* to compare the workmen's compensation law before him with a wrongful-death statute. Had he done so he might have found it difficult to draw a distinction. He did remark that commerce would be burdened far more by workmen's compensation than by the law struck down in *The Roanoke*, but he did not discuss *The Hamilton*. Perhaps it is true that more losses are incurred by reason of injuries during the loading or operation of a vessel than by the disappearance of contractors who have neglected to pay for ordered supplies. Yet any force in such an estimate of the probabilities seems clearly overcome by the substantially greater interest of the state in the application of its workmen's compensation statute. If it is true that the state's interest in safety and compensation is sufficient to support the application of its wrongful-death statute, the similar policy of recovery for industrial accident as embodied in a workmen's compensation law appears equally strong. As for the federal interest, workmen's compensation is a less drastic liability than wrongful death, since it does not include all of the ele-

---

[157] Baltimore & Ohio R.R. v. Baugh, 149 U.S. 368 (1893). The dissent was by Mr. Justice Field. Professor Black has called the maritime contract the central part of the shipping business, "*par excellence* the concern of the admiralty tribunal." Black, *supra* note 65, at 277. In a view which he later described as "somewhat mellowed," GILMORE & BLACK 28 n. 98, he suggested that maritime contract be made an exclusively federal subject and maritime personal injury be given exclusively to the states, for substantive purposes.

[158] Green, *Freedom of Litigation (III)*, 38 ILL. L. REV. 355, 379 (1944).

ments of damage found in the indemnity provisions of a wrongful-
death law.[159] On the other hand, workmen's compensation is an absolute liability. Such laws impose liability in many more situations than
does the wrongful-death act, and in many situations in which there is
no violation of a duty recognized by the maritime law. Only with
respect to pilotage had the states ever been permitted to do that, and
pilotage was a matter involving the maintenance of order as well as
safety in the ports of the state. The peculiar remedial process of
workmen's compensation also may have been a stumbling block. Actions for wrongful death could be brought in any court; workmen's
compensation was generally an administrative remedy.[160] This meant
that the action in which liability was imposed on the shipowner might
be taken out of the power of the federal courts, except for ultimate
review by the Supreme Court; and this was a more serious matter.[161]

The demand for uniformity was so great in the days of Mr. Justice
McReynolds that not even an act of Congress could make the workmen's compensation laws of the states applicable in admiralty. Congress amended the saving clause after *Jensen* to preserve to suitors not
only common-law remedies but also their rights under the state compensation statutes.[162] In *Knickerbocker Ice Co. v. Stewart*[163] the Court
struck down the amendment: The Constitution itself demands uniformity, and Congress cannot alter the matter by delegating its lawmaking powers to the states. Congress chose to interpret this opinion
as having declared the statute unconstitutional simply because it applied to seamen as well as to longshoremen and harbor workers. Accordingly, Congress tried again, this time limiting the saved workmen's compensation remedy to persons other than the crew of a vessel.[164] Again, in *Washington v. W. C. Dawson & Co.*,[165] Mr. Justice

195

---

[159] See 1 LARSON, WORKMEN'S COMPENSATION 9–11 (1952).

[160] See 2 *id.* at 252, 288. In Louisiana the compensation system is administered by the courts.

[161] *Cf.* Panama R.R. v. Johnson, 264 U.S. 375, 390 (1924), where the Supreme Court tortured the Jones Act to permit suits under that statute to be brought in admiralty as well as at law, in order to avoid "a grave question . . . respecting its constitutional validity," which would have been presented if the Act had been construed as removing these cases from the admiralty jurisdiction.

[162] Act of Oct. 6, 1917, ch. 97, 40 Stat. 395.

[163] 253 U.S. 149 (1920).

[164] Act of June 10, 1922, ch. 216, 42 Stat. 634.

[165] 264 U.S. 219 (1924).

McReynolds held unconstitutional the delegation of power to the states. Again the decision drew a sharp dissent in which Mr. Justice Brandeis relied on several decisions in which Congress had been permitted to leave a subject otherwise requiring uniformity under the Commerce Clause to the diverse regulations of the states.

Such extreme insistence upon uniformity is puzzling. In many areas of the law the Court has upheld acts of Congress tying federal law to the changing laws of the several states.[166] In many instances there is utility in having federal laws correspond with those of the state in which a transaction takes place; and because of the state interest in these matters, and the declaration by Congress that uniformity is not of grave importance, even the Commerce Clause's injunction of uniformity has been overridden. Again the insistent question is posed: Why is uniformity any more critical in maritime matters? One might have thought the important thing, as in the Commerce Clause area, was simply that the states ought not to be able to disrupt commerce to the prejudice of other states' interests by the enactment of disuniform or otherwise burdensome regulations. It is difficult to understand why the federal interest in a free commerce, whether land or sea, is in need of protection from the action of the very body to whose care it is intrusted.[167] The question presented by the *Knickerbocker* and *Dawson* cases has not been re-examined by the Court. In all probability they will be treated as aberrations. In a footnote dictum, Mr. Justice Black recently rejected a suggestion that a state law would be invalid even if sanctioned by Congress as "so lacking in merit that it need not be discussed."[168]

Mr. Justice McReynolds was sufficiently deferential to precedent, however, to hold in *Western Fuel Co. v. Garcia*[169] that a state wrongful-death statute might validly be applied in a court of admiralty. For

196

[166] *Cf.* In re Rahrer, 140 U.S. 545 (1891); Clark Distilling Co. v. Western Md. Ry., 242 U.S. 311 (1917). See also the Assimilative Crimes Act, 18 U.S.C. § 13 (1958); the Prison Made Goods Act, 45 Stat. 1084 (1929), 49 U.S.C. § 60 (1958). See Whitfield v. Ohio, 297 U.S. 431 (1936). For the development of the conformity principle in procedure and its abandonment in 1934, see HART & WECHSLER, *op. cit. supra* note 138, at 581–89.

[167] See Morrison, *supra* note 138, at 480–81, condemning the *Knickerbocker* and *Dawson* cases on this ground.

[168] Wilburn Boat Co. v. Fireman's Fund Ins. Co., 348 U.S. 310, 321 n. 29 (1955). Professors Hart and Wechsler, *op. cit. supra* note 138, at 482–83, declare that "There seems to be small chance" that the principle of these decisions would be accepted today.

[169] 257 U.S. 233 (1921)

reasons which he did not elaborate, a death statute was "local" in
character in a way that workmen's compensation was not. What the
Court meant by "local" in this case was not that the nature of the
injured party's employment and the business of his employer made
uniformity necessary.[170] In *Garcia* the wrongful-death act was declared
to be local because of something in the nature of the cause of action
itself. The state law was allowed to apply to a stevedore killed on
board a vessel, to whom workmen's compensation would clearly have
been denied by precedents directly in point.[171]

Mr. Justice McReynolds' recognition of the continued vitality of
state law in maritime affairs was made somewhat less unpalatable for
him by a second holding in *Garcia*. Since the right created by the state
wrongful-death act was a right asserted under state law, he reasoned,
that right must be enforced in accordance with any limitations or conditions imposed by that state's law. In the case before him the state
statute of limitations had run while the unfortunate administrator was
pursuing a state compensation remedy later annulled on the authority
of *Jensen*. Some support for this holding was found in *The Harrisburg*,[172] which had denied the application of state wrongful-death
statutes on the ground that the statute of limitations was a condition
of the right and therefore extinguished the cause of action.[173] But Mr.

197

[170] *E.g.*, Grant Smith-Porter Ship Co. v. Rohde, 257 U.S. 469 (1922).

[171] This distinction was pointed out by Mr. Justice Harlan in Hess v. United States,
361 U.S. 314, 329 n. 11 (1960) (dissenting).

[172] 119 U.S. 199 (1886).

[173] There has been considerable difficulty in the conflict of laws in determining whether
a statute of limitation simply closes the doors of the state which enacted it, or whether it
is a "condition of the right" and therefore applicable in other forums as well. See, *e.g.*,
Bournias v. Atlantic Maritime Co., 220 F. 2d 152 (2d Cir. 1955); Lorenzen, *The Statute of
Limitations and the Conflict of Laws*, 28 YALE L. J. 492 (1919). The "general rule" has been
that limitation statutes are "procedural" and therefore apply only in the courts of the state
of enactment. But in recognition of considerable criticism of this rule, numerous exceptions have grown up, notably in actions for wrongful death. In part this attitude toward
wrongful death seems to have been the result of a conservative judicial antipathy toward
the new right of action; it is also in part attributable to the fact that usually a distinct
period of limitation is prescribed for wrongful-death actions. This latter circumstance was
thought to indicate a legislative intention that the expiration of the period terminates not
only the remedy but also the right. The distinctions that have been drawn seem highly
artificial. The proper inquiry should be whether the state legislature's purpose in limiting
death actions was simply to keep the courts of the state free for more recent business or to
protect defendants from the prosecution of claims based on stale and unreliable evidence.
See Magruder & Grout, *Wrongful Death within the Admiralty Jurisdiction*, 35 YALE L. J.

Justice Bradley's opinion had gone on to equivocate on the question whether a federal court had power to extend the statutory period on equitable grounds. Mr. Justice McReynolds did not refer to this, but it was to crop up again some thirty-odd years after *Garcia* in a dissenting opinion which would have changed the relationship between state and federal law substantially by applying federal standards and duties in wrongful-death cases.[174]

IV. SUBSTANTIVE STANDARDS IN WRONGFUL-DEATH CASES

In 1920 Congress, in the Jones Act,[175] provided remedies for the wrongful death of seamen and, in the Death on the High Seas Act,[176] for death occurring beyond the territorial waters of the states; but much room was left for the operation of state death statutes. Where federal law gave no remedy and state statutes were held to apply, lower courts long differed over whether the standard of care to be applied in an action for maritime wrongful death was to be determined by federal or state law, and whether the state law of contributory negligence might be applied to defeat recovery.[177] In *The Tungus v. Skovgaard*[178] the Supreme Court recently decided the issue in favor

198

395, 397 n. 12 (1926). In the usual case probably both purposes are relevant, and therefore no suit should be allowed in any forum after the expiration of the prescribed period. This has been the assumption in wrongful-death cases in admiralty, as exemplified by *Garcia* and *The Harrisburg*, and it seems also to lie behind the holding that federal courts must follow state statutes of limitation in the enforcement of rights created by state law under the *Erie* doctrine. Guaranty Trust Co. v. York, 326 U.S. 99 (1945). Lorenzen, *supra*, at 495–97, approves this practice.

[174] See text *infra*, at notes 179–93.

[175] 41 Stat. 1007 (1920), 46 U.S.C. § 688 (1958).

[176] 41 Stat. 537 (1920), 46 U.S.C. § 761 (1958).

[177] *Compare*, *e.g.*, O'Leary v. United States Lines Co., 215 F. 2d 708 (1st Cir. 1954), *cert. denied*, 348 U.S. 939 (1955) (dictum) (federal law), *with* Byrd v. Napoleon Ave. Ferry Co., 125 F. Supp. 573 (E. D. La. 1954), *affirmed*, 227 F. 2d 958 (5th Cir. 1955), Curtis v. A. Garcia y Cia, Ltda., 241 F. 2d 30 (3d Cir. 1957), *and* Puleo v. H. E. Moss & Co., 159 F. 2d 842 (2d Cir. 1947), *cert. denied*, 331 U.S. 847 (1947) (state law). The weight of authority clearly favored state law, as did most of the commentators. *But see* La Bourgogne, 210 U.S. 95 (1908), in which state law was ignored in applying a French wrongful-death remedy in a case involving a French vessel. In that case, however, the question was simply whether the French remedy was available. Neither state law nor the question of substantive standards was at issue.

[178] 358 U.S. 588 (1959). A companion case was United N.Y. & N.J. Sandy Hook Pilots Ass'n v. Halecki, 358 U.S. 613 (1959).

of state law. Mr. Justice Stewart's opinion for five members of the
Court was brief and to the point. Finding consistent authority to support him in Supreme Court decisions from *The Harrisburg* to the
present, he quoted Mr. Chief Justice Waite:[179] "If the admiralty
adopts the statute as a rule of right to be administered within its own
jurisdiction, it must take the right subject to the limitations which
have been made a part of its existence." Mr. Justice Stewart then discussed the *Garcia* case,[180] in which similar statements had been made
and recovery for wrongful death again barred by a state statute of
limitations; and *Levinson v. Deupree*,[181] in which Mr. Justice Frankfurter had written that the federal admiralty court was free to permit
amendment of a complaint to cure the defective appointment of an
administrator under state law, and thus to avoid the state statute of
limitations. That, said Mr. Justice Frankfurter, was "a procedural
nicety"; in any matter of substance state law governed. "The power
of a State to create such a right," said Mr. Justice Stewart in *The
Tungus*, "includes of necessity the power to determine when recovery
shall be permitted and when it shall not."[182] Nor was there any question of the state law's interference with uniformity: "Even *Southern
Pacific Co. v. Jensen*, which fathered the 'uniformity' concept, recognized that uniformity is not offended by 'the right given to recover in
death cases.'"[183] He then went on to say that he would not disturb the
holding of the Court of Appeals that the New Jersey statute incorporated maritime standards and, therefore, that recovery had properly
been granted for death caused by unseaworthiness.

This logical holding, although supported by ample precedent, was
disputed by four members of the Court in an opinion written by Mr.
Justice Brennan. The minority concurred in the result, since the Court
ultimately held that New Jersey would apply federal standards of
liability; but they argued that federal standards should be applied
regardless of state law. "The Court has simply failed to grasp the important distinction here between duties and remedies; between the
law governing the details of human behavior and the law governing

199

[179] The Harrisburg, 119 U.S. 199, 214 (1886).
[180] Western Fuel Co. v. Garcia, 257 U.S. 233 (1921).
[181] 345 U.S. 648 (1953).
[182] 358 U.S. at 594.
[183] *Ibid.*

the specific application of judicial sanctions for breach of duty. . . .
The duty claimed to have been broken here was one grounded in
federal law."[184] Rather forcefully, Mr. Justice Brennan argued that it
was a "strange principle that the substantive rules of law governing
human conduct in regard to maritime torts vary in their origin depending on whether the conduct gives rise to a fatal or a nonfatal
injury."[185] This is of course true, but it is the result of the unfortunate
holding in *The Harrisburg* some eighty years before, that there is no
federal remedy for wrongful death. That case should have been overruled. It is not altogether clear whether Mr. Justice Brennan would
have granted relief as a matter of state remedial law or by the creation of a federal remedy by analogy. Although the result is the same,
only the latter is logically consistent. To maintain that state law is
being applied, and then to apply a state remedy in a case in which the
state gives no recovery, is not to apply state law at all. If, as may be
suggested elsewhere in Mr. Justice Brennan's opinion, the federal
court does not adopt the state remedy but rather fashions its own by
analogy,[186] his approach would be a decided step forward in the creative development of maritime law, and it finds a parallel in the field of
labor relations.[187] But we are not told why it would not be equally
possible—and indeed more desirable—for the Court to fashion its
own rule by analogy to the Death on the High Seas Act,[188] which
would have furnished a uniform rule. In part the minority seem to
have been influenced by a few remarks on the floor of Congress which
indicated some concern over the states' rights to name the beneficiaries. But, under Mr. Justice Brennan's solution, recovery for wrongful death would still be at the mercy of the states; it is only because of
the fortuity that each state at present affords some relief for death[189]
that there is any uniformity at all.

200

[184] *Id.* at 600–601.

[185] *Id.* at 611.

[186] *Id.* at 604.

[187] See Textile Workers Union v. Lincoln Mills, 353 U.S. 448 (1957); Mishkin, *The Federal "Question" in the District Courts,* 53 COLUM. L. REV. 157 (1953); Meltzer, *The Supreme Court, Congress, and State Jurisdiction over Labor Relations: II,* 59 COLUM. L. REV. 269 (1959); Bickel & Wellington, *Legislative Purpose and the Judicial Process: The Lincoln Mills Case,* 71 HARV. L. REV. 1 (1957).

[188] 41 Stat. 537 (1920), 46 U.S.C. § 761 (1958).

[189] See The Tungus v. Skovgaard, 358 U.S. 588, 600 (1959) (Brennan, J.).

Thus neither the majority nor the minority solution is entirely satisfactory. Several state death acts have been construed not to afford relief for death caused by unseaworthiness;[190] others allow contributory negligence as a complete defense[191] rather than in mitigation of damages, as would be the rule under maritime law. Thus, under *The Tungus*, a party may be denied recovery for death resulting from the violation of a duty recognized by federal law, despite universal acceptance of the policy that it is as much a tort to kill a man as to maim him. This is intolerable. There is no reason for the absence of a federal wrongful-death remedy. The overruling of *The Harrisburg* should have presented no difficulty. There can hardly be any substantial reliance interest in preserving an absence of liability when the defendant has concededly violated a duty. The existence of the Death on the High Seas Act also should present little obstruction. In providing for a federal remedy for death occurring beyond the waters of the states, Congress left some traces in the legislative history of an intention to leave other death actions to the states.[192] These stray remarks, none of which were indorsed by the committees themselves, have not been enacted into law. The failure of the Congress to deal with a situation with which it was not confronted and which was being developed by the courts should not be taken to indicate a ban on judicial modification of maritime law in this area.[193]

201

[190] *E.g.,* Graham v. A. Lusi, Ltd., 206 F. 2d 223 (5th Cir. 1953) (Florida).

[191] *E.g.,* Niepert v. Cleveland Elec. Illuminating Co., 241 F. 2d 916 (6th Cir. 1957), *cert. denied,* 354 U.S. 909 (1957) (Ohio); Curtis v. A. Garcia y Cia, Ltda., 241 F. 2d 30 (3d Cir. 1957) (Pennsylvania); Byrd v. Napoleon Ave. Ferry Co., 125 F. Supp. 573 (E. D. La. 1954), *aff'd,* 227 F. 2d 958 (5th Cir. 1955) (Louisiana); Graham v. A. Lusi, Ltd., 206 F. 2d 223 (5th Cir. 1953) (Florida). *Contra:* Holley v. The Manfred Stansfield, 269 F. 2d 317 (4th Cir. 1959), *cert. denied,* 361 U.S. 883 (1959) (Virginia); and *The Tungus* and *Halecki* cases as decided by the Third and Second Circuits, respectively (New Jersey).

[192] The Senate Committee which recommended the bill did not state any reasons for the omission. The report did reprint without comment two letters advocating passage which stated that it would leave "unimpaired the rights under State statutes" and avoid "conflict with State statutes." S. Rep. No. 216, 66th Cong., 1st Sess. (1919). Some indication was given during debate of a desire to preserve the jurisdiction of the state courts— which would in no way have been affected by an overruling of *The Harrisburg*—and the state schemes of beneficiaries. 59 CONG. REC. 4484–85 (1920).

[193] A more complete statement of the arguments regarding the Death on the High Seas Act is to be found in 73 HARV. L. REV. 84, 152 (1959).

At least one court has held that state statutes providing for survival of claims for pain and suffering and expenses prior to the death of the injured party, unlike wrongful-death

Less than a year after *The Tungus* doubt was cast on its vitality. In *Goett v. Union Carbide Corp.*,[194] five justices voted to vacate and remand a decision of the Fourth Circuit to insure, as required by *The Tungus*, that state standards of liability had been applied. The four justices who had disagreed with the application of state law in *The Tungus* were among these five; they reserved their opinions as to whether that case should be overruled, stating that at least its doctrine should be applied evenhandedly.[195] Justices Harlan, Frankfurter, and Stewart, in dissent, insisted that the opinion of the court below left little doubt that in fact state law had been applied as it should have been.[196] But the interesting facet of the case was the dissent by Mr. Justice Whittaker, who argued that the Court of Appeals had applied federal law and that the decision ought, therefore, to be affirmed. *The Tungus*, he said, did not decide that state standards applied; it decided that federal standards applied. The state wrongful-death statute, he said, was used remedially only; the duty was one created by federal law. The dissent in *The Tungus* makes this clear, he continued, for that opinion would have permitted the federal court to fashion its own remedy for wrongful death by analogy to state law.[197]

The Whittaker opinion is in substance indistinguishable from the argument advanced by Mr. Justice Brennan in *The Tungus*. Mr. Justice Whittaker would denominate the law applied as state rather than federal, but he would define the duty by federal standards. This is a clear repudiation of what *The Tungus* stood for, and a very strong indication that now Mr. Justice Whittaker would be willing to join with the four who disagreed with that decision to overrule it should it

202

---

claims for loss of support, are "remedial" and therefore to be governed by federal substantive law; since no new cause of action is created, federal law is the source of the right. Curtis v. A. Garcia y Cia, Ltda., 241 F. 2d 30 (3d Cir. 1957). The metaphysics of this distinction are elusive. It seems evident that if no relief is available in the absence of state law, relief can be granted only where the state law affords it, whether the state statute be termed remedial or substantive. But these difficulties illustrate even more emphatically the need for overruling the misguided decision in *The Harrisburg*.

[194] 361 U.S. 340 (1960).

[195] *Id.* at 344 n. 5.

[196] *Id.* at 344, 350–51. The lower court had said: "The right to maintain such a suit can be enforced in admiralty only in accordance with the substantive law of the state whose statute is being adopted. The endowment must be taken *cum onere*." 256 F. 2d 449, 453 (4th Cir. 1958).

[197] 361 U.S. at 345–48.

be presented again. One paragraph of Mr. Justice Whittaker's opinion appears to rest on an interpretation of the West Virginia statute as referring to duties under federal law, and thus to be consistent with *The Tungus*.[198] But the general tenor of his opinion is the same as that which was rejected by the Court in that case: that federal standards govern liability in a maritime action for wrongful death under a state statute.

The Tungus was carried to what Mr. Justice Stewart considered its logical consequence in his brief opinion for the Court in *Hess v. United States*.[199] To him the application of Oregon's Employers' Liability Law in a maritime death action was not a serious problem. *The Tungus* had already decided the question. In a death action there is no federal remedy; state wrongful-death statutes may be enforced; and state standards determine the extent of the defendant's duty. There was no constitutional impediment to the application of the Oregon law; apparently *The Tungus* had decided this, too, by its dictum that "uniformity is not offended by 'the right given to recovery in death cases.' "[200] The Court left open the possibility that some state laws might be so offensive to maritime principles that they would be struck down even in death cases. This statute, however, was quite unobjectionable; indeed, it contained "many provisions more in consonance with traditional principles of admiralty than the State's general wrongful death statute."[201]

203

This is altogether too facile to be convincing; it may fairly be said that the Court dodged every issue. Surely there is a difference between permitting a state to supply a remedy for the breach of a duty recognized by maritime law and permitting it to increase the maritime standard of care. The Court's conception of what makes state law offensive to maritime law ignores the policies underlying the rejection of state law. No sense of theoretical beauty of similarity prompts the courts to deny state law. The reasons are the burden imposed on the enterprise of maritime commerce, the disuniformity of duties and liabilities in various locations, and the undermining of federal substantive policies. What consolation is it to the defendant that the liability

---

[198] *Id.* at 346–47.

[199] 361 U.S. 314 (1960).

[200] *Id.* at 320.

[201] *Id.* at 320–21.

imposed by the Oregon law is one reminiscent of the familiar maritime remedy of unseaworthiness, if that remedy is extended to an area unknown to maritime law, with a corresponding rise in his liabilities and a substantial effect on the conduct expected of him?

The requirement that a person use every precaution, device, or care practicable for the protection of life and limb may be a more extensive duty than that entailed by the warranty that a ship and its equipment are reasonably fit for the use to which they are intended.[202] The Oregon law appears to require not just good, average devices but the best that it is reasonable to expect the defendant to use, without regard to price.[203]

It is not suggested that the decision in *Hess* was wrong but only that the issue was far more complex and difficult than it was considered to be by the Supreme Court. Whenever a state law is sought to be applied there are two distinct questions: whether the state law creates a right, and, if it does, whether it is constitutionally applicable to the maritime situation. To afford recovery under state law for death caused by unseaworthiness in no way affects the conduct of a shipowner, and the application of state death statutes can only work to the benefit of the victim's dependents, even if the duties recognized are not so extensive as those of the maritime law. In the absence of a federal remedy for wrongful death, plaintiffs can hardly complain if the state law without which no remedy would exist is not uniformly favorable to their cause. Thus the sole feature of the death statute applied in *The Tungus* that might have been objectionable to federal interests was the increase in the monetary liabilities of defendants for death caused by violation of a duty established by federal law. On the other hand, the Employers' Liability Act has a decided effect on the standard of conduct. Mr. Justice Harlan in his dissent cited three personal-injury cases in which state laws purporting to create a new

204

---

[202] Although the Court in Mitchell v. Trawler Racer, Inc., 362 U.S. 539 (1960), disposed finally of the notion that negligence might be requisite to transitory unseaworthiness, that opinion recognized that a ship need only be "reasonably suitable for her intended service." *Id.* at 550.

[203] The Court of Appeals, while giving equally little attention to the conflicting interests involved or to the treatment of precedent, at least was able to perceive that it is the practical effect of the statute on the outcome of cases rather than the theoretical similarity between state and maritime law that is the significant consideration. That court held the statute a violation of the *Jensen* principle. 259 F. 2d 285, 291–92 (9th Cir. 1958). See 73 HARV. L. REV. 1363, 1364–65 (1959).

maritime standard of care were struck down.[204] The Court gave no
policy justification for ignoring them.

All these points were forcefully argued by Mr. Justice Harlan in a
dissent joined by Mr. Justice Frankfurter and, with reservations, by
Mr. Justice Whittaker. Superficially it may be said that the position
of the *Hess* dissent is similar to the minority position in *The Tungus*.
That is, Mr. Justice Brennan in *The Tungus* would have permitted the
utilization of a state death remedy whenever a federal duty was violated; Mr. Justice Harlan would have permitted the enforcement of a
state death claim only if a federal duty was violated. Both, in other
words, drew a sharp distinction between duties and remedies. But,
both in theory and in practical result, the two opinions are polar op-
posites. While Mr. Justice Harlan accepted the principle of *The
Tungus*, that the right to be enforced must be created by state law, he
insisted that such a right is unconstitutional if it imposes a duty
greater than the federal. Mr. Justice Brennan argued that no right
need be created by state law at all. As to the outcome of the cases, Mr.
Justice Harlan would have denied recovery unless both a federal and a
state duty had been violated, while Mr. Justice Brennan would have
permitted recovery at least whenever federal duties were violated,
whatever the state law. Further, there is nothing in Mr. Justice
Brennan's opinion in *The Tungus* to suggest that he would have voted
the other way in *Hess* had his earlier view prevailed. There is nothing
inconsistent in holding that a state remedy may be utilized whenever
there is a breach of a federal standard and also that a state statute may
be permitted to increase the standard. Thus it is strongly arguable
that Mr. Justice Brennan and those who agreed with him in *The
Tungus* would have permitted recovery for wrongful death whenever
either a federal or a state duty was violated, while Mr. Justice Harlan
would clearly have required the violation of both federal and state
duties. To emphasize the similarity between the two positions in their
separation of duty and remedy, therefore, is to distort the impression
conveyed by two opinions sharply at variance both in theory and in
practical result.

The result in *Hess* is not objectionable. The Employers' Liability
Law is supported by Oregon's policies of safe working conditions and
indemnity for injury. That state's connection with the injury was sub-

---

[204] 361 U.S. at 324–26.

stantial: the death occurred in Oregon and the deceased had lived and worked within the state. Oregon's interest was strong. Despite the degree of disuniformity and the substantive burden which the statute would have imposed, persons engaged in business activity can readily obtain liability insurance to spread their tort liabilities over a period of time, and the burden then seems comparable to that which may be imposed by the exaction of payments for unemployment compensation.[205] No substantial reason appears, in fact, for denying the states power to impose any liability they see fit for maritime personal injury or death as long as there is no discrimination against maritime commerce. The interest in uniformity simply is not as great as the states' interest in preventing or compensating for death. Payment of such sums may reasonably be considered a part of the cost of doing business, and the burden of knowing the laws of the various states a cost of doing business among the several states.[206] But this is not what the Court held. It mentioned neither policy nor interest but seems to have drawn a distinction between fatal and nonfatal injuries. Whatever the proper result, the issue deserved more attention than it received.

Interestingly enough, the issue of Oregon's power to create wrongful-death remedies in the face of maritime policy should never have been reached in *Hess*. The plaintiff was the employee of a local contractor whose activities were centered in the region of the Columbia River. The fact that he might occasionally have worked on the Washington side of the water does not seem to make his rights so uncertain and unpredictable as to demand the exclusive application of federal law. Certainly that fact cannot be used to deny the power of the state to help him by affording additional relief. The defendant was the United States, which has expressly disclaimed, by the very terms of the Tort Claims Act,[207] any need for uniformity in the law governing its tort liability. Thus the United States is in the position of a businessman who, in addition to engaging in numerous and varied other activities all over the globe, is the proprietor of a number of dams scattered throughout the nation, one of which is the Bonneville Dam on the Columbia River. Although there is something to be said for a uniform

206

---

[205] Standard Dredging Corp. v. Murphy, 319 U.S. 306 (1943).

[206] It has been suggested that the case in support of the Oregon statute was somewhat weaker than that in favor of the typical wrongful-death statute. See 73 Harv. L. Rev. 1363, 1366 (1959).

[207] 28 U.S.C. § 1346(b).

law to govern the rights and duties of all persons who engage in business activity in more than one state, the need is drastically reduced
when, as in *Hess*, the activities are stationary and each portion of the
enterprise localized. The Government's activities in regard to Bonneville Dam are centered in the Columbia River area. Government
employees on the dam are subjected to none of that uncertainty of
changing liabilities and duties that attends the voyage of a ship from
New York down the Atlantic coast and to New Orleans. The imposition of state law on such a localized defendant cannot subject him to
great problems of unpredictability. It only requires a certain localization of the planning of costs and the observance of determinate standards of care. Such minimal interference with the operations of a far-
flung business or industrial organization cannot be fairly said to neces-
sitate the rejection of a state law supported by strong policy and designed to protect Oregon workmen from unsafe working conditions,
or to compensate them for injury, even if that law might, as suggested
by Mr. Justice Harlan, interfere unduly with the certainty of maritime law if it had been applied against a shipowner in interstate or
foreign commerce.[208] There was no federal interest of substance to
weigh against the state policy in *Hess*.

V. Occupation of the Field by Federal Law: Personal-Injury Litigation and the Hess Case

A question perhaps more difficult than whether state law can
be applied in a maritime action to reduce or deny relief which the
general maritime law would grant is whether a state may add to the
duties imposed by federal law in an area in which maritime law recognizes some duty. For example, does the doctrine of unseaworthiness
express not only a federal policy that recovery shall be allowed an injured seaman or marine worker in certain cases but also a negative
policy that recovery shall not be allowed in other situations? It may
be argued that the law of recovery for personal injury represents the
result of a deliberate balancing of the conflicting interests of freedom
of action and of compensation for injury. Under this view, a rule of
liability prescribes both a minimum and a maximum, and state law

[208] See 72 HARV. L. REV. 1363, 1369 (1959). The fact that for other purposes Bonneville
Dam has been termed an "aid to navigation," 259 F. 2d 285, 289 n. 4, is patently irrelevant.

cannot be permitted to enlarge duties created by federal law. But this
is not a necessary inference. A rule may well be provided as an absolute minimum, with no policy expressed as to cases not included.
Many federal statutes, for example, deal only with a limited situation
in which a problem is particularly acute. Congressional silence on
analogous issues is not necessarily to be taken as indicating a contrary
policy in the omitted cases.[209] Similarly, it seems, the existence of a
duty to provide a seaworthy ship but not to observe due care toward
seamen might be attributable simply to history, to a simple lack of
prior adjudication on the subject, or to the absence of a compelling
policy in favor of relief, as easily as to any negative policy.

In the case of injury to the seaman, the maritime law in 1918 provided for an award of maintenance and cure, without regard to fault,
for injury or illness suffered while in the service of the vessel. Such an
award did not include sums for loss of earning power or for pain and
suffering but simply for medical expenses and sustenance, at best until
the point of maximum cure, and wages to the end of the voyage. In
addition to this remedy, the seaman was permitted to recover full indemnity, including sums for loss of earning power and for pain and suffering, if his injury was caused by the unseaworthiness of the vessel or
the defective condition of its equipment. In those days this liability for
unseaworthiness was often unavailable in cases of injury attributable
to the negligence of the crew in the operation of the vessel.[210] Maritime law, even after Congress' abolition of the fellow-servant rule,[211]
imposed no duty of due care toward the seaman on the owner of a
vessel. In that year the Supreme Court, in a notable decision by Mr.
Justice McReynolds, held in *Chelentis v. Luckenbach S.S. Co.*[212] that,
in a seaman's state court action to recover for personal injuries incurred on the high seas, the maritime law furnished the sole governing
duties, and that state law could not constitutionally be applied to af-

[209] See, *e.g.*, San Diego Bldg. Trades Council v. Garmon, 359 U.S. 236 (1959);
Meltzer, *supra* note 187.

[210] The scope of the warranty of seaworthiness was greatly expanded by the decision
in Mahnich v. Southern S. S. Co., 321 U.S. 96 (1944), and again in Mitchell v. Trawler
Racer, Inc., 362 U.S. 539 (1960), and extended to stevedores as well as seamen in Seas
Shipping Co. v. Sieracki, 328 U.S. 85 (1946). Before *Mahnich* the important case for the
definition of seamen's rights was The Osceola, 189 U.S. 158 (1903). See generally GILMORE
& BLACK ch. VI.

[211] Act of March 4, 1915, ch. 153, § 20, 38 Stat. 1185.

[212] 247 U.S. 372 (1918).

208

ford a remedy for injury caused by the negligent orders of the seaman's superior officer. His language was characteristically broad in holding that the saving clause's preservation of a "common-law remedy" does not authorize the state to create rights of action arising out of transactions or events within the admiralty jurisdiction: "We find nothing therein which reveals an intention to give the complaining party an election to determine whether the defendant's liability shall be measured by common-law standards rather than by those of the maritime law."[213] This was a clear repudiation of the language of Mr. Justice Holmes in *The Hamilton*[214] eleven years earlier. By the time *Chelentis* was decided, Holmes's view had already been interred by the McReynolds Court in the *Jensen* case, and Mr. Justice Holmes had ceased to protest every decision. In *Chelentis* he merely "concurred in the result" without opinion.

Mr. Justice McReynolds seems to have considered the provision by the maritime law of remedies for maintenance and cure and unseaworthiness as intended to be exclusive. "No state," he declared, "has power to abolish the well recognized maritime rule concerning measure of recovery and substitute therefor the full indemnity rule of the common law."[215] Thus in his eyes the maritime law, by providing certain remedies, had entirely pre-empted the field of shipowners' liabilities toward seamen; the states would infringe federal policy, and therefore the supremacy principle, by imposing additional duties. He also invoked at great length the policy of uniformity developed in *The Lottawanna* and first applied in *The Roanoke:* if the states are free to add to the duties of the shipowner in the various waters which the vessel plies on its voyage, he will be unable to plan his conduct or predict the extent of his liabilities.

Only infrequently has the Supreme Court encountered the issue of the state's power to create additional duties for a person already subject to some obligation imposed by maritime law. Far more often state law is urged where federal law is altogether silent. In both kinds of cases the real questions of policy and interest are the same. The decisions have tended to treat the provision for a duty relative to a particular set of facts as pre-empting everything about those facts, to a

209

---

[213] *Id.* at 384.

[214] 207 U.S. 398, 404 (1907).

[215] 247 U.S. at 382.

far greater extent than they have held a rule of nonliability preclusive. Where maritime law was operative but insufficient, the Supreme Court of the 1920's twice followed *Chelentis*. In *Carlisle Packing Co. v. Sandanger*[216] the Court declared it error to instruct a jury in a maritime case with regard to the state law of negligence as applied to an injury to a member of a ship's crew, but the error was held harmless because unseaworthiness was clear. In *Robins Dry Dock & Repair Co. v. Dahl*[217] the Court, again in an opinion by Mr. Justice McReynolds, rejected the application of state law. There, a New York statute imposing an absolute duty to provide a safe place to work had been held applicable by a state court to a worker injured while repairing a vessel in navigable waters. State law, said the Court in its brief opinion, can neither impair nor enlarge the duties imposed by general maritime law.

210

   This statement appears to declare a general rule that when maritime law makes any provision for a particular case or class of cases state law must be disregarded; that every maritime rule of recovery expresses a negative as well as a positive policy. At least in the area of personal-injury litigation, the issue has not been passed on by the Court since the *Dahl* case was handed down in 1925. A recent decision, however, appears to indicate that the Supreme Court still views the question in terms of whether the entire area is governed by state or federal law. Without first attempting to determine the content of the state or federal laws, Mr. Justice Stewart, in *Kermarec v. Compagnie Generale Transatlantique*,[218] cited *Sandanger* in holding maritime rather than state law applicable to determine the liability of a shipowner to a social guest of a crew member, injured in a fall aboard the vessel. In *Kermarec* the state rule would have denied relief afforded by the maritime law, but this does not appear until the end of the opinion, and there is nothing in the language of the Court to indicate that state law might have been applied had the laws been reversed. *Kermarec* in its actual decision is only a reaffirmation of *Garrett* and *Hawn*, but its reasoning is an adoption of the principle of *Chelentis* and *Dahl*: where the maritime law provides a duty in a particular situation, state law can neither add to nor detract from that duty.

[216] 259 U.S. 255 (1922).
[217] 266 U.S. 449 (1925).
[218] 358 U.S. 625 (1959).

It would be dangerous in light of the still more recent decision in *Hess v. United States*,[219] however, to predict that *Dahl* would be followed today. Again, in *Hess*, Mr. Justice Stewart talked in terms of entire areas of the law: "In an action for wrongful death . . . conduct said to give rise to liability is to be measured . . . under the substantive standards of the state law. . . . Uniformity is not offended by the 'right given to recover in death cases.' "[220] As in *Kermarec*, the interests of state and nation were balanced before the content of the opposing rules was discussed. It is submitted, however, that without knowing the substance of a rule it is impossible to discover either its policy or the degree of its interference with uniformity, and no satisfactory accommodation of conflicting interests can be made. Thus, to hold across the board, as Mr. Justice Stewart apparently has done, that actions for personal injury are governed by federal law and actions for wrongful death by state law, is to give inadequate consideration to the competing national and local interests.

211

In *Hess* the Court permitted the application of state law in an action for wrongful death under a statute quite similar to that struck down in a personal-injury suit in *Dahl*.[221] Both statutes imposed a duty not satisfied by due care. In both cases the state-created duty was considerably greater than that imposed by maritime law. To be sure, there are some slight differences between the two statutes, but the Court did not even cite *Dahl* or in any way seek to justify the distinction that was drawn. In no case prior to *Hess* had the Court ever permitted the application of a state law increasing tort duties, even in a death action; in fact, *Jensen* itself was a death case. It is difficult, to say the least, to maintain that the maritime law is opposed to the imposition of a duty on shipowners to provide a safe place to work, so that a state may not provide relief when failure so to provide causes

---

[219] 361 U.S. 314 (1960).

[220] *Id.* at 319–20.

[221] The New York law in *Dahl* provided: "A person employing or directing another to perform labor of any kind in the erection, repairing, altering or painting of a house, building or structure, shall not furnish . . . contrivances which are unsafe, unsuitable, or improper, and which are not so constructed, placed, and operated as to give proper protection to . . . life and limb. . . ." N.Y. Labor Law of 1909, ch. 36, § 18 (3 Consol. Laws of N.Y., 1909, pp. 3016–17), as amended, now found with minor changes in N.Y. CONSOL. LAWS ANN., ch. 31, art. 10, § 240(1) (McKinney 1948). In *Hess*, Oregon law required: "Persons having charge of, or responsible for, any work involving a risk or danger to the employes or the public, shall use every device, care and precaution which it is practicable to use for the protection and safety of life and limb. . . ." ORE. REV. STAT. § 654.305 (1959). If anything, the Oregon statute seems to impose a greater burden.

personal injury, and yet that because there is no federal policy against actions for wrongful death the state may impose a substantially identical duty enforceable only in death cases. It is the duty, not the remedy, that may be objectionable to federal principles. If federal law has balanced the interests of the shipowner in freedom of action and of the workman in indemnity for injury and determined that due care is the sole standard of conduct, that policy determination is no less infringed by an award in a death action than in one for a nonfatal injury. The uniformity of duty and liability of the maritime defendant is disturbed substantially in both cases. In some ports he will be subjected to liability beyond that expected of him by maritime law, and he will have to conform his activities to an increased standard of care. Further, it is not easy to perceive that the interest of the state in requiring a safe place to work is either more or less acute when the beneficiaries of this duty are the dependents of the workman rather than the workman himself. *Hess* is not an inevitable result of the holding that there is no maritime remedy for wrongful death. If *Dahl* is right, that the state's interest is not sufficient to overcome the lack of uniformity that might be produced by applying an absolute duty of safety to afford recovery for personal injury, the supposed inability of a federal court to fashion a remedy for wrongful death neither diminishes the federal interest nor enhances that of the state. Therefore, it cannot justify contrary results in a death action. Conversely, if *Hess* is right in holding that the state's interest is sufficient to permit the imposition of a high standard of safety in a death case despite the burden on the defendant, there is no greater federal interest in uniformity and no less state interest in the application of the same law in a suit for personal injuries, and *Dahl* should no longer be followed. Despite the clear language of the Supreme Court in two of its most recent pronouncements, it is not safe to predict that a consistent Court would adhere to its apparently firm distinction between personal-injury and death cases to deny the application of the Oregon Employers' Liability Law in a hypothetical action for maritime personal injury. Properly interpreted, therefore, *Hess* ought to stand for the view that prescription of a tort duty by federal maritime law should be taken only as requiring a certain minimum and not as expressing also a policy against increasing that duty if state law so provides.[222]

212

---

[222] See generally the dissenting opinion of Mr. Justice Harlan in *Hess*, 361 U.S. at 322, which faced the relevant issues squarely but would have reached the opposite result in that case.

VI. The Last Twenty Years: Long Live the Plaintiff!

In *Just v. Chambers*[223] in 1941 the Court upheld the application of a Florida statute under which an action for personal injuries survived the death of the tort-feasor. The Court of Appeals had been impressed by the argument that, while the absence of wrongful-death recovery in maritime law was the result of a gap or untouched area in which there was no maritime rule, there was a "positive rule" of admiralty against the survival of action.[224] But in neither situation does the maritime law provide relief; in both, the state law can be said to supplement the maritime law or to modify it, depending on whether the admiralty law is stated in positive or negative terms. The provision for survival would upset uniformity no more than a wrongful-death act; no essential features of an exclusive federal jurisdiction were involved. There were no dissents.

Some commentators attempted to draw fine distinctions between wrongful-death and survival statutes on the ground that the latter, whether preserving a right of action in the representative of a deceased victim or against the estate of a deceased tort-feasor, did not create a new right of action but rather purported to "preserve the right which the maritime law takes away."[225] But the Supreme Court was properly unimpressed. After the acceptance of wrongful death this case was easy. Not only does the survival statute not affect the conduct required of persons engaging in maritime commerce; it does not substantially affect planning for maritime operations, since it does not affect measurably the liabilities of a going concern. Further, there was no more policy behind the absence of a rule of survival than there was behind the absence of relief for wrongful death; it was an historical anomaly. On the other hand, the interest of the state in preserving liability in order that the injured party may be compensated has been recognized.[226]

213

---

[223] 312 U.S. 383 (1941).

[224] The Friendship II, 113 F. 2d 105 (5th Cir. 1940). One argument given by the court in rejecting the state rule was that a uniform rule was needed because it was often impossible to ascertain in which state an offshore tort occurred. This statement assumes that the discredited territorialist doctrine still is the *summum bonum* of choice of law and affords the only guides to decision. In any event, the avoidance of difficult questions of choice of law is no justification for ignoring a substantial state interest in cases in which only a single state is involved.

[225] See Stevens, *supra* note 11, at 257.

[226] The policies embodied in survival statutes are discussed in B. Currie, *Survival of Actions: Adjudication versus Automation in the Conflict of Laws*, 10 Stan. L. Rev. 205 (1958).

It is rather surprising and disappointing that the Court was content to leave the matter to the whim of the states rather than create its own maritime rule of survival.[227] There seems to be little doubt that, similarly, the Court will permit the application of state law providing that rights of action for personal injury survive the victim, and several lower federal courts have permitted its application.[228] The Court's rejection of the suggested gap-theory distinction between "untouched areas" and "positive rules of law" does not seem to indicate that the states are free in every case to add to maritime remedies. Rather it seems to be a recognition that it is not whether admiralty courts have previously passed on the issue, but whether there is any maritime policy opposed to the state law, that ought to be determinative. In *Just* the holding was clear;[229] but surely there are some cases in which the denial of maritime liability is based upon a policy against recovery, and clearly such a policy is as much entitled to respect as one embodied in a rule allowing recovery.

214

Further inroads on the *Jensen* principle were made in *Standard Dredging Corp. v. Murphy.*[230] There the Court, without dissent, upheld a state law exacting unemployment compensation contributions from the employers of a cook on a dredge in navigable waters and a grain worker employed on a floating elevator. The Court did not approach the problem in terms of the local nature of the work and the consequent absence of a need for uniformity on the particular facts. Indeed, the earlier cases would probably have denied that the transaction was local at all, at least in regard to the cook, who was probably classifiable as a seaman.[231] Rather, Mr. Justice Black took the opportunity to throw more stones at the unhappy *Jensen* decision. Even in its glory *Jensen* would not have covered this case, he wrote, since unemployment insurance was "markedly different" from workmen's

[227] See 40 COLUM. L. REV. 1439 (1940).

[228] Curtis v. A. Garcia y Cia, Ltda., 241 F. 2d 30 (3d Cir. 1957); O'Leary v. United States Lines Co., 215 F. 2d 708 (1st Cir. 1954), *cert. denied*. 348 U.S. 939 (1955) (dictum); Holland v. Steag, 143 F. Supp. 203 (D. Mass. 1956), 70 HARV. L. REV. 1095 (1957). The problem of whether state or federal standards of liability should apply under either "active" or "passive" survival statutes has not been specifically answered by the Supreme Court, but any attempt to distinguish *The Tungus* would necessarily be artificial.

[229] Even strenuous advocates of maritime supremacy have applauded *Just*. Dickinson & Andrews, *supra* note 129, at 216–17.

[230] 319 U.S. 306 (1943).

[231] See London Guar. & Acc. Co. v. Industrial Acc. Comm'n, 279 U.S. 109 (1929); Carlisle Packing Co. v. Sandanger, 259 U.S. 255 (1922).

compensation in its effect on maritime law. Moreover, "the *Jensen* case has already been severely limited, and has no vitality beyond that which may continue as to state workmen's compensation laws."[232] This levy was analogous to a property tax on vessels, and such taxes had long been upheld.[233]

Mr. Justice Black's depreciation of *Jensen* is difficult to understand. He cannot have meant that the door is now open to the states to apply their own laws in any maritime case. Only the year before he had written an opinion for the Court holding that a state might not impair the right of a seaman to recover under the general maritime law or the Jones Act by shifting the burden of proof.[234] Perhaps he meant that now the states were free to add to, but not to subtract from, the remedies given by the admiralty. But the Second Circuit declared that uniformity was dead, that *Jensen* would now be enforced only with "reluctance," and that even during the days of *Jensen* state law would have been permitted to make irrevocable an offer for a maritime contract.[235] This interpretation seems unfortunate. The advantages of a uniform law are particularly great in contract, since contracts are the core of planning for the conduct of business.[236] With the exception of the unsatisfactory *Wilburn Boat* decision,[237] later cases have not generally supported this extension of state law to maritime contracts.[238] But the policy of uniformity may very well have been overcome in the area of personal injury and death. Even before *Just v. Chambers*, the Supreme Court had not struck down a state law

215

---

[232] 319 U.S. at 309.

[233] Southern Pacific Co. v. Kentucky, 222 U.S. 63 (1911).

[234] Garrett v. Moore-McCormack Co., 317 U.S. 239 (1942).

[235] Jarka Corp. v. Hellenic Lines, Ltd., 182 F. 2d 916 (2d Cir. 1950).

[236] "Determining the validity of a maritime contract by varying state law is out of line both with precedent and with modern commercial needs." 36 CORNELL L. Q. 355, 360 (1951).

[237] Wilburn Boat Co. v. Fireman's Fund Ins. Co., 348 U.S. 310 (1955).

[238] The Supreme Court ignored state law and applied its own, often without the benefit of real precedent, in Ryan Stevedoring Co. v. Pan-Atlantic S.S. Corp., 350 U.S. 124 (1956); Bisso v. Inland Waterways Corp., 349 U.S. 85 (1955); and American Stevedores, Inc. v. Porello, 330 U.S. 446 (1947). The Second Circuit has recently recognized that maritime contracts are predominantly to be governed by federal law, restricting the *Wilburn* case to marine insurance. A/S J. Ludwig Mowinckels Rederi v. Commercial Stevedoring Co., 256 F. 2d 227 (2d Cir.), *dismissed per stipulation,* 358 U.S. 801 (1958). *Jarka* was brushed aside as "inapposite"—i.e., discarded. See MacChesney, *Marine Insurance and the Substantive Admiralty Law,* 57 MICH. L. REV. 555 (1959).

that added to the remedies available for personal injury. Not only is it unlikely that *Jensen* would itself be followed if it were possible for that case to arise today; even *Chelentis* would likely go by the boards.

The late 1940's were the nadir of federal maritime supremacy. The Supreme Court had applied state law in *Just*, in *Murphy*, in *Caldarola*, and in the workmen's compensation case of *Davis v. Department of Labor and Industries*.[239] *Murphy* throws an interesting light on the *Jensen* line of decision. Some systems of workmen's compensation, like that apparently involved in *Jensen* itself, provide for an award to be paid by the employer, and the enforcement procedure is analogous to that in tort litigation. The chief differences are absolute liability and the administrative rather than judicial procedure prevailing in most states. In six states, however, the employer is assessed sums payable to a state compensation fund out of which injured employees are given compensation.[240] His liability is thus measured by the number of his employees rather than by the incidence of injury; awards are made from the state fund and do not directly burden the employer. Under such a system it is difficult to see that the effect on maritime commerce is "markedly different" from that of an assessment for unemployment insurance. In both the employer is assessed a sum dependent on the number of his employees; the actual incidence of accident or of unemployment does not affect his liabilities at all.[241] It is possible that the impact of multiple taxation by the several states on an employer engaged in interstate operations for contributions for members of the crew of a vessel might unduly burden commerce and thus be void. But the burden would appear equally great in either case,

216

---

[239] 317 U.S. 249 (1942).

[240] Nevada, North Dakota, Ohio, Washington, West Virginia, and Wyoming. See Note, 53 YALE L. J. 348, 356 n. 35 (1944). A statute of this type was denied maritime application in Washington v. W. C. Dawson & Co., 264 U.S. 219 (1924). While the West Virginia and Ohio acts permit an employer to choose self-insurance under some circumstances, this fact does not make the statutes any more burdensome to the employer who is given an election. A similar choice—to insure or to be subjected to common-law actions without benefit of the usual defenses—is available to West Virginia and Nevada employers.

[241] The similarity to the workmen's compensation law struck down in *Dawson* was utilized prior to *Murphy* to argue for unconstitutionality of the Illinois unemployment insurance statute in maritime applications. Deutsch, *Constitutionality of State Unemployment Legislation as Applied to Dredge Boat Crews*, 15 TUL. L. REV. 241, 260 (1941). The similarity seems no less significant when it is invoked in support of the opposite conclusion on the basis of *Murphy*.

and *Murphy* did not distinguish *Jensen* on the local nature of the facts. Rather, to quote a remark made by the late Professor Powell in another context, "The ruling distinction between the two cases is the intervening change in the composition of the Court."[242]

Confronted by another situation such as *Just* in which no federal precedent was squarely in point, Mr. Justice Black, in *Halcyon Lines v. Haenn Ship Ceiling & Refitting Corp.*,[243] dismissed an action brought for contribution by a shipowner, held liable to a stevedore for unseaworthiness, against the workman's employer, who was alleged to have been equally at fault. State law was not mentioned by the Court or pressed by counsel.[244] But it is interesting to note that the law of Pennsylvania, in whose waters the injury took place, provided for contribution under these circumstances.[245] The Court's refusal to fashion a federal right of contribution—a right generally considered a desirable advance in distributive justice—is made more difficult to understand in light of the existence of such relief in collision cases.[246] The Court offered no reasons for drawing a distinction between cases of collision and of personal injury. Since the employer was exonerated by the Longshoremen's and Harborworkers' Compensation Act from liability for injury beyond the amount of federal workmen's compensation,[247] the Court of Appeals had limited contribution, as would Pennsylvania law, to that amount.[248] But the Court did not decide on this ground. Only the legislature, said the Court, can accommodate the diverse interests in this type of case.[249] This attitude is in marked contrast to the willingness exhibited by the Court in *Kermarec* to create a standard of care for a shipowner to a social guest

217

---

[242] POWELL, VAGARIES AND VARIETIES IN CONSTITUTIONAL INTERPRETATION 110 (1956).

[243] 342 U.S. 282 (1952).

[244] See Petition for Certiorari; Respondent's Memorandum on Petition for Certiorari, pp. 2–3; Respondent's Brief on the Merits, p. 6.

[245] Pennsylvania has adopted the Uniform Contribution among Tort-feasors Act, 12 PURDON'S PA. STATS. §§ 2082–89 (1959 Supp.). This 1951 enactment superseded a 1933 act, which was construed in Maio v. Fahs, 339 Pa. 180 (1940), to permit partial recovery of contribution from a tort-feasor protected against full liability by a state workmen's compensation statute.

[246] E.g., The Chattahoochee, 173 U.S. 540 (1899).

[247] 44 Stat. 1426 (1927), 33 U.S.C. § 905 (1958).

[248] Baccile v. Halcyon Lines, 187 F. 2d 403 (3d Cir. 1951).

[249] 342 U.S. at 285–87 (1952).

injured aboard the vessel, when the state law would apparently have
denied relief by virtue of the distinction between a licensee and a
business visitor.[250] It is also in marked contrast to the willingness of
the Court to adopt a state law when it is unable or unwilling to
fashion its own rule, as in the wrongful-death and survival cases and
in the creation of the home-port lien.[251] The unexpressed reasoning
behind the *Halcyon* opinion may be found in Mr. Justice Black's dissent from a later decision, permitting the shipowner in such a case to
recover indemnity from the stevedore's employer in a case in which
the latter was solely at fault.[252] The chance of recovery against the
employer, he explained, would diminish the employer's desire to aid
the injured party in his action against the shipowner. Without the
risk of indemnity or contribution, the employer, liable to the stevedore under the federal compensation statute, was encouraged to aid
him because he was entitled to reimbursement from the employee out
of sums received. The allowance of indemnity, however, would destroy any advantage to him in the suit against the third party, and the
purpose of the compensation act would be frustrated. The application
of state law would have had the same effect. Thus, perhaps, even if
state law had been argued, it would have been rejected as contrary to
the policy of the federal act.

218

---

[250] Kermarec v. Compagnie Generale Transatlantique, 358 U.S. 625 (1959). That the
problem of contribution is not too complex to be worked out by the courts is evidenced by
a Pennsylvania decision prior to the enactment of that state's contribution statute, affording relief as a matter of common law. Goldman v. Mitchell-Fletcher Co., 292 Pa. 354
(1928). For its "making law by refusing to make law," the *Halcyon* case has been roundly
condemned by Professors Hart and Sacks, who inquire whether the decision is perhaps
"false to the most basic presuppositions of Anglo-American law, constituting, in effect,
an abdication of judicial responsibility?" HART & SACKS, THE LEGAL PROCESS: BASIC PROB-
LEMS IN THE MAKING AND APPLICATION OF LAW 515 (tentative ed. 1958). "At one stroke
the Court (1) reached an unsound conclusion in the case before it; (2) destroyed the harmony of the underlying maritime law in this general area; and (3) established a precedent
which puts in question the continued vitality in the federal courts of the whole Anglo-
American tradition of growth of decisional law." *Id.* at 535.

[251] A New Jersey court recently applied that state's contribution statute in a maritime
case, distinguishing *Halcyon* because no employment relationship was involved. Fruch v.
Kupper, 54 N.J. Super. 296 (1959), 13 RUTGERS L. REV. 718 (1959). This decision is markedly preferable to *Halcyon*, although one might still wish for the enunciation of a federal
rule.

[252] Ryan Stevedoring Co. v. Pan-Atlantic S.S. Corp., 350 U.S. 124, 144–46 (1956). The
treatment given this reasoning by Professors Hart and Sacks is scathing. HART & SACKS, *op.
cit. supra* note 250, at 541.

In 1954, Mr. Justice Black declared for the Court, in *Madruga v. Superior Court*,[253] that no principle of uniformity barred a state from applying its own laws to partition a vessel. He spoke in terms of a gap in the maritime law, referring to the absence of an admiralty rule or of a need for uniformity. Not only was this not an action in rem but no federal rule was required. None existed, and none would be created by the Court. This decision has had little effect on subsequent cases and represents no serious invasion of the principle of uniformity. Property matters have seldom been the subject of Supreme Court action in the state-federal admiralty mélange. When they have arisen the issue has been resolved in favor of state authority,[254] and this is probably justifiable in view of the substantial state interest that has always been recognized.

In *Maryland Casualty Co. v. Cushing*[255] in 1954 the Court held, five to four, that no action could be maintained against an insurer under the Louisiana direct-action statute[256] during the pendency of proceedings for limitation of a shipowner's liability arising out of a collision. To permit the action would drain off assets which otherwise would inure to the benefit of the shipowner and thus deprive him of the benefit of his insurance, as well as inducing a rise in the insurance rate, both to the detriment of the policy of shipowner protection expressed in the Limitation Act. Four dissenters joined in an opinion by Mr. Justice Black. Mr. Justice Clark concurred with the statement of these four that after termination of the limitation proceeding, when the claims which the shipowner was required to pay had been satisfied out of the proceeds of insurance, the direct action might be pursued without infringing upon either the Limitation Act or the Constitution. "No reason has been advanced," said Mr. Justice Black, "why marine insurance, long the province of the states, so imperatively requires uniformity that we should now hold that Congress alone can regulate it."[257]

219

---

[253] 346 U.S. 556 (1954).

[254] *E.g.*, Crapo v. Kelly, 16 Wall. 610 (1872), upholding the power of the state to order the transfer of a vessel in an insolvency proceeding on the ground that a rule of property was involved and the case was therefore not even within the admiralty jurisdiction.

[255] 347 U.S. 409 (1954).

[256] LOUISIANA INSURANCE CODE § 655, La. Rev. Stat. § 22:655 (West 1959).

[257] 347 U.S. at 430–31. The McCarran Act, 59 Stat. 34 (1945), 15 U.S.C. § 1012(b) (1958), was also invoked by the Court of Appeals as a ground for upholding the state

The intimation in *Cushing* that a state direct-action statute might validly be applied in a maritime litigation is not startling; the statute is remedial. Rather than being required to sue the shipowner himself and thus cause multiple suits, or to sue both in a single action, the injured party is permitted to short-cut delays by recovering directly against the insurer, whose liability for the eventual burden is recognized even in the absence of the statute. Like the provision of a maritime lien for home-port supplies, and like the statutory remedy of specific enforcement of agreements to arbitrate, both of which had earlier been upheld in admiralty suits,[258] the direct-action statute creates no new duties but only an additional remedy for a duty recognized by the maritime law. It is true that the statute may deprive the insurer of certain personal defenses of the insured, *e.g.*, interspousal immunity.[259] But this relatively small substantive change seems justified, in the light of such decisions as *Murphy* and *Hess*, by the state's interest in providing a quick and certain remedy for the injured party.

220

A more serious issue of state and federal law in the area of marine insurance was presented to the Court in 1955 in *Wilburn Boat Co. v. Fireman's Fund. Ins. Co.*[260] Suit was brought to recover on a fire insurance policy for the loss of a houseboat. The company pleaded breach of two warranties in the policy: 1) the vessel had been used for commercial purposes; 2) it had been transferred to a dummy corporation. Under the law of Texas, a breach of warranty is no defense to recovery on a policy of insurance unless the breach contributed materially to the loss;[261] in this case the breaches were harmless. The Court of Appeals held that the rule in admiralty required strict compliance with all terms of a marine insurance policy, that state law

law. Mr. Justice Frankfurter, speaking for four members of the Court, rejected this ground, stating that the statute had nothing to do with maritime substantive law but only permitted the states to continue regulating the insurance business as they had done before insurance was held to be interstate commerce in United States v. South-Eastern Underwriters Ass'n, 322 U.S. 533 (1944). Mr. Justice Black, on the other hand, for the four dissenters, accepted the lower court's argument, declaring that the McCarran Act in "unambiguous language" compelled the application of state law. 347 U.S. at 437. Mr. Justice Clark, who cast the deciding vote, did not mention the statute.

[258] The Lottawanna, 21 Wall. 558 (1875) (lien); Red Cross Line v. Atlantic Fruit Co., 264 U.S. 109 (1924) (arbitration).

[259] See 103 U. Pa. L. Rev. 263 (1954); 10 Tul. L. Rev. 312 (1936).

[260] 348 U.S. 310 (1955).

[261] Vernon's Tex. Civ. Stat. arts. 5.37, 6.14 (1952).

could not be applied, and that recovery was barred.[262] The judgment was reversed in an opinion by Mr. Justice Black. The Supreme Court had never said that strict compliance was required; therefore there was no such rule in admiralty, and therefore state law was determinative. There was no need for uniformity here; traditionally, the states have had great power over the regulation of insurance. Nor would the Court create its own rule; insurance law is for a legislature, not for a court, since a court cannot choose among the several possible lenient rules in regard to breaches of warranty.

This decision caused great stir. Mr. Justice Frankfurter concurred on the ground of the local nature of the particular transaction in *Wilburn*.[263] But he, as well as Mr. Justice Reed in dissent, argued that "If uniformity is needed anywhere, it is needed in marine insurance."[264] Shipmasters must know what they must do to retain insurance protection, and insurers must know if they are to set premiums with any degree of accuracy. The dissenting justices would have been willing to overrule what they considered authority for a federal rule of strict compliance. The effect of provisions in a contract, said Mr. Justice Reed, is a matter "which the Court is particularly equipped to handle."[265] The general reaction to *Wilburn* was highly negative.[266]

Mr. Justice Black was careful, however, to preserve the effect of his holding in *Garrett v. Moore-McCormack Co.*[267] that the state law cannot derogate from a right given by maritime law. His opinion in *Wilburn* seems to be a combination of the theory that the federal law has left the area untouched and a recognition of a strong state interest in insurance. The suggestion in *Wilburn* that the frequency of prior

221

---

[262] 201 F. 2d 833 (5th Cir. 1953).

[263] 348 U.S. at 323. Mr. Justice Frankfurter doubted that the Court would permit an insurance policy covering the Queen Mary to be subjected to the vagaries of state laws.

[264] *Id.* at 333.

[265] *Id.* at 334.

[266] Professors Gilmore and Black stated that "the decision seems to make serious inroads on the uniformity of the maritime law," GILMORE & BLACK 44 (1957), echoing Mr. Justice Reed's conviction that "marine insurance is the world-wide maritime subject *par excellence*." *Ibid.* Further, "the implication of Wilburn would appear to be that marine insurance law as a whole is to be excised from the general maritime law. . . ." *Id.* at 63. An excellent note, 29 So. CAL. L. REV. 359, 360 (1956), declares that *Wilburn* "illustrates the post-*Jensen* erosion of the *Jensen* Court's views on maritime uniformity." Professor MacChesney, *supra* note 238, concludes with relief that *Wilburn* will probably not be extended.

[267] 317 U.S. 239 (1942).

litigation might be determinative of the applicability of state law has been aptly termed "a nightmarish solution" which "would make a sheer crazy quilt of the subject."[268] Fortunately, it had been rejected earlier by the Supreme Court in *Just v. Chambers*.[269] In later decisions, the Court has not taken the trouble to determine whether prior adjudications constitute a "rule." Nor has the Court abandoned the entire area of maritime contract to state law. Not long after *Wilburn* the Court applied federal law to determine the validity of a provision in a towage contract exculpating a tugboat company from negligence.[270] It did so again on the question of the shipowner's right to recover indemnity from a stevedoring company whose injured employee had recovered damages for unseaworthiness caused by the negligence of the employer.[271] These rules were no more "established" than was the rule of strict compliance, ignored in *Wilburn*. And in the field of personal injuries the Supreme Court's decision in *Kermarec* eliminates any possibility that state law will be applied across the board. Even lower federal courts have refused to extend *Wilburn* in the area of contract.[272]

For obvious reasons, the antiquated and unjust rule of strict compliance was unacceptable to Mr. Justice Black. The clear solution would have been that suggested by the dissent: to hold as a matter of general maritime law that no breach of warranty shall defeat recovery unless it contributes materially to the loss. This hardly seems an unjustified exercise of power for a Court which did not hesitate a year later to declare that a provision in a contract of towage, purporting to absolve the towing company from liability for negligence, was invalid as a matter of court-made maritime law. Nor does it seem a function less suited to the judiciary than the Court's action in *Kermarec*, abolishing any distinction between the duties owed an invitee and a licensee by a shipowner, or than the extensive lawmaking in which the Court has indulged in the development of the law of recovery for unseaworthiness.[273] On the contrary, it seems an eminently judicial

[268] GILMORE & BLACK 62, 63.

[269] 312 U.S. 383, 391 (1941).

[270] Bisso v. Inland Waterways Corp., 349 U.S. 85 (1955).

[271] Ryan Stevedoring Co., v. Pan-Atlantic S.S. Corp., 350 U.S. 124 (1956).

[272] *E.g.*, A/S J. Ludwig Mowinckels Rederi v. Commercial Stevedoring Co., 256 F. 2d 227 (2d Cir. 1957), *dismissed per stipulation*, 358 U.S. 801 (1958).

[273] This remedy was created out of whole cloth in The Osceola, 189 U.S. 158 (1903), and then stretched beyond recognition to encompass many types of negligence. See note 210, *supra*.

function to declare the effect to be given to contractual provisions and to declare illegal those which are unduly oppressive and which result from the superior bargaining position of one of the parties.[274] A solution in terms of a federal rule would have produced uniformity in an area in which the need for it appears strong.[275] In many states a backward rule prevails;[276] the ability of the insured to recover will vary according to the forum. In the interpretation and effect of a contract, the states apply innumerable and varying choice-of-law rules which unpredictably refer to the law of the place of the contract's making or performance, as variously defined; the law intended by the parties; or some other chosen from a bag of infinite variety, with the inevitable effect of confusion.[277] The refusal to create a federal rule, even at the expense of overruling a few decisions by lower federal courts, is difficult to explain. In this respect the decision is similar to that in *Just v. Chambers*.

Mr. Justice Black's easy conclusion, that since no federal rule could be found state law must govern, should be contrasted with his action in *Halcyon*. There the case was dismissed because of the Court's deference to congressional prerogative, although state law might have been utilized exactly as it was in *Wilburn* to give the relief sought. Perhaps the answer lies simply in the failure of counsel in *Halcyon* to argue the state law. But it is noteworthy that in *Halcyon* the state rule, like a federal rule of contribution, would have impaired the position of the injured longshoreman, while in *Wilburn* the liberal warranty rule helped a policyholder at the expense of an insurance company. In case after case in recent years, the Supreme Court appears to have found state law acceptable when it helped that favored litigant, the personal-injury claimant,[278] and rejected it when it would in any way work to his detriment. *Kermarec* and *Hess* are examples; in the latter

223

---

[274] Bisso v. Inland Waterways Corp., 349 U.S. 85 (1955); Railroad Co. v. Lockwood, 17 Wall. 357 (1873).

[275] A number of commentators favored the creation of a federal rule. *E.g.*, MacChesney, *supra* note 238, at 564–68; 40 MINN. L. REV. 168 (1956); 29 So. CAL. L. REV. 359, 362 (1956); Note, 50 Nw. U. L. REV. 677, 682–83 (1955).

[276] See MacChesney, *supra* note 238, at 569–71. That the law of Illinois requires strict compliance was said to be "quite clear, if not conceded," by the Court of Appeals after remand in *Wilburn*. 259 F. 2d 662, 663 (5th Cir. 1958).

[277] For an extensive analysis of the intricate problems of international choice of law in marine insurance, see Griese, *Marine Insurance Contracts in the Conflicts of Laws: A Comparative Study of the Case Law*, 6 U.C.L.A. L. REV. 55 (1959).

[278] Note, 50 Nw. U. L. REV. 677, 688–89 (1955).

case, the Court permitted unprecedented disuniformity to allow recovery under state law, and in the former it made a point of fashioning its own new rule imposing liability when state law would have denied relief. *Wilburn* represents another situation in which sympathies are strongly in favor of one of the parties.

In his dissent in *Hess*[279] Mr. Justice Harlan replied to a suggestion[280] that the Court was applying state law when it was in line with enlightened views of modern justice but rejected it when it imposed outmoded restrictions. He explained the acceptance of some state laws as the result of a determination that the state's interest in those areas outweighed the federal demand for uniformity. Although one would like to believe with Mr. Justice Harlan that what the Court should not do it does not do, it is difficult to describe the haphazard course of decision in recent years as the result of a neutral and objective balancing of the interests of the states and of the federal government. An examination of the Court's treatment of maritime cases in the past twenty years leaves little room for any explanation other than that the Court is seeking the best of both worlds: it makes use of state law when it feels that law desirable as a supplement to maritime law. If the maritime rule is undesirable, the Court is usually reluctant to change it; often the reason is that the decision would be "legislative." If the state law would impair a federal right, as in *Garrett*, it is never applied. If it would create a right that is undesirable for other reasons, it will be ignored, as in *Halcyon*. If it creates a right that is desirable, as in *Wilburn* or *Just* or *Hess*, it will be applied; the interest in uniformity will be ignored, a contrary federal rule will be conveniently slipped under the rug, the wrongful-death and home-port lien cases will be earnestly cited, and the subject will be declared "untouched" by maritime law. If, as in *Kermarec*, state law is not favorable and the old maritime rule is inadequate, the Court will resort to judicial creativity.

In no case since 1940 has the Supreme Court denied the applicability of a state law on constitutional grounds when the law favored the plaintiff. With the exception of the decision in *Maryland Casualty Co. v. Cushing*, that Louisiana's direct-action statute interfered with the policies of the Limitation of Liability Act if suit was brought prior to the termination of the limitation proceeding, no Supreme Court case

---

[279] 361 U.S. at 330.

[280] See Note, 73 Harv. L. Rev. 84, 148 (1959).

224

since 1940 has refused on any grounds to apply a state law favorable to
the plaintiff; and in that case five justices agreed that the state law
might be applied validly following final judgment in the limitation
proceeding. In contrast, in no case since 1940 has the Supreme Court
permitted the application of state law when it would have been less
favorable to the plaintiff than the maritime law, with the exception of
Caldarola v. Eckert; and even the author of that opinion has abandoned
it. This may be mere coincidence; but the principle of uniformity for
the protection of shipping interests from varying liabilities has not
been enforced since 1940, although the cases have involved such matters as the effect of harmless warranty breaches in contracts of marine
insurance and the standard of care in cases of wrongful death. If the
policy of uniformity is ever to be given effect it seems that it would
have been observed in at least one of these cases. Nor since 1940 has
the existence of a maritime rule been held to express a negative policy   225
prohibiting the addition of duties by a state. It seems safe to say,
therefore, that no longer, as in the days of Mr. Justice McReynolds,
is it true that a state may neither impair nor enlarge the rights given
by the maritime law; the states may never impair those rights, but
they have certainly been permitted in recent years to enlarge them.

VII. CONCLUSION

It cannot be gainsaid that the area of federalism and the admiralty is plagued with inconsistencies. This is, in part, the unfortunate result of the Court's being called upon to determine, as in numerous other areas of constitutional litigation, the relative strengths of
competing interests—often clearly a matter of preference rather than
of reasoning from established premises. Moreover, in searching for a
touchstone to aid in the process of decision, the Court has developed
diverging lines of precedent which obscure the necessity for an earnest inquiry into the merits of the state and federal interests in new
cases. Still worse, the ancient decisions which form the base of each
line were often the products of entirely distinct theories of legal
reasoning.

Thus two criticisms seem warranted: the Court should assume a
more creative role in formulating a cohesive maritime law, and it
should pay more attention to the competing policies of nation and
state. As to the first, if there is any vitality in the principle that it is a
function of the federal admiralty courts to enunciate and to apply a

common law of the sea in the interests of the uniform, orderly governance of maritime commerce—and I believe there is—then that law ought not to be left incomplete and incapable of fulfilling its function on the ground of absence of precedent or an unnecessarily abject deference to the powers of Congress. If there is a "void" in the maritime law it is the duty of the Supreme Court to ascertain the federal policy by a balancing of the interests of the parties, as was done in formulating a standard of care toward shipboard guests in *Kermarec*; not, as was suggested by Mr. Justice Black in *Wilburn*, to turn automatically to state law. As for the second suggestion, it may very well be that the states ought to be free to apply their own laws to increase the standard of care in all cases of death or personal injury. It is obviously more important in *Hess* that the dependents of the deceased recover for the loss of their provider than it is to the United States that liability be avoided. As the impact on the plaintiff is greater than that on the defendant, so perhaps it may be argued that the interest of the state in granting relief is greater than that of the maritime law in denying it, especially if the only federal policy is that of uniformity for planning purposes. As long as the maritime worker is guaranteed his federal remedies against state impairment, as he clearly is under present decisions, and as long as the shipowner is free to insure against the imposition of additional liability under state laws, the increase in the cost of operations ought no more to be held to outweigh the state's humanitarian interest than to burden interstate commerce; and that there is no undue burden on commerce is clear. But if this is what the Court means to do in *Hess*—to permit the state to create whatever liability it wishes for maritime death or personal injury—it ought to say so. It ought to describe the various interests involved and tell why that of the state is greater. It is not very persuasive to say simply that "uniformity is not offended by 'the right given to recover in death cases.' "[281]

When the Supreme Court takes a more active view of its responsibilities in developing a rational common law of the sea, and when it pays more attention to relevant state and federal interests and to consistency between decisions, it may escape the tangle and seaweed which has long obstructed the development of this branch of the law, as it has doomed the hapless wild duck.

226

---

[281] The Tungus v. Skovgaard, 358 U.S. 588, 594 (1959).

Commentaries on *The Federalist*

The Federalist on Federalism: "Neither a National Nor a Federal Constitution, But a Composition of Both"

Martin Diamond†

Something surprising confronts the contemporary reader who turns to *The Federalist* to see what it has to say about federalism. Expecting to find the original source of his view of American federalism, he finds instead a very different understanding from ours of the nature of federalism and of the federal character of American government. We think that the invention of federal government was the most important contribution made by the American founders to the art of government and we thus regard the system they devised as the very paradigm of what we call "federal government." Indeed, as we shall see, most contemporary definitions of federalism are little more than generalized descriptions of the way we Americans divide governing power between the states and the central government. It is surprising, therefore, to discover that *The Federalist* does not likewise characterize the American constitutional system as a "federal government." Instead, it tells us that the "proposed Constitution . . . is in strictness neither a national nor a federal constitution; but a composition of both."[1]

This formulation is typical of the way the entire founding generation saw the matter. For example, the proceedings of the Federal Convention—especially in the famous compromise regarding the House and Senate—show that the delegates likewise understood the terms federal and national in a way that required characterizing the Con-

† Leavey Professor of the Foundations of American Freedom, Georgetown University. The Editors regret the passing of Professor Diamond not long after this essay was completed. All students of the Constitution are greatly indebted to him for what he taught us about the thought and aspirations that inspired our existing form of government.
    1. THE FEDERALIST No. 39, at 257 (J. Cooke ed. 1961) [hereinafter cited to this edition without reference to editor]. Professor Cooke's edition is the definitive modern edition of *The Federalist*.

227

stitution as a compound or composition of both elements. But what Madison and the founding generation carefully distinguished as partly federal and partly national, we have for a long time blended or blurred under the single term federal. Alexis de Tocqueville saw this happening: "Clearly here we have not a federal government but an incomplete national government. Hence a form of government has been found which is neither precisely national nor federal; but things have halted there, and the new word to express this new thing does not yet exist."[2] Although it may well have been politically salutary that things "halted" at the old word federal, much may thereby have been lost in precision. And that is the concern of this review of what *The Federalist* teaches about federalism, namely, to suggest that it would be analytically useful to restore *The Federalist*'s "strict" distinction between the federal and the national elements in our compound political system, and therewith to restore also *The Federalist*'s understanding of federalism in general.

228

The Federalist was operating with a typology, so to speak, composed of two fundamental modes of political organization, the federal and the national. The founders thought that they had combined these two fundamental modes or "elements" into a "compound" system. We disagree and think, instead, that they invented a third fundamental mode or element, which we call federal government. In so thinking, we are operating with a typology composed of three elemental forms: confederation, federal government, and national or unitary government. The difference between our thinking and that of the founders evidently turns on the distinction that we make, and they did not, between confederalism and federalism. That familiar distinction will be found in almost all contemporary writing on federalism. But *The Federalist* and the whole founding generation saw no more difference between confederalism and federalism than we see, say, between the words inflammable and flammable; nothing more was involved than the accidental presence or absence of a nonsignifying prefix. For the founders, then, there were only two basic modes to choose from: confederal/federal as opposed to national/unitary; confederal/federal being that mode which preserves the primacy and autonomy of the states, and the national/unitary being that mode which gives unimpeded primacy to the government of the whole society. Given their bipartite typology or framework, the founders had to view the Constitution as being a "composition" of the two elemental modes

2. A. DE TOCQUEVILLE, DEMOCRACY IN AMERICA 143 (J. Mayer & M. Lerner eds. 1966).

and, given our tripartite one, we have to see the Constitution as elementally fedefal. The question is who is right, we or they? Which is the more useful mode of analysis?

It is instructive, and perhaps disconcerting, to learn that our modern distinction between confederalism and federalism derives from John Calhoun. His *Discourse on the Constitution and Government of the United States* begins with a severe and systematic attack on *The Federalist*'s view of federalism. In particular, Calhoun argues that its view of American government as compoundly federal and national is a "deep and radical error."[3] Now Calhoun had some very practical reasons for rejecting the "compound" view. He could not admit that there was anything national at all about the central government because that would open the door to an effective national jurisdiction over South Carolina's slave interests. Yet, because the central government under the Constitution was so palpably stronger than under the Articles of Confederation, Calhoun could not characterize it as confederal/federal, which was the only category left to him according to the bipartite typology then still universally accepted. Moreover, Calhoun did not really want to return to the old Articles; he was not averse to having a government as powerful as that under the Constitution, provided it could be rendered safe for southern interests. Calhoun solved all of his problems by inventing a new category of "federal government" which he contradistinguished from both a confederacy and a national government.

Not surprisingly, Calhoun saw "federal government" as differing rather more from the national form, which posed the threat to southern interests, than from the confederal form. Indeed, Calhoun's new "federal government" turns out to be nothing but a confederacy in all respects save one; unlike a confederacy, which has at its center "a mere congress of delegates,"[4] it has a real central government to carry its powers into execution. This becomes clear if we examine his famous and shrewdly labeled theory of the "concurrent majority." The concurrent *majority* is in fact a system of *unanimous* concurrence; according to Calhoun's scheme, the central government can act only when its measures have the unanimous concurrence of majorities in every sovereign sub-unit of the system. This requirement of unanimity (an exaggeratedly confederal requirement) guaranteed that nothing could be done without the voluntary concurrence of South Caro-

229

3. J. CALHOUN, A DISQUISITION ON GOVERNMENT AND A DISCOURSE ON THE CONSTITUTION AND GOVERNMENT OF THE UNITED STATES 156 (R. Cralle ed. 1851).
4. *Id.* at 163.

lina. Whatever South Carolina concurred in, however, would then be executed, not with confederal weakness, but directly upon individuals throughout the country with the full force of a national government. Is it not clear, then, that far from being contradistinguished from confederation and national government, Calhoun's "federal government" is in fact nothing but a compound of these two fundamental forms? He combined an exaggeratedly confederal/federal means of arriving at central decisions with a wholly national means of execution, and then arbitrarily assigned to his peculiar compound the new label of federal government.

This appears to have been an important source of our contemporary understanding of federalism. While we have largely rejected his theory of the concurrent majority, we have nonetheless taken over Calhoun's tripartite framework and the elemental status it assigns to federal government. Many scholars have, of course, been perfectly aware that the founding generation conceived their handiwork differently than Calhoun did and we do. But the difference has not been taken seriously. Either there has been a patronizing assumption that our understanding has scientifically superseded theirs, or the difference has been shrugged off as a mere matter of their having their terminology and we ours.[5] But this is surely too serious a matter to be so quickly dismissed; if *The Federalist* is analytically right in its compound view, then we have lost ground in our understanding of federalism. After all, is it not as obscurantist in political things, as it would be in, say, physics or chemistry, to confuse as a new element what in fact is only a compound? In both cases, it would be rendered difficult if not impossible to see how the essential parts of the compound worked and, thereby, to know how to achieve, preserve, or improve it.

To resolve our dispute with *The Federalist*, as to whether our political system is compoundly federal and national or integrally federal, we need a satisfactory definition of federalism. Unfortunately, the current conventional definition will not do. Consider the following from the standard contemporary work on federalism by Professor K. C. Wheare. Like Calhoun, Wheare disagrees with *The Federalist*'s compound theory and also sees federal government as a distinctive form differing from both the confederal and the national forms. He defines this distinctive federal principle as "the method of dividing powers

5. A recent example of the latter is Gunther, *Toward "A More Perfect Union": Framing and Implementing the Distinctive Nation-Building Elements of the Constitution*, 2 STAN. LAW., Fall 1976, at 5. In this otherwise very thoughtful essay, Professor Gunther takes note of *The Federalist*'s compound theory, but then treats it only as belonging to "the terminology of that day." *Id.*

so that the general and regional governments are each, within a sphere, co-ordinate and independent."[6] Nearly all contemporary definitions concur in the single point of this one, namely, the reduction of federalism solely to the idea of the division of the governing power.[7] Indeed, the "division of power" definition of federalism is so familiar that it is hard to force ourselves to examine it closely. But its shortcomings will become evident if we ask precisely what is federal about such a division of power. Clearly there is nothing federal at all about the "general" government; it is just a national government like every other one, save that its jurisdiction is not complete. The only thing federal, then, is the retention by the "regional governments" of some portion of the governing power. But this is manifestly nothing more than to define arbitrarily as uniquely federal what is merely the combination of an incomplete national government with the retention in the member units of a confederal/federal autonomy in some respects. In short, the modern theory turns out to be an arbitrarily unacknowledged and hence obscuring version of *The Federalist*'s compound theory. *The Federalist* openly alerts us to the national and federal elements in the compound, enabling us to see when it is becoming more simply national or more simply federal, and thereby enabling us to take appropriate action. By lumping together under the term federal government what *The Federalist* keeps separately visible, the modern definition makes it harder for us to see and evaluate such changes in the compound system.

231

But more importantly, the modern definition is a badly truncated version of *The Federalist*'s compound theory. It blinds us to a whole range of federal phenomena that *The Federalist*'s understanding of federalism properly comprehends. A moment's reflection reminds us what is left out. Consider the Senate; every school child knows (or at least used to be taught) that the Senate is a peculiarly federal part of American government. *The Federalist*, as we shall see, can readily explain what is federal about the Senate. And so can we all, unless we take seriously the modern definition of federalism, which makes the

---

6. K. WHEARE, FEDERAL GOVERNMENT 11 (3d ed. 1953).
7. An example in a recent American textbook can be found in M. CUMMINGS & D. WISE, DEMOCRACY UNDER PRESSURE (3d ed. 1977): "[T]he United States has a *federal* system of government, in which power is constitutionally shared by a *national* government and fifty state governments." *Id.* at 63 (emphasis added). *See also* W. BENNETT, AMERICAN THEORIES OF FEDERALISM 10 (1964) (The "essence of federalism" is evidenced by any "political system in which there is a constitutional distribution of powers between provincial governments and a common central authority."); W. RIKER, FEDERALISM 5 (1964) ("The essential institutions of federalism are, of course, a government of the federation and a set of governments of the member units . . . .")

federalness of the Senate quite inexplicable. After all, the Senate has nothing to do with the reserved powers of the states, which is the sole federal desideratum according to the modern definition. The Senate is a part of the general government of the whole society. But it is a *federal* part of that government. And that is what the truncated modern definition cannot reach—the federal elements in the structure and procedures of the central government itself. By limiting federalism to the reserved jurisdiction of the states, the modern definition obliges us, insofar as we take it seriously, to conceive the central government as purely national. It thus contradicts what our commonsense tells us about the federal character of the Senate and, as we shall see, it tends to blind us to other federal elements in the design of our central government.

232
    The Federalist's compound theory offers a clearer and fuller account of federalism, albeit not in the handy form of a definition. We must glean that definition from the various ways *The Federalist* replies to the main charge made by the opponents of the proposed Constitution, namely, that it had departed from the federal form in favor of the "consolidated" national form. In *Federalist* 39, where the charge is most systematically dealt with, Madison examines five ways to "ascertain the real character of the government" relative to the federal-national question.[8] By examining them closely, we will be able to piece together *The Federalist*'s understanding of federalism.

    First, the mode by which the Constitution is to be ratified, Madison argues, is federal and not national, because only the voluntary assent of each state, taken as a distinct and independent body politic, joins it to the Union. Second, Madison examines the sources of the legislative and executive branches of the central government. The House of Representatives is national because it derives from the whole people treated as a single body politic; the people will be represented in it, Madison says, exactly as they would be in any unitary state. Contrarily, the Senate is a federal element in the central government because it derives from, and represents equally, the states treated as "political and coequal societies." The Presidency has a "very compound source" because the electoral votes allotted to the states "are in a compound ratio, which considers them partly as distinct and coequal societies, partly as unequal members of the same society." The presidential aspect of the central government thus "appears to be of a

---

8. The quotations in the analysis that follows are taken from THE FEDERALIST No. 39, at 250-57. The concept of federalism is discussed throughout *The Federalist*; other papers that are especially relevant are numbers 15-17, 23, 27, 45, and 46.

mixed character presenting at least as many *federal* as *national* features."[9] Third, the government's mode of operation, in exercising its enumerated powers, is national because it reaches directly to individual citizens like any other national government (like any *government*, one might say). Fourth, as to the extent of its powers, Madison cautiously says that the government "cannot be deemed a national one," because it has a limited, enumerated jurisdiction. Madison means that the new system is national as to the extent of powers entrusted, but is federal insofar as a substantial portion of the governing powers autonomously remains with the states as distinct political societies. (Notice that Madison is here treating as but one aspect of federalism what the modern definition treats as the whole of it. In his first three considerations, Madison had been inquiring into what was federal in the formation, structure, and operation of the central government, that is, into crucial aspects of federalism which the modern definition excludes from its purview.)

233

Fifth, and finally, Madison judges the amending process to be neither wholly federal nor wholly national. His argument on this brings to the fore the logic and language of his theory of federalism.

> [Were the amending process] wholly national, the supreme and ultimate authority would reside in the *majority* of the people of the Union; and this authority would be competent at all times, like that of a majority of every national society, to alter or abolish its established Government. Were it wholly federal on the other hand, the concurrence of each State in the Union would be essential to every alteration that would be binding on all. . . . In requiring more than a majority, and particularly in computing the proportion by *States*, not by *citizens*, it departs from the *national*, and advances toward the *federal* character: In rendering the concurrence of less than the whole number of States sufficient, it loses again the *federal*, and partakes of the *national* character.[10]

This is the way the federal principle was understood in 1787 and, for that matter, in all earlier political writings. We are now in a position to summarize it. Having the nature of a "league or contract,"[11] federalism is a relation of independent, equal bodies politic that join

9. THE FEDERALIST No. 39, at 255 (emphasis in original).
10. *Id.* at 257 (emphasis in original).
11. Samuel Johnson's dictionary defined "confederacy" as: "A league; a contract by which several persons or bodies of men engage to support each other; union; engagement; federal compact." The definition of "federal" said: "Relating to a league or contract." The entry for "federate" said: "Leagued; joined in confederacy." 1 S. JOHNSON, A DICTIONARY OF THE ENGLISH LANGUAGE (Philadelphia 1818) (1st Amer. ed. from 11th London ed.).

together for limited purposes and carry those out, as the Latin root (*foedus, fides*) of the word reminds us, only by the obligation of good faith, rather than by governmental, which is to say coercive, authority. Insofar as any governmental structure, process, power, or practice conforms to the primacy of the separate bodies politic, to their equal status within the federal association, to the limited nature of that association, and to its operational dependence upon faithful compliance rather than political coercion, the structure, process, power, or practice is federal; insofar as it departs toward the principle of a complete, coercive government of a single body politic, it is national. Indeed, one may even contrast federalism, not only with national government, but with government as such. This is in fact what Alexander Hamilton argues in *Federalist* 15. The Constitution differs from the Articles of Confederation, he argues, because it incorporates "those ingredients which may be considered as forming the characteristic difference between a league and a government."[12]

234

Because they thus understood federalism, the leading Framers of the Constitution were convinced that no "merely federal" system would suffice for the purposes of union.[13] For those purposes, the federal principle of voluntary association was inadequate; a true government of the whole was required. "Mr. Govr. Morris explained the distinction beween a *federal* and *national, supreme,* Govt.; the former being a mere compact resting on the good faith of the parties; the latter having a compleat and *compulsive* operation."[14] Accordingly, in the Virginia Plan, the leading Framers proposed "a *national* Government . . . consisting of a *supreme* Legislative, Executive & Judiciary."[15] Happily, as we may now say, they did not wholly succeed in their plan to institute "one supreme power, and one only";[16] federal elements were worked back into their national design. Had the nationalists wholly succeeded, the Preamble of the Constitution would have had to read "in order to form a perfect Union," not just a "*more* perfect" one. Had the opponents of the Constitution succeeded, the country would have remained under the radically imperfect Union provided by the Articles of Confederation. The phrase "a more perfect Union" is no grammatical solecism, but an accurate description of the compromised, compoundly federal and national system that resulted from

---

12. The Federalist No. 15, at 95.
13. 1 M. Farrand, The Records of the Federal Convention of 1787, at 33 (rev. ed. 1937).
14. *Id.* at 34 (emphasis in original).
15. *Id.* at 33 (emphasis in original).
16. *Id.* at 34 (remark of Gouverneur Morris).

the Convention and that Madison had the theoretical apparatus to analyze so precisely.

The Federalist's theory of federalism is not only analytically superior to our contemporary approach in explaining the American political system as originally devised, but it also better illuminates the federal-national balance of the system as it has developed historically. The Senate is again a good case in point. It has developed in some respects into a more nationally oriented body than the House, where localist tendencies are very strong. Yet why should this be so if the Senate, because of the equal suffrage of the states, is the formally federal branch of the legislature? Should that not have made the Senate primarily parochial rather than national in outlook? It could be suggested that its not having become so is but one more example of the way formal, institutional factors propose, while underlying historical and behavioral forces informally dispose in unanticipated ways. We need not have recourse to the mysterious working of such forces in order to explain why the Senate developed both federal and national characteristics. Using *The Federalist*'s compound theory, we can see that the Senate was formally constituted in a more compound manner than is usually appreciated. Now the leading Framers had always intended some sort of senate to balance and moderate the more immediately democratic House of Representatives; as the democratic analogue of the traditional upper or aristocratic house, it was intended to be the branch that took the longer and more systematic, as it were, the more national view. But the Connecticut Compromise (national House, federal Senate) threatened to balk that intention. The leading Framers feared that the Senators, as had been so many delegates to the Confederal Congress, would be too closely bound by state interests and views to function, as desired, on behalf of long-run national considerations. They succeeded in mitigating the federal character of the Senate by means of four subtle formal departures from the practice under the Articles of Confederation. One was the provision for per capita voting ("each Senator shall have one Vote"). The Articles had required each state's delegates to cast a single ballot as a delegation; this forced them to form, as it were, an ambassadorial judgment on behalf of the state. The constitutional per capita provision invites and enables Senators to form individual legislative judgments just as do members of the national House of Representatives.

The other departures were three closely linked provisions, all of which likewise tended to lessen the federal control of the states over the Senators. One disallowed the states the power they had under the

235

Articles to recall their delegates at any time. Another provided for the six-year senatorial term; and the third permited indefinite and uninterrupted eligibility for re-election. The Articles had provided that no person could serve more than three years during any six-year period, the aim being to keep the delegates on a short leash with frequent rustication, so to speak, back to the states.

It is easy to summarize the significance of all these departures. The *federal* aim of the Articles was to reduce the delegates as much as possible to the status of agents of their states. The *national* aim of the Constitution was to make the Senators, despite the federally equal suffrage of the states, more nearly into representatives in the Burkean sense, free to serve long-run national interests as the deliberative process suggested. To appreciate the effectiveness of these provisions in permitting the Senate to develop a national outlook despite its partly federal basis, think how very much more federal (like Congress under the Articles) it would have been had the state delegations been obliged to vote as a unit and had the Senators been obliged to function under the threat of state recall. By contrast, imagine that the states had not been made the electoral districts for the Senate and, as was strongly urged at the Convention, that districts had been based upon the same national population principle as the House of Representatives. How very much *less* federal—how very much less committed to the primacy of state interests and views—the Senate and all of American politics would then have become. The peculiarly mixed character of the Senate as it actually developed becomes more visible and intelligible when we understand it in the light of *The Federalist*'s theory of a compoundly federal and national constitutional basis.

Indeed, that theory of federalism can make more visible and intelligible the compound complexity of the whole American political system. It is thus especially valuable to those who treasure the federal elements in the compound and who fear that those elements are weakening, because it enables them to see more clearly what and where the sources of federal vitality are throughout the whole political system. As we have seen, these are of two fundamental kinds: everything connected with the division of governing power, and everything connected with the federal elements in the central government. The importance of the first source, the balance between state power and the enumerated powers of the central government, is understandable enough under the modern theory of federalism; indeed, that is all it comprehends. It also is that source or aspect of federalism most familiar and intelligible to students of

236

constitutional law. Ever since *McCulloch v. Maryland,* the question of the extent of the enumerated powers has been, to use Marshall's phrase, "perpetually arising."[17] In any event, it happens to be a question that is perpetually gratifying to lawyers and the courts because it is so amenable to legal disputation and judicial determination. But *The Federalist,* as this review has argued, directs our attention to what may be called the political rather than the legal side of federalism. It emphasizes that other and neglected source of federalism, namely, the federal elements in the design of the central government itself and in its politics. Both sources of federalism, not just the one emphasized in the modern theory and in constitutional law, sustain the federal vitality of American government and political life, a vitality achieved by keeping interest, affection, power, and energy alive and well at the state level of politics in an otherwise homogenizing and centralizing age. Neither source should be neglected.

237

The status of the first of these two has been rendered increasingly problematic since the time of the New Deal. For decades the limiting doctrine of delegated and enumerated powers has been eroded, and the scope of national government has been vastly expanded. True, the strength of the states in the system has not been weakened to a corresponding degree. This is because the states have likewise vastly increased the scope of their activities. Although perhaps not an unmixed blessing, it means that the state is still that government which most affects citizens in their daily lives. Heedless of many learned pronouncements on their obsolescence, the states have thus stubbornly retained more of their federal vigor than might have been expected. Nonetheless, those who are concerned to preserve the federalism in the American compound remain concerned to limit the growth of national government relative to the states, as one indispensable support for that federalism. To this end, it is especially necessary to restore the moral and intellectual *bona fides* of the constitutional doctrine of enumerated powers as a crucial resource for limiting that growth.

But those concerned to preserve federalism must also devote their energies to that other support of American federalism to which *The Federalist* alerts them, namely, the federal elements in the central government. One such element now under heavy attack is the Electoral College. But the federal aspect to the Electoral College controversy has received relatively little attention: indeed, it is regarded as irrelevant to it. The argument has been that because the President is the rep-

---

17. 17 U.S. (4 Wheat.) 316, 405 (1819).

resentative of "all the people," he should be elected by them in a wholly national way, unimpeded by the interposition of the states through the Electoral College. Given the prevailing understanding of federalism, the "general" government is supposed to be purely national; from this perspective, the participation of the states in presidential selection does indeed seem to be an unjustifiable intrusion, and the potential "mischiefs" resulting from that intrusion seem insupportable. But from the perspective of *The Federalist*'s compound theory of American government, there is no reason why the President, admittedly the representative of "all the people," cannot represent them and, hence, be elected by them in a way corresponding to the American government's compoundly federal and national character.

238 The Presidency, especially the modern Presidency, is no doubt the most nationalizing single element in the American political system, and quite rightly so. Yet the method by which the President is elected has also operated for years in a countervailing federalizing fashion, and just as rightly so. Every Presidential election—the nominating campaigns as well as the electoral campaign itself—is a dramatic reaffirmation that the states are the basis of American political life. Nothing is more vigorously federal than this informal manifestation of federalism in political practice. But it all depends upon the formal structure of the Electoral College as originally conceived and as subsequently statutorily modified by the states. The informal federalizing effect of the Electoral College derives in the first instance from the "compound ratio" by which the states figure in the original constitutional design. Still more federalizing is the general ticket or unit-rule system (the state's entire electoral vote goes to the popular vote winner in the state) which, for nearly a century and a half, almost all the states have employed. Any removal of these federalizing elements, any change toward a purely national mode of Presidential election, would have a corresponding nationalizing effect on the spirit and practice of American politics. The nominating process—primaries and national party conventions—now is radically decentralized by force of the Electoral College's use of the states as states; the nominating process naturally takes its cues from the electing process. If the President were elected in a single national election, the same "cuing" process would continue, but in reverse.

However unproblematic such a centralizing effect might have seemed to partisans of electoral reform some years ago, it seems very problematic indeed now when circumstances are so changed. The thrust of much recent social and political criticism has been against the homogenizing and centralizing tendencies of mass society and its tendency to diminish political participation. *The Federalist* alerts us to the federal implications of the Electoral College and its potential for countervailing those tendencies. To nationalize the Presidential election, especially in this age of electronic media, is to reduce Presidential politics to a single arena with room for little participation. By preserving the federal importance of the states in the process, the Electoral College scatters the Presidential contest into fifty-one arenas (the states and the District of Columbia), with correspondingly enlarged opportunity for a vastly greater number of political participants.

The modern theory of federalism tends to blind us to such peripheral possibilities of federalism in the Presidential election process and throughout our political system. *The Federalist*'s theory is superior in clarity and comprehensiveness. The reason this can be so, despite nearly two centuries of eventful history since *The Federalist* was written, is that its political understanding was not limited to the historical period within which it was produced. Rather, it speaks to perennial political issues and, especially, to those peculiar to the genius of American politics. Publius (the pen name Hamilton, Madison, and Jay used in writing the essays) remains our most instructive political thinker. Making accessible to contemporary use his subtle understanding of federalism and of the compoundly federal and national American republic has been the intention of this review.

239

CONGRESS, THE STATES AND COMMERCE

Allison Dunham*

IN THE 1870's THE NATIONAL GRANGE, with a membership of over one and one-half million persons interested in agriculture, sought to defend its members and the public against the greatly feared power of monopolies, particularly against excessive rates exacted by railroads and grain elevators.[1] Its political power was so extensive that it induced a number of state legislatures to enact statutes limiting the rates to be charged by these businesses. It was almost unbelievable in the economic climate of the time that government could regulate the price at which private property or its services were sold. In 1876 operators of grain elevators in the Chicago area challenged the Illinois statute. They claimed that the statutes constituted a deprivation of private property without due process of law. Secondarily, they asserted that the Commerce Clause gave exclusive regulation to Congress. In a series of cases sometimes known as the *Granger Cases* and sometimes by the name of the spearhead case, *Munn v. Illinois,*[2] the Supreme Court upheld the validity of the Illinois statute.[3] Chief Justice Waite wrote for the majority and concentrated on the due process argument. This case has been said to belong among the dozen or so most important cases in our constitutional history.[4] It gave constitutional warrant to economic regulation of private property and opened new vistas to legislative majorities. Although a misuse of Waite's inept expression "business clothed with a public interest" was for a time turned to restrict rather than permit regulation of business enterprise, the main doctrine of that case is firmly established in the constitutional law of state and nation.[5]

* Professor of Law, University of Chicago Law School; co-editor (with Kurland), Mr. Justice (1956).

Note by Professor Dunham: "Four of my colleagues and I were invited to prepare individual papers on selected issues of federalism for the August 1958 meeting of the Conference of State Chief Justices. This article is a revision of the paper which I submitted to the Conference. Naturally, the Conference is not responsible for the views expressed here; nor are we responsible for the views expressed in the Conference Report."

[Editors' Note: The other four articles submitted to the Conference of State Chief Justices are also being published in legal periodicals. The Report of the Conference of State Chief Justices has been published in pamphlet form by the Council of State Governments. It may also be found in U.S. News & World Report, p. 92 (Oct. 3, 1958).]

[1] Consult 2 Warren, The Supreme Court in United States History 574-91 (rev. ed., 1926).

[2] 94 U.S. 113 (1876). The cases decided at the same time as Munn v. Illinois were concerned with state regulation of railroad rates. Chicago, B. and Q. R. R. Co. v. Iowa, 94 U.S. 155 (1876); Peik v. Chicago, etc. and N.W. Railway, 94 U.S. 164 (1876); Chicago, Milwaukee and St. Paul R.R. Co. v. Ackley, 94 U.S. 179 (1876); Winona and St. Peter R.R. Co. v. Blake, 94 U.S. 180 (1876); and Stone v. Wisconsin, 94 U.S. 181 (1876).

[3] For a discussion of the significance of these cases, consult Frankfurter, The Commerce Clause 83-90 (1937); Trimble, Chief Justice Waite 175-84 (1938).

[4] 2 Warren, op. cit. supra note 1, at 574, 581.

[5] Nebbia v. New York, 291 U.S. 502 (1934).

Seventy years later, in 1947, this same Illinois statute regulating rates of grain elevators was again in the United States Supreme Court. The elevator operators again were objecting to the Illinois statute but they did not claim to be free of regulation; nor did they claim as they did in 1876 that the dormant Commerce Clause excluded state regulation. They claimed that the United States Warehouse Act[6] which admittedly regulated them in some respects had superseded the authority of the Illinois Commerce Commission to regulate the commercial matters in question.[7] The Supreme Court of the United States, speaking through Mr. Justice Douglas, upheld this contention and affirmed a decree enjoining a proceeding before the Illinois commission under this venerable and famous statute. *Rice v. Santa Fe Elevator Corporation*[8] thus buried the first major statutory regulation of private industry in the United States. This remarkable sequence aptly makes the point of the major area of constitutional controversy outside of the personal liberty field. Today we seldom ask, *can* government regulate; we ask a little more often, *can* a state government regulate interstate commerce; we ask almost every day, *has* federal legislation superseded state legislation in any particular field.

241

The legislative and administrative history of the United States Warehouse Act is also indicative of the developing problem and it indicates that current constitutional controversy is also ancient controversy. The first United States regulation of warehouses came in 1916 as a part of a rash of regulations of the Wilsonian era. That act carefully provided that it should in no way be construed to conflict with or limit state acts.[9] In 1931, the Secretary of Agriculture asked Congress to amend the act so that the federal act should be "exclusive" with respect to all persons securing a federal license.[10] Presumably in 1931 no one knew what this really meant or that it meant anything more than the supremacy of the federal act wherever there was a direct conflict with a state act.[11] But after 1940 this older statute was challenged as one among many state statutes alleged to have been displaced by federal law.

This summary history of warehouse legislation contains the elements of my subject—the power of the states to regulate economic activity of persons where the transaction touches more than one state. A dispute which starts as a question of whether any government may regulate private

---

[6] 39 Stat. 486 (1916), as amended, 7 U.S.C. §§ 241-273 (1952).
[7] L. Ill. (1871) p. 762, repealed by Ill. Rev. Stat. (1955) c. 114, §§ 214.1-214.27.
[8] 331 U.S. 218 (1947).
[9] 39 Stat. 490, § 29 (1916). "[N]othing in this Act shall be construed to conflict with ...or ...to impair or limit the effect or operation of the laws of any State."
[10] 46 Stat. 1465 (1931), 7 U.S.C. § 269 (1952) ("the power, jurisdiction, and authority conferred upon the Secretary of Agriculture . . . shall be exclusive").
[11] In his book on the Commerce Clause, Professor Frankfurter, as he then was, noted that the federal act had assumed partial control "and to some extent dislodged the states" but he refused to speculate on the extent of the supersession. In Rice v. Santa Fe Elevator Corp., 331 U.S. 218 (1957) Justice Frankfurter thought the 1931 amendment only outlawed "conflicts" between the two statutes.

property in *Munn v. Illinois* must of necessity become, once an affirmative answer has been given, a question of which government may regulate. The answer to the question of which government may regulate is controlled or shaped by the entire constitutional history of this country. To understand this we should recall that the Constitution neither refers to "interstate commerce" nor does it prohibit the states from doing anything with respect to "commerce" (a term which is used) except laying imposts or duties on imports or exports.[12] All that the Commerce Clause says is that Congress has the power "[t]o regulate Commerce with foreign nations, and among the several states and with the Indian tribes."[13]

As an original proposition concerning this clause it could be argued, as my colleague Professor Crosskey argues in his monumental history of the constitutional convention and times,[14] that this clause gave to Congress complete power over regulation of commerce, whether interstate or intrastate. It could likewise be argued as Chief Justice Taney urged in his opinion in the *License Cases* in 1847, that

> the mere grant of power to the general government cannot . . . be construed to be an absolute prohibition to the exercise of any power over the same subject by the States. . . . [I]n my judgment, the State may . . . make regulations of commerce . . . unless they come in conflict with a law of Congress.[15]

Neither Professor Crosskey's theory nor Chief Justice Taney's has ever been successfully urged in the Supreme Court, although they have been asserted from time to time since *Cooley v. Board of Wardens*[16] established a different or third proposition. All modern cases say something similar to Chief Justice Stone's statement in *Southern Pacific Co. v. Arizona* in 1945:

> Ever since . . . Cooley v. Board of Wardens, 12 How. 299 it has been recognized that, in the absence of conflicting legislation by Congress, there is a residuum of power in the state to make laws governing matters of local concern which nevertheless in some measure affect interstate commerce or even, to some extent regulate it. . . . But ever since Gibbons v. Ogden, 9 Wheat. 1, the states have not been deemed to have authority to impede substantially the free flow of commerce from state to state, or to regulate those phases of the national commerce which, because of the need of national uniformity, demand that their regulation, if any, be prescribed by a single authority.[17]

---

12 U.S. Const. Art. 1, § 9.
13 U.S. Const. Art. 1, § 8, cl. 3.
14 Consult Crosskey, Politics and the Constitution 17-363 (1953).
15 5 How. (U.S.) 504, 579 (1847).
16 12 How. (U.S.) 299 (1851).
17 Southern Pacific Co. v. Arizona, 325 U.S. 761, 767 (1945). For other expressions of this doctrine, see California v. Zook, 336 U.S. 725, 728 (1949); Cities Service Co. v. Peerless Co., 340 U.S. 179, 186 (1950).

Chief Justice Stone continued:

> For a hundred years it has been accepted constitutional
> doctrine that the commerce clause, without the aid of Congres-
> sional legislation, thus affords some protection from state legisla-
> tion inimical to the national commerce, and that in such cases,
> where Congress has not acted, this Court and not the state legis-
> lature is under the commerce clause, the final arbiter between
> competing demands of state and national interests.[18]

Mr. Justice Black has from time to time attempted to revive the Taney
view that there is no negative implication from the Commerce Clause[19]
but it would appear that since *Morgan v. Virginia*[20] in 1946, where the
Court held unconstitutional under the Commerce Clause the Virginia
statute requiring separation of passengers on a color basis, he has
acquiesced in the Court's phrasing of the power of the states over interstate commerce. The late Mr. Justice Jackson tried in *Hood and Sons v.
DuMond*[21] to revive an idea from the Marshall era that the Commerce
Clause of its own effect prohibited regulation by the states of certain subjects concerning commerce. He also was unsuccessful. Thus we may
say as the Court says almost every term—the Commerce Clause of its
own force inhibits to some extent the power of the states—and we may
further say that it is the Supreme Court, not the state legislature, which
determines the extent of this inhibition.

243

To say that the states are to some extent inhibited by the Commerce
Clause from regulating or even to say that federal legislation sometimes
displaces state legislation does not tell us how much nor does it give us
a real picture of the impact of Supreme Court decisions on our federal
system. Historically (and I think correctly) critical appraisal of the
Court's work has assumed that the doctrine of federalism does not permit
a quick and easy conclusion that state power was inhibited by the Constitution or restricted by the passage of an act by the national legislature.
Thus it was that critics of the Supreme Court before 1940 thought that
the Court was unduly restricting state power under a theory that congressional power under the Commerce Clause was exclusive.

In this time when it is easy to criticize the Supreme Court for weakening the states, it is pleasant to report that as far as the dormant Commerce Clause is concerned the Supreme Court since the late 1940's has
considerably enhanced the power of the states to regulate economic
activity which touches more than one state. As far as the Commerce

---

[18] Southern Pacific Co. v. Arizona, 325 U.S. 761, 769 (1945).
[19] Consult the dissenting opinions in Gwin, White & Prince, Inc. v. Henneford, 305
U.S. 434, 442 (1939); Southern Pacific Co. v. Arizona, 325 U.S. 761, 784 (1945); and
concurring opinion in Morgan v. Virginia, 328 U.S. 373, 386 (1946).
[20] 328 U.S. 373 (1946).
[21] 336 U.S. 525 (1949). Consult also his concurring opinion in Duckworth v. Arkansas,
314 U.S. 390, 397 (1941).

Clause is concerned "to some extent" in the quoted phrase means "very little."

But if the doctrine of federalism requires us to believe that a heavy burden of persuasion should be on him who asserts that an act of Congress displaces state exercised power, then we must assert that since 1940 the Supreme Court and Congress between them have drastically reduced a state's ability to deal with its own social order and economic enterprise as it wishes. The congressional contribution to the consequent decline of federalism has been the expansion of the exercise of federal power. The Court's contribution has been to find from vague inferences concerning the· exercise of federal power that Congress intended by such legislation to displace state law.

Two matters will be described in this article: (1) the factors which the Supreme Court appears to consider in arbitrating the competing demands of state and national interests under the Commerce Clause when Congress has not acted; and (2) the factors which the Court appears to consider in determining whether congressional regulation of a matter precludes state regulation of a related matter or field. State taxation of interstate commerce[22] and federal and state regulation of labor will not be considered.

244

At first thought it might appear incongruous to combine in one paper a consideration of the factors which determine the constitutionality of a state statute under the Commerce Clause with a consideration of factors which govern the construction of an act of Congress.[23] One justification for this combination of subjects comes from the fact that whether it be the negative implication of the dormant Commerce Clause which voids a state statute or it be a conclusion that congressional statutes have occupied the field, the decision of the Supreme Court is subject to the control of Congress. As the Supreme Court has said on numerous occasions and held several times, "Congress has undoubted power to redefine the distribution of power over interstate commerce."[24] Congress may either permit the states to regulate the commerce in a manner which would otherwise not be permissible under Court decisions or it may exclude state regulation even of matters of local concern if it believes interstate commerce is affected. Thus it may be said that whether the Court is arbitrating between state and federal power under. the Commerce Clause or whether it is construing a federal statute to determine whether Congress intended that state law be superseded, the problem is basically the

---

[22] State taxation of interstate commerce is more difficult than regulation because there are usually many other sources of revenue available. See Frankfurter, J., dissenting in Hood & Son v. DuMond, 336 U.S. 525 (1949).

[23] Consult Stern, Commerce and Due Process, 4 Vand. L. Rev. 446, 460 (1951).

[24] Southern Pacific Co. v. Arizona, 325 U.S. 761, 769 (1945). The leading case sustaining the power of Congress to authorize state regulation of interstate commerce is Prudential Ins. Co. v. Benjamin, 328 U.S. 408 (1946).

same. In the former case the question before the Court is the significance to be attached to congressional silence or failure to act; in the latter case the question before the Court is the significance to be attached to the fact that congressional legislation regulated only a limited amount of that which could have been regulated. In both cases the Court must decide for itself, without much help from Congress, whether an industry or activity should be left in some respect unregulated. In *California v. Zook* in 1949 the Court equated the two problems thus: "[W]hether Congress has or has not expressed itself, the fundamental inquiry . . . is the same: does the state action conflict with national policy." [25]

While attempts have been made from time to time to work with mechanistic formulae and thus to avoid making a judgment, it is now clear that in this area at least a court cannot avoid judging. The attempt to determine whether a state act is a regulation of commerce and therefore void or is an exercise of the police power and therefore good;[26] the attempt to determine when interstate commerce ends, for example, after the original package is broken[27] or when interstate commerce begins, for example, after natural gas is pressurized for transmission in pipes;[28] the attempt to determine whether a burden on interstate transactions is direct and therefore bad or indirect and therefore good[29] have each ended in failure. As Justice Stone said in his dissent in the *DiSanto* case over 30 years ago, the judges who make this attempt "are doing little more than using labels to describe a result rather than any trustworthy formula by which it is reached."[30] Something more substantial is needed and courts should avoid searching for the unobtainable in this field. There is no substitute for hard analysis, mustering of facts and ultimately, the making of judgments hard to make.

245

Although not foolproof in predictability, the judicial method used and suggested in *Southern Pacific Co. v. Arizona*,[31] decided in 1945, offers real suggestions for courts struggling with this difficult problem. The facts of the case were these: In 1912, Arizona made it unlawful to operate within the state a railroad train of more than 14 passenger or 80 freight cars. In 1941, the state brought suit against the Southern Pacific Company to recover the statutory penalties for violation of the statute. The Supreme Court of Arizona upheld the act as a safety measure designed to reduce the number of accidents. The Supreme Court speaking through

---

[25] 336 U.S. 725, 729 (1949).
[26] See Gibbons v. Ogden, 9 Wheat. (U.S.) 1 (1824).
[27] Brown v. Maryland, 12 Wheat. (U.S.) 419 (1827).
[28] Discussion in Interstate Gas Co. v. Power Comm'n, 331 U.S. 682 (1947).
[29] The best attack on the mechanistic formulae is found in the dissent of Stone, J., in Di Santo v. Pennsylvania, 273 U.S. 34 (1927) and his discussion of the formulae in Parker v. Brown, 317 U.S. 341, 360 (1943); Illinois Natural Gas Co. v. Central Illinois Public Service Co., 314 U.S. 493, 504 (1941). Consult also Freund, Umpiring the Federal System, 54 Col. L. Rev. 561, 567 (1954).
[30] Di Santo v. Pennsylvania, 273 U.S. 34, 44 (1927).
[31] Southern Pacific Co. v. Arizona, 325 U.S. 761 (1945).

Chief Justice Stone reversed. In this opinion he outlined various steps in analysis leading to exercise of judgment.

First he required that any asserted violation of the Commerce Clause be supported by relevant factual material which "will afford a sure basis" for an informed judgment. This is another way of putting the usual presumption of constitutionality, but the similarity with the presumption rule ends at this point for as the Chief Justice said:

> [I]n considering the effect of the statute as a safety measure, therefore, the factor of controlling significance for present purposes *is not whether there is basis for the conclusion of the Arizona Supreme Court* that the increase in length of trains beyond the statutory maximum has an adverse effect upon safety of operation. The decisive question is whether in the circumstances the total effect of the law as a safety measure in reducing accidents and casualties is so slight or problematical as not to outweigh the national interest in keeping interstate commerce free from interferences which seriously impede it and subject to local regulation which does not have a uniform effect.[32]

246

Where did the Supreme Court get the idea that this was a safety measure? Chief Justice Stone said that while he accepted the Arizona conclusion in this case that there was a need for safety and that the measure served this purpose, this conclusion is not binding on the Supreme Court. In other words the legislative recital that this is a safety measure does not bind the Supreme Court in Commerce Clause cases; the Court must analyse the statute and its effect to determine this for itself. *Hale v. Bimco Trading Co.*,[33] decided in 1939, is illustrative of this part of the Court's function. A Florida statute recited that the poor quality of foreign cement jeopardized public safety and that, therefore, inspection of the quality of such cement was required, and a substantial fee was charged for the inspection. The recital in the statute seemed to bring it within the traditional subject matter of local regulation. But the Supreme Court did not stop with the recital. It noticed that the statute by its terms was applicable only to imported cement. Justice Frankfurter pointed out that if public safety was the real objective of this inspection fee, that objective demanded equal application of the quality and inspection requirements to all cement used in construction in Florida. From this analysis the Court concluded that this law was really a restraint on competition and therefore an invalid discrimination against foreign commerce.

The Court's statement in *Southern Pacific* that it was accepting the regulation as a safety measure, and the Court's analysis in *Hale* to conclude that this was a measure regulating competition indicate another factor of significance. It would appear from the decided cases that the

---

[32] Ibid., at 775 (italics added).
[33] 306 U.S. 375 (1939).

extent of the permissible burden on interstate commerce varies with the objective of the state statute. There may be some objectives which are not permissible whatever the effect on commerce. Mr. Justice Jackson attempted to carve out such an area in *H. P. Hood and Sons v. DuMond*[34] in 1949. Petitioner was a milk distributor in Massachusetts who operated three licensed receiving stations in New York. It applied for a license for an additional receiving station, but the New York authorities denied the application on the ground that expansion of facilities would reduce the supply of milk for local markets and would result in destructive competition. Speaking for a majority of five, Justice Jackson held the refusal to license petitioner an unconstitutional burden on interstate commerce. He said:

> This distinction between the power of the State to shelter its people from menaces to their health or safety and from fraud, even when those dangers emanate from interstate commerce and its lack of power to retard, burden or constrict the flow of such commerce for their economic advantage, is one deeply rooted in both our history and our law.[35]

247

If Justice Jackson meant to establish an absolute principle concerning economic regulation, the cases before and after the *Hood* case do not support it. A producing state has been given considerable leeway in fixing prices to be paid producers even when the bulk of the product is sold in interstate commerce, and even when the purpose of the regulation is to improve the economic well-being of the producers at the expense of the out-of-state consumers. Thus in *Milk Control Board v. Eisenberg*,[36] sustaining an order fixing the price to be paid milk producers by a dealer selling the product out of the state; *Parker v. Brown*,[37] sustaining an elaborate scheme to control the supply of raisins sold primarily to out of state consumers; and in *Cities Service Co. v. Peerless Co.*,[38] sustaining an order of the Oklahoma Corporation Commission fixing a minimum wellhead price, regulations designed to protect the competitive position of sellers against resident and nonresident buyers were upheld. In the *Cities Service Case* the Court distinguished the *Hood* case on the ground that New York was, in that case, trying to protect the supplies needed for local consumers to the disadvantage of the nonresident consumers rather than to protect the competitive position of suppliers. In the following year, the Supreme Court upheld a Michigan requirement that an interstate natural gas pipeline obtain a certificate of necessity and convenience before selling gas directly to industrial consumers in competition with a local supplier who purchased his gas from an interstate pipeline. *Panhandle Eastern Pipeline Co. v. Michigan Public Service Commission*.[39]

---

[34] 336 U.S. 525 (1949).
[35] Ibid., at 533.
[36] 306 U.S. 346 (1939).
[37] 317 U.S. 341 (1943).
[38] 340 U.S. 179 (1950).
[39] 341 U.S. 329 (1951).

This line of cases cast considerable doubt on *Buck v. Kuykendall*,[40] decided in 1925, where the Court held that a state could not deny a permit to an interstate truck line on the ground that such service was unnecessary in view of existing facilities. On the other hand, the Court as late as 1948 exhibited this hostility to a regulation designed to control the competition of outsiders in *Toomer v. Witsell*.[41] In this case a regulation about licenses, berthing and other matters appeared to the Court to have as a primary purpose the preference of local commercial fishermen over nonresidents, and the Court had no difficulty in striking it down. But the two chances which the Court had to reconsider *Buck v. Kuykendall* since the *Panhandle* case and explain its position have been dodged. In *Fry Roofing Co. v. Wood*,[42] where an interstate motor carrier was required to obtain a certificate of convenience and necessity, the Court upheld the regulation, but on the basis that the Arkansas commission had, as the commission interpreted the statute, no right to refuse the certificate. Thus the certificate was for identification purposes and not for economic regulation. In *Chicago v. Atchison, T. & S. F. R. Co.*,[43] decided in June, 1958, the licensing statute clearly gave the city power to refuse the certificate on economic considerations, and the Court held the ordinance bad, not on the basis of the Commerce Clause, but on a conclusion that the Interstate Commerce Act precluded the city from exercising any veto power on economic considerations over the interstate transfer service.

While we can say that if the purpose and effect of the regulation is to restrict seriously the competition between local and interstate competitors for a particular supply or consumers market, the Court will closely scrutinize the regulation, we cannot from this factor alone predict with accuracy the outcome of the case. At this point a very significant factor is the tradition or convention of regulation. Thus in the raisin case, *Parker v. Brown*,[44] the state regulation was in the pattern of a previously approved congressional policy; in the interstate pipeline cases the congressional regulation was built upon certain assumptions as to what the states could do and were doing. National regulation of railroads is old and strong; state regulation of trucks is equally strong. It is this long standing conventional pattern of regulation, almost as much as the financial stake of the states in ownership of the highways, which explains why the regulation of trucks and motor buses seems to be treated so much differently from regulations of similar matters with railroads. The Court usually emphasizes this point by saying that "there are few subjects of state regulation affecting interstate commerce which are so peculiarly of local concern as the use of the state's highways." The Court has, of course, in no small part

---

[40] 267 U.S. 307 (1925).
[41] 334 U.S. 385 (1948).
[42] 344 U.S. 157 (1952).
[43] 357 U.S. 77 (1958).
[44] 317 U.S. 341 (1943).

contributed to the truth of this statement by allowing the states more power over trucks than over trains.

But having determined that the subject matter of the regulation is a clearly permissible local subject is not enough to sustain the validity of the state regulation. The next step is to determine the extent of the burden on interstate commerce. At one extreme are the situations where the regulation wholly prohibits the interstate activity or transaction; at the other are the situations in which the regulation is at most a certain amount of paper work, red tape and predetermination of the action to be taken. The seriousness of the burden also is involved, and this varies with the need for uniformity and the strength of the interests of the states.

Two cases will illustrate the applicability of these considerations and how the seriousness is estimated.

In *Clason v. Indiana*[45] in 1939, a comprehensive Indiana statute dealing with the disposal of the bodies of large dead animals required the bodies to be disposed of by the owner either at the place of death or by transportation to a disposal plant licensed and inspected by the state. Thus the statute prohibited the export of such bodies and also the import of them. The conviction of a person transporting such a body without a license to a disposal plant out of the state was upheld as a health and safety measure which could be enforced only if transportation was limited to delivery to licensed and inspected disposal plants. Here it appeared to the Court that the only method of achieving the legitimate state objective was the prohibition of interstate commerce altogether. It further appeared that the state interest outweighed any national interest in the free transportation of such bodies.

249

This case may be contrasted with *Dean Milk Co. v. Madison*[46] in 1951. A Madison, Wisconsin ordinance made it unlawful to sell milk in Madison unless it had been processed and bottled at an approved pasteurization plant within a radius of five miles from the center of Madison. The objective of the ordinance was obvious, and the problem of inspecting milk processed at a distance away from the location of the inspectors was recognized. The majority concluded, however, that the ordinance was invalid because there were alternative methods of securing the legitimate local interest. In short, the state may exclude an interstate transaction in order to achieve a serious local objective if it appears that there is no reasonable way to achieve the objective other than the one selected. *Castle v. Hayes Freight Lines Inc.,*[47] also belongs in this category. The question was whether Illinois could bar an interstate motor carrier from use of state highways for interstate purposes as punishment for repeated violations of

---

[45] 306 U.S. 439 (1939).
[46] 340 U.S. 349 (1951).
[47] 348 U.S. 61 (1954).

the state highway weight regulations. The Supreme Court agreed with the Illinois Supreme Court that it could not. Not only did the state fail to show that suspension of intrastate business rights would not be sufficient to secure compliance, but also that the federal motor carrier act provided the state a procedure whereby it could secure suspension of the federal certificate to operate in interstate commerce by the Interstate Commerce Commission. The available alternatives made the selected regulations seem drastic.

At the other extreme from complete prohibition of interstate commerce is the situation where the burden seems so infinitesimal as to be almost *de minimis*. Of the cases in recent years which fall in this category, *Fry Roofing Co. v. Wood*[48] in 1952, *Terminal R.R. Ass'n of St Louis v. Brotherhood*[49] in 1943, and *Carter v. Virginia*[50] in 1944, are illustrative. In the first, an interstate motor carrier was required to obtain a certificate called a certificate of convenience and necessity, but one which the Arkansas commission conceded it had no right to refuse. The Court held that Arkansas could require interstate motor carriers to identify themselves. In the *Terminal Railroad* case, the state commerce commission ordered a terminal railroad operating in East St. Louis to provide cabooses on its trains. This was upheld even though some of the runs went across state lines and back. In the *Carter* case, the Virginia Alcoholic Beverage Act required transporters of liquor through Virginia to file a paper designating the consignee and the direct route through the state and a bond assuring performance. This was upheld as a necessary adjunct of the state regulation of liquor within the state.

250

In between these two extremes — complete prohibition and a requirement of notices and other minimal activity — we have the great bulk of the cases and also the area of most difficult judgment. It is here that the courts must assess the relative weights of state and national interests. The cases also indicate significant factors here. One broad category (which is perhaps a continuation of the one suggested above) is distinguishing between a regulation which is in the nature of a physical obstruction to the free movement of goods and one which imposes only greater financial costs. This contrast is seen in the *Southern Pacific* case involving the Arizona train limit law, and *Collins v. American Buslines*,[51] involving the applicability of an Arizona workmen's compensation law to the death in Arizona of a nonresident employee of an interstate bus company. The train crew law not only imposed greater costs on interstate commerce, it necessitated conversion and reconversion of train lengths with consequent delay in traffic time and diminution of volume moved in a given time. The

---

[48] 344 U.S. 157 (1952). See also Railway Express v. New York, 336 U.S. 106 (1949) (state statute prohibited advertising on trucks).
[49] 318 U.S. 1 (1943).
[50] 321 U.S. 131 (1944).
[51] 350 U.S. 528 (1956).

Court regarded this burden in the physical sense to be extremely significant in balancing the state's interest in safety against the national interest
of free movement of commerce. It thus distinguished the train-size cases
from state laws prohibiting the car stove, requiring locomotives to be supplied with headlights and the like, which at most increased the financial
costs of commerce. These did not affect uniformity of train operation. In
the *Collins* case, the Court pointed out that the *Southern Pacific* case was
not at all applicable, because here the burden on interstate commerce was
at most financial.

When the Court is acting as arbiter under the Commerce Clause, it
uses many factors which in varying combinations produce varying results.
Underlying almost all factors is the Court's assessment of the ability of
normal political processes to correct any excess in regulation. Thus in the
Southern Pacific case, the Court in explaining the differences between truck
and railroad regulation made this observation: "The fact that they [regu-
lations of trucks on highways] affect alike shippers in interstate and in-   251
trastate commerce in great numbers, within as well as without the state,
is a safeguard against regulatory abuses."[52] The milk cases and the Oklahoma regulation of the price of natural gas at the wellhead also contain
this element. Because of the large number of local as well as out-of-state
consumers, an abusive regulation designed to increase the price which a
local seller may charge to all of his customers may be corrected by the
electoral process. On the other hand, if a state seeks to give its suppliers
a competitive advantage in the market for the custom of local consumers,
the out-of-state producer does not have as effective a political process to
obtain an elimination of the competitive advantage.

The factors which seem most significant for a state court judge in making this arbitration in the first instance seem to be these: (1) Whether
the field of state regulation is one which the states have traditionally occupied. Highway regulations are an example. (2) What, considering the
effect of the statute as well as its recited purpose, seems to be its true
objective. A presumption of constitutionality is not to be used as a substitute for thorough analysis of the situation. (3) Assuming the objective of
the legislation to be within permissible bounds such as protecting the
health and safety of the state citizens, are there any relevant data for an
informed judgment as to the seriousness of the burden of the regulation on
commerce. If there is not, the state legislation should not be invalidated.
(4) Assuming the objective of the regulation to be in the field of regulating the position of competitors, the state court should examine carefully

---

[52] Southern Pacific Co. v. Arizona, 325 U.S. 761, 783 (1945). For other motor carrier
cases, see S.C. Hwy. Dept. v. Barnwell Bros., 303 U.S. 184 (1938); California v. Thompson,
313 U.S. 109 (1941), licensing of transportation agents for motor carrier travel; Railway
Express v. New York, 336 U.S. 106 (1949), prohibition of advertising on trucks; Buck
v. California, 343 U.S. 99 (1952), permit required for a taxicab operating through
licensing authority but not discharging there.

the effect of the regulation and should require rather persuasive reasons to find the effect of no significance.

Although there may be some inconsistency in the cases, such as the tolerance of state regulation of interstate pipelines and interstate purchasers from farmers, in the main, the Court in the past twenty years has exhibited no marked tendency to depart from traditional approaches to an ancient problem. The Court is making a value judgment, and in so doing it has expanded state power under the Commerce Clause.

At the same time that this expansion of state power has occurred, the Supreme Court has been increasingly concerned with the question of whether a federal act in the field of commerce regulation supersedes a state act in the same field. This is to be expected for no other reason than that Congress is legislating in many more areas of economic life than it did when *Munn v. Illinois* was decided in 1876. So are the states legislating in more areas than in 1876. More cases involving the supremacy of federal statutes over state statutes should therefore be expected.

252

It requires no disagreement with the doctrine of federalism under our Constitution to say that when a state and federal act covering the same general subject puts the regulated person in the position that if he complies with one act he must defy or violate the other, then the federal act controls or supersedes or displaces the state act. The Union could not hold together without such a rule as the supremacy clause which makes the Constitution and the laws of the United States supreme over state laws. This kind of conflict between federal and state law seldom arises since most regulation is prohibitory or negative in form and does not require that which is permitted. Thus a federal law prohibiting truck bodies greater than ten feet in width on an interstate motor truck would not conflict, in this sense, with a state law prohibiting truck bodies greater than eight feet in width. Compliance with the eight-foot law of the state would not require a violation of the federal ten-foot law.

It requires no discussion to show that when Congress has provided all of the regulation it deems desirable for a given bit of commerce, state action is excluded. The problem is the factors to be used to determine when Congress intends there to be no further regulation. The factors used depend, in no small part, on the attitude of the judges toward centralism and federalism. In the past, and today by a minority of the Court, we have been reminded that respect for the federal system requires a belief that federal acts do not displace state acts unless Congress says so.[53] The rule prior to *Hines v. Davidowitz*, in 1941, seemed to be that state law was not displaced "unless the statute plainly and palpably . . . encroaches upon the exercise of some authority delegated to the United States"

[53] See Frankfurter, J., dissenting in Bethlehem Steel Co. v. State Labor Relations Board, 330 U.S. 767, 780 (1947).

(Stone, J., dissenting).[54] Prior to 1940 the bloc on the Court who believed that there was little in the Constitution restricting the states under the Fourteenth Amendment or Commerce Clause also believed that the Court should not infer that Congress intended to displace state law when it legislated. Since 1940 the dominant majority, while finding little in the Constitution restricting state economic regulation, has been quick to find that state law is displaced.

The Court has never taken the position that there is no displacement unless Congress expressly directs supersedure or unless there is an essential conflict. It has always drawn inferences from the policy and effect of the state and federal laws in question. The result is that we have had the decision described by Justice Butler in 1939: "Our decisions provide no formulae for discovering implied effects of federal statutes upon state measures." [55]

Two cases under the Federal Pure Food and Drug Act[56] in 1912 and 1913 illustrate the problem. The federal act prohibits, among other things, interstate shipment of food and drugs if misbranded by bearing any statement, design or device which is false or misleading. An Indiana statute required the labels on certain food offered for sale in that state to disclose the formula for the food. A Wisconsin statute required glucose mixtures offered for sale to contain on the label one designation "glucose flavored with ..." and prohibited any other designation. As an original proposition it could be argued that since the federal act dealt with statements on the labels of food and drugs, any state law dealing with statements on the package was displaced. At the other extreme it could be argued that until the state acts required a statement on the package which the federal act called misleading the state acts should be allowed to stand since there was no conflict. The Supreme Court upheld the Indiana act in 1912[57] and struck down the Wisconsin Act in 1913.[58] In the latter case the Court found an inconsistency in policy between the federal act which permitted any label or statement as long as not misleading and the state act which permitted only one type of label.

Over time the Court has used a number of tests or doctrines which become so confused in statement and application that it is often difficult to decide which test is being used. The simplest test is that of conflict between state and federal act but this test has been referred to in recent years only when the Court upholds the state legislation. The highwater mark of this test is *Maurer v. Hamilton*[59] decided in 1940. The question was whether a Pennsylvania statute prohibiting the operation on its high-

253

---

[54] 312 U.S. 52, 75 (1941).
[55] Welch Co. v. New Hampshire, 306 U.S. 79, 84 (1939).
[56] 34 Stat. 768 (1906), as amended, 21 U.S.C. § 1 et seq. (1952).
[57] Savage v. Jones, 225 U.S. 501 (1912).
[58] McDermott v. Wisconsin, 228 U.S. 115 (1913).
[59] 309 U.S. 598 (1940).

ways of motor vehicles carrying other vehicles over the cab was superseded by rules concerning safety of equipment promulgated by the Interstate Commerce Commission.

After extensive hearings, the Commission had issued a report in
which it concluded that there was no evidence of the load over the cab
being unsafe and it issued rules concerning safety of truck equipment
which omitted regulation of the load over the cab. The Supreme Court
upheld the state statute against a claim of supersedure. It analysed the
legislative history and the federal statute to find that Congress was
hesitant to enter the field of weight regulation in which the states had a
special interest because of their investment in the highways. The Court
refused to infer that the Congress intended to displace state regulations
by its own entry into regulation of safety and operation and equipment.
The Court said that "As a matter of statutory construction Congressional
intention to displace local laws in the exercise of its commerce power is
not, in general, to be inferred unless clearly indicated by those considerations which are persuasive of the statutory purpose." In assessing today's
critical comment, note should be taken that the Court was criticized as
having gone too far in upholding state action.[60]

The shift in emphasis began the next year in 1941 in *Hines v. Davidowitz*,[61] which is not a Commerce Clause case. The United States had an
alien registration act which did not require the alien to carry his identification card. Pennsylvania had an alien registration act which did. The
majority of the Court held that the state act was superseded because it
served the same general policy and purpose as the federal act. Unless
the state action serves some independent purpose within its province,
coincidence of the state and federal regulation will require the state act
to give way. That the shift in emphasis is not complete and that it is
difficult to find a consistent policy can be seen from *California v. Zook*[62]
in 1949. California had a statute which imposed a penalty for sale of
transportation by a carrier which had no permit from the Interstate
Commerce Commission or the California commission. A regulation of
the Interstate Commerce Commission covered this type of unscheduled
transportation. The question was whether the federal statute superseded
the state act. The majority of the Court found that it did not. It stated
that the coincidence of the two acts is not enough absent some evidence
of conflict of policy. This case should be compared with *Pennsylvania v.
Nelson*[63] involving the Pennsylvania sedition act where the result was
the opposite and the common personnel in the two split-decision cases
shifted sides.

254

---

[60] Consult Power of States to Regulate Interstate Motor Carriers, 39 Mich. L. Rev.
631, 633-37 (1941).
[61] 312 U.S. 52 (1941).
[62] 336 U.S. 725 (1949).
[63] 350 U.S. 497 (1956).

Just as the Court attempted to restate the factors involved in a "dormant" Commerce Clause case in *Southern Pacific Co. v. Arizona* so it also sought to restate the law in *Rice v. Santa Fe Elevator Corp.*[64] as to the significant factors in a displacement or supersedure case. Mr. Justice Douglas listed as his first factor the historical or conventional classification of the subject: is it a matter which Congress has historically legislated about or is it one in which the states have traditionally acted. If the case falls into the latter category the Court is less likely to read federal legislation as precluding any state regulation. In *California v. Zook*, Mr. Justice Murphy refers to the "usual police power of the states" as a useful factor in displacement questions. What does the Court mean by "traditional" or "usual"? Apparently, not first in the field. In *California v. Zook* it would appear that Murphy really meant, protection of health, safety and protection against fraud. This point of health and safety is also emphasized in *Mauer v. Hamilton* as subjects traditionally belonging to the states. In the *Rice* case the states were clearly first in time yet the Court found displacement of state law. The regulation was of prices, selling practices and other factors commonly found in highly regulatory economic statutes.

255

Particularly significant in this historical approach to the problem is the question whether the subject became national because of earlier Supreme Court decisions excluding the states from regulation. If earlier Supreme Court decisions had precluded the states under the Commerce Clause and if Congress thereupon began regulating the matter, then state regulation is thereafter precluded even though subsequent interpretations of the Constitution would allow the states to regulate. Likewise if the earlier decisions had carved out an area of permissible state regulation then subsequent federal legislation designed to fill in the gaps will not be interpreted as ousting the states. Many of the supersedure cases under the Natural Gas Act are illustrative of this principle.[65] Prior to this act, the Supreme Court had held that the states could not regulate the sales for resale by interstate pipelines and gas companies, but the states could regulate direct sales of such companies to local consumers. The Supreme Court has suggested that the states could now regulate both types of sales. But in the meantime the Natural Gas Act of 1938 was passed for the purpose of regulating activity which in 1938 the Court had said the states could not regulate. The cases fairly consistently hold that Congress has occupied the field which the old Supreme Court said the states could not regulate, but that the federal act does not occupy the field which the old Supreme Court said the states could regulate.

---

[64] 331 U.S. 218 (1947).
[65] Consult Public Utilities Comm'n v. Gas Co., 317 U.S. 456 (1943); Interstate Natural Gas Co. v. Federal Power Commission, 331 U.S. 682 (1947); Panhandle Pipe Line Co. v. Comm'n, 332 U.S. 507 (1947); Power Comm'n v. East Ohio Gas Co., 338 U.S. 464 (1949); Panhandle Co. v. Michigan Comm'n, 341 U.S. 329 (1951); Phillips Petroleum Co. v. Wisconsin, 347 U.S. 672 (1954); Natural Gas Co. v. Panama Corp., 349 U.S. 44 (1955).

Parker v. Motor Boat Sales[66] in 1941 is an extreme illustration of the significance of this factor. The Longshoremen's Act specifically said that the federal act should not apply where recovery under local workmen's compensation acts could validly be had under state law. In 1917 in *Southern Pacific v. Jensen*[67] the Supreme Court had decided that the jurisdiction of Congress over admiralty was so exclusive that a state workmen's compensation law could not be applied to those employees in admiralty, such as longshoremen, not covered by the federal act concerning seamen. Subsequently the Congress filled up this gap between the Jones Act, applicable to seamen, and state workmen's compensation laws by enacting the longshoremen's act but with the proviso mentioned above. In the *Parker* case an office employee of a boat dealer was drowned on inland navigable waters while demonstrating a boat. The Virginia workmen's compensation act was in terms applicable and under constitutional doctrine current by 1941 could constitutionally be applied. The Supreme Court held that the federal law occupied the field. It interpreted the proviso as meaning state law was applicable to the extent *Southern Pacific v. Jensen* and its doctrine would have permitted.

If the field of regulation is one traditionally occupied by the states, then a further question concerning displacement is necessary, and that is: whether it can be inferred that the congressional intent is to displace state law. Four factors are here relevant according to the *Rice* case. The pervasiveness and scope of the federal act is significant. The more it appears to be a complete system of regulation the more likely state acts are to be displaced. Although there are no cases under the act, it is doubtful that state law touching atomic energy, even the extent of tort liability, can survive the Atomic Energy Act for this reason.

Cloverleaf Butter Co. v. Patterson[68] in 1942 is illustrative both of this principle or factor and the difficulty of its application. The federal act in question regulated the processing of renovated butter for health and sanitation purposes, admittedly a purpose traditionally within the state police power. It was a comprehensive statute which dealt with renovated butter at two points in the processing and distribution system: it imposed rigid sanitary procedures on the manufacture and distribution of such butter; and it subjected butter approved by the federal inspectors to the laws of the importing state. The Alabama act in question, for the same objectives, regulated the other end of the process which the federal act had left unregulated: the packing stock butter from which the finished product subject to federal and state regulation came, and to which the manufacturing process subject to federal regulation was applied. The majority of the Supreme Court thought that the all pervasive federal

256

---

[66] 314 U.S. 244 (1941).
[67] 244 U.S. 205 (1917). See also Knickerbocker Ice Co. v. Stewart, 253 U.S. 149 (1920); Washington v. Dawson & Co., 264 U.S. 219 (1924).
[68] 315 U.S. 148 (1942).

scheme supported an inference that Congress wanted the raw material left unregulated. The minority thought this inference was not overwhelmingly supportable and it relied on a presumption of no displacement.

Secondly, said Justice Douglas in the *Rice* case, the federal act may touch a field in which the federal interest is so dominant that the federal system will be assumed to preclude enforcement of state laws on the same subject. This, according to Douglas, is the basis of *Hines v. Davidowitz* to which reference has been made. The Alien Registration Act touched an area in which the federal interest was dominant—the field of foreign affairs; power over immigration, naturalization and deportation. A similar case is *Pennsylvania v. Nelson.*[69]

Thirdly, the object of the federal act and the character of the obligation imposed thereby may reveal a purpose to supersede the states. Examples of this type of supersedure are instances where federal legislation was avowedly passed to obtain uniformity such as the Safety Appliance Act.[70]

Finally, state policy may produce a result inconsistent with an objective of the federal act. Many of the labor supersedure cases are of this variety. *Hill v. Florida*[71] in 1945, where a Florida law requiring registration of union business agents was found to conflict with the policy of the National Labor Relations Act, is illustrative.

After listing these factors Mr. Justice Douglas adds that the cases which do not fall into any of these categories are "difficult" cases. As examples of "difficult" he cites two cases where state power was upheld: *South Carolina Highway Department v. Barnwell Bros.*[72] (width and weight regulation of interstate trucks); and *Union Brokerage Co. v. Jensen*[73] (federal license of a customs broker as opposed to qualification under a Minnesota foreign corporation act). Unless the Justice is cavalier in his citations, the reference to these cases as "difficult" is really revealing of an intent on Douglas' part to sweep aside past law and indeed to change the rule of construction. The areas of law referred to in these cases have traditionally been regulated by the states even though there is also some federal regulation and the Court has seldom had sharp divergence of views on these matters. This reference may well mean that Douglas is prepared to sweep all other rules aside and apply only one test to which he refers in the *Rice* case. He summarizes the matter by saying:

257

---

[69] 350 U.S. 497 (1956).
[70] 27 Stat. 531 (1893), 45 U.S.C. § 1 et seq. (1952). Douglas, J., cites for this proposition Southern Ry. Co. v. R.R. Comm'n, Indiana, 236 U.S. 439 (1915) (Safety Appliance Act); Charleston & Car. R.R. v. Varnvelle Co., 237 U.S. 597 (1915) (Carmack Amendment on liability of carrier for damage to goods); New York Central R.R. Co. v. Winfield, 244 U.S. 147 (1917) (Federal Employers' Liability Act); Napier v. Atlantic Coast Line, 272 U.S. 605 (1926) (Federal Locomotive Boiler Inspection Act).
[71] 325 U.S. 538 (1945).
[72] 303 U.S. 177 (1938).
[73] 322 U.S. 202 (1944).

The test, therefore, is whether the matter on which the State asserts the right to act is in any way regulated by the Federal Act. If it is, the federal scheme prevails though it is a more modest, less pervasive regulatory plan than that of the State.[74]

The latest case on displacement of state law, *City of Chicago v. Atchison Topeka and Santa Fe Ry. Co.*,[75] would seem to indicate that the Court has about reached this point. In that case the city proposed to require a certificate of necessity from the carrier selected by the railroads to provide transfer service between stations in Chicago. Without reference to any legislative history or any of the tests referred to in the *Rice* case, the majority concluded that two general sections of the Interstate Commerce Act imposing a duty on carriers to establish through routes and passenger interchanges made Chicago impotent to license the transfer agent. These seem to have eliminated a search for congressional intent as to supersedure and substituted the Court's judgment whether the state act might be inconsistent with some unexpressed congressional policy. The only search for congressional intent seems now to be a search for an intent not to displace. Thus in *Rice v. Chicago Board of Trade*,[76] Justice Douglas found no displacement of state regulation of boards of trade by the Commodity Exchange Act[77] which had an express reservation of state power in some sections. Douglas reasoned that if Congress used such care to preserve state authority where conflict was possible, there is no displacement where there is no conflict.

There is a definite trend in the Court toward a reversal of the historic attitude toward this problem. The reversal of attitude can only mean that the doctrine of federalism has suffered. A *true* federalist cannot regard state exercise of power as unique where Congress has also acted. A nationalist cannot expect the states to legislate on many subjects without the consent of Congress. But the important point is that the problem is one for Congress. If it expresses itself either generally or specifically as to its desires on the displacement question, there is little indication that the Court will ignore a congressional mandate.

[74] Rice v. Santa Fe Elevator Corp., 331 U.S. 218, 236 (1947).
[75] 357 U.S. 77 (1958).
[76] 331 U.S. 247 (1947).
[77] 49 Stat. 1491 (1936), as amended, 7 U.S.C. § 1 et seq. (1952).

CIVIL WAR AND THE PRESERVATION OF AMERICAN FEDERALISM *

Daniel J. Elazar

Temple University

The problem of political unification is one of the most pressing and intriguing ones of twentieth century politics. One of the most frequently tried devices for unifying diverse politics and populations is the device of federalism. The results have been mixed, with at least as many failures as successes on the record.[1] The United States is one of the great—if not the greatest—successes. Its nearly two centuries of stability under a federal form of government represent a modern record.[2] Yet the United States went through a period of civil war when its survival as a single nation was in grave doubt. It may be that the survival of the nation and its federal form of government through a major conflict couched in terms of federalism itself, and its bitter aftermath, can throw some light on the uses and limits of federalism as a device for political unification.

To the perceptive student of American politics in our time, the most intriguing aspect of the American Civil War is not that it occurred in the first place, not that Americans on both sides of the Mason-Dixon line responded to it with a fervor that was to continue to surround that conflict for one hundred years, not that the Union prevailed. The most intriguing thing about the Civil War is that

259

*This article is based on the writer's study of the impact of the Civil War on American government, state and national, now in preparation as part of the United States Civil War Centennial Commission's series on the impact of the Civil War on American life. Much of the interpretation developed here is based on a reanalysis of the voluminous literature on the War in light of the literature on American federalism that has emerged in recent years. Special acknowledgement is due the Henry E. Huntington Library, San Marino, California, whose collections offered the writer an opportunity to expand his analysis by reviewing significant documents of the war period and whose financial assistance enabled the author to make use of its superb facilities.

[1] See, for example, Amitai Etzioni, *Political Unification* (New York: Holt, Rinehart & Winston, 1965); William Riker, *Federalism: Origin, Operation, Significance* (Boston: Little, Brown & Co., 1964); K. C. Wheare, *Federal Government* (New York: Oxford University Press, 1964); Carl Friedrich, *Trends of Federalism in Theory and Practice* (New York: Praeger, 1968); and Daniel J. Elazar, "Federalism" in *International Encyclopedia of the Social Sciences* (New York: Macmillan, 1969).

[2] See, in particular, Morton Grodzins, *The American System: A New View of Government in the United States* (Chicago: Rand McNally, 1966) edited by Daniel J. Elazar.

American federalism emerged from it intact as a system and substantially as it was before the war began. It is all the more intriguing when one stops to consider that whatever the composite of causes leading to war, it was the existence of federalism—of the structural division of the nation into 31 states, each a civil society in its own right as well as an integral part of the national civil society—that gave the Southern secessionists the form through which to mount their rebellion and the arguments by which to justify it. Moreover, the secessionists' misuse of the federal system over the years and especially after 1861 gave the Northern revolutionaries who emerged as the dominant power in the Union at the end of the war every reason to try to eliminate Southern political influence (the "slave power" they called it) locally and nationally by eliminating or at least drastically altering the system that had given the South with only one third of the nation's population its power to veto measures perceived to run contrary to its interests in the antebellum period and which would automatically restore that power to it.[3]

260

All these pressures weighed against a system of government which is in many ways a fragile one by virtue of the very moderation and forebearance which is demanded of those who would maintain it. For a federal system is one which requires, above all things, a sense of restraint on the part of the powerholders. Indeed, the more power that is held exclusively, the greater the restraint that must be exercised. At the same time, the value of federalism is hard to dramatize, especially in the face of a moral crusade, since the mechanisms of federalism will often appear to obstruct justice while the benefits of federalism are usually difficult to visualize—until the system is subverted and they no longer exist.

Yet, when viewing the course of American governmental history from today's perspective, it is almost as reasonable to view the war as an unfortunate interruption in the continued development of the American federal polity as it is to view it as a great epochal crisis in American history. From that larger perspective, the war was almost a digression in a period which saw the federal, state, and local governments of the United States first rise to the challenges of industrialization and first demonstrate that the American system could meet those challenges without abandoning its highly valued tradition of non-centralization.[4]

[3] Herbert Agar, *The Price of Union* (Boston: Houghton Mifflin Co., 1950), provides an excellent analytic review of the American political process in the nineteenth century which illustrates how the Southern veto power could be used.

[4] For a discussion of the meaning of noncentralization as a basic principle of American federalism, see Daniel J. Elazar, *Federalism and the Community* (Pittsburgh: University of Pittsburgh, 1968).

I

It is not surprising that the war came. With all the acknowledged foolishness, misjudgments, and even knavery of the antebellum era that contributed to the crisis, the weight of the evidence as it is understood today reveals that the war was still an "irrepressible conflict," the most logical culmination of the fundamental struggle over slavery and the whole thrust of events and attitudes that shaped intersectional rivalries from colonial days on into the 19th century.[5]

Revolutions are not mounted on single issues and civil wars are not the end result of single causes. The years after 1847 saw a convergence of a number of issues and trends which not only reenforced each other but which divided the country along sectional lines which more or less followed the boundaries of the states in one way that could lead to a serious disruption of the American federal union. One of the great strengths of the American federal system has been the rarity with which problematic issues have divided the country along state lines. Rather, they have tended to cut across boundaries on the basis of other kinds of interest alignments that are perpetually shifting from issue to issue thereby reducing pressure upon the system as such. In the 1850's, this pattern was disrupted for the first and only time in American history. One by one, the slavery issue, the problem of diverging socio-economic systems, the breakdown of communication in regard to the meaning of America's basic political consensus, all aligned themselves with one another along state and sectional lines so as to cut off the cross-pressures which normally prevent such issues from destroying political systems. In other times, those cross-pressures could have prevented any single one of the divisive issues from disrupting a Union, which as Lincoln said, was bound by "The mystic chords of memory, stretching from every battlefield, and patriot grave, to every living heart and hearthstone, all over this broad land."[6]

As the bonds of union snapped during the 1850's, Northerners and Southerners found themselves facing each other on several fronts in a

---

[5] Avery Craven is the foremost exponent of the theory that the war need not have taken place. See his *The Coming of the Civil War* (Chicago: University of Chicago Press, 1957), 2nd ed. [1st ed., New York: C. Scribner & Son, 1942]. More recently, Allan Nevins has taken the lead in recognizing the irrepressible character of the conflict. See his magnum opus, *Ordeal of the Union:*
    Ordeal of the Union (New York: Scribners, 1947)
        Vol. 1 "Fruits of Manifest Destiny (1847—1852)"
        Vol. 2 "A House Dividing (1852—1857)"
    The Emergence of Lincoln (New York: Scribners, 1950)
        Vol. 3 "Douglas, Buchanan, & Party Chaos (1857—1859)"
        Vol. 4 "Prologue to Civil War (1859—1861)"
[6] Abraham Lincoln First Inaugural Address, March 4, 1861.

"cold war." As the cold war increased in intensity, the two sections
became further polarized. And, as their respective demands for
guaranteed security increased, it finally became necessary for the one
most likely to lose the competition within the nation, to test its
ability to destroy a nation.

It is not surprising that the war should have stirred the spirits of
the American people the way it did and the way it has. There is a
horrible fascination in a brothers' war, particularly one with the
revolutionary implications of our civil war. There is the hypnotic
element of being drawn into an unwanted conflict which is in no way
diminished by the fact that the war may have been inevitable. There
is the moral fervor generated by the central issue of the war—
slavery—which touches the greatest and most persistent of all
American dilemmas. There is the troubled Lincolnesque reaction of
knowing that both sides had so much in common, even as they
viewed the world so differently; that both could honestly believe
their causes to be right in the best American sense. There is the great
constitutional question of using extra-constitutional means to fight
war to save a political system rooted in constitutionalism without
allowing unconstitutional acts necessary in time of crisis to become
precedents for future violations.

It is not surprising that the Union triumphed. It is not necessary to
recount statistics so well documented from every angle by generations of Civil War experts that demonstrate the inherently superior
physical and material capabilities of the North, all other things being
equal (as they were). The Southerners, indeed, banked on their
mistaken belief that all other things were not equal, that they had a
natural superiority in morale because they were fighting for home
and fireside and a moral superiority arising from their defense of
traditional liberties; and consequently that they were favored with
God's special providence. They forgot that "Yankees" were also
Americans and did not reckon with the Northerners' equally firm
belief that they were fighting for the principles of the American
Revolution and the larger moral good; and that the Union was
endowed with God's special providence.

II

What may be surprising is the way in which the American system
of government survived the conflict. The very assertion that the
federal system survived intact runs against the conventional wisdom
about the war. The most widely read history books assert a very
different conclusion, generally proclaiming that the United States
started the war a loose confederation and emerged from it a

262

centralized union.[7] In this they are supported by certain generally accepted facts:

1) The Civil War was, as the Southerners have characterized it, a "war between the states," at least to the extent that it was precipitated by the attempted secession of eleven states as states, and to the extent that the overwhelming majority of their citizens, most of whom probably did not wish their states to secede, placed state loyalty above national allegiance and contributed in positive ways to the Confederate war effort once the decision was made. Most Northerners were aware of this choice of state loyalty over national allegiance and most did not want to allow state loyalties to be used to foster treason ever again.

2) The Radical Republicans were anxious to restore the Union only if they could extirpate what they believed to be the major cause of secession—slavery—once and for all. They understood (as did their opposite numbers in the South) that slavery was more than "Negroes-held-in-bondage," that it was the foundation stone of a socio-economic system that fostered values, mores, and patterns of behavior which they believed to be not only different from their own, but evil. They not only wanted to eliminate enslavement of blacks but the "slavocracy"—the leaders of Southern society—the "slave system"—the whole antebellum Southern way of life insofar as it was based on slavery as an institution—and the "slave power"—the political influence of the slave-centered South in national affairs. The Radicals' aims were not popular at first but, as the war stretched on, began to attract more and more support from other Northerners. After the war, the struggle for the control of the state governments in the South became a major aspect of the struggle between Northerners and Southerners over this very point.

3) The actual fighting was followed by a very difficult period of Reconstruction, three times the length of the war itself, during which all the issues of the war except the already-settled secession question were really fought out. The Southern states were occupied by Union troops for all or most of that period and were treated as conquered territory for much of it. Restoration of internal self-government in the South was contingent upon the states' ratification of three amendments to the United States Constitution—the Thirteenth, Fourteenth, and Fifteenth—which were designed to deny them the

263

[7] The common pattern in American history courses and textbooks is to use the Civil War as the dividing line between the United States as a "federal republic" and a "national union." This division has been institutionalized in the textbooks. See, for example, John Donald Hicks, *The Federal Union: A History of the U.S. to 1865* (Boston: Houghton Mifflin Co., 1948) and *The American Nation: A History of the U.S. From 1865 to the Present* (Boston: Houghton Mifflin Co., 1941).

right to maintain slavery, to discriminate against the ex-slaves in their civil rights, or to prevent the freedmen from voting, and which gave Congress the power to enforce those provisions through legislation.[8]

III

Moreover (and this is not noted in the standard histories) during the war, the North had passed through a period of domestic reform with revolutionary implications that in the long run would do at least as much to transform the country as any actions on the battlefield. The election of a Republican President was in one sense, revolution enough. A new party, dedicated to limiting slavery with a view toward encouraging its ultimate extinction and representing an alliance of the promoters of industrialization with the promoters of commercial agriculture, had to be a harbinger of changes to come, especially since the country was ripe for new departures.[9] A full generation had passed since Andrew Jackson had mounted the last great national reform movement and a half generation had elapsed since the pressures of industrialization had begun to awaken people to new problems requiring government action.[10]

Revolutionary domestic reform in the North took three paths. There was the effort on the part of Republican political leaders to make the GOP the nation's majority party, through identification of their party with the preservation of the Union and the Democrats with treason, and through destruction of the Southern "slave power" which had dominated the nation before the war. There was the effort on the part of influential Republican members of Congress to make that body—which could most easily be dominated by Republican votes—supreme, through close supervision of the President in all his activities, through reduction of the power of the Supreme Court, and through reorganization of Congress itself into an almost parliamentary system. Finally, there was the effort on the part of the Republican coalition of interests to secure the benefits for which they had fought, through emancipation of the slaves, through the enactment of new programs to benefit industry, and through the

---

[8] See Eric McKitrick, *Andrew Johnson and Reconstruction* (Chicago: University of Chicago Press, 1960); Kenneth M. Stampp, *The Era of Reconstruction* (New York: Knopf, 1965); John Hope Franklin, *Reconstruction After the Civil War* (Chicago: University of Chicago Press, 1961); and E. Merton Coulter, *The South During Reconstruction* (Baton Rouge: Louisiana University Press, 1947) for discussion of this from various angles.

[9] For a history of this alliance, see Agar, *op. cit.*

[10] The theory of generational change implicit here is expressed more elaborately in Daniel J. Elazar, *Toward A Generational Theory of American Politics* (Philadelphia: Center for the Study of Federalism, 1969).

enactment of new programs to benefit the yeomen farmers of the North's West.

The first and second of these revolutions were to lead to the bitter experiences of Reconstruction. The first was to be sufficiently successful to give the GOP majority status in the nation as a whole until the New Deal, though the matter would be touch and go until 1896.[11]

The second was to come close to succeeding and then fail, leaving a residue which was to plague Presidents for a generation and which even today helps Congress maintain itself in the face of just the opposite kind of pressure.

The third was expressed through a veritable "New Deal" of concentrated expansion of the role of government; to paraphrase Lincoln, a "New Birth" of the 1860's. In the short span of Lincoln's administration, the American people gave their system a push into the new industrial age, a push felt in Washington, in the state capitols, and, after the war, in the local communities as well.

The changes wrought by this "New Birth" involved a substantial increase of governmental activities on all planes, in the manner to which the American system had already become accustomed. Here we can only chronicle the most important actions on the federal plane which opened this new era of government activity.

The first area of priority for federal action involved reorganization of the nation's fiscal system which, after the demise of the subtreasury system in 1846, had been rudderless, with no federal structure or program to guide it. In 1861, it was confronted with the task of financing a major war while still reeling from the Depression of 1857.[12] Early that year Congress enacted an income tax and established a national currency, primarily to finance the war. The next year a national banking system was created and with it a national monetary system. Taken together these measures would restore to the federal government the major role in the nation's fiscal affairs which it had had until the 1840's and also form the basis for the great political conflicts of the next generation.

Agriculture, commerce, and industry were attended to in turn, responding to the Republican Party's campaign promises and its vision of the political constellation that would govern America in the future. A second major area of federal activity was connected with the nation's expansion westward. In 1862, the land grant college

---

[11] V. O. Key, Jr. discusses this in *Parties, Politics and Pressure Groups* (New York: Thomas Y. Crowell, 1942).

[12] Bray Hammond, *Banks and Politics in America: From the Revolution to the Civil War* (Princeton: Princeton University Press, 1957).

system was inaugurated with the Morrill Act, to enable the states to train men for the new age. That same year, the Homestead Act was passed to provide free land for settlers in the West; and grants were made to foster construction of the great transcontinental railroads to open that west. Congress even set what is now the world's standard railroad gauge when it established the 4'8" gauge for the transcontinental railroads. Taken together these measures would make the post-war conquest of the last land frontier possible and inevitable.

Existing programs of vital importance to the nation's industrial and commercial development were altered or expanded. Congress opened the U. S. mails to merchandise in 1861. Two years later free mail carrier service was inaugurated in cities of 50,000 or more, a service which was expanded to include 51 cities by 1871. Railway mail service and the money order system were made operational in 1864. The Morrill Tariff of 1861 restored the protectionist approach to tariff policy and inaugurated two generations of that form of federal subsidy for domestic manufacturing. In 1864 the Contract Labor Act was passed, providing for licensed recruitment of European laborers to man the nation's new industrial plants and further stimulate the influx of Europeans to American shores.

Congress even initiated the nation's active conservation efforts. In 1864, it granted California the Yosemite lands for the express purposes of creating a public nature reserve, the first to result from federal action.

The very structure of the government was changed. Aside from the great, though temporary, expansion of the federal bureaucracy in connection with war effort, a number of permanent new federal bureaus were created during the war years and immediately after. Each of them represented a crystallization of the expanded federal role in various important fields. Among them were the Department of Agriculture (1862), and Bureau of Printing and Engraving (1862), the Office of Comptroller of the Currency (1863), and the Office of Immigration (1864). In 1863, Congress created the National Academy of Sciences, initially to screen technological innovations to ascertain their usefulness for the war effort. In 1867, a Federal Office of Education was established to round out the period.

Finally, the nation filled in the remaining gaps on the country's political map. Between 1861 and 1868, eight new territories were organized and endowed with Republican-dominated territorial governments, all but completing the political organization of the west. Four new states were created, all but one of which fell into the regular Republican column. Alaska was purchased, virtually rounding out the territorial integrity of the nation.[13]

Thus, after 1865, when the South had to be brought back into the Union, the Union itself was changed. Slavery was no more; a new political party with no roots in the South was in power for the foreseeable future; and the role of government in the nation's life had been substantially enlarged.

IV

With all the pressures of sectional polarization, national disruption, domestic reform, and popular emotionalism regarding the war and the slavery issue expressed in the strongest religious terms, we can look back at the federal system of 1880 and find that it conveys much the same sense of operational reality to us as the federal system of 1840. Though two changes were evident—the theory of secession had been buried and government activities had expanded on all planes and in all sections of the country—a closer look reveals that the federal system in its essence and in its crucial details had been restored, even after the tribulations of War and Reconstruction.

In the first place, the boundaries of ten of the eleven seceding states were completely intact. Virginia, the one state that suffered territorial loss, was also the only one that had a substantial Unionist population located in a large contiguous bloc of territory bordering on free soil and susceptible of detachment and admission to the Union as a state in its own right. Western Virginia became West Virginia primarily because its people wanted it to become a separate state. Pleased as were the Northern Republicans at the prospect of dismembering Virginia and acquiring two more votes in the Senate, they would not have initiated the action. Indeed, all that Lincoln did to interfere with those people west of the Virginia tidewater who wished to remain Virginians, was to attach two secessionist counties along the Maryland line to the new state in order to protect the Baltimore and Ohio Railroad. And, it must be remembered that even this dismemberment of Virginia was completed in 1863 when the outcome of the war was still in doubt and the North was still willing to use extraordinary measures to assure a Union victory. The harshest days of Congressional Reconstruction saw nothing remotely comparable to it, though in theory the most radical members of Congress would have accepted changes in the boundaries of the Southern states.

[13] Nevins discusses all of this in Volumes 5, 6 and 7 of *Ordeal of the Union*.

267

The restoration of boundaries alone would prove little; what is more important is that all eleven states of the former Confederacy were restored to their full positions in the Union. Though Lincoln's rather conservative efforts to restore the states reoccupied during the war came to naught, after April 1865, there was a rapid restoration of the states' internal self-government. By the end of July of that year, provisional governors of local origin and holding the confidence of the local population had been appointed in all eleven. By December, 1865, new state governments had been elected under newly framed constitutions, all under the aegis, protection and encouragement of Andrew Johnson and the federal occupying troops taking orders from him as commander-in-chief. Though Congress refused to accept these governments as legitimate by refusing to seat their representatives, it did nothing to interfere with their basic internal functioning for three years. By 1868, when the radicals moved to impose military reconstruction, the states had been effectively reconstituted and were no longer candidates for destruction. Though their duly (if discriminatorily) elected leaders were thrust into political exile, in some cases for as long as eight years, their restoration at the end of that period was virtually assured.

Even the imposition of the Thirteenth, Fourteenth, and Fifteenth Amendments had little effect on the position of the states themselves. The Thirteenth Amendment abolished slavery and in the sense that it denied to the states the right to legalize a slave system, their powers were restricted. As subsequent events were to show, it did not prevent the states from imposing systems of virtual bondage on blacks after 1877.[14] The Fourteenth Amendment, whatever the intentions of its framers, was soon used for purposes of limiting government powers in the field of commerce regulation but was barely used until our own day to deal with war-generated problems of Negro rights. State powers over minority rights were virtually unlimited until well into the 20th century. Even the use of the Fourteenth Amendment to prevent the states from regulating business was hardly more of a restriction of their powers than were the decisions of John Marshall in the great commerce cases of the 1820's. The enforcement of the Fifteenth Amendment (which incidentally, applied equally in a very real sense, to the Northern states, most of which disenfranchised Negroes until it was ratified) was also left to the states after 1877, more or less until the 1950's.

These three amendments represent the most tangible centralizing

[14] See C. Van Woodward, *Reunion and Reaction: The Compromise of 1877 and the End of Reconstruction* (Garden City, N.Y.: Doubleday, 1956).

developments of the war period. Their long term impact should not be minimized. Indeed one hundred years later they may well be providing the grounds for truly unprecedented changes in the relationship between the federal government and the states. But their short term role should not be exaggerated either. In part, they simply ratified constitutional doctrines long since accepted in the North. Even in their innovative aspects, they would be more appropriately termed nationalizing rather than centralizing since what they did was to raise minimum national standards in certain selected fields (just as the Constitution did in its original form in 1789). They did not really alter the structure or the mechanisms of federalism as civil rights workers active in the South in the 1960's discovered.[15]

Moreover, there is considerable evidence that, much as they tried, the Northern radicals were unable to change the structure of leadership in the South, the central reason for their imposition of a harsh Reconstruction after the war. The continuity of Southern leadership took on three dimensions:

1) In the first place, even in the earliest days of military occupation, the North found that it had to rely upon ex-Confederates to provide local leadership. The roster of the provisional Governors of the states, appointed directly by President Johnson revealed this fully. This was so for the very same reason that after World War II the Allied armies occupying Germany and Japan had to rely upon local people identified with the defeated regimes (no invidious comparison intended) in both countries to form the basis for local self-government. They were the only people sufficiently skilled in governing to succeed and sufficiently acceptable to their communities to command popular respect and obedience. Most authentic Unionists in the South, who had refused to support the Confederacy, like most real anti-Nazis in Germany, did not have the confidence of Southerners because they were considered traitors, renegades who had refused to accept the cause of their people as their own. This was particularly true in the post Civil War South because the Confederacy had no serious moral taint in the eyes of most of the world and certainly none in the eyes of most Southerners. Thus the occupation authorities were forced to turn to those who held the public's confidence and simply tried to pick the ex-Confederates who appeared most willing to accept the new order of things and to cooperate with the North. The later failure of Congressional Reconstruction, which relied so heavily upon "carpet-baggers,

269

[15]See Joseph Bliss James, *The Framing of the Fourteenth Amendment* (Urbana: University of Illinois Press, 1956); William Gillette, *The Right to Vote* (Baltimore: John Hopkins Press, 1965); and McKitrick, *op. cit.*

scalawags, and freedmen," none of whom had the confidence of the local whites, only demonstrated how true this was.

2) Even during the worst period of Congressional Reconstruction, there apparently were not enough carpet-baggers, scalawags, and freedmen to fill all the government positions in the Southern states. There is evidence that in many of the counties in the South the ex-Confederates remained in power throughout Reconstruction by default. In these cases, local governmental institutions provided a basis from which to launch an assault on carpet-bag government as the 1870's wore on.[16]

3) Finally, after the Compromise of 1877 in which the Northern Republicans took the Presidency by promising to leave the Southern states alone to work out their own destinies, the Southerners responded by making Confederate service the normal pre-requisite for public office for at least the next generation. The records of the Confederate "brigadiers," in national life as well as in the politics of their states are well-known. Ex-Confederates from "high privates in the rear rank" to full generals, served in the offices of government in the South ranging from the most local to the Senate of the United States and even the U.S. Supreme Court. A small but significant number of Southerners who had held federal office before the war and had then "gone South," even resumed their public careers after a decent interval.[17]

The Compromise of 1877 restored the states of the South to their full rights. From then on, though occasional efforts were made to conduct inquiries into the ways the Southern states were handling the race issue, they were left substantially alone until after World War II.[18] Not only that, but Southerners were given full freedom to advance in national life—up to a point—and once again became highly influential in the nation's government. Even the presidency fell to a man of Southern birth (Woodrow Wilson) in 1912—not fifty years after Appomatox—though it was to be a full century before a full-fledged resident of one of the ex-Confederate states was elected to that high office.

V

All this points to the conclusion that the Southern States emerged from the war having suffered only one major loss and that was the

[16]This theme is treated in greater detail in the author's forthcoming book, *Partnership in Crisis: The Impact of the Civil War on American Government, State and National.*

[17]William Hesseltine, *Confederate Leaders in the New South* (Baton Rouge: Louisiana State University Press, 1950).

[18] For a constitutional history of federal actions in the civil rights field between 1877 and 1954, see Paul L. Murphy and James M. Smith, eds., *Liberty and Justice* (New York: Knopf, 1958).

right to maintain a slave system.[19] But this does not tell us the entire story. Two questions still remain: Why did the federal system survive and how was its survival engineered?

An answer to both questions can be found in an examination of six factors: 1) the continuity of ordinary governmental concerns even in the face of a crisis; 2) the rapid restoration of Southerners' unionist inclinations and the absence of any serious secessionist sentiment after 1865; 3) the existence of a substantial bloc of people, many occupying key civil and military positions in the North, who wished to restore the federal system even to the point of repealing the obvious changes wrought by the war; 4) the reemergence of the United States Supreme Court as a bulwark of federalism after the heyday of Congressional Reconstruction; 5) the continued existence of the Union of States in the North which made the reconstitution of the state system in the South a prerequisite for the restoration of the citizenship of Southern whites or the acquisition of citizenship by Southern blacks; and 6) the deeply imbedded political consensus of the American people, North and South, which is founded on commitment to the federal principle. All of these bear close examination but space limitations will limit the focus of this article to the first two and the last.

271

It is only human that popular fascination with the Civil War is founded on the glamour of crisis and conflict. Yet the fascination with crisis has obscured the great measure of continuous cooperative national activity even during a great and difficult crisis which culminated in a restoration of the normal partnership of governments and interests that has characterized American federalism since the founding of the Republic.[20] In comparison with the drama of the war itself, this side must necessarily appear humdrum and ordinary in its outlines but, to those interested in the maintenance of political systems in general—and the American system in particular—it has a fascination all its own.

Today, historians and political scientists generally agree that: 1) The Constitution as written and understood by the founders of the Republic created a strong, if non-centralized national

[19]This was a great loss and should not be minimized since it disrupted an entire way of life for the Southern ruling elite, changing power structures throughout the Southern states, but, in terms of federalism, it must be understood as a relatively modest consequence since it left the states themselves quite intact as civil societies. It could be argued that loss of the right of secession was an even more decisive change but the very existence of such a "right" was a matter of dispute long before the war. Majority constitutional opinion denied that such a right ever existed, hence it can honestly be argued that it was never there to be lost.

[20]See Daniel J. Elazar, The American Partnership (Chicago: University of Chicago Press, 1962).

union with a potentially powerful national government and was not designed to create a limited confederacy.[21] 2) The American federal system before 1860 was one in which the federal government played an active, if still limited role in the development of the nation, a role which included strong and vital financial and technical support for state and local activities within the context of their common interests and national politics and problems. While the founders' view of the Union as a strong agent of the people was replaced by the "states-rights" position after 1835, the role of the federal government, though reduced, remained substantial and even began to grow again after 1848. Consequently, until the old ties of politics and sentiment were finally torn asunder, North and South alike remained bound by a system of federal services and rewards that made union worthwile until all else failed and which would ultimately do much to make union possible once again.

272

Furthermore, while the war was being waged, the national, state, and local governments of both sides continued to govern. They did so by interfering as little as possible with the accepted structure of government even in their most revolutionary moments. That, in itself, is fascinating. Here was the South, endeavoring to mount a rebellion for the sake of independence yet at the same time making every effort to avoid any consciously revolutionary changes in the political institutions inherited from the "Old Union." (The contemporary observer must add "any changes except one great one" because today we know as they did not that their very conception of the Union as a state-centered confederacy was a revolutionary interpretation of the Constitution.) And here was the North, endeavoring to preserve the Union but using the opportunities of the war to initiate a number of well-nigh revolutionary actions designed to redistribute political power and to lead government into paths untrod since the days of the founding fathers themselves, without disturbing the structure of the federal system in any significant way.

When the South seceded, the eleven states of the Confederacy continued their state governments as before, except for assuming jurisdiction over some previously federal activities within their boundaries, mostly in the judicial realm. Even as the war continued, the states were reluctant to alter traditional patterns and their leaders denounced the Richmond government whenever Jefferson Davis or his colleagues appeared to be departing from the precedents set after

[21]See, for example, David G. Smith, *The Convention and the Constitution* (New York: St. Martin's, 1965) and Martin Diamond, "What the Framers Meant by Federalism," in Robert A. Goldwin, ed., *A Nation of States* (Chicago: Rand McNally, 1961).

1840 in the "Old Union". The Confederate Government, by the same token, only exerted the powers granted it under its constitution very gingerly. For example, the record of the Davis administration in protecting civil liberties and free speech during the war was much better than that of the Lincoln administration. Lincoln rejected the idea that the Constitution could not be bent to save the Union, placing first things first as he saw them. Davis could not accept the idea that a constitution could be bent, even to save the Confederacy.[22]

But the continuity of government in the South went beyond that. When the Confederacy was formed, federal officers in the Southern states and Southerners holding federal offices in Washington were co-opted *en masse* to form the basic cadres for Confederate civil, political, and military services. The conventional histories all relate how this was so among the politicians. The war did not produce new leaders in the South so much as it elevated Southern leaders with national reputations to new posts in the Confederacy. Just as the continuity of Southerners' political career lines was not broken by secession so was the continuity of the public administration maintained as much as possible. Postmasters, customs officials, Indian agents, judges, marshals, military and naval officers of the "Old Union" took up commensurate positions in state or Confederate service with hardly a pause to take new oaths of office.[23]

The laws of the United States were also adopted *en masse*, with but a few modifications needed to suit a nation based on the slave system, and were, in most cases, retained for the duration. Even pending Federal court cases were simply transferred to the new jurisdictions and tried on schedule as if nothing had happened. The extent to which this was so is in no way better revealed than in the case of *United States* v. *David L. Martin* in the District Court of the Confederate States for the District of Georgia. Martin, the Captain of the slave ship *Wanderer* had been indicted in 1860 under U.S. law for smuggling slaves into the South and was in jail when Georgia seceded. He was tried by a Confederate judge during the war for that offense, convicted, sentenced to prison and held in jail until the fall of the Confederacy when he was turned over to federal authorities.

[22]See, for example, E. Merton Coulter, *The Confederate States of America 1861−1865* (Baton Rouge: Louisiana State University Press, 1950); Clifford Dowdey, *Experiment in Rebellion* (Garden City, N.Y.: Doubleday, 1946); Edward Younger, ed., *Inside the Confederate Government* (New York: Oxford University Press, 1957); and Curtis A. Amlund, *Federalism in the Southern Confederacy* (Washington, D.C.: Public Affairs Press, 1966). The autobiographies of the Confederate leaders attest to this as well.

[23]See *Partnership in Crisis, op. cit.*; Coulter, *Confederate States, op. cit.*, Chapter VI, "Consolidating the Government"; and Charles P. Roland, *The Confederacy* (Chicago: University of Chicago Press, 1960), II, "Birth of the Confederacy."

The political revolution in the South was not to come until after
the war, when the former Union officials who had "gone secesh"
were turned out of office "for good" (at least for a while) and the
North extended its own revolution southward. Here we come
directly to the problem of restoration. It is certainly clear that by the
end of the war all normal channels of collaboration between North
and South were cut off. The problem of the Northern victors in May
1865 was threefold. Most immediately, the Union Army had to
restore order to a vanquished territory whose lawful civil government
had been all but destroyed and somehow feed a starving population
which included several million recently freed slaves. Then the
Northern authorities had to restore normal governmental services in
the South with the ultimate goal of restoring local self-government to
the Southern people. Finally, it was recognized that there would
have to be full restoration of the rights due Southerners as Americans
before too long, with proper safeguards for the freed Negroes and
full security against further rebellion by Southern whites. These goals
could be achieved in a variety of ways but the very nature of
American democracy precluded anything less than ultimate restoration of rights of all but a very few of the most prominent
secessionists.

274

As it turned out, the first steps taken by federal authorities were
decisive in determining the ultimate outcome of all three tasks,
though many trials and tribulations would occur before that became
clear. Within weeks, federal relief was pouring southward. Mail
service had been restored in Union-occupied territory even as the
fighting continued. In June, President Andrew Johnson lifted the
blockade of Southern ports, opening them up to commerce and
economic restoration. By May, enterprising Southerners were applying for bank charters under the national banking act passed "in their
absence." Most were to receive those charters without serious
difficulty. By summer, then, the federal government was not only
resuming its interrupted services in the Southern States but was
extending its revolution southward in ways more acceptable to the
ex-Confederates than Negro emancipation. As mentioned above, by
summer there was already substantial restoration of state and local
self-government in the conquered section. Ultimately, all the "New
Birth" programs were extended to the Southern states even before
federal troops were withdrawn[24]

Yet a third modification of traditional views is called for once it is
recognized that the ordinary activities of government, those activites

[24] See Coulter, *The South During Reconstruction, op. cit.* and Paul H. Buck, *The Road to
Reunion 1865–1900* (Boston: Little, Brown & Co., 1938).

which offer a community and the individuals within it an opportunity to relate to the national governing authority—and even encourage its leadership to attempt to influence public policy in small ways—were restored to the South with amazing speed. Moreover, they were to be maintained even while Congress was doing all in its power to deny most Southern whites the fundamental rights of citizenship. Willy-nilly, the old system was restored almost before a conscious decision as to its future had been made.

VI

The careful student, upon reviewing the actions that led to this dual restoration of the South and the federal system, is drawn to the inescapable conclusion that, even as the existence of federalism provided the framework for the disruption of the Union, it also made possible the reunification of the nation as a stronger and "more perfect" political order. The full meaning of this cannot be explored here. It is only possible to allude to its high points.

275

The crucial point in this analysis is the fact that the existence of federalism prevented the victorious North from confronting the defeated South with an "either-or" proposition, namely, demanding that the Southerners accept reunification on the North's terms alone or forever be denied their rights as Americans, this despite the desire of some Northern radicals to do just that. The existence of federalism made it possible for the South to accept those minimal terms which the North could not help but demand—abjuration of secession and slavery and minimal recognition of the Negroes' civil rights while retaining much of its own way of life and regaining the right to be the master of its future.

More specifically the fact that the Southern states were left intact allowed Southerners to reidentify with the Union which had humbled them, destroyed their institutions and property, and killed their sons, without accepting the Northern interpretation of the meaning of the war. They could do this by reidentifying through their beloved states whose continued existence as civil societies made possible the legitimate perpetuation of the record of their heroic sacrifices in the late war, and the theories by which the war was justified, within the Union. (Even the Confederate flag could be preserved in this way, by incorporating its design into their state flags.) Ultimately, this enabled them to make the Confederate myth a legitimate part of the whole nation's heritage, adding to their "comfort" as restored members of the Union. (Given the popular response to Confederate symbols in the intervening century, the South may even have won the war of myth and interpretation.)

Moreover, by acquiring a stake in the Union through their states they could transfer their bitternesses and hatreds to the "Yankees" rather than continue to direct them toward the United States as a whole or even toward the federal government.

The fact that the continued existence of federalism in the nation as a whole meant the ultimate restoration of local self-government in the South not only allowed a generation of "rebels" to restore significant elements of the way of life which they valued but, as their most astute leaders realized, enabled them to better maintain it within the framework of the Union than they could have done outside of it. This did much to blunt residual secessionism as a political idea. In addition, restoration of the states allowed a generation of rebel leaders to successfully pursue public careers within the national political system, removing a potential threat to reunification of major proportions. These talented ex-Confederates could aspire to office only because they could stand for election in constituencies that were also ex-Confederate. Moreover, those constituencies had high and powerful offices at their disposal. It was unnecessary and unwise for the South's "national" leadership to remain disgruntled outsiders. Their acceptance of the war's outcome, because it was to their benefit, meant that their publics could accept that outcome as well. If, however, a whole generation of these "national" leaders would have been excluded from positions of national power they might have made serious efforts to encourage separatist sentiments among the Southern people.

Federalism as the basis for reunion offered the North certain advantages as well. Northerners could afford to accept the Southerners as partners in a restored union while closing their eyes to the latter's insistence on the perpetuation of the Southern myth within it. In this way, they could avoid the necessity of enforcing an impossible orthodoxy on the vanquished or the alternative of denying themselves the fruits of their victory. Moreover, once they had tired of ruling the South, they had little choice but to restore to the residents of that section the degree of self-government needed to satisfy their political demands as Americans.

VII

No conscious decision to restore the federal system had to be made because the federal principle was so deeply embedded in the American consensus. This consensus, which gives form to the basic ideals of the American people and translates them into terms which are manageable in the maintenance of a political system, is most immediately a procedural one. That is to say, Americans agree on the rules of the game and through them are able to make their political system work. But the consensus goes beyond the procedural in two ways. First of all, Americans agree on the nature of the game to be played. So, for example, Americans agree that every four years there shall be a presidential election and that the winner shall take office freely, but they agree to this because of a prior agreement that there is a virtue in a kind of government which limits the tenure of presidents and requires them to be chosen by the people in a fair contest—in short, in a kind of democratic government. Without the second level of agreement, the first would not long survive.

Beyond that second level, there is still a third. Ultimately Americans are tied together by a common perception of the nature of man and government that leads them to "consent" to democracy. There is some question in this writer's mind as to how concrete this ultimate consensus—which is a highly substantive consensus indeed— must be. It may be that it need only take on a certain very general content. It is reasonably certain that it must remain open to broad variations in interpretations—up to some limit. It was the breakdown of this third level of consensus which led to the Civil War and it was its restoration that made the restoration of the federal system possible.

The American consensus is, in its ultimate ideational form, a federal consensus. This may seem to be a surprising statement to those schooled only in the terminology of today. The definition of federalism commonly used by students of government today has diminished the original meaning of the term, to make it virtually synonymous with intergovernmental relations. This is not how federalism was conceived by American political theorists in the past. There is some evidence to show that it is not how the American people conceive of the federal principle today, except that they do not articulate their conception and it is commensurately difficult to isolate.

The term *federal*, which was not invented until the beginning of the modern era, (it was first used in 1645) is derived from the Latin word meaning covenant. Originally a theological concept which described the basic relationship between man and God, by extension it also defined the proper relationship between man and man. In the time of the founding fathers, it was used to describe an arrangement or system (not necessarily political) created by free men who freely entered into a lasting yet limited compact to achieve certain ends or to protect certain rights. Though the federal compact might be perpetual, it not only guaranteed the unity of the whole in perpetuity but also the integrity of the parts. In this, the federal principle stands as the very antithesis of the totalitarian conception of an organic society based on some general will which inheres in the society regardless of the rights or interests of the individuals who (or the communities which) compose it and which takes full precedence over all its individual parts.

Thus federalism stands in contradistinction to collectivism which is based on the myth of the organic society. The great myth of federalism is that society is a compact between individuals, a compact that is binding, lasting, permanent, but one which by its very nature recognizes the value of individual liberty and the legitimacy of the survival of the parties to it as separate entities with inalienable rights.

With this understanding of the federal principle in mind, we can understand the social compact theories of the founding fathers more clearly. We can understand how it was natural for the founders to transform the idea of a social compact among individuals establishing a civil society into the idea of a similar compact among individuals and states establishing a federal union. We can also understand how the federal principle, which Americans have applied in some way to almost every aspect of their public life, would be so strong in 1865 that it could override the pressures of civil war to restore the "federal" rights of the vanquished, thus preserving its political manifestation in an "indestructible Union of indestructible States."

FEDERAL-STATE COLLABORATION IN THE NINETEENTH-CENTURY UNITED STATES *

FEDERALISM: COOPERATIVE OR DUAL

THE operation of the American federal system in the nineteenth century has been the subject of much discussion and some examination since the New Deal and the so-called "rise of cooperative federalism." It has generally been assumed that federalism in practice, like federalism in theory in the nineteenth century (which is here taken to include the entire period between 1790 and 1913) has been dual federalism, in which the federal and state governments pursued virtually independent courses of action during a period when government activity was, in any case, minimal.[1]

Dual federalism has been defined by Clark, among many others, as "two separate federal and state streams flowing in distinct but closely parallel channels." Perhaps the best definition of the term was that given by Chief Justice Roger B. Taney in the name of the United States Supreme Court, in *Ableman* v. *Booth* (21 Howard 506), at the height of the era

* This essay is based on a study of intergovernmental collaboration in the nineteenth-century United States, conducted under the auspices of the Workshop in American Federalism, University of Chicago, and financed by the Ford Foundation. The major product of the study is the writer's book, *The American Partnership* (Chicago, 1962) which presents the data summarized below in greater depth and detail. Particular acknowledgment is due the Institute of Government and Public Affairs, University of Illinois, which provided me the time and facilities with which to prepare this essay.

1 This thesis has been most persuasively stated by George C. S. Benson in *The New Centralization* (New York, 1941) and Jane Perry Clark in *The Rise of a New Federalism* (New York, 1938), and has been repeated by such eminent authorities as Arthur N. Holcombe in *Our More Perfect Union* (Cambridge, Mass., 1950). A variant thesis, which argues that federal-state administrative cooperation existed in the early days of the Republic and was then replaced by strict dual federalism, has been advanced by Edward S. Corwin (inventor of the term "dual federalism") in *The Twilight of the Supreme Court* (New Haven, 1934) and in other books and by Leonard D. White in his great four-volume study of American administrative history, *The Federalists* (New York, 1948), *The Jeffersonians* (New York, 1951), *The Jacksonians* (New York, 1954) and *The Republican Era* (New York, 1958).

of dual federalism, in 1858: "The powers of the general government, and of the state, although both exist and are exercised within the same territorial limits, are yet separate and distinct sovereignties, acting separately and independently of each other, within their respective spheres." Dual federalism as a doctrine has been expounded at various times by presidents of the United States (particularly while vetoing federal aid measures); [2] by the United States Supreme Court (particularly in opinions restricting the powers of government—federal or state—to act); [3] by spokesmen for the South (particularly when justifying slavery, segregation, or secession); [4] and by conservative business interests (particularly when seeking to avoid government regulation). The doctrine has been expounded as representing classic American federalism so long and so forcefully that it has been accepted, by students of American institutions and others, as fact.

The central hypothesis of this study is that the traditional picture of nineteenth-century American federalism is unreal, that federalism in the United States, in practice if not in theory, has traditionally been cooperative, so that virtually all the activities of government in the nineteenth century were shared activities, involving federal, state, and local governments in their planning, financing, and execution. The pattern of sharing in American federalism was established, in its essentials, in the first decades after the adoption of the Constitution. This study seeks to explain how that pattern has continued to evolve since then. Its central conclusions are that the theory of dual federalism was not viable when applied to concrete governmental problems in specific situations even in the early days of the Republic; that dual federalism when interpreted to mean demarcation of responsibilities and functions has never worked in practice; and that,

280

2 See James D. Richardson (ed.), *Messages and Papers of the Presidents* (Washington, D. C., 1908), for exemplary statements by Thomas Jefferson, James Madison, James Monroe, Andrew Jackson, Franklin Pierce, James Buchanan, and Grover Cleveland, among others.

3 See, for example, *Collector* v. *Day* (11 Wallace 113), the Slaughterhouse Cases (16 Wallace 36), *Munn* v. *Illinois* (94 U.S. 113), *Hammer* v. *Dagenhart* (247 U.S. 251), and *Ponzi* v. *Fessendan, et al.* (258 U.S. 254).

4 The classic statement of the Southern viewpoint is that of Alexander H. Stephens, *A Constitutional View of the War Between the States* (Philadelphia, 1868).

while the amount of governmental activity on all planes in
relation to the total activity of American society (the "velocity of government") has increased, the governmental activity
that existed in the nineteenth century was shared in much
the same manner as governmental activity in the twentieth
century. All this is true despite formal pronouncements to
the contrary, made by the political leadership of the day
who spoke in terms of demarcation but practiced cooperation.

THE ELEMENTS OF COOPERATIVE FEDERALISM

The roots of cooperative federalism are entwined with the
roots of federalism itself. It was during the colonial period
that the four elements which later coalesced to form the pattern of intergovernmental cooperation first appeared on the
American scene. Among these elements were a federalist
theory of government,[5] a dual governmental structure, some
specific cooperative programs, and some administrative techniques for intergovernmental collaboration.[6]

These four elements of theory, structure, program, and
technique can be traced through the subsequent evolution of
the American governmental partnership. They were first
combined under a general American government by the
Second Continental Congress after the declaration of American independence in 1776. Consequently, the patterns of
intergovernmental cooperation that developed informally
during the Revolutionary War antedate even the Articles of
Confederation. That document, the first written constitution of the United States, implicitly provided for collaboration in a manner highly reminiscent of the then recently
sundered relationship between colonies and crown, as it had
been viewed in American political theory and as it was embodied in the structure of colonial government institutions.

[5] For a discussion of this theory of federalism, see Carl Becker, *The
Declaration of Independence* (New York, 1958), Chap. III. Part of the theoretical debate over the nature of the British Empire prior to 1776 centered
on specific cases of parliamentary agents engaging in unconstitutional uni-
lateral action within the colonies rather than conforming to the constitutional patterns of crown-colonial cooperation as they were conceived by the
colonists, though the discussions were not phrased in those terms.

[6] For a discussion of land grants in the colonial period, see Mathias N.
Orfield, *Federal Land Grants to the States, With Special Reference to Minnesota* (Minneapolis, 1915), Part I, 5–30.

Even the programs requiring collaboration (defense, taxation) were much the same. With the development of a national policy of grants-in-aid based on the Western lands in the Northwest Ordinances of 1785 and 1787, the creation of the Confederation-sponsored Bank of North America in 1784, and the general reliance of the Confederation Congress on state officials to execute its actions, the colonial techniques of collaboration were also embraced by the Confederation.

It is unquestionably true that collaboration under the Articles was over-dependent on the actions of the states and often failed in practice. This was, of course, purposely changed with the adoption of the Constitution in 1789 and in the course of its translation into action during Washington's first administration. While the "intentions of the framers" are always subject to dispute, it seems safe to say that the Constitution is oriented to neither cooperative nor dual federalism per se. It provides for dual institutions, some cooperative programs, and a wide range of concurrent powers which can either be divided between the federal government and the states or shared by them in various cooperative programs. By and large, the decision of the American people has not been to separate functions by government but to maintain dual institutions which share responsibility for the implementation of specific functions. This "decision" has not been made through a prior conscious design but through a continuous series of specific decisions involving concrete programs. The continuing evolution of the theories, structures, programs, and techniques of the federalism that emerged from this process is what we today term cooperative federalism.

THE ARCHITECTS OF COOPERATIVE FEDERALISM

Just as the founding fathers did not perceive the future role of political parties in the United States, it seems that they did not plan on the development of cooperative federalism as we know it. The majority of the theoretically-oriented founding fathers either viewed the federal system as dual and separate with the states having the dominant role and the powers of the federal government confined to those objects specifically enumerated in the Constitution or as one in which the national government would have the dominant

role while the states were to become relatively weak reposi-
tories of residual local powers.

The men who became the architects of American federalism did not view the federal system as one in which there
was to be either a perpetual struggle between the federal
and state governments for dominance or an irrevocable separation of their respective functions for the sake of amity
between them. Avoiding the premises of legalistic thought,
they did not view the two planes as rivals, but as partners
in government who were to share responsibility for a wide
range of activities for the mutual benefit of the nation as a
whole and for its constituent states.

These architects did not leave a formally organized and
recognized body of theory behind them because they wrote
of their theories almost exclusively in response to specific
practical problems. Nevertheless, examination of their official reports and other documents which they produced during their public careers does reveal some coherent patterns
of thought on the proper nature and goals of American federalism.[7]

Foremost among the men who led the movement toward
intergovernmental cooperation to meet the problems of a
dynamic society were Albert Gallatin and John C. Calhoun,
who pioneered the formulation and implementation of cooperative programs during the first four decades of the Republic. Aside from these two principal architects of American federalism, many people made major contributions to
the development of the federal system as we know it. Other
top-ranking officials in the federal executive branch, particularly in the Treasury, War, and Interior Departments, led
the federal government into the field of specific cooperative
activities when cooperation, as such, was not popular as a
doctrine. The professionals in the federal and state govern-

283

[7] Some of the most important of these documents setting forth the cooperative approach are: Albert Gallatin, "Report on Roads and Canals,"
American State Papers: Miscellaneous, I, 724–921 (April 4, 1808); John C.
Calhoun, "Report on Roads and Canals, Communicated to the House of
Representatives, January 14, 1819," in Calhoun, *Works* (New York, 1855), V,
40–54; Calhoun, "Report on the Condition of the Military Establishment
and Fortifications, Communicated to Congress by the President, December
7, 1824," *ibid.*, 141; Mahlon Dickerson, *Report on the President's Message
as Respects the Distribution of the United States Surplus*, 21st Congress, 1st
Session, December 1830.

ments, who were interested in promoting specific programs for the benefit of the whole nation and its constituent parts, provided cadres for the initiation and implementation of cooperative programs in undramatic ways while the rest of the country virtually ignored them and the governments they served. The advocates of specific programs, who were not in or of government at any level but who wanted to see the development of certain public activities at all levels (or regardless of level), provided a basis for the mobilization of popular support in those cases where government did take part. Finally, much of the development of the system was stimulated by the members of the Congress of the United States and the several state legislatures who, because of their interest in the general welfare or as an outgrowth of their local concerns, supported intergovernmental cooperation in those fields of endeavor which seemed most necessary to them despite an overall theoretical disposition to limit government in general and to separate by level those few activities that were considered to be of legitimate governmental concern.

COOPERATIVE FEDERALISM BETWEEN 1789 AND 1848

American federalism has evolved over three historical periods, all bound together by the thread of intergovernmental collaboration. A strong case can be made to demonstrate that the three periods of federalism correspond to the three major periods in post-colonial American history generally. The particular characteristics of federalism in these three periods can be identified by the forms of intergovernmental collaboration that predominated in each, though in every period the other forms of cooperation existed alongside the predominant ones. The difference between the three periods is not a difference in the nature of intergovernmental cooperation but in the predominant forms by which such cooperation was effected.

The first period encompassed the formative years of the American nation and its federal system, including the Revolutionary and Federalist eras, the flourishing and subsequent decline of the Jeffersonians, and the rise of "Jacksonian Democracy." When it came to a close in the mid-eighteen-forties, the United States had fought its second war of independence, turned its back on Europe to concentrate on westward expansion, and was just completing the continental expansion of the nation's boundaries.

This was also the period in which the mercantilist orientation of the American economy which openly allotted to government a major share in the economic development of the nation persisted and finally declined, to be replaced by the laissez-faire persuasion which, at least in theory, denied government any but a minimal role.[8] In fact, the last decade of this period was marked by the fluidity and confusion characteristic of a change in eras, both in the economic and governmental realms, since the changes in the forms of federalism coincided with the changes in economic organization.

This first period contributed refined versions of the vital ideas of natural law and constitutionalism to the American mystique, as expressed in the basic documents that emerged from the Revolutionary era. As part of this set of ideas, the concepts of federalism were defined and refined as well. Dominant in this formative period were the activities of the major architects of pre-twentieth-century cooperative federalism, Gallatin near the beginning and Calhoun near the end.

The major vehicles of intergovernmental cooperation in this period were the joint stock company (in which federal, state, and local governments, as well as private parties, joined to invest in corporations established to undertake specific projects, usually in the realm of internal improvements and banking) for long-term cooperative projects, and the cooperative survey (in which the federal government would send or lend Army Engineers to the states to survey and plan internal improvement projects) coupled with the widespread use of federal technicians by the states as a means of providing federal services-in-aid to the latter. During this period the majority of the states then in the Union did not have extensive federal lands within their boundaries, so the tone of cooperation was set by programs designed for the states without public lands. Cooperation in the field of banking was the most formally structured on a nationwide basis. Internal improvement programs usually involved formal arrangements, but were almost always tailored to specific situations

285

---

[8] For a discussion of the mercantilist approach in American political economy during this period, see Curtis P. Nettels, "British Mercantilism and the Economic Development of the Thirteen Colonies," *The Journal of Economic History*, XII (1952), 105–14.

in each state and even for each project. Federal aid to education was vital, but generally consisted of "back-door financing" through federal "reimbursement" of certain state-incurred expenditures with the implicit understanding that the funds would be used for education. The major continuing programmatic concerns of American government had already emerged during the first period. They were the extension of internal improvements, the maintenance of a sound nationwide fiscal system, the establishment of appropriate educational facilities, and, to a more limited extent, the provision of necessary public welfare aids.

In the field of internal improvements, the first period was given over, in the main, to water transportation, primarily through canals, and, to a lesser extent, to overland transportation via wagon roads. One of the best examples of federal-state collaboration in canal construction was the opening of the Dismal Swamp Canal, connecting Norfolk, Virginia, with Albemarle Sound in North Carolina. In 1816, after several abortive local attempts to construct a canal through the Great Dismal Swamp of Virginia, the State of Virginia joined the State of North Carolina, the City of Norfolk, and private investors in the creation of a joint stock company to implement a canal plan prepared by the Army Engineers in 1808 as part of a national blueprint for internal improvement.

Informal cooperation between state and federal officials was developed to advance construction. This included federal assistance in securing a supervising engineer for the state (1816), as well as a second survey by qualified federal engineers (1817). This cooperation involved the highest administrative levels of both the federal government and the state, including the President of the United States; the Secretaries of State, Treasury, and War; the diplomatic corps; government bureaus such as the Army Engineers, the governor of Virginia, his agents, and the Virginia Board of Public Works. Some of this cooperation came about through direct interlevel contracts made through the normal administrative channels. Part of it came about through the state officials' use of the services of their senators and representatives in Washington.

Ten years later, despite the company's efforts and further informal federal-state collaboration, the canal had still to be completed. Despite periodic state subsidies, the company still lacked the requisite funds. In 1826, the Virginians, with the active assistance of the War Department, were able to persuade Congress to invest $150,000 in the project and, in that way, to acquire 600 (out of a total of 1,240) shares in the company. Once the federal government became a partner in the enterprise, it provided the additional professional and administrative services, as well as the needed funds, for the completion of the project. Despite the oratorical denunciations of "states'-rights" Virginians, this federal "intervention" succeeded in bringing the canal to a state of readiness by 1828. For the next three decades the federal government and the State of Virginia continued their cooperative efforts to maintain and improve the canal. Though the formally cooperative aspects of the program came to an end with the coming of the Civil War, the canal is still in use as an important part of the intracoastal waterway system.

287

Closer examination of the details of this program reveals the three major areas of federal-state cooperation characteristic in projects of this nature: construction of the canal, maintenance and improvement of its facilities, and control over the administration of its operations. The first two areas involved both fiscal aid and the services of governmental personnel. The third involved cooperation between federal and state officials. While the federal government did not become a full partner in this enterprise until it was already under construction, once it did enter the partnership its role became a crucial and even dominant one. Yet this did not come about through the lessening of the state's power but through a coincidence of interest (often made explicit in the correspondence between state and federal officials at the time) between the state and federal governments. To ensure this coincidence of interest the state as a whole and the locality involved both had means of influencing federal policy and actions through their senators and representatives.

Administration of the canal was a joint federal-state venture. The federal executive delegated the power of proxy (to represent the federal interest in the project's administration) to the Collector of the Port of Norfolk and detailed other federal personnel to aid in the construction of the canal. The state executive, pursuant to earlier acts of the

Legislature, provided for the State Board of Public Works to act as proxies and supervisors for the state which, through its greater direct role in the company (which was a quasi-official state agency) became primarily responsible for actual construction. Cooperative procedures were then developed by the two sets of officials involved. Construction and, later, maintenance proceeded under the direction of the company, supervised by the State Board of Public Works and utilizing federal engineers and equipment. The company reported to the state and to the federal government and the State Board also reported to the Treasury and War Departments. Company policy was decided by its board of directors dominated by the United States and the State of Virginia, whose representatives operated in concert within a community of interest. The few attempts to change company policy that were made were in every case directed against both governments by the non-governmental shareholders rather than by one against the other.

The case of the Dismal Swamp Canal is typical. By the third decade of the nineteenth century, the pattern of intergovernmental cooperation was already clear in projects such as this one, of which there were many. Changes were indeed made in subsequent years but they were changes designed to improve the mechanisms rather than to modify the basic relationships. While federal control over standards tended to grow, state control over processes grew as a counterbalance.

Collaboration under the Constitution in the fiscal field may be said to have begun with federal assumption of the states' Revolutionary War debts in 1790. During the seventeen-nineties, federal reimbursement of state debts already paid, coupled with the sale of state lands, furnished sufficient income for most of the states to maintain themselves without resorting to taxation.[9] Though the level of state governmental activities was low prior to 1816, the states began to develop a tradition of spending money with relatively little responsibility for raising revenues. This was coupled with a developing, albeit unrecognized, reliance on the federal government for funds to initiate and support the major pro-

[9] William J. Shultz and M. R. Caine, *Financial Development of the United States* (New York, 1937), 117–18.

grams of each era. While it may be argued that the reimbursement funds "rightfully" belonged to the states in the first place, in the last analysis they came from the federal treasury and were used for projects which the states would not have been able to finance alone because of local opposition to increased taxation.

Two other major cooperative fiscal programs were established by the first Congress. The first involved the levying of a direct tax among the states, which were given quotas based on the constitutional formula and required to raise and deliver the taxes to the federal government. Direct taxes were levied in the above manner intermittently over the next century. The second program involved the inauguration of a central banking system for the United States through the chartering of the first Bank of the United States as a federal-controlled agency.

289

Federal involvement in the banking system is almost as old as banking as an institution in this country. When the first Bank of the United States was established in 1791, only four other banks existed in the entire United States and one of these four, the Bank of North America, had been chartered by the Confederation Congress as a quasi-national bank.[10]

In the early period, the great majority of banks were either state-owned, joint stock companies in which the state was a major shareholder, or controlled by the state through special charter provisions. The Bank of the United States, a government-controlled bank under federal auspices, served as the fiscal and banking arm of the federal government and manager of the federal deposits. In this capacity it dominated the American financial scene prior to 1800. According to Shultz and Caine, "Through its branch organization it cooperated with and to some extent controlled the newly-created state banks throughout the country."[11]

Under this first and subsequent national banking programs, a significant amount of intergovernmental cooperation developed. Some of this cooperation was formally written into law by both nation and state, while some of it evolved informally in response to obvious situations and

[10] Bray Hammond, *Banks and Politics in America, from the Revolution to the Civil War* (Princeton, 1957), 144.

[11] Shultz and Caine, 125.

needs. The directors of the Bank, which was located in Philadelphia, did not originally intend to establish branches in other parts of the country, but pressures from stockholders in other cities soon forced them into widespread branch banking, primarily because so few banks existed outside of the Northeast. Four branches were opened in the spring of 1792 after some attempts were made to absorb the four existing state banks. This latter move was resisted by many of the same people who had previously supported creation of the national bank against those who felt it to be a threat to states' rights as well as a corrupting influence in an agrarian society. Just as they recognized the need for some centralized banking institution, they also feared too much centralization and resisted any attempts to eliminate the system of dual institutions which makes cooperative federalism possible.

290

The United States Bank soon began to function as a clearing house and source of capital for the various state banks, as well as serving as fiscal arm of the federal government. As such it was accepted as an asset by the more conservative banks and as an undesired threat by the more reckless and speculative ones. Hammond describes its operation in these words:

> Being the main government depository and having offices in the principal commercial cities, the Bank was the general creditor of the other banks. It had the account of the largest single transactor in the economy—the federal government— and the receipts of the government being mostly in the notes of state banks and these notes being deposited in the Bank, it could not help being their creditor. By pressing them for payment of the notes and checks received against them, the Bank automatically exercised a general restraint on the banking system. . . . This restraint upon bank lending came later to be designated central bank control of credit.[12]

Congress allowed the Bank's charter to expire in 1811, despite administration support for its renewal, as a result of the opposition generated by a coalition of extreme states'-rights conservatives and spokesmen for Eastern businessmen interested in speculation on the frontier, where less control over fiscal matters would aid their highly speculative ventures. As in the debate of 1791 and in many subsequent debates

[12] Hammond, 198–99.

over similar subjects, the arguments this coalition used against the Bank were those of constitutionality, but the motivations were those of business. On the other hand, the new agrarians, primarily Westerners, wanted to maintain the National Bank precisely because the state banks had already proved their inability to meet what were, in essence, national needs, in particular those related to westward expansion.

The nation soon discovered how useful the central bank had been. The War of 1812 brought with it serious fiscal problems for the federal government and the states, many of which could have been avoided had a central bank been in existence. In 1816 Congress reversed itself and voted the establishment of the second Bank of the United States. The reversal was made possible by a parting of the speculator–states'-rights coalition. While the speculators continued to oppose central banking as interfering with their opportunity to manipulate the nation's fiscal affairs, a number of states'-rights advocates supported the new federal bank as an aid to the states in their struggle, often against the speculation interests, for fiscal solvency. They were led to take this position as a result of the contrast between their experiences with the intergovernmental collaboration that had developed between the states and the first Bank and their experiences with "free" banking between 1811 and 1816. Indeed, their major demand in preparing the charter for the second Bank was that its collaborative aspects be strengthened. Cooperative federalism in the banking field was already being used to develop a system in which the duty and ability of the states to take action was both stimulated and guaranteed by the federal government.

The most forceful argument for federal responsibility in monetary matters, from the constitutional point of view, came from John C. Calhoun, who had assumed Gallatin's role as leading architect of cooperative federalism in his generation. His statement, in this case as in so many others, has a most modern ring. It was Calhoun's view that when any private enterprise (in this case the financial interests) grows strong enough to exercise a power granted to the federal government under the Constitution (in this case, control over the soundness of the currency) it must be subject to regulation in the public interest. This regulation is best

291

achieved by reassumption of the power by the federal government, in the interests of the public and of the states.[13]

The charter that was finally enacted made it quite clear that the second Bank was a continuation of the first. Thus it may be said that the same national banking system served the country for forty of the forty-five years between 1791 and 1836. The new charter gave the federal government the power to require the Bank to establish at least one branch in each state, under certain conditions. In addition, the bank was specifically designated as the principal depository of the United States Treasury, though the state banks, which had inherited the federal deposits after the demise of the first Bank, under a different cooperative program were allowed to keep some deposits because they were so dependent on them to stay solvent.

Even without the National Bank, cooperative relationships had developed between the U. S. Treasury and the state banks. The latter served as federal depositories and disbursing agents during periods when the National Bank did not exist and also parallel to it when it did. As long as the mercantilist view of the role of government in the economy prevailed for a majority of the nation, this cooperation continued. It was only when this view was abandoned due to changing times that the forms of cooperation created under it became inadequate.

After 1828 the operations of the U. S. Bank centered around forcing the state banks to adopt more conservative banking practices. This attempt came just as the more radical and speculative business elements were attaining political power under the Jacksonian Democracy. As a result, their cries that the Bank was strangling business expansion in the interests of a few wealthy Eastern capitalists fell on willing ears and doomed the second Bank in much the same manner as the first had been. Even so, the political struggle that led to Jackson's veto of the recharter bill in 1832 sealed the fate of the Bank more because of conflicts between persons in the political arena than for reasons of principle, and certainly did not imply a rejection of federal-state collaboration.

Beginning in 1833 the $6,500,000 in federal deposits were gradually withdrawn as the funds were spent (gradually, to

[13] Calhoun, *Works*, II, *passim*.

prevent a sudden collapse of the nation's finances, a tribute to the role played by the Bank as the central force in the national monetary system). Newly received funds were deposited in the state banks once again, as they had been after the demise of the first Bank, where they remained until the establishment of independent federal depositories in the eighteen-forties.

The first century of the American Republic witnessed a struggle between advocates of a national banking system designed to bring some measure of national order to the fiscal scene and advocates of maximum local control over the money system. For forty years prior to the administration of Andrew Jackson, the nationalists were successful in perpetuating a centralized, cooperative, banking system. In the eighteen-thirties the tide turned and the localists were able to decentralize the system. During the Civil War, the passage of the National Banking Act of 1863 signified another turn in the direction of order through the creation of a uniform national currency and nationally applied bank standards which in themselves gave rise to a new cooperative regulatory program in which the federal and state governments shared in the regulation of the newly created national banks. Finally, the creation of the Federal Reserve System in 1913 brought both the national and local approaches together in a workable compromise.

293

Collaboration in the field of education in the states without public lands was less direct in the early period. Before 1837, one major means by which federal assistance for the establishment of public schools was made available was through the reimbursement process. It has already been indicated that federal assumption of the states' Revolutionary War debts and the general government's reimbursement of those debts already paid by the states provided the bulk of the states' revenues prior to the War of 1812. During that conflict, and subsequent ones through the Spanish-American War, the federal government again had to rely upon the states for a major share of the immediate financing of the nation's war effort. Whenever necessary, the states raised, equipped, and supplied their troops with the promise of federal reimbursement after the cessation of hostilities. While the War of 1812 marked the high point in the role of the states in financing a war effort, reimbursable state defense expenditures continued to be made for Indian conflicts, international border disputes, and even for major national wars, throughout the nineteenth century.

Federal reimbursement of war expenditures provided the states with larger amounts of revenue for use in providing domestic services than would otherwise have been possible for the states to raise through universally unpopular taxation. Furthermore, in the negotiations for reimbursement, the states' Washington agents and congressional delegations were often able to have expenditures of less than strict legitimacy included in the final accounting. This was possible because it soon became widely understood and accepted that federal reimbursement funds would be used by the states wholly or partly to finance the establishment of free public educational systems. Here, as in the case of internal improvement and fiscal organization, the problem of education was simultaneously of both local and nationwide concern and, consequently, was attacked by all planes of government. In the public land states, the federal-state-local partnership could operate through the medium of the land grant by which the federal government provided potentially handsome endowments for public education from elementary school through the university. Constitutional scruples on the part of a strong and determined minority prevented the direct, overt extension of federal aid to those states without public lands. However, since the felt need for federal assistance and stimulation in the field of education remained, the reimbursement system was seized upon to provide an acceptable alternative to formal grants-in-aid.

Thus it was that the states would file claims for reimbursement with the War Department, with the necessary substantiating documents, and then would secure congressional approval for any out-of-the-ordinary claims by letting it be understood that the funds involved would be used to promote education, often through the creation of a permanent fund that would provide annual benefits. In some states, such as Virginia, the interest on the invested reimbursement funds provided the state's sole contribution to public education for decades. Even in New England they were influential and important, particularly in stimulating the states to

enforce their own compulsory school laws which were often
ignored when left entirely to the local communities.

In 1837, the United States Treasury surplus was distributed among the states by a formula based on each state's
population. While the strict constructionists prevented formal earmarking, a provision was inserted in the act of Congress making the distribution a loan and providing for recall
of the funds should the federal government deem it advisable
(that is, if the funds were used by the states for purposes
other than the two implicit options of education or internal
improvement). Though the Panic of 1837 ended the surplus distribution in less than a year, and the one attempt to
revive it in 1841 also failed in a year's time, the amount of
funds accruing to the more populous Eastern states did much
to offset the national imbalance that resulted from federal
grant-in-land assistance to the Western states. Furthermore,
by federal and state law as well as through local custom, the
surplus distribution monies, like the proceeds of the land
grants (and, in most cases, the reimbursements), were placed
in earmarked permanent investment funds whose incomes
were used for the support of education year after year. In a
majority of the states, these permanent funds have remained
in existence, albeit with the original federal funds diluted
by other increments. During the nineteenth century they
became administrative devices which stretched the impact of
federal aid to education over the years, renewed its impact
annually, and gave the states a lever by which to gain control
over school systems and educational endeavors in order to
raise educational standards.

While social welfare programs were fewer in the early
period, significant advances in that field were also made
through federal-state-local collaboration. A few examples
will suffice. Government support for education for the handicapped had its origins in the Hartford Asylum for the Deaf
and Dumb founded in 1817 under private, church-supported,
auspices and transformed into a public institution in 1819
through a federal land grant and cooperative arrangements
with the six New England states. The successful federal-
state partnership in this pilot project stimulated the creation
of schools for the deaf and dumb in other sections of the nation. The drive for better treatment for the insane led to

295

the development of state insane asylums in the mid-nineteenth century, many of which were initially constructed through the use of federal land grants, reimbursement funds, or the surplus distribution. Veterans of the nation's wars were awarded lands, the pre-Civil War equivalent of pensions, through federal-state cooperative projects. Less formally, a network of marine hospitals for the nation's seamen was constructed and maintained along the sea coasts and inland waterways by joint federal-state action. Each of these early welfare programs involved not only a sharing of fiscal responsibility, but the development of routinized administrative collaboration to bring the programs to fruition. It was this routinized administrative collaboration which set the tone and the pace for cooperative federalism in the period.

296

COOPERATIVE FEDERALISM BETWEEN 1848 AND 1913

The landmark that comes closest to marking the end of the formative period and the beginning of the second era in American federalism was the Mexican War. After the war the questions of manifest destiny, commercial expansion, and political democracy that had provided the impetus for government activities during the first period gave way to concern over slavery, industrialization, and the settlement of the newly acquired Far West, opening up a new set of problems for government.

While the great land grant programs which dominated the second period were created during the formative period, and even antedated the other forms of cooperation, they were almost entirely confined to the public land states, which did not become major factors on the American political scene until the Age of Jackson and did not begin to set the national pace until the middle of the nineteenth century. The second period can be considered to begin from the time when land grant programs became the predominant form of intergovernmental cooperation, that is, when their impact on government became greater than any other form of cooperative federalism and other forms of cooperation began to be measured in relation to the level of collaboration in the public land states. The transition from the formative period began during the Jackson administration, with the demise of the U. S. Bank, the greatest of all the joint stock companies, and the distribution of the surplus revenue in 1837 which was partly designed to balance the land grants to the Western states. By mid-century, the states admitted to the Union after ratification of the Constitution outnumbered the original thirteen. Though not all of the former were public land states, the majority shared in the problems of the West. They provided the support necessary for the establishment of the land grant as a major means of implementing national policy. The Land Grant College Act of 1862 marks the triumph of this policy, in that it was applied without distinction to all the states, east and west.

The second period lasted for the remainder of the nineteenth century. During this period the patterns of American democracy evolved after 1775 were subjected to their greatest domestic tests. In the political realm, there was the challenge of classical states'-rights, secession, disunion, and reconstruction. In the economic realm the complex of radical individualist and anti-government doctrines known as laissez-faire was the order of the day. The slavery issue and its outgrowth, segregation of the Negroes, tore at the fabric of American democratic ideals. Politically, this was the Republican era. The Democratic party, in power as the nation's majority party at mid-century, was already declining. During the first decade of the second period, the Republican party wooed and won more or less of a majority of the voters who turned to it as the best vehicle available to respond to the era's major issues. Though challenged by Populists from its own ranks and by a Democracy led by the resurgent South, the Republican party managed to maintain its position throughout the period.

Between 1848 and 1913 the hope of the American people lay in the West as never before or since. The West, whatever it may have been in reality, became the shining haven of the American dream. It was this period that added the refined idea of the frontier to the American mystique and, in reality, it was in the West that cooperative federalism flourished and matured. The great land grant programs set the tone for intergovernmental cooperation in the older states because of their expansion in the new ones. Uniformly structured land grants for internal improvements and

297

education dominated the stage, supplemented by various types of federal subsidies, new cooperative developments in the regulatory field, and by an increasing amount of informal cooperation among professionals on all levels of government. Through the land grant the impact of the federal government was felt in almost every field of activity throughout the West and in most of the East.

During the second period, as in the first, problems of internal improvement, fiscal organization, education, and public welfare were the dominant continuing concerns of government on all planes. However, during this period, there was a paradoxical intensification of support for the theory of dual federalism simultaneous with a sharpening of the structures and techniques of cooperative federalism and an expansion of collaborative programs into new fields.

298

The actual transfer of federal lands to the states under the terms of a grant-in-land was begun in 1802, with Ohio's achievement of statehood. Under the terms of the Northwest Ordinance of 1785, Ohio received a grant of one section of land per township, designed to go directly for the establishment and support of public schools. This school grant was subsequently extended, with some modifications, to every new public land state. Experience soon demonstrated that the purposes of the grant would be better achieved if it were administered by the states rather than by local government and if a minimum price for the lands were established in the federal grant. The grant was also expanded to include up to four sections per township by the end of the century. Later conditions imposed by Congress included the requirement that any lands sold be disposed of at advertised public sales only.

This first land grant program contained within it the seeds of many of the principles and procedures that were evolved in later federal grants-in-aid, both land and cash. The grant was a general one, applicable to all states carved out of the public domain as a matter of course, though, because it was applied to new states only as they were organized, specific legislation was necessary to apply the grant in each case. The amount of the grant was set down in the general law and was uniform for all the states organized while the general law was in effect. Finally, the grant was not a gift. It came with specific conditions attached, including an obligation on the part of the state to create township or state-administered permanent trust funds based on the proceeds of the sale or leasing of the granted lands to be used exclusively for the promotion of public elementary education and an obligation on the part of the federal government to provide indemnity lands where the designated school sections were otherwise pre-empted. It is true that the conditions attached to this first grant were rudimentary; however, these rudimentary conditions were expanded and tightened as experience proved necessary.

Ohio also received the first land grants for higher education and for internal improvements. As the first state to be carved out of the federal public domain, it was the testing ground for many of the early land grant programs. Yet Ohio was only the first of the thirty public land states to receive grants-in-land for programs falling within the scope of all four continuing concerns of government. Of the other twenty states, all, with the possible exception of Hawaii, have received land grants for programs in two or more categories. It would not be amiss to say that virtually every major governmental function in the public land states benefited from federal land grants directly or indirectly. The grants directly stimulated, financed, or helped to finance vital governmental operations. Indirectly, the pervasiveness of the public domain, and the need for its proper disposition to enable a state to grow, served to involve the state government either formally or informally through the political process in all federal land activities that took place within its boundaries. In this manner the public domain came to serve as the integrating factor in the development of cooperative action between the federal government and the states.

Federal land distribution programs fell into three basic categories. First was the system of land grants made by the federal government to the various states to aid them in developing education, internal improvement, and welfare programs. Over the years grants were made to the states for elementary education, higher education, general internal improvements, land reclamation, river and harbor improvements, public buildings, public institutions, and veterans' benefits. These grants were designed to make basic contri-

299

butions to the growth of vital public services in the various states in a manner closely resembling the monetary grants-in-aid of the twentieth century.

There was also a system of federal land grants for education and internal improvements made through the states to private companies, primarily for roads, canals, and railroads, but also for academies and colleges. Under such arrangements, the states became the implementing agencies for the federal government administering the distribution and proper use of the grants.

Finally there were the federal programs designed to dispose of the public domain without formally including the states. These programs in the main consisted of the various homestead, mineral, and tree culture acts; grants to certain Western railroads primarily situated outside of state boundaries at the time of the grants; and some townsite and local improvement grants that generally were made to embryonic towns prior to statehood. Even those programs did not function outside of the sphere of federal-state cooperation, since the states either developed concurrent "matching" programs of their own which were then coordinated with the federal grants or were able to gain a say in the formulation and execution of the federal programs through their influence in Congress.

The real import of cooperative federalism in the second period can best be understood when the full impact of federal-aided programs in a single state is assessed as a unified whole. Minnesota is a case-in-point. Federal land grant programs encompassed almost every field of governmental activity in Minnesota. There were grant programs for education (common school, university, agricultural, and mechanical college grants); internal improvements (general internal improvements, railroad construction, river and harbor improvements, and public buildings grants); welfare (salt spring and public institutions grants); reclamation (swamp and overflowed land grants); and conservation (Itasca State Park grant). In addition, funds from the unearmarked federal land grants were instrumental in the founding and maintenance of almost every public institution in the state.

Though few cash grants were in existence, Minnesota did receive money for internal improvements (from the Five Per

Cent Fund); [14] welfare (grants for the support of the Minnesota Soldiers Home); defense (militia grants); and education (the Hatch Act and the second Morrill Act). Goods and materials were granted to the state for programs in science (weights and measures, specimens from U. S. scientific expeditions); agriculture and conservation (seed distributions, fish stocking); education and welfare (distribution and exchange of documents for libraries, schools, and public institutions). Cooperative activities involving coordination of services included the fields of education (exchange of information); science (meteorological reports, geological surveys); law enforcement (cooperation in hunting law violators, jailing of federal offenders); conservation (protection of forests); land settlement (homestead and tree culture programs); and agriculture (cooperation in grasshopper eradication, exchange of experiment station research reports, exchange of information).

The financial impact of these programs on the State of Minnesota was generally greater than that of the mid-twentieth-century grants-in-aid. In the latter third of the nineteenth century, a greater portion of the state's revenues came from federal sources than in any subsequent period. At times, revenues from federal sources, including direct federal payments to the state and income from federal grants, represented over forty per cent of the total annual revenue of Minnesota, and after 1865, never fell below twenty per cent.[15] The analogous percentage in 1959 was 25.3, actually somewhat lower than the apparent annual average in the late nineteenth century.

In the nineteenth, as in the twentieth century, federal aid stimulated matching state contributions. In some cases there were formal matching requirements attached to the federal grants. For example, the first Morrill Act required the states to appropriate funds for construction of buildings for their agricultural colleges in order to retain the principal of the federal grant intact for the support of actual instructional

301

[14] The Five Per Cent Fund was an annual federal grant of five per cent of the proceeds from the sale of federal lands within the state to the state for internal improvements. This grant was originated in 1802.

[15] The percentage of income from federal sources between 1865 and 1900 at selected intervals was: 1866, 37.6; 1875, 38.0; 1880, 38.6; 1885, 41.8; 1890, 22.2; 1895, 30.6; 1900, 30.6.

activities. In this way, federal-originated funds involved state funds in the development of joint collaborative programs. Between 1862 and 1900, identifiable cooperative programs claimed an apparent average of fifty per cent of the state's total expenditure, excluding amounts spent by the state in informal collaborative arrangements and for the general expenses of executives, such as the governor, who were directly and continuously involved *ex officio* in the administration of cooperative programs.[16]

The impact of federal aid was state-wide and federal funds penetrated into every county. The state's major activities were clearly dependent on federal aid. Minnesota's military establishment, important in defending the state's settlers against marauding Indians, relied heavily on federal funds. State and local internal improvements were almost entirely federal-supported. Minnesota's railroads were almost entirely the products of formal federal-state collaboration and even the Northern Pacific Railroad, recipient of a direct federal land grant that ostensibly by-passed the state, was brought into the sharing arrangement in several ways.

At the instigation of the territorial legislature, Minnesota's major roads were constructed by the Army Engineers even prior to statehood and were then transferred to state control, while the federal Five Per Cent Fund furnished most of the money for county roads and bridges before the advent of the automobile. In 1875, for example, the Five Per Cent Fund paid for twenty-seven internal improvement projects in twenty counties. Ten years later, the annual distribution of the Fund was used for fifty-one projects in thirty-eight counties. At the same time, the land grant endowed internal improvement permanent fund was also being used for local roads, bridges, and like improvements.

Minnesota's school system benefited greatly from the semi-annual subsidy distributed from the earnings of the common school land grant. In 1866 schools in forty-two counties with a total enrollment of 50,564 met the state educational requirements and received grants from the permanent school fund. Subsequently, schools in every county in the state

---

[16] The percentage of total state "matching" expenditures between 1862 and 1900 at selected intervals was: 1862, 47.6; 1866, 49.1; 1875, 44.7; 1880, 52.4; 1885, 51.3; 1890, 50.1; 1895, 44.3; 1900, 48.3.

shared in the annual distributions from the funds. By 1895, some 276,000 students were benefiting from the federal grant. In addition, the Permanent School Fund was used as a revolving fund to provide capital loans for the construction of elementary and high school buildings in every school district and town in the state. In 1895, loans totaling $224,906 were made to 249 school districts in seventy-two counties. The State University's operating costs were almost entirely borne by the earnings of the University land grants and direct federal appropriations, including the budgets of the Agriculture Experiment Station and the State Geological Survey. A major proportion of the operating costs of the Minnesota Soldiers' Home also came from direct federal matching grants. Intermittent but vital aid was also given to the state normal schools and public institutions from the various permanent funds and land grants.

303

Perhaps the major cooperative effort in nineteenth-century Minnesota, as in all the public land states created after 1816, revolved around the construction of railroads, designed to open up the interior of the state for settlement and to connect the state with the outside world. Between 1857, when the first federal grants were made, and 1907, when the last link in the state's internal railroad network was completed, supervision of the railroad land grants was a major activity of the state government, one which involved almost daily contacts with the appropriate federal officials and departments. On the basis of federal and state legislative authorizations, federal and state administrators shared responsibility for approving the railroads' construction plans; supervising the selection of railroad lands along the federally prescribed rights-of-way; securing federal patents for the selected lands; transferring the lands to the railroads as they met the conditions laid down in the federal and state legislation; harmonizing the interests of the railroads and beneficiaries of other land grant programs when they came into conflict; and supervising the relinquishment and replacement of improperly transferred lands. In each case, the Commissioner of the General Land Office and his deputies in Washington and in the field were required to oversee the actions of the governor and his agents to insure compliance with the conditions set down in the land grant legislation by Congress.

All six major railroads operating in present day Minnesota were beneficiaries of federal-state land grants, receiving, all told, 11,173,920 acres valued at approximately $48,812,000. Even the Northern Pacific Railway, which received 1,905,-897 acres in Minnesota from a direct federal land grant, was the recipient of 2,167,918 acres through the federal-state program as it absorbed smaller land grant railroads. In addition, the federal grants were matched with bonds valued at $5,875,000 issued by the state and its local governments. Some idea of the magnitude of the cooperative railroad construction program may be gathered from the percentage of the state's total revenue paid by the railroads in taxes between 1875 (over ten per cent) and 1900 (over fifteen per cent).[17]

The types of cooperative activities and the means of their administration in Minnesota were familiar in the other states as well. All the land grant programs except those designed to aid in the reclamation of arid lands were in operation. Direct federal aids to individuals and groups were subject to state influences much as elsewhere. Cooperative exchanges of goods and services in Minnesota were recognizable as parts of the national pattern. So were the paraphernalia of administration—in land grant matters an *ex officio* State Land Board and its agents; the General Land Office and its local land officers; local school and county officials. Indeed, it seems that very few federal and state offices in Minnesota were not involved in the cooperative programs.

Since the scope of cooperative programs and the administration of sharing were no different from the standard nationwide pattern, it is reasonable to project the Minnesota pattern of fiscal sharing onto other states as well. This does not mean that all states benefited equally from federal financial support. As in the twentieth-century grant-in-aid programs, federal aid provided a proportionately larger share of the budgets of the smaller states, the newer states, and the poorer states, though the differences between states may actually have been less pronounced than in the twentieth

304

[17] The land grant railroads' share of the state's total revenue for selected years between 1875 and 1900 was:

	1875	1880	1885	1890	1895	1900
Total state revenue (thousands)	$981	$1,417	$2,078	$3,296	$5,427	$6,903
Land grant railroad tax (thousands)	107	209	673	621	729	1,106

century because of greater state reluctance in the nineteenth century to finance local programs with tax money obtained locally.

The central fact that emerges from an analysis of the development of sharing in a single state over several decades is the sheer weight of political time devoted to intergovernmental cooperation. Not only were the administrators heavily involved in cooperative activities, but the programs that were most highly developed as shared programs also preempted the bulk of the policy-makers' time. Minnesota governors and legislatures together were preoccupied with the cooperative programs throughout this entire period. The already enumerated programs should indicate why this was so, since no aspect of internal improvements, education, or general disposition of the public domain in the state escaped involvement in the sharing process. Furthermore, even defense against the Indians and the recruitment of an army for the defense of the Union during the Civil War became shared functions. By the end of the second decade of statehood, the regulatory functions of government were also being shared, partly because the fields of regulation were tied to already cooperative programs (as in the case of railroad regulation) and partly because it was simply more convenient to cooperate (as in the case of regulating state and federal-chartered banking institutions). A survey of the governors' messages, the legislative journals, the statute books, and the attorney generals' opinions reveals the extent of this concern with programs that were cooperative in character, a concern not over the general theory of collaboration but over the procedural aspects of the various programs. Federal-state cooperation was a fact of life, hence the policy-makers rarely referred to it directly in their deliberations. The system of sharing is all the more impressive because of its implicit acceptance as part of the process of government.

COOPERATIVE FEDERALISM SINCE 1913

The last major land grant program was inaugurated in 1894. Selection of lands under the land grant acts has persisted through the mid-twentieth century and the extension of the traditional grants to Alaska upon its admission as a state in 1958 has revived the land grant era in one state.

Nevertheless, since 1913 the cash grant, coupled with the rising impact of cooperation among professionals at all levels of government, has become the dominant form of intergovernmental cooperation. The modern cash grants had their origins in the later years of the land grant period. They rose to predominance with the adoption of the specific programs embodied in Woodrow Wilson's New Freedom and were notably extended with the rise of the New Deal. The third period of American federalism does not fall under the purview of this study. Beginning in 1913, it is generally considered to be the era of cooperative federalism. In this period, formally structured grant-in-aid programs of internal improvement have had to share the center of the stage with the "new federalism" of welfare. The less visible areas of intergovernmental collaboration expanded apace. As government has become more pervasive, so has intergovernmental cooperation, to the point where the twentieth century has been labeled the century of cooperative federalism, while the intergovernmental cooperation of the nineteenth century has faded into obscurity.

306

THE ROLE OF THE PUBLIC DOMAIN

As long as the land frontier lasted, the public domain served as the greatest single source of national wealth, the foundation of the American economy. Even the development of major industries of the nineteenth century, agricultural implements, railroads and telegraphs, machines for processing the produce of the land, and the like, was directly tied to the development of the public domain. It is not surprising, then, that the land, owned, as most of it was, by the federal government, should have served as the foundation for intergovernmental cooperation in the expanding nation.

The public land states differed from their non-public land counterparts in the nature of their cooperative relationships with the federal government only insofar as the existence of the public domain within their boundaries made it less difficult to justify major cooperative programs under the strict constructionist terms then dominant in constitutional interpretation. Certainly the states without public lands were at no time excluded from the operations of cooperative fed-

eralism. Considering only formal grants-in-aid, it is possible that the public land states did receive more benefits
than the others, and so it was argued on the floors of Congress when the states possessing no public lands wanted to
gain additional benefits from the federal government for
themselves. Yet, when the benefits derived from the other
forms of intergovernmental cooperation and direct federal
aid to localities are included, the balance seems to have been
rather adequately redressed and the amount of cooperation
generally equalized. To take but one example, the protective tariff was unquestionably a great aid to Eastern manufacturing interests, often to the detriment of the West and
the South. It was as much a subsidy as a government defense
contract is in 1964, and was so considered by both its proponents and opponents.[18] The Eastern railroad companies
coupled benefits gained from the protective tariff (or exemptions from the tariff, as was sometimes the case) with federal
mail subsidies (whose cooperative impacts were great, particularly in those Eastern states, north and south, which
participated in the construction of their railroads as owners
or investors, during the era of railroad building) and more
direct state and local subsidies to construct the network of
railroads east of the Great Lakes. They began to take advantage of these benefits even before the major railroad land
grants were made and continued to do so subsequently as
well.

Frederick Jackson Turner, in stating his renowned frontier hypothesis, made a major point of the influence of the
West, the states carved out of the public domain, in the development of nationalism and governmental centralization.
He maintained that the growth of the federal government
was greatly fostered by the demands of the Western settlers
and their early experiences with federal officials, who
preceded state governments in almost every new territory.[19]
Turner's point is generally valid, but it is considerably more
accurate to say that not only did westward expansion increase central government activity in Washington, but that
it did so primarily by increasing intergovernmental coopera-

---

[18] For a discussion of this aspect of the protective tariff, by one of the
men who best understood its nature, see Charles Wiltse, *John C. Calhoun*
(New York, 1944, 1949), Vols. I and II.
[19] Frederick Jackson Turner, *The Frontier in American History* (New
York, 1920).

tion, formal and informal, thus also increasing the central governmental activities of the states. The public domain served as a vehicle for the development of the role of the federal government in promoting national expansion while at the same time providing a means for the states and localities to share in this task. The pattern of relationships that emerged from the cooperative manipulation of the public domain was carried over into the twentieth-century cooperative programs. It was the prior existence of this pattern that made it possible to integrate the increased velocity of government into the federal-state framework without major alterations in the operation of the federal system.

Indeed, the newer states developed a tradition of intergovernmental cooperation that antedated their admission to the Union. If the federal government did not always precede the first settlers into new territory, it almost invariably preceded the state government. From this arrangement emerged an implicit conception of the rightness of the role of the federal government as a major participant in the development of new territories and new frontiers. This conception was carried over within each state after statehood was achieved and, ultimately, became dominant in a majority of the states in the Union. The movements to attain statehood reflected the impact of the land grant and the general tradition of intergovernmental cooperation upon the newly settled territories of the West. On one hand they were certainly attempts to gain more power for local self-government. Even more important, the desire for statehood was linked to the perceived greater ability of states than territories to gain more benefits from Washington. In almost all cases, land grants were not available until statehood was achieved. Lack of voting power in the national elections and full representation in the Congress meant that a territory would be dependent on favors from Washington over which its citizens had only a minimum of influence and control. Statehood came to mean the right to participate in national policy formation as much as the right to manage one's local affairs.

CONTROL OVER THE GRANT PROGRAMS

The organization of control over the grant programs was

308

another matter that tended to obscure the nature of the cooperative relationships in the nineteenth century. The evolution of formal federal controls did not signify changes in the fundamental policy of congressional supervision of the programs, but did indicate that the Congress and the states represented in it learned from experience. The principle of federal control existed from the days of the earliest grants. At first it was assumed that mere incorporation of certain principles into the state constitutions in order to secure congressional approval prior to achieving statehood would be sufficient to ensure compliance with the spirit of the program in question. To some extent, this method was successful and has continued to be so. If for no other reason than the continued increase in the scope of government activity, this method came to be too cumbersome. As it was seen that more specific controls were necessary, they were added by the representatives of the very states that would receive the grants. In addition, as administrative complexities increased and new methods of enforcement outside the courts had to be found, they too were added, not as changes in policy but as improvements in method.

309

The question still arises as to the degree of enforcement of these provisions. There is no doubt that grants were not often revoked, or lands often withheld, though enough cases of revocation and withholding lands can be found to indicate that federal control could be carried to its ultimate implications in this manner. The absence of large-scale revocation programs is due less to the failure of the federal government to enforce the terms administratively than to the political power of the states in the halls of Congress. This is no less true in 1964 than in 1864. Students of government have noted that since the rise of the great cash grant programs following the New Deal, little money has been withheld from any of the states for maladministration or violation of the terms of the program in question. Attempts have been initiated by the federal executive to withhold funds from individual states for a number of reasons. In almost every case these attempts have been overruled in the Congress or suitable compromises have been negotiated with congressional help. When state violations of federal regulations do occur, they are dealt with in less drastic ways because the Congress will not often allow the drastic solution and the federal bureaucrats know this.

Only once in American history was massive revocation of federal grants because of misuse even considered. Between 1870 and 1900 the question of revoking some of the unfulfilled transportation land grants became a matter of some political importance. Congressional investigations into the uses of land grants by railroad companies were widespread during this period. Ultimately, federal-state land grants to eight railroad companies were revoked in whole or in part and steps were taken to withhold lands from the great transcontinental railroads as well.[20]

While other federal grants to the states were not often revoked, specific lands within the different land programs were frequently withheld by the federal government. Not infrequently, the states were even forced to re-cede lands already patented to them because of conflicts with other federal grant programs or land policies. As the available public domain diminished and the number of land grant programs increased, the amount of control and intensity of supervision grew also, leading to greater exercises of federal authority, subject always to the formal and informal limitations attached by Congress. Ultimately these controls were transferred, modified, and expanded to provide adequate supervision for cash grants-in-aid as they began to emerge.

COOPERATIVE FEDERALISM: THE ALTERNATE HYPOTHESIS

Cooperative, or collaborative, federalism can be defined as the sharing of responsibilities for given functions by the federal and state governments. In this sense it is conceived to be the opposite of dual federalism which implies a division of functions between governments as well as a division of governmental structures. While the theory of cooperative federalism assumes a division of structures, it also implies a system of sharing that ranges from formal federal-state agreements covering specific programs to informal contacts on a regular basis for the sake of sharing information and experience.

Even during the nineteenth century, when the ethos of

[20] Federal Coordinator of Transportation, *Public Aids to Transportation* (Washington, D. C., U.S. Gov't. Printing Office, 1938), Vol. II, Part I, Sect. A.

the times called forth a theory of dualism that was based on a functional demarcation between governments, the actual exigencies of the operation of the system of necessity demanded cooperation. Consequently, federal-state cooperation was developed in a wide variety of cases. Though it was usually opposed in theory, it persevered in many forms and under different guises. Its procedures were refined through trial and error, often subtly since it was, in the main, unrecognized. Officially recognized or not, a system of intergovernmental collaboration was evolved to serve the dual purpose of maintaining the federal balance while providing needed governmental services. Where cooperation did not develop and should have, both the system and the programs in question suffered. In a sense, a substantial share of the history of American government has been the search for methods to provide for the necessary collaboration of the various parts of the federal system while at the same time preserving and strengthening those parts as separate bases for such collaboration. Much of what historians have mistaken for rejection of intergovernmental cooperation in the nineteenth century was, in reality, the rejection of certain methods of interaction as failing to meet one or both of these criteria.

311

On the basis of this evidence, it would seem necessary to develop a new theory to explain the nature of the American federal system and its character over time, a theory which takes into account the continuous existence of an amount of intergovernmental collaboration equal to, and in fact greater than, the amount of separation (as traditionally defined) in the federal system. Within the large area of concurrent powers provided, explicitly or implicitly, by the federal constitution, the federal and state governments have been able either to divide responsibility among their separate jurisdictions, with each responsible only for its own share of the divided responsibility ("dual federalism"), or to divide the works of government cooperatively, sharing responsibility in specific programs, with all units directed toward common goals that extend along the entire chain of concurrent powers ("cooperative federalism") and generally overflow into the ostensibly "exclusive" preserves.

The actual division of responsibility under the concurrent powers is primarily determined anew for each case through the political process, rather than through legal decisions. That is, the decisions as to the distribution of the areas of concurrent powers are made either on the political level or by constitutional interpretations based on political realities. Such decisions are recognized in constitutional law either after a political decision has been made or as a result of a constitutional interpretation that, sooner or later, must follow the polls.

In understanding our federal system, there is a basic conflict between simple rationalities and the logic of political experience. Simple rationalities demand a federal structure with a clear-cut division of powers that can easily be measured, while political experience, dealing with reality, demands a concurrent approach to problem solving. While the conflict between rhetoric and practice has to a certain degree obscured the image of federalism, the result has nevertheless been the development of that complex mechanism of intergovernmental relations, characteristic of the American federal-state-local partnership, known today as cooperative federalism.

DANIEL J. ELAZAR

UNIVERSITY OF MINNESOTA

Federalism in the Progressive Era:
A Structural Interpretation of Reform

WILLIAM GRAEBNER

T HE Progressive era has long been recognized as one of substantial contribution to social legislation. Working through state and national legislatures, reformers rewrote child labor laws and safety and factory inspection statutes. They cast the society's response to industrial accident and death into the new form of workmen's compensation. They limited working hours for some women and, in a few cases, for men. In some states night work became illegal. By 1915 several states had passed minimum wage legislation. Of the major reform goals of the period, only compulsory health insurance failed to win enactment. The history of this avalanche of social legislation has been described as a struggle between social justice progressives and conservative state and national court systems;[1] as a conflict between ideas of voluntarism and compulsion and individual and collective responsibility;[2] and as a political process involving interest groups, particularly business and labor.[3]

313

A structural approach, emerging from the work of historians of child labor reform, is as yet neither fully articulated nor tested. According to this model, legislative social reform suffered from a temporary incongruity between economic and political systems. While business increasingly operated in both national and regional markets, the political

William Graebner is associate professor of history in State University College, Fredonia.

[1] Harold Underwood Faulkner, *The Quest for Social Justice, 1898-1914* (New York, 1931), 79; Samuel P. Hays, *The Response to Industrialism, 1885-1914* (Chicago, 1957), 80; Eric F. Goldman, *Rendezvous with Destiny* (New York, 1953), 133.

[2] Roy Lubove, *The Struggle for Social Security, 1900-1935* (Cambridge, 1968), 4; Hace Sorel Tishler, *Self-Reliance and Social Security, 1870-1917* (Port Washington, N.Y., 1971), viii, ix.

[3] James Weinstein, *The Corporate Ideal in the Liberal State: 1900-1918* (Boston, 1968); Gabriel Kolko, *The Triumph of Conservatism: A Reinterpretation of American History, 1900-1916* (New York, 1963); Robert H. Wiebe, *Businessmen and Reform: A Study of the Progressive Movement* (Cambridge, 1962); Jeremy P. Felt, *Hostages of Fortune: Child Labor Reform in New York State* (Syracuse, 1965); Robert F. Wesser, "Conflict and Compromise: The Workmen's Compensation Movement in New York, 1890s-1913," *Labor History*, XI (Summer 1971), 345-72; William Graebner, "The Coal-Mine Operator and Safety: A Study of Business Reform in the Progressive Period," *Labor History*, XIV (Fall 1973), 483-505; Forrest A. Walker, "Compulsory Health Insurance: The Next Great Step in Social Legislation," *Journal of American History*, LVI (Sept. 1969), 290-304.

system remained federal, its authority residing theoretically in two levels of government but practically in the states.[4] Federalism, in conjunction with national markets, meant that the states were part of the economics of competition. Key business groups, largely from highly competitive industries with interstate markets, opposed most state social legislation on the grounds that it would place their firms at a competitive disadvantage in relationship to firms operating in states with less advanced, and therefore less costly, programs.[5] A wide range of reformers and reform groups, from William Howard Taft and the National Civic Federation (NCF) to Florence Kelley and the National Consumers League, from John Mitchell and the United Mine Workers (UMW) to John R. Commons and the American Association for Labor Legislation (AALL) accepted this structural model and interpretation of business attitudes.

314

Progressive reformers who were interested in welfare measures and labor legislation wanted to eliminate the structural incongruities within the political economy. Since no reformers seriously considered returning the economy to localism,[6] they focused on the political system. The laws had to be nationalized to conform to a national economy. The most obvious solution—national legislation—had limited appeal to a generation accustomed to working through local political frameworks and influenced by a mythic concept of local self-government. In addition, the United States Supreme Court presented its own obstacles to national legislation in social reform areas.

While one group of politicians, social reformers, and businessmen insisted that only national legislation could solve the structural problems posed by state laws and a national business system, another, even larger group, embraced uniform state legislation as an acceptable, even superior, alternative. Uniform state legislation may have been the political system's single most important structural and procedural problem-solving mechanism from 1900 through 1914, and it continued to be a viable approach to social legislation in the 1920s and 1930s. Despite its origins in the 1870s and continued viability, uniform state legislation was one of the progressives' distinctive contributions to reform. Whereas the nineteenth century was characterized by state

---

[4] Municipal and county governments are not discussed here largely to simplify the model.

[5] Walter I. Trattner, *Crusade for the Children: A History of the National Child Labor Committee and Child Labor Reform in America* (Chicago, 1970), 82-83; Stephen B. Wood, *Constitutional Politics in the Progressive Era: Child Labor and the Law* (Chicago, 1968), 24-25, 32-33, 80. Jeremy Felt recognizes the existence of this business argument but remains unconvinced of its validity, let alone its centrality. Felt, *Hostages of Fortune*.

[6] The anti-trust campaign might be seen as a symbolic effort along these lines.

legislation and the New Deal by national legislation, the Progressive era represented a compromise, tied to the past yet anticipating the future.

Two areas to be affected by the argument that competitive disadvantage precluded state-by-state reform were factory inspection and industrial and mine safety. As widely accepted functions of state police power, they were perhaps relatively unaffected by hostile judicial decisions. The announced purpose of the nation's factory inspectors, meeting in convention for the first time in 1887, was "to produce something like uniformity, both in the laws and in the practice of the inspectors."[7] Uniformity was deemed especially important in contiguous states.

Even Kelley, one of the few factory inspectors to criticize the competitive advantage argument, conceded its validity in situations where the conditions in a trade were so depressed that improvement in one place resulted "in banishing the manufacture to *other* places. . . ."[8] Her example was tenement house manufacture, an area that received considerable attention from the factory inspectors and other agencies of reform. Since the passage of sweating laws in New York, John Franey, president of the International Association of Factory Inspectors (IAFI), noted that the promoters of the sweating system "have sent some of their victims across the North River over to the state of New Jersey. . . . Some had moved into Connecticut, others into the small towns of Pennsylvania, and still others had parcelled out bundles for the farm districts of Maine, Vermont, New Hampshire, and the Massachusetts interior."[9] The U.S. Industrial Commission, investigating tenement manufacturing in 1900, recommended uniform legislation—the adoption of the factory act of New York or Massachusetts by New Jersey and other affected states. The commission, recognizing that uneven enforcement could nullify uniform legislation, felt that administrative uniformity was essential to legislative uniformity and was dependent upon the quality of the inspector and his freedom from outside influence.[10] This was a problem

315

[7] *National Convention of Factory Inspectors in the United States, held at Philadelphia, June 8-9, 1887* (Columbus, Ohio, 1887), 3. The organization was later renamed the International Association of Factory Inspectors (IAFI).

[8] *Ibid.*, 20; International Association of Factory Inspectors, *Eighth Annual Convention of International Association of Factory Inspectors of North America, Held at Philadelphia, Pennsylvania, September 25-28, 1894* (n.p., n.d.), 23; International Association of Factory Inspectors, *Proceedings of the Seventh Annual Convention of the International Association of Factory Inspectors of North America, Held at Chicago, Illinois, September 19-22, 1893* (Cleveland, n.d.), 5.

[9] International Association of Factory Inspectors, *Eighth Annual Convention*, 101; International Association of Factory Inspectors, *Seventh Annual Convention*, 111.

[10] U.S. Congress, House, Industrial Commission, *Final Report of the Industrial Commission* (Washington, 1902), 743-44, 950.

that affected business relationships within the same state as well as between firms in different states, and one for which the factory inspectors had no solution.[11]

In the area of safety, inspectors and manufacturers of industrial equipment advocated uniform legislation. The boilermakers' national association pointed out that manufacturers were faced with a multiplicity of state and municipal boiler inspection laws, so that boilers built, for example, in Chicago, under the regulations of that city, would not pass inspection in Ohio or Massachusetts. The argument also was made that manufacturers of machinery often failed to attach appropriate safeguards to the machinery during the manufacturing process because the safeguards added excessively to the cost of production and lessened the competitive bidding capacity of the manufacturer. In this instance, the purpose of uniform state legislation was to protect workers by safeguarding machinery at the point of manufacture rather than at the factory where the machinery was used.[12]

316

During the nineteenth century, analyses based on competitive disadvantage in a federal system were the province of a limited number of groups, most notably the factory inspectors and the [National] Conference of Commissioners on Uniform State Laws (NCCUSL), which developed in the late 1880s out of the American Bar Association.[13] In 1900, however, such analyses received endorsement by the United States Industrial Commission. Created by an act of Congress, the commission was mandated to "furnish such information and suggest such laws as may be made a basis for uniform legislation by the various States of the Union."[14] After hearing testimony from business, labor, and public officials on every current variety of labor legislation, the commissioners concluded that a major obstacle to productive legislation

[11] The factory inspectors were troubled internally by a conflict over national legislation. L. A. Havens of New York presented a plan for a federal factory act in 1910. International Association of Factory Inspectors, *Twenty-fourth Annual Convention of International Association of Factory Inspectors Held at Hendersonville, N.C. and Columbia, S.C., August 23, 24, 25, 26, 1910* (Columbia, S.C., n.d.), 73, 76.

[12] Conference of Commissioners on Uniform State Laws, *Proceedings of the Twenty-second Annual Conference of Commissioners on Uniform State Laws, Held at Milwaukee, Wisconsin, August 21, 22, 23, 24 and 26, 1912* (n.p., n.d.), 26, 35, 36, 57-59. The organization was later renamed the National Conference of Commissioners on Uniform State Laws. International Association of Factory Inspectors, *Eighth Annual Convention*, 93; National Civic Federation, Department on Compensation for Industrial Accidents and Their Prevention, *Proceedings of Meeting Held December 8, 1911, New York* (n.p., n.d.), 57.

[13] W. Brooke Graves, *American Intergovernmental Relations: Their Origins, Historical Development, and Current Status* (New York, 1964), 588-89.

[14] U.S. Congress, House, *Report of the Industrial Commission on Prison Labor* (Washington, 1900), 5.

was the federal system. "Employers and employees who have appeared
before the commission," stated the final report, "have quite generally
agreed upon the usefulness and the importance of factory legislation and
its strict enforcement. The main criticism brought out is that of the lack
of uniformity."[15]

The commission took a selective, rather than indiscriminate, approach
to the problem of competitive advantage. Within limits, the commission
said, statutory reductions in working hours for women and children
would not place a state at a competitive disadvantage, but for
Massachusetts to reduce its working hours to forty-eight per week while
other competitive states remained at sixty, would indeed place the state
at a competitive disadvantage. The commission believed that some
degree of uniformity was "an urgent requirement."[16] The
commission's investigations, whether of hours, child labor, safety, or
tenement manufacture, focused on those geographic areas, such as New
England and New York City, and those industries, such as coal mining
and cotton textiles, where competition was most severe and market
structures were most competitive.[17] The commission anticipated the
clash between textile manufacturers of New England and the South
over many legislative issues in the second decade of the century and
the major efforts of the coal industry, assisted by inspectors, operators,
and union officials, to spread the burdens of safety and workmen's
compensation evenly over competitive areas.[18]

In the textile industry, the sectional war was hard fought; the battles
were child labor, night work, and other varieties of labor legislation.
Massachusetts operators, noting declining profits since the 1890s as a
result of southern competition, and Massachusetts politicians, observing
the state's declining industrial fortunes,[19] made and listened to the
argument that the state was suffering because of its relatively advanced
labor legislation. There were, of course, many reasons for New
England's decline, but sectional differences in labor legislation were one

317

[15] Congress, *Final Report of the Industrial Commission*, 901.

[16] *Ibid.*, 788.

[17] U.S. Congress, House, *Report of the Industrial Commission on the Relations and Conditions of
Capital and Labor Employed in the Mining Industry, including Testimony, Review of Evidence,
and Topical Digest* (Washington, 1901), 29, 48, 56, 88-89, 103, 164-65, 175, 190-91; U.S.
Congress, House, *Report of the Industrial Commission on Labor Legislation* (Washington, 1900),
522, 75-6; Congress, *Final Report of the Industrial Commission*, 545, 744.

[18] William Graebner, "Great Expectations: The Search for Order in Bituminous Coal,
1890-1917," *Business History Review*, XLVIII (Spring 1974), 49-72; Graebner, "The Coal-
Mine Operator and Safety."

[19] This decline was relative to other states and regions rather than absolute.

factor—and there is some evidence that they were a critical factor—in the ongoing transfer of capital from the North to the South.[20]

A handful of child labor reformers rejected this argument, arguing that child labor was not cheap labor but expensive. Its abolition would confer a competitive advantage upon the mill owners. "Recent reports from cotton manufacturing towns in New England," concluded one critic, "show that there is not a cotton mill that has been injured or put out of business by the enactment of rigid child labor laws."[21] Even those who denied the validity of the argument, and they were few, were aware of its continued influence. "The point we make," said Owen Lovejoy of the National Child Labor Committee (NCLC), "is that there are a great many manufacturers who believe that they are injured by the adoption of such laws, who believe that they work to their disadvantage, but we have been seeking to show them that when such laws are adopted in other states their competitors will be under the same conditions as they are and they will not suffer at all. Because employers regard this inequality of law as a handicap they impress legislative committees, and this fact stands as a great obstacle to our work."[22] At the very least, New England's industrial decline left economic and political leaders vulnerable to arguments and issues that otherwise might have seemed of less consequence. New Englanders were convinced that labor legislation was a factor in their economic problems, and that perception lent urgency and credibility to the argument.[23]

Southerners, of course, could not argue from the premise of industrial decline, but this did not prevent them from using variations on the same theme. In one case, southern mill owners opposed national eight-hour

318

[20] On this point economic historians are not in complete agreement, but the majority supports the interpretations presented here. See Thomas Russell Smith, *The Cotton Textile Industry of Fall River, Massachusetts: A Study of Industrial Localization* (New York, 1944), 94-95; R. C. Estall, *New England: A Study in Industrial Adjustment* (New York, 1966), 53; R. C. Estall and R. Ogilvie Buchanan, *Industrial Activity and Economic Geography: A study of the forces behind the geographical location of productive activity in manufacturing industry* (London, 1961), 106; Seymour E. Harris, *The Economics of New England: Case Study of an Older Area* (Cambridge, 1952), 18, 22, 23, 161, 163; Ben F. Lembert, *The Cotton Textile Industry of the Southern Appalachian Piedmont* (Chapel Hill, 1963), 79-80, 170, 173; Richard M. Abrams, *Conservatism in a Progressive Era: Massachusetts Politics, 1900-1912* (Cambridge, 1964), 226-34, 290-94; Wood, *Constitutional Politics*, 9; and Congress, *Final Report of the Industrial Commission*, 923.

[21] Conference of Commissioners on Uniform State Laws, *Proceedings of the Twentieth Annual Conference of Commissioners on Uniform State Laws, Held at Chattanooga, Tennessee, August 25, 26, 27 and 29, 1910* (n.p., n.d.), 67.

[22] Ibid.; "Proceedings of the Sixth Annual Meeting of the National Child Labor Committee," *Supplement to the Annals of the American Academy of Political and Social Science*, XXXIII (1909), 7, 254.

[23] For a similar argument made for the antebellum South, see Charles Grier Sellers, Jr., "The Travail of Slavery," Charles Grier Sellers, Jr., ed., *The Southerner as American* (Chapel Hill, 1960), 40-71.

legislation on the grounds that southern operations could not survive foreign competition.[24] Intoxicated with their new-found economic success after so many years of stagnation, southern businessmen argued that the competitive advantages in labor legislation that had supported it must also continue. Northern textile manufacturers, claimed the southerners, were promoting uniform and national legislation in order to retard the region's growth by eliminating the South's competitive advantage. The federal argument also was applied within the southern states, where manufacturers in Alabama and the Carolinas asked that their child labor laws not be enforced since their competitors in Georgia had no similar legislation.[25] Arguments such as these convinced the United States Industrial Commission that although competitive conditions in textiles allowed southern mills to impose restrictions on working hours beyond those currently employed, "it would be too much to expect the Southern States to prohibit child labor at once under the age of 14, as is done in Massachusetts and Connecticut, at least until the remaining New England States have set an equally high standard."[26] Although a few influential southerners advocated national labor legislation, the idea of uniformity, whether achieved through state or national legislation, was not popular in the South.[27] Lobbyists from the southern textile states, reflecting the views of their industrial constituents, opposed national child labor legislation in Congress.[28] If the southern argument seems less compelling and less discriminating than that of New England, one must remember that the debate took place within an intensely competitive national industry, whose southern future was not clearly evident in 1900 or 1915.

319

That arguments based on interstate competition were employed in industries where they made some sense and in which they were in some

[24] Wood, *Constitutional Politics*, 39.

[25] "Proceedings of the Annual Meeting of the National Child Labor Committee, Held in the City of New York, February 14-16, 1905," *Annals of the American Academy of Political and Social Science*, XXV (May 1905), 149-71; Congress, *Report of the Industrial Commission on Labor*, 530, 42.

[26] Congress, *Final Report of the Industrial Commission*, 922.

[27] Congress, *Report of the Industrial Commission on Labor*, 784, 522, 530; "Proceedings of the Sixth Annual Meeting of the National Child Labor Committee," 201-02. See also Florence Kelley, "What Should We Sacrifice to Uniformity?" *Supplement to the Annals of the American Academy of Political and Social Science*, XXXVIII (1911), 24-30.

[28] Wood, *Constitutional Politics*, 47-55; Cotton Manufacturers' Association of North Carolina, *Proceedings of the Eleventh Annual Convention, 1917* (Charlotte, N.C., 1917); John Porter Hollis, "Child Labor Legislation in the Carolinas," *Supplement to the Annals of the American Academy of Political and Social Science*, XXXVIII (1911), 116-17; David Clark, "A Demand for a Square Deal," *Child Labor Bulletin*, IV (May 1915-Feb. 1916), 43. On the degree of progress toward uniformity in child labor legislation in the southern states, see "Child Labor," *American Labor Legislation Review*, I (Oct. 1911), 71. The South lagged even in commercial uniformity.

degree valid is confirmed in a number of other industries. Without question, the major opponents of state legislation for minimum wage, child labor, and hours for women were small businessmen in atomistic industries operating in an interstate market.[29] The New York State Fruit Growers' Association, representing some 1,300 fruit growers, opposed legislation regulating the hours of women and children, charging that if the bill became law it would "seriously cripple the fruit-growing industry and drive out of the state the canning industry."[30] When New York considered minimum wage legislation in 1915, public opposition came from retailers, shirtmakers in New York City and Long Island, and a boxmaker who sold his product in interstate markets.[31] At public hearings on a prospective minimum wage in Michigan that same year, the interstate competition argument was made by businessmen from the candy, shirtwaist, and laundry industries, and by a representative of the garment trades. By far the most vocal opposition to minimum wages came from the cigarmaking industry, which most economists would describe as a low level oligopoly with a large competitive fringe.[32]

The glass industry, which, next to the textile industry, provided the most consistent opposition to child labor legislation, largely, though not completely, conforms to the model. A commerce department report claimed that the industry not only had to meet intense foreign competition but also suffered more from domestic competition than any other industry. Information indicates low profits in two of the three areas of the glass industry employing large numbers of children.[33] Glass manufacturers in New Jersey opposed passage of an act that would have

[29] To some extent these arguments depended upon increasingly sophisticated methods of cost accounting, which made possible isolation of various production costs. See A. C. Littleton, *Accounting Evolution to 1900* (New York, 1933), 322, 352-53, 357-58; J. Hugh Jackson, "A Half-Century of Cost Accounting Progress," Michael Chatfield, ed., *Contemporary Studies in the Evolution of Accounting Thought* (Belmont, Cal., 1968), 223-27.

[30] New York, Factory Investigating Commission, *Second Report of the Factory Investigating Commission, 1913. Transmitted to the Legislature January 15, 1913* (4 vols., Albany, 1913), IV, 2261 and II, 1300. For the responses of the needle trades, see *ibid.*, 1332-37.

[31] New York, Factory Investigating Commission, *Fourth Report of the Factory Investigating Commission, 1915. Transmitted to the Legislature February 15, 1915* (5 vols., Albany, 1915), V, 2712, 2731.

[32] *Report of the Michigan State Commission of Inquiry into Wages and the Conditions of Labor for Women and the Advisability of Establishing a Minimum Wage* (Lansing, Mich., 1915), 234-35, 251-52, 256-57, 280-82, 291-92; The American Cigar Company controlled only 25 percent of industry capacity at its greatest extension; in 1909 the industry contained over 15,000 independent firms. Willis N. Baer, *The Economic Development of the Cigar Industry in the United States* (Lancaster, Pa., 1933), 99-105.

[33] U.S. Department of Commerce, Bureau of Foreign and Domestic Commerce, *The Glass Industry, Report on the Cost of Production of Glass in the United States* (Washington, 1917), 51, 46.

banned night work in factories for persons under sixteen years of age, and in Illinois they threatened to move out of the state if pending child labor legislation were passed.[34] This, however, is not the whole story. The lighting goods segment of the industry, which employed many children, had a comparatively high profit rate.[35] A 1911 study of glass industry mobility revealed that in Illinois and Ohio, where the child labor laws were relatively advanced and well enforced, the industry had not been damaged. "Not a single plant," reported the study, "has left either state or has failed because of these laws."[36] In fact, eight plants had moved into Ohio or Illinois from Indiana and West Virginia, states with less developed legislation.[37]

Only twice did highly concentrated industries employ the interstate competition argument in opposing social legislation. In each case the target was the eight-hour day, and the opponents were the steel and paper industries. But this deviance from the model is superficial. Paper and steel were continuous process industries, operating around the clock on twelve-hour shifts. There could be no gradual reduction of hours in such industries, and a change to eight-hour shifts imposed a particular burden. Commons, labor economist and leader of the American Association for Labor Legislation, accepted the argument. "Eight hours in continuous industries," he said, "cannot be brought about by state legislation."[38]

321

The Massachusetts experience with minimum wage legislation in the 1910s provides evidence of the power of the competitive advantage argument in a state undergoing relative industrial decline. Although the state was, in 1912, the first to create a minimum wage commission, in five years the commission had imposed minimum wages in only four industries—retail stores, brushes, laundries, and women's clothing. The women's clothing industry was regulated only after the commission acknowledged that state action risked driving the industry from the

[34] Ransom E. Noble, Jr., *New Jersey Progressivism before Wilson* (Princeton, 1946), 124; "Proceedings of the Seventh Annual Meeting of the National Child Labor Committee," 186; Samuel McCune Lindsay, "Child Labor a National Problem," *Annals of the American Academy of Political and Social Science*, XXVII (1906), 331-41. See also *Report of the Michigan State Commission of Inquiry into Wages*, 311.
[35] Department of Commerce, *Glass Industry*, 46.
[36] Charles L. Chute, "The Glass Industry and Child Labor Legislation," *Supplement to the Annals of the American Academy of Political and Social Science*, XXXVIII (1911), 123-32.
[37] *Ibid.*, 123, 126; Owen R. Lovejoy, "Some Unsettled Questions About Child Labor," *Supplement to the Annals of the American Academy of Political and Social Science*, XXXIII (1909), 56.
[38] John R. Commons, "Eight-Hour Shifts by Federal Legislation," *American Labor Legislation Review*, VII (March 1917), 144. See also Henry R. Seager, Charles A. Gulick, Jr., eds., *Labor and Other Economic Essays* (New York, 1931), 172-73.

state. The wage board established to deal with the brush industry described it as too poor and too competitive to pay as high a minimum wage as some other industries in the state, and premised its recommendation for minimum wages for this industry on the assumption that higher wages would actually aid the industry by regularizing its labor supply. The cotton textile industry, employing 25 percent of the female manufacturing workers in Massachusetts in 1912, was investigated but no wage board called, and the state's boot and shoe industry was never investigated, although it employed 30,000 women. "In the cotton industry," the commission concluded, "which is not only interstate but international, and whose costs are determined by severe competition with the cheapest labor in Europe and Asia, it may be that there is little room for improvement in the wages, or for a steadying of employ. Thus the industry may be one in which the employees will eternally be at a disadvantage, and in which it must be conceded the application of a minimum-wage level will be peculiarly baffling."[39]

322

Massachusetts was unique only in the extent of its reaction. A moderate parallel emerged in New York, where the state's workmen's compensation commission recommended legislation covering a limited rather than inclusive list of dangerous trades. The New York commission, explained one of its members, Crystal Eastman, had treated interstate competition as a real and difficult issue. "Our reason in selecting these dangerous trades instead of all dangerous trades," she said, "was a purely utilitarian opportunist reason. . . . We thought it would be a good plan to get our entering wedge in on the industries which did not directly compete with other industries outside of the State."[40]

[39] Quoted in Elizabeth G. Evans, "Report on Cotton Industry," [Massachusetts] *Report of the Commission on Minimum Wage Boards, January, 1912,* House No. 1697 (Boston, 1912), Appendix C., 208; [Massachusetts] *Fourth Annual Report of the Minimum Wage Commission For the Year Ending December 31, 1916.* Public Document 102 (Boston, 1917), 23, 48-49; Massachusetts, Minimum Wage Commission, *Statement and Decree Concerning the Wages of Women in the Brush Industry in Massachusetts,* Bulletin 3, August 15, 1914 (Boston, 1914), 23-24; Massachusetts, Minimum Wage Commission, *Third Annual Report* (1915), 12; National Industrial Conference Board, *Minimum Wage Legislation in Massachusetts* (New York, 1927), 21-22, 154, 157, 157n-58n; [Massachusetts] *Report of the Special Commission on Social Insurance, February, 1917,* House No. 1850 (Boston, 1917), 130-45. The California garment industry probably escaped early minimum wage regulation because of similar apprehensions. See California Industrial Welfare Commission, *Second Biennial Report, 1915-1916* (Sacramento, 1917), 77-168.

[40] *Workmen's Compensation for Industrial Accidents, Third National Conference, Chicago, June 10-11, 1910, Proceedings* (n.p., n.d.), 18, 17, 59.

Concentration on the issue of interstate competition led reformers to consider economic regionalism. They attempted to define natural economic regions and to bring the relevant political units together in legislative conferences. Lovejoy, Jane Addams, Eastman, and others were intrigued with the idea of the Pittsburgh District, defined as eastern Ohio, western Pennsylvania, and northern West Virginia. Others were attracted to notions of Ohio or Mississippi Valley regionalism and to several conceptions of southern regionalism.[41] But the promise of regionalism was, with one exception, not fulfilled before World War I. The exception was the western states generally, and particularly the coastal states, where social legislation was relatively advanced. In 1916, for example, the eight-hour day was limited to Washington, D.C., and a small group of western states, including California and Washington. Workmen's compensation in the Pacific states was relatively progressive, and the basic occupations, with the exception of agriculture, were covered. The Pacific states were all receptive to minimum wage legislation for women. Although Massachusetts was responsible for the first such law in 1912, in 1913 five western states, including the three Pacific ones, were among the eight that enacted laws. In that year, California and Oregon were two of only four states that had commissions with power to regulate working hours of women and children. California, Oregon, and Washington were among nine states that employed the commission method of fixing minimum wage rates for women and children.[42]

323

Because of the absence of industries offering employment to women and children, western progressive legislation has usually been seen as a result of an absence of opposition. This explanation is valid but

[41] Owen R. Lovejoy, "The Test of Effective Child-Labor Legislation," *Annals of the American Academy of Political and Social Science*, XXV (May 1905), 450-52; Jane Addams, "Child Labor Legislation—A Requisite for *Industrial Efficiency*," *Annals of the American Academy of Political and Social Science*, XXV (May 1905), 547; Crystal Eastman, *Work-Accidents and the Law* [one of six volumes of the Pittsburgh survey] (New York, 1910); Dorothy W. Douglas, "American Minimum Wage Laws at Work," *American Economic Review*, IX (Dec. 1919), 701-38. Illinois manufacturers were responsible for a 1913 conference of manufacturers' associations in the Mississippi Valley. See Illinois Manufacturers' Association, *Proceedings of the Sixteenth Annual Meeting, 1913* (n.p., n.d.), 7, 23, 41, 43, 54, 74-75. Although the conference acted to create a General Conference Committee to pursue uniformity, evidence of further activity is lacking.

[42] "Legislation for Women in Industry," *American Labor Legislation Review*, VI (Dec. 1916), 361, 384, 390-91; John H. Wallace, "Compulsory State Insurance from the Workman's Viewpoint," *American Labor Legislation Review*, II (Feb. 1912), 22; U.S. Congress, Senate, *Workmen's Compensation Laws of the United States and Foreign Countries* [Prepared Under the Direction of Royal Meeker, Commissioner of Labor Statistics] (Washington, 1914), 376 and chart facing 48; U.S., Department of Labor, Bureau of Labor Statistics, Hugh S. Hanna, *Labor Laws and Their Administration in the Pacific States* (Washington, 1917), 38.

insufficient. Western progressivism also must be seen as the product of
regional isolation from competition, an economic condition that freed
California, Washington, and Oregon producers from the real or
imagined liabilities accruing to states with strong legislation. Freight
rates partially protected Washington boxmakers and California garment
workers from eastern competitors.[43] The industries opposing western
minimum wage legislation were those that came into direct competition
with the products of eastern sweatshops—cracker and candy producers
and elements of the garment and box trades.[44]

The problem of intra-regional competition remained in several
industries, but since there were only three states involved, adjustments
were possible. Intense intra-regional competition in the fruit-canning
industry was responsible for the Oregon minimum wage rulings that
brought the state's law more into line with California's. The lists of
hazardous occupations under workmen's compensation were virtually
identical in Oregon and Washington. And in September 1919,
recognition of the need for regional uniformity in the areas of wages,
cost of living, the six-day week, apprenticeship periods, enforcement,
night work, and women's dependents brought the industrial welfare
commissions of California, Oregon, Washington, and British Columbia
together in a regional conference.[45]

The force of the interstate competition argument can also be
measured by observing its reception among those committed to social
legislation. Wisconsin's Charles McCarthy, deeply concerned over the
continued presence and vitality of that viewpoint, told a national
conference on workmen's compensation in 1910 "not to fear this
bugaboo of interstate competition."[46] Child labor reformers studied the

[43] [Washington] *First Biennial Report of the Industrial Welfare Commission, 1913-1914*
(Olympia, Wash., 1915), 14; Bertha Von Der Nienburg, "Employment of Women and Minors in
the Garment Trades of California," California Industrial Welfare Commission, *Second Biennial
Report*, 84-85.
[44] California Industrial Welfare Commission, *Second Biennial Report*; Victor P. Morris, *Oregon's
Experience with Minimum Wage Legislation* (New York, 1930), 29-30; California, Industrial
Welfare Commission, Bulletin No. 1, *Report on the Regulation of Wages, Hours and Working
Conditions of Women and Minors in the Fruit and Vegetable Canning Industry of California, May,
1917* (Sacramento, 1917).
[45] [Washington] *Fourth Biennial Report of the Industrial Welfare Commission* (Olympia,
Wash., 1920), 11; U.S. Senate, *Workmen's Compensation Laws*, 376; Douglas, "American
Minimum Wage Laws," 737; Morris, *Oregon's Experience with Minimum Wage Legislation*,
205-07. See also John M. Peterson, "The Employment Effects of a Minimum Wage" (doctoral
dissertation, University of Chicago, 1956), 87-88.
[46] *Workmen's Compensation, Third National Conference*, 88-89. Charles McCarthy
acknowledged that businessmen continued to view social legislation in the context of interstate
competition. Charles McCarthy, "Need of Information About Interstate Competition," *Survey*
(Aug. 21, 1909), 696-97.

silk and glass industries to challenge claims of forced migration.[47] The
New York Factory Investigating Commission and Mitchell of the United
Mine Workers contended that uniformity in social legislation was of
limited value in the great majority of industries in which other basic
conditions, especially wages, also were not uniform.[48]

Nonetheless, the outright critics of the competitive disadvantage idea
were few, and those who counseled rejection of it often did so with
ambivalence or trepidation. For example, Kelley told the New York
investigators in 1912: "I have looked into that now for about thirty-five
years. The experience of the States and countries which put restrictions
on working hours is that the industry adapts itself to those working
hours."[49] Kelley, in short, asked the commissioners to disregard the
idea of interstate competition while accepting its premise; affected
industries would survive by adapting. Isaac Rubinow testified before the
New York commissioners in 1915 that "The prophecies in regard to
the economic effects of legislative enactment have had such a bad
reputation in the past that I am not willing to put much faith in them."
Fears of a "wholesale emigration" of firms from New York to New
Jersey following passage of workmen's compensation in New York had
not been fulfilled. "I have failed to hear of a single case," he observed,
"where that prophecy has taken place." Yet Rubinow asserted a
"certain theoretical basis for the fear of possible interstate
competition," and he concluded his testimony with rumors of New
York manufacturers gradually extending their operations in other
states.[50]

325

The basic response of the Progressive era to the specific problem of
interstate competition and, indeed, to its general economic and political
environment, was uniform state action. It is not difficult to locate
advocates of strictly national programs of workmen's compensation,
health insurance, child labor and mine safety legislation, and factory
inspection, but only in the case of child labor did these sentiments

[47] Eleanor H. Adler, "Children Who Weave Silk," *Child Labor Bulletin*, III (Nov. 1914), 52,
59, 60; and Chute, "Glass Industry and Child Labor Legislation," 123, 126.
[48] *Workmen's Compensation, Third National Conference*, 127-28; National Civic Federation
Review, IV (May 1914), 9; New York, Factory Investigating Commission, *Fourth Report*, I,
42-43, 564; and *Report of the Michigan State Commission of Inquiry into Wages*, 11. Actually,
the New York Factory Investigating Commission was considerably more interested in reducing
overlapping jurisdictions within the state—especially the disparity between upstate and New York
City inspection, than in interstate competition.
[49] New York, Factory Investigating Commission, *Preliminary Report of the Factory Investigating
Commission, 1912. Transmitted to the Legislature March 1, 1912* (3 vols., Albany, 1912), III,
1603.
[50] New York, Factory Investigating Commission, *Fourth Report*, V, 2842, 2846; Wesser,
"Conflict and Compromise," 365.

produce legislation directly affecting a significant number of employers or employees.[51] Because of constitutional limitations, uniform state legislation reached its fullest development in the areas of child labor, workmen's compensation, and mine safety, yet uniformity was also suggested for, or applied to, a broad spectrum of subjects, including anti-trust, incorporation, road building, life insurance, inheritance and corporate taxation, conservation, food and drugs, motor vehicles, marriage and divorce, credit, vital statistics, the professions of medicine, law, and public accounting, and numerous legal and commercial procedures.[52]

Certainly uniformity had its critics. Progressive Senator Albert J. Beveridge indicted uniformity "because [the states] cannot act uniformly, and do not—*never have on any subject*...." McCarthy insisted that uniformity in pure food laws would restrict the legislation of the more progressive states such as Wisconsin to some low common denominator. Uniformity also came to be seen as a centralizing agent. "Each and every piece of uniformity jockeyed through the dull legislatures of the several states," wrote Philadelphia attorney John Hemphill in the 1920s, "is in the final analysis, an attack upon

326

[51] Demands for national legislation included the following: *Report of the Michigan State Commission of Inquiry into Wages*, 281, 307, 311, 316-17; Morris, *Oregon's Experience with Minimum Wage Legislation*, 207; Congress, *Report of the Industrial Commission on Prison Labor*, 15; Congress, *Report of the Industrial Commission on Labor Legislation*, 530; Congress, *Report of the Industrial Commission on . . . the Mining Industry*, 103; U.S. Congress, House, *Report of the Industrial Commission on the Relation and Conditions of Capital and Labor Employed in Manufactures and General Business* (Washington, 1901), 585, 591, 569, 578, 562; Charles Sumner Bird, "An Employer's View of Factory Inspection," *American Labor Legislation Review*, III (Feb. 1913), 22; [Massachusetts] *Report of Special Commission on Social Insurance*, 41; Curtis Guild, Jr., "Child Labor Legislation in Massachusetts," *Supplement to the Annals of the American Academy of Political and Social Science*, XXXV (1910), 7; Tennessee Manufacturers' Association, *Report of Officers and Committees at the Annual Meeting, May 27, 1915* (n.p., n.d.), 4.

[52] See National Association of Manufacturers, *Proceedings of the Eleventh Annual Convention of the National Association of Manufacturers of the United States of America, Held at New York, N.Y., May 14, 15 and 16, 1906* (New York, n.d.), 94-95; National Civic Federation, *Tenth Annual Meeting of the National Civic Federation Held at New York, November 22 and 23, 1909* (New York, 1910), 4-5; National Civic Federation *Review*, III (March 1, 1909), 4, 10; *ibid.*, IV (March 1, 1910), 18; National Civic Federation, *Eleventh Annual Meeting of the National Civic Federation Held at New York, January 12th, 13th, and 14th, 1911* (New York, n.d.), 60, 120; Conference of Commissioners on Uniform State Laws, *Twentieth Proceedings*, 111; Conference of Commissioners on Uniform State Laws, *Proceedings of the Twenty-first Annual Conference of Commissioners on Uniform State Laws, Held at Boston, Massachusetts, August 23, 24, 25, 26 and 28, 1911* (n.p., n.d.), 117, 180.

The framework of competition-avoidance and state-avoidance that Gabriel Kolko developed is generally valid, but Kolko fails to appreciate that uniformity was designed to accomplish these objectives without vesting so much authority in the national government. Kolko, *Triumph of Conservatism*, 3.

decentralized government and to that extent a theft from the States."[53]
The equivalent of Hemphill's criticism during the Progressive era was
the complaint that legislation, which was genuinely uniform, would
violate the needs and requirements of different states and regions. Yet in
retrospect, uniformity was neither a purely negative variant of localism
nor the advance guard of centralization. It was a mainstream
methodology. Occupying a middle ground, uniformity was the
Progressive era's answer to the need for a political device that would
take a variety of questions beyond the states but keep them from the
national government.

The methodology of uniformity had its origins in the last quarter of
the nineteenth century, and in concerns only tangentially related to
social legislation and interstate competition. As of 1880, popular faith
in federalism remained strong.[54] John Fiske, a well-known historian,
wrote that federal government was "the sublime conception of a nation
in which every citizen lives under two complete and well-rounded
systems of law . . . moving one within the other, noiselessly and without
friction."[55] The rather minimal additions to national powers in most
areas of government in the two postwar decades did not, however,
assuage the fears of those who claimed to observe a strong tendency
toward centralization. This combination of reality and myth was
responsible for much of the early interest in uniformity. The first
attempts at uniformity in commercial codes were led in the 1870s by
David Dudley Field, whose strong states' rights views allowed
recognition of the need for dealing with the new national corporations in
an area larger than the cities and states.[56]

The legal profession, confronted with a proliferating common law and
wary of centralization, established in 1878 a national organization, the
American Bar Association (ABA), dedicated, according to its
constitution, to promoting "the administration of justice and uniformity

327

[53] Albert J. Beveridge, "Child Labor and the Nation," *Annals of The American Academy of Political and Social Science*, XXIX (Jan. 1907), 118-19; Conference of Commissioners on Uniform State Laws, *Twentieth Proceedings*, 47, 50-51; and John Hemphill, "The Uniform Laws Craze," *American Mercury*, V (May 1925), 60.

[54] Phillip S. Paludan, "John Norton Pomeroy, State Rights Nationalist," *American Journal of Legal History*, XII (1968), 279.

[55] Quoted in J. A. C. Grant, "The Search for Uniformity of Law," *American Political Science Review*, XXXII (Dec. 1938), 1082.

[56] David Dudley Field, "Centralization in the Federal Government," *North American Review*, CXXXII (May 1881), 407-26; W. Brooke Graves, *Uniform State Action: A Possible Substitute for Centralization* (Chapel Hill, 1934), 33.

of legislation throughout the nation.''[57] ABA showed no interest in implementing that objective for almost ten years, when interest in and passage of the Interstate Commerce Act revived the issue of federalism among lawyers and political scientists, and in 1889 ABA established a special committee on uniform state laws. An act of the New York legislature, requiring appointment of three commissioners to promote uniform state legislation, determined that the future organization of the Commissioners on Uniform State Laws would be at least nominally separate from the bar association and dependent upon the legislatures of the states. During the 1890s, the commissioners were limited not only by the failure of many state legislatures to create, and governors to appoint, commissioners, and by the failure of all states to salary their commissioners, but also by self-imposed limitations on the subject matter of uniformity. New York's original call had proposed marriage and divorce, insolvency, and notorial certificate form as possible subjects. The thrust of early uniformity was toward elimination of obstacles to trade, such as uncertainty, confusion, needless litigation, and long delays, and toward the maintenance of the states as the loci of legislative activity. Uniform legislation usually was presented as a way of restructuring the law while maintaining a federalism that idealized local self-government,[58] although in response to the dislocation of the 1890s, uniformity was also seen as a means of promoting social stability and affirming the absence of sectional prejudices.[59]

[57] American Bar Association, *Report of the American Bar Association, Held at Saratoga Springs, New York, August 20th and 21st, 1879* (Philadelphia, 1879), 20; American Bar Association, *Report of the Fourth Annual Meeting of the American Bar Association, Held at Saratoga Springs, New York, August 17th, 18th, and 19th, 1881* (Philadelphia, 1881), 172-74; American Bar Association, *Report of the Seventh Annual Meeting of the American Bar Association, Held at Saratoga Springs, New York, August 20, 21, and 22, 1884* (Philadelphia, 1884); American Bar Association, *Report of the Ninth Annual Meeting of the American Bar Association, Held at Saratoga Springs. New York, August 18th, 19th, and 20th, 1886* (Philadelphia, 1886); and Grant, ''Search for Uniformity,'' 1088.

[58] American Bar Association, *Report of the Thirteenth Annual Meeting of the American Bar Association, Held at Saratoga Springs, New York, August 20, 21 and 22, 1890* (Philadelphia, 1890), 30, 336-37; American Bar Association, *Report of the Sixteenth Annual Meeting of the American Bar Association, Held at Milwaukee, Wisconsin, Aug. 30, 31 and September 1, 1893* (Philadelphia, 1893), 346; American Bar Association, *Report of the Fourteenth Annual Meeting of the American Bar Association, Held at Boston, Massachusetts, August 26, 27 and 28, 1891* (Philadelphia, 1891), 365-75; American Bar Association, *Report of the Fifteenth Annual Meeting of the American Bar Association, Held at Saratoga Springs, N.Y., August 24, 25 and 26, 1892* (Philadelphia, 1892), 287-311; American Bar Association, *Report of the Sixteenth Meeting,* 210-11.

[59] American Bar Association, *Report of the Twenty-First Annual Meeting of the American Bar Association, Held at Saratoga Springs, New York, August 17, 18 and 19, 1898* (Philadelphia, 1898), 315-33; American Bar Association, *Report of the Twentieth Annual Meeting of the American Bar Association, Held at Cleveland, Ohio, August 25, 26 and 27, 1897* (Philadelphia, 1897), 239.

Uniformity remained the solution of a few until Secretary of State Elihu Root, speaking to the Pennsylvania Society of New York in late 1906, presented his analysis of the nation's latest constitutional crisis. Responding to the national legislation of 1906, which included railroad, food and drug, meat inspection, and employer's liability laws,[60] to the threat of national child labor legislation, and, more generally, to what he described as "a development of business and social life which tends more and more to the obliteration of State lines and the decrease of State power as compared with National Power," Root suggested the one way that the powers of the states could be preserved. That way, he said, "is by an awakening on the part of the States to a realization of their own duties to the country at large. Under the conditions which now exist, no State can live unto itself alone and regulate its affairs with sole reference to its own treasury, its own convenience, its own special interests." States that maintained legislation that promoted child labor, that encouraged the formation of trusts and monopolies, or that promoted overcapitalization of corporations were "promoting the tendency of the people of the country to seek relief through the National Government. . . ." The people, Root emphasized, "will have the control they need either from the States or from the National Government; and if the States fail to furnish it in due measure, sooner or later constructions of the Constitution will be found to vest the power where it will be exercised—in the National Government. The true and only way to preserve State authority is to be found in the awakened conscience of the States. . . ."[61]

This speech, now almost forgotten by historians of the Progressive era, was the intellectual trigger for an intensive, decade-long debate on the federal system.[62] Though this debate produced a wide variety of analyses and solutions, two elements of consensus emerged. First, the current reliance on the independent states was not adequate to deal with a twentieth-century business system. In combination with interstate competition, this system militated against a variety of reforms. Alone, it

329

[60] John Braeman, "The Square Deal in Action: A Case Study in the Growth of the 'National Police Power,' " John Braeman, Robert H. Bremner, and Everett Walters, *Change and Continuity in Twentieth-Century America* (Columbus, Ohio, 1964), 35, 43, 57, 75.

[61] Quoted in Graves, *American Intergovernmental Relations*, 798-99.

[62] For reactions to Elihu Root's address, see Charles F. Amidon, "The Nation and the Constitution," American Bar Association, *Report of Thirtieth Meeting*, 463-85; National Civic Federation, *Tenth Annual Meeting*, 2-3; Henry Wade Rogers, "The Constitution and the New Federalism," *North American Review*, CLXXXVIII (Sept. 1908), 329; David Graham Phillips, "Secretary Root and His Plea for Centralization," *Arena*, 37 (Feb. 1907), 120-25; Edmund J. James, "Conflicts of Federal and State Authority," *Independent*, LXIII (Sept. 19, 1907), 655-56; Frank J. Goodnow, *Social Reform and the Constitution* (New York, 1911).

encouraged the states to compete for corporate wealth by offering tax
and other advantages, resulted in needless conflicts of authority, and
proved to be overly complex and inefficient. Woodrow Wilson called
attention to this when he wrote: "the enforcement of the laws of the
States in all their variety threatens the country with a new war of
conflicting regulations as serious as that which made the Philadelphia
convention of 1787 necessary. . . . This conflict of laws . . . constitutes
the greatest political danger of our day."[63] The second element of
consensus was on the virtue of federalism. Henry Wade Rogers, dean of
Yale University Law School, argued that local self-government—the
symbol of federalism—developed "an energetic leadership" that existed
for the benefit of the people. "The noblest system of political
institutions the world has known," Rogers concluded, "and the most
conducive to the happiness and welfare of mankind, is that of local self-
government." Federalism, wrote political scientist John W. Burgess,
"produces a political civilization which is not only unique but which is
of a far higher order than any other form can create." President Charles
Thaddeus Terry of the Conference of Commissioners carried the federal
vision to new heights. Having presented the view that the Constitution
barred national legislation in a number of areas, he turned to the duty of
the commissioners.

This duty is, among other things, to set our faces, inflexibly and sternly . . .
against the onrushing horde of those who would overthrow our system of
government and reverse the precepts of the fathers . . . have we any good reason
for believing that the principles laid down by the founders of our unique plan of
government, conceived in profound study and insight and put forth in the most
exalted and inspired spirit of prophecy, have proved themselves inadequate to
meet and solve the problems of these latter days?[64]

[63] Woodrow Wilson, "The States and the Federal Government," *North American Review*,
CLXXXVII (May 1908), 693. See also Rogers, "Constitution and the New Federalism," 324-25;
Charles Merz, "Growth of Federalism," *New Republic*, X (March 31, 1917), 257.
[64] Rogers, "Constitution and the New Federalism," 334, 335; John W. Burgess, *Germany and
the United States, An Address Delivered Before the Germanistic Society of America, January 24,
1908* (New York, 1908), 15; Conference of Commissioners on Uniform State Laws, *Proceedings of
the Twenty-third Annual Conference of Commissioners on Uniform State Laws, Held at Montreal,
P.Q., Canada, August 26, 27, 28, 29 and 30, 1913* (n.p., n.d.), 98, 96.
   For other opinions of federalism, see Edgar Davies, Chief Factory Inspector for Illinois, in
International Association of Factory Inspectors, *Twenty-fourth Proceedings*, 76; Walter George
Smith, Presidential address, in Conference of Commissioners on Uniform State Laws, *Twenty-
second Proceedings*, 93; Conference of Commissioners on Uniform State Laws, *Twentieth
Proceedings*, 109-10; National Association of Manufacturers, *Proceedings of Eleventh Annual
Convention*, 38; "Federal Power and Child Labor," *Nation*, 98 (Feb. 12, 1914), 150-51; Simeon
E. Baldwin, "The Progressive Unfolding of the Powers of the United States," *American Political
Science Review*, VI (Feb. 1912), 1-16.
   Two scholars of federalism have noted the mythical properties of the American version. See
Arnold Brecht, "American and German Federalism: Political Differences," Aaron Wildavsky, ed.,

Root's address was important because it contained both of these elements of consensus—the necessity of dealing with national problems and the value of federalism—and because it anticipated a solution— uniform state legislation—that appeared to bring these elements of consensus into harmony. In the decade after 1906, that solution was accepted and developed by a wide variety of groups, each with its own particular emphases and needs.[65] The American Association for Labor Legislation (AALL) was established in 1906, a spin-off from the International Association for Labor Legislation which was organized in part to bring uniformity to European social legislation.[66] Although uniformity was from the beginning a constitutional objective of AALL, it was not until 1909 that the organization, overwhelmed by the argument of interstate competition and convinced that the Constitution was unamendable,[67] turned to uniform state legislation as its basic policy.[68] Working through the Minnesota Workmen's Compensation Commission, AALL succeeded in calling an Interstate Conference on Workmen's Compensation in 1909 and two in 1910. At each of these conferences, uniformity received a mixed reception. When the third conference closed, uniformity remained a viable policy alternative, but it was increasingly suspect as the state commissioners subjected the interstate competition argument to closer scrutiny.[69] AALL, however,

331

American Federalism in Perspective (Boston, 1967), 185, and William Anderson, *Federalism and Intergovernmental Relations: A Budget of Suggestions for Research* (Chicago, 1946), 32. Frank J. Goodnow premises his arguments on the "almost superstitious reverence" in which Americans held the federal Constitution. Goodnow, *Social Reform and the Constitution*, 9-10. Loren Beth discusses the power of the "received" theory of federalism in these years, a related myth that emphasized the strict division of sovereignty between national and state governments. Loren P. Beth, *The Development of the American Constitution, 1877-1917* (New York, 1971), 49-53.

[65] 1908 appears to have been the year in which interest in uniformity increased in a variety of organizations and over a number of issues. At least two events played a role—the invalidation by the Supreme Court of the national Employers' Liability Act of 1906 and the reversal of the fine against Standard Oil Company of Indiana. Richard Leopold completely ignores Root's contribution to the debate over federalism and the critical position of that debate in the history of the Progressive period. See Richard W. Leopold, *Elihu Root and the Conservative Tradition* (Boston, 1954), 8, 15, 70, 73.

[66] International Labour Office, *First Comparative Report on the Administration of Labour Laws: Inspection in Europe* (London, 1911), iii-viii; International Labour Office, *Factory Inspection: Historical Development and Present Organisation in Certain Countries* (Geneva, 1923), 59, 73, 86; Lloyd F. Pierce, "The Activities of the American Association for Labor Legislation in Behalf of Social Security and Protective Labor Legislation" (doctoral dissertation, University of Wisconsin, 1953), 1-2.

[67] William S. Livingston, *Federalism and Constitutional Change* (Oxford, 1956), 242; John A. Lapp, "Uniform State Legislation," *American Political Science Review*, IV (Nov. 1910), 576; J. Allen Smith, *The Spirit of American Government* (New York, 1907).

[68] Pierce, "Activities of the American Association for Labor Legislation," 155, 39.

[69] American Association for Labor Legislation, *Third Annual Meeting, New York, N.Y., Dec. 28-30, 1909* (New York, 1910), 19-20; Pierce, "Activities of the American Association for Labor Legislation," 155; *Atlantic City Conference on Workmen's Compensation Acts, Held at Atlantic City, N.J., July 29-31, 1909, Report* (n.p., n.d.), 7-8; *Workmen's Compensation, Third National Conference*, 77-78, 88-89, 126.

remained committed to uniformity, partly as a result of the efforts of Henry R. Seager, who led the organization for four of the five years after 1910.[70] Under Seager, the organization drafted a model workmen's compensation law and helped to prepare state legislation based on it. Uniform reporting of industrial accidents and notification of occupational diseases and, in the 1920s, uniform mine safety legislation, were other important projects of this broad-based reform group.[71]

The National Civic Federation (NCF), a theoretically tripartite (business, labor, public) but actually business-dominated organization, became committed to uniform state legislation at about the same time as AALL and over the same issue—compensation of workmen for industrial accidents. Within the organization, the movement was spearheaded by its president, Seth Low, and National Civic Federation *Review*'s editor, Ralph Easly. Together they managed to present all the major arguments for uniform legislation but their frequent eulogistic references to Root reveal opposition to centralization as their fundamental motivation.[72] The interest of NCF leaders led to a national conference. Held in Washington, D.C., in 1910, the National Civic Federation Conference on Uniform State Legislation attracted 750 delegates representing the governors of forty-four states, over 100 representatives of civic, labor, professional, agricultural, and business organizations, as well as President Taft, who joined Low in warning against the centralization of power in the national government. The conference passed resolutions calling for uniform state legislation in fifteen areas, including workmen's compensation, mine safety, child labor, taxation, and pure food and drugs.[73] This promise was never fulfilled, for NCF soon narrowed its interest in uniformity to a few issues. By 1911 the organization had produced a relatively liberal model workmen's compensation bill, which for several years was in great demand in state legislatures. NCF's Committee on Improvement of State Inspection of Factories developed a model safety and inspection bill.

[70] Henry R. Seager was once a student of Simon N. Patten, an early critic of federalism, at the University of Pennsylvania. Henry Rogers Seager, "Introductory Address," *American Labor Legislation Review*, II (Feb. 1912), 12, 14. Seager, *Labor and Other Economic Essays*, ix-xiv.

[71] John B. Andrews, "Report of Work 1910," *American Labor Legislation Review*, I (Jan. 1911), 97; Henry Baird Favill, Frederick L. Hoffman, David L. Edsall, Frederick N. Judson, and Charles R. Henderson, "Memorial on Occupational Diseases," *American Labor Legislation Review*, I (Jan. 1911), 37.

[72] National Civic Federation, *Tenth Annual Meeting*, 2-5, 46, 332-35; National Civic Federation *Review*, III (March 1, 1909), 15. The interstate competition argument was presented at National Civic Federation (NCF) meetings and at the 1910 Washington conference, so it should not be dismissed.

[73] National Civic Federation *Review*, III (March 1, 1910), 1-3, 18.

Efforts on behalf of uniform food and drug legislation appear to have accomplished little, and in 1917 war-related problems vitiated any lingering interest in uniformity.[74]

The most consistent advocate of uniform legislation in the Progressive era was the National Conference of Commissioners on Uniform State Laws. Although this organization's primary interests were in commercial and legal uniformity, the commissioners moved tentatively into workmen's compensation and child labor[75] and dealt briefly with boiler inspection, and reporting and prevention of occupational diseases. A Special Committee on Child Labor, working with Lovejoy of the National Child Labor Committee and impressed, as Lovejoy was, with the political power of the interstate competition argument, developed in 1911 a model bill based on the provisions of laws already in force in a number of states. As of 1915 no state or jurisdiction had adopted it.[76] NCCUSL's involvement in workmen's compensation grew out of a request from August Belmont, who supervised workmen's compensation for the National Civic Federation. Because of the projected high cost of insurance under the new compensation systems, wrote Belmont, "it is rendered doubly essential that there be legislation practically uniform, especially in the industrial, competitive states.'"[77] The new Special Committee on Workmen's Compensation concluded that compulsory plans were superior to elective plans, but after three years the organization's conservative membership, led by its southern wing, approved only a model bill based on elective principles, and efforts to secure its adoption were no more successful than in the child labor areas.[78] The commis-

333

[74] National Civic Federation, Department on Compensation for Industrial Accidents and Their Prevention, *Proceedings of Meeting Held December 8, 1911, New York* (n.p., n.d.), 30, 38, 41; National Civic Federation, *Eleventh Annual Meeting*, 2-3, 140-42, 118-21, 148-49, 187, 202, 207, 209, 215, 228; National Civic Federation, *Proceedings of the Twelfth Annual Meeting of the National Civic Federation, Held in Washington, D.C., March 5-7, 1912* (New York, n.d.), 150; National Civic Federation *Review*, III (Feb. 15, 1912), 10-11; *ibid.*, IV (Dec. 1, 1913), 5; *ibid.* (March 1914), 7, 16-19, 22; *ibid.* (May 1914), 7.

[75] Conference of Commissioners on Uniform State Laws, *Twenty-second Proceedings*, 26, 35-36, 57-59; Conference of Commissioners on Uniform State Laws, *Twenty-third Proceedings*, 24; and Conference of Commissioners on Uniform State Laws, *Proceedings of the Twenty-fourth Annual Conference of Commissioners on Uniform State Laws, Held at Washington, District of Columbia, October 14, 15, 16, 17 and 19, 1914* (n.p., n.d.), 277.

[76] Conference of Commissioners on Uniform State Laws, *Twentieth Proceedings*, 64-65, 67, 193-214; National Conference of Commissioners on Uniform State Laws, *Twenty-fifth Proceedings of the National Conference of Commissioners on Uniform State Laws, Held at Salt Lake City, Utah, August 10, 11, 12, 13, 14 and 16, 1915* (n.p., n.d.), 140-41.

[77] Conference of Commissioners on Uniform State Laws, *Twentieth Proceedings*, 104-05, 98-99.

[78] Conference of Commissioners on Uniform State Laws, *Twenty-first Proceedings*, 45-46, 49-50; Conference of Commissioners on Uniform State Laws, *Twenty-third Proceedings*, 67-74; and National Conference of Commissioners on Uniform State Laws, *Handbook of NCCUSL & Proceedings of Thirty-fifth Annual Meeting, Held in Detroit, Michigan, Aug. 25-31, 1925* (n.p., n.d.), 36-37.

sioners approached uniformity from a variety of philosophical perspectives, yet most believed strongly in the advantages of a decentralized
system of government while recognizing that "the boundaries of the
states have become, from the point of view of the business man [sic],
merely geographical expressions."[79] Legal order, conducive to commercial and industrial growth, and within the context of traditional
federalism, was the aim pursued by the conference.[80]

Was uniformity a reasonable response to political and economic conditions in the Progressive era? Was it capable of overcoming the political
diversity inherent in a federal system and reinforced by arguments based
on interstate competition? In the peripheral areas of social legislation,
the answer is usually no. Night work was subject to regulation in only

[79] Quotation from Walter George Smith, President of NCCUSL, Conference of Commissioners on Uniform State Laws, *Twenty-first Proceedings*, 119.

[80] Conference of Commissioners on Uniform State Laws, *Twentieth Proceedings*, 108-10; Conference of Commissioners on Uniform State Laws, *Twenty-first Proceedings*, 117, 119; Conference of Commissioners on Uniform State Laws, *Twenty-second Proceedings*, 91, 93, 95; Conference of Commissioners on Uniform State Laws, *Twenty-third Proceedings*, 59, 88-94, 96, 98; and Conference of Commissioners on Uniform State Laws, *Twenty-fourth Proceedings*, 119-21.

Foremost among the remaining organizations with an interest in uniform social legislation was the National Child Labor Committee (NCLC). From its formation in 1904 until 1913, the NCLC remained essentially committed to state, as opposed to national, legislation. After 1913 the organization's major commitment was to national legislation, but to the extent that national legislation was frustrated by the Congress and the courts, uniformity remained the only workable solution.

Questions of social legislation were of secondary importance to the National Association of Manufacturers (NAM), yet that organization endorsed uniform workmen's compensation legislation on the basis of interstate competition. National Association of Manufacturers, *Proceedings of the 15th Annual Meeting of the National Association of Manufacturers held in New York, N.Y., May 16-18, 1910* (New York, n.d.), 280, and National Association of Manufacturers, *Proceedings of the 16th Annual Meeting of the National Association of Manufacturers, held in New York, N.Y., May 15-17, 1911* (New York, n.d.), 109. NAM's committee on incorporation favored national legislation but found the constitutional obstacles insuperable and was willing to settle for uniform state action. National Association of Manufacturers, *Proceedings of the 14th Annual Meeting of the National Association of Manufacturers, held in New York, N.Y., May 17-19, 1909* (New York, n.d.), 179-80.

The Governors' Conference, a Theodore Roosevelt-inspired institution, was conceived in part as an agent of uniformity. National Civic Federation *Review*, III (March 1, 1909), 4; A. H. Birch, *Federalism, Finance and Social Legislation in Canada, Australia, and the United States* (Oxford, 1955), 23; Conference of Commissioners on Uniform State Laws, *Twenty-fourth Proceedings*, 112; and "Uniform State Legislation," *Outlook*, 105 (Sept. 13, 1913), 57-58.

Of more benefit to the movement was the Legislative Drafting Association, designed to assist the states in writing quality legislation, and the growing number of state legislative reference bureaus, intended to insure that state legislators knew what other states were doing or had done when they considered new legislation. Conference of Commissioners on Uniform State Laws, *Twentieth Proceedings*, 111; John A. Lapp, "Work of a Legislative Reference Department," Ohio State Board of Commerce, *Proceedings of the Sixteenth Annual Meeting, 1909* (Columbus, n.d.), 346-51; Parkinson, "Problems and Progress of Workmen's Compensation Legislation," 59-60.

Following the defeat of a number of state eight-hour bills in 1916 on the grounds of interstate competition, the National Consumers' League and the Women's Trade Union League began a campaign for a uniform eight-hour day, introducing legislation into forty states in 1917. "Legislation for Women in Industry," 362.

eleven states between 1890 and 1916. Minimum wage legislation for women and children in 1918 covered workers in only twelve states and the District of Columbia, and uniformity was apparent only in West Coast legislation. Because only three states specified the minimum rates in their legislation, leaving final determination to commissions, the potentiality of uniformity was further restricted.[81] More progress had been made in uniform regulation of hours of working women. In 1916 twenty-eight states had a nine- or ten-hour day and weekly maximums of fifty-four to sixty hours. Statistical uniformity, especially in state accident reporting, was also advancing.[82] In the highly technical area of coal mining safety, uniformity was approximated only in the industrial states with well-established mining regions—Pennsylvania, Illinois, and Ohio. Factory inspectors expressed continual frustration over the absence of uniformity in their area of operation. Indeed, the inspectors, while remaining committed to some kind of national solution to factory inspection problems—either national legislation or uniform state legislation—experienced great difficulty in establishing workable mechanisms for presenting their case. It was 1913 before the organization had even a standing committee to survey factory laws in the preparation of model legislation.[83]

335

Where uniformity was consistently pursued, as in workmen's compensation and child labor, there was substantial progress, but complete success remained elusive. In 1918, workmen's compensation was the law in thirty-eight states. Waiting periods and amounts of compensation as a percent of wages were roughly similar.[84] Yet ten states, nine of them southern, had no compensation legislation, and many confined their coverage to especially hazardous employments.[85] Child labor

[81] "Legislation for Women in Industry," 371. For minimum wages, see *ibid.*, 384, 390-91; "Minimum Wage Legislation in the United States," *American Labor Legislation Review*, VIII (Dec. 1918), 355.

[82] "Legislation for Women in Industry," 361; Pierce, "Activities of the American Association for Labor Legislation," 111-12.

[83] International Association of Factory Inspectors, *Tenth Annual Convention of the International Association of Factory Inspectors, Held at Toronto, Canada, September 1-3, 1896* (Chicago, n.d.), 11; International Association of Factory Inspectors, *Twenty-fourth Annual Convention . . . Factory Inspectors*, 73; International Association of Factory Inspectors, *Proceedings of the Twenty-fifth Annual Convention of the International Association of Factory Inspectors, Lincoln, Nebraska, September 18, 19, 20 and 21, 1911* (St. Louis, n.d.); International Association of Factory Inspectors, *Proceedings of the Twenty-seventh Annual Convention of the International Association of Factory Inspectors, Held May 6-9, 1913, Chicago, Illinois* (n.p., n.d.), 131-32.

[84] See "Minimum Wage Legislation in the United States," 293.

[85] U.S. Senate, *Workmen's Compensation Laws*, chart facing 48, 226, 254, 325, 341-42, 376. Neither NCCUSL nor AALL was successful with its model bill. See National Conference of Commissioners on Uniform State Laws, *National Conference of Commissioners on Uniform State Laws, Twenty-sixth Proceedings, Held at Chicago, Illinois, August 23, 24, 25, 26, 28 and 29, 1916* (n.p., n.d.), and Pierce, "Activities of the American Association for Labor Legislation," 173-74. The AALL's standards are available in "Standards for Workmen's Compensation Laws," *American Labor Legislation Review*, IV (Oct. 1914), 585-94.

legislation also was moving toward uniformity. As of 1909, almost all states, even in the South, had fourteen-year age limits; most of the progress in the direction of uniformity occurred after 1904. Enforcement systems also became more uniform over the same period. Uniformity in hours of labor, however, declined during the ten-year period before 1909, and here the southern states were primarily responsible for the regression.[86] After 1910, the general trend was toward uniformity, even if one takes into account the continued backwardness of southern legislation. Major advances in uniformity occurred in night work and hours limitations for children and in recognition of hazardous occupations.[87] Uniform child labor legislation was not, as one southern inspector and NCLC member, said, "one of the impossible things."[88] Not impossible, but difficult.

336

These approaches to uniformity notwithstanding, one can hardly avoid historian William O'Neill's conclusion that "the failure of the movement for uniformity is all the more interesting when measured against the apparent enthusiasm for it."[89] Why did uniformity so disappoint its advocates? Was the methodology itself flawed, or did Americans simply expect too much from it? To some extent, uniformity was doomed by its origins. Interstate competition at once made uniformity an urgent need and encouraged resistance to state legislation. Where interstate competition was the most severe, in textiles, coal mining, glass, cigars, and clothing, for example, the need for protective legislation was the greatest and the opposition to it the strongest. Southern resistance to uniform state legislation was less the result of sectional differences in ideology than of the presence of competitive interstate industries, only lately developed and entrepreneurial in quality. Conversely, uniformity was most attractive to, and most successfully applied to, established industrial areas and their industries—New England textiles, Ohio glass, Pennsylvania, Illinois, and Ohio coal mining.

The development of uniformity as part of the federal myth was also harmful, since it encouraged a correspondingly emotional view of uniform state legislation. Federalism, an American religion, required a

[86] William F. Ogburn, *Progress and Uniformity in Child-Labor Legislation: A Study in Statistical Measurement* (New York, 1912), 72-76, 94, 96, 108-09, 124, 194-95.

[87] Raymond G. Fuller, "Progress in Standards of Child Labor Legislation," *Proceedings of the National Conference of Social Work, 49th Annual Session, 1922* (Chicago, 1922), 281-82; "Child Labor," 71.

[88] International Association of Factory Inspectors, *Twenty-fourth Annual Convention . . . Factory Inspectors*, 48. Stephen B. Wood assesses uniformity more negatively. Wood, *Constitutional Politics*, 24-26.

[89] William L. O'Neill, *Divorce in the Progressive Era* (New Haven, 1967), 244.

savior, not a political adjustment; and uniformity was, therefore, usually accepted as a panacea.

The uniformity movement also suffered from structural and organizational deficiencies. Its success depended upon legislation, and yet with few exceptions, it was not organized to secure legislation. The Commissioners on Uniform State Laws were charged, as individuals, with procuring enactment of legislation in their home states, and they maintained a close relationship with the state bar associations. This arrangement, however, was largely limited to projects for commercial uniformity; when NCCUSL turned to social legislation, the alliances with bar associations broke down. In factory and mine inspection, inspectors were left to their own economic resources and political devices in securing state legislation. In contrast, AALL and NCLC maintained relatively strong state branches that paid off in legislative gains.[90]

337

Organizational deficiencies within private and quasi-public groups were matched by an absence within the states of any consistent enthusiasm for cooperative action. The Conference of Governors was a public relations success but a political failure. Interregional conferences were few. Even the conservative commissioners were hampered by the refusal of states to send representatives or provide reasonable expense allowances.[91] In 1911 the commissioners tabled the published proposal of an Oklahoma Supreme Court Justice for a permanent salaried interstate legislative commission supported by the states not because the idea seemed unappealing, but because it seemed manifestly impossible.[92] The states behaved like "island communities."[93]

This study of interstate competition and uniformity in the context of social reform has several implications for the history of the Progressive era. First, it is essential that historians recognize that the process of reform took place within a framework that was both economic and political, within a political economy, whose major components were interstate competition and federalism, working at cross purposes. Although the constitutional obstacles to social reform were not minimal, the political economy of these years was at least as important.[94]

[90] Conference of Commissioners on Uniform State Laws, *Twentieth Proceedings*, 14; International Association of Factory Inspectors, *Proceedings of the Seventeenth Annual Convention of the International Association of Factory Inspectors, held in Montreal, Canada, August 25-27, 1903* (n.p., n.d.), 19; Andrews, "Report of Work 1910," 105; Pierce, "Activities of the American Association for Labor Legislation," 16-17, 32.

[91] Conference of Commissioners on Uniform State Laws, *Twentieth Proceedings*, 107-08.

[92] Conference of Commissioners on Uniform State Laws, *Twenty-first Proceedings*, 77.

[93] Robert H. Wiebe, *The Search for Order, 1877-1920* (New York, 1967), 111.

[94] For this thesis see Abrams, *Conservatism in a Progressive Era*; Kolko, *Triumph of Conservatism*; Oscar E. Anderson, Jr., *The Health of a Nation: Harvey W. Wiley and the Fight for Pure Food* (Chicago, 1958).

Opposition to social legislation on the grounds of interstate competition was often a valid argument; when not valid, it was usually perceived as valid by those who made it and by those charged with evaluating it. Even under attack, the argument was influential. This amalgam of politics and values—sometimes raised to mythic proportions—was demonstrably dysfunctional in the late-nineteenth and early twentieth centuries, incapable of effective response to the problems created by a national economy. That so much social legislation became law in the Progressive era was due to the extraordinary pressure and need for it and to the ability of uniformity, however limited, to transcend the artificial geography of state boundaries. Federalism had proven to be a good deal more than a massive laboratory of political experimentation.[95]

The second point concerns the place of uniformity in the structure of politics in the Progressive era. The search for a structural definition of progressive politics traditionally has been conducted within the duality of Wilson's New Freedom and Theodore Roosevelt's New Nationalism, with some scholars emphasizing progressivism's reliance on national solutions and its anticipation of the reforms of the New Deal.[96] These

[95] George Mowry offers the strongest statement of the laboratory idea by an historian. George Mowry, *The Era of Theodore Roosevelt, 1900-1912* (New York, 1958), 80. George Benson recognizes the potency of interstate competition and questions whether decentralization has actually operated as an "experimental laboratory." George C. S. Benson, *The New Centralization: A Study of Intergovernmental Relationships in the United States* (New York, 1941), 22-40. André Maurois argues that the federal system, in dividing political and judicial authority and fragmenting power, created an environment in which businessmen could prosper without controls. André Maurois, *From the New Freedom to the New Frontier: A History of the United States from 1912 to the Present* (New York, 1962), 7. This reverses the position taken in this paper, which is in part that businessmen found federalism an inefficient and unproductive system.
     The emphasis on cooperative federalism (the growing ties between national and state governments in the nineteenth and twentieth centuries) which emerges from Daniel J. Elazar, *The American Partnership: Intergovernmental Co-operation in the Nineteenth-Century United States* (Chicago, 1962); Beth, *The Development of the American Constitution* and Morton Grodzins, *The American System: A New View of Government in the United States* (Chicago, 1966), complements this study but focuses on administration rather than politics. In social reform areas, cooperative federalism was considerably less important than dual federalism with cooperation (uniformity in various forms) at one level of the duality.
[96] The national content of progressive reform is emphasized in Braeman, "Square Deal"; Faulkner, *Quest for Social Justice*, 124; Wood, *Constitutional Politics*, ix; Sidney Fine, *Laissez Faire and the General-Welfare State: A Study of Conflict in American Thought, 1865-1901* (Ann Arbor, 1956), 367; James H. Timberlake, *Prohibition and the Progressive Movement, 1900-1920* (Cambridge, 1963), 159; Anderson, *Health of a Nation*; Andrew M. Scott, "The Progressive Era in Perspective," *Journal of Politics*, 21 (Nov. 1959), 689; Kolko, *Triumph of Conservatism*; Wiebe, *Search for Order*, 185, 198. William Leuchtenburg argues that "the New Nationalism would be the most fruitful doctrine of the Progressive era. . . ." Theodore Roosevelt, *The New Nationalism*, ed. by William Leuchtenburg (Englewood Cliffs, N.J., 1961), 16. Otis Graham, Russel Nye, Richard Hofstadter, and James Patterson are among those emphasizing progressivism's ties to the states. Otis L. Graham, Jr., *An Encore for Reform: The Old Progressives and the New Deal* (New York, 1967), 10, 36, 38, 93, 125-26, 121, 124, 182-83, 185-86; Russel B. Nye, *Midwestern Progressive Politics: A Historical Study of Its Origins and*

scholars offer an either/or fallacy, a choice between the states or the national government as the essential progressive political methodology. In reality, the period employed its own distinctive methodology, uniform state legislation. This methodology was, it is true, strongly identified with the Taft wing of the Republican party. Nonetheless, uniformity held some attraction for Wilson and the Democrats and for a wide range of social reformers, many of whom were identified with the New Nationalism of Roosevelt. The New Nationalism in many respects went beyond uniformity, but it did not reject it.[97] The central place of uniformity also offers some perspective on issues of chronology. If uniformity was crucial to progressive methodology, then, methodologically, the progressive period extended back into the 1880s, reached a peak between 1908 and 1914, and continued vital through the 1930s.[98] Again, methodologically, its basic ties were to the past, its basic vision one of building a state-centered system that would handle the obviously national problems of the present and future.

339

Development, 1870-1950 (East Lansing, Mich., 1951), 381-82; Richard Hofstadter, *The Age of Reform: From Bryan to F.D.R.* (New York, 1955), 320-26; and James T. Patterson, *The New Deal and the States: Federalism in Transition* (Princeton, 1969), 24-25.

[97] For Roosevelt's receptive attitude to the workmen's compensation program of the National Civic Federation, see Weinstein, *Corporate Ideal in the Liberal State*, 54-55. On the New Nationalism, see Roosevelt, *New Nationalism*, 34-36. According to Sidney Fine, the New Nationalism included standardization of mine and factory inspection by federal statute or by interstate agreement. Fine, *Laissez Faire and the General-Welfare State*, 390. Democrat Alton B. Parker was chairman of the session on uniform state legislation at an NCF meeting in 1911.

[98] Graves, *American Intergovernmental Relations*, 582-93; Jane Perry Clark, "Interstate Compacts and Social Legislation," *Political Science Quarterly*, 50 (Dec. 1935), 502-24; Jane Perry Clark, "Interstate Compacts and Social Legislation II: Interstate Compacts after Negotiation," *Political Science Quarterly*, 51 (March 1936), 36-60.

Unite to Divide; Divide to Unite: The Shaping of American Federalism

By William T. Hutchinson

By the late nineteenth century the American West had apparently exhausted itself as a provider of new frontiers; today it probably has yielded its last state to the Union. With the admission of Alaska, the United States has no organized territory on the North American mainland for the first time in 170 years. Between the beginning of territorial government in the oldest Northwest in 1788 and its end in the newest Northwest in 1959, each of thirty states evolved out of a territorial stage, and most of the remaining six underwent a somewhat equivalent experience.[1] Although historians a generation or more ago wondered how the disappearance of the frontier might affect America's future, their successors today seem unlikely to feel a similar concern over the end of state-making. To close the circle of states can hardly deprive any one of them of power or hasten the concentration of authority at Washington. The strength of the nation no longer hinges upon its capacity for territorial growth. On the other hand, the opening of the original circle of thirteen to new members, thereby joining expansion with union, was a matter of first importance in our history. To suggest how an environment stretching wide into the West and a heritage running deep into colonial history may have helped to determine the nature of early American federalism is the subject of this essay.

Our federal union has two dimensions — the one horizontal to link together its more or less autonomous parts, and the other vertical to connect each of these parts and its citizens with a central government, made by and stretching over all of them. Although a

EDITOR'S NOTE: — This paper was presented as the presidential address at the Fifty-second Annual Meeting of the Mississippi Valley Historical Association in Denver, Colorado, on April 23, 1959.
[1] Vermont, Kentucky, Maine, Texas, California, and West Virginia.

considerable degree of comity prevailed among the courts of the
different colonies, and although their governors usually co-operated
in extraditing fugitives from justice or forced labor,[2] the more obvious evidence of a nascent federalism within the British Empire
by the eve of the Revolution was the division of governmental fields
between the Empire's center and the American colonies. This
separation of functions, along with the Privy Council's role as re-
viewer both of colonial legislation and of the appealed decisions of
colonial courts, made the Empire federalistic in its structure and
mode of operation, no matter what it may have been in correct constitutional theory.[3] If the colonies did not possess rightful powers
of their own, much of Jefferson's indictment of King George III in
the Declaration of Independence had no validity either in law or in
history.

341

Measured against the form of the later American union, however, the Empire lacked at least three important features to be truly
federal. It had no written Constitution with which the many official
documents of high authority must conform. At best, too, it was a
topsy-turvy sort of federalism because the home government participated directly in the rule of most of the colonies but they shared
not at all in the administration of the home government. Moreover,
the legal ties between the colonies were few and their official relationships were often far from amicable. Their chronic un-
neighborliness, manifest even as late as the Revolution, began as
early as the 1630's when two of them had come into geographic
proximity for the first time.

This discord mainly stemmed from either the diverse modes of
settlement and economic life or from the competition between
individuals of adjacent colonies seeking financial profits in the same
areas and in identical ways. The American environment, traversing
fifteen degrees of latitude and contrasting belts of climate, soil, and
topography, contributed much to the molding of dissimilar societies,
frequently in closer touch with people in England than with one
another. Although drawn together by the highway of commerce
and communication provided by their ocean frontier, they were

[2] Shirley A. Bill, "The Meaning and Background of the Interstate Comity Clause of
the Constitution" (Ph.D. dissertation, University of Chicago, 1950), 92-93, 148-51.
[3] Andrew C. McLaughlin, "The Background of American Federalism," *American
Political Science Review* (Baltimore), XII (May, 1918), 215-40.

almost continuously estranged by disagreements over the ownership and exploitation of their land frontier. Of ill omen, also, to future success in politically uniting these societies were the prevalent beliefs, born of experiences under British dominion, that a merger of neighboring colonies meant autocratic rule, a division of one large colony into two colonies marked a gain in self-government, and that the protection of individual liberty required slack control by England and a powerful local legislature.

By 1760, for periods ranging in duration from only thirty years in Georgia to much over a century longer in Virginia, these thirteen provincial societies had felt the thrust and counter-thrust of opposing forces — of logic and a cultural heritage from Great Britain impelling them to unite, and of economic and political differences, often aggravated by the mother country, spurring them to maintain their separation. Beneath the stormy surface of intercolonial affairs, however, ran a strong undercurrent of mutuality, frequently unrecognized and sometimes scorned. Until the onset of the Revolution the personal bonds between colonists, rather than the shadowy legal connections between the colonies, comprised the best earnest of their eventual co-operation.

Lacking an intercolonial union or a single community, the Americans were obliged to rest their case against the new measures of the Crown after 1760 upon the rights of each colony and the rights of individual colonists. To all except the most radical and most conservative of their leaders, joint action recommended itself merely as a temporary device to be employed only because it appeared best calculated to gain a speedy redress of grievances. The First and Second Continental Congresses, and the Continental Association, represented the maximum in the way of common endeavor that many of the moderates had dared to hope for and more than some of them desired to have. These united efforts came as an expedient response to an instant emergency and not as the natural outcome of a long historical development.

The patriots blamed the central government overseas for precipitating this crisis by exercising unconstitutional and unaccustomed power to their detriment and to that of the colonies. Arrogating complete sovereignty to itself in the Declaratory Act, Parliament thereby shattered the base of the Empire by reducing

342

these colonies, at least on paper, to something like the lowly status of municipal corporations. Ten years later the Continental Congress, by its resolution of independence, completed the demolition of the constitutional structure of the Empire, in so far as the thirteen colonies were concerned, by lopping off its apex.

Viewed in this way, the history of the United States began with the destruction of a federalistic union. The subsequent political transition involved a shift from control by each colony over some fields of power to control by each state over all of them. As heir of the Crown, every state in its constitution expanded its former claim to limited rights of self-government into an assertion of complete sovereignty.[4] Comity relationships, if any, between these self-styled sovereigns moved, logically it would seem, into the realm of international law. Without a legally established central government to guarantee support of the Declaration of Independence, its signers could only "pledge . . . each other" to uphold it with their "Lives . . . Fortunes and . . . sacred Honor."

343

The adoption of the resolution of independence reversed the chief constitutional issue of the preceding decade. The problem of transferring power downward from a sovereign central authority to each colonial government changed to one of moving power upward from thirteen sovereign units to a central government not yet formally created. Men who had argued valiantly in defense of the rights of a colony were suddenly confronted with the need to give reasons, often contradictory in tenor to those they had advanced not long before, why a vigorous over-all administration would not endanger individual liberties or state independence. Although a few leaders turned this constitutional somersault with ease, many of them were unable on short notice to muster the requisite agility.

Their will to join hands in rebellion did not signify their willingness to compromise interstate differences sufficiently to agree upon articles of union. On the contrary, spokesmen for one state or another asserted its rights as against a sister state with the same vehemence which, as colonists, they had manifested in resisting encroachments by Parliament. The weakness of their nationalism is not surprising. If their loyalty to Great Britain, centuries-old in the background of many of them, could not outlast a decade of dis-

---

[4] Claude H. Van Tyne, "Sovereignty in the American Revolution: An Historical Study," *American Historical Review* (New York), XII (April, 1907), 529-45.

content charged against their mother country, it could hardly be transformed overnight into a heartfelt allegiance to a newly-born United States of America. People in arms against one central government naturally hesitated to replace it with another.

Fear of a common danger probably served as a stronger force than love of a common country to hold most of these men together in this "worst of times." If the principal tie between the states was the war, its termination would also end their co-operation through a central congress. Among others, James Madison expressed concern lest winning the prize of independence might have the union as its price.[5] To preserve this union in the face of the enemy and to define its terms in an official document were separate and even conflicting tasks. The course of the conflict itself hampered the leaders who strove to form a durable central government. The readiness of patriots to confer more power upon the Continental Congress frequently varied directly in its intensity with the nearness of the foe to their own state. For this reason the staggered nature of Britain's main military effort, ranging southward from Boston to Philadelphia between 1775 and 1778, and northward from Savannah to Yorktown during the next three years, fostered disagreements about the scope of authority to be entrusted to Congress.

Until 1781, however, if not until 1789, the horizontal problem of allaying discord between states eclipsed in persistence and probably in importance the vertical problem of persuading all of them to yield powers to a central government. To water down drastically, in deference to state sovereignty, the original version of the Articles of Confederation was less of a task than to induce states at odds with one another to associate within a "perpetual union." No one of the first state constitutions contained any provision for interstate comity.[6] A section on this subject, so essential to a harmonious confederation, was added to the Articles almost as an afterthought.[7] A main stumbling block in the long road leading

344

[5] James Madison to Thomas Jefferson, November 18, 1781, Julian P. Boyd (ed.), *The Papers of Thomas Jefferson* (15 vols. to date, Princeton, 1950-   ), VI, 131-32.

[6] Perhaps this statement needs one slight qualification. When the Connecticut legislature declared the Charter of 1662 to be the "Civil Constitution of this State," it adopted a resolution making at least a gesture in the direction of interstate comity.

[7] Article IV, on interstate comity, was added in November, 1777, just before the document was sent to the states for ratification. Comparing this Article with the Federal Constitution's Article IV, sections 1 and 2, on the same subjects, reveals a significant addition to the horizontal dimension of federalism.

to their adoption by Congress and their ratification by each state was the insistence that the document be unambiguous on all important matters in controversy. The troubles caused by this demand for definiteness may have convinced the makers of the Federal Constitution that an organic law gains both in virtue and in durability by dealing vaguely with divisive subjects.

The equality of individuals, which had been proclaimed in the Declaration of Independence and affirmed somewhat equivocably in many of the state constitutions, yielded place to the equality of states as the central issue in the drafting and acceptance of the Articles of Confederation. To attain political equality with his more affluent neighbor, a "landless man" had to build himself up by acquiring enough property to qualify for the privileges of voting and officeholding. Among the ways to help achieve state equality, the "landless states" demanded that their big neighbors scale down in size by divesting themselves of their acreage west of the Appalachians.[8] Great Britain was not the only sovereign which lost territory as a result of the American Revolution. Victory and union each took its toll in land.

345

Marylanders had no relish for a confederation which would merely substitute a master close at hand in the form of an overtowering Virginia for a master on the far side of the Atlantic Ocean. Although twelve states had ratified the Articles by early 1779, Maryland remained immovable for two more years until the "Big Knife," as Virginia was sometimes called, offered to cede most of its land north and west of the Ohio River to the United States. New York had already made a similar promise and the lead of these two states would eventually be followed by the other five states with territory west of the mountains. How the conflicting interests of speculators in western lands had prolonged the deadlock between Maryland and Virginia over this issue, and how the British military threat to both of these states and the pressure exerted upon Maryland by the French minister, Luzerne, led them to yield in early

[8] On March 23, 1776, in a letter to Horatio Gates, John Adams lamented that agreement upon a "continental constitution" would be impeded by the avarice for land "which has made . . . so many votaries to Mammon, that I sometimes dread the consequences." Edmund C. Burnett (ed.), *Letters of Members of the Continental Congress* (8 vols., Washington, 1921-1936), I, 406. Early in the struggle Congress and eight of the states made this land hunger an instrument of war by offering land bounties to stimulate enlistments in the armed forces.

1781, are too well known to bear repetition here.[9] Although speculators in public securities would help to bring about the adoption of the Constitution, rivalry between speculators in public lands slowed up the ratification of the Articles of Confederation.

These Articles guaranteed in perpetuity the sovereignty of each state but their acceptance depended upon an action permitting a nationalistic shift of major proportions. Unlike the Federal Constitution, which added much to national power but went into effect only after amendmen.s had been pledged to prevent its abuse, the Articles hedged the central government within more constricted limits than before, but became operative only by widely expanding the potential authority of Congress. In days when the close of armed conflict and the news of a victor's peace broke the principal bond between the states, freed some of them to renew their acrimonious disputes over boundaries and trade, and led prominent leaders like George Clinton almost to forget that there was a United States,[10] the common possession of a "West" by all the states served importantly to hold them together, to instill confidence that the huge war debt could be paid without encroaching seriously upon tax sources used by the states, and to keep Congress alive and busy whenever it could muster a quorum. Without the western lands and the foreign issues arising from their possession, a sufficient central government to bridge the years between the end of the Revolution and the opening of the Constitutional Convention would have been far more difficult, if not impossible, to maintain.

Thus the West, once a main source of intercolonial discord, became a chief link between the states. Easterners who had feared that success in the war might be followed by a dissolution of the Confederation into its thirteen units or at least into several smaller leagues, now voiced grave concern lest the westerners transfer their allegiance to Spain or Great Britain. In his "Farewell Orders to the Armies of the United States," on November 2, 1783, Washington mentioned America's land and sea frontiers as the areas where

346

[9] Merrill Jensen, "The Cession of the Old Northwest," *Mississippi Valley Historical Review* (Cedar Rapids), XXIII (June, 1936), 27-47, and "The Creation of the National Domain," *ibid.*, XXVI (December, 1939), 323-42; St. George L. Sioussat, "The Chevalier De La Luzerne and the Ratification of the Articles of Confederation by Maryland, 1780-1781," *Pennsylvania Magazine of History and Biography* (Philadelphia), LX (October, 1936), 391-418.

[10] E. Wilder Spaulding, *New York in the Critical Period, 1783-1789* (New York, 1932), 160, 163.

youthful veterans would find the greatest economic opportunities.[11]
Through emigration from the East to the West and through the
development of trade routes between them, he sought as earnestly
to end the dangerous isolation of the West as in his better known
Farewell Address of 1796 he sought to persuade his fellow citizens
to insulate themselves from Europe's politics and wars.

While agreeing with Washington, Jefferson endeavored in the
1780's to solve the western problem by a constitutional plan destined to become basic to the history of American federalism. Building upon earlier congressional guarantees, he proposed a policy of
transient colonialism whereby the frontiersmen themselves might
create sovereign states like those on the seaboard. By emancipating
the West at an early date from the rule of a distant Congress and
dividing the area into states, he would foster the patriotism of its   347
people.[12] By refusing to be as generous in making colonialism
merely a forerunner of federalism, Britain had driven her colonists
to unite. The outcome of their union had been a division of the
Empire. In its stead the Americans were to create a markedly different Empire, designed to disappear as soon as all of its subordinate
parts qualified for admission to the parent Union.

Although Washington and Jefferson took for granted that the
weak Congress of the Confederation had ample power to govern
whatever western region a state might cede to the United States,
they could not cite the Articles of Confederation in justification of
their stand. And yet, as Madison wrote later in *The Federalist*, No.
38, "no blame" was "whispered, no alarm . . . sounded" when Congress "without the least color of constitutional authority" exercised
as complete dominion over the Old Northwest as Parliament had
claimed for itself over the colonies. This western region, being
beyond the jurisdiction of Congress or of any state, was a power
vacuum. Counted upon to furnish the income needed to establish
public credit, the territory clearly could not fulfill this mission until
it had a government and a land system. Congress provided both of
these and, in doing so, went far toward offsetting the sovereignty

[11] John C. Fitzpatrick (ed.), *The Writings of George Washington from the Original Manuscript Sources, 1745-1799* (37 vols., Washington, 1931-1940), XXVII, 222-27.
[12] Jefferson's Ordinance of 1784 reflected his belief that a state could exist under
the flag but outside of the Union. Although Vermont and Kentucky were hardly of
that status during the 1780's, North Carolina and Rhode Island would be between
March, 1789, and the date when each of them ratified the Constitution.

of each state on the seaboard by making itself sovereign over a vast area west of the Appalachians. As the assumption of state debts by the federal government a few years later would win for it the support of many influential holders of public securities, so the assumption of control over the Old Northwest led men of economic and political weight to look to the Congress of the Confederation for favors. Although almost pitiably ineffective within the domain of its delegated powers, this body acted with bold statesmanship within a sphere outside its legal competence to enter. Its western policy contributed largely, and for long in the future, to the constitutional development of American colonialism, federalism, and nationalism.

348

Controversies between the states, the failure of some of them to pay Congress either money or respect, Shays' Rebellion in Massachusetts, continuing unrest among the western settlers, threatened Indian wars, and the shattered hope of making the public domain north of the Ohio River a ready source of revenue, are all well-known aspects of the situation leading to the Constitutional Convention of 1787. What its members did to strengthen the United States by transforming it from a confederation into a federal union was paralleled that same summer by what Congress did to furnish the Old Northwest with a government.[13] Members of Congress and of the Convention agreed that the time had come to curb localism, rule by irresponsible majorities, and other "excesses of democracy."

Although the Ordinance of 1787 embodied Jefferson's earlier proposals in general, it also greatly modified them by imposing an authoritarian government upon the frontiersmen until they became numerous enough to qualify for a legislature, by requiring land ownership for voting and officeholding, by transferring primary control over the state-making process from the settlers to Congress, and by reducing the number of states to be formed in the Old Northwest from ten to a maximum of five. On the other hand, the Ordinance included most of the individual guarantees associated with a bill of rights and, above all, an orderly method whereby the union of equal states could expand. The new Constitution, to the

[13] Eleven men, including Rufus King, James Madison, and William S. Johnson, were members of both assemblages. Whether the makers of the Constitution, in deciding what to put into it about the West, were much influenced by the Ordinance, enacted over two months before they adjourned, is not certainly known.

meager extent that it mentioned the territories, contained nothing which ran counter to the provisions of the Ordinance.[14] The First Congress of the United States re-enacted the measure and soon extended it, except for its antislavery stipulation, to apply to the Territory South of the River Ohio.

The West figured importantly in some of the state contests over the ratification of the Constitution. In the tenth *Federalist*, which was probably his most noteworthy essay in that series, Madison argued, in effect, that the admission of new states from the West would be a prime assurance against arbitrary rule by the central government and a firm guarantee that the federal union would endure. His reading of David Hume[15] had persuaded him that, contrary to the view commonly held, a representative government would operate more successfully in a big country than in a small one. The wider its expanse the larger the number of competing economic interests it would embrace; hence the less the likelihood that any one of them would gain control of the government. By having all of these groups represented in the central administration, clashes within the social order would be neutralized and the tyranny of a selfish majority or of an oligarchy would be avoided. Pride in bigness would be consonant with faith in its efficacy. Madison, as well as other strong-government advocates, believed that a spacious West and its administration under a policy of "Divide to Unite" would aid greatly in making a republican government equivalent to a just government.

349

During the 1790's the adjustment of the seaboard states to the requirements of the new Constitution and the adjustment of the West to the legislation enacted for its governance proceeded in opposite directions. In the East the Constitution obliged each state to relinquish some of its fields of power to the central government while at the same time, as ruler of the territories, Congress passed power downward to regions which were in process of becoming

[14] Territorial officials soon called the Ordinance "the Constitution" of their jurisdictions. It may also have been so ·-garded by the framers of the Federal Constitution. In other words, they may have limited their mention of the West to a few clauses, not solely because they could not agree about the subject, but also because the Ordinance covered the matter fully.

[15] Douglass Adair, " 'That Politics May Be Reduced to a Science': David Hume, James Madison, and the Tenth Federalist," *Huntington Library Quarterly* (San Marino, Calif.), XX (August, 1957), 348-49, 351, 353, 359. See also the *Federalist*, Nos. 7, 9, 14, and 51.

states. Too little attention, I believe, has been given to the governmental changes which the original thirteen states necessarily made as a consequence of ratifying the Constitution. Under only slight pressure from the Washington and Adams administrations to hurry, these states integrated themselves more closely with the national government at varying rates of "deliberate speed," the slowest requiring nearly ten years to complete the process.[16] The rise of the Jeffersonian opposition reflected not only a mounting dislike of the Federalists' domestic and foreign policies but also a sharpened realization by state-centered politicians that the new Constitution deprived them of jobs and prestige in addition to taking from them areas of government once under their control. The constitutional reasons for the Democratic-Republican victory in 1800 will be better understood if the emergence of the party is viewed from the bottom as well as from the top.

350

Both the liberal and the illiberal aspects of territorial administration by Congress helped to determine the form and future of American federalism.[17] When the settlers challenged the prerogatives of their appointed rulers, they were mainly striving for autonomy rather than for political democracy.[18] By resisting the autocratic regime imposed by Congress during the earliest phase of territorial development, they were enabled to discover their leaders and gain experience in political debate and tactics. This training served them well as soon as the population of their territory increased sufficiently to entitle it to an elective house of representatives. Frontier conditions, including the huge and partially inaccessible areas to be governed, blunted the real authority of even

[16] Frank L. Esterquest, "State Adjustments to the Federal Constitution, 1789-1800" (Ph.D. dissertation, University of Chicago, 1940).

[17] Congress delegated much of the business of territorial administration to the President and several members of his cabinet. Probably the most extensive treatment of the reactionary aspects of the Ordinance of 1787 is Francis S. Philbrick, "Introduction," *The Laws of Illinois Territory, 1809-1818* ([Illinois State Historical Library, *Collections*, Vol. XXV], Springfield, 1950), cxxvi-ccclxxvii.

[18] Thomas P. Abernethy, *From Frontier to Plantation in Tennessee: A Study in Frontier Democracy* (Chapel Hill, 1932), 359, 362; William B. Hamilton, "Politics in the Mississippi Territory," *Huntington Library Quarterly*, XI (May, 1948), 290. As Professor Carl Becker once commented about many patriot leaders seeking autonomy for their colony on the eve of the Revolution, the territorial politicians strove earnestly for home rule but they were determined to "rule at home." Carl L. Becker, *The History of Political Parties in the Province of New York, 1760-1776* ([*Bulletin of the University of Wisconsin*, No. 286, History Series II, No. 1], Madison, 1909), 22.

the most dictatorial governor. The security and good order of an isolated community depended far more upon extra-legal regulations made by itself than upon the proclamations and laws of duly constituted authorities residing at the distant territorial or national capital. The resulting clash of the legal with the extra-legal led the settlers to cherish home rule. Not a few opposed statehood, equating it with higher taxes, more rather than less interference in their local affairs, and domination by the politicians of the larger towns. These townsmen usually led in the drive for what they liked to call an "emancipation" from territorial status. Sometimes, no doubt, they masked a desire to open up to themselves more public offices and more opportunities for land speculation behind high-level declarations about their "natural right" of self-government.[19]

The sincerity of their plea, however, can readily be granted without concluding that tyranny had wrung it from them. On the contrary, supervision of the territories by Congress relaxed rather than tightened between 1789 and 1820. It taxed the settlers lightly if at all, seldom disallowed the acts of territorial legislatures, eased the terms of buying government lands, and often condoned involuntary or even deliberate infractions of its laws. As the First Congress under the Constitution had drawn the support of wealthy easterners to the new central government by assuming the debts owed to them by the states, so Congress in 1821 allayed the ill will of many westerners toward Washington by providing an easy means whereby they could clear their debts to the United States incurred through purchases of the public domain.

During the second decade of the nineteenth century, slowness in surveying this domain or the delinquency of its buyers in paying their installments resulted in several territories having enough people to entitle them to legislative assemblies, but with either too small a landowning constituency to make their election practicable or with so few voters that the assembly was patently unrepresentative. Under these circumstances, Congress in a series of acts abolished the property qualifications for suffrage. In other words, a Congress largely dominated by easterners granted universal white manhood suffrage to the frontiersmen, not wholly and, in at least

351

[19] In general, pro-statehood westerners called upon history and, above all, "the principles of the Revolution" in support of their stand, while the anti-statehood men stressed the hazards and primitiveness of their environment.

one instance, not mainly because they had demanded it.[20] Rather, this important step toward political democracy was taken, in considerable measure, because the basic laws relating to land survey and sale blocked the operation of the equally basic laws relating to government, thus preventing a territory from moving toward statehood as its white population increased. Prior to the Missouri-Maine issues, furthermore, Congress rarely raised serious objection to the admission of a new western state and usually took for granted that its constitution provided the republican form of government required by the Federal Constitution.

The emphasis of the settlers upon the rights of a territory, reminiscent of the rights-of-a-colony position on the eve of the Revolution, expanded after statehood into a stress upon state sovereignty. Only by selecting with great care and rejecting with abandon can the westerner be fashioned into a constitutional nationalist. On matters of banking and currency the well-known cases before the Supreme Court of the United States in the 1820's probably are sufficient evidence of the characteristic western attitudes on these issues.[21] Unless the westerner came from Kentucky he lived in a state where the United States was by far the biggest landowner. Partly for this reason but also because his state was sparsely populated and weak in financial resources, he looked to the central government for much help. To this extent he was a nationalist. But the arguments he often advanced to justify this assistance, and the goals he always sought from its extension, were decidedly of a state-rights or state-sovereignty tenor. Although he expected the federal government at its expense to provide him with roads or canals, he demanded on constitutional grounds, once an internal improvement reached completion, that it be turned over to his state. He commonly urged the United States to sell its domain more rapidly or to cede it to the state in which it was located; otherwise the sovereignty or equality of that state would be unconstitutionally impaired for an intolerable length of time. When eight eastern

352

[20] Ninian Edwards to Richard M. Johnson, March 14, 1812, Clarence E. Carter (ed.), *Territorial Papers of the United States* (23 vols. to date, Washington, 1934–   ), XVI (1948), *Territory of Illinois, 1809-1814*, pp. 199-200. Congress extended universal white manhood suffrage to Indiana Territory, March 3, 1811; to Illinois Territory, May 20, 1812; to Missouri Territory, June 4, 1812; to Mississippi Territory, October 23, 1814; and to Arkansas Territory, March 2, 1819.

[21] As examples, see Osborn *v.* Bank of the United States, 9 *Wheaton* 738 (1824); Craig *v.* Missouri, 4 *Peters* 410 (1830).

states and Kentucky in the early 1820's asked Congress for grants
from the public domain to support their public schools, westerners
retorted that if these requests were honored the sovereignty of their
states would be further breached by the intrusion within them of
land titles held by sister commonwealths.[22] For a like reason, it
was contended, the central government should either relinquish its
jurisdiction over the Indians within a western state or, better still,
remove them beyond its borders.

In a word, the acquisition and administration of the West was
an incalculably great nationalizing force in American federalism,
making the United States government sovereign over the territories
and also obliging it to exercise within the public-domain states
many powers implied only vaguely, if at all, in the Constitution.
On the other hand the politicians from those states were rarely   353
nationalistic in aim. If for no other reason, their firm belief in state
sovereignty had been nurtured by their dislike of the rule imposed
by Congress during the territorial period.[23]

This rule had been about the only part of their environment
which they noticeably reflected in their first state constitutions.
In their provisions for curbing the power of the executive branch
and exalting that of the legislative, these documents harked back
to their counterparts drafted during the Revolution by easterners
who had just rid themselves of governor-centered colonial regimes.
Of far greater constitutional importance, however, is the fact that,
no matter to what extent the frontier may have shaped the social
and economic views of the settlers, it did not make them adventur-
ous in the realm of political institutions. Their constitutions and
codes of law were little more than copies or composites of earlier
American models.[24] Perhaps regrettably from the academic stand-

[22] The state legislatures which petitioned in 1821-1822 were those of Maryland, New
Hampshire, Rhode Island, Connecticut, New Jersey, Delaware, Maine, Vermont, and
Kentucky. *American State Papers, Public Lands* (8 vols., Washington, 1832-1861),
III (1834), 499-501, 509-11. For western opposition, see especially the speech of Senator
Ninian Edwards (Illinois) on March 1, 1822, *Annals of Congress*, 17 Cong., 1 Sess.
(1821-1822), I, cols. 247-68. The lead taken by Maryland in seeking these grants is
interesting because of her reverse stand during the Revolution when she insisted upon
land cessions *by states to* the central government.

[23] For evidence, other than constitutional, of the westerners' absorption in local
issues or of their conscious efforts to be autonomous, see R. Carlyle Buley, *The Old
Northwest: Pioneer Period, 1815-1840* (2 vols., Indianapolis, 1950), II, 9, 17, 27, 30,
87, 164, and David Donald and Frederick A. Palmer, "Toward a Western Literature,
1820-1860," *Mississippi Valley Historical Review*, XXXV (December, 1948), 414-23.

[24] Max Farrand, *The Legislation of Congress for the Government of the Organized*

point, the westerners neglected their opportunities to experiment with new constitutional forms. Fortunately, however, in light of the need to lay a firm and uniform foundation for an expanding federalism, they were content to be imitative rather than creative. In the constitutional history of the early West, the appropriate point to stress, if choice must be made, is the influence of heredity rather than of the physical environment.

Men in the Constitutional Convention of 1787 had doubted whether a central go /ernment could be created strong enough to maintain itself effectively without crushing the states under the weight of its authority. Although the Hamiltonian measures and the Alien and Sedition laws appeared to justify their fears of centralization, the constitutional influence of the West soon helped to quiet them. The admission of nine Mississippi Valley states by 1821, as well as of two others in New England, continuously recruited state strength with an attendant emphasis upon state sovereignty. Thus, the West aided greatly in preserving a workable equilibrium between the center and the parts, between nationalism and state rights, so difficult to attain and retain in a federal union. Moreover, even before 1820, the favor of western congressmen was being sought by their eastern colleagues in order to redress the balance on issues dividing them.

In our early history the formation and success of the Union depended upon its ability to grow. For its growth the West was essential. The flow of power from the original states to the central government and from it to the new states, and the transfer of land from seven of the original states and as many foreign countries to the central government and from it to individuals, groups of individuals, corporations, and new states, have been vital forces in the development of the American federal union. They brought it into being, enabled it to expand, caused many of its most serious problems, and largely accounted for its survival. With the admission of Alaska, the first of these processes in all likelihood has terminated on this continent, and the second reached its climax in the pledge by the national government to give this new state during the next

354

Territories of the United States, 1789-1895 (Newark, 1896), 54; Bayrd Still, "An Interpretation of the Statehood Process," *Mississippi Valley Historical Review*, XXIII (September, 1936), 189-90; Earl Pomeroy, "Toward a Reorientation of Western History: Continuity and Environment," *ibid.*, XLI (March, 1955), 581-82, 585-86.

twenty-five years about 103,000,000 acres of public domain, an area larger than California.[25] Thus the policy and the promise made by the Second Continental Congress over 175 years ago in order to unite the thirteen states under the Articles of Confederation now attain their ultimate fulfillment on the shores of Bering Strait within sight of Asia. In our day of retreating colonialism, often accompanied by bloodshed, a territorial system of "Unite to Divide; Divide to Unite," under which American federalism with little violence has spanned a continent, merits commemoration as it passes into history.

[25] 72 *Stat.* 339, Act of July 7, 1958. This law also guarantees to Alaska 5 per cent of the proceeds of the sale of the public domain within the state as a fund for the support of its public schools.

Toward a Reappraisal of the 'Federal' Government: 1783-1789

by HERBERT A. JOHNSON*

A S THE WRITING AND TEACHING OF HISTORY is a verbal, and at times verbose, occupation, it is not surprising to find historians misled by the very words which are the basis of their art. Such a deceptive term is "constitutional history" which for many students of American history entails the study of the Constitution of 1787 and the subsequent decisions of the Supreme Court of the United States which pertain to, or interpret, the clauses of the 1787 Constitution. Yet the scope of "constitutional history" is much broader than the analytical study of a written constitution or judicial precedents. Constitutional history is concerned with the relationships between sovereign power and the individuals subject to that power; it treats the techniques utilized by the state to secure tranquillity through regulation of societal activities; and finally, it is the narrative of the gradual evolution of political institutions from those of monarchy to those of representative democracy. Our associates in the field of British constitutional history are well aware of the many facets of the term "constitutional history"; lacking a document analogous to the Constitution of 1787, they do not suffer from the malady of "Constitution" fixation which burdens their fellows in American history with the handicap of being unable to distinguish between "constitutional history" and "the history of the 1787 Constitution".[1]

Perhaps this chronic illness is not of the fatal order, for certainly other fields of American history complement the work of the constitutional historian, filling in the areas of administrative, social and intellectual history considered so essential to the understanding of British constitutional history. Nevertheless there are two areas in American history where the broader British approach is not only desirable, but also essential. The first, of course, is the entire colonial period; the second, not quite as obvious, is the period during and after the American Revolution. This article will deal with the second

---

* Member of the New York Bar and lecturer in history, Hunter College.

[1] See J. Franklin Jameson, ed., in his preface to *Essays in the Constitutional History of the United States in the Formative Period 1775-89* (Boston: 1889), ix, vii.

of these periods of critical constitutional development, with particular emphasis upon the years 1783-1789.

Neglect in the area of post-Revolutionary development of the constitution stems not only from a failure to follow the more expansive British approach, but also from the pervasive and continuing influence of John Fiske. It is not without significance that his *Critical Period in American History* wedges the true meat of the book between the peacemaking of 1783 and the Constitutional Convention of 1787.[2] Between two such formidable pieces of bread, the meat of the Confederation Period is but a niggardly slice. Subsequent historians have decried Fiske but persist in following his literary example. Merrill Jensen, impressed by the political cycles of the American Revolution and the philosophy of the Articles of Confederation, approaches the Confederation Period from the viewpoint of the American Revolution, and develops some remarkable conclusions.[3] Andrew C. McLaughlin, a far more able scholar than Fiske, follows Fiske's example in looking back at the Confederation Period from the vantage point of the Constitutional Convention of 1787.[4] To me, both positions are unbalanced; Jensen is running at full speed when he reaches the turn in the track represented by the Confederation Period, hence he is drawn off his true course by centrifugal force; McLaughlin is attempting to run a true course while looking backward over his shoulder, and thus may be in danger of missing the turn altogether. Is it not about time that the "sandwich technique" of Fiske be discarded, along with the "open sandwich" technique of Jensen, and that attention be directed toward the Confederation Period *per se?* In short, what *were* the constitutional developments during the years 1783-1789?

357

One of the most telling charg s made by Richard B. Morris against Jensen's interpretation is tł t the failure of the Confederation government is seen as a resul느 of the inability of the radical

---

[2] In his *Critical Period of American History 1783-1789* (Boston: 1888).

[3] Jensen's major works on the period are *The Articles of Confederation: An Interpretation of the Social-Constitutional History of the American Revolution, 1774-1781* (Madison, Wisc.: 1940), and *The New Nation* (New York: 1950). Two shorter interpretive essays setting forth Jensen's point of reference are "The Articles of Confederation: A Re-Interpretation," *Pacific Historical Review*, VI (1937), 120-142, and *The American Union: Its Interpretation and Its Historical Origins* (An Inaugural Address delivered before the University of Oxford on 21 February 1950, Oxford: 1950).

[4] *The Confederation and the Constitution 1783-1789* (New York: 1905).

leaders to maintain their power rather than the actual inadequacy of the government itself.[5] Indeed when one objectively considers the evidence of inefficiency, there are undeniable signs that the oil of patriotic fervor no longer was capable of easing the clashing gears of an imperfect political system.[6] Congress itself met irregularly in 1783 and quorums did not assemble for weeks at a time; as the years passed the length of time between successful quorum calls became more extended.[7] Lack of a quorum resulted in unpaid officials, lack of instructions to ministers abroad, and the neglect of pending legislation and petitions.[8] While it is possible to debate the need for a federal rather than a confederate government, the contending historians should not lose sight of the elementary fact that the lethargy of Congress made impossible the effective implementation of the Articles of Confederation.

While Congress helplessly debated, certain institutions of government had evolved that served to continue the functions of government in the absence of a quorum as well as could be expected without the supervision and direction of the governing body. Without these subordinate bodies there can be little doubt that the "Critical Period" would have been no less than catastrophic.[9] The development of these institutions was one of the principal achievements of Congress, and it is surprising that this evolution has not occupied the attention of the historical profession.[10]

Among these subordinate institutions, the first in time and eminence was the presidency of the Continental Congress. Extreme

358

---

[5] "The Confederation Period and the American Historian," *William and Mary Quarterly*, 3rd Ser., XIII (1956), 150, 151. This is essentially the position of McLaughlin, see *Steps in the Development of American Democracy* (New York: 1920), 62. See also Harry Ward, *The Department of War, 1781-1795* (Pittsburgh: 1962), 85.

[6] One might cite the long delays in obtaining Congressional action on routine requests, the failure promptly to ratify the 1783 treaty, and inactivity in the face of Shay's Rebellion, as examples of inadequacy.

[7] Thomas Jefferson, *Autobiography* (New York: 1959), 65; McLaughlin, *Confederation and . . . Constitution*, 48.

[8] McLaughlin, *ibid.*, 87; see also Jefferson, *ibid.*, 71, commenting, "That one hundred and fifty lawyers should do business together, ought not to be expected." Secretary at War Knox vainly waited for a quorum before taking action in the case of Shay's Rebellion, Ward, *Department of War*, 77, 78.

[9] The very existence of the executive departments resulted in a continuity of government even amidst the lack of direction from a lethargic Congress. This was sensed by McLaughlin in his *Confederation and Constitution*, at xv.

[10] Jensen notes this achievement in *The New Nation*, 360.

distrust of any grant of executive power to a single individual caused the Congress to limit the President's powers to those of a presiding officer. Despite the colorful incumbents of the presidential chair,[11] the office never became endowed with any more prerogatives than originally bestowed. Of course the burden of correspondence was considerable, and the President who became the master of the terse phrase was a most fortunate individual.[12] Sanders tells us that the President's signature was required on all official papers, that the President frequently acted as an expediter of legislative matters, and that his home was the site of many extra-cameral caucuses.[13] With the end of the war and the rise of the executive departments the administrative duties of the President were lessened, leaving more time for performing the various social duties which attached to the office.[14] Although the President of Congress was predominantly a legislative official, it is not accurate to ignore entirely the contributions of his office to the development of national executive authority, as does Charles C. Thach in his study of *The Creation of the Presidency 1775-1789.*[15] When the framers of the 1787 Constitution thought of executive authority on the national level, their practical experience with the Presidency of the Continental Congress served as both a foundation upon which to build and a warning against an improper dilution of executive authority.

359

Beyond any doubt the central figure of the Confederation government was Charles Thomson, Secretary of Congress from 1775 to 1789. Thomson has been unwisely neglected by historians and biographers; the most recent full-length biography by Lewis R. Harvey, printed in 1900, was in a limited edition of 500 copies.[16]

[11] A colorful group they were indeed, John Hancock with his aristocratic demeanor, quarrelsome Henry Laurens threatening to kick Secretary Thomsom off the rostrum, and the pro-consular proclivities of Arthur St. Clair!

[12] Jennings B. Sanders, *The Presidency of the Continental Congress, 1774-89; A Study in American Institutional History* (Chicago: 1930), 34, 36.

[13] *Ibid.*, 34, 56, 57. For use of patronage to obtain control, see Herbert Sanford Allen, *John Hancock, Patriot in Purple* (New York: 1948), 217.

[14] Sanders, *The Presidency*, 13, 24, 41; see also Edmund C. Burnett, "Perquisites of the President of Continental Congress," *American Historical Review*, XXX (1929), 69-76; and Edmund C. Burnett, ed., *Letters of Members of the Continental Congress*, VIII (Washington: 1936), 270.

[15] In *Johns Hopkins University Studies in Historical and Political Science*, XL (Baltimore: 1922).

[16] *Life of Charles Thomson, Secretary of the Continental Congress* (Philadelphia: 1900). A later sketch by Charles William Heathcote, "Charles Thomson," *General Magazine and Historical Chronicle*, XLVII

Thomson's principal duties were recording the minutes of the Congress, and he rarely missed a session of Congress during his term of office.[17] In the early years he had performed functions which later would have been assigned to the Secretary for Foreign Affairs or the Secretary at War.[18] Some official correspondence was signed by Thomson on behalf of the Congress, but a major portion of the correspondence was sent over the signature of the President. Quite possibly a detailed study of the functions of the Secretary of Congress will reveal that the executive departments were evolved to reduce the burdensome duties of the secretary's office, as well as to replace the inefficient committees of Congress which had originally been entrusted with administrative details.[19] When the executive departments were established Thomson transmitted papers from Congress to the department heads.[20] Although Thomson does not appear to have acted as a supervisor of the department heads, he did rank above them in matters of protocol, and had at times served as chairman of Congress' deliberations in the absence of its President.[21] More than any other official Thomson represented continuity in the service of the government, and his pleas for concerted effort frequently had a salutary effect upon the dilatory members of Congress. To ignore the "Sam Adams of Philadelphia" is to overlook an important key to the intricacies of government in the Confederation Period.

360

(Autumn 1944), 46-55, and a superb piece on Thomson's early career by John J. Zimmerman, "Charles Thomson, 'The Sam Adams of Philadelphia,'" *Mississippi Valley Historical Review*, XLV, 464-485, add little to our knowledge of his activities as Secretary of Congress, although Zimmerman gives a valuable insight into the political abilities of Thomson.

[17] Jennings B. Sanders, *Evolution of the Executive Departments of the Continental Congress, 1774-1789* (Chapel Hill: 1935), 173; Harvey, *Life of Charles Thomson*, 93, 95.

[18] Thomson was well aware of the value of his broad and undefined powers, and considered an attempt to state his powers to be malicious in intention, Burnett, *Letters*, VIII, 84 (Charles to Hannah Thomson, April 3, 1785). For functions in foreign affairs see Harvey, *Life of Charles Thomson*, 104, 105; for war department functions see Sanders, *Executive Departments*, 179.

[19] Alexander De Conde, *The American Secretary of State: An Interpretation* (New York: 1962), 16, notes that the office of Secretary of Foreign Affairs grew directly from the Committee of Secret Correspondence of 1775, and the office of the Secretary of the Continental Congress. Thach, *Creation of the Presidency*, p. 68.

[20] Sanders, *Executive Departments*, 179.

[21] For precedence see *ibid.*, 181; as temporary chairman, see *ibid.*, 174, 175.

The creation of the three major executive departments in 1781 represents what is probably the outstanding constitutional achievement of the years before 1789. Comparatively little scholarly work has been done concerning the functions of the individual departments,[22] and even less attention has been paid to the question of the relationships between the departments. Students of other departments have noted the deference paid to the wishes of Robert Morris by the other department heads, and Clarence Ver Steeg notes that a "semi-official cabinet" meeting was held every Monday evening in which the department heads, the Secretary of Congress, and the Commander-in-Chief participated.[23] Sam Adams may not have been wrong when he feared that the Superintendant of Finance would eventually assert the same influence over Congress that the First Lord of the Treasury exercised over the British Parliament.[24] The relatively short existence of the post of Superintendent of Finance should not obscure the possible contribution this informal arrangement may have made to the American constitution of the day; in short there is need to examine the possibility that a cabinet system of government, patterned to a degree after the British model and even closer to the modern French constitutional pattern, actually pre-dated the creation of an executive branch of the government.

361

In addition to his informal duties as leader in discussions of the "semi-official" cabinet, Robert Morris instituted reforms within the Office of Finance. These included the creation of an office which audited the accounts of the old Treasury Board and other fiscal agencies required to settle accounts with the Superintendent of Finance. Serving in this post with the title of Treasurer to the Superintendent of Finance, John Swanwick performed yeoman service in untangling the war-time financial records.[25] New audit procedures were introduced, and the Superintendent initiated economies in his own, as well as in the other, executive departments.[26] When

---

[22] Specific works and articles will be discussed below; the sole work devoted exclusively to all of the executive departments is Sanders, *Executive Departments*, which is a good guide, but too brief on the individual departments to be considered a definitive monograph.

[23] Clarence L. Ver Steeg, *Robert Morris, Revolutionary Financier: With Some Account of His Earlier Career* (Philadelphia: 1954), 83. See also suggestion of Harry Ward, *Department of War*, 15, that there were probably oral communications between the Secretary for Foreign Affairs and the Secretary at War.

[24] Sanders, *Executive Departments*, 4, 121; Sanders, *Presidency of Congress*, 42.

[25] Ver Steeg, *Robert Morris*, 81.

[26] *Ibid.*, 80; Sanders, *Executive Departments*, 139.

Alexander McDougal refused to accept the post of Secretary of Marine, the proposed functions of that office were assigned to Robert Morris, who became Agent for Marine while retaining his position as Superintendent of Finance.[27] The fiscal functions of the Office of Finance are well explored in Ver Steeg's outstanding study[28] but some attention should be given to the administrative developments within the department and the impact which its new audit procedures had upon the other branches of government.

Next in order of national importance to the Finance Department, was the Office of Foreign Affairs. There is some disagreement among historians concerning the influence of the first Secretary, Robert R. Livingston. While Milledge L. Bonham, Jr., would have us believe that Secretary Livingston was a forceful administrator who demanded respect for his office and enhanced the powers of the Secretariat,[29] George C. Wood considers Livingston's administration a period of transition between the chaos of committee superintendence of foreign affairs, and the vigorous administration of the second Secretary, John Jay.[30] Both interpretations are subject to criticism; that of Bonham is but a minor part of his discussion of foreign affairs in the last years of the Revolution, hence it suffers from oversimplification. On the other hand the viewpoint of Wood, which is surprisingly pro-Jensen for its day, is based upon what appears to be inadequate research in the manuscripts of the Continental Congress and the Office of Foreign Affairs.[31] Furthermore the "chaos" before

---

[27] Jay Caesar Guggenheimer, "The Development of the Executive Departments 1775-1789", in J. Franklin Jameson, ed., *Essays in the Constitutional History of the United States in the Formative Period 1775-1789* (Boston: 1889), 160. Unlike Sanders, Guggenheimer approached this study from a consideration of the Federal government under the 1787 Constitution; he then proceeded to trace the functions of the Federal government departments to their predecessors in the Confederation Period. The result is most unsatisfactory.

It is interesting to speculate what effect the Marine Agency in the Finance Department may have had. Perhaps it is in part responsible for the placement of the U. S. Coast Guard in the Treasury Department.

[28] *Robert Morris*, 12.

[29] "Robert R. Livingston," Samuel Flagg Bemis, ed., *The American Secretaries of State and Their Diplomacy*, I (New York: 1958), *passim*.

[30] George Clayton Wood, *Congressional Control of Foreign Relations During the American Revolution 1774-1789* (Allentown, Pa.: 1919), 107. See also De Conde, *American Secretary of State*, 9, 12.

[31] Wood claims to have consulted many more sources than are indicated in his one page bibliography. While the treatment seems to be thorough the lack of scholarly documentation is noteworthy, and no manuscript sources are indicated.

the creation of the Foreign Affairs Office could not have been as bad as Wood indicates, for before 1781 James Lovell was frequently the only member of the Committee on Foreign Affairs present at Philadelphia.[32] As a result Lovell was a *de facto* Secretary for Foreign Affairs.

The Secretary for Foreign Affairs was early granted the privilege of attending Congress and participating in debate, and this may be attributed to Livingston's persistence in this regard.[33] On the other hand Livingston did not insist that all communications pertaining to foreign affairs be referred to his office, and frequently lost track of diplomatic dispatches.[34] Jay, on the other hand, insisted that his office be the channel of communications with Congress, thus insuring a knowledge of all transactions concerning international diplomacy.[35] The Secretaries for Foreign Affairs provided channels for communications between Congress and the governors of the several states, usually by means of "circular letters." [36]

While Jay's extensive experience in foreign missions caused his opinion to be highly regarded by Congress,[37] all important matters had to be referred to Congress for their consent. Thus the operations of the Secretary were severely hampered when there was no quorum in Congress.[38] So limited were the discretionary powers of the Sec-

363

---

[32] While De Conde describes his little monograph as merely an introduction to the field, it is notable that despite several errors in historical detail, his is the only published reference I have found to James Lovell's role as unofficial secretary of foreign affairs, *American Secretary of State*, vii, 2, 3.

[33] Sanders, *Executive Departments*, 114; Bonham, "Robert R. Livingston," 123.

[34] Livingston transmitted documents to military and naval commanders as well as diplomats, see Bonham, "Robert R. Livingston", 132.

[35] Samuel Flagg Bemis, "John Jay," Samuel Flagg Bemis, ed., *The American Secretaries of State and Their Diplomacy*, I (New York: 1958), 200.

[36] *Ibid.*, 203.

[37] *Ibid.*, 202, see also McLaughlin, *Confederation and Constitution*, 51. During his term as Secretary for Foreign Affairs, Jay may have laid some basis for Clause 8, Section 9 of the 1787 Constitution by insisting upon the consent of Congress before he would accept the gift of a stallion from the Spanish *chargé d'affaires*, Bemis, "John Jay," 242. It is said that, like Thomson, Jay's long tenure in office was a strong symbol of the continuity of the government, Jensen, *The New Nation*, 366.

[38] Sanders, *Executive Departments*, 96, 97, 114, 115, 126. De Conde, *American Secretary of State*, 7. In the series of reports submitted during the last few months of the Confederation government the Department of Foreign Affairs was commended for its ". . . neatness, method and

retary that Jay was unable to agree to a leave of absence requested by Thomas Jefferson early in 1788; after several months passed without a quorum, Jay informed Jefferson unofficially that he might begin making preparations to return because Jay did not believe the request would be denied. Indeed it is in the area of international relations where the need for continuous executive authority becomes most apparent.[39]

A notable exception to the dearth of monographic studies of governmental operations in the Confederation Period is Harry Ward's well-researched study of the Department of War.[40] He notes that during the last two years of the Revolutionary War the Secretary at War,[40a] Benjamin Lincoln, acted as a center of military information for Congress. Lincoln acted in partnership with the Commander-in-Chief, being content to accept those duties which Washington did not wish to handle.[41] With the end of the war and the resignation of General Washington, the Secretary at War assumed the duties of a peace-time commander-in-chief and also those of a judge advocate general and comptroller of accounts.[42] Ward further

364

---

perspicuity, . . .", Edmund C. Burnett, *The Continental Congress* (New York: 1941), 721.

[39] An attempt to create a Committee of the States to exercise the executive functions of Congress between sessions was made in 1784. Although the original proposal of Jefferson was considerably weakened before being enacted, the Committee never functioned because it was unable to obtain a quorum of members. The only discussion I have found of the Committee is in Edmund C. Burnett, "The Committee of the States," *American Historical Association Report for 1913*, I, 141-158. It is mentioned in Harry Ward, *Department of War*, 48, but I have not found it mentioned in Jensen, *The New Nation*. See also the notice in Jefferson, *Autobiography*, 66-67.

[40] Harry Ward, *Department of War*.

[40a] The author's researches reveal the use of Secretary at War rather than the current form, Secretary of War, during this period, and hence, he prefers the former term.—Editor.

[41] *Ibid.*, 11, 14, 18, 32. Generally a well presented study, it is likely that some students of military history will object to Ward's use of the term "general staff" to refer to a staff of generals who consulted with the Commander-in-Chief, see page 12.

[42] *Ibid.*, 54, 56, 58. Ward notes that the Secretary's most important task was coordination. One hesitates to accept his assertion that the Secretary at War served as a check on the assumption of unwarranted authority by the military in time of peace, see page 19. The inaction of Secretary Knox in the crisis of Shay's Rebellion, indicates a mentality far from that of the vigilant guardian of civilian supremacy over the military; and the very fact that both Secretaries were military men also causes some doubt in this regard.

notes that the principal activity of the Department of War in the post-war period was the supervision of Indian affairs.[43] In addition there is an interesting discussion of the role of the Secretary in the War Office, who handled petitions and requests, and the remarkable record of one incumbent, Joseph Carleton, who was probably the best accountant in government service.[44] Ward's work has filled many areas left unexplained in an earlier sketch by Jennings B. Sanders;[45] although it would be valuable to have a more thorough analysis of the functions of the Department of War and how they affected the later War Department, this study is an example of the work which must be done before the significance of the Confederation. Period can be fully appreciated.

While the executive departments have been given little attention by historians, another area of governmental action has been nearly totally ignored. The cession of western lands was one of the large issues of the period, and has been rather thoroughly treated.[46] However the authority of Congress, such as it was, also extended to the settlement of boundary disputes between the states. Among the disputed boundaries treated by the procedures set up in the Articles of Confederation were those of New York and Massachusetts (1784), and the dispute over Wyoming Valley lands between Connecticut and Pennsylvania (1782). Although the Congress was unable to enforce the arbitration awards, the very submission of the disputes to arbitration was a step toward the creation of a sentiment favorable to a national judiciary.

Even more conducive to the erection of a national judiciary was the precedent of the Committee on Appeals on Cases of Capture, and the later Court that served the same function.[47] Restricted to appel-

365

---

[43] *Ibid.*, vii, 56.

[44] Serving as Secretary in the War Office from 1778 to 1785, Carleton accounted for all but $320.00, and Congress gratefully credited this amount to him, *ibid.*, 46, 47. A 1788 report on the War Department commended the office for the economical changes instituted in its operations, Burnett, *Continental Congress*, 720.

[45] In attempting to cover all of the departments Sanders of necessity was less exhaustive than Ward.

[46] Two articles of interest are Merrill Jensen, "The Creation of the National Domain, 1781-1784," *Mississippi Valley Historical Review*, XXVI, 323-342, and Herbert Baxter Adams, *Maryland's Influence upon Land Cessions to the United States* (Baltimore: 1885).

[47] J. Franklin Jameson notes the possible origin of the Committee on Appeals in the Lords Commissioners of Appeal in Prize Cases, to which colonial vice-admiralty cases were referred, "The Predecessor of the Supreme Court," J. Franklin Jameson, ed., *Essays in the Constitu-*

late jurisdiction and hampered by the inability of Congress to enforce the Court's decisions, the Court nevertheless heard 110 cases before it was disbanded in 1782.[48] J. Franklin Jameson notes that the appellate procedure was generally acquiesced in by the states, and that the concept of a superior judiciary hearing appeals from state courts was probably derived from this experience during the Revolution.[49]

With the advent of peace there was need for another national court that would be capable of enforcing the law of nations. Edwin D. Dickinson has noted the impact of the De Longchamps case (1784), which indicated the need for a national tribunal to punish criminal assaults upon the persons of foreign diplomatic officials.[50] Such a court was also needed to facilitate collection of debts owed by Americans to British merchants, and which the Treaty of 1783 guaranteed collectible. Another reason for a federal court was that Congress needed a forum in which to try federal officers, to hear appeals from state courts in cases bearing on international treaties, to consider cases involving the federal revenue and to adjudicate those cases in which the United States was a party.[51]

All of the foregoing areas require extensive study before we can truly assess the contribution which the Articles of Confederation have made to the constitutional history of the United States. It is just as unscientific to assign ulterior conspiratorial motives to the

366

tional History of the United States During the Formative Period, 14. The existence of the Court and its jurisdiction is noted inaccurately in Fiske, *Critical Period*, 97; see also Robert J. Steamer, "The Legal and Political Genesis of the Supreme Court," *Political Science Quarterly*, LXXVII (1962), 559-565 at 565.

[48] On inability to enforce decisions see Jameson, *ibid.*, 19. John C. B. Davis, *The Committees of the Continental Congress, Chosen to Hear and Determine Appeals from Court of Admiralty, and the Court of Appeals in Cases of Capture Established by that Body* (New York: 1888), 10; Jefferson, *Autobiography*, 88, 89; Jensen, "The Articles of Confederation," *passim*.

[49] Jameson, "Predecessor of the Supreme Court", 11, 44. It is interesting to note that the records and proceedings of the Court of Appeals in Prize Cases were ordered deposited in the office of the Supreme Court of the U. S. in 1789, *ibid.*, 42.

[50] In "The Law of Nations as Part of the National Law of the United States," *University of Pennsylvania Law Review*, CI (1952), 26-56, at 36. He thus restates the 1783 suggestion by Hamilton, "Proposals to Amend the Articles of Confederation 1781-1789," in Albert B. Hart and Edward Channing, eds., *American Historical Leaflets: Colonial and Constitutional*, No. 28 (New York: 1896), 16.

[51] Jensen, *The New Nation*, 419-420.

framers of the Constitution as it is to mark their achievement as a new departure in the field of national government. Once in power the Federalists seem to have borrowed rather freely from the governing practices of the earlier government. There is a continuity, and although Jensen criticizes Leonard D. White for not recognizing the relationship,[52] no historian of the Confederation Period has accepted the challenge which this comment presents.

Amidst the heat produced by the friction of conflicting interpretations, historians have tended to reinterpret the old isues in new ways. It is about time that the enormous collection of Continental Congress Papers, now available in a microfilm publication, be utilized for the study of governmental operations. Admittedly the result of this study may be less spectacular than that yielded in other research areas, but it is the only reliable source upon which to write a constitutional history of the earliest period of our existence as a nation. Perhaps in the examination of endorsements to letters and reports there is valuable material for the imaginative reconstruction of the long-forgotten tale of how the United States became a nation even before the binding chain of the Constitution of 1787 was forged.

367

---

[52] *Ibid.*, 360.

THE BACKGROUND OF AMERICAN FEDERALISM

ANDREW C. McLAUGHLIN

University of Chicago

The purpose of this paper is to make plain two facts: first, that the essential qualities of American federal organization were largely the product of the practices of the old British empire as it existed before 1764; second, that the discussions of the generation from the French and Indian war to the adoption of the federal Constitution, and, more particularly, the discussions in the ten or twelve years before independence, were over the problem of imperial organization. The center of this problem was the difficulty of recognizing federalism; and, though there was great difficulty in grasping the principle, the idea of federalism went over from the old empire, through discussion into the Constitution of the United States. By federalism is meant, of course, that system of political order in which powers of government are separated and distinguished and in which these powers are distributed among governments, each government having its quota of authority and each its distinct sphere of activity.[1]

We all remember very well that, until about thirty years ago, it was common to think of the United States Constitution as if it were "stricken off in a given time by the brain and purpose of man." About that time there began a careful study of the background of constitutional provisions and especially of the specific make-up of the institutions provided for by the instrument.[2] It is probably fair to say that the net result of this investigation was the discovery that the Constitution was in marked degree

[1] This paper is limited to the subject stated above. It does not pretend to assert or deny economic influences. It confines itself to the intellectual problem of imperial order. Only one other subject vies with this in importance—the problem of making real the rights of the individual under government.

[2] The first of these studies, as far as I know, was Alexander Johnston's "First Century of the Constitution" in the *New Princeton Review*, IV, (1887), 175.

founded on the state constitutions, and that they in turn were largely a formulation of colonial institutions and practices; the strong influence of English political principles and procedure was apparent, though commonly that influence had percolated through colonial governments and experiences.

In such studies as these just mentioned, we do not find, nor have recent works furnished us, any historical explanation of the central principle of American federalism.[3] And still, one may well hesitate to give the historical explanation, because, when stated, it appears as obvious as it is significant. No better occasion than this, however, is likely to arise for acknowledging the fact that out of the practices of the old empire, an empirical empire, an opportunistic empire, an empire which today is seeking formulation in law or in public acknowledgment of institutional coördination, an empire which the Englishmen even of a century and a half ago did not understand—no better time than now to acknowledge that to the practices of English imperialism we owe the very essence of American federalism. It is a striking fact that there are two great empires in the world: one the British empire based on opportunism and on the principles of Edmund Burke; the other the American empire based on law, the law of imperial organization. The first of these, an empire without imperial law, was profoundly influenced by the experiences of the American Revolution and by slowly developing liberalism; the other—an empire with a fundamental law of coördination, also influenced by its experiences and by Revolutionary discussion—institutionalized and legalized, with some modifications and additions, the practices of the prerevolutionary imperial system of Britain.[4]

369

If we go back to the old empire as it was, let us say in 1760, we find that it was a composite empire, not simple and centralized.

[3] One of the books which does in some degree recognize the nature of the Revolutionary discussion is Holland, *Imperium et Libertas.*

[4] So successful has been the empire of opportunism, of operation and coöperation based on understandings, not on fixed law, that we find ourselves looking with some misgiving on discussions now in progress at Westminster, lest, through well intentioned effort to reach definiteness, fluidity be changed to rigidity.

We are not speaking of any theory of the law of the empire but of its actual institutions and their practical operation.

First: The active instrument or authority of imperial government was the crown. It operated of course most immediately and effectively in the royal colonies. It operated by the appointment of some officials, by instructions, and by disallowance of colonial acts. The generalization is probably just, that instruction and disallowance were exercised chiefly for essentially nonlocal, imperial purposes, the maintenance of the character and aim of the empire. The process of review of cases appealed from the colonies can probably be similarly classified—its operation was for homogeneity in part but substantially for imperial purposes. This central authority of the empire had charge of foreign affairs, navy and army, war and peace, subordinate military authority being left to the individual colonies.[5] It managed the post office; it was beginning to take charge of Indian affairs and trade with the Indian tribes; it had charge of the back lands and of crown lands within the limit of the colonies; it was preparing to take in hand the building up of new colonies (our territorial system); it exercised executive power in carrying out the legislation of Parliament which was chiefly concerned with trade and navigation.

Second: Parliament had legislated little if at all for strictly local internal affairs of the colonies. If we omit for the moment acts of trade and navigation, we should find the act making colonial real estate chargeable with debts, the post office, the Naturalization Act of 1740, the Bubble Act, the act against the land bank, the act against paper money. Each one of these acts was of imperial scope or nature, because it was directed against an evil of more than local extent, or because, as in the case of the post office, it was of more than local interest. The acts of trade and navigation were in some instances, for example the act against the smelting of iron, a somewhat rude intrusion

[5] Working out the principle of federalism in military affairs was a big problem in the French and Indian war, in the decade before independence, in the Revolution, in the Federal Convention, in the War of 1812, in the Civil War, in the Congress of 1916, in the War of 1917.

upon the sphere of local action; but to see these things properly, we must associate them together with the general policy of mercantilism, and see them as a part of a system, not always wisely developed, of making a self-sustaining empire. On the whole, Parliament, as was perfectly natural, had to a very marked extent interested itself in regulation of trade; it was perfectly natural that the empire as far as Parliament was concerned should have been largely a commercial empire; the part played by mercantilistic doctrine in the seventeenth and eighteenth centuries made such parliamentary interests and activities inevitable.[6]

Third: The colonies managed their own "internal police," some of them under charters, all by governments in which there were representative assemblies. They levied taxes for local purposes, and voluntarily contributed, after a wholesome or a ramshackle manner, to the defense of the empire. They managed local trade, and in short did the thousand and one things— sometimes under pressure from the representatives of the royal prerogative—that concerned the daily life of the colonist.

Any one even slightly familiar with American constitutional system will see at once that to a very marked degree we have here the distribution of powers characteristic of American federalism. In fact if we add to the powers of the central authority in the old empire the single power to obtain money by direct or indirect taxation immediately from the colonists for imperial purposes, we have almost exactly the scheme of distribution of our own constitutional system.[7]   Of course there had

371

6 I have left out of consideration the question of the absorption by the colonies of common law and the acceptance of legislation modifying common law, especially criminal law. It is a big and complicated question. Limited space does not permit the treatment. I content myself with a general picture of the make-up of the empire, which I believe is substantially correct. It is also noteworthy that there was in the empire national or imperial and local citizenship, and that naturalization by colonial authorities was after 1740 under imperial law.

7 The reader may object that Congress can now provide for standards of weights and measures, patents, and copyrights. He might point out, possibly with justice, that coining money and regulating the value thereof did not belong in the old empire to the central authority; but I leave the old practice to justify my assertion and refer again in passing to the act against paper money. The bankruptcy power, as a part of the general power of our central government, probably can be traced back with certainty at least to colonial conditions, and the Bubble Act and its extension to the colonies must not be forgotten.

to be found a thorough working legal basis and a legal method of operation. The legal basis was found when the constitutional convention of 1787 declared that the Constitution should be law. The operation of the central government directly upon its own citizens, a most important quality of our own federalism, probably came in part from the old empire, but was distinctly worked out in the debates of the convention.

If any one wishes to criticize unfavorably some detail of the scheme of empire which has just been sketched, he will still scarcely deny that Britain had a working federal empire by the middle of the eighteenth century. If Great Britain, in 1760, had reached out and said, "this is the law of the empire; thus the system is formed," she would have seen herself as the most considerable member of a federal state based distinctly on law and not on practice alone. If Britain by a formal constitution could have formulated the empire she had, if the imperial order could have been frozen, petrified, in the form that time had made for it, the British empire would have been legally a federal empire. But though she did not, she made her contribution; her imperial history had selected and set apart the particular and the general, according to a scheme which was of lasting significance in the development of American imperial order. On that general scheme of distribution the Constitution of the United States was founded.

Let us now discuss this subject more in detail and with some consideration for chronological sequence, with some deference, that is to say, to the order and time in which events occurred and arguments were put forth. The scheme of imperial order presented by the Albany congress is so well-known, that it does not need extended comment; it is of interest as a plan for redistribution of powers in certain essential particulars and it is of lasting significance as an effort to select certain things of extra-colony rather than intra-colony importance, those things which needed general control by a colonial representative body. It tried chiefly to solve the problem of imperial order as far as that centered in the need of securing men and money for imperial security; and for the time the plan failed.

This matter of imperial security, augmented in weight by the experiences of the war, became the center of dispute in the decade or so after the peace of 1763. Could England by parliamentary enactment secure money for imperial defense? While this question was the center of dispute, the discussion was soon narrowed, or, if you like, broadened, to this: Did the colonies, as constituent parts of the whole, possess certain indefeasible legal rights and especially the right to hold on to their own purse strings? The dispute was narrowed because it came to be confined to the field of theory; it was not a question as to whether Parliament could get money from the colonies but whether they would acknowledge the abstract legal right to get it. The dispute was broadened, because it involved the whole question of interdependence and relationship.

373

Any amount of argument over the theoretical legal right to exercise sovereignty in the empire does not get one very far. There is no great practical value in trying to determine whether the colonies by the principles of English law were subject to taxation by Parliament. It may not be amiss, however, to point out that most of this argument, as far as it seeks to make out that Parliament did have the taxing power, whether that argument was made in 1765 or in 1917, has for its basis the constitution of the island and not that of the empire. It is largely insular argument, based on insular experience and founded on insular history. The unwritten constitution of the empire is the other way, and that is just what the men, especially the Englishmen, of a hundred and fifty years ago could not see. They could not think and talk imperially, when it came to a matter of constitutional law. If the practical working empire of 1760 had been frozen into recognizable legal shape, the right to tax the colonies would not have been within the legal competence of Parliament, even as an imperial legislature. And because the Englishmen did not think imperially, because they did not realize that time had wrought out for them a composite federal empire, because they insisted on the principle of centralization in theory, they failed patiently to set about the task of determining some way by which, while recognizing federalism and colonial integrity, they could on a basis of justice and consent obtain authoritatively an acknowledged legal right to tax for strictly imperial purposes. Men that could not comprehend federalism, who denied the possibility of its existence, were incapable of dealing with a crisis of an imperial system in which federalism already existed.[8]

Some one may say, and with considerable justice, that the colonists were also incapable, quite as incapable as the parliamentarian and the British pamphleteer, of understanding the nature of a composite empire. It long remained true as Franklin said in disgust after the failure of the Albany plan: "Everybody cries, a Union is absolutely necessary, but when they come to the Manner and Form of the Union, their weak noddles are perfectly distracted."[9] That was the trouble—weak noddles. But, withal, the idea was hard to grasp, simple as it may appear to us; and it took the discussions and experience of a generation to find the manner and form of imperial order, though, when they did find it, it was the old scheme only in part modified, representing in its method of distributing powers the familiar practices of the empire.[10]

374

[8] This statement needs modification; for Burke, rejecting legalism, still displayed statesmanship of the highest order. He resented any attempt to fossilize or ossify the empire and sought to hold out the idea of parliamentary duty rather than legal power. In these latter days it would be stupid to declare that one must grasp and apply legal federalism if he is to deal with the elements of a composite empire; Burke's principles of duty and of freedom have been proved to be the cement of the British empire. But, withal, it is quite plain that the statesmen of the Revolution on both sides thought there was need of fixing legal authority; and those incapable of seeing the principle of distributed authority—federalism—were in a bad way.

[9] Writings, ed. by A. H. Smyth, III, p. 242.

[10] It is worth noticing that at a later time Franklin himself after reading a considerable portion of Dickinson's Farmer's Letters is evidently at a loss; and he at a comparatively early day, about 1768, found no middle ground between complete independence of the colonies and complete power of Parliament. Speaking of the Farmer's Letters Franklin wrote: "I have read them as far as No. 8. . . . I am not yet master of the idea they and the New England writers have of the relation between Britain and her colonies. I know not what the Boston people mean by the 'subordination' they acknowledge in their Assembly to Parliament, while they deny its powers to make laws for them, nor what bound the Farmer sets to the power he acknowledges in Parliament to 'regulate the trade of the colonies' it being difficult to draw lines between duties for regulation and those for revenue; and if the Parliament is to be the judge, it seems to me that establishing such principles of distinction will amount to little." Quoted in note in Memoirs of the Historical Society of Penn., XIV, 281.

And yet it is not quite correct to say that colonial noddles utterly failed. It is true that the colonists often spoke as Englishmen, they claimed rights as Englishmen, they, too, argued on the basis of insular law; and indeed the principles of insular law were not at variance with the rights which they set up as citizens in the empire. But some of them went further, and defended the rights of the colonies, as distinguished from the rights of Englishmen; they defended, to use later phraseology, states rights as distinguished from individual rights; they argued from the structure of the empire rather than from the principles which aim to protect the individual from governmental wrong. As far as they did this, they grasped the nature of an imperial system in which the outlying portions had their own indefeasible share, legal share, of political authority.

375

If there were space to examine critically the whole mass of constitutional arguments, we should see a groping after the idea of classification of powers, and on the other hand the emphatic declaration that to deny to a government the right to make any particular law or any special kind of laws is to deny all power and authority—government must have full sovereign power or none. In examining some of the materials throwing light on the nature of the arguments, it will be well on the whole to exclude those assertions from which we can gather only inferentially that the writer or speaker grasped the principle of differentiation. As we have already seen, the Albany plan was distinctly based on the idea of classification and distribution. The controversy of 1764 regarding the revenue act brought out occasional indications that certain distinctions were close at hand, if not as yet fully comprehended; at least there was a recognition of the old exercise of power over trade and an objection to the newly proposed schemes of revenue. In the main, however, the American opposition at that time was not clearly and precisely directed against taxation because it violated a principle of imperial structure, but rather because it violated a principle of English personal liberty. Otis, in his *Rights of the Colonies Asserted*, denies the authority of Parliament to tax, and admits their right to regulate trade; but his argument against taxation is English not imperial argument, on the whole.   It is probably safe to say he relied on personal right rather than on the principles of empire.[11]

Still in these early days of 1764 and '65 certain fundamentals did appear, even when lines were not drawn with the precision of later days.   Dulaney recognized a supreme authority in Parliament to preserve the dependence of the colonies; he spoke of the subordination of the colonies, which still however retained rights despite their inferiority; for "in what the Superior may rightly controul, or compel, and in what the Superior ought to be at Liberty to act without Controul or Compulsion, depends upon the nature of the dependence, and the Degree of the Subordination."[12] He suggests that a line may be drawn "between such Acts as are necessary, or proper, for preserving or securing the Dependence of the Colonies, and such as are not necessary or proper for that very important Purpose."[13]   He thus clearly points to the possibility of an empire managed in the large by a central authority but in which the outlying parts are possessed of indefeasible authority on subjects belonging of right to them, subjects which do not contravene the general superintending power lodged in the central authority.   He naturally dwells on those particular exercises of authority then under dispute, and declares that there is "a clear and necessary Distinction between an Act imposing a Tax for the single Purpose of Revenue, and those Acts which have been made for the Regulation of Trade, and have produced some Revenue in Consequence of their Effect and Operation as regulations of Trade."[14]   This pamphlet of Dulaney's was a states-

[11] This interpretation of Otis is of course strengthened by the fact of his belief in the representation of the colonists in Parliament and his reliance on the right of a court to declare an unjust act void; but, after all, Otis did distinguish between powers, and did believe in the constitutional restraints on Parliament.

[12] *Considerations on the Propriety of Imposing Taxes in the British Colonies for the purpose of raising a revenue, by act of Parliament,* (London, 1766), p. 16. Tyler says that there was an American edition of 1765.   This I have not seen.

[13] *Ibid.,* p. 17.   See for an early statement of federalism, Ann Maury, *Memoirs of a Huguenot Family,* 425–426; letter of Maury to Fontaine, December 31, 1765. Portions of Patrick Henry's resolutions of 1765 have the federal argument.

[14] *Considerations on the Propriety of Imposing Taxes in the British Colonies,* etc., (London, 1766), p. 46.

manlike production, and contained at least the foundations for the conception of federalism.[15]

Unhappily in 1766, Franklin in his examination before the committee of commons does not indulge in clear and precise thinking. Had he then enlarged on the character of the imperial structure, and had he sharply drawn the lines of demarcation between imperial superintendence and colonial legal right, possibly the listening commons might have understood the vital distinctions. Franklin's examination admirably discloses the opportunistic and nonlegalistic nature of his statesmanship. In this examination he does, of course, emphasize the colonial objection to revenue acts; but he became hopelessly confused in discussing the basis for trade regulation, and impressed on his listeners that what was objectionable was internal taxation as distinguished from external; he appears to have impressed this distinction so firmly, that the Englishmen never lost the notion that it was peculiarly dear to the American heart; and, when within a year or two external taxes were levied, the English administrators were hurt in their minds by the prompt rejection of their schemes. It is true that Lyttleton (1766) called the attention of the lords to the fact that the Americans made no such distinction and that it could not be found in Otis's pamphlet;[16] but the idea seems to have persisted, aided probably by the loose use of terms by occasional American writers.

377

It was partly to clear up such confusion as this and to draw the line properly, that John Dickinson penned his *Farmer's Letters*. The thinking of Dickinson was plain, straightforward and able. Possibly in his first letter he enters upon indefensible ground; for, having in mind the effort to compel the New York legislature to furnish quarters for troops and thereby to incur certain expense, he insists that an order to do a thing is the imposition of a tax. But in no other place does he become

[15] See also Stephen Hopkins, *Grievances of the American Colonies Candidly Examined*, p. 19.
[16] "Mr. Otis, their champion, scouts such a distinction." *Parl. Hist.*, XVI, col. 167.

entangled in dubious assertions.[17] Dickinson spoke as an imperialist, as one who saw and felt the empire; he is hardly less
emphatic in his declarations concerning the imperial power of
Parliament and the existence of a real whole of which the colonies
are parts, than in defending the indefeasible share of empire
which the colonies possessed. Hitherto the colonies, save as
they had been restrained in trade and manufacture by parliamentary legislation under the general principles of mercantilism, had been regulated even for purposes of empire largely by
the exercise of the royal prerogative. Dickinson realized the
necessity of parliamentary control and guidance; he saw as did
Dulaney the need of a superintending authority, and he openly
acknowledged that it lay with Parliament. It was perfectly
inevitable that a statesman—colonial or English—should think
of the control of trade as the big duty, and thus Dickinson
emphasized that duty and the right of Parliament to direct the
trade of the whole system. He saw an empire, composite and
not simple or centralized, with a Parliament possessed of indubi-
table power to maintain the whole and chiefly to look after the
interests of the whole by the regulation of trade.[18]

It was just because Dickinson was thinking imperially and
was doing more than to acknowledge that Parliament might
regulate trade, that his words deserve especial weight. He was
not speaking as a disgruntled colonist merely finding fault; he
was not setting up purely insular constitutional principles; he
was not talking as a frontier individualist; he saw the existence
of an imperial reality and he presented strongly certain principles
of imperial structure. He denied that Parliament had the right
to tax; scouting the supposed distinction between internal and

[17] For a sharp statement of Dickinson's position of empire consistent with
colonial freedom—freedom of the colonies—see the early parts of Letter II of
the *Farmer's Letters*.

[18] The distinction between regulation of commerce and taxation never, I think,
entirely disappeared from the colonial mind, though after about 1772 some leaders
came to the point of openly asserting complete freedom from parliamentary
control. See for the distinction *Letter from the Massachusetts House to Dennis
de Berdt*, (London, 1770), p. 16. It is possible that this letter was written earlier
than 1770. I have been unable to find it in the *Mass. State Papers*.

external taxation, he openly admitted the authority of Parliament to regulate trade.

Taxation is an imposition for the raising of revenue; it at times seems strange, not that Dickinson should have made the distinction between taxation and regulation, but that men at all experienced with actual practices of the empire and familiar with mercantilistic doctrine should not have readily accepted it. That distinction had been touched on before Dickinson wrote; but he made the thing so evident that men ought to have been able to see it. Still it is not plain that men did see it. At least they were not quite able to see that he was proposing not only a perfectly valid distinction between powers, but a real theory of imperial structure. Consequently Dickinson's words did not have the weight they deserved in pointing the way to composite empire, an empire in which there was an indefeasible participation of the parts under a government charged with the maintenance of the whole. Federalism, we must remember, necessitates singling out of specific branches of authority, which we commonly call "powers." Nothing is simpler in the primer of our constitutional law than the distinction between the taxing power and the power to regulate interstate and foreign commerce. Any person, though he be unlearned in jurisprudence, will talk glibly of the commerce power, the treaty making power, the taxing power and many other powers, fully realizing that we take certain authorities of government and label them, put them in certain receptacles, and leave to our astute courts the duty of deciding whether a legislative act is to be classified thus or so and whether it is a due exercise of "powers" that have been authoritatively granted. And so it is amazing to us, this difficulty in seeing the validity of this most commonplace distinction, and that writers should still think Dickinson was speaking in confusion instead, as was the fact, talking the A, B, C of American constitutional law.

Dickinson's position distinguished the power to regulate trade from the power to tax. The distinction deserves to be called proper, because we have had it in active operation under our Constitution for a century and over. But it was proper also,

379

because it carried on the practices of the old empire. Parliament had regulated trade; it had not taxed. For a century or more the empire had acknowledged in practice, not to speak of in charters and commissions and instructions, the existence of colonies with the authority to tax for local concerns, and had refrained from taxation for imperial purposes. To a marked degree we may say again the empire was a commercial empire. Its commercial purposes were expressed in navigation acts, and a large portion even of the administrative control by the Royal council had been directed to the support of those enactments and that commercial policy.

Before passing on to other and particularly later appreciations of federalism, let us turn to the other side of the matter. Englishmen, whether they defended the colonists or opposed them, were likely to take refuge in insular (i.e., English) law, not discussing the question openly as to whether Parliament had become imperial, or whether, if it had, its power was unlimited; blank assertion took the place of argument.[19] They occasionally spoke learnedly or superficially of whether places without the realm could be taxed, or whether such places must be brought within the realm and given representation before they could be taxed; and thus, in referring to past conditions in the history of Britain, they really recognized the fact that even Britain herself had been a growth and had been compounded, but curiously enough they were blind to the composite empire already in existence and to the practices of a century. The freedom from taxation they discussed from the viewpoint of insular institutions, and, as the world knows, made the ludicrous blunder of attempting to impute the insular system of representation to the whole empire. They fumbled with the whole principle of representation; but their chief error was the insistence on applying to the whole empire certain rigid principles which they believed were logically irrefutable. Scarcely any one of them

[19] Special exceptions should of course be made. Thomas Pownall, in his *Administration of the Colonies* (London 1764 and later amplified editions), struggles to find expression. Of course there were others. Vide, for example, *Johnstone's Speech on . . . . recommitting the address*, etc., (London, 1776).

saw that, in the development of empire, had arisen new principles of law and organization. Of course they rejected the distinction between internal taxation and external taxation, as there may have been reason for doing on practical as well as theoretical grounds; from the beginning they denied the possibility of classification of powers; they asserted the indivisible character of legislative power, and almost at once took a position which, if insisted on in practice, left nothing to the colonists but a choice between acceptance of an absolute government at the head of a centralized empire on the one hand, and the total denial of all parliamentary authority on the other.[20]

The pamphlet entitled *The Controversy Between Great Britain and her colonies*, commonly attributed to the pen of William Knox, probably deserves the praise bestowed upon it as being the best presentation of Britain's case.[21]   It is true that in one flagrant instance it falsely juggles with Locke's second essay, and it shows more than usual cunning in making Locke's theories support governmental authority; but the argument from the history of Parliament and the empire to support the claim for imperial authority is able and has the strength of historical statement as contradistinguished from bald assertion and adroit legalism. Knox, however, has a merry time with Dickinson, proving to his own satisfaction the folly of distinguishing between taxation and regulation of commerce; and he thus fails utterly to see anything but a centralized empire with all authority in Parliament. "There is no alternative: either the colonies are a part of the community of Great Britain, or they are in a state of nature with respect to her, and in no case can be subject to the jurisdiction of that legislative power which represents her community, which is the British Parliament." Nothing could more fully discredit legalism when dealing with a practical problem of statesmanship; this was denying that Parliament could not recognize the illegality of doing what in practice it actually had

381

[20] Pitt's statement distinguishing taxation from legislation is omitted from this discussion in the text. See for partial support of position above Grenville, Speech of January 14, 1766. *Parl. Hist.*, XVI, 101. See also *Ibid.*, 167.

[21] Except Hutchinson's speeches of 1773.

not done and what the passing years were proving it could in reality not do.[22]

Even before 1770, many American opponents of parliamentary taxation had been hurried along to the position in which they denied that Parliament possessed any power over them.[23] It would appear, however, that the more sober-minded did not as yet openly go so far; it was easy for the thoughtless to resent British assertion of authority by the simple denial of all authority. There is no such declaration, however, in the American state papers. There was still readiness, as there continued to be after 1770, to acquiesce in British regulation of the trade of the empire, and in such royal control as was consistent with practice and the charters.

382

In 1770 when the long controversy arose between Hutchinson and the Massachusetts legislature over the right to remove the legislature to Cambridge, Hutchinson declared that the Boston men, having denied the power of Parliament over them, were now prepared to deny the power of the crown. It is perfectly true that that controversy concerned the power of the crown; it involved the question whether the prerogative could be used freely and arbitrarily and in disregard of established laws and the charter; but certainly till that time the colonists had not committed themselves to the doctrine that Parliament was totally powerless, nor did they then deny *in toto* the authority of the crown. As before 1770 they had asserted that there were bounds to the authority of Parliament, so now they rejected the notion that sufficient excuse for a governor's acts was his simple declaration that he had received orders from Westminster. Even in the exercise of the prerogative, there must be recogni--

[22] In a pamphlet attributed to Phelps, *The Rights of the colonies and the extent of the legislative authority of Great Britain briefly stated and considered*, (1769), pp. 11 and 12, we find: "The colonies, therefore, must either acknowledge the legislative power of Great Britain in its full extent, or set themselves up as independent states; I say in its full extent, because if there be any reserve in their obedience, which they can legally claim, they must have a power within themselves superior to that of the mother country; for her obedience to the legislature is without limitation." Winsor says Phelps was Under-Secretary to Lord Sandwich. *Narr. and Crit. Hist.*, VI, 85.

[23] See for example J. K. Hosmer, *Life of Thomas Hutchinson*, 134.

tion of the legal entity and the legal competence of the colony as an integral portion of an integral empire; that was the position of the Massachusetts legislature translated into modern terms.

Students of the Revolution that believe the movement was economic in origin, character and purpose, may not deny that, after 1768, Parliament had no express hope or intention of obtaining revenue from America. From that time on, British interest was largely, if not wholly, confined to asserting parliamentary omnipotence, or, if this seems too strong, confined to an insistence upon the supreme power of Parliament and to resisting what they believed, under the tutelage of American governors, was a conscious tendency toward independence. Indeed, especially after 1768, but to a considerable extent from 1766, the question was not so much whether the colonies would pay taxes as whether they would acknowledge the legal obligation; and to an amazing extent the conflict was over the existence or nonexistence of an abstract right. As we have already seen, much of the colonial argument was in defense of individual liberty, not of states rights; but the center of the controversy was whether or not Parliament was possessed of limitless authority.

The colonists at least claimed to be satisfied with the old régime, in which power had been divided, and in which Parliament had chiefly shown its power by the regulation of trade.[24] The parliamentarians insisted that in the law of the empire the will of Parliament was nothing more nor less than supreme and

383

[24] "Every advantage that could arise from commerce they have offered us without reserve; and their language to us has been—'Restrict us, as much as you please in acquiring property by regulating our trade to your advantage; but claim not the disposal of that property after it has been acquired—Be satisfied with the authority you exercised over us before the present Reign.'" *Additional Observations on the nature and value of Civil Liberty, and the War with America*, by Richard Price.

"And when men are driven for want of argument, they fly to this as their last resource—'acts of parliament (say their advocates) are sacred, and should be implicitly submitted to—for if the supreme power does not lodge somewhere operatively, and effectually, there must be an end of all legislation.'" *Lord Chatham's Speech on the 20th of January, 1775.* Taken by a member, page 9, (1775).

all-inclusive. The colonists insisted, though they did not use this phraseology, that old practices of the empire were the law of the empire and thus, in modern phraseology, they demanded the recognition of a composite empire based on law. Even if we admit the presence of many economic and social forces, we find in actual conflict two theories of imperial order; and in this discussion after 1768, if not before, the English parliamentarians and pamphleteers were victims of certain dogmas of political science, curiously similar to the doctrine of indivisible sovereignty.[25] How often did Burke deprecate the continual harping on Parliament's authority, on the necessity of acknowledging the theoretical supremacy of Parliament![26] He deplored the common talk about the legal rights. Beyond Burke's speeches little needs be cited to show the essentially legalistic character of the whole discussion.

It may be rash to assert that the colonists were less insistent upon knowing what the constitution of the empire was than were

384

[25] "If, intemperately, unwisely, fatally, you sophisticate and poison the very source of government by urging subtle deductions and consequences odious to those you govern from the unlimited and illimitable nature of sovereignty, you will teach them by those means to call that sovereignty itself in question. When you drive him hard the boar will turn upon the hunters. If that sovereignty and their freedom cannot be reconciled, which will they take? They will cast your sovereignty in your face, nobody will be argued into slavery." Burke, Speech on American Taxation, *Works*, vol. II, p. 73. See also *Ibid.*, pp. 141–142, for Burke's wishing to see the colonies admitted to an interest in the constitution, an evidence that he too recognized in some measure the need of formal statement.

[21] An illustration of the same thing may be seen in an American source:

"Moreover, when we consider that Parliamentary taxations are not as to their present value, a matter of moment, either to the mother country, or the colonies; that the contention between us, is upon the points of principle and precedent; that it is not the quantum, but the manner of exacting our unconstitutional impost, which is the bone of contention, our public jealousies must necessarily be increased.

"When the taxation was more general, there was some colour for the assertion in the Revenue Act, that it was intended for the safety and defence of the colonies. But it is not only true, that this cannot be asserted of the paltry duty on tea; we know, we were assured by our enemies, that when the other articles charged by the Revenue Acts were exempted by the partial repeal, the duty on tea was left as a standing memorial of the right of Parliament to tax Americans." Force, *Archives*, Fourth Series, I, 256 note—copied from the *New York Gazetteer*, May 12, 1774.

the Englishmen, though there seems no reason to doubt that the colonists would have willingly accepted the old practice as sufficient, if it were not threatened. Still, the colonists desired to know precisely what were American rights; and in this respect possibly America was more legalistic than Britain, because Parliament insisted on the existence of unlimited power—asserted, one might not unjustly say, that Parliament was above the law—while the colonists asserted that Parliament was bound by rigid law. "The patchwork government of AMERICA," wrote Bernard in 1765,[27] "will last no longer; the necessity of a parliamentary establishment of the governments of AMERICA upon fixed constitutional principles, is brought out with a precipitation which could not have been foreseen but a year ago; and is become more urgent, by the very incidents which make it more difficult."   At this time, it will be remembered, he proposed an extraordinary Parliament, in which there were to be American representatives, which should form and establish "a general and uniform system of American government;" "and let the relation of America be determined and ascertained by a solemn Recognition; so that the rights of the American governments, and their subordination to that of Great Britain, may no longer be a subject of doubt and disputation."   In 1766 he declares that "the Stamp Act is become in itself a matter of indifference; it is swallowed up in the importance of the effects of which it has been the cause. . . . And as the relation between Great Britain and the colonies has not only been never settled, but scarce even formally canvassed, it is the less surprising, that the ideas of it on one side of the water and on the other are so widely different, to reconcile these, and to ascertain the nature of the subjection of the colonies to the crown of Great Britain, will be a work of time and difficulty."

385

There can be little doubt that Bernard was right; the problem of the day was the problem of imperial organization: were Englishmen or Americans capable of finding a law of the empire?[28]

[27] *Select Letters*, p. 33.
[28] By "law" I do not mean that there was a demand for a parliamentary act; I mean at the least an evident understanding, at the most a formal acknowledg-

If so, that law must be consonant with practical realities; it must be a formulation of the principles of relationship which recognized not centralization but distribution.[29] As an indication of the fact that men were discussing legal rights, and losing sight of financial returns, it may be sufficient for the earlier days to refer to the comments in the *Parliamentary History*[30] on the debate about the Circular Letter. It was insisted by opponents of the ministry in debate on the Massachusetts Circular Letter and in respect to the revenue laws "that the inutility of these laws was so evident, that the ministers did not even pretend to support them upon that ground, but rested their defence upon the expediency of establishing the right of taxation." And if we turn again to Dickinson, we find the same thing in a different guise—the necessity of law in the empire—not a law securing centralized authority but freedom. There could be no freedom without legal restriction: "For who are a free people? Not those, over whom government is reasonably and equitably exercised, but those, who live under a government so constitutionally checked and controlled that proper provision is made against its being otherwise exercised."[31]

386

ment of power and the extent of it, a formal recognition of the complete authority of Parliament or, on the other hand, of the width and depth of the actual colonial legal competence.

[29] It is plain, too, that Hutchinson, a legal-minded man, also felt in the days of Bernard's governorship, as later, that the constitution must be settled. "I wish to see known established principles, one general rule of subjection, which once acknowledged, any attempts in opposition to them will be more easily crushed." Letter of April 21, 1766, quoted in *Quincy Reports*, 443-444. "Our misfortune is the different apprehension of the nature and degree of our dependence. I wish to see it settled, known, and admitted; for while the rules of law are vague and uncertain, especially in such fundamental points, our condition is deplorable in general." Letter of December 31, 1766, Hosmer's *Hutchinson*, p. 121.

Only one other question—and that intimately associated with the first—vied with it in importance: Were there or were there not rooted in the British constitution fundamental principles of individual liberty superior to legislative authority and must they be recognized in the British legislation for colonial affairs?

[30] XVI, p. 488.

[31] *Memoirs of the Historical Society of Penn.*, XIV, p. 356.

We might wisely spend much time in considering the dispute in 1770 already referred to—the dispute as to whether instructions could *ipso facto* dispose of all matters of constitutional right of the colonies, or whether even the crown was limited in imperial authority by the fact of the existence of competent and legally recognized colonial legislatures. But passing over those three years or so of legalistic dispute, let us come to "the great controversy" of 1773. In considering this we can echo John Adam's expression of amazement at Hutchinson's audacity in throwing down the gauntlet. The truth probably is that Hutchinson had been grievously tried for years, not alone by what he considered the unmannerly conduct of the rabble, but by the doctrines which he heard in the market place and perhaps in legislative halls. He believed that the theories of the malcontents were unsound and that he in the plenitude of his wisdom could establish their invalidity; and he prepared therefore to bring his heaviest artillery to bear upon the unreasoning followers of Samuel Adams and against the arch agitator himself. What he wished to do, be it noticed, was to demolish a false theory of the empire and bring every one to acknowledge, not the wisdom of obnoxious legislation, but the legal authority of Parliament. By this time doubtless there was much talk about complete freedom from parliamentary control, but there had been little if any formal public announcement by the radicals of anything more than a freedom from taxation.

Hutchinson, it must be said, had considerable reason for having confidence in his massed attack; for his argument was able and compelling, serving by its weight to bring into play all the open and masked batteries of the opposition. He finally reached in his first paper a position from which he believed he could discharge one final and conclusive volley; he was prepared to use an undeniable principle of political science; he believed he could silence his enemies with its mere pronouncement: "It is impossible there should be two independent Legislatures in the one and the same state."[22] Despite all the discussion that had gone on,

---

[22] *Mass. State Papers*, p. 340.

387

despite the fact that Britain had been practicing federalism, Hutchinson could see nothing but the theory of centralized legislative omnipotence and could not conceive of distribution of power between mutually independent legislative bodies. And yet this undeniable axiom of political science was to be proved untrue in the course of fifteen years by the establishment of fourteen independent legislatures in the single federal state, the United States of America.

The two branches of the legislature met Hutchinson's general argument somewhat differently. The house argued valiantly for complete freedom from parliamentary control; in facing the alternative of complete freedom from Parliament and complete subservience, they unhesitatingly chose the former, though they did seem to recognize the possibility of drawing a line between the supreme authority of Parliament and total independence.[33] The council, wiser and more conservative than the house, announced federalism; they contended that the colony had "property in the privileges granted to it," i.e., an indefeasible legal title: "But, as in fact, the two powers are not incompatible, and do subsist together, each restraining its acts to their constitutional objects, can we not from hence, see how the supreme power may supervise, regulate, and make general laws for the kingdom, without interfering with the privileges of the subordinate powers within it?"[34] This is a clear, precise and thorough description

[33] That is to say, they did not deny the possibility of distribution and a line of distinction between governments in the empire. "And, indeed, it is difficult, if possible, to draw a line of distinction between the universal authority of Parliament over the colonies, and no authority at all." "If your Excellency expects to have the line of distinction between the supreme authority of Parliament, and the total independence of the colonies drawn by us, we would say it would be an arduous undertaking, and of very great importance to all the other colonies; and therefore, could we conceive of such a line, we should be unwilling to propose it, without their consent in Congress." Hosmer, *Hutchinson*, pp. 382, 395.

[34] Hosmer, *Hutchinson*, p. 412. It will not do, to argue that they meant, by "subordinate," subject to the whim and control of Parliament; for that is just what they were arguing against. They denied that supremacy meant complete unlimited power, or that subordination meant unlimited submission. Of course "coordinate" is more nearly expressive of federalism than "subordinate;" but the principle these men had in mind is that of distribution, legal distribution, by

of federalism. It is plain enough, then, that there were some clear-headed men, who, in the years just before the final break with England, were not silenced by the fulminations of British pamphleteers or the dogmatic assertions of Hutchinson into a belief that the empire was simple and unitary; nor were they as yet ready to accept the learned and technical argument of John Adams, though buttressed by pedantic reference to Calvin's case, that the empire was held together by the king, a personal union only.

The American theory of federalism is stated with such amazing accuracy in an answer to Doctor Johnson's *Taxation No Tyranny*,[35] that it deserves quotation at considerable length:

"Now this, in abstract, sounds well. When we speak of the Legislature of a community, we suppose only one Legislature; and where there is but one, it must of necessity have the right you speak of; otherwise, no taxes at all could be raised in that community. . . . Now the present dispute is not with respect to this Island alone, which certainly has but one Legislature, but with respect to the *British* Empire at large, in which there are many Legislatures; or many Assemblies claiming to be so. . . . From the state of the *British* Empire, composed of extensive and dispersed Dominions, and from the nature of its Government, a multiplicity of Legislatures, or of Assemblies claiming to be so, have arisen in one Empire. It is in some degree a new case in legislation, and must be governed therefore more by its own circumstances, and by the genius of our peculiar Con-

389

which the parts legally control local affairs, a general government regulates and safeguards general affairs.

I omit, to save space, the extended argument, but I must call attention to their assertion of legal possession of constitutional right by the colonies as integral portions of the empire, and also to their declaration, in a delicate manner, that Hutchinson was dealing with theories and disregarding the fact, and that fact was the distribution of powers not centralization: "What has been here said [i.e. by Hutchinson], concerning supreme authority, has no reference to the manner in which it has been, in fact, exercised; but is wholly confined to its general nature." *Ibid.*, p. 413. These arguments are also to be found in *Mass. State Papers*, as well as in the appendix to Hosmer's *Hutchinson*.

[35] *An Answer to a Pamphlet entitled "Taxation No Tyranny,"* found in Force's *American Archives*, Fourth Series, I, 1450, latter part of paragraph on p. 1451.

stitution, than by abstract notions of Government at large. Every Colony, in fact, has two Legislatures, one interiour and Provincial, viz: the Colony Assembly; the other exteriour and imperial, viz: the *British* Parliament. . . . Neither will the unity of the Empire be in danger from the Provincial Legislature being thus exclusive as to points. It is perfectly sufficient, if the *British* Legislature be supreme as to all those things which are essential to *Great Britain's* being substantially the head of the Empire; a line not very difficult to be drawn, if it were the present subject. Neither is there any absurdity in there being two Assemblies, each of them sufficient, or, if you will, supreme, as to objects perfectly distinct; for this plain reason, that the objects being perfectly distinct, they cannot clash. The Colonist, therefore, allowing that the supreme power or Legislature, where there is but one, must have the right you speak of, will say that with respect to him, there are two, and that the Provincial Legislature is the supreme power as to taxation for his Colony. And so the controversy, notwithstanding your position, will remain just where it began."

The discussions in the Continental Congress of 1774 show us the trouble that the colonists had in reaching a satisfactory theory. By that time, many had come to the conclusion that Parliament possessed no power to pass laws governing the colonies. But the situation and the experience were too plain, and Congress "from the necessities of the case" announced that parliamentary regulation of trade would be accepted, but not taxation external or internal. They proposed as a working basis for the whole system—perhaps no longer to be termed an empire if there was no legislature with any imperial power legally speaking—the distinction between taxation and regulation of commerce, and they really put themselves back, as far as practice was concerned, nearly if not quite in the position of eleven years before. It cannot be supposed, as they accepted the king as their king, that the Congress of 1774 would deny the general right of the mother country, through the executive head, to make war and peace, manage diplomacy, hold the back lands, control Indian affairs and probably the post office—in other words, to exercise the significant powers bestowed on the central government of the United States under our Constitution. They were prepared to acknowledge a political order, in which all the great powers bestowed on our central government under the Constitution with the exception of the power to tax should be in the hands of the central authorities at Westminster; and they evidently accepted and promulgated the possibility of distribution of power.[34]

In drawing up the Declaration of Independence the Continental Congress accepted the theory that Parliament had had no legal authority over them; but the Articles of Confederation were drawn on the principle of distribution of powers. Of course it may properly be said that the Articles did not provide for the creation of an imperial state. If, however, we look to see how far they carried on the actual distribution which had existed in practice in the old empire, we see much in common between the empire and the Confederation. We do not find in the new system, of course, any right in the Congress—the new central authority—to exercise some of the functions formerly exercised by the crown in council; there was no right to appoint governors, or to instruct them, or to disapprove of the state laws. But the

391

[34] I have not attempted in this paper to cite all the instances of an appreciation of the fact that the discussion was over the possibility of distribution of power in the empire. Let me refer to a letter of Gouverneur Morris to Mr. Penn, May 20, 1774. It speaks of the danger of America's falling "under the worst of all possible dominions . . . the domination of a riotous mob," and then proposes "a safe compact" between the colonies and the mother country, "internal taxation i.e. to be left with ourselves," "the right of regulating trade to be vested in *Great Britain.*" Of course the compact was to form the legal and binding authority for the exercise of power. Force, *American Archives,* Fourth Series, I, 342–343.

Notice also that the Pennsylvania Convention of 1774 speaks of the desirability of agreements with Great Britain; she is to renounce certain claims and America is to accept certain statutes; money is to be given to the king. It also dwells on the compact which has to do largely with trade: "With such parts of the world only as she has appointed us to deal, we shall continue to deal; and such commodities only as she has permitted us to bring from them, we shall continue to bring. The executive and controlling powers of the crown will retain their present full force and operation." *Ibid.,* 561. Vide also among other plans, *Proposal for a Plan toward a Reconciliation and Reunion,* etc., by one of the Public (London, 1778).

I omit in this paper mention of various plans of imperial order. They are important as disclosures of effort to distribute powers on a legal basis.

great powers of war and peace, foreign affairs, the post office
and Indian affairs belonged to Congress; and it was understood
before adoption that the tremendously important matter of the
ownership of the back lands, and the administration of the back
settlements—in other words the extension of the empire—was
to be in the hands of Congress.   Only a detailed examination
would show how much of the old practical system of the empire
was formulated in the Articles.   It is sufficient now to say, and
it is quite unnecessary to say it, that very much of the old
system was there formulated, and the Articles carried on very
distinctly the principle of distribution of powers and on the whole
provided for governments with distinct spheres of action.[17]
A student of the Articles will of course be carried back to the Albany plan and even to the New England Confederacy of 1643;
but he will be hopelessly at sea unless he grasps the fact that the
contents of the document are distinctly the products of imperial
history, and they constitute, (1) the first quasi-legal formulation
of imperial existence, (2) the immediate preparation for ultimate real and full formulation in the Constitution.

The two powers of which there had been much discussion in
the ten years before independence were not adequately provided
for in the Confederation.   Congress, the new general government,
was not given the right to raise money by taxation, the Articles
accepting the principle of requisitions which the colonists as part
of the British empire had insisted on.   Everybody knows that
requisitions proved a failure in the new system, and this fact in
a way gave a tardy justice to the arguments of the parliamentarians in the days before the Revolution.   It is more surprising,
however, that Congress was not given the right to regulate trade,
inasmuch as, almost to the last, the colonies had either openly
acknowledged parliamentary authority in the matter or openly
professed a willingness to acquiesce in the practical exercise of
such authority.   The failure to grant the authority to Congress
shows how particularism had grown, or it discloses an inability
to see that the need of imperial regulation of trade was just as
vital in the new system as in the old.   Because Congress did not

392

[17] Even the system of admiralty jurisdiction was carried forward through the
Articles into the Constitution of the United States.

possess these two powers, taxation and regulation of commerce, the Confederation proved a failure.

The Confederation might very well, we may suppose, have proved a failure even if Congress had been given these two essential powers. As to that little or nothing need be said; it is a very old story; the states suffered from the natural effects of a Revolution, and, had Congress had authority on paper, license and particularistic folly might have made it impossible to go on, until the natural reaction in favor of nationalism and order set in. However that may be, these two powers had to be bestowed, conditions proved it; and in the new Constitution Congress was given power to tax for national purposes and to regulate commerce. The principle of federalism was recognized, formulated and legalized in the Constitution; the new government was given its distinct sphere of action and was made the recipient of a body of powers, carefully named and carefully deposited in their proper places; but in the selection and deposition little needed to be done but to follow the practices of the old British colonial system.

393

The Convention of 1787 had difficulty in seeing the whole complicated scheme as a working mechanism; but how could the members possibly have imagined it at all, or provided for the scheme which in its essentials was the basis of federalism the world over, without the aid of the historical forces and the old practices? Save perhaps with the old troublesome problem of the militia, the military question in the federal state, they had little trouble in determining what should be the distribution and classification of powers. Their chief difficulty was again the old one—colonial disobedience, which was now state willfulness; and this difficulty was surmounted, as we know, by firm adherence to the principle of distinction between local and general authority, and by recognizing that each governmental authority was competent and supreme within its own sphere and had the legal power to enforce its lawful acts on its own citizens. Perhaps both parts of this principle of cohesion and of authority— of cohesion because of division, and of authority because of immediate operation—were inherited from the old empire; certainly the former one was.

Toward Federalism:
Virginia, Congress, and the Western Lands

Peter Onuf

O n March 1, 1784, Virginia ceded its vast charter claims north of the Ohio River to the Continental Congress. This epochal transaction resolved the protracted dispute over western claims between the landed states and Congress. It secured the first strong congressional claim to a national domain and set in motion a liberal territorial policy which led to the formation of new western states. Little can be added to the history and background of the cession, covered in masterful detail by T. P. Abernethy and Merrill Jensen, or to Francis Philbrick's exhaustive discussion of its legal and constitutional implications for the territories.[1] But these writers have focused on congressional land and territorial policy or on the machinations of land company speculators. Virginia's reasons for ceding its northwestern claims have not been fully explored.

The 1784 cession climaxed Virginia's decade-long pursuit of policy goals in the West deemed vital to its sovereign pretensions. Virginia did not intend to retain jurisdiction across the Ohio. It did require that state claims there, based on the 1609 charter, be recognized by Congress and the other states.

Mr. Onuf is a member of the Department of History at Columbia University. An earlier version of this paper was delivered at a meeting of the Southern Historical Association in Atlanta, November 1973. The author is indebted to Richard Ryerson, Rosalind Rosenberg, Stuart Bruchey, and particularly Eric McKitrick for helpful criticism. Mr. Onuf's doctoral dissertation, "Sovereignty and Territory: Claims Conflict in the Old Northwest and the Origins of the American Federal Republic" (The Johns Hopkins University, 1973), is an extended treatment of the subject of this article.

[1] Thomas Perkins Abernethy, *Western Lands and the American Revolution* (New York, 1937); Merrill Jensen, "The Cession of the Old Northwest," *Mississippi Valley Historical Review*, XXIII (1936), 27-48; Jensen, "The Creation of the National Domain, 1781-1784," *ibid.*, XXVI (1939), 323-342; Jensen, *The Articles of Confederation: An Interpretation of the Social-Constitutional History of the American Revolution, 1774-1781* (Madison, Wis., 1948); Jensen, *The New Nation: A History of the United States during the Confederation, 1781-1818* (New York, 1950); Francis S. Philbrick, *The Laws of Illinois Territory, 1809-1818* (Illinois State Historical Library, *Collections*, XXV [Springfield, 1950]); Philbrick, *The Rise of the West, 1754-1830* (New York, 1965). See also Robert F. Berkhofer, Jr., "Jefferson, the Ordinance of 1784, and the Origins of the American Territorial System," *William and Mary Quarterly*, 3d Ser., XXIX (1972), 231-262.

Though it acknowledged that abridgement of those claims was ultimately necessary, it insisted that this be done on terms the General Assembly itself should dictate. A cession of Virginia's western claims to Congress, under express stipulations, was the logical culmination of this policy.

Seen as a vindication of state claims—and state sovereignty—the Virginia cession illuminates a hitherto neglected aspect of state-congressional relations. Though the cession transaction did benefit Congress—indeed, it was one of the few significant congressional triumphs in domestic diplomacy—it did not do so at Virginia's expense. Both parties gained by the cession. Virginia was secured within manageable, permanent, and—more important—undisputed bounds, drawn at its own sovereign discretion. Congress gained control over the immense, largely undeveloped Northwest. Such mutually beneficial transactions were necessary before substantive constitutional reform, giving new powers to a dangerously feeble Congress, could even begin to take place.

The Virginia cession of 1784 vindicated the state's claims and eliminated one of the chief threats to its sovereignty. Though constitutional historiography has correctly emphasized the contest for authority among states and Congress over such questions as taxation and commerce, it has failed to recognize the threat to state jurisdiction posed by unresolved and overlapping boundary claims.[2] Revolutionary statesmen were concerned with rights to be defended as much as with powers to be exercised. Both in a symbolic and in a real sense, challenges to territorial jurisdiction were challenges to the existence of the new states. British tampering with colonial boundaries was seen as one of the reasons for revolution.[3] Similarly, new state leaders had to fend off threats by domestic separatists, local and out-of-state land claimants (including loyalists), the conflicting claims of other states, and, for those states with western claims, counter-claims by Congress or other nations.[4]

Virginia faced imperial boundary changes, implied in the Proclamation of 1763 and subsequent Indian boundaries, and explicitly in the proposed new colony of Vandalia and the Quebec Act in the 1770s. Separatists challenged colony and state jurisdiction in Transylvania (Kentucky) and in southwest Virginia. Private land companies, including the Ohio and Loyal companies

395

[2] Boundary disputes absorbed much of the Confederation Congress's time and energy. Edmund Cody Burnett, *The Continental Congress* (New York, 1941). Decisions in some of these cases are conveniently collected in James Brown Scott, ed., *Judicial Settlement of Controversies between States of the American Union: Cases Decided in the Supreme Court of the United States* (New York, 1918).
[3] This was one of the chief objections to the Quebec Act of 1774, attaching the trans-Ohio region to Canada.
[4] Abernethy, *Western Lands;* Frederick Jackson Turner, "Western State-Making in the Revolutionary Era," *American Historical Review,* I (1895-1896), 70-87, 251-269; Samuel Cole Williams, *History of the Lost State of Franklin,* rev. ed. (New York, 1933).

of Virginia, in addition to the Indiana, Illinois, and Wabash companies, all dominated by out-of-staters, sought to establish property claims within Virginia's charter lines.[5] Meanwhile Pennsylvania asserted its claim in the contested Pittsburgh region.[6] In the farther West, England, Spain, and the United States Congress promoted various title pretensions, as did Connecticut and Massachusetts on the basis of their charters, and New York State on the strength of its suzerainty over the Iroquois—all within the limits of the Virginia charter.[7]

Whatever the source of such threats, whatever the motives of their promoters—to enrich speculators, spread republicanism to the West, or strengthen the Union—and however they combined to support or oppose one another, they all constituted challenges to Virginia's territorial jurisdiction. They all endangered the state's territorial integrity, the security of its boundaries, and its control over private property titles and the distribution of its public lands. In response, Virginians pursued a policy designed to vindicate and secure the state's claims. The cession of the Northwest under specific conditions emerged as the main feature of this policy.

Virginia's western policy, and the claims cession first offered in 1781, aroused suspicion and hostility in other state governments. The opposition included speculators who had a material interest in the disposition of claims. But it also included landless state governments, led by Maryland, which feared that Virginia's boundary proposals would leave that state too large and powerful. They believed that recognition of Virginia's claims would jeopardize the sovereignty and survival of their own states.[8]

396

[5] On the Indian boundaries see Louis De Vorsey, Jr., *The Indian Boundary in the Southern Colonies, 1763-1775* (Chapel Hill, N.C., 1961), and John Richard Alden, *John Stuart and the Southern Colonial Frontier: A Study of Indian Relations, War, Trade, and Land Problems in the Southern Wilderness, 1754-1775* (Ann Arbor, Mich., 1944). Literature on the land companies includes Shaw Livermore, *Early American Land Companies: Their Influence on Corporate Development* (New York, 1939); George E. Lewis, *The Indiana Company, 1763-1798: A Study in Eighteenth-Century Frontier Land Speculation and Business Venture* (Glendale, Calif., 1941); K. L. Bailey, *The Ohio Company of Virginia and the Westward Movement, 1748-1792* (Glendale, Calif., 1939); and Lois Mulkearn, ed., *George Mercer Papers Relating to the Ohio Company of Virginia* (Pittsburgh, Pa., 1954). Land company membership lists may be found in the Thomas Jefferson Papers, VII, 1164 (Vandalia), 1166 (Indiana and Illinois-Wabash), Library of Congress.

[6] Neville B. Craig, ed., *The Olden Time*, I (Cincinnati, Ohio, 1876), 433-519; Boyd Crumrine, "The Boundary Dispute between Pennsylvania and Virginia, 1745-1785," Carnegie Institute, *Annals of the Carnegie Museum*, I (Pittsburgh, Pa., 1901), 505-524.

[7] The various state claims are outlined in the cession proposals reprinted in Thomas Donaldson, *The Public Domain: Its History with Statistics . . .* (Washington, D.C., 1884), 82, 86-88.

[8] Maryland's key role in opposing the Virginia claims is discussed by Herbert B. Adams, *Maryland's Influence upon Land Cessions to the United States*, The Johns

Beginning in 1776, Virginia's leaders showed a willingness to abridge the state's claims. The Virginia constitution provided for the creation of "new governments" in the West.[9] In 1778 Richard Henry Lee proposed "the Ohio as a boundary to the Westward." The Northwest could be "settled for common good and ma[d]e a new State."[10] A defense of Virginia's claim, drafted in 1782, argued that it was impossible for East and West to "remain under one government."[11] Some kind of division was inevitable, and Virginia was as interested as the other states in creating a national domain. National interests were not in clear opposition to state interests. The struggle was over the terms on which one state would be secured in its claims and the impact of those guarantees on the security and survival of the other states.

A successful reconciliation of the states' various interests and policies was vitally important to the future health of Congress and the Union. If Virginia failed to gain guarantees from Congress and the other states for its territorial claims, it would be perpetually exposed to encroachments from its neighbors—and from Congress. Congress might assert its jurisdiction in the West on its own initiative. This would "introduce a most dangerous precedent which might hereafter be urged to deprive [any state] of territory or subvert [its] sovereignty."[12] Yet if state rights and sovereignty were secured, it would be possible to entrust Congress with larger powers, even in such ambiguous areas as commerce and taxation where it was much less certain what state rights or powers were or should be. The vindication and guarantee of state rights had to precede the enlargement of congressional powers.

This view of the significance and meaning of the land cession suggests a

397

Hopkins University Studies in Historical and Political Science, 3d Ser., I (Baltimore, 1885), 1-54. The arguments against those claims are developed in the Maryland legislature's declaration and delegate instructions of Dec. 15, 1778, which were laid before Congress on May 21, 1779. Worthington C. Ford et al., eds., Journals of the Continental Congress (Washington, D.C., 1904-1937), XIV, 619-622, hereafter cited as Jour. Cont. Cong.; the Declaration is reprinted in William Waller Hening, ed., The Statutes at Large: Being a Collection of all the Laws of Virginia, From the First Session of the Legislature, in the Year 1619 (Richmond, 1809-1823), X, 549-552.

[9] Ordinances Passed at a General Convention of delegates and representatives . . . (Williamsburg, Va., 1776), 5-13. In an earlier draft of the constitution Thomas Jefferson used even stronger language, calling for "new colonies" which "shall be free and independent of this colony and all the world" (Julian P. Boyd et al., eds., The Papers of Thomas Jefferson [Princeton, N.J., 1950-   ], I, 362-363).

[10] Richard Henry Lee to Patrick Henry, Nov. 15, 1778, James Curtis Ballagh, ed., The Letters of Richard Henry Lee, I (New York, 1911), 452-453.

[11] "Outline and Preamble of Argument on Virginia's Claim," Boyd et al., eds., Jefferson Papers, VI, 665. Virginians would not stand in the way of "their Western brethren" when they thought themselves "able to stand alone." James Madison to Jefferson, Mar. 24, 1782, ibid., 170-171.

[12] Remonstrances of the Virginia General Assembly, Dec. 14, 1779, Hening, ed., Statutes at Large, X, 557-559.

more general reinterpretation of Confederation politics. Issues which have
been considered peripheral, such as land and territorial policies and claims,
may deserve considerably more attention. The politics of this period has often
been reduced to two opposing positions or persuasions, variously identified as
nationalist and states' rights, or cosmopolitan and localist.[13] But a third
position was possible. Defense of state rights and claims, particularly against
other states, could be perfectly consistent with support for a strengthened
Congress—if the states were adequately guaranteed against congressional
encroachments. The states and Congress were not necessarily competing for
the same sovereign powers. State and federal sovereignties were not mutually
exclusive. Many Americans believed that both could be secured in a proper
constitutional settlement that would create a strong union on the foundation
of strong states, secure in their rights.[14]

Before the Revolution colonists shared a sense of community or "union,"
nurtured in British imperial patriotism and consummated in united resistance
to British tyranny. Continental patriotism was reinforced by economic ties
and family connections, and by the millennial expectations of evangelical
Protestants.[15] But the Revolution also promised to secure local rights and
interests, and the autonomy and independence of the American states.
Cosmopolitan and localist tendencies coexisted in Revolutionary politics.
They were held in check by the recognition that national union and state

398

[13] For the most recent and sophisticated formulation of the "cosmopolitan-
localist" dichotomy see Jackson Turner Main, *Political Parties before the Constitution* (Chapel Hill, N.C., 1973).

[14] One of the leading Federalist arguments was that a stronger national government would strengthen the states: Congress and the states would all benefit by
constitutional reform. "The peace and independence of each state, will be more fully
secured . . . than they will under a constitution with more limited powers." Noah
Webster, *An Examination into the leading principles of the Federal Constitution
proposed by the late Convention held at Philadelphia . . . ,* in Paul Leicester Ford,
ed., *Pamphlets on the Constitution of the United States, Published during Its
Discussion by the People, 1787-1788 . . .* (Brooklyn, N.Y., 1888), 46. It was "very
evident" to Pelatiah Webster "that the Constitution gives an establishment, support,
and protection to the internal and separate police of each State, under the superin-
tendency of federal powers, which it could not possibly enjoy in an independent
state" (*The Weakness of Brutus exposed: or, some Remarks in Vindication of the
Constitution proposed by the late Federal Convention . . . , ibid.,* 128).

[15] See, for example, Alan Heimert's discussion of the Calvinist-evangelical idea
of union in *Religion and the American Mind: From the Great Awakening to the
Revolution* (Cambridge, Mass., 1966), 95-158. The impact of ideas on the Revolution
has been demonstrated by Bernard Bailyn, particularly his *The Ideological Origins
of the American Revolution* (Cambridge, Mass., 1967). The connection between
these ideas and behavior has puzzled historians; some provocative suggestions have
been made by Gordon S. Wood, "Rhetoric and Reality in the American Revolution," *WMQ.* 3d Ser., XXIII (1966), 3-32.

sovereignty were politically, if not logically, inseparable. Most Americans thought they could have both. This was the third position, distinct from localism or cosmopolitanism—and pervasive to a greater or less degree in both camps. Its proponents sought an equilibrium of interests and a balance of state and congressional powers. A stronger national government was imperative; but this government had to be disinterested, insulated from the ambition of speculators and promoters, and immune to the influence of state and sectional interests.[16] It was this third position which the rebellious colonists had sought to achieve when they declared their independence: they wanted both strong, sovereign states and a perpetual league among them, with its own full complement of sovereign powers.

Did this third position actually determine policy in the Confederation period? Jackson Turner Main has persuasively demonstrated the bipolarity of state politics before the Constitution. But was it logically necessary for the policies of the various localist or cosmopolitan parties either to limit or to enlarge national power? Did opposition to Congress *as it was then constituted* always indicate opposition to a stronger national government on any terms?

399

There were limits to even the most extreme cosmopolitanism. State legislators would predictably resist any radical derogation of their own privileges and powers: the instinct for institutional self-preservation was universal. Nor could the most advanced nationalist happily countenance insults or injuries to the honor, dignity, or essential interests of his own state. Depending on circumstances, a nationalist might feel compelled to advocate his state's rights. On the other hand, legislators were able to support measures enlarging and strengthening the national power, provided certain essential state rights were secured. Indeed, such ambivalence was typical.

An examination of the territorial question in Virginia will illuminate some of these essential rights—what Americans conceived to be the nature of state sovereignty—and show how even cosmopolitan-nationalists came to their defense. A successful adjustment of state and congressional claims was a *sine qua non* of enlarging congressional power. In the cession of 1784, Virginia asserted and secured its jurisdictional limits at the same time that it granted the vast trans-Ohio region to Congress. The national domain was to be (or so it was thought) a source of virtually unlimited financial and political power for Congress. Virginians were convinced that this power, limited by the terms of the cession, would not be turned against them.

[16] Checks and balances or interest group pluralism as delineated in Madison's Federalist No. 10 might accomplish this; so too would a redirection of this ambition from interest to the "quest for glory." According to Gerald Stourzh, "this passion topped all others in the eighteenth-century hierarchy of passions, since it was the only one to comprehend private and public, individual and general interest" (*Alexander Hamilton and the Idea of Republican Government* [Stanford, Calif., 1970], 106).

The American idea of state sovereignty, and Virginia's claims to territorial integrity, were based on concepts of colonial distinctness and autonomy. On the eve of the Revolution leading Virginians argued that colonial boundaries could not be altered without the consent of the people of the colony and that, within those boundaries, public lands were held in trust for the community. Concern with territorial integrity and the inviolability of Virginia's boundaries preceded the Revolution, anticipating the state's more extensive claims to sovereignty at independence.

The source of territorial title in Virginia and other colonies was fraught with ambiguity. Broad and dubious territorial claims antedated colonization.[17] Thereafter the precise nature of English territory in America and its relation to English territory at home was never satisfactorily defined.[18] Sir William Blackstone wrote in his *Commentaries* that colonies "were no part of the mother country, but distinct, though dependent dominions." [19] At the very least, this meant that parliamentary authority in the colonies was not the same as at home. The colonial dominions were not part of the realm. And, taken to the extreme, this distinctness—the peculiar legal, political, and territorial position of each colony—could be held inviolable, beyond the power of Parliament to alter. Imperial administrators were more concerned with the "dependent" than the "distinct" status. The idea of colonial distinctness could not be abandoned, however, because it meant that colonies

[17] Hugo Grotius contended that a "new people arises possessed of its own rights" with the establishment of a colony. Grotius, *De Jure Belli Ac Pacis*, trans. Francis W. Kelsey, II (Oxford, 1925), 264. Another great law-of-nations writer, Samuel von Pufendorf, argued that with the planting of a colony, "in the place of one state we have two" (*De Jure Naturae et Gentium Libri Octo*, trans. C. H. and W. A. Oldfather [Oxford, 1934], 1363). These suggestions were based on classical precedents; they were balanced by the contrary doctrine that a sovereign's laws were binding on his subjects not only within his own jurisdiction but where no jurisdiction had been established—areas subject to colonization.

[18] This question has been considered by historians solely on the limited and technical point of the differential impact of "realm" and "dominion" on parliamentary authority. The king's dominions outside Great Britain were not bound by parliamentary legislation for the realm, of which Parliament was the legislature, according to the famous argument of Charles Howard McIlwain, *The American Revolution: A Constitutional Interpretation* (New York, 1923), 20. McIlwain's claims are anachronistic, suggesting that the rise of Parliament was confined to the insular not imperial constitution, and that colony connections with the mother country were to be delineated according to the constitution as it existed at the time of colonization. This narrow, legalistic distinction was exploded by other writers (see, for example, Robert Livingston Schuyler, *Parliament and the British Empire: Some Constitutional Controversies Concerning Imperial Legislative Jurisdiction* [New York, 1929]), yet this did not mean that there were no distinctions at all between colonies and mother country.

[19] William Blackstone, *Commentaries on the Laws of England* (Oxford, 1765), I, 112.

were not part of the British state. Colonists were subject to the absolute control of Parliament because they were dependent, yet had no reciprocal claims because they were distinct. They were not represented in Parliament, fictions of virtual representation notwithstanding. The whole spectrum of constitutional possibilities was latent in Blackstone's dictum. In one extreme or the other, "distinctness" was alternatively "slavery" or independence. Naturally, colonists supported the latter version. And this distinctness, construed as community integrity, was the conceptual foundation for the ultimate defense of local rights in the Revolution.[20]

The American idea of state sovereignty developed out of claims of distinct and irreducible rights and the integrity of colonies as territorial communities. But such a definition was radically different from the English idea of sovereignty as the ultimate and indivisible locus of legitimate authority in the state.[21] The English maintained that the King-in-Parliament was sovereign.[22] The English idea of sovereignty was institutional; it grew out of the separate claims, rights, privileges, prerogatives, and immunities of the three branches. English sovereignty, seen as the synthesis of the branches in Parliament, never extended to America. Prerogative, in theory if not in practice, remained unbounded.[23] The adversary relationship that once typi-

401

[20] Thomas Pownall's *The Administration of the Colonies* ... (London, 1766 [orig. publ. London, 1764]), 158, 201-202, 291, argued that citizens of each colony constitute "a community—they are a society, and have a fixed property in their lands, have a fixed permanent interest, which must subsist under a continued series of security." He advocated constitutional reform to provide the colonies with that security. See also Edward Bancroft, *Remarks on the Review of the Controversy between Great Britain and her Colonies* (London, 1769), 13, 29, 111: *because* the colonies were distinct communities, Parliament should desist "from all future Impositions ... till they are united to Great Britain in a civic capacity," that is, until the empire itself constituted a single community. American authors also frequently claimed community status for their colonies. According to Moses Mather, "a state is a country or body of people that are connected under one and the same constitution of civil government" (*America's Appeal to the Impartial World. Wherein the Rights of the Americans ... are Stated and Considered ...* [Hartford, Conn., 1775], 47). The empire was not such a state; the American colonies were. Reformers who recognized colony community status argued that the empire could be preserved if Great Britain and its colonies were connected by international agreements or treaties. See Malachy Postlethwayt, *The Universal Dictionary of Trade and Commerce, translated from the French of the Celebrated Monsieur Savary* (London, 1766), lviii, and James Wilson, *Considerations on the Nature and the Extent of the Legislative Authority of the British Parliament* (Philadelphia, 1774), 34n.

[21] F. H. Hinsley, *Sovereignty* (New York, 1966), 152; Peter S. Onuf, ed., *Maryland and the Empire, 1773: The Antilon-First Citizen Letters* (Baltimore, 1974), 4-11.

[22] Blackstone, *Commentaries*, I, 94, 112; David Lindsay Keir, *The Constitutional History of Modern Britain Since 1485-1951*, 5th ed. (London, 1953), 271.

[23] Bernard Bailyn, *The Origins of American Politics* (New York, 1968), 59-105.

fied the English constitution—the hostility and suspicion among the branches that regularly immobilized government before the Glorious Revolution—continued to exist in America thereafter.

Colonial legislatures, acting on behalf of their constituents, began to assert their own legitimacy in order to justify resistance to prerogative (which, if alone legitimate, could not be limited). This was the source of the American Revolutionary idea of sovereignty.[24] Legitimate authority was transferred from the institutions of government to the people of the new states. American sovereignty, unlike English, was extra-institutional, outside of government.[25]

The American concept of state sovereignty reflected its peculiar historical development, in the defense of the colonial constitutions. Because Americans juxtaposed sovereignty and actual governing authority, they were particularly sensitive to encroachments on their individual and collective rights. They were less interested in vesting their governments with powers than with protecting themselves—and their sovereignty—from their governments. Virginians rushed to the defense of the state's territorial claims and its right to determine land policy and titles within its sovereign jurisdiction. Yet these same Virginians remained divided on what the state's rights were or should have been in such areas as regulation of commerce and taxation, which, from our modern perspective, are far more important to the sovereignty of a political community. Contemporary ideas of state sovereignty were much better defined at the periphery, on questions of rights, than at the center, in determining the exercise of sovereign powers.

[24] Colonial constitutions, in which legitimate English authority was balanced and limited by the legitimate rights and privileges of the colonists acting through their assemblies, were entirely different from, and bore only a superficial resemblance to, the English constitution. First, English sovereignty was outside of, and abstracted from, the colonial constitutions. It acted through the prerogative branch of colonial governments. Second, English authority in America was limited by the "independence" or legitimacy of the peculiarly American branches of government. Many writers regretted the difference between the colonial and English constitutions. Onuf, ed., *Maryland and the Empire*, 21-22. The self-conscious imitation of the House of Commons by colonial lower houses was not likely to eliminate but rather increase the distinction. Jack P. Greene, "Political Mimesis: A Consideration of the Historical and Cultural Roots of Legislative Behavior in the British Colonies in the Eighteenth Century," *Am. Hist. Rev.*, LXXV (1969), 337-360. As Americans began to claim parity for their communities as distinct bodies politic with irreducible rights and privileges, colonial and English constitutions progressively diverged. On the eve of independence, colonial constitutions—if they could be said to exist at all—were radically different from the English model.

[25] Balance in the colonial constitutions was an *effect* of a working balance between English and American sovereignties expressed through, but not contained in, those constitutions. It was not inherent in the mutual relations of the branches themselves.

The preservation of state sovereignty, as Americans defined it, was not necessarily incompatible with strengthening and securing national authority.[26] State sovereignty was not like British sovereignty, nor did the states necessarily seek powers which they felt belonged in Congress, under certain conditions: that is, *if* the colony-state rights they had sought to vindicate in the Revolution were respected and secured. We have been too prone to consider the defense of these rights peripheral to the constitutional struggle over powers. Yet these questions may seem peripheral precisely because they were so successfully resolved. Many controversial issues had already been laid to rest before the Philadelphia convention was called to order; and these issues shed as much light on state-federal relations as do the more familiar struggles over taxation, commerce, or representation.

The western lands claims were one such issue. Until 1784 it repeatedly threatened the harmony and even the existence of the Continental Congress. The controversy could be resolved, however, because the aims of the participants were, finally, not mutually exclusive. Congressional authority could be enhanced, and Virginia's sovereignty secured, through completion of a territorial cession on mutually satisfactory terms. This solution was possible because one of the most important characteristics of state sovereignty—which cosmopolitan and localist Virginians combined to defend—was control over public lands within firmly secured state boundaries.

403

The Virginian concern with territory was an important issue in the Revolution itself. The state's position on its territorial claims was fully developed by the time of independence, and that position was maintained and defended until the successful conclusion of the cession in 1784. The territorial issue emerged fully only when it could be argued that colonial Virginians possessed the exclusive, preemptive right to crown lands within their charter

[26] The need for a superintending authority was recognized by American writers before and after independence. Onuf, ed., *Maryland and the Empire*, 11-12n. The problem of establishing such an authority on a sound and safe basis, preserving peace among the American states and securing them in their rights, led American theorists into the literature on world federalism, embodied in "peace plans" that sought to prevent war and preserve separate sovereignties. This body of thought was most easily available to Americans through such law-of-nations writers as Emerich de Vattel, who called for limited regional federations that would preserve smaller states in the larger balance of power. Vattel, *The Law of Nations, or, Principles of the Law of Nature, Applied to the Conduct and Affairs of Nations and Sovereigns*, trans. of the 1758 ed. by Clarke G. Fenwick (Washington, D.C., 1916), 47-49, 251. Americans such as Benjamin Franklin, who sponsored publication of one obscure plan, were conscious of the peace plan tradition and saw the Federal Constitution as its culmination in America. Franklin to Ferdinand Grand, Oct. 22, 1787, U.S. Bureau of Rolls and Library, *Documentary History of the Constitution of the United States of America*, IV (Washington, D.C., 1900), 341-342.

limits. These charter claims began to assume a new significance for the colony at the conclusion of the French and Indian War.[27] The divergent interests of Virginia settlers, land company speculators, Indians, and imperial administrators made the jurisdictional question—who would control the Ohio Valley and for what purposes?—a vitally important one. Subsequent British policy intensified the conflict of interests. White settlement was prohibited beyond the Atlantic watershed by the Proclamation of 1763; negotiations with Indians from 1768 to 1770 pushed the line considerably to the west.[28]

After the French and Indian War, new colony proposals focused on the Illinois and Great Lakes region, where the Illinois and Wabash companies maintained extensive claims based on Indian purchases of doubtful legality. But the Indian boundaries confined most speculators and promoters to Virginia's immediate hinterland. A group of Philadelphia traders claimed the Indiana tract in present-day West Virginia under a deed granted by Indians at Fort Stanwix in 1768. The Indiana group combined forces with politically powerful English speculators in 1769 to form the Walpole Company. The new company ultimately proposed to establish the colony of Vandalia, covering all of modern West Virginia and part of Kentucky. The Loyal and Greenbrier companies of Virginia claimed land in the same area. Gov. Robert Dinwiddie had promised colonial soldiers bounty grants in the West; hundreds of Virginia families, encouraged by a series of colony laws, had already settled in the Vandalia region.[29]

The clash of interests and claims in the nearby frontier region produced the first hints of Virginia's claims defense. William Nelson, president of the royal council and acting governor, defended the colony's interests against the Vandalia plan in a long letter to the colonial secretary, Lord Hillsborough, in 1770. Nelson suggested that the people of Virginia had earned a preemptive right to extend their own frontiers. Though he would "not presume to say to whom our Gracious Sovereign shall grant his vacant lands," he was confident the secretary would recognize that "the weight prevails" on the side of Virginians "who have run great hazards during the course of the war, many

[27] For Virginia's increasingly extensive claims in the West see the governors' reports to the Board of Trade for 1742, C.O. 5/1325, 113-119, Public Record Office; for 1743, 1744, and 1747, C.O. 5/1326, 12-19, 103-110, 234-244; for 1749 and 1750, C.O. 5/1327, 778-783, 105-112; for 1755, R. A. Brock, ed., *The Official Records of Robert Dinwiddie, Lieutenant-Governor of the Colony of Virginia, 1751-1758,* I (Richmond, 1883), 381; and for 1763, King's Manuscript 205, 255-276, British Library.
[28] De Vorsey, *Indian Boundary in Southern Colonies,* 48-92.
[29] The Virginia Burgesses passed acts in 1752, 1753, and 1754 "encouraging persons to settle on the waters of the Mississippi." Hening, ed., *Statutes at Large,* VI, 258, 355-356, 417-420.

of whom lost their lives and fortunes." If vacant lands were still crown lands, at least the king could be expected to protect the interests of his loyal subjects in Virginia.[30]

Demands for limitations on the disposal of crown lands became more explicit as the Revolutionary crisis approached. In his *Summary View*, written in 1774, Thomas Jefferson anticipated the colony's response to proposed changes in the land grant system. "Kings are the servants, not the proprietors of the people," he wrote; changes in land policy that made "acquisition of lands . . . difficult" were unconstitutional. Jefferson did not evade the logical conclusion that the king had "no right to grant lands of himself," without the colony's approval or acquiescence.[31] In 1775 the Burgesses registered similar objections to the new land policy, announced by Governor Dunmore's proclamation of March 21. They doubted the king's "right" to make these changes but, more cautious than Jefferson, relied merely on "the established usage of granting lands." [32]

Imperial policy created a congestion of conflicting interests on the near frontier, involving Indians, local and foreign speculators, and settlers. In the midst of this confusion, audacious Virginians began to assert the rights of the colony to control the disposition of land, first against competing interests and later, while relying on a title based entirely on the royal charter, even against the crown itself. And logically, if Virginia could control the disposition of vacant lands as they were granted, the colony's title included all the territory within its charter lines. Thus when land policy became an issue, jurisdiction likewise became an issue. Virginians were prepared not only to battle competitors for vacant lands but also to deny the right of the crown to alter old boundaries or erect new colonies within its western claims. These claims included Kentucky and much of the old Northwest

Up to the outbreak of the Revolution, the Vandalia new colony proposal made progress in British government circles. In response, Virginians developed a sophisticated defense of their own claims in the same region. This defense, first outlined in 1773 by George Mason, argued that the colony's charter lines were inviolable.[33] Together with an anonymous "Vindication"

405

---

[30] William Nelson to Hillsborough, Oct. 18, 1770, C.O. 5/1348, 321-330. The plight of actual settlers had been periodically invoked in Virginian objections to the Proclamation of 1763. Gov. Francis Fauquier to Lords of Trade, Feb. 13, 1764, C.O. 5/1345, 319; Fauquier to Shelburne, Nov. 18, 1766, *ibid.*, 313-314; May 20, 1767, King's MS 206, 141-157.

[31] Thomas Jefferson, *A Summary View of the Rights of British America* . . . (Williamsburg, Va., 1774), 21.

[32] Resolution on Land Grants, Mar. 27, 1775, Boyd *et al.*, eds., *Jefferson Papers*, I, 162.

[33] "Extracts from the Virginia Charters, With Some Remarks on Them Made in the Year 1773," in Kate Mason Rowland, *The Life of George Mason, 1725-1792*, I (New York, 1892), 393-414.

of the Virginia claims—possibly also by Mason—and Jefferson's *Summary View,* this document stated the colony's mature title defense.[34] This same defense survived intact as the bulwark of the Virginia position until the successful completion of the second cession offer in 1784. Mason's "Remarks" of 1773 touched on the key points: first, that charter rights inure to the benefit of Virginians "forever, notwithstanding the dissolution of the Virginia Company"; and, second, that the territory of the colony was not confined to the area "purchased from or ceded by the Indians." In other words, charter lines created the colony's jurisdiction, and Indian rights had no effect on them. The basis for Mason's claim was that Virginians "have enjoyed these rights and privileges from time Immemorial."[35] This was an appeal to prescription; prescription also explained the creation of Maryland, North Carolina, and Pennsylvania within the charter lines. Jefferson maintained that those proprietaries had been erected "into distinct and independent governments . . by an assumed right of the crown alone," and he warned that though Virginians had acquiesced in these changes, they would allow no others. "No exercise of such a power, of dividing and dismembering a country, has ever occurred in his majesty's realm of England, . . . nor could it be justified or acquiesced under there, or in any other part of his majesty's realm."[36]

This prescriptive right applied not only to settled areas but also to undeveloped western claims. It was an exclusive preemptive right to Indian

406

[34] The "Vindication of Virginia's Claims Against the Proposed Colony of Vandalia" is printed in Boyd et al., eds., *Jefferson Papers,* VI, 656-662. The text is often identical with Mason's "Remarks."
[35] Rowland, *Life of Mason,* I, 398n-399, 410-411n. If Indian treaties were invoked in support of Virginia's title, a basis would be established for promoting land company claims. The Fort Stanwix Treaty of 1768, for instance, apparently supported the colony's claims south of the Ohio; yet the Indiana Grant had been transacted at the same treaty. Thus reliance on the treaty would confirm the Indiana Company's claims. See Carter Braxton, "Address to the Convention of Virginia," *Virginia Gazette* (Dixon and Hunter), Oct. 8, 15, 1776. Arthur Lee premised his defense of state claims in part on Indian cessions at Lancaster and Loggs-town in 1744 and 1752. See Lee, "Concise View of the Title of Virginia to the Western Lands in Refutation of the Pamphlet called Public Good" (ca. 1782), in Paul P. Hoffman, ed., *The Lee Family Papers, 1742-1795,* Reel 7, 280 (microfilm publication, Charlottesville, Va., 1966). But such a defense only served to make company pretensions, also based on Indian transactions, all the more plausible. Edmund Randolph thought it "rank suicide to oppose the title of the natives to the claims of the companies," and such dangerous doctrines were generally suppressed. Randolph to James Madison, Robert A. Rutland, ed., *The Papers of James Madison* (Chicago, 1962-   ), IV, 226.
[36] Jefferson, *A Summary View,* 8. For a similar argument against the Quebec Act see Edmund Randolph's brief on territorial claims, Aug. 20, 1782: "even if it [that act] had been designed to abridge the boundaries of the colonies, the right of the British parliament to do so must be denied" (*Jour. Cont. Cong.,* XXIII, 510-511).

lands within the charter lines, according to the "Vindication." Indian purchases had kept pace with the expansion of settlement, first to the fall line, "then to the blue ridge of Mountains; afterwards to the Alleghany Mountains, and lately to the River Ohio."[37] It was a central point in subsequent Virginian arguments that the state's title was equally good in settled and unsettled areas anywhere within the charter lines. Kentucky was as much part of Virginia as Williamsburg, Edmund Pendleton maintained, "for she can't distinguish upon what ground she may claim the one and not the other."[38]

The outlines of Virginia's western policy were stated in the constitution of 1776.[39] Specific land policy and determination of Indian and land company rights were worked out in resolutions and legislation over the next three years. The constitution appealed specifically to the charter in defining state boundaries, limited on the west at the Mississippi River by the Peace of Paris in 1763 and by the creation of new colonies to the north—Pennsylvania and Maryland—and south—Carolina. The constitution suggested that even these new colonies were usurpations of its charter rights but still "ceded, released, and forever confirmed" to those colonies the Virginia territory. This insistence on charter rights, however, was joined by another provision that "one or more Territories shall hereafter be laid off, and Governments established Westward of the *Alleghany* Mountains." Virginians were aware of the difficulties in administering the state's extensive territorial claims. But any separation had to be "by act of [this] legislature."[40] Significantly, Edmund Pendleton felt that such separation could be effected only after "all Land titles are Adjusted by Us, and the Several Purchases from the Crown or the Indians either confirmed or set aside."[41] The boundary question was inextricably bound up with recognition of private titles within those boundaries, and so too was inseparable from the state's sovereignty. "If the disposition of our Lands be not Local," Pendleton declared, "there can be nothing so."[42]

407

The link between charter lines and private titles was forged in 1778 and 1779 with passage of the Land Office and Land Title bills by the Virginia

[37] "Vindication," Boyd et al., eds., *Jefferson Papers*, VI, 656-662.
[38] Edmund Pendleton to Joseph Jones, Feb. 10, 1781, David John Mays, ed., *The Letters and Papers of Edmund Pendleton, 1734-1803* (Charlottesville, Va., 1967), I, 334.
[39] *Ordinances Passed at a Convention,* 5-13.
[40] See n. 10 above. Boyd et al., eds., *Jefferson Papers*, I, 383. See also Berkhofer, "Jefferson, the Ordinance of 1784, and the Origins of the American Territorial System," *WMQ*, 3d Ser., XXIX (1972), 233.
[41] Pendleton to the Virginia delegation, July 14, 1776, Boyd et al., eds., *Jefferson Papers*, I, 462-464.
[42] Edmund Pendleton to Jefferson, Aug. 3, 1776, *ibid.*, 484.

assembly.[43] A "torrent" of new settlers had already spread west.[44] As Edmund Randolph later suggested, Virginia "had hardly a choice between an acquiescence in the rights acquired by the hardihood of occupancy to the vacant western lands and the daily diminution of that important fund for her public debt."[45] At the least, the state had to preserve public authority. Adjusting its sovereign authority to the rapid expansion of settlement by determinations on titles, conditions on land sales, and the creation of new counties—and ultimately new states—in the West was the underlying theme of Virginia's western policy. In any case, there would be no attempt to imitate British policy and retard or prohibit frontier development.

The Land Title Bill was designed to assure that there remained something to protect from either Congress or the separatists in Transylvania, Kentucky, or Franklin. George Mason, author of the bill, was faced with numerous colonial grants to land companies, unauthorized Indian purchases, and "thousands of entries for lands with surveyors of counties, which covered the whole Western country."[46] The title bill was stalled in the house until deliberations on the Henderson, Loyal, Illinois-Wabash, and Indiana claims were completed. The two former claims were recognized according to a formula of equitable compensation which acknowledged both state sovereignty and a real investment by the companies.[47] The Indiana and Illinois-

408

---

[43] For the land office bill see Hening, ed., *Statutes at Large*, X, 50-65. It may be compared with Jefferson's original draft in Boyd *et al.*, eds., *Jefferson Papers*, II, 139-142. The title bill is in Hening, ed., *Statutes at Large*, X, 35-50; Mason's original draft is in Boyd *et al.*, eds., *Jefferson Papers*, II, 155-160. As early as Oct. 1776 the Virginia assembly identified two of the chief sources of apprehension in the state over its distant claims. Resolutions of Oct. 28, 1778, *Journals of the House of Delegates* (Richmond, Va., 1827-1828), 31. These resolves, drawn up in response to the Transylvania separatists, warned Congress "against dismembering the state of that or any other part of its ancient territory, or forming any new government within its limits." The assembly also warned Virginians against "any attempt to form themselves into a distinct or independent government."

[44] Jefferson to Samuel Huntington, Feb. 9, 1780, Boyd *et al.*, eds., *Jefferson Papers*, III, 286-289.

[45] Edmund Randolph, *History of Virginia*, ed. Arthur H. Shaffer (Charlottesville, Va., 1970), 272-273.

[46] Jefferson's note, Boyd *et al.*, eds., *Jefferson Papers*, II, 138.

[47] On the Henderson claim see *Jour. of Delegates*, Oct. and Nov. sess., 1778, 36, 42, 79, 91, 100, 105, and Hening, ed., *Statutes at Large*, IX, 571-572. On the Loyal claim see *Jour. of Delegates*, Oct. 1778 sess., 53-54, 88. The claim was confirmed by decision of the Court of Appeals in 1783. Daniel Call, ed., *Reports of Cases Argued and Adjudged in the Court of Appeals of Virginia*, IV (Richmond, 1824), 21-37. The resolution of Nov. 4, 1778, voiding "all purchases of lands made or to be made of the Indians, within the chartered boundaries of this Commonwealth," constituted a rejection of all company claims, including Illinois-Wabash. *Jour. of Delegates*, 36.

Wabash companies were unwilling to compromise, however, and their claims were disallowed.[48]

By 1779 the main lines of Virginia's western policy had emerged. Subsuming all other issues was the demand that the state's charter claims be recognized. The state was willing to divide itself, but only at its own initiative and provided that its determination of private titles were recognized. The cession idea had already been recognized by this time as a possible device for securing these policy goals.[49] Charters, Edmund Pendleton wrote, "are the only Criterion by which the distinct Territorial Claim of each State, can be ascertained." Virginia set forth its boundaries in the 1776 constitution and, in joining the Confederation, had reserved her "distinct rights of Sovereignty and Soil." Here was the leading implication of the claims dispute for the Confederation: Virginia insisted on a "strict regard to the Separate rights of each State [as] the only means of preserving and Cementing the Union." The "dismembering of the State . . . could not be made without the Assent of it's legislature." If this territorial dispute could be resolved, Congress could have its national domain. Virginia would be all the more interested in supporting congressional power if its rights were secured. This was the true principle of "balance" in the United States: it did not matter, Pendleton wrote, "*whether Virginia be a little larger than Pennsylvania,* or ten times as large."[50] Questions of land title, boundaries and other state rights (many of which were much less well defined) were to be decided according to legal right, not according to some arbitrary formula for balancing state size and power.[51] No

409

[48] The final vote on the Indiana claim was 50 to 28 for rejection, according to Samuel Wharton, *Plain Facts: Being an Examination into the Rights of the Indian Nations of America, to their Respective Countries* . . . (Philadelphia, 1781), 145. Prominent Virginians who supported the claim included Patrick Henry, Edmund Randolph, James Mercer, and Edmund Pendleton. See Pendleton's "Opinion Relating to George Croghan's Title to Lands Purchased from the Six Nations," July 19, 1777, Mays, ed., *Pendleton Papers*, I, 216-217, and Randolph's comments at the ratifying convention in 1788, Jonathan Elliot, ed., *The Debates in the Several State Conventions on the Adoption of the Federal Constitution* . . . , III (Philadelphia, 1876 [orig. publ. 1863]), 574.

[49] Cessions were suggested by the Congressional Finance Committee, Sept. 19, 1778, *Jour. Cont. Cong.*, XII, 931. The idea of making Virginia policy objectives explicit cession conditions emerged only after Congress failed to agree that private property determinations of the states would be confirmed. James Madison to Joseph Jones, Sept. 11, 1780, Edmund C. Burnett, ed., *Letters of Members of the Continental Congress* (Washington, D.C., 1921-1936), V, 245. An attempt to circumvent cession conditions was made Sept. 6, 1782, in a motion by John Witherspoon of New Jersey to uphold state findings on private property. The motion was narrowly defeated on Sept. 25. *Jour. Cont. Cong.*, XXIII, 552-555, 604-605.

[50] Pendleton to Joseph Jones, Feb. 10, 1781, Mays, ed., *Pendleton Papers*, I, 328-338.

[51] Arbitration procedures for territorial disputes were set up in Article IX of the Articles of Confederation. James D. Richardson, *A Compilation of the Messages and*

American state need sacrifice its essential sovereign rights in the Union. State claims, if overlapping, could be resolved according to their merits by an impartial arbitration process. The central questions were whether the states could remain secure in their sovereignty, regardless of size or supposed power, and whether it was possible to erect a vigorous national authority on this basis.

The western boundary question became controversial because charter claims could not be dissociated from determinations on private property claims. The Indiana and Illinois-Wabash claims were built on pre-Revolutionary purchases or grants from the Indians. To Maryland and other small landless states, Virginia's disallowance of these claims—in which many of their leading citizens were interested—meant that Virginia intended to exploit the disputed land for its own benefit. Maryland objected that Virginia, "by selling on the most moderate terms a small proportion of the lands in question, would draw into her treasury vast sums of money, and . . . be enabled to lessen her taxes." This would lead to the "depopulation, and consequently the impoverishment," of neighboring states.[52]

With the companies' failure in the Virginia assembly, the focus of the western lands controversy shifted to Congress. The speculators had powerful friends among materially interested delegates and among representatives of the small landless states who feared Virginia's overwhelming size and independent land policy. Congress itself, which had been seeking a national domain since 1776, was a potential ally. But this shift in focus solidified opinion in Virginia on the related issues of territorial integrity. While a sizeable minority in the assembly could support the Indiana claim as long as there was no threat to state authority, the new land company-small state campaign in Congress challenged Virginia's jurisdiction, and therefore, many Virginians felt, the state's sovereignty.

From 1777 to 1784 the western lands question exacerbated relations among Virginia, Congress, and the landless states. At times it appeared that the issue would destroy the already fragile union. Congress struggled over how the Articles of Confederation would deal with western lands and whether or not it would assert its own claims, as specified in the Dickinson draft of 1777.[53] Virginia and the other landed states were able to dictate the

---

Papers of the Presidents, 1789-1902, I (Washington, D.C., 1905), 13-15. Only one case was fully adjudicated under this article: Connecticut v. Pennsylvania over the Wyoming Valley.

[52] Instructions to the Maryland delegation, laid before Congress May 21, 1779, *Jour. Cont. Cong.,* XIV, 619-622.

[53] For the Dickinson draft see *ibid.,* V, 546-551. Its provisions followed the outline proposed by Benjamin Franklin in his Confederation Plan of 1775, *ibid.,* II, 195-199. See also Jensen, *Articles of Confederation,* 126-139.

terms of the Articles, but they could not force other states to assent to them. Maryland withheld its approval until 1781, registering strong objections to the extensive Virginia claims which the Articles apparently secured.

In 1780 Congress adopted resolutions calling for cessions of state claims in the West. Such cessions were consistent with Virginia policy, under certain explicit conditions. Virginia's opponents argued, however, that its terms were unacceptable: the cession proposed by the Virginia assembly in 1781 stipulated that all private claims in the ceded area be invalidated, and that the state's remaining claims—south of the Ohio—be guaranteed.[54] The landless states, commanding congressional majorities for the next two years, succeeded in blocking the cession.[55] Meanwhile in Virginia, anticongressional sentiment reached a peak. Arthur Lee felt that Congress had "insulted" the state by refusing the cession.[56] Otherwise temperate politicians alluded darkly to the imminent collapse of the Union and asserted that Virginia should pursue its western policy independently of Congress. James Madison predicted that "the present union will but little survive the present war."[57]   411
Virginians believed that if the state's claims were not guaranteed—if the cession could not be made on terms determined by the assembly—there would be no protection against unlimited congressional encroachments on the state's sovereignty.

The congressional record in the claims controversy up to 1784 was a disaster. Successive attempts to assert congressional authority in the West were stalemated. The different claims arguments made on behalf of Congress against Virginia during this period have a certain theoretical interest. But these arguments—that Congress succeeded to crown jurisdiction and that western boundaries had been set by the Proclamation of 1763; or that the "common blood and treasure" of all the states had secured the West as

[54] The first cession was passed on Jan. 2, 1781, *Jour. of Delegates*, 80-81; the second cession during the Oct. 1783 session, *ibid.*, 148. The principal conditions were approved by a congressional committee on Sept. 13, 1783, *Jour. Cont. Cong.*, XXV, 554-564; and the act was finally accepted by Congress on Mar. 1, 1784, *ibid.*, XXVI, 113-116.

[55] The landless bloc combined to urge acceptance of the New York cession of 1781 of its northwestern claims, as recommended in a committee report of Nov. 3, 1781, Papers of the Continental Congress, Item 30, foll. 1-13, National Archives. The New York cession was finally accepted on Oct. 29, 1782, but the landless victory was an empty one; Virginia continued to insist on the validity of its claims. *Jour. Cont. Cong.*, XXIII, 694.

[56] Lee's comments referred to the congressional committee report of Nov. 3, 1781, which recommended against accepting the cession. "Concise View," Hoffman, ed., *Lee Family Papers*, Reel 7, 601-602.

[57] Madison to Edmund Pendleton, Oct. 30, 1781, Burnett, ed., *Letters of Members*, VI, 252. See also Virginia delegates to Gov. Thomas Nelson, Oct. 23, 1781, *ibid.*, 246-247.

national territory; or that a cession by New York, based on its presumed jurisdiction over the Iroquois, had given Congress a valid title[58]—only stiffened Virginia's resolve. They made support of the state's charter claims a test of state sovereignty. After the land companies hired Thomas Paine to attack Virginia's title in his pamphlet *Public Good* (1780), Virginians rose in defense. Edmund Pendleton and Arthur Lee both drafted replies to Paine.[59] In May 1782, the House of Delegates named Edmund Randolph to head a title defense committee including Lee, Mason, Jefferson, and Thomas Walker. After a series of delays, Randolph readied the committee's report for the printers in 1783. The successful completion of the cession made publication unnecessary.[60]

Forebodings of doom and disaster on the territorial question—whether from Congress, Maryland, or Virginia—may appear to have been exaggerated rhetorical posturings. But we have recently come to understand more clearly the ideological orientation of the Revolutionary generation and the continuing impact of that orientation on early American politics. It no longer required a "long train of abuses" to arouse patriotic Americans. Behind even the most innocuous policies Americans were able to discover insidious designs against their liberties. Thus Marylanders were convinced that Virginians, with their vast open lands, resources, and population, were determined to impoverish their state and reduce it to satellite status. At the same time, congressional delegates could see Virginia plotting the destruction of the Union; and Virginians could see Congress aiming at nothing less than the destruction of state claims, state sovereignty, and even the state itself.

412

The cessions idea, first discussed in Congress in 1778 and formally proposed in the congressional resolutions of 1780, provided a means to resolve the controversy. The Virginia claims would be vindicated by the cession, and the state's remaining claims would be secured. But it was on the question of

---

[58] All these arguments are outlined in Edmund Randolph's brief on territorial claims submitted to Congress on Aug. 20, 1782, as suggested guidelines for American peace negotiators at Paris. The report generated intense debate because of its bearing on the states' western claims controversy. *Jour. Cont. Cong.*, XXIII, 473-476, 487-522. For a congressional title based on the provisional peace articles see Madison's notes on debates of Ar. 9, 18, 1783, Rutland, ed., *Madison Papers*, VI, 442-443, 471.

[59] They remained unpublished. Pendleton to Joseph Jones, Feb. 10, 1781, Mays, ed., *Pendleton Papers*, I, 328-338; "Concise View," Hoffman, ed., *Lee Family Papers*, Reel 7, 601-602.

[60] For a discussion of the history of the committee see Boyd et al., eds., *Jefferson Papers*, VI, 653. On the delays see Randolph to Madison, June 1, July 15, and Aug. 13, 1782, Rutland, ed., *Madison Papers*, IV, 305, 395-396, V, 50; and Randolph to Arthur Lee, July 18, 1782, and Mar. 21, 1783, Hoffman, ed., *Lee Family Papers*, Reel 7, 247, 260, 370. Randolph wrote to Jefferson, then in Paris, that he would forward a copy of the committee report (May 14, 1784). Boyd et al., eds., *Jefferson Papers*, VII, 259-260. The manuscript has not survived.

conditions that opposing interests in Congress were deadlocked. Small-state representatives early recognized that the terms on which Congress received state claims would have a profound impact on the development of the West, as well as on the continued prosperity and security of the eastern states. And one condition in the Virginia cession offer was especially obnoxious to the landless bloc: the condition invalidating company claims in the Northwest. Not only was this condition contrary to the interests of the many company shareholders in these states, but it was viewed as a challenge to private property and contract rights. It would deprive the landless states of a chance to participate in the development of the West. The balance of power in the Confederation would be destroyed. New states would be drawn into the orbit of their neighboring, large, powerful ceding states.

Yet Virginians believed that invalidation of company claims was vital to the future of the American republics. Denial of these claims would prevent the diversion of the revenue from land sales into private pockets and foreclose the possible development of a landed aristocracy and special privilege in the West. Indeed, the fears of the landless states were unfounded. The Northwest was a magnet for a truly national emigration; the new western territories and states proved to be all too independent.

413

Resolution of the claims deadlock resulted from the failure of Congress to make good an alternative title claim and establish control over a national domain. Various policy considerations, including migration to the West, the threat of Indian trouble, and the need to implement congressional policy after the peace settlement of 1783, made an end to the dispute imperative.[61] In the ultimate resolution, intended as a compromise, Congress accepted Virginia's disallowance of land company claims, and Virginia retreated from earlier demands that its remaining claims be recognized. But all other cession conditions, including provisions for new states and use of national lands for the common benefit of the states, were confirmed. On these terms, set forth in a congressional committee report in September 1783, the second cession offer was sent to Congress in 1784 and confirmed by a narrow vote on March 1.[62]

An important, and little recognized, effect of this cession was that it began the practical work of implementing Virginia's goal of territorial integrity, by securing the state's permanent boundaries. In keeping with its cessions policy, Congress did not specifically validate Virginia's Kentucky

[61] Peter Stevens Onuf, "Sovereignty and Territory: Claims Conflict in the Old Northwest and the Origins of the American Federal Republic" (Ph.D. diss., The Johns Hopkins University, 1973), 355-368.

[62] Report of June 6, 1783, agreed to Sept. 13, and cession accepted Mar. 1, 1784, *Jour. Cont. Cong.*, XXV, 559-564, XXVI, 111-121. Cession offer adopted by Virginia house and senate Dec. 18, 20. 1783. *Jour. of Delegates,* Oct. 1783 sess., 97, 115, 119, 123, 129, 130, 131, 148.

claims. The congressional committee indicated that the Articles of Confederation guaranteed the region to Virginia, *if* its claims were valid.[63] But the burden of proof was on counter-claimants, and Congress was not sympathetic to separatists. Congressional failure—or prudence—in not challenging the Kentucky claims was interpreted as a tacit recognition of Virginia title. The Kentucky question remained unresolved, however, until the ultimate goal of creating a new state there was achieved through the precarious tripartite negotiations—involving the state, the Kentucky district, and Congress—which were completed in 1792. Virginia had no intention of maintaining its jurisdiction in the district, but extensive settlement and land grants under Virginia authority made it was necessary for the legislature to set specific guidelines for separation. Though some of these conditions evoked negative response in Kentucky, the chief obstacles to statehood were the violent factional politics of the district and the hesitation of the dying Confederation Congress to authorize admission of Kentucky to the Union.

414

The future of the republic seemed doubtful in the early 1780s. Attendance at Congress fell off alarmingly. The impost of 1781 and finance plan of 1783 failed to gain the unanimous vote required for amendments to the Articles. Congressional requisitions were rarely met. Several states began to take over the continental debt held by their citizens. And, just as political and financial power shifted from Congress to the states, localism and separatism challenged state authority. Inveterately suspicious of partisan, interested activity—and of each other—many Americans harbored misgivings about the future of their republics. Cosmopolitans may have shared a dream of continental greatness, but their opponents saw only a continental self-interest. And localists' attention to their own, more narrowly defined interests earned an equal measure of suspicion in return.

The Virginia cession exemplifies the kind of transactions, submerged from view by their very success, that secured the foundations of American federalism and helped Americans—with continental or local perspectives, interested or disinterested patriotism—discover a common ground. The possibility of a successful adjustment of state and federal powers and rights set the limits and goals for the dialogue between localists and nationalists and gave meaning to their all-too-justified mutual suspicions.

The political history of the western land claims does not fit into the usual categories of Confederation history. It has been considered important for the subsequent development of the territories. Against a monotonous backdrop of failure, the creation of a national domain has been seen as a triumph of congressional politics. Yet the cession of 1784 was most significantly a vindication of Virginia's long-standing western policy. Further, the cession

[63] Report of June 6, 1783. *Jour. Cont. Cong.*, XXV, 559-563.

was vitally important in facilitating the coexistence of the states with one another and with the federal government. Only with such previous success could the more familiar debate over the limits of national power begin. And only then did the distinction between localists and cosmopolitans become relevant.

Virginia's western policy was not necessarily opposed to the interests of the United States government. The principles delineated in the cession facilitated the establishment of new states and their admission to the Union. The Virginia claims were validated through the cession. Congress was able to quiet all outstanding claims in the West through successive cessions, and so establish its national domain. Most important, Virginia was secured in permanent boundaries, and the uncertainty and danger to the Confederation of conflicting claims were at last overcome. In this significant area—the jurisdictional question in its largest sense, encompassing both the feasibility of maintaining inherited colony bounds, defining the jurisdictions of old and new states, and specifying the nature of that jurisdiction in terms of land policy in the ceded territory and within new state boundaries—the cessions transaction eliminated a major source of friction among the American states and an impediment to the institution of a stronger central government.

415

THE
WILLIAM AND MARY
QUARTERLY
A MAGAZINE OF EARLY AMERICAN HISTORY, INSTITUTIONS, AND CULTURE

| THIRD SERIES | *January, 1946* | Vol. III No. 1 |

THE BASES OF AMERICAN FEDERALISM

By JOHN C. RANNEY*

Ever since the founding of the American union, it has been something of a national custom to inquire why other nations—or for that matter the entire world—do not unite in the same way. Benjamin Franklin was asking as early as 1787 whether the time had not come for Europe to form "a Federal Union and One Grand Republick of all its different States and Kingdoms; . . . for we had many Interests to reconcile."[1] And the present generation of his countrymen abounds in enthusiasts who maintain that, if anything, conditions today are more favorable for an international federal union than they were for the union of the American colonies in 1787.[2]

There is, of course, the greatest variety among their plans. Some envisage a world union; some, a union of the democracies or the United Nations; and some, a union of particular areas such as Western or Central Europe. But for the most part they share in common a tendency to make certain explicit or implicit assumptions:

(1) That the American experience provides an impressive precedent for the reconciling of differences in culture, religion,

416

---

*The author, Assistant Professor of Government at Smith College, received his doctorate from Harvard in 1942 (October) and continued to teach there and at Radcliffe for several months before going to Smith in 1943.

[1] Benjamin Franklin to Mr. Grand, Philadelphia, October 22, 1787 in Max Farrand, ed., *The Records of the Federal Convention of 1787* (Revised edition, New Haven, 1937), III, 131.

[2] The most famous of these plans, Clarence Streit's *Union Now* (New York and London, 1939) frankly draws its inspiration from the American experience. For other plans, see P. E. Corbett, *Post-War Worlds* (New York, 1942); Edith Wynner and Georgia Lloyd, *Searchlight on Peace Plans* (New York, 1944), 83-180.

way of life, and political outlook within a common governmental
framework;

(2)   That the formation of the American union, achieved as
it was through peaceful deliberation and voting, indicates that union
is primarily a matter of reason and that it will be adopted once
its logic and necessity are made apparent;

(3)   That the importance of considerations of defense in
promoting American union makes it probable that the intense
present-day longing for "freedom from fear" will provide a strong
and enduring basis for union;

(4)   That the same economic forces which contributed so
prominently to American union are present in the world in intensified form: for international economic interdependence is greater
than was ever the case with the American colonies, and transportation and communication have made the world a smaller place than
was the America of 1787; and

(5)   That national patriotism as an obstacle to union is less
important today, when no country is safe from aggression and
when most countries cannot even maintain their independence
without foreign aid, than was state patriotism in colonial America.

In the light of the importance of these assumptions, it is remarkable that so little systematic effort has been made to test their
validity; and this omission is all the more striking because of the
very abundance of the evidence.   For Americans have never been
noted for reticence in political matters, and the years from 1787 to
1789 were no exception.   "Docti indoctique scribimus," the appre-
hensive Jay wrote Jefferson; and learned and unlearned alike sat
"in Council and in Judgment, both within and without Doors."[3]   If
ever, therefore, the circumstances leading to the formation of a
federal union were exhaustively expounded, the occasion was the
acceptance of the American Constitution.

What were these circumstances, and to what extent do they
bear out the assumptions of the international federal unionists?

I

The first thing which strikes one, in considering this evidence,
is that the American union was based on a remarkably high degree
of cultural, social, and political community.

Most of the colonists, it is true, were not themselves aware of
this fact.   Separated as they were by vast distances and abomi-
nable roads, unaccustomed to travel in other states or to communicate with their inhabitants, living in isolated communities

417

---

[3] New York, September 8, 1787 in *Documentary History of the Constitution of the United States of America, 1786-1870* (Washington, 1894-1905).
IV, 276.

which of necessity approximated to self-sufficiency, they had little
interest in and little knowledge of their neighbors. When the first
Continental Congress assembled in Philadelphia in 1774, many
of the delegates spent the opening days in acquiring the most elementary information about the attitudes, political divisions, and
forms of government of the other colonies.[4] As late as 1786,
Madison could write to Jefferson "Of the affairs of Georgia I
know as little as of those of Kamskatska."[5]

Moreover, what knowledge the colonists had of one another
was likely to emphasize what was different and distinguishing—
the variations in climate and crops, the divergences in nationality,
religion, and social structure, and the presence or absence of institutions like slavery and primogeniture. Prerevolutionary trav-
elers like Burnaby confidently reported that "fire and water are not
more heterogeneous than the different colonies in North America.
Nothing can exceed the jealousy and emulation which they possess
in regard to each other."[6] And even after the Revolution, the
French chargé d'affaires could cite the opinion of a powerful
group that

418

> In the present state of affairs, it is impossible to unite under
> a single head all the members of the Confederation. Their
> political interests, their commercial views, their customs and
> their laws are so varied that there is not a resolution of Con-
> gress which can be equally useful and popular in the South
> and in the North of the Continent. . . . [7]

Yet such differences were obvious rather than profound.

In nationality, although America already showed signs of its
heterogeneous destiny as the world's melting pot, the non-British
elements were in the minority in each colony; and the governing
class in particular, save for the readily assimilable French Hugue-
nots and Dutch, was almost purely English and maintained the

---

[4] Charles Francis Adams, ed., *The Works of John Adams* (Boston,
1850-1856), II, 357-402, 421-431. See also Evarts Boutell Greene, *The
Revolutionary Generation, 1763-1790* (New York, 1943), 185-186, 431-432;
Merrill Jensen, *The Articles of Confederation* (Madison, 1940), 56, 117-118,
163-164; Allan Nevins, *The American States during and after the Revolution, 1775-1789* (New York, 1924), 544-552; Claude H. Van Tyne, *The
Causes of the War of Independence* (Boston and New York, 1922), 75.

[5] Philadelphia, August 12, 1786 in Gaillard Hunt, ed., *The Writings of
James Madison* (New York, 1900-1910), II, 261.

[6] Andrew Burnaby, *Travels through the Middle Settlements in North
America, in the Years 1759 and 1760; with Observations upon the State of
the Colonies* (3rd edition, London, 1798—reprinted New York, 1904), 152-153.

[7] Mr. Otto to the Comte de Montmorin, New York, June 10, 1787, in
Farrand, *Records*, III, 42.

predominance of the English language, English customs, and English political traditions.[8]

In religion diversity was somewhat more apparent; and feeling among the different denominations was often bitter, with Quakers, Baptists, Anglicans, and Catholics being especially resentful of the treatment of their coreligionists in certain colonies.[9] Each colony, however, was stanchly Protestant and, especially after the passage of the Quebec Act of 1774, shared a fear of Catholic neighbors in Canada and the Spanish colonies which was stronger than any dislike of other Protestants.[10] Most denominations, moreover, were intercolonial in their constituency; and in many churches a strong movement for ecclesiastical unity, regardless of state lines, developed concomitantly with the movement for national political unity.[11]

As for way of life, the great majority of the people in each of the colonies was engaged in some extractive occupation, more especially farming. Few of them had attained great wealth, and few suffered from dire poverty. Long before Tocqueville had discovered the "prodigious influence" of "the general equality of conditions" on the whole course of American society, his compatriot Crèvecoeur was pointing out that

419

> The rich and the poor are not so far removed from each other as they are in Europe. Some few towns excepted, we are all tillers of the earth, from Nova Scotia to West Florida. . . . If [an enlightened Englishman] travels through our rural districts he views not the hostile castle, and the haughty

---

[8] Although the Germans accounted for one-third of the population of Pennsylvania, they comprised only ten per cent of the population of the colonies as a whole. The Scotch-Irish, the only other powerful minority, shared a common language with the English majority. Merle Curti, *The Growth of American Thought* (New York and London, 1943), 4-12; Greene, *Revolutionary Generation*, 70-72; Curtis P. Nettels, *The Roots of American Civilization* (New York, 1938), 392-393.

[9] The protest of the Quakers and Baptists to the Massachusetts delegates to the Continental Congress is described in Adams, *Works*, II, 397-400.

[10] Even Maryland, founded as a Catholic haven, had a Protestant majority. For anti-Catholic feeling, see Philip Davidson, *Propaganda and the American Revolution, 1763-1783* (Chapel Hill, 1941), 122, 125-128; Van Tyne, *Causes*, 403-405.

[11] This was particularly true of Presbyterians, Methodists, Baptists, Episcopalians, and Quakers. George Bancroft, *History of the Formation of the Constitution of the United States of America* (New York, 1882) I, 210; Curti, *Growth*, 12-13, 58; Greene, *Revolutionary Generation*, 99-116, 180-181, 195-196; Edward F. Humphrey, *Nationalism and Religion in America, 1774-1789* (Boston, 1924), 167-356, 440-486; J. Franklin Jameson, *The American Revolution Considered as a Social Movement* (Princeton, 1940), 95-98; Michael Kraus, *Intercolonial Aspects of American Culture on the Eve of the Revolution* (New York, 1928), 64-90.

mansion, contrasted with the clay-built hut and miserable cabbin, where cattle and men help to keep each other warm, and dwell in meanness, smoke, and indigence. A pleasing uniformity of decent competence appears throughout our habitations. The meanest of our log-houses is a dry and comfortable habitation. Lawyer or merchant are the fairest titles our towns afford; that of a farmer is the only appellation of the rural inhabitants of our country. . . . We have no princes, for whom we toil, starve, and bleed; we are the most perfect society now existing in the world.[12]

Differences in climate and geography were, of course, reflected in variations in the type of farming; and opponents of union liked to emphasize that class distinctions were greater in the South than in New England and that the prevalence of slavery in the southern states indicated a fundamental moral and political divergence.[13] But whatever the differences in their crops and methods, the great majority of the farmers in all states, and the majority of the slaveholders as well, belonged to the middle class and shared its way of living and thinking. Charles Pinckney could tell the Federal Convention that

> The people of the U. States are perhaps the most singular of any we are acquainted with. Among them there are fewer distinctions of fortune & less of rank, than among the inhabitants of any other nation. Every freeman has a right to the same protection & security; and a very moderate share of property entitles them to the possession of all the honors and privileges the public can bestow: hence arises a greater equality, than is to be found among the people of any other country. . . . [14]

This equality was intensified by the departure of the Tories and the confiscation of their estates; while to the extent that a new

---

[12] J. Hector St. John Crévecoeur, *Letters from an American Farmer* (London, 1782—reprinted New York, 1908), 49-50. See Charles M. Andrews, *The Colonial Background of the American Revolution* (New Haven, 1924), 195; Jameson, *American Revolution*, 28-30; Alexis de Tocqueville, *Democracy in America* (New York, 1838), xi and *passim;* Van Tyne, *Causes*, 313, 318-319.

[13] See the speech attributed to Luther Martin in the Federal Convention, June 19, 1787, Farrand, *Records*, IV, 24-25. See also, below, p. 22.

[14] Farrand, *Records*, I, 398. See also Pinckney's speech in Jonathan Elliot, ed., *The Debates in the Several State Conventions on the Adoption of the Federal Constitution* (2nd edition, Philadelphia, 1896), IV, 232: Richard Henry Lee, "Letters from the Federal Farmer," in Paul Leicester Ford, ed., *Pamphlets on the Constitution of the United States* (Brooklyn, 1888), 321; Greene, *Revolutionary Generation*, 17; Arthur N. Holcombe, *The Middle Classes in American Politics* (Cambridge, 1940), 4-6, 136-137, 153-155.

commercial, manufacturing, and speculating class appeared, it constituted a relatively small part of the population.[15]   It was particularly significant, moreover, that those class and economic distinctions which did exist—whether between the farming majority and the commercial minority or between seaboard and frontier —tended to cut across rather than to coincide with state lines and thus to build up a common outlook among men of similar interest in different states.[16]

It was in political outlook, however, that intercolonial harmony was most conspicuous. Once the Revolution had done away with the differences among proprietary, royal, and charter colonies, the same type of government prevailed in each, with the result that, among the colonies as a whole, written constitutions, the separation of powers, representative government, trial by jury, and legislative bicameralism were characteristic and almost inevitable.[17] The principles of the common law of England won increasingly general acceptance;[18] and the widespread movement toward social and economic reform which accompanied the Revolution lessened many of the outstanding institutional differences, easing the acquisition of property and the vote, disestablishing the church outside of New England, and eliminating primogeniture and entail almost entirely.[19]

In political ideas, the uniformity was even more striking. The British political and legal tradition gave a common background to colonial thought, and leaders throughout the colonies were deeply influenced by their reading in Locke and Montesquieu, Blackstone and Coke. Moreover, the propaganda of the Revolution had spread a common gospel of liberty among the people as a whole with such success that by 1787 these ideas had acquired an

421

[15] Thomas C. Cochran, New York in the Confederation (Philadelphia, 1932), 64; Greene, Revolutionary Generation, 336; Jameson, American Revolution, 32-35; Nevins, American States, 444.

[16] For the growth of commerce and manufacturing as an interstate interest, see Greene, Revolutionary Generation, 35-66; Kraus, Intercolonial Aspects, 17-41; Nettels, Roots, 669-670; Nevins, American States, 572-574.

[17] Only Pennsylvania departed significantly from the general pattern, and this difference in institutions was used as an argument against ratification in that State. John Bach McMaster and Frederick D. Stone, eds., Pennsylvania and the Federal Constitution, 1787-1788 (Philadelphia, 1888), 21, 457-459, 626. For the general similarity of institutions, see Andrews, Colonial Background, 35, 37; Greene, Revolutionary Generation, 180; Andrew C. McLaughlin, The Confederation and the Constitution, 1783-1789 (New York and London, 1905), 46; Robert Livingston Schuyler, The Constitution of the United States (New York, 1923), 18-20.

[18] Kraus, Intercolonial Aspects, 208-212; Richard B. Morris, Studies in the History of American Law (New York, 1930), 9-68.

[19] See the testimony of Charles Pinckney, Farrand, Records, I, 400. See also Jameson, American Revolution, 27-40; Nevins, American States, 430-445, 602.

almost unchallengeable sanctity. In each of the state conventions praises of inalienable rights and denunciations of unchecked power recurred with a monotonous inevitability.[20] When there were differences in attitude between radicals and conservatives, as in assessing the relative merits of liberty and order, the difference was one which overrode state and sectional lines. Only in the case of slavery and the slave trade was there a conflict of principle which divided the states into opposing groups, and even here the line was by no means clearly drawn. Some Northerners profited from the slave trade, while many Southern leaders were strongly opposed to slavery. In fact, the intellectual defense of slavery had still to be developed, and the conflict at this time was one of economic interest rather than of political theory.[21]

The degree of intercolonial community, in short, was much greater than that existing even among the world's democracies today. It may be that people now know more of what is happening in other lands and travel to them with greater ease and speed. But once they are there, they find differences in language and level of civilization, in national consciousness and political outlook which exceed anything to be found in the American colonies. These are fundamental differences, and they are exceedingly difficult for human beings to remove or reconcile or control. Any effective co-operation requires understanding and an ability to work together, and these qualities in their turn are dependent to a large extent on a common type and level of civilization and perhaps even more (since union is a political arrangement) upon a common political outlook. Pennsylvania's political differences from the other colonies contributed to her reluctance to accept the Constitution. Yet the difference between her government and those of her neighbors was slight in comparison with the differences between constitutional republics and constitutional monarchies or between parliamentary and congressional democracies.[22] These differences become all the more basic if one attempts to extend the union to authoritarian countries. For both experience and logic indicate that when the political difference is a fundamental one, it is impossible for either party to agree to a strong union embodying those principles to which it is opposed at home without discrediting

422

---

[20] The reading of the debates in these conventions provides an impressive demonstration of the general acceptance of the same ideas and symbols. Elliot, *Debates, passim.*

[21] In the North, only New Hampshire and Massachusetts were free states, while Connecticut, Rhode Island, and Pennsylvania had taken steps for gradual emancipation. Some Northern delegates to the Federal Convention condoned the slave trade while delegates from the upper South were eager to abolish it.

[22] See footnote 17 above.

the whole system of institutions and ideas on which its government is based.   It would be ridiculous, for example, to suppose
that the Union of Socialist Soviet Republics or Spain could permit
free and competitive elections for delegates to an international
legislature while forbidding such elections for a national assembly.

In this sense, Clarence Streit has been wiser than many others
in limiting his hopes for the immediate future to a union of those
countries which are already democratic and in particular to those
which are Anglo-Saxon.   But even this limited union would require
the reconciliation of political differences greater than any which
separated the American colonies.

II

The second factor which stands out is the unusually large
amount of experience, frequently of a federal pattern, which the
colonies had had in co-operating with one another.

For one thing, federal ideas were a natural outgrowth of the
relationship of the colonies within the British empire.   The division
of functions between imperial and local bodies, which developed as
a matter of convenience, came to be regarded as a matter of right
as well and suggested the later division between state and federal
authorities.[23]   Similarly, the power of the imperial government,
acting through the royal governors and the Privy Council, to disallow colonial legislation accustomed men to the idea of interests
which were shared in common and which had an importance
superior to local interests.[24]

The colonists, of course, often differed among themselves as
to the precise boundaries of the respective interests and authorities,
and logic frequently yielded to strategy in an attempt to meet the
changing requirements of political warfare.   But even this had
its advantages.   Hundreds of people who would never have interested themselves in theories which served no practical purpose

423

[23] Randolph G. Adams, *Political Ideas of the American Revolution* (Dur-
ham, 1922), 69; Andrew C. McLaughlin, "The Background of American
Federalism," *American Political Science Review*, XII, 217, 224-227, 238
(May, 1918) and *A Constitutional History of the United States* (New York,
1936), 70-71; Nettels, *Roots*, 276, 546-548.
[24] This executive veto has sometimes, and inaccurately, been regarded
as a form of judicial review.   Charles M. Andrews, "The Royal Disallowance," American Antiquarian Society, *Proceedings*, new series, XXIV (October, 1914), 342-362; Oliver M. Dickerson, *American Colonial Government,
1696-1765* (Cleveland, 1912), 228-234; Elmer B. Russell, *The Review of
American Colonial Legislation by the King in Council* (New York, 1915),
221, 227; Arthur M. Schlesinger, "Colonial Appeals to the Privy Council,"
Political Science Quarterly, XXVIII (June and September, 1913), 279-297,
433-450; Benjamin F. Wright, *The Growth of American Constitutional Law*
(Boston, 1942), 13.

acquired proficiency in arguments which assumed the existence of
two sets of governmental institutions, each limited to a definite
and inviolable sphere of activity. With this foundation, the concept
of federalism was one which could be accepted easily and naturally.[25] In fact, it was the most natural thing in the world for the
delegates to the Continental Congress, once the question of independence arose, to feel the need for some new organization to fill
the vacuum left by the breaking of the British connection.

Even more significant was the development of spontaneous
intercolonial co-operation. In addition to the New England Confederation (whose success was something less than spectacular but
whose memory continued to exert an important influence), there
was a long succession of intercolonial conferences, generally concerned with problems of defense; and a good deal of colonial
intellectual activity from 1690 on was accounted for by projects
of confederation of one sort or another, although this speculation
was limited to a comparatively few statesmen and intellectuals.
Popular interest in union did not arise until the quarrel with
Britain; and the organization of Sons of Liberty throughout the
colonies and the holding of the Stamp Act Congress in 1765
marked the first general awareness of common interests and the
first popular willingness to take joint action to promote them.[27]
The Committees of Correspondence also promoted the spread of
common ideas and the taking of united action, and their activities
were largely responsible for the apparent spontaneity of the movement for a Continental Congress in twelve of the thirteen colonies.[28]

For a time, the political maneuvering incidental to the struggle
between radicals and conservatives in the Congress prevented the
acceptance of any definite plan of union; and even after the
outbreak of hostilities and the adoption of the Declaration of Independence, the Articles of Confederation were accepted slowly
and reluctantly and only after the powers granted Congress had
been drastically curtailed.[29] Yet it would be hard to exaggerate

---

[25] R. G. Adams, *Political Ideas*, 27-28, 69, 101-108; Davidson, *Propaganda*, 110.

[26] Richard Frothingham, *The Rise of the Republic of the United States*
(Boston, 1890), 33-66, 109-122, 132-150; Mrs. Lois K. Mathews, "Benjamin
Franklin's Plan for a Colonial Union, 1750-1775," *American Political Science
Review*, VIII (Aug., 1914), 396, 405-406.

[27] John C. Miller, *Sam Adams, Pioneer in Propaganda* (Boston, 1936),
50-80; Arthur M. Schlesinger, *The Colonial Merchants and the American
Revolution, 1763-1776* (New York, 1918), 62-75; Van Tyne, *Causes*, 182.

[28] Edward D. Collin, "Committees of Correspondence of the American
Revolution," *Annual Report of the American Historical Association for the
Year 1901*, I, 245-271; Miller, *Sam Adams*, 262-271; Schlesinger, *Colonial
Merchants*, 393.

[29] Edmund Cody Burnett, *The Continental Congress* (New York, 1941),
33-59; 90-92; Jensen, *Articles*, 68-72, 91-92, 110-111, 124-163.

the importance of the Articles in the development of American federalism.

In the first place, men live largely by symbols; and the Confederation was a symbol of unity, making ordinary people aware of interests and activities shared in common with the other colonies.

In the second place, the Articles prepared people's minds for the strengthening of the common institutions. To a large extent, the powers of Congress under the new Constitution were a continuation or amplification of powers which already existed under the Confederation. Madison was able to argue that "The truth is, that the great principles of the Constitution proposed by the convention may be considered less as absolutely new, than as the expansion of principles which are found in the articles of Confederation."[30] and that "If the new Constitution be examined with accuracy and candour, it will be found that the change which it proposes consists much less in the addition of New Powers to the Union, than in the invigoration of its Original Powers."[31] This meant that Americans, in considering the new Constitution, did not need to adjust themselves to a series of shocking and sudden innovations. Instead, they were asked to render more effective the powers of a central government which already existed and to expand and invigorate principles to which men were already accustomed. To those who know the conservatism of the human spirit, the advantages of this situation are obvious.

425

A third service of the Articles of Confederation was the provision of invaluable experience in the technique of operating joint institutions of government, with the result that the plans for the new government were not drawn up by a group of amateurs but by men who had had the most direct and personal experience with the institutions and problems of federal government.

And fourthly, the Congress under the Confederation brought together the most influential statesmen of the individual colonies, made them acquainted with one another, and gave them an understanding of national interests and, in many cases, a national loyalty.

The importance of this last function can scarcely be overestimated. When the delegates first assembled at Philadelphia in 1774, many of them still thought of their states as their "countries" and of themselves as "ambassadors."[32] Most of them had never seen one another before, and many of them had never even heard of one another.[33] But in the course of the years, Congress-

---

[30] *The Federalist*, XL.
[31] *Ibid.*, XLV.
[32] Jensen, *Articles*, 56.
[33] Burnett, *Continental Congress*, 27-28, 58; Curti, *Growth*, 143; Greene, *Revolutionary Generation*, 282, 300-301; Nevins, *American States*, 554-555.

men and other officials, by the very nature of their associations and work, were under tremendous pressure to think in national terms and to moderate their provincial outlook. Because of this, Charles Pinckney could tell the Federal Convention: "There is an *esprit de corps* which has made heretofore every *unfederal* member of congress, after his election, become strictly *federal,* and this I presume will ever be the case in whatever manner they may be elected."[34] Not every Congressman yielded to this pressure, and many who were vigorous advocates of a closer union were moved by other considerations. But it was more than coincidental that of the fifty-five men who went to Philadelphia to frame the Constitution thirty-nine had seen service in Congress and that all ten of those who were most active in determining its form came from this group.[34a]

426

Any comparison between this experience and the co-operative experience of modern nations is necessarily complex. On the one hand, even the United Nations have had no uniform political experience comparable to the colonial unity within the British empire. On the other hand, there have been many more plans for international co-operation and many more international conferences. Particularly in the economic and social fields, there has been a great natural growth of functional organizations like the Universal Postal Union and the International Labor Organization.[35] In fact, in absolute terms it could be maintained that there is more international government and administration today, especially as an outgrowth of the war, than was ever the case in the American colonies.[36] Yet the extent of this activity has received little popular attention and has made little popular impression.

Neither the League of Nations nor the United Nations have yet provided so effective a symbol of unity as the Articles of Confederation. Too many of the great powers abstained from membership in the League, which in any case was never entrusted with work of such consequence as the Confederation Congress's direc-

---

[34] Farrand, *Records,* I, 365.

[34a] Charles Warren, *The Making of the Constitution* (Boston, 1937), 55-57. The ten men whom Warren lists are Madison, Randolph, Franklin, Wilson, Gouverneur Morris, King, Rutledge, Charles Pinckney, Ellsworth, and Sherman.

[35] Frederick L. Schuman, *International Politics* (3rd edition, New York and London, 1941), 198-229.

[36] Henri Bonnet, *The United Nations—What They Are—What They May Become* (Chicago, 1942) ; Paul Reynaud, "Program for Peace," *Atlantic Monthly,* CLXV (April, 1940), 445-448; Payson S. Wild, Jr., "Machinery of Collaboration between the United Nations," *Foreign Policy Reports,* XVIII (July 1, 1942), 94-108.

tion of the colonial war effort. And the United Nations, although having many instruments of co-operation, are only now creating a continuing symbol of unity by establishing a permanent assembly and council.

Nevertheless both the League and the United Nations have performed a service similar to that of the Confederation in providing institutions capable of continuation and expansion as part of a more intimate union.[37] In addition, the men who have had to carry on these joint activities have gained experience in the techniques of co-operation and perhaps in an even more important sense have come to know one another much as did the delegates to the Continental Congress. The ease and frequency with which the topmost officials have met at Moscow, Washington, Quebec, Cairo, Casablanca, Teheran, Yalta, and Berlin provides a vivid illustration of what in a more humble way has been going on constantly among lesser officials who have kept in touch by telephone and conference with their "opposite numbers" in other governments. Churchill's comments concerning the Combined Chiefs of Staff could be applied to many other joint commissions and indicate one of the most striking parallels with colonial experience:

> This committee with its elaborate organization of staff officers of every grade disposes of all our resources, and in fact it uses British and American troops, ships, aircraft, ammunition just as if they were the resources of a single state or nation. . . . All these men now know each other. They trust each other. They like each other and most of them have been at work together for a long time. . . . Now, in my opinion, it would be a most foolish and improvident act on the part of our two Governments, or either of them, to break up this smooth-running and immensely powerful machinery the moment the war is over.[38]

III

The Confederation made another and unintentional contribution to the movement for a "more perfect union" simply through the breakdown of its governmental machinery.

The story of the defects of the Articles of Confederation is a familiar one: the desperate position of governmental credit, the inability of the Congress to maintain order or even to protect itself, its weakness in the face of foreign commercial discrimination and treaty violation, its failure to maintain the quorum neces-

[37] Henri Bonnet, *Outlines of the Future* (Chicago, 1943), and Wild, "Machinery."
[38] *New York Times,* September 7, 1943, 14.

sary to do business, the cumbersomeness of its machinery of government, and, most fundamental, its dependence on the individual states for the carrying out of its decisions and its inability to make the states live up to their obligations.[39]

So far as the people as a whole were concerned, however, these deficiencies aroused little interest. Living in an extractive economy, with little need for or contact with the national government and with adequate if not opulent standards of living, they were likely to think of the Confederation, when they thought of it at all, as performing its functions fairly well.[40]

But among the statesmen who had to work the machinery of government, and among the propertied classes which suffered most from its inadequacy, the defects were obvious and the demand for reform insistent. James Wilson complained that "Congress may recommend; they can do no more: they may require; but they must not proceed one step further. . . . Can we perform a single national act? Can we do any thing to procure us dignity, or to preserve peace and tranquillity? . . . The ,powers of our government are mere sound."[41] And Washington called the Confederation "a half-starved, limping government, that appears to be always moving upon crutches, and tottering at every step."[42]

It was those who knew the government best who were most aware of the need for drastic reform; and, since many of them were leaders in their own states, it was precisely this group which was most strategically placed for the promotion of its desires. The significarice of the breakdown of the Confederation, therefore, was not that it persuaded the mass of the people of the need for fundamental change—for it did not—but that it persuaded practical men of politics and affairs to use their talent and influence in the fight for the new Constitution.

This was of basic importance. For generations men of exceptional vision had turned out plans for union, but these blueprints had never won the serious consideration of any substantial number of colonial leaders. Even the outbreak of the war with England found the bulk of colonial politicians unwilling to create a really strong government in common. But their direct ex-

428

---

[39] See Madison's "Preface to Debates in the Convention of 1787" in Farrand, Records, III, 542-544. See also, The Federalist, XV, XX.

[40] Robert A. East, Business Enterprise in the American Revolutionary Era (New York, 1938), 238, 261-264; Max Farrand, The Fathers of the Constitution (New Haven, 1921), 23, 30-31, 34; McLaughlin, Confederation, 69-71, 78; Arthur M. Schlesinger, New Viewpoints in American History (New York, 1928), 186-187.

[41] Elliot, Debates, II, 525-526.

[42] Washington to Benjamin Harrison, Mount Vernon, January 18, 1784, in John C. Fitzpatrick, ed., The Writings of George Washington from the Original Manuscript Sources, 1745-1799 (Washington, 1931-1944), XXVII, 305-306.

perience with the failures of the Confederation achieved what no
intellectual argument could; and once the "practical" men were
ready to throw their influence and energy into the movement for
reform, what had been a visionary hope became the most immediate of possibilities.[43]

If one were to look only at this factor, one might draw the
rather strange lesson that the worse the preliminary instruments
of co-operation the better the ultimate prospects for federal union.
Actually, of course, there must be other and forceful motives for
at least some co-operation. But if there are important needs which
can be met only through co-operation, and if the looser forms of
co-operation prove utterly inadequate, the result must inevitably
be a demand for more effective and intimate union. Men will
notoriously put up with a moderately bad political structure where
they would insist on sweeping reform of one which was a total
failure, and because of this the very defectiveness of the earlier
instruments of co-operation may hasten the achievement and increase the completeness of the final union. It was, for example,
the hope of Clarence Streit that the very extent of the failure of
the League of Nations would make men aware that piecemeal
reform would do no good and that only a fundamental change in
structure could prove adequate.[44]

429

In this connection, it is important that, apart from a few
intellectuals and scholars, the first people to become aware of the
defects of a co-operative organization are likely to be the practical
political leaders who are expected to make it work and who generally have considerable influence over public opinion in their own
countries. But there are few signs today that any considerable
number of statesmen have yet been influenced by previous international failures to look upon federal union as a practical and immediate solution.

IV

Probably the most persistent of the active factors promoting
co-operation in America was military necessity. From the New
England Confederation to the Albany Conference, each of the
early attempts at union was the direct consequence of some military threat—from the Indians, the Dutch, or the French; and
although economic considerations were of fundamental importance
in the quarrel with Great Britain, the strength of the intercolonial

---

[43] In several States, it was the influence of this group, whose power far
exceeded its numbers, which determined the outcome of the contest over
ratification. See below, pp. 27-30.

[44] *Union Now*, 199.

organization increased in direct relation to the seriousness of the military danger. The greatest steps toward an active and united government were taken when hostilities broke out, and military necessity played an essential part in speeding the framing of the Articles of Confederation and in providing the final impulse for ratification both by Congress and by the most reluctant of the states.[45]

Even after the war, foreign dangers provided a leading argument for unity, although an occasional anti-Federalist insisted that the peril was sufficient in itself to hold the colonies together:

> Disunion is impossible. The Eastern States hold the fisheries, which are their cornfields, by a hair. They have a dispute with the British government about their limits at this moment. Is not a general and strong government necessary for their interest? . . . New York and Pennsylvania anxiously look forward for the fur trade. How can they obtain it but by union? . . . Is there not a strong inducement to union, while the British are on one side and the Spaniards on the other? Thank Heaven, we have a Carthage of our own![46]

But the Federalists were the principal beneficiaries of such arguments, and in each of the states they took care to point out the perils of disunion.[47]

These arguments, however, had relatively little effect on the mass of the people. Only in Georgia, which was engaged in an Indian war, was defense an important motive for ratification. Elsewhere, fear of attack was at a minimum, and it was a commonplace of the time to attribute to this safety the lack of federal sentiment. "These republicans no longer have a Philip at their gates," wrote Otto in explaining the weakness of the Confederation;[48] and Governor Randolph reminded the Virginia Convention that "our perilous situation was the cement of our union. How different the scene when this peril vanished, and peace was restored!"[49] David Ramsay could write in 1786 that "In 1775 there was more patriotism in a village than there is now in the

---

[45] Burnett, *Continental Congress*, 236-237, 248, 257, 344; Jensen, *Articles*, 228.

[46] Grayson in the Virginia Convention, Elliott, *Debates*, III, 278.

[47] *The Federalist* placed special emphasis on this danger: III, IV, V, VII, XI. The type of threat emphasized varied from state to state. New England centering its attention on the possibility of attack from Canada, New York on the British control of frontier posts, the South on the Spanish and Indian danger, and coastal areas on the possibility of foreign naval attacks. Elliott, *Debates*, II, 21, 43, 67, 129, 143, 185-186, 212, 217, 379, 526; III, 71-74, 239, 276-278, 309, 633; IV, 17, 284.

[48] Otto to the Comte de Montmorin, New York, April 10, 1787; Farrand, *Records*, III, 16-17.

[49] Elliot, *Debates*, III, 27.

13 states."[50]   John Jay, the Confederation's foreign secretary, went so far as to advocate war against the "Algerines" to restore the flagging national spirit.[51]

Some people, in fact, were more afraid of civil than of foreign war.   The colonial period of American history had been marked by territorial and boundary disputes in which practically all of the states had taken part at one time or another, and a leading concern of the more conservative members of the first Continental Congress was the fear that any move toward independence would free the thirteen colonies from the restraining hand of British control and permit them to spring at one another's throats.   The subsequent clashes over Vermont and the Wyoming Valley seemed to confirm these fears, and the authors of *The Federalist* even foresaw the development of a balance of power system in which New England, New Jersey, and Maryland would join to restrict the growing power of New York.[52]   In addition, there were warnings that states like New Jersey and Connecticut, which suffered from intercolonial trade barriers, would eventually resort to violence.[53]

As in the case of foreign dangers, however, these fears were restricted to a comparatively few men of foresight and imagination; and however real the danger may have been, its influence on public opinion as a whole was a very minor one.

431

Probably the greatest contrast between the colonial experience and that of our own time is the incomparably greater role of military considerations in promoting union today.   It is "freedom from fear" which before all else appeals to public opinion, and the core of each plan for international federation is a proposal for defense against aggression or for some kind of international police force.[54]   Yet the colonial experience gives some reason for

---

[50] Ramsay to Benjamin Rush, New York, February 11, 1786, in Edmund C. Burnett, ed., *Letters of Members of the Continental Congress* (Washington, 1921-1936), VIII, 301.

[51] Bancroft, *History*, I, 474-475.

[52] VII.   See also, Burnett, *Continental Congress*, 540-546; Nevins, *American States*, 578-583.

[53] Elliot, *Debates*, II, 186, 212; Paul Leicester Ford, ed., *Essays on the Constitution of the United States* (Brooklyn, 1892), 180, 404, and *Pamphlets*, 84; E. Wilder Spaulding, *New York in the Critical Period, 1783-1789* (New York, 1932), 156-159.

[54] Harrop Freeman, *Coercion of States in International Organization* (Philadelphia, 1944); Frederick L. Schuman, "The Dilemma of the Peace-Seekers," *American Political Science Review*, XXXIX (Feb., 1945), 12-30; Wynner and Lloyd, *Searchlight*.   The preamble to the new United Nations Charter makes no fewer than five references to the maintenance of peace and begins with the words "We, the peoples of the United Nations, Determined to save succeeding generations from the scourge of war, which twice in our lifetime has brought untold sorrow to mankind . . . ." *New York Times*, June 27, 1945, 12.

doubting the ultimate efficacy of this motive. It is clear that a great and immediate military danger can be extremely effective in promoting union for defense; and the greater the danger, the more effective the union is likely to be. But unless other motives are present, the decline in danger is likely to bring an equally sharp decline in desire for union. It was for this reason that Wendell Willkie and Sumner Welles were so insistent that an international Organization should be established before the end of hostilities and while nations still needed one another and would be willing to make concessions. And just as in colonial times, the recent outbreak of quarrels over Poland, Greece, and Syria has heightened the desire for effective organization to keep the peace by indicating how real is the danger of conflict among the victorious allies themselves. Yet paradoxically, to the extent that the United Nations organization eliminates these dangers without making itself indispensable in other ways, it will eliminate much of its own *raison d'être*.

432

There is another and more enduring way, however, in which military danger can contribute significantly to union. Men are largely creatures of inertia, and if a habit of co-operation is sufficiently well developed as a response to military peril, it may survive the disappearance of the peril. The importance of the very existence of the Confederation in developing a national loyalty among Congressmen, administrators, and diplomats has already been noted.[55] And the soldiers of the Revolutionary armies were subjected to the same influence. At first, it is true, the common service in the intercolonial army seemed, if anything, to intensify the antagonism among men from different colonies; and all that was novel and different in their new companions appeared inferior and disagreeable. There were frequent charges and countercharges of corruption, cowardice, and inefficiency; and there were reports that some of the colonial troops would as willingly fight each other as the British.[56] But after the common triumph at Saratoga and the common suffering at Valley Forge there arose something of a national pride and loyalty. Northerners joined in the universal respect for Washington, and Southerners recognized the ability of a commander like Greene. Ultimately it was no accident that much of the most vigorous support for union came from veterans, and especially officers, of the Continental army.[57]

---

[55] See above, pp. 10-12.
[56] Nevins, *American States*, 548-551; Van Tyne, *The War of Independence—American Phase* (Boston and New York, 1929), 62-63, 302-309.
[57] Bancroft, *History*, I, 89, 370; Greene, *Revolutionary Generation*, 300-301; Nevins, *American States*, 554. Both, of course, were likely to have a financial interest in union as well.

Even among the people as a whole, the war contributed to the breaking down of provincialism. In particular, the propaganda of the Revolution, through its attacks upon the British and its glowing statement of colonial rights, built a consciousness of a common cause and, what was equally important, of a national difference between the colonists and the inhabitants of the mother country.[58]

Thus, if the military factor did not provide a widespread popular motive for the ratification of the Constitution, it did contribute to the building of institutions and habits of mind which endured even after the military threat had vanished.

If one seeks for a modern parallel, it is significant that both the League of Nations and the United Nations grew out of wartime alliances and that some of the machinery of the United Nations represents a continuation of institutions designed to meet military needs.[59] Yet it would be a decided exaggeration to claim that the experience of the men who are fighting the war or of the statesmen who are directing it is anything more than the faintest shadow of the Revolutionary experience, in the sense of building an international patriotism.

433

V

Thanks to Charles Beard, the dynamic role of economic influences in the movement for closer union needs little amplification.[60] The Constitution, it is obvious, had the support of merchants eager for a sound currency and the removal of barriers to trade, of manufacturers desiring protection for their enterprises, of propertied men fearing paper money and "desperate debtors," and of holders of government obligations and speculators in western lands.

The incidence and importance of these considerations, however, varied a good deal from state to state. On the surface, concern for commerce was the most important of the economic motives. The Federal Convention grew directly out of meetings at Mount Vernon and Annapolis which were commercial in their inspiration, and Madison later noted as a chief reason for calling the Convention "the want of authority in Congress to regulate commerce" which "had produced in Foreign nations particularly Great Britain a monopolizing policy injurious to the trade of the United States and destructive to their navigation; the imbecility

---

[58] Davidson, *Propaganda*, 139-152, 410; Greene, *Revolutionary Generation*, 303-304.

[59] Bonnet, *Outlines*, and Wild, "Machinery." See also Churchill's statement, above, p. 12.

[60] Charles A. Beard, *An Economic Interpretation of the Constitution of the United States* (New York, 1914).

and anticipated dissolution of the Cenfederacy extinguishing all apprehensions of a Countervailing policy on the part of the United States."[61] In Massachusetts in particular the commercial provisions of the Constitution appealed not only to the great merchants and manufacturers but also to the working classes in the towns and were influential in winning the rather reluctant support of men like Sam Adams;[62] and in all of the commercial towns, from Portsmouth and Portland in the North to Charleston in the South, union sentiment was also strong.[63] When these sections could, they carried their states with them, and when they feared they could not, as in the cases of New York and Rhode Island, there were threats that they would secede.[64]

But commerce and manufacturing were both very limited in their appeal and, especially in the states south of Delaware, there were important sections where the promotion of these interests could have very little importance as a motive for union.[65] The desire to protect and promote property interests, on the other hand, was much more general. From the earliest days of colonial independence, men of property had dreaded the possibility that "radicals" would get out of hand and had, accordingly, sought strength through union with conservatives in other colonies. This was especially apparent when the Articles of Confederation were being framed, although the conservatives were defeated at this time and the Dickinson draft, sponsored by them, drastically modified.[66] Subsequent events like the triumph of the paper money party in certain states seemed to confirm their worst fears;[67] and in their eagerness for a stronger government capable of preventing such developments they found support from those who hoped that a firm government would enhance the value of government obligations and that it would raise the value of western lands.

434

---

[61] Farrand, *Records*, III, 547.

[62] Miller, *Sam Adams*, 377, 379. For the clearest statement of this interest, see Elliot, *Debates*, II, 57-58. See also, *ibid.*, 58, 67, 82, 106-107, 124, 130, 139, 170.

[63] Orrin Grant Libby, *The Geographic Distribution of the Vote of the Thirteen States on the Federal Constitution, 1787-1788* (Madison, 1894), 29, 49; Farrand, *Records*, III, 18-19.

[64] *Documentary History*, IV, 687; V, 226; Spaulding, *New York*, 253-255.

[65] Concern for manufacturing was greatest in Massachusetts and Pennsylvania, Beard, *Economic Interpretation*, 41-46; East, *Business Enterprise*, 310-315; Elliott, *Debates*, II, 59; Jameson, *American Revolution*, 53-60; Spaulding, *New York*, 10.

[66] Conservatives who were firmly in control of their own States were naturally less eager for union. Jensen, *Articles*, 91-92, 124-163.

[67] This group triumphed to some extent and temporarily in seven States, and its activities in Rhode Island were looked on with special horror. Even Jefferson referred to the State as the "little vaut-rien." *Documentary History*, IV, 522, 566, 615, 716, 764, 808; V, 212.

But although many men of influence belonged to these groups, a large number of them were relatively apathetic toward union until a more spectacular threat to their interests appeared. In Massachusetts this spur was provided by Shays's rebellion and particularly by the growth in the radical vote in the state elections of 1787;[68] and despite the ease with which the rebellion and other minor disorders in New Hampshire and Vermont were suppressed, they provided an excellent talking point for Federalists outside the state. Washington's letters reveal the intense impression made upon him by the somewhat hysterical information he received from Massachusetts;[69] and in every state there were men like James Wilson to spread the alarm by proclaiming that "The flames of internal insurrection were ready to burst out in every quarter; . . . and from one end to the other of the continent, we walked on ashes, concealing fire beneath our feet. . . ."[70] Probably the greatest tribute was paid to the efficacy of the argument by Jefferson when he warned that "our Convention has been too much impressed by the insurrection of Massachusetts: and in the spur of the moment they are setting up a kite to keep the hen-yard in order."[71]

Whatever the precise form it took, therefore, the economic interest has naturally been regarded as "the dynamic element" in the movement for the new Constitution.[72] In fact, the great bulk of the members of the Federal Convention had some personal financial interest in the outcome of their deliberations; and although it is possible to exaggerate the importance of this fact (since in some instances this personal stake was quite small and since some of the wealthiest of the delegates had little influence on, or even opposed, the Convention's work), it is important that the small farmers and artisans, who comprised the overwhelming majority of the people, had little personal representation.[73]

It would be an oversimplification, however, to see in the contest over ratification a clear-cut struggle between "desperate

---

[68] Robert A. East, "The Massachusetts Conservatives in the Critical Period" in Richard B. Morris, ed., *The Era of the American Revolution* (New York, 1939) ; Joseph P. Warren, "The Confederation and Shays' Rebellion," *American Historical Review*, XI (Oct., 1905), 42-67.

[69] *Writings*, XXIX, 52, 122.

[70] Elliot, *Debates*, II, 521; see also, *ibid.*, III, 180; IV, 20, 281-282; Spaulding, *New York*, 150-151. There was also some fear of violence on the part of Southern slaves, *The Federalist*, XLIII and Elliott, *Debates*, III, 73.

[71] Jefferson to Colonel Smith, Paris, November 13, 1787, *Documentary History*, IV, 378.

[72] Beard, *Economic Interpretation*, 149.

[73] It is worth noting that Hamilton, whose speeches are always quoted to indicate the conservatism of the Convention, was very far from having his way. See also, E. S. Corwin's review of Beard's book in *History Teacher's Magazine*, V (February, 1914), 65-66.

debtors" and the *beati possidentes*. For one thing, the bulk of the people in the country belonged to neither of these classes but were members of a middle class which owned property but which was far from opulent.[74] And in the second place, the men of wealth, although generally standing to profit from union, were not unanimous in this respect. Landholders feared that the burden of taxation would fall on them under the new government, and no section of the Constitution roused more universal protest than the provision for direct taxation.[75] Many purchasers of Tory property were afraid that their titles might be held invalid by federal courts, and well-to-do debtors feared that creditors abroad or in other states would use the federal courts to obtain payment. In the South there was general apprehension that the federal power over commerce would be used to give the North a monopoly of the carrying trade and to increase its cost. Plantation owners in South Carolina and Georgia disliked the provisions for the taxing and the eventual abolition of the slave trade. In Kentucky, citizens thought the federal government might surrender the right to navigate the Mississippi. In New York, taxpayers regretted the loss of the "tribute" which they received from Connecticut and New Jersey. And in all of the states officeholders might be expected to resist any loss of power and prestige.[76]

On the other hand, particularly in the large towns, a good many of the members of the middle and lower classes, the artisans and mechanics, identified their interests with those of the merchants and manufacturers and gave their support to the Constitution.[77] And even among the farmers there were those who desired the security and order they expected the new government to bring.[78]

Many of these interests, in fact, were sectional or functional rather than class in character; and even when men of wealth united

436

[74] See above, pp. 4-6; Holcombe, *Middle Classes.* 4-6. 136-137, 153-155; Lee, "Letters", 321.

[75] Every one of the States which asked for amendments asked for a return of the requisition system. Elliot, *Debates*, II, 41, 76, 101-102, 132, 330-331, 356-357, 501; III, 248, 264, 285, 327; IV, 80, 289. Yet some of the greatest landholders also had heavy investments in public securities. Cochran, *New York in the Confederation*, 17; Spaulding, *New York*, 71-74, 83.

[76] For examples of such opposition in the South, see Elliot, *Debates*, III, 151, 325, 333-349, 574-575, 581, 616; IV, 286; Farrand, *Records*, I, 566-567; II, 364, 371, 631. For New York see Nevins, *American States*, 556-560 and Spaulding, *New York*, 153-154. For the expected opposition of office holders, see Farrand, *Records*, I, 284, 379, 555; II, 89, 478; and below, pp. 28-29.

[77] Miller, *Sam Adams*, 377, 379; Ulrich B. Phillips, "The South Carolina Federalists," *American Historical Review*, XIV (Apr., 1908). 542; Spaulding, *New York*, 10.

[78] See the testimony of a Massachusetts "ploughjogger," Elliot, *Debates*, II, 102.

to promote union, there was no reason for thinking that they did so from an impression that the interests of a wealthy South Carolina planter were identical with those of a wealthy Boston merchant. But fortunately for the Federalists, this sectional division of interest was a complicated one. Commercial interests were concentrated in the North, but many Northerners had no direct interest in the carrying trade; and states like Connecticut and New Jersey had little more to gain from "navigation laws" than did Virginia or the Carolinas. Similarly, the southern states were divided among themselves on the issue of the slave trade; while the middle states shared interests with both sections and were reluctant to cast in their lot exclusively with either. In consequence of these sectional divisions within the sections, it was considerably easier to work out compromises which could attract the support of the great majority of the states.[79]

In short, if the Constitution represented in general the interests of the wealthier classes, it represented a compromise of their interests and not a single homogeneous interest. And if it won the support of most of the men of wealth, it had also to win the support of at least a minority of the other classes. For, as Otto pointed out, "The men of wealth, the merchants, the public officials, the Cincinnati are all eager for a more absolute government, but their number is quite small when compared with the mass of the citizens."[80] And although the men of wealth may have prevailed in the Federal Convention, the actual ratification of the Constitution was up to state conventions in which the other classes had an important if not a decisive representation. In some states, as in Massachusetts and New Hampshire, the Constitution could not have been ratified without the conversion of some of their representatives through the winning of some of their leaders (by the use, it must be admitted, of rather questionable means), through reassurance about civil liberties and the rights of the states, and through the recommendation of amendments eliminating the power of direct taxation and restoring the system of requisitions. And in general, although the wealthier classes provided an influence and enthusiasm quite out of proportion to their numbers, at least the passive consent and tolerance of other elements was necessary.

There are obvious differences between this pattern of economic interests and the one which prevails in the modern world. For one thing, the industrial revolution has brought enormous changes in our economy and, as federal unionists like to point out, the

437

[79] Farrand, *Records*, II, 220-223, 359-365, 414-417, 449-453.
[80] Otto to Montmorin, June 10, 1787, Farrand, *Records*, III, 45.

world is far more interdependent economically than the thirteen colonies ever were. In addition, the cost of warfare and the extension of governmental control which is its inevitable consequence is likely to make businessmen sympathetic to any federal plan which could guarantee peace; and it has even been suggested that the movement for federal union is intended to promote joint imperialist ambitions and to win the support of other countries for the British empire.[81]

Yet on the other hand, the few intercolonial barriers to trade represent only the faintest foreshadowing of the elaborate structure of economic nationalism which prevails today; and the interests which profit from the wide variety of protective devices are incomparably more potent politically and have far more to lose than did those which profited from the trade barriers of 1787. In many countries, including to some extent the old free-trade stronghold of Great Britain, there has been an increasing fear of foreign competition and a desire to turn to cartel and marketing agreements and to political direction of the flow of trade, while there is a certain fantasy in talking of freedom of trade with a state-directed economy like that of the Union of Socialist Soviet Republics.[82] In short, any plan, like that of Clarence Streit, which calls for free trade as an essential ingredient of international union will inevitably have a large and powerful part of the vested economic interests opposed to it.

But while some of the strongest property interests are fundamentally opposed to closer international economic ties, it is significant that an influential part of the working class favors them, as evidenced by the C. I. O.'s support of the reciprocal trade agreements in this country and by the interest in European federation evinced by the Labor and Socialist Parties in England and on the Continent.[83] If the movement for international federal union proves successful, the historian of the future may well discern a pattern precisely the reverse of Charles Beard's and discover the "dynamic element" in its achievement to be not the influence of the men of wealth but the political power of the organized workers.

VI

It is paradoxical that a feeling of nationalism was important as a motive both in favor of and in opposition to union. To most people, the nation, in so far as it existed at all, was

---

81 D. N. Pritt, *Federal Illusion?* (London, 1940).

82 See the comments of Arthur Krock, *New York Times,* July 29, 1945. IV, 3.

83 H. N. Brailsford, "Federation for Europe," *New Republic,* CI (December 13, 1939), 227; E. L. P., "European Federation," *New Republic.* CXII (June 11, 1945), 814-825.

the state; but to a small and highly influential group, it was the United States.

The French and Indian War had built a certain amount of intercolonial pride even before the outbreak of the Revolution;[84] and the Revolutionary War, as already noted, made some breaches in colonial provincialism.[85] In particular, the propaganda of patriotism, with its bitter denunciation of British tyranny and British atrocities, served the important purpose of distinguishing Americans from Englishmen; while the need for joint effort if the war was to be a success encouraged some conception of a common interest.[86] Indeed, in the first flush of enthusiasm for resistance and independence, certain colonial statesmen went so far as to proclaim that state boundaries had ceased to exist and that henceforth there were neither Virginians, Pennsylvanians, New Yorkers, or New Englanders but only Americans.[87]

Such sentiments, however, represented oratorical fancy rather than any fundamental shift in the thinking of the bulk of the people. To them the realities were still Massachusetts and Pennsylvania, Virginia and Carolina. When they thought of the inhabitants of other colonies at all, their attitude has been compared to that of a modern Australian toward a Canadian or South African.[88] Only in the case of a few statesmen was there an exception. Franklin wistfully hoped that the members of the new Congress under the Constitution would think of themselves as representatives of the nation rather than the states.[89] James Wilson declared he "could not persuade himself that the State Governments and sovereignties were so much the idols of the people, nor a National Government so obnoxious to them, as some supposed. . . . Will a citizen of *Delaware* be degraded by becoming a citizen of the *United States?*"[90] Madison confessed that he did not think it a terrible thing for the federal government to swallow up the states and maintained that too much emphasis was laid on the states as political societies.[91] And George Read of Delaware opposed a guarantee of the territory of the states because "it abetted the idea of distinct States which would be a perpetual

439

[84] Greene, *Revolutionary Generation*, 181.
[85] See above, pp. 17-18.
[86] Davidson, *Propaganda*, 139-152, 365-375, 410; Greene, *Revolutionary Generation*, 303-304.
[87] Patrick Henry, as quoted by John Adams, *Works*, II, 367.
[88] Nevins, *American States*, 544-545. See also, Andrews, *Colonial Background*, 26-27; Van Tyne, *War of Independence*, 271, 299-301.
[89] Farrand, *Records*, I, 197.
[90] *Ibid.*, 253.
[91] *Ibid.*, 463.

source of discord. There can be [no] cure for this evil but in doing away States altogether and uniting them all into [one] great Society."[92]

But such feelings were highly exceptional. The Federalist leaders were obliged to recognize that a union which abolished the states would never win acceptance. As Hamilton told the Federal Convention, all governments require an "habitual attachment of the people. The whole force of this tie is on the side of the State Government. Its sovereignty is immediately before the eyes of the people: its protection is immediately enjoyed by them."[93] And so, when advocates of compromise like Johnson of Connecticut pointed out that the chief objections to the Constitution would be removed if the existence of the states could be guaranteed, the necessary concessions were forthcoming.[94] Once these concessions were made, it is notable that it was the smaller states (except for Rhode Island) which tended to ratify the Constitution most promptly and by the largest majorities.[95] Under the circumstances, General Knox, ardent Federalist that he was, reflected something of the unenthusiastic tolerance which prevailed among his party when he wrote: "Although I frankly confess that the existence of the State governments is an insuperable evil in a national point of view, yet I do not well see how in this stage of the business they could be annihilated."[96]

440

The making of the concessions, however, did not eliminate all apprehension on this score. No objection to the Constitution enjoyed greater currency than the charge that the new government would accomplish a "consolidation" of the states and that the phrase "We the people" in the preamble (a wording chosen to avoid the problem of predicting which states would adhere to the new government) meant the destruction of state sovereignty.[97] Melancthon Smith told the New York convention that all important matters would now be handled by Congress and asked how the state legislatures could retain the respect of the people when they met "once in a year to

---

[92] Farrand, *Records*, I, 202.
[93] *Ibid.*, 284.
[94] Such stanch nationalists as Hamilton, Madison, Wilson, and King admitted that the abolition of the states would be a profound shock to public opinion. *Ibid.*, 283, 284, 287, 322-324; see also Madison, *Writings*, II, 337-339. For Madison's explanation of the compromise, see Farrand, *Records*, III, 133-134.
[95] *Ibid.*, III, 538.
[96] Knox to Washington, New York, August 14, 1787, *Documentary History*, IV, 251.
[97] Elliot, *Debates*, II, 45-46, 60, 99, 134, 201, 241-242, 312, 334, 338, 403, 438, 455; III, 22, 29, 61, 171, 327, 395, 444, 500, 522; IV, 16, 50, 57, 164, 170, 303.

make laws for regulating the height of your fences and the repairing of your roads."[98]   And Patrick Henry asked the Virginia convention:

> What shall the states have to do? Take care of the poor, repair and make highways, erect bridges, and so on, and so on? Abolish the state legislatures at once. What purposes should they be continued for? Our legislature will indeed be a ludicrous spectacle—one hundred and eighty men marching in solemn, farcical procession, exhibiting a mournful proof of the lost liberty of their country, without the power of restoring it.[99]

One of the chief occupations of the Federalist leaders was explaining the extent of the guarantees and powers given the states; and every state which asked for any amendment at all asked for further protection of the states. In the two states which temporarily rejected the Constitution—North Carolina and Rhode Island—state patriotism was an important factor.[100]

In short, so far as the bulk of the people were concerned, any sentiment of patriotism was likely to be an obstacle rather than an aid to union because such loyalties were attached to the states and not to the country as a whole. On the other hand, among the wealthier classes a shrewd calculation of personal economic interest frequently created a willingness to work for national union at the expense of state authority.[101] But what was most important was the fact that among a very small minority, which included men of the highest prestige like Washington and Franklin and of the highest political ability like Madison and Wilson, there had developed a genuine and lofty patriotism.[102]   Often this took the form of identifying America with the cause of liberty throughout the world;[103] and occasionally it even anticipated the creation of a

441

---

[98] Elliott, *Debates*, II, 312.

[99] *Ibid.*, III, 171. This reference to Virginia as his "country" forms an interesting contrast to his statement to the First Continental Congress in 1774: "I am not a Virginian, but an American." Adams, *Works*, II, 367.

[100] Frank Greene Bates, *Rhode Island and the Formation of the Union* (New York, 1898), 74, 105, 174, 207-211; Henry McGilbert Wagstaff, "State Rights and Political Parties in North Carolina—1776-1861" *Johns Hopkins University Studies in Historical and Political Science*, Series 24, Numbers 7-8 (July-August, 1906), 28.

[101] See above, p. 19.

[102] Claude H. Van Tyne, "Sovereignty in the American Revolution," *American Historical Review*, XII (April, 1907), 529-545.

[103] Davidson, *Propaganda*, 131-137; Elliot, *Debates*, II, 529; IV, 319-320; Hans Kohn, *The Idea of Nationalism* (New York, 1944), 290-300.

distinct national language and character.[104] The enormous influence and political skill of these few who were consciously American nationalists moved a far broader public which had no share in the national spirit. In this sense, nationalism must rank as one of the important motives in creating the federal government.

Today, far more than in colonial times, it would be extremely difficult to find an extensive "United Nations patriotism." The present war with its accumulation of bitter memories seems to have intensified the feeling of particularistic nationalism rather than to have moderated it.[105] The spectacular revival of patriotism in the Union of Socialist Soviet Republics, the nationalistic attitudes of some of the newly liberated countries like Yugoslavia and Czechoslovakia (in their respective demands for Trieste and the elimination of the Sudeten Germans), and General de Gaulle's preoccupation with France's *gloire* all indicate that even in those countries whose political ideas have been most opposed to nationalism or whose experience in the war has indicated their inability to survive without foreign aid, there is a strong emotional obstacle to any effective loyalty to a higher entity. Irrational barriers are often the most enduring, and today they offer what is undoubtedly the greatest obstacle to international federal union. In comparison with their strength, the patriotism of the American states, whose independent existence had been so short in duration, whose history had been relatively so free from bitter memories of strife and conquest, and whose political boundaries were not reinforced by differences in language and culture. was so different in degree as really to be different in kind.

VII

It has repeatedly been apparent in the course of this paper that the leading motives for union, whether military necessity, economic advantage, or national feeling, influenced only a minority—and in some cases a very small minority—of the population. As a result it is essential to ask how this minority was able to prevail over the majority of those who were hostile or indifferent; and this brings us to a consideration of the two

---

[104] Elliot, *Debates,* II, 527.
[105] For conflicting views on this subject, see D. W. Brogan, "The Power of Nationalism," *New Republic,* CIX (December 27, 1943), 916-918, and Albert Guérard, *Europe Free and United* (Stanford University, California, 1945), 49-121.

methods by which minorities may hope to prevail: political influence or adroitness, and coercive power.

In the American colonies, political influence and adroitness were especially important as a function of the unusually able Federalist leadership. Of all the colonial leaders, the two who inspired the greatest veneration were Washington and Franklin, and it was the good fortune of the Federalists that both of these men were strong advocates of union before, during, and after the Convention. The fact that they had been present at the debates (which had been secret and were therefore open to popular suspicion) and advocated ratification of the Constitution with all the force at their command did much to silence criticism and inspire confidence; for no one could believe seriously in the sinister character of proposals which had been framed with the help of the two national heroes. Washington's support was particularly active. A friend wrote of him in 1787: "I never saw him so keen for any thing in my Life, as he is for the adoption of the new Form of Government."[106] And the effects of his support may well have been decisive. James Monroe, who was himself opposed to the Constitution, attributed its acceptance primarily to Washington's influence;[107] and Hamilton placed his prestige first among the factors favoring ratification.[108] The Comte de Moustier, writing to the Comte de Montmorin, declared:

> The opinion of General Washington was of such weight that it alone contributed more than any other measure to cause the present constitution to be adopted. The extreme confidence in his patriotism, his integrity, and his intelligence forms to-day its principal support. It has become popular much more out of respect for the chief of the republic than by any merit of its own. All is hushed in presence of the trust of the people in the savior of the country.[109]

Within the states, the pattern of leadership was somewhat more confused. There was only one Washington and only one Franklin; but there were many statesmen of local importance who were divided in their attitude. Office holders in particular had a vested interest in the *status quo,* and those who doubted their

443

---

[106] A. Donald to Jefferson, Richmond, November 12, 1787, *Documentary History,* IV, 375.

[107] Monroe to Jefferson, Fredericksburg, July 12, 1788, Bancroft, *History,* II, 474.

[108] *Documentary History,* IV, 288.

[109] New York, June 5, 1789, in Bancroft, *History,* II, 495-496.

ability to win prominence on the national scene were likely to
conclude that it was better to rule in Seriphus than to be a
citizen in Athens.[110] In several states they were the dominant
factor in the opposition; and in Massachusetts the Federalists
were sure of victory only after they had tempted Governor
Hancock with the suggestion that he might be the first president of the new government.[111] In general, however, the
Federalists drew their supporters from the class which was
more highly educated and more powerful; and it was sometimes complained, as in Massachusetts, that they had a monopoly of talent and knowledge: "The Opposition complain that
the Lawyers, Judges, Clergymen, Merchants, and men of
Education are all in Favor of the Constitution, and that for
this reason they appear to be able to make the worst, appear
the better cause."[112] In states like Massachusetts, New Hampshire, Connecticut, New Jersey, and Pennsylvania, the Federalists had the great advantage in the quality of their leadership, both in power to debate and in knowledge and use of
political strategy. In New York and Virginia, however, the
talent was far more evenly divided. And in Rhode Island and
North Carolina, it rested conspicuously with the anti-
Federalists.[113]

Of course, everything cannot be explained in terms of
leadership and political influence. For Connecticut, New Jersey, and Georgia, the advantages of union were so apparent
that ratification would have been won even without particularly able leadership. In Rhode Island, the opposition to
union was so overwhelming that even the ablest leadership
would probably have failed. But in critical and doubtful
states, the superior skill of the Federalist leadership did much
to determine the outcome; and in some cases, as in Massachusetts and New Hampshire, unusually effective leadership
was even able to turn defeat into victory.

The importance of this factor of leadership in achieving
union in America is one of the more hopeful indications so far
as contemporary international federal unionists are concerned,
and it is somewhat surprising that more emphasis has not
been placed upon this consideration. For it indicates that it

444

---

[110] See Otto to the Comte de Montmorin, New York, July 25, 1787,
Farrand, *Records*, III, 61-62; *ibid.*, I, 284, 379, 513-514, 555; II, 89, 478.

[111] Miller, *Sam Adams*, 374-384.

[112] Rufus King to Madison, Boston, January 27, 1788, *Documentary
History*, IV, 459.

[113] Bates, *Rhode Island*, 174; Nevins, *American States*, 225, 305, 342,
352; Henry McGilbert Wagstaff, "Federalism in North Carolina," *The James
Sprunt Historical Publications* (Chapel Hill, 1910), IX, 8, 12-13; "State
Rights," 15.

is not essential for union to be based upon the deliberate consent of the mass of the people. Particularly in a day when,
even in the democracies, political leaders are likely to control
highly disciplined followings and to be able to deliver the
votes of legislatures according to their desires, there is a real
possibility that unusually enlightened, imaginative, and cour-
ageous leaders can use their strategic position to speed the
acceptance of union. An almost spectacular instance of this
was Winston Churchill's offer of union to France in the disas-
trous summer of 1940 and the narrowness of the margin by
which the French cabinet rejected the offer.

Far less important than the role of leadership in achieving
American union was the role of coercion. In a few states and
to a minor degree, however, it did play a part. In Pennsylvania in particular there was some bitterness because anti-
Federalist members of the state legislature, deliberately ab-
senting themselves to prevent a quorum, were dragged into
the legislative chamber. In addition, the time set for the
election of members of the state convention was strikingly
brief and left little opportunity for the Constitution to be
studied or for a campaign against ratification to be carried on.

R¹ ɔde Island, moreover, entered the union not from conviction so much as from fear of economic disadvantage and
the possibility that force might be used to collect its unpaid
requisitions;[114] and North Carolina entered because she recognized the economic impracticability of isolation from the other
colonies.[115]

Taken all in all, however, these instances are relatively
mild. What is striking is the fact that the overwhelming majority of the states accepted the Constitution, some enthusiastically, some reluctantly, but freely and in good faith. On
the whole, the traditional picture of the founding fathers meeting in peaceful assembly and deciding through discussion and
compromise to adopt the new form of government is not
greatly exaggerated and, in fact, tribute was paid to this
factor in state after state.[116] If one seeks for examples of military force as the basis of American federal union, he must turn
to the Civil War and not to the making of the Constitution.

The American experience would seem to indicate that
union cannot be founded upon the coercion of any of its important members but that if the most important members can

---

[114] Bates, *Rhode Island*, 192-195.
[115] Wagstaff, "Federalism," 17-18.
[116] Elliot, *Debates*, II, 170, 173, 182-183, 200, 422; IV, 331.

come to peaceful agreement, the smaller states, because of their economic and military weakness, will scarcely dare to stand aside. This conclusion found considerable support at the San Francisco conference when it became obvious in many instances that once the great powers had reached an agreement, the small powers, in spite of their greater voting potentiality, would have to accept it.

VIII

The pattern of federal motivation in the United States is badly complicated by the presence of forces which themselves had nothing to do with the simple issue of federalism. In particular, the absence of a Bill of Rights (which might just as well have been included in the Constitution from the beginning) roused the distrust of many people who had no objection to union in itself. There was, it is true, some feeling common to the political thought of the time, that any centralized government extending over a large territory would necessarily be tyrannical. But the greatest opposition was based not so much on this theory as on the very practical fact that the gospel of liberty, as preached during the Revolution, seemed to have found no place in the Constitution. Once the Federalists indicated their willingness to accept amendments on this subject, many anti-Federalists were won over, as in Massachusetts and New Hampshire, and many others gained some reassurance.[117]

The tremendous amount of feeling aroused on this score and the extent to which it surprised the framers of the Constitution indicates the degree to which the fate of any proposal of international union may depend upon considerations which, on the surface, are quite irrelevant. During the past months, there has been a noteworthy parallel to this concern in Senator Vandenberg's successful fight to include in the United Nations Charter a pledge "to establish justice and to promote respect for human rights and fundamental freedoms."[118] Without such a provision the Charter would scarcely have been ratified so easily.

IX

In assessing the relative importance of the motives and forces involved in the struggle for a more perfect union, there is a constant danger of placing the chief emphasis upon a

---

[117] Evidence of the uneasiness aroused by this omission is omnipresent in Elliot's *Debates* and in Ford's *Essays* and *Pamphlets*.

[118] *New York Times*, April 2, 1945, 11; April 11, 1945, 1.

single factor or of assuming that each individual was monistic in his motivation. Actually there was a serious mixing or interpenetration of motives. In different parts of the country greater emphasis might be given different issues: in Georgia defense against Indians, in Massachuetts the promotion of the carrying trade, and in Connecticut and New Jersey the elimination of interstate trade barriers. But the same Boston merchant who gazed enviously at British control of the South-'ern trade was likely to be appalled by the threat of Shays's rebellion and by the radical successes in the election of 1787. His commercial contacts with other colonies would have made him aware of a community of interest and culture of which the more self-sufficient frontiersman and the isolated farmer would have little conception. He might be strongly under the influence of men like Washington and Knox, and he might be humiliated by American military weakness in rivalry with Great Britain.

Among the opponents of the Constitution, there was a similar blending of motives, and perhaps an even commoner experience was to have motives conflict. Some men would gladly have followed the leadership of Washington who were distressed by the absence of a Bill of Rights, and owners of both land and securities feared taxation at the same time that they hoped for an increase in the value of government obligations.

447

To select any of these motives as crucial would be superficial. The community in language, religion, type and level of civilization, and political forms and ideas provided a remarkably favorable basis for understanding. The fact that military necessity had driven the colonies to co-operate, from the New England Confederation to the Revolution, accustomed people to the idea of common action, gave common experience in the practice of co-operation, and developed a national outlook and in some cases a national devotion. Without these basic factors, the commercial discrimination of Great Britain, the trade barriers, the fears of foreign attack, the economic failures of the government, and the alarm caused by Shays's rebellion and the paper money fever would have had quite different consequences. And even with all of these factors, such essentially unmeasurable and unpredictable elements as the personal prestige of Washington or even of John Hancock had at times a decisive influence. Moreover, a great deal depended on skill in making concessions without which failure would have been inevitable and on meeting objections, such as the absence of a Bill of Rights, which were not an integral part of the federal issue.

How sound, then, are the generalizations on which international federal unionists tend to base their hopes?

(1) Beyond all doubt, the cultural, social, and political differences among the colonies have been enormously exaggerated. The American experience offers no real precedent for the reconciliation of fundamental differences in way of life, level of civilization, and political outlook. The colonies, it is true, were not homogeneous, and there was a large amount of mutual misunderstanding and bitterness. But there was no difference in culture which remotely approached that between Great Britain and China; and there was no difference in political outlook which approximated that between the United States and the Union of Socialist Soviet Republics. If one limits one's hopes, as does Clarence Streit, to a union of those democracies which already have much the same level of civilization and political ideology, it is still true that the differences in culture and in political forms are far greater than anything which separated the American colonies.

448

(2) In the second place, although many of the motives which contributed to American union were eminently rational, there is a real distortion in any supposition that American union was the consequence simply of a logical process of reasoning. The long tradition of co-operation, the feeling of nationalism, and the loyalty to certain colonial leaders were all essential ingredients in the pattern of union; and they were the result of habit, emotion, and a dependence upon symbols rather than of hard-headed calculation. Moreover, the strongest obstacles to union, in the shape of sectional animosity and state patriotism, were largely a matter of feeling. Yet it was precisely these emotional forces which it was hardest to overcome.

(3) Military necessity, far from being a decisive element in the final achievement of union, was of remarkably little consequence. The great contribution of this motive was the earlier building of institutions and habits of co-operation and the stimulating of a national patriotism which endured longer than the military threat itself. But fear of attack was not strong enough even to maintain the loose Confederation, and it had only a minor part in the struggle for the Constitution.

(4) Economic forces undoubtedly played a leading part in the movement for federal union, but the economic forces which were important then were very different from those which are dominant today. In so far as communication and transportation are essential to union, the world is in a better

position than were the colonies. But the increase in international economic interdependence has been accompanied by an increase in international economic rivalry far more intense than anything characteristic of America in 1787; and today there are powerful economic interests which look on union with the gravest apprehension.

(5) Lastly, although there was every logical reason for expecting the harrowing experiences of the last years to weaken the feeling of nationalism in countries which were conquered by the enemy and which received the most searing proof of their inability to stand alone, the suffering and humiliation of these experiences has had much the opposite effect. Indeed, much of the bitterest resistance to Hitler's forces was called forth not by a devotion to democracy or justice in the abstract but by a devotion to the fatherland when it was in danger. Nationalism is today a far more powerful force than was any loyalty in America to states which had been independent for so short a time and which had never suffered so cruelly at the hands of their neighbors.

449

Yet the American precedent is not a completely discouraging one. There are certain elements—in particular the factor of leadership and the development of common loyalties and experience through participation in earlier and looser forms of co-operation—which are full of hope for the future. In addition, certain influences, such as the amount of international government in actual existence today, the growth of international economic interdependence, the improvement in means of communication and transportation, and the strong popular determination to prevent the recurrence of war, are far more powerful than any corresponding influences in colonial history.

However, these positive forces are confronted by stronger obstacles than the colonists ever had to face, in the form of nationalism, cultural and political diversity, and economic interests which profit from disunion. In particular, it is important to remember that colonial union was the result of a long succession of efforts at intercolonial co-operation, that its growth was gradual, and that modern nations, while engaging in more extensive social and economic co-operation, have had far less *political* co-operation. There has been no tradition of union like that of the colonies under the British empire, and there has been no collective enterprise so intense in character as the fighting of the Revolution. Under the circumstances it would be naïve to suppose that the world is ready for its Constitution; but it is not so fantastic, perhaps, to think that parts of it are getting ready for their Articles of Confederation.[119]

---

[119] Although this article was written in July, 1945 (before the announcement of the invention of the atomic bomb) subsequent events have tended to bear out its conclusions. The fear of the consequences of another war, already the most powerful of the motives for international union today, has been greatly increased by the atomic bomb. Not only has another call for "World Federal Union" been issued by a group of "prominent Americans" meeting at Dublin, New Hampshire, on October 16, but, far more significantly, several influential statesmen have joined the demand for effective world government. In the United States, Captain Stassen has declared that "This new development is one additional powerful reason for developing a new and higher level of Government to serve mankind . . . . The world needed government on a world level before the atomic bomb. Now it has become an imperative." And in Great Britain, official spokesmen for both of the great parties, Ernest Bevin and Anthony Eden, have asked for a real strengthening of the United Nations Organization and for an abatement of "present ideas of sovereignty" as the only solution to the problem created by the atomic bomb.

Yet Eden was obliged to remark that "It is yet true that national sentiment is still as strong as ever, and here and there it is strengthened by this further complication—the differing conceptions of forms of government and differing conceptions of what words like freedom and democracy mean." And it is significant that even the "prominent Americans" at Dublin were divided as to the desirability of an immediate attempt at world union, since a minority of those attending the conference believed that a union should first be formed among "nations where individual liberty exists."

In short, the pressure for union as the only path to security has been enormously increased; but—as the failure of the London conference of foreign ministers indicated in September—even the threat of the atomic bomb has not overcome the basic obstacles of nationalism and a difference in political outlook. See the *New York Times* for October 17 and for November 9, 23, and 24, 1945.

WAYNE LAW REVIEW

VOLUME 4   SPRING, 1958   NUMBER 2

"STATES' RIGHTS" AND THE ORIGIN OF THE SUPREME COURT'S POWER AS ARBITER IN FEDERAL-STATE RELATIONS

John R. Schmidhauser[†]

The ideological content of states' rights doctrine has, over the past century and one half, undergone so fundamental a transformation[1] that a resurrected John Taylor of Caroline probably would cheerfully embrace the nationalistic welfare state. For the modern states' rights philosophy, with its primary objective the protection of vested interests, could hardly be acceptable to a political theorist who sought to defend the rights of the many against political and economic power in the hands of the few.

451

Despite the remarkable changes affecting the purposes of states' rights doctrine in American history, the methods of achieving these purposes have remained essentially the same. Political argument based upon alleged constitutional scruples has been for over sixteen decades the big gun in the states' rights polemical arsenal.

One of the most important of the states' rights constitutional arguments concerns the legitimacy of the Supreme Court's power to render definitive decisions in conflicts between the federal government and the states, or between individuals and states which denied them rights guaranteed by the Federal Constitution. Whether the decisions were those in the notable *M'Culloch* or *Cohens*[2] cases in the early nineteenth century or those of the "Tidelands Oil" or racial segregation cases[3] in the middle of the twentieth century, the consistent states' rights reaction has been to deny that the Supreme Court had constitutional authority to render such decisions.[4] The continued vitality of this old constitutional argument was strikingly illustrated on March 12, 1956, when Senator Walter George introduced a manifesto signed by nineteen Senators and seventy-seven Representatives from the Southern states.[5] The manifesto referred to the Supreme Court's decision in *Brown v. Board of Education*[6] as "judicial usurpation," a substitution of "naked power for

---

[†] Assistant Professor, Department of Political Science, State University of Iowa.
1. Harris, States' Rights and Vested Interests, 15 J. of Politics 457-71 (1953).
2. M'Culloch v. Maryland, 17 U.S. (4 Wheat.) 415 (1819), and Cohens v. Virginia, 19 U.S. (6 Wheat.) 264 (1821), respectively.
3. United States v. Louisiana, 339 U.S. 699 (1950), and Brown v. Bd. of Educ., 347 U.S. 483 (1955), respectively.
4. 1 Warren, The Supreme Court in United States History 487-88, 495 (1937); Dodd, Chief Justice Marshall and Virginia, 1813-1821, 12 Am. Hist. Rev. 782-85 (1907).
5. 102 Cong. Rec. 3948 (1956).
6. 347 U.S. 483 (1955).

established law" and an "unwarranted exercise of power . . . contrary to the Constitution."[7]

Although the supporters of this manifesto made no attempt to formulate serious theoretical or historical arguments to buttress their charge of judicial usurpation, they may properly be considered the intellectual heirs of the constitutional argument of John C. Calhoun. For in advocating the repeal of the twenty-fifth section of the Judiciary Act of 1789, Calhoun unequivocally denied that the framers of the Constitution had chosen the Supreme Court as federal umpire.[8]

The challenges of judicial usurpation of the power to arbitrate in federal-state relations, whether made by a Calhoun or one of his modern successors such as Byrnes or Talmadge, are susceptible to historical examination. The record of history unequivocally demolishes these challenges.

452

The conception of a powerful judicial body maintaining a division of powers between a government of a whole nation and governments of its parts or sections did not appear miraculously to the Justices of the Supreme Court after the adoption of the Constitution. It was clearly understood and partially applied during the period when America was a colony of Great Britain and under the old Articles of Confederation.

The British Empire maintained the fiction that it was a unitary system until after the American Revolution, but the Empire's relationships with the thirteen colonies had, in reality, become essentially federal. The government of the whole Empire, that of Great Britain, had been forced by the pressure of European wars and great distances to leave most problems of domestic legislation and administration to the governments of the "parts" of the Empire, notably the American colonial governments. Naturally enough, the development of local autonomy in the colonies led to conflicts of authority between the mother country and the colonies as well as among the colonies themselves. It was a quasi-judicial institution of the British Empire, the Committee on Trade and Plantations of the British Privy Council, which resolved such conflicts.[9]

After the American colonies broke with Great Britain, a new problem arose, that of balancing the powers of the states and the new central government in North America. A temporary solution was found in the creation of a confederate system. The old Articles of Confederation established a very limited form of judicial arbitration in two narrow fields, the settlement of disputes between the states and the settlement of disputes between the Confederation Congress and the states concerning cases of capture at sea.

The first category of disputes was to be settled in accordance with

---

7. 102 Cong. Rec. 3948 (1956).
8. Discourse on the Constitution and Government of the United States, 1 Works of John C. Calhoun 238 (Cralle ed. 1851).
9. The Committee later became the Board of Trade. Dickerson, American Colonial Government, 1695-1765, at 225 (1912); McLaughlin, The Background of American Federalism, 12 Am. Pol. Sci. Rev. (May 1918).

the ninth article of the Articles of Confederation. This provided that
"the united states in Congress assembled shall also be the last resort on
appeal in all disputes and differences now subsisting or that hereafter
may arise between two or more states concerning boundary, jurisdiction
or any other cause whatever. . . ." The parties to a dispute could be
directed by Congress "to appoint by joint consent, commissioners or
judges to constitute a court for hearing and determining the matter in
question." Or if the disputing parties could not agree, Congress could
itself make the appointments. The article further provided that "the
judgment and sentence of the court . . . shall be final and conclusive. . . ."[10] A serious land dispute was peacefully resolved under this
article in 1782.[11] Yet such a court of arbitration lacked permanence.
Consequently, it was probably the second judicial institution created under the Confederation which was more influential in the evolution of the
judicial arbiter concept in American federalism. For the Court of Appeals in cases of capture was a permanent judicial body which heard
118 cases before the Articles of Confederation were replaced by the new
Federal Constitution. A member of this court, Judge John Lowell, made
the experiences of this judicial body available to the constitutional
framers in 1787 and to the Senate in 1789, sketching a plan for a federal
judiciary in a letter to some of the framers and later, in 1789, giving his
counsel and advice to the Senate Judiciary Committee.[12]

453

During the waning years of the Confederation itself, serious attention was given to various proposals to establish a more powerful central
judiciary capable of putting an end to state encroachments on or defiance
of the authority of the Confederation government. Although these
proposals never were adopted by the Confederation, they do provide
unmistakable evidence that political leaders of this era were fully aware
of the potentialities of a judicial arbiter in confederate or federal governmental systems. A confederation congress committee report, submitted in 1786 by Charles Pinckney, contained, in essence, a complete
arrangement for creation of a federal court capable of umpiring federal-
state disputes. Pinckney's committee suggested that the Confederation
Congress be authorized:

> . . . to institute a federal judicial court for trying and punishing
> all officers appointed by congress for all crimes, offenses, and mis-
> behavior in their offices, and to which court an appeal shall be al-
> lowed from the judicial courts of the several states in all causes
> wherein any question shall arise on the meaning and construction
> of treaties entered into by the United States with any foreign
> power, or on any law of nations, or wherein any question shall arise
> respecting any regulations that may hereafter be made by congress

10. Documents of American History 113 (Commager ed. 1934).
11. Jensen, The New Nation: A History of the United States During the Federation,
1781-1789, at 335-37 (1950).
12. Jameson, The Predecessor of the Supreme Court, in Essays in the Constitutional
History of the United States in the Formative Period, 1775-1789, at 3-44 (1889).

relative to trade and commerce, or the collection of federal revenues pursuant to powers that shall be vested in that body, or wherein questions of importance may arise, and the United States shall be a party. . . .[13]

Similar ideas for strengthening the confederation government through creation of some sort of federal judicial arbiter were formulated or discussed by Rufus King,[14] James Madison,[15] and Nathan Dane.[16] Just prior to the Philadelphia Convention of 1787, however, a significantly different argument was discussed widely. Instead of viewing a federal judicial arbiter as primarily a defender of the central government, a broadly circulated pamphlet proposed that:

> In order to prevent an oppressive exercise of powers deposited with Congress, a jurisdiction should be established to interpose and determine between the individual States and the Federal body upon all disputed points, and being stiled The Equalizing Court, should be constituted and conducted in the following manner. . . .

454

This proposal appeared in the *Pennsylvania Gazette* in Philadelphia on June 6, 1787 and was republished in the leading newspapers during the early days of the Convention.[17] Thus, while supporters of the idea of a strong national government had begun to favor the judicial arbiter concept as a means of restraining the states, those who feared the encroachments of a strong national government had begun to look upon a strong judicial system as a protector of individual and states rights. Recognition of this development makes more understandable the absence of states' rights or anti-Federalist opposition to most of the proposals made in the Convention which strengthened the federal judiciary.

One of the major reasons for holding the Philadelphia Convention had been the necessity to find a remedy for the evils arising from state legislation which hurt or interfered with the interests of other states, infringed treaties made by the Confederation Congress, oppressed individuals, or invaded the sphere of authority of the confederation government. The convention delegates were faced with the task of finding suitable means of restraining such state legislation or action. Despite the fact that the idea of a judicial arbiter was understood and widely discussed before the opening of the Convention, the creation of a high federal court to solve this problem was by no means a foregone conclusion. Years after the close of the Convention, James Madison referred

13. Quoted in 2 Bancroft, History of the Formation of the Constitution, 376-77 (1903).
14. Letter to Jonathan Jackson, September 3, 1786, as quoted by Warren, op. cit. supra note 4, at 5.
15. Letter to George Washington, April 16, 1787, as quoted by Carson, The History of the Supreme Court 88 (1891). Madison deemed the judicial arbiter of secondary importance to a congressional negative of state laws; however, see Rufus King's letter referred to in note 14 supra.
16. Published in the Independent Gazetter, November 30, 1786, as quoted by Warren, The Making of the Constitution 319 (1929).
17. Id. at 169.

to the situation in the following manner: " . . . [T]he obvious necessity of a control on the laws of the States so far as they might violate the Constitution and laws of the United States left no option, but as to mode . . . ," noting as the three possible choices "a veto [executive] on the passage of the State laws, a Congressional repeal of them, a judicial annulment of them."[18]

Analysis of the record of the Philadelphia Convention underscores the fact that the granting of power to the Federal Supreme Court to arbitrate finally in federal-state relations came about through a complex series of developments. Basically they represented a compromise between the strong nationalists who originally wanted a veto over the states vested in the new national legislature or executive and the states' righters who either opposed such supervision of the states or preferred that such power be vested, in what they considered, a weaker and more impartial agency, notably the supreme federal court suggested in the original Paterson Plan.

455

Among the more important of these developments were (a) the repudiation of coercion of the states by force and the adoption of coercion of individuals by law, (b) the readiness of every major bloc in the Convention to set up a federal judiciary, (c) the demands of one powerful group for a system of inferior federal tribunals, (d) the defeat of the congressional negative proposals and the substitution by Luther Martin of a supremacy clause, and (e) the tendency to look upon a federal judiciary as a protector of individual and states rights which was reflected in the proposals for a Council of Revision. Very often these developments seemed totally unrelated, but their cumulative effect was the granting of final interpretive powers in federal-state relations to a supreme federal tribunal.

A provision for a congressional veto of state laws was prominent among the resolutions for the Union presented by Edmund Randolph at the opening session of the Convention. It provided "That the national legislature ought to be empowered . . . to negative all laws, passed by the several States, contravening, in the opinion of the national legislature, the articles of union." Later, on May 31, the Convention, in committee of the whole house, amended it by addition of the phrase "or any treaties subsisting under the authority of the Union." The entire resolution was agreed to by the committee without debate or dissent.[19]   However, when this resolution was reported from the committee to the Convention on July 17, it met with violent opposition. Gouverneur Morris thought such power "likely to be terrible to the States"; Luther Martin considered it improper; and Sherman believed that since the state courts would hold invalid any laws contravening the authority of the Union, such a veto would be unnecessary. Madison and Charles Pinckney did not share Sherman's confidence in the state courts, however, and held

---

18. Letter to Nicholas P. Trist, 1831, as quoted by id. at 318.
19. 1 Records of the Federal Convention 54 (Farrand ed. 1911).

that the congressional negative was necessary as, in the words of Madison, "the most mild and certain means of preserving the harmony of the system." In spite of Madison's appeal, the Convention defeated the proposal for a congressional negative on state laws by a vote of seven to three.[20]

Even before the rejection of the congressional negative by the Convention on July 17, there was clear-cut evidence that the advocates of a strong central government were prepared to limit the congressional negative by providing for final appeal to a national judiciary. As early as July 10, Randolph had sent Madison a list of concessions to be used "as an accommodating proposition to small states" which then were bitterly opposed to the principle of representation based upon population.[21] In terms of the judicial arbiter concept, the fourth and fifth of Randolph's proposals were particularly significant, because they clearly anticipated the Supreme Court's modern role as both a federal umpire and as a defender of individual rights against state infringement. His suggestions provided:

456

> IV.   That although every negative given to the law of a particular state shall prevent its operation, any state may appeal to the national judiciary against a negative, and that such negative if adjudged to be contrary to the powers granted by the articles of the Union, shall be void.
>
> V.   That any individual, conceiving himself injured or oppressed by the partiality or injustice of a law of any particular state, may resort to the national judiciary, who may adjudge such a law to be void, if found contrary to the principles of equity and justice.[22]

Randolph was prepared to offer these conciliatory proposals to the Convention on July 16, but did not do so because of the victory of the small states, on that day, in securing equal voting rights in the Senate.[23]

Throughout the course of the Philadelphia Convention the major discussions of the federal judicial arbiter were generally related to the nationalists' attempts to gain approval for the congressional negative of state laws. However, other discussions in the Convention also contributed to the evolution of the supreme federal tribunal. The proposals for a council of revision, composed of the chief executive and judges of the highest national court, while eventually defeated, stimulated discussion of the power of judicial review.[24] Rejection by the Convention of

---

20. 2 id. at 27-28.
21. 3 id. at 55; see also Brant, James Madison, Father of the Constitution, 1781-1800, at 63-100 (1950).
22. Published in 5 Elliot, Debates of the State Ratifying Conventions 579-80 (1901).
23. 2 Farrand, op. cit. supra note 19, at 17-18.
24. During these debates, Mercer of Maryland unequivocally opposed "the Doctrine that the judges as expositors of the Constitution should have authority to declare a law void." 2 id. at 298-99. Mercer's stand represents the only instance within the Convention of direct opposition to the granting of power to judges (but not a council of revision composed of the judges and the executive) to negative unconstitutional laws. 1 id. at 93-94, 96-97, 138-40 and 2 id. at 73, 76, 298-99.

the proposals to coerce the states by force, contained in both the Randolph and Paterson Plans, were followed by adoption of the principle of direct coercion of individuals by the national government itself. This solution reflected the recognition by Convention leaders of the need to discover a peaceful mode of limiting state interference with national authority.[25] The initiative in finding such a solution was now taken by the leaders of the small states bloc in the Convention, many of whom were of states' rights persuasion.

Using as their starting point a clause from the Paterson Plan guaranteeing the supremacy of the national government within the sphere of its legitimate authority, states' rights supporters attempted to placate the nationalists who were bitterly disappointed by the defeat of the congressional negative proposal on July 17. Luther Martin submitted what he undoubtedly considered a mild substitute for such a negative.[26] His original proposal stated:

457

> ... [T]hat the Legislative acts of the United States made by virtue and in pursuance of the Articles of Union, and all treaties made and ratified under the authority of the United States shall be the supreme law of the respective States, as far as those acts or treaties shall relate to the said states, or their citizens and inhabitants—and that the Judiciaries of the several States shall be bound thereby in their decision, anything in the respective laws of the individual States to the contrary notwithstanding.[27]

Later, the nationalists in the Convention changed this relatively mild resolution in several important respects. These amendments were made in the closing days of the Convention in August and September. On August 5, 1787, the Convention's committee on detail had compressed Martin's resolution and made two significant changes—federal laws were declared supreme over state constitutions as well as state laws, and the duty to uphold the supreme law was imposed on "the Judges in the several States" instead of on "the Judiciaries of the respective states." On August 23, John Rutledge proposed the following important addition: "This Constitution and the laws of the United States made in pursuance thereof . . . shall be the supreme law of the several states."

---

25. 1 id. at 21, 34, 54, 165, 245, 256, 320, 339-40.
26. Later, in his "Reply to the Landholder," March 18, 1788, Martin pointed out, bitterly, that, "When this clause was introduced, it was not established that inferior continental courts should be appointed for trial of all questions arising on treaties and on the laws of the general government, and it was my wish and hope that every question of that kind would have been determined in the first instance in the courts of the respective states; had this been the case, the propriety and the necessity that treaties duly made and ratified, and the laws of the general government, should be binding on the state judiciaries which were to decide upon them, must be evident to every capacity, while at the same time, if such treaties or laws were inconsistent with our [i.e. the state] constitution and bill of rights, the judiciaries of this state would be bound to respect the first and abide by the last, since in the form I introduced the clause, notwithstanding treaties and laws of the general government were intended to be superior to the laws of our state government, were [sic] they should be opposed to each other, yet that they were not proposed nor meant to be superior to our constitution and bill of rights. It was afterwards altered and amended to the form in which it stands in the system now published . . . ." 3 id. at 287.
27. 2 id. at 28-29.

Thus the Constitution was made judicially enforceable law. The Convention adopted his proposal without debate.[28] Finally, on September 12, the committee on style completed the final draft of the Constitution. Luther Martin's resolution had become a part of Article VI. From the point of view of federal-state relations this was the crucial provision in the fundamental document. Section three of that article read:

> This Constitution, and the laws of the United States which shall be made in pursuance thereof; and all treaties made, or which shall be made, under the authority of the United States, shall be the supreme law of the land; and the judges in every state shall be bound thereby, anything in the Constitution or laws or any state to the contrary notwithstanding.

Defeat of the congressional negative plan left the Convention with two institutional alternatives for the enforcement of national supremacy. The first was an ultra-nationalistic suggestion put forth by Alexander Hamilton in his plan for union. Section ten of the plan provided that "all laws of the particular States contrary to the Constitution or laws of the United States to be utterly void; and the better to prevent such laws being passed, the Governour or president of each state shall be appointed by the General Government and shall have a negative upon the laws about to be passed in the state of which he is Governour or President."[29] Hamilton's alternative was not even seriously considered by the Convention. The second was the judicial arbiter which had been an integral part of the original Paterson Plan. Section five had provided "that a federal judiciary be established to consist of a supreme tribunal the judges of which to be appointed by the Executive. . . ." Section two of the same plan proposed that violations of acts of the federal congress be tried in the first instance in "the superior Common Law Judiciary" of the state concerned, "subject . . . for the correction of all errors, both in law and fact . . . , to an appeal to the Judiciary of the United States."[30]

Actually, every major plan for union—Randolph's, Hamilton's and Paterson's—had provided for a national judicial system. The essential difference between the nationalistic plans of Randolph and Hamilton and the states' rights plan of Paterson is that the latter failed to provide a system of inferior federal courts.[31] The nationalists did not actually oppose the adoption of a judicial arbiter, but merely felt, as James Wilson later indicated, that a judicial check on the states would not be sufficient to maintain a strong central government. On August 10, 1787, Charles Pinckney grudgingly admitted that the federal judges "will even be the Umpires between the United States and individual states as well as between one State and another."[32] However, a few days later, on August 23, he tenaciously sought to reinstate the congressional negative, but was

458

28. 2 id. at 389.
29. 1 id. at 293.
30. 1 id. at 243-44.
31. 1 id. at 21, 243-44, 292.
32. 2 id. at 248.

defeated by a six to five vote. In urging support for Pinckney's motion, Wilson recognized impliedly that in the absence of a congressional negative, the national judiciary would seek to maintain the supremacy of the national government. This he felt was not enough because "the firmness of Judges is not of itself sufficient. Something further is requisite—it will be better to prevent the passage of an improper law, than to declare it void when passed."[33]

A letter exchange between Thomas Jefferson and James Madison concerning the relative merits of the congressional negative and the judicial arbiter illustrates clearly the contrasting positions of the states' righters and the nationalists. Although he did not attend the Convention, Jefferson was representative of those who, while they feared establishment of a national government in which all authority would be centralized, realized quite clearly that some degree of centralized control was necessary to bring stability to the then chaotic thirteen states. In his reply to Madison's inquiry concerning a congressional negative on state laws, Jefferson presented a viewpoint which might be taken as indicative of the attitude of other advocates of strictly limited government. He wrote:

459

> The negative proposed to be given them on all the acts of the several Legislatures is now for the first time suggested to my mind. Prima Facie I do not like it. It fails in an essential character, that the hole and the patch should be commensurate; but this proposes to mend a small hole by covering the whole garment. . . . Would not an appeal from the state judicatures to a federal court in all cases where the act of Confederation controlled the question, be as effectual a remedy, and exactly commensurate to the defect?[34]

On the other hand, the advocates of a strong central government, while favoring the granting of broad judicial powers, had realized that judicial nullification of state laws was possible only when federal questions arose in bona fide cases before the new Supreme Court. Madison's letter to Jefferson after the close of the Convention indicated that the lack of assurance he shared with other strong government advocates. He wrote:

> It may be said that the Judicial authority under our new system will keep the states within their proper limits and supply the place of a negative on their laws. The answer is that it is more convenient to prevent the passage of a law than to declare it void, after it is passed; that this will be particularly the case, where the law aggrieves individuals who may be unable to support an appeal against a state to the Supreme Judiciary, that a state which would violate the legislative rights of the Union would not be very ready to obey a Judicial decree in support of them, and that a recurrence to force, which in the event of disobedience would be necessary, is an evil which the new Constitution meant to exclude as far as possible.

---

33. 2 id. at 390-91.
34. To Madison, June 20, 1787, as quoted by Warren, op. cit. supra note 16, at 168-69.

A Constitutional negative on the laws of the states seems equally necessary to secure individuals against encroachments on their rights. The mutability of the laws of the States is found to be a serious evil.[35]

After the final defeat of the congressional negative in the Convention on August 23, the nationalists determined to make the best of an unhappy situation by strengthening the federal arbiter by means of grants of broad constitutional jurisdiction and through institution of a complete system of inferior federal courts. The extension of the Supreme Court's jurisdiction to all cases, state and federal, arising under the Constitution was made without states' rights argument. But the attempt at creation of a system of inferior federal courts aroused such fierce opposition that the nationalists were compelled to accept a compromise by which the establishment of such courts was left to the discretion of the new Congress.[36]

Nationalist bitterness at the substitution of a judicial arbiter for their cherished congressional negative persisted to the end of the Convention. For example, on September 12, James Madison supported a motion by Mason which provided that the clause relating to export duties be amended to allow the states to lay such duties for "the sole purpose of defraying the charges of inspecting, packing, storing and indemnifying the losses in keeping the commodities in the care of public officers before exportation." Gorham and Langdon had asked: "How was redress to be obtained in case duties should be laid beyond the purpose expressed?" Madison coldly replied that "[t]here will be the same security as in other cases—The jurisdiction of the Supreme Court must be the source of redress. So far only had provision been made by the plan against injurious acts of the States. His own opinion was, that this was insufficient,—A negative on the State laws alone could meet all the shapes which these could assume. But this had been overruled."[37]

The Philadelphia Convention record indicates unmistakably that the new Supreme Court had been clearly designated the final judicial arbiter in federal-state relations and that it was primarily the states' righters in the Convention who had brought this to pass. The nationalists had not opposed the creation of the judicial arbiter, but had felt strongly that a national judiciary would not, by itself, be strong enough to cope with state encroachments on national authority.

In spite of their misgivings, the advocates of strong central government did not let lack of confidence in a federal judiciary weaken their efforts to secure ratification of the Constitution. Two of the contributions to the *Federalist* by Madison and Hamilton were devoted to an examination of the proposed judicial arbiter, its purposes and its impartial character.[38] Within the state ratifying conventions, the national-

35. To Jefferson, October 24, 1787, as quoted by id. at 324.
36. Id. at 326, 334-38.
37. 2 Farrand, op. cit. supra note 19, at 588-89.
38. The Federalist No.'s 39 & 80, at 238, 494-95 (Lodge ed. 1904).

ists frequently found themselves the staunchest defenders of the same judicial arbiter for which they had indicated only luke-warm enthusiasm during the Philadelphia Convention; for serious states' rights objections were raised to certain provisions of the judicial clauses in the new Constitution, notably those concerning the possible establishment of a system of inferior federal courts and those extending federal jurisdiction to suits between a state and individuals.[39] In five of the more important of the state ratifying conventions—Connecticut,[40] North Carolina,[41] Virginia,[42] Pennsylvania,[43] and South Carolina[44]—the new Supreme Court's function of resolving state and federal conflicts was discussed clearly and ultimately was accepted. In virtually all of the ratifying conventions some jurisdictional grants to the new federal court system were subjected to severe criticism. Out-and-out opponents of the Constitution, such as Robert Yates of New York, recognized the scope of the Supreme Court's power and made the judicial grants a major point for attack on the proposed new system of government. Under the pseudonym of "Brutus," Yates wrote that "the opinions of the Supreme Court . . . will have the force of law; because there is no power provided in the Constitution that can correct their errors or control their jurisdiction. From this court there is no appeal."[45] But in the end, the nationalists managed to secure early ratification in all of the most important states.

461

These facts stand out as a result of this analysis of the Philadelphia Convention and the state ratifying conventions. Both the nationalists and the states' righters were in substantial agreement on the need for a supreme judicial arbiter in federal-state relations. By 1789 it was clearly understood that the Supreme Court of the United States was to fulfill that role. Naturally enough, the nationalists tended to emphasize the aspect of judicial arbitership concerned with the protection of national supremacy against state encroachments. However, both nationalists and states' righters explicitly recognized that the Supreme Court's role was that of an *impartial* arbiter. Thus, it was also anticipated that federal laws violative of states' rights were to be declared unconstitutional. The prevailing contemporary conception of the new Supreme Court's role is best illustrated by Oliver Ellsworth's description in the Connecticut Ratifying Convention of January, 1788:

> This Constitution defines the extent of the powers of the general government. If the general legislature should at any time overleap their limits, the judicial department is a constitutional check. If the United States go beyond their powers, if they make a law which the Constitution does not authorize, it is void; and the

39. Willoughby, The Supreme Court 20-21 (1890).
40. 2 Elliot, op. cit. supra note 22, at 196.
41. 4 id. at 155.
42. 3 id. at 532.
43. 2 id. at 408-09, 439-40, 445-46, 468-69, 478, 480-81.
44. 4 id. at 257-58.
45. As quoted by Davis, Annulment of Legislation by the Supreme Court, 7 Am. Pol. Sci. Rev. 577 (Nov. 1913).

judicial power, the national judges, who, to secure their impartiality, are to be made independent, will declare it to be void. On the other hand, if the states go beyond their limits, if they make a law which is a usurpation upon the general government, the law is void; and upright, independent judges will declare it so.[46]

On March 4, 1789, the wheels of the new central government began to turn; but for eleven months after the United States came into existence, it lacked a judicial branch of government. Although the first judiciary bill was introduced the very next day after the new Senate was organized, it was six months before the bill became law and before President Washington could appoint members to the first Supreme Court.[47]

While the constitutional framers had drawn the broad outlines of the judicial power, they had left to congressional discretion the composition of the federal courts, the extent of the appellate jurisdiction of the Supreme Court, the existence or nonexistence of any inferior federal courts and the extent of their jurisdiction. Consequently, the manner in which the first Congress dealt with these problems in the Judiciary Act of September 24, 1789, set the pattern for subsequent development of the federal judicial system. This act was especially important because without broad grants of appellate jurisdiction to the Supreme Court by Congress, the entire judicial arbiter plan would have fallen into abeyance for lack of implementation.

The first judiciary act was largely the product of the Senate Judiciary Committee, and within the committee, Oliver Ellsworth and William Paterson took leading roles in drafting the bill. In the early stages of this drafting, Ellsworth sought to establish a complete network of inferior federal courts and to extend their jurisdiction to the limits set by the Constitution. However, to secure the concurrence of Richard Henry Lee, Ellsworth apparently had to accept a more limited inferior federal court system. This setback was mitigated by inclusion of a provision which allowed a defendant sued in a state court in a case involving a federal question to remove the case to a federal circuit court, or to appeal to the Supreme Court, by writ of error, after trial in the highest court of law or equity in a state in which a decision in the suit could be had.[48]

When debate on the draft bill began in the Senate in committee of the whole, on June 22, the issue centered around the question whether there should be any district courts at all or whether the functions of executing federal laws should be left in the first instance to the state courts. Ellsworth had been opposed to giving the state courts such power on the grounds discussed in a letter he wrote later on the subject. He felt that "to annex to State Courts jurisdiction which they had not before, as of admiralty cases, and perhaps, of offenses against the

462

---

46. 2 Elliot, op. cit. supra note 22, at 196.
47. Warren, The First Decade of the Supreme Court of the United States, 7 U. Chi. L. Rev. 631 (1940).
48. Warren, New Light on the History of the Federal Judiciary Act of 1789, 37 Harv. L. Rev. 49 (1923).

United States, would be constituting the Judges of them, *pro tanto*, Federal Judges, and of course they would continue such during good behavior, and on fixed salaries, which in many cases, would illy comport with their present tenure of office. Besides, if the State Courts, as such, could take cognizance of those offenses, it might not be safe for the General Government to put the trial and punishment of them entirely out of its own hands."[49]

Debate over the various proposals in the bill raged for three months in the Senate and the House. The crucial issues were whether there should be any inferior federal courts, and, if there were to be any such courts, whether the Constitution required that they be vested with the full jurisdiction which the Constitution permitted. In its final form the bill was a compromise. The nationalists were forced to abandon their contention that the federal courts be granted the broadest jurisdiction possible under the Constitution, while the states' righters were unable to confine federal cases to state courts, subject only to final appeal to the new federal Supreme Court. Section twenty-five, which became the very cornerstone of federal judicial supremacy, established the appellate jurisdiction of the Supreme Court over state courts where such courts decided against a claimed federal right. Significantly, the states' righters in Congress actually advocated this crucial grant of jurisdiction in 1789.[50]

463

In sum, the modern states' rights charges of federal "judicial usurpation" of power to arbitrate in federal-state relations may be viewed as a particularly persistent bit of political mythology. For examination of the Philadelphia Convention, the state ratifying conventions, and the legislative history of the first judiciary act indicates unmistakably that the framers clearly intended that the Supreme Court be given responsibility for umpiring the federal system,[51] that the federal judicial arbiter was

49. To Law, August 4, 1789 as quoted by Warren, id. at 66.
50. Id. at 102-05.
51. For arguments in opposition to this interpretation see Harris, Judicial Review in the United States of America, 56 Dick. L. Rev. 177 (1952), and 2 Crosskey, Politics and the Constitution, at 1008-1046 (1953). Harris alleged that the constitutional framers denied to the Supreme Court the power of judicial review. His account of the Philadelphia Convention is, however, inaccurate because it overlooks a great deal of evidence contradicting his thesis and misinterprets major developments in rather startling fashion. Professor Crosskey's position may be summed up as follows: With a single exception, "Our *entire* record of what was said on the subject of judicial review, in the Federal Convention, consists of parts of James Madison's notes . . . since the man in question was not . . . a very credible witness on this particular subject, the possibility that his testimony may have been, not inadvertently, but deliberately, false and misleading . . . is one that cannot lightly be passed over . . . ." Later Crosskey asserted that "apart from Madison's own notes, [there is] virtually no known evidence relating to the Convention which even vaguely suggests" the view that the Supreme Court was granted power to act as an "ultimate guardian" between the nation and the states. (2 Politics and the Constitution at 1009-10.)

Madison's reliability as a recorder of the proceedings of the Philadelphia Convention remains unshaken by Crosskey's attack at least with regard to his notes relating to the judicial powers. For even if one were to disregard Madison's notes on the evolution of the judicial arbiter in federal-state relations, the letters and public statements of opponents (such as Luther Martin and Robert Yates), and supporters (such as Charles Pinckney, James Wilson, Alexander Hamilton, William Davie and Oliver Ellsworth) indicated unmistakably a conception of the judicial arbiter similar to Madison's. (See notes 26, 40-44

understood and accepted by the more important of the state ratifying conventions, and that appellate jurisdiction necessary for the fulfillment of its responsibilities was granted the Supreme Court by the first Congress.

Ironically, it was the states' righters of that era—the anti-Federalists —who were largely responsible for the acceptance of the judicial arbiter in the Philadelphia Convention. Similarly, they strongly supported its implementation in the first Congress. Later their basic assumption, gloomily shared by many nationalists, that the federal judicial arbiter would be a rather mild check on state authority proved to be false. And later, the confidence of the states' righters in the impartiality of the Supreme Court was shaken, particularly during the tenure of Chief Justice John Marshall. But during the formative period, 1786-1789, both the states' righters and the nationalists, the former with confidence, the latter with grave misgivings, had accepted the new Supreme Court as the arbiter in federal-state relations.

464

---

supra.) Significantly, all of these individuals were, like Madison, members of the Philadelphia Convention.

REVOLUTIONARY ORIGINS OF THE SOUTH'S CONSTITUTIONAL DEFENSES

By David L. Smiley*

"The American Revolution, with its foreign and future consequences," James Madison declared in 1790, "is a subject of such magnitude that every circumstance connected with it, more especially
every one leading to it, is already and will be more and more a matter
of investigation." For that reason he regarded the proceedings in
Virginia during the Stamp Act crisis a quarter-century earlier as
peculiarly significant. Information about those events, he said, was
"a sort of debt due from her contemporary citizens to their successors."
He asked elder statesman Edmund Pendleton, therefore, to write out
his recollections of the Stamp Act resolves of 1765—"by whom and how
the subject commenced in the Assembly; where the resolutions proposed by Mr. Henry *really* originated; what was the sum of the arguments for and against them, and who were the principal speakers on
each side." [1]

Madison's interest in 1790 in the background to the Revolution
was no idle antiquarian speculation. Expressed when Congress was
debating the question of state debt assumption, and only a few months
prior to adoption of the Virginia Resolutions on that subject, it was
an implied recognition of the continuity of constitutional arguments
in America. As Madison came to realize, there were fundamental
similarities between the legal defenses employed to justify opposition
to Acts of Parliament in the Revolutionary generation and those heard

465

---

* Dr. Smiley is professor of history at Wake Forest University, Winston-Salem.
This paper was read at a meeting of the Southern Historical Association in Richmond, Virginia, November 18, 1965.
  [1] Madison to Pendleton, April 4, 1790, in Gaillard Hunt (ed.), *The Writings of
James Madison* (New York: G. P. Putnam's Sons, 9 volumes, 1900-1910), VI, 9-10,
hereinafter cited as Hunt, *Writings of James Madison.* Compare the opinion of the
editor of the *Times* (London): "The rebels or patriots of 1772 [*sic*] invoked rights
and asserted principles which could not fail to be serviceable to any rebels or patriots
of future times." Noting that the Revolutionaries of 1776 searched diligently through
Puritan histories seeking the "forms of revolution," he said that "the Seceders of the
present day may turn to the records of the American Revolution with far greater
success. . . . We think the Seceding States might appeal with some plausibility in
defense of their proceedings to the precedents of the Revolutionary War. . . ."
Times (London, England), May 24, 1861, hereinafter cited as *Times* (London).

under the Constitution in supporting resistance to national legislation. Though it would be years before James Madison used constitutional contentions with which he had become familiar in 1776, others were already renewing the struggle.

As the timing of Madison's request to Pendleton indicated, the Virginia Assembly's response to the Stamp Act in 1765 and to the assumption of state debts in 1790 offered an example of such continuity. In the earlier year Patrick Henry's resolutions marked the prologue to the Revolution; twenty-five years later the same man's resolutions, addressed to a similar grievance and couched in comparable language, sounded the alarm which initiated a new conflict over constitutional interpretation and expressed a philosophy which in the nineteenth century became characteristically southern. Far from being original in their efforts to circumvent a hostile majority, the apologists for southern rights from 1790 to 1860 were but adapting a constitutional mechanism which had served Americans once before. The intellectual preparation and legal vindication of resistance in the War for American Independence supplied the origins of the Old South's constitutional rationale. The leaders of the Revolution evolved a set of constitutional principles which patriots in all parts of the country could accept as a means of preserving human liberty, and these same principles were adapted by a sectional minority in defense of states' rights and southern institutions, including slavery. This shift in attitudes was a significant development in American thought.

Those impassioned southerners who chose secession in 1860 were fully aware of the similarities between their actions and those of the Revolutionary patriots. As they saw themselves, they were but following in the footsteps of the Founding Fathers. A New Orleans editor contended that "the Confederate States are acting over again the history of the American Revolution of 1776."[2] The South Carolina Convention of 1860 declared that the South stood "exactly in the same position toward the Northern States that our ancestors did toward Great Britain,"[3] and a delegate to that convention evoked patriotic emotions when he shouted that "the tea has been thrown overboard; the Revolution of 1860 has begun."[4] Even volunteer versifiers, answer-

---

[2] *Daily Picayune* (New Orleans, Louisiana), hereinafter cited as *Daily Picayune*, in Frank Moore (ed.), *The Rebellion Record* (New York: G. P. Putnam and D. Van Nostrand, 11 volumes and supplement, 1861-1868), II, 252.

[3] "Address of the People of South Carolina, Assembled in Convention, to the People of the Slaveholding States of the United States," in *Journal of the Convention of the People of South Carolina* (Columbia, S.C.: Gibbes, 1862), 467-476. The quotation is on page 468.

[4] Quoted in Alan Barker, *The Civil War in America* (Garden City, N.Y.: Doubleday and Company, Inc., 1961), 93.

ing the call to the colors with poetry, often bad, sang of the resemblances between 1776 and 1860. As one expressed it:

> Yes, call them rebels! 'tis the name
> Their patriot fathers bore,
> And by such deeds they'll hallow it,
> As they have done before.[5]

But for all their proud assumption of the patriots' mantle, the nineteenth century defenders of local autonomy would have strengthened their case had they known and followed Madison's injunction to study carefully the coming of the American Revolution. Every one of their constitutional arguments had its counterpart in the Revolutionary quarrel with Britain. Even the editor of the London *Times*, with an ill-concealed malicious glee, noted the comparisons clearly. The North had a good case, but it was "surprisingly like the cause of England," he said. "By substituting the words 'British Empire' for 'American Union' we shall get very nearly the case of George III and his ministers." Defenders of the Union had not advanced a single argument against secession, he asserted, "which could not have been employed with equal justice by Lord North."[6]

In spite of the proud southern recognition and the somewhat spiteful English corroboration of the similarities between 1776 and 1860, there were basic differences between the two American "secessions" and the two civil wars for independence. Beyond the fact that each historical event is unique, perhaps the most obvious disparity was the difference between the constitutions to which each group appealed. The British Constitution and the United States Constitution were alike in that each was susceptible to different interpretations so that each side in both conflicts could clothe itself in the garments of legality. But the nebulous nature of the British Constitution as compared to the definite written instrument of 1787 made the tasks of the Revolutionary generation more difficult. Though they remained convinced that they were preserving ancient English rights granted under a specific and long-established Constitution against the perversions of a tyrannical King and Parliament, ultimately the 1776 rebels reduced their emphasis upon the Constitution in favor of an equally nebulous doctrine

467

---

[5] *Daily Picayune*, May 26, 1861, quoted in E. Merton Coulter, *The Confederate States of America, 1861-1865*, Volume VII of *A History of the South*, edited by Wendell Holmes Stephenson and E. Merton Coulter (Baton Rouge: Louisiana State University Press [projected 10 volumes, 1948—], 1950), 60.
[6] *Times* (London), May 24, 1861. For a dissenting view of the two rebellions, see George Fitzhugh, "The Revolutions of 1776 and 1861 Contrasted," in *Southern Literary Messenger*, XXXVII (November and December, 1863), 718-726.

of "natural rights" as their primary defense. There were other important differences. Changes in communications, in values, and in personalities contributed unique characteristics to each event.

Still, stripped of their superficial trappings, the two sets of American rebels gave considerable substance to the observations of the London editor. The constitutional bases of both civil wars were arguments which displayed similar verbiage if not always exactly comparable meanings. Each contended that legitimate governments were compacts between principals; that certain legislation had violated fundamental charters—the products of compact agreements—and was therefore null and void; that local governments were supreme in their political spheres and could judge the actions of the general government in the light of the fundamental law; and that any change in the essentially federal nature of government was destructive of human liberty. Considered broadly, even the grievances voiced in the two rebellions—tariffs or commercial regulation, taxation, home rule and individual rights, and the control of western territory—demonstrated a startling similarity. Constitutional theorists and publicists in both camps, confronted with a hostile majority whether in the British Parliament or in the United States Congress and the Electoral College, fell back upon arguments and devices which had much in common.

Each group began with the compact theory of government. The colonials, utilizing European political writers such as John Milton and John Locke, James Harrington and Algernon Sidney, had long asserted the contractual nature of the state. To the Puritans it was but the extension of covenant Calvinism into the secular sphere. "It is of the nature and essence of every society," John Winthrop declared, "to be knitt together by some Covenant, either expressed or implyed." [7] Similar views appeared in the Mayflower Compact, the Fundamental Orders of Connecticut, and in the frontier charters such as that of Watauga. Patrick Henry, in his argument—or that of his biographers— in the Parson's Cause, extended the compact idea to include the colony's connection with Britain. [8] James Otis declared that "the form and mode of government is to be settled by *compact*," and Samuel Adams was sure that "whatever Government in general may be founded in, Ours was manifestly founded in Compact." [9] In 1776 the

468

---

[7] Quoted in Edmund S. Morgan, *The Puritan Dilemma: The Story of John Winthrop* (Boston: Little, Brown & Company, 1958), 93.

[8] William Wirt, *The Life of Patrick Henry* (Hartford, Connecticut: S. Andrus and Son [Tenth Edition], 1850), 46-47.

[9] James Otis, *The Rights of the British Colonies Asserted and Proved* (Boston: n.p. [Third Edition, Corrected], 1766), 22; this pamphlet is reprinted in Charles F. Mullett, "Some Political Writings of James Otis," *University of Missouri Studies*, IV (July 1, 1929), 45-101. Harry A. Cushing (ed.), *The Writings of Samuel Adams* (New York: G. P. Putnam's Sons, 4 volumes, 1904-1908), I, 29, hereinafter cited as Cushing, *Writings of Samuel Adams*.

Continental Congress was therefore on familiar ground when it declared that governments were instituted among men, "deriving their just powers from the consent of the governed." [10]

The compact theory of government was a part of the Americans' heritage from the eighteenth century, and they continued it in the process by which the state conventions ratified the Constitution of 1787. That method of approval, together with the fact that the Constitution itself established a government partly national and partly federal, made the compact idea a fundamental defense in later opposition to national legislation. "By compact under the style and title of a Constitution for the United States," ran Jefferson's classic statement in 1798, "they constituted a general government for special purposes. . . . To this compact each State acceded as a State, and is an integral party, its co-States forming, as to itself, the other party." [11]

In Jefferson's verbal footsteps followed other publicists who found acts of national legislation distasteful. Defined as an agreement between coeval states united in a league or confederation, the phrase "compact theory" rolled easily off the tongues of southern leaders. In 1831 John C. Calhoun declared that "the Constitution of the United States is, in fact, a compact, to which each State is a party." [12] And in a Senate speech in 1860 Jefferson Davis demonstrated the tenacity of the idea: "the States were the grantors," he said; "they made the compact; they gave the Federal agent its powers." [13] So close were the theoretical connections between the two revolutions that in 1798 Jefferson could assert that he had not departed from the principles he followed in 1775, and in 1831 Calhoun could claim that he was true to the republican spirit of 1798. [14]

If the compact idea gave continuity to a set of constitutional arguments, in other aspects of the minority's defenses the nineteenth cen-

469

---

[10] *Journals of the Continental Congress* (Washington: Government Printing Office, 34 volumes, 1904-1937), V, 510, hereinafter cited as *Journals of the Continental Congress*. See Andrew C. McLaughlin, "Social Compact and Constitutional Construction," *American Historical Review*, V (April, 1900), 467-490, for an argument that the idea of compact underwent a change in meaning between 1776 and 1860.

[11] "The Kentucky Resolutions of 1798," in Saul K. Padover, *The Complete Jefferson* (New York: Duell, Sloan and Pearce, 1943), 128-129.

[12] Richard K. Crallé (ed.), *The Works of John C. Calhoun* (New York: Appleton, 6 volumes, 1853-1855), VI, 60, hereinafter cited as Crallé, *Works of Calhoun*. See also Calhoun's statement in the *South Carolina Exposition*, quoted in Crallé, *Works of Calhoun*, VI, 36.

[13] Jefferson Davis, *The Rise and Fall of the Confederate Government* (New York: Appleton, 2 volumes, 1881), I, 585, hereinafter cited as Davis, *Rise and Fall*.

[14] Jefferson to Samuel Smith, August 22, 1798, in Henry Augustine Washington (ed.), *The Writings of Thomas Jefferson* (Washington: Taylor & Maury, 9 volumes, 1853-1854), IV, 254; Calhoun to Christopher Van Deventer, August 5, 1831, in J. Franklin Jameson (ed.), *Correspondence of John C. Calhoun* (Washington: Government Printing Office [*Annual Report of the American Historical Association for the Year 1899*, Volume II], 1899), 296.

tury drew heavily upon Revolutionary pamphleteers. Upon the premise of the compact theory, expanded to include the local government's relationship to the general, both groups defined their union as a
federal one of political members possessing certain features of sovereignty. Federalism, the idea that there were two levels of government, one general and the other local, lay at the roots of Colonial
resistance to Parliament. However real may have been the economic
pressures, the heady content of the intellectual currents sweeping out
of Enlightenment Europe, or the popular demands for social change,
Colonial American spokesmen were careful to express their opposition
to British legislation in constitutional and federal terms.[15]

The defenders of Colonial rights asserted that their charters granted
them legislative supremacy over their internal matters. "By this Charter," said Samuel Adams in Massachusetts, "we have an exclusive
Right to make Laws for our own internal Government and Taxation."
Distance rendered it impractical for Americans to be represented in
Parliament, he continued, speculating that it was "very probable that
all subordinate legislative powers in America, were constituted upon
the Apprehension of this Impracticability."[16] The American governments, Massachusetts' Governor Francis Bernard confirmed, "claim to
be perfect states, not otherwise dependent upon Great Britain than by
having the same king."[17] Rhode Island's Governor Stephen Hopkins,
defining the Empire as a federal union, declared that "each of the
colonies hath a legislature within itself, to take care of its Interests...
yet there are things of a more general nature, quite out of reach of
these particular legislatures, which is necessary should be regulated,
ordered, and governed."[18]

Colonial opposition to imperial taxation brought forth only an
immediate manifestation of a prior belief in a federal Empire. The
Massachusetts House of Representatives, in a debate with Governor

470

[15] Daniel J. Boorstin, *The Genius of American Politics* (Chicago: University of
Chicago Press, 1953), Chapter III. In Chapter IV Professor Boorstin argues, in
general terms, the continuity of constitutional thought between the Revolution and the
Confederacy. See also Thad W. Tate, "The Coming of the Revolution in Virginia:
Britain's Challenge to Virginia's Ruling Class, 1763-1776," *William and Mary
Quarterly*, XIX (July, 1962), 323-343, for an argument that constitutional issues
combined with a threat to Virginia's power structure brought on revolution—a thesis
which might apply with equal force to the Confederates. Additional interpretive
matter on this point is in R. G. Adams, *Political Ideas of the American Revolution*
(New York: Facsimile Library, 1939) and Charles F. Mullett, *Fundamental Law
and the American Revolution, 1760-1776* (New York: Columbia University Press,
1933).
[16] Cushing, *Writings of Samuel Adams*, I, 29.
[17] Quoted in Claude H. Van Tyne, *The Causes of the War of Independence* (Boston:
Houghton Mifflin, 1922), 218.
[18] Quoted in Alfred H. Kelly and Winfred A. Harbison, *The American Constitution*
(New York: W. W. Norton, 1948), 69-70.

Bernard over the Stamp Act, asserted "that the charter of this province invests the General Assembly with the power of making laws for its internal government and taxation"—obviously taking its language from Samuel Adams.[19] Perhaps the clearest Colonial statement of federalism appeared in the Declaration and Resolves of the First Continental Congress. In an appeal based upon "the immutable laws of nature, the principles of the English constitution, and the several charters or compacts," they petitioned for redress of grievances "as Englishmen their ancestors in like cases have usually done." They declared that the foundation of English liberty was the right of popular participation in government. Since they could not properly be represented in the British Parliament, they asserted their right to a "free and exclusive power of legislation in their several provincial legislatures, where their right of representation can alone be preserved, in all cases of taxation and internal polity, subject only to the negative of their sovereign, in such manner as has heretofore been used and accustomed." But at the same time they would "cheerfully consent" to Parliamentary regulation of external commerce. In these resolutions the Continental Congress explicitly stated its view of the Empire as a federal, rather than a unitary, political organization.[20]

471

The states' rights dogma, characteristically a fundamental element in the Old South's constitutional defenses, thus had roots in Revolutionary thought. Though most southern spokesmen went no further back than the Constitutional Convention of 1787, a few recognized the Colonial origins of American federalism. Governor Littleton W. Tazewell of Virginia was one who did. "In their colonial state, they constituted several distinct Societies, whose affairs were regulated by governments absolutely independent of each other," he said. "In throwing off their former governments they did not dissolve their former associations—the Societies remained, after the governments were no more." The Declaration of Independence, Tazewell declared, "far from proclaiming that they were One People or One Nation, in its own terms declared them to be free and Independent States."[21]

---

[19] Alden Bradford (ed.), *Speeches of the Governors of Massachusetts from 1765 to 1775* (Boston: Russell and Gardner, 1818), 45, quoted in Edmund S. Morgan and Helen M. Morgan, *The Stamp Act Crisis: Prologue to Revolution* (Chapel Hill: University of North Carolina Press, 1953), 101, hereinafter cited as Morgan, *Stamp Act Crisis*.

[20] *Journals of the Continental Congress*, I, 67-69. For a discussion of the implications of the Declaration and Resolves, see Charles H. McIlwain, *The American Revolution: A Constitutional Interpretation* (New York: Macmillan Company, 1923; and Ithaca: Cornell University Press, 1958), 114-137.

[21] Littleton W. Tazewell, *A Review of the Proclamation of President Jackson of the 10th of December, 1832* (Norfolk, Virginia: J. D. Ghiselin, 1888), 53. See also Crallé, *Works of Calhoun*, I, 188-193.

Other opponents of national power also called upon the pre-Revolutionary past to justify their present contentions. James Madison, a youthful participant in the Revolution, saw the continuity between Colonial theory and states' rights under the Constitution. "The fundamental principle of the Revolution was, that the Colonies were co-ordinate members with each other and with Great Britain, of an Empire united by a common executive sovereign, but not united by any common legislative sovereign," he said in 1800. "The legislative power was maintained to be as complete in each American Parliament, as in the British Parliament. . . . A denial of these principles by Great Britain, and the assertion of them by America," Madison concluded, "produced the Revolution."[22] In 1844 Robert Barnwell Rhett praised the sense of independence "which prompted our ancestors to enter the field in 1776," and said the same spirit would make southerners "warm now, and watchful, to resent every assault upon the province of our local government and from whatever quarter it may come."[23]

472

Building upon the conviction that local governments were supreme in their own domains, the next step in the minority's defense was to assert the limited nature of the general government. In placing limitations upon the legislative powers of their unions, both groups urged a strict construction of their constitutions. The claim that the British constitution put limits upon the powers of Parliament appeared frequently in the quarrel with the mother country. It was heard in Virginia in 1753, when the Assembly declared that "the Rights of the Subject are so secured by Law, that they cannot be deprived of the least Part of their Property, but by their own Consent: Upon this excellent Principle is our Constitution founded."[24] In Massachusetts Samuel Adams could become quite academic in expounding the idea of constitutional limitations. "If then according to Lord Coke, *Magna Charta* is declaratory of the principal grounds of the *fundamental* laws and liberties of the people, and Vatel is right in his opinion, that the supreme legislature cannot change the constitution," he wrote, "I think it follows, whether Lord Coke has expressly asserted it or not, that an act of Parliament made against *Magna Charta* in violation of its essential parts, is void."[25]

[22] Hunt, *Writings of James Madison*, VI, 373.
[23] *Mercury* (Charleston, S.C.), August 1, 1844, quoted in William R. Taylor, *Cavalier and Yankee* (New York: George Braziller, 1961), 265. In "The Spirit of '76," 262-270, Professor Taylor discusses efforts of South Carolinians to relate themselves to the Revolutionary patriots.
[24] Quoted in David J. Mays, *Edmund Pendleton, 1721-1803* (Cambridge: Harvard University Press, 2 volumes, 1952), I, 76, hereinafter cited as Mays, *Edmund Pendleton*.
[25] Cushing, *Writings of Samuel Adams*, II, 325-326.

Other Colonial leaders agreed that the British Constitution placed limits upon Parliament and thereby substantiated their claims to English political rights. John Rutledge of South Carolina assured the First Continential Congress that "our claims, I think, are well founded on the British Constitution." And to the same gathering Joseph Galloway of Pennsylvania said that he had sought the basis of American rights "in the constitution of the English government, and there found them. We may draw them from this source securely." [26]

British taxation of their American colonies brought forth the most vigorous appeals to the Constitution. The Virginia Assembly attacked the Stamp Act as contrary to a "fundamental principle of the British Constitution, without which Freedom can no Where exist." [27] The Massachusetts House of Representatives went even further. "It by no means appertains to us to presume to adjust the boundaries of the power of Parliament; but boundaries there undoubtedly are," its members declared. "We beg leave just to observe that the charter of this province invests the General Assembly with the power of making laws for its internal government and taxation, and that this charter has never yet been forfeited." [28] In a protest to the Townshend Acts the Massachusetts House resolved that "In all free states, the constitution is fixed; it is from thence, that the legislative derives its authority; therefore it cannot change the constitution without destroying its own foundation." [29] Samuel Adams defined the Townshend duties as "Infringements of their natural and constitutional Rights," and James Otis expressed the opinion that "there are Limits, beyond which if Parliaments go, their Acts bind not." [30]

473

With these constitutional appeals as precedents, after 1789 it was easy for the opponents of national legislation to continue the tradition. In 1790 the Virginia delegates could "find no clause in the constitution authorizing Congress to assume the debts of the states," and a decade later asserted "the authority of constitutions over governments, and . . . the sovereignty of the people over constitutions." [31] Thomas Jef-

---

[26] Quoted in Mays, *Edmund Pendleton*, I, 287-288. See also Andrew C. McLaughlin, *The Foundations of American Constitutionalism* (New York: New York University Press, 1932), 140-142, hereinafter cited as McLaughlin, *Foundations of American Constitutionalism*.

[27] Mays, *Edmund Pendleton*, I, 158.

[28] Quoted in Morgan, *Stamp Act Crisis*, 101.

[29] Massachusetts House to the Earl of Shelburne, January 15, 1768, in Alden Bradford (ed.), *Massachusetts State Papers*, reprinted in Henry S. Commager, *Documents of American History* (New York: Appleton-Century-Crofts [Fourth Edition], 1948), 65, hereinafter cited as Commager, *Documents*, as a convenient source for pertinent materials.

[30] Cushing, *Writings of Samuel Adams*, I, 184-185, reprinted in Commager, *Documents*, 66; Otis quoted in Morgan, *Stamp Act Crisis*, 140.

[31] "Virginia Resolutions on Debt Assumption," in W. W. Hening (ed.), *Statutes at*

ferson regarded it as axiomatic that acts of the general government not specifically granted in the constitution were without authority.[32] Into the nineteenth century the minority, whether in New England after 1801 or later in the South, insisted upon retaining the letter of the Constitution as the preserver of their liberties. John C. Calhoun, who had learned his constitutional theory in Tapping Reeve's law school in Litchfield, Connecticut, in the days of Federalist eclipse, based his complicated minority-defense mechanism upon the Constitution, which he declared had established a federal union of sovereign entities. To prevent the dread alternatives of centralization or disunion, he set himself the objective "that the government of the United States should be restored to its federal character. Nothing short of a perfect restoration," he said, "as it came from the hands of its framers, can avert them."[33] After Calhoun many others, including Jefferson Davis and Alexander H. Stephens, employed similar arguments. Their thinking, however, was original not so much in their basic premises as in their adaptation of a well-defined Revolutionary constitutional interpretation to meet their contemporary needs.[34]

474

In their appeal to the Constitution the colonials anticipated an idea later celebrated as the doctrine of state interposition. In 1771 Samuel Cooper said of the people of Boston that "the greater Part have a settled persuasion . . . that our Parliament here ought to come between the sovereign and the American subject, just in the same Manner that the British Parliament does with respect to the British subject. . . ."[35] Nineteen years later, when the Virginia delegates opposed the assumption of state debts, they declared themselves the "guardians then of the rights and interests of their constituents, as sentinels placed by them over the ministers of the federal government, to shield it from their encroachments." Twenty-seven years later, when the Virginians objected to the Alien and Sedition Acts, they declared that the states "have the right and are in duty bound to interpose for arresting the

Large of Virginia (Richmond: Printed for the editor at Franklin Press, 13 volumes, 1819-1823), XIII, 238, hereinafter cited as Hening, Statutes. The resolutions also appear in Commager, Documents, 155. The "Virginia Report of 1800," is in Hunt, Writings of James Madison, VI, 352.

[32] Dumas Malone, Jefferson and the Ordeal of Liberty, Volume III of Jefferson and His Time (Boston: Little, Brown [projected multivolume work, 1948—], 1962), 403-404, hereinafter cited as Malone, Jefferson and the Ordeal of Liberty.

[33] Margaret L. Coit, John C. Calhoun, American Portrait (Boston: Houghton Mifflin, 1950), 42. The quotation is in Crallé, Works of Calhoun, I, 381. For a study of differences between Madison's and Calhoun's concepts of the Union, see Edward S. Corwin, "National Power and State Interposition, 1787-1861," Michigan Law Review, X (May, 1912), 535-551.

[34] Davis, Rise and Fall; Alexander H. Stephens, A Constitutional View of the Late War Between the States (Philadelphia: National Publishing Co., 2 volumes, 1868).

[35] Samuel Cooper to Thomas Pownall, November 14, 1771, in Frederick Tuckerman (ed.), "Letters of Samuel Cooper to Thomas Pownall, 1769-1777," American Historical Review, VIII (January, 1903), 325.

progress of the evil. . . ."[36] Under the Constitution the defense ma-
neuver of state interposition to protect the citizens from outside encroachments was an important aspect of the South's particularistic
philosophy, but it had roots in the earlier debate with Britain.

Along with interposition went the claim that a state had the power
to judge the constitutionality of national legislation and to nullify
within its borders measures which a strict reading of the fundamental
law did not justify. Usually regarded as having its beginnings in the
South Carolina Nullification Convention of 1832, or in Calhoun's
Exposition of 1828, or even in the Kentucky Resolutions of 1799, the
doctrine of nullification had its counterpart in the prologue to the
Revolution. However often the colonials may have nullified commercial measures by smuggling, it was the Stamp Act which brought from
them statements of the constitutional idea of nullification.

The Stamp Act was the first British effort to tax the colonists directly, so it was an open challenge to American constitutional theories.
Though Colonial agents and assemblies petitioned against the measure, they had no vote in Parliament. Subjected to the legislation of
an unfriendly majority, they fell back upon constitutional defenses.
Patrick Henry, a newcomer to the Virginia House of Burgesses, introduced a set of resolutions designed to nullify the act within the province. The right of the people to determine their own taxes, he said,
"is the only security against a burdensome taxation, and the distinguishing characteristick of British freedom, without which the ancient
constitution cannot exist." According to tradition, one of his resolutions included the assertion that the Virginians were "not bound to
yield obedience" to an unconstitutional law.[37]

Colonial response to Henry's resolutions was important not only in
the coming of the Revolution but also in later constitutional defenses.
Regardless of what actually happened in the Virginia House in May,
1765—and the truth may never be known—the doctrine of nullification
spread rapidly in newspaper accounts. Upon publication of the Virginia "Resolves," groups in other colonies endorsed them and issued
statements often bolder in tone. The Sons of Liberty in Portsmouth,
New Hampshire, for example, declared that the Stamp Act violated
fundamental rights of British subjects and was "Therefore void of all
Lawfull Authority, so that depending upon Meer Force it may Law-

475

---

[36] "Virginia Resolutions on Debt Assumption," in Hening, *Statutes*, XIII, 238;
"Virginia Resolutions of 1798," in Hunt, *Writings of James Madison*, VI, 326,
and reprinted in Commager, *Documents*, 182-183. See also the *South Carolina Exposition*, in Crallé, *Works of Calhoun*, VI, 55-57.
[37] "Virginia Stamp Act Resolves," in Morgan, *Stamp Act Crisis*, 91-92, and also in
Commager, *Documents*, 56. For confusion over the resolves, see Morgan, *Stamp Act
Crisis*, 89-94.

fully be oppos'd by Force."[38] The Northampton County Court in Virginia asserted that "the said act did not bind, affect or concern the inhabitants of this colony, in as much as they conceive the same to be unconstitutional. . . ."[39] The Rhode Island Assembly appealed for resistance to the Act and directed the colony's officials to ignore it.[40] John Adams in Massachusetts defined the Act as "utterly void, and of no binding Force upon us."[41] With their leaders expressing such views, Colonial mob violence effectively nullified the offending Act. Non-importation agreements and the Continental Association intended similar treatment for other British imperial actions.

From these beginnings the doctrine of nullification emerged as a weapon of the minority under the Constitution. As Madison's 1790 letter to Edmund Pendleton implied, there was a close theoretical relationship between Patrick Henry's resolutions on the Stamp Act and his remarks on the assumption of state debts. A few years later, when the Alien and Sedition Acts extended the powers of the federal judiciary to include common law jurisdiction in criminal cases, Thomas Jefferson wanted his state to declare that the "acts are, and were ab initio, null, void, and of no force or effect." The 1799 Kentucky Resolutions made it explicit that the states "being sovereign and independent, have the unquestionable right to judge of the infraction," and that a "nullification" of the offending measures "is the rightful remedy." It was on the basis of these precedents, reaching back to pre-Revolutionary ideas, that John C. Calhoun recommended that South Carolina could constitutionally nullify a tariff measure.[42]

Thus, from compact theory and strict construction to nullification and secession, there were close similarities between the constitutional defenses of both the Revolutionary generation and the planter-politicians of the Old South. In both cases, when men judged the power at the center to be too great, they declared the compact to be broken. And in each instance they employed similar devices to correct the errors they decried. Each, acting upon constitutional premises, sought to block the majority by a literal interpretation of the fundamental law; each solemnly declared "unconstitutional" legislation to be null and void. When their petitions failed to bring redress, each turned to secession and a movement for independence as the means of preserv-

---

[38] Quoted in Morgan, *Stamp Act Crisis*, 203.
[39] Quoted in McLaughlin, *Foundations of American Constitutionalism*, 126n, and in Commager, *Documents*, 59.
[40] Morgan, *Stamp Act Crisis*, 98-99.
[41] Morgan, *Stamp Act Crisis*, 140.
[42] Malone, *Jefferson and the Ordeal of Liberty*, 407; Crallé, *Works of Calhoun*, VI, 159. See also Chauncey S. Boucher, *The Nullification Controversy in South Carolina* (Chicago: University of Chicago Press, 1916), 33, 105-106.

ing—or of restoring—constitutional liberties. Given the opportunity to draw up a frame of government according to their own standards, each group—one in the Articles of Confederation of 1781 and the other in the Confederate Constitution of 1861—closely copied what it imagined or desired the original constitution to be.

The close agreement between the two sets of constitutional defenses did not mean that the nineteenth-century defenders of the plantation and slavery possessed more patriotism or longer memories than did their northern opponents. It did suggest that they, like their eighteenth-century predecessors, were in a minority. It meant that in the Anglo-Saxon tradition there had developed an orthodox process by which a minority could protect itself:[43] Any group of leaders, powerful in its own region but a minority in the larger political unit, immediately adopted a program to restrict the majority's actions. It contained the ideas of local sovereignty, or federalism; strict construction of the Constitution which bound the union together; the doctrines of sentinelship and interposition; nullification; and secession. Against these minority defenses the majority in both cases also followed a recognizable pattern of action: national sovereignty, loose construction of the Constitution, and the coercion of rebellious or dissident elements.

There were other reasons, apart from the Anglo-Saxon tradition of constitutionalism, which lay behind the southern emulation of Revolutionary opinions. The rural nature of the planters' society, and their insistence upon clinging to a Colonial economy and an outdated labor system, made them sensitive to outside criticisms. Outstripped in the population race and with the frontier closed by what they regarded as "natural limits" to slavery expansion,[44] they emphasized the federal aspects of the Union as a means of preserving their regional way of life. But more important was a continuity of leadership which served as a bridge between the two American rebellions. The same men— Patrick Henry, Thomas Jefferson, and James Madison, among others— appeared as contributors in the formulation of both constitutional defenses. Memories of the methods of one revolutionary era served as guideposts for another, and subsequent southern leaders adopted the weapons and philosophy of government of an older generation. In 1800, when Madison attacked the claim that a law could be "binding on these States as one society" as a doctrine "evidently repugnant to the fundamental principle of the Revolution,"[45] he was but trans-

477

---

[43] See John C. Calhoun, *Address to the People of South Carolina*, in Crallé, *Works of Calhoun*, VI, 136, 139, for evidences of minority sentiment. For a discussion of the Anglo-Saxon tradition of rebellion, see Roy F. Nichols, "1461-1861: The American Civil War in Perspective," *Journal of Southern History*, XVI (May, 1950), 143-160.
[44] Charles W. Ramsdell, "The Natural Limits of Slavery Expansion," *Mississippi Valley Historical Review*, XVI (September, 1929), 151-171.
[45] Hunt, *Writings of James Madison*, VI, 374.

mitting a minority constitutional defense from the Revolutionary generation to its successors.

478

The Concept of a Perpetual Union

KENNETH M. STAMPP

THE American Civil War, whatever else it may have been, was unquestionably America's most acute constitutional crisis. Viewed from this perspective, the fundamental issue of the war was the locus of sovereignty in the political structure that the Constitution of 1787 had formed. Did this document create a union of sovereign states, each of which retained the right to secede at its own discretion? Or did it create a union from which no state, once having joined, could escape except by an extra-constitutional act of revolution? In a Constitution remarkable for its ambiguity on many substantive matters, none was more fateful than its silence on this crucial question. Even the Articles of Confederation, which the nationalists despised, were unequivocal in defining the Union of the states. Their title was "Articles of Confederation and Perpetual Union," and Article XIII stipulated that their provisions "shall be inviolably observed by every state, and the Union shall be perpetual. . . ." Whether the incorporation of these words in the Constitution of 1787 would have been sufficient to prevent the crisis of 1861–1865 is problematic, but at the very least we would have been spared the prolix and convoluted debate over the legality of secession.

479

In returning to the old controversy about the nature of the Union, I am not, of course, exploring one of the neglected problems of American history. The evolution of the doctrine of state sovereignty, from the protests against Alexander Hamilton's economic program to the southern movement for secession, has been thoroughly examined.[1] The growth of American nationalism in the nineteenth century has also been the subject of numerous studies.[2] However, one aspect of nationalist

This essay, in an abridged form, was delivered as the presidential address of the Organization of American Historians at New York, April 13, 1978. Kenneth M. Stampp is the Morrison Professor of American History in the University of California, Berkeley.

[1] In addition to the numerous special studies of these constitutional crises, the evolution of the state-rights and secessionist arguments can be traced in Jesse T. Carpenter, *The South as a Conscious Minority, 1789–1861: A Study in Political Thought* (New York, 1930).

[2] For background see Paul C. Nagel, *One Nation Indivisible: The Union in American Thought, 1776–1861* (New York, 1964) and Alpheus Thomas Mason, "The Nature of Our Federal Union Reconsidered," *Political Science Quarterly*, LXV (Dec. 1950), 502–21.

thought—the origin of the concept of a perpetual union and of the complex argument that supported it—has received surprisingly little critical analysis and is not, I think, very well understood. Since the Union's perpetuity was rather firmly established at Appomattox and has rarely been disputed since, this antebellum topic of debate lacks the urgency of a still relevant political issue. Nevertheless, it is worth noting that the unionist case was sufficiently flawed to make it uncertain whether in 1865 reason and logic were on the side of the victors—indeed, whether, in the tangled web of claims and counterclaims, they were indisputably on either side.

480

Lacking an explicit clause in the Constitution with which to establish the Union's perpetuity, the nationalists made their case, first, with a unique interpretation of the history of the country prior to the Philadelphia Convention; second, with inferences drawn from certain passages of the Constitution; and, third, with careful selections from the speeches and writings of the Founding Fathers. The historical case begins with the postulate that the Union is older than the states. It quotes the reference in the Declaration of Independence to "these united colonies," contends that the Second Continental Congress actually called the states into being, notes the provision for a perpetual Union in the Articles of Confederation, and ends with the reminder that the preamble to the new Constitution gives as one of its purposes the formation of "a more perfect Union." In 1869, when the Supreme Court, in *Texas* v. *White*, finally rejected as untenable the case for a constitutional right of secession, it stressed this historical argument. The Union, the Court said, "never was a purely artificial and arbitrary relation." Rather, "It began among the Colonies. . . . It was confirmed and strengthened by the necessities of war, and received definite form, and character, and sanction from the Articles of Confederation."[3] Abraham Lincoln, in his first inaugural address, summarized this part of the unionist case most succinctly:

[We] find the proposition that, in legal contemplation, the Union is perpetual, confirmed by the history of the Union itself. The Union is much older than the Constitution. It was formed in fact, by the Articles of Association in 1774. It was matured and continued by the Declaration of Independence in 1776. It was further matured and the faith of all the then thirteen States expressly plighted and engaged that it should be perpetual, by the Articles of Confederation of

[3] *Texas* v. *White*, 7 Wall. 700 (1869) at 724–25.

1778. And finally, in 1787, one of the declared objects for ordaining and establishing the Constitution, was *"to form a more perfect union."*[4]

In the secessionists' interpretation of history, the states are older than the Union—in fact, they created the Union, but without yielding any part of their sovereignty. According to South Carolina's secession convention, the colonies in 1776 had declared "that they are, and of right ought to be, FREE AND INDEPENDENT STATES." The quotation is inaccurate, of course, for it substitutes "they" for "these united colonies." Similarly, the South Carolina convention ignored the reference in the Articles of Confederation to a perpetual Union, but it made the most of Article II: "each State retains its sovereignty, freedom and independence, and every power, jurisdiction and right which is not . . . expressly delegated. . . ."[5] Both Lincoln and the Supreme Court left this article unexplained.

481

As a matter of logic, however, the long debate over the state of the Union prior to 1787 was rather pointless, because the action of the Constitutional Convention made it irrelevant to any convincing case for or against a perpetual union. When the Confederation Congress agreed that the states should send delegates to the Philadelphia Convention, it stipulated that the "sole and express purpose" was to revise the Articles of Confederation. The revisions, or amendments, were to be submitted to the state legislatures for ratification, each requiring unanimous consent. But the delegates ignored their instructions, wrote an entirely new Constitution, and specified ratification by specially elected state conventions rather than by the legislatures. Most important, they abandoned the requirement that ratification be unanimous. Instead, when nine states had approved, the Constitution would at once become operative for them, leaving any states that declined to ratify outside and independent.

By these acts, the Philadelphia Convention made the historical argument for perpetuity invalid, because the Convention and the ratifying states destroyed the existing Union. Every state had the option

[4] Roy P. Basler, Marion Dolores Pratt, and Lloyd A. Dunlap, eds., *The Collected Works of Abraham Lincoln* (8 vols., New Brunswick, N.J., 1953), IV, 265. Abraham Lincoln's historical case for a perpetual Union is amplified and affirmed in Curtis Putnam Nettels, "The Origin of the Union and of the States," *Proceedings of the Massachusetts Historical Society*, LXII (1963), 68–83.

[5] Frank Moore, ed., *The Rebellion Record: A Diary of American Events* (12 vols., New York, 1861–1868), I, 3–4.

of *not* ratifying, and as many as four might have remained independent (as two did for a time) while the other nine entered a new union.[6] The result of this dismantling of the "perpetual" union created by the Articles of Confederation is a break in historical continuity. The preamble to the Constitution, be it noted, does not propose to make the old Union more perfect but to "*form* a more perfect Union"—that is, to create a new and better one.

That the old Union would be dissolved was acknowledged occasionally at the Philadelphia Convention, in the state ratifying conventions, and during the public debates. James Madison, in one of his contributions to *The Federalist*, agreed that if some states refused to ratify, "no political relation can subsist between the assenting and dissenting States," but he hoped for "a speedy triumph over the obstacles to *re-union*."[7] In Philadelphia, Elbridge Gerry of Massachusetts, stressing the disunion implicit in requiring ratification by only nine states, "urged the indecency and pernicious tendency of dissolving . . . the solemn obligations of the articles of confederation." He warned that if nine of the thirteen states could abolish the old Union, six of the nine might just as easily abolish the new.[8] At the North Carolina ratifying convention, William Lenoir accused the authors of the Constitution of dissolving the Union and foresaw the possibility that at some future time "it may be thought proper, by a few designing persons to destroy [the new Union] . . . in the same manner that the old system is laid aside."[9] In Pennsylvania, antifederalist Robert Whitehill objected that "it never was in the contemplation of any man" that the delegates to Philadelphia "were authorized to dissolve the present union "[10] However, George Clymer, a Federalist, insisted that the Confederation Congress could not prevent the states from entering the new Union "separately and independently" if they wished.[11] Indeed, Thomas Fitzsimons believed that the proposed Constitution "presupposes . . . that no Confederation exists."[12]

Some Federalists, attempting to escape responsibility for destroying the old Union, claimed that it already had been destroyed by the failure

---

[6] One might argue that for a time in 1788 two unions existed. The first nine states to ratify formed a new union, while the other four (New York, Virginia, North Carolina, and Rhode Island) remained in the old union under the Articles of Confederation.

[7] Jacob E. Cooke, ed., *The Federalist* (Cleveland, 1961), 298. Italics added.

[8] Max Farrand, ed., *The Records of the Federal Convention of 1787* (4 vols., New Haven, 1937), II, 561.

[9] Jonathan Elliot, ed., *The Debates in the Several State Conventions on the Adoption of the Federal Constitution* (5 vols., Philadelphia, 1861), IV, 203.

[10] Merrill Jensen, ed., *The Documentary History of the Ratification of the Constitution* (2 vols., Madison, Wisc., 1976–   ), II, 394.

[11] *Ibid.*, 86.

[12] *Ibid.*, 89.

of certain states to respect their obligations under the Articles of Confederation. Madison charged that state violations of the Articles "had been numerous and notorious." Considering the Union as "analogous . . . to the conventions among individual states," he believed "that a breach of any one article, by any one party, leaves all the other parties at liberty to consider the whole convention as dissolved. . . ."[13] In the South Carolina legislature, Charles Cotesworth Pinckney argued that the old compact "had been repeatedly broken by every state in the Union; and . . . when the parties to a treaty violate it, it is no longer binding. This was the case with the old Confederation; it was virtually dissolved. . . ."[14] James Iredell of North Carolina asserted that the failure of several states to comply with the requisitions of Congress meant that the "Articles of Confederation are no longer binding."[15] John Jay contended that no union in fact existed and that none would exist until the Constitution was ratified. Meanwhile, the states were not only without money or credit but also "without Union, without Government."[16]

483

Arguments such as these might have relieved the Founding Fathers of responsibility for abolishing the old Union; but those who advanced these arguments were playing a dangerous game, for they were explaining to posterity how even a perpetual union might be dissolved. As a matter of fact, the secessionists of 1860–1861 used precisely this logic to justify their action. Oliver Ellsworth of Connecticut, concerned about the consequences, told the delegates at Philadelphia that he "could not admit the doctrine that a breach of (any of) the federal articles could dissolve the whole. It would be highly dangerous not to consider the Confederation as still subsisting."[17] But in avoiding that trap, Ellsworth, in effect, simply placed the onus of terminating the old Union on his fellow delegates. Either way, the break in historical continuity undermines the case for a perpetual union based on the country's political condition before 1787. Hence, the only relevant arguments are those derived from the language of the Constitution and from the statements of the Founding Fathers about their intentions.

When they turned to the Constitution for supporting evidence, the nationalists were confronted with the problem of ambiguity. At one

[13] Farrand, *Records of the Federal Convention of 1787*, I, 314–15.
[14] Elliot, *Debates in the Several State Conventions*, IV, 308.
[15] *Ibid.*, 230.
[16] John Jay, "An Address to the People of the State of New-York On the Subject of the Constitution, Agreed upon at Philadelphia," Paul Leicester Ford, ed., *Pamphlets on the Constitution of the United States, Published During Its Discussion by the People, 1787-1788* (Brooklyn, 1888), 83.
[17] Farrand, *Records of the Federal Convention of 1787*, I, 335.

point during the Philadelphia Convention, a Committee of Detail had
before it a number of draft resolutions, one of which, written by Charles
Pinckney of South Carolina, contained the provision of the Articles of
Confederation that "the Union shall be perpetual."[18] However, the
subject was never brought before the general body for discussion.
Apparently the Articles, which guaranteed the states their sovereignty
and independence, could speak boldly of perpetuity; but the Founding
Fathers, who endowed the federal government with substantial power,
thought such language too risky. Perhaps they also found it slightly
embarrassing to declare their intention to build a new perpetual union
on the wreckage of the old.

Eventually those who developed the case for perpetuity claimed that
the equivalent of the wording in the Articles had been incorporated into
the preamble of the Constitution—that is, in its stated aim "to form a
more perfect Union." As Lincoln argued in his first inaugural address,
"if destruction of the Union, by one, or by a part only, of the States, be
lawfully possible, the Union is *less* perfect than before the Constitution,
having lost the vital element of perpetuity."[19] The Supreme Court found
the preamble decisive on this point: "It is difficult to convey the idea of
indissoluble unity more clearly than by these words. What can be indissoluble if a perpetual Union, made more perfect, is not?"[20] But
Lincoln and the Court, by linking the Articles and the preamble, were
again assuming continuity, and my contention is that there was no
continuity—that the aim announced in the preamble is not to strengthen
the old Union but to form a new, "more perfect Union." Therefore, a
valid case for perpetuity cannot lean on the terms of the Articles but
must demonstrate that it is clearly articulated in the Constitution itself.

Taken alone, the language of the preamble fails to solve the problem
of ambiguity, for the phrase "a more perfect Union" does not
inescapably evoke the idea of a perpetual union. It is more than a
mere metaphysical quibble to question whether, in a political system,
perpetuity is a necessary attribute of perfection. Before 1861, many
thoughtful people in all sections understood a perfect union to be one to
which the citizens of each state belong by their own consent, and they
regarded a union held together by military force as decidedly less than

---

[18] *Ibid.*, II, 134–36; Charles C. Tansill, ed., *Documents Illustrative of the Formation of the
Union of the American States* (Washington, 1927), 964–66; Max Farrand, *The Framing of the
Constitution of the United States* (New Haven, 1913), 71–72; [Andrew C. McLaughlin] "Sketch
of Pinckney's Plan for a Constitution, 1787," *American Historical Review*, IX (July 1904),
735–47.

[19] Basler, Pratt, and Dunlap, *Collected Works of Abraham Lincoln*, IV, 265.

[20] *Texas* v. *White*, 7 Wall. 700 (1869); at 725.

perfect. In 1814, Joseph Lyman of Massachusetts contended that a "Union founded upon submission is the Union of slaves."[21] Years later, a southern editor opined that the term *union* "implies voluntary association" and that "a compulsory compact . . . would cease to be a Union, and would become a despotism."[22] As late as 1861, this alternative concept of perfection still troubled some northern Unionists.

Apart from the preamble, the body of the Constitution contains its own ambiguities. Clearly, some delegates to the Philadelphia Convention wanted to take from the states every vestige of sovereignty and create a consolidated national government. The Virginia Plan would have denied the states equal representation in either branch of Congress, endowed Congress with power to veto the acts of state legislatures, and authorized federal military coercion of any state that failed to fulfill its duties. A few delegates would have gone further and either abolished the states or converted them into mere administrative districts. But these were the very issues on which the nationalists suffered their most severe defeats. The rejection of the veto power in the Virginia Plan and the provision for equal representation of all states in the Senate, together with the subsequent adoption of the Tenth Amendment, preserved the principle of state sovereignty to some indeterminate degree. Thus, as Alpheus T. Mason observes, the nationalists had failed "to stave off what they thought would vitiate the nationalizing features of the new system." They had protested that equal representation "would infect the new government with the same disease that plagued the Articles," for it "would make the states a constituent part of the national government," thus permeating it with "the very infirmity which the new system was designed to correct. . . ."[23]

In the end, "We the People," in whose name the Constitution was framed, created a union of states—to be sure, a union with the powers of the federal government significantly augmented and the powers of the states curtailed, but a union rather than a consolidated nation nonetheless. Only uncertainty about which states would ratify prevented the delegates from writing the preamble to read "We the People of the States of New Hampshire, Massachusetts, Rhode Island," etc., rather than "We the People of the United States."[24] Moreover, Article VII

485

[21] Samuel Eliot Morison, *The Life and Letters of Harrison Gray Otis: Federalist 1765-1848* (2 vols., Boston, 1913), II, 188.
[22] New Orleans *Bee*, Jan. 22, 1861, quoted in Dwight Lowell Dumond, ed., *Southern Editorials on Secession* (New York, 1931), 410.
[23] Alpheus Thomas Mason, *The States Rights Debate: Antifederalism and the Constitution* (Englewood Cliffs, 1964), 46.
[24] Farrand, *Framing of the Constitution*, 190-91.

declares that "The Ratification of the Conventions of nine States, shall be sufficient for the Establishment of this Constitution between the States [not the people of the states] so ratifying the Same." Following this article, a concluding statement compounds the ambiguity: "Done in Convention by the Unanimous Consent of the States present. . . ."

Needless to say, the defenders of state sovereignty suffered their own damaging defeats. They lost equal state representation in the House of Representatives. The portentous "supreme law of the land," "necessary and proper," and treason clauses, as well as the requirement that state officers take an oath of allegiance to the federal Constitution, were powerful weapons in the hands of nationalists in subsequent years. But none of these provisions is fatal to the logic of the case for state sovereignty. For example, secessionists could argue that the Constitution is the "supreme law" and that state officers take an oath of allegiance only so long as their state chooses to remain in the Union. Nationalists made much of the fact that popularly elected state conventions, not the legislatures, ratified the Constitution, but secessionists could contend that what the sovereign people of a state had done they could also undo. To quote Alpheus T. Mason again, "What emerged from this often ambiguous interplay was a document no less ambiguous. The Constitution reflects the conflicting influences and drives of latter-day Federalists and Antifederalists alike."[25]

In truth, the wording of the Constitution gives neither the believers in the right of secession nor the advocates of a perpetual union a case so decisive that all reasonable persons are bound to accept it. Lincoln, in his first inaugural address, offered the most persuasive constitutional argument for perpetuity ever devised, but at the same time he virtually

[25] Mason, *States Rights Debate*, 55. See also Alpheus Thomas Mason and Richard H. Leach, *In Quest of Freedom: American Political Thought and Practice* (Englewood Cliffs, 1959), 110–14. Other constitutional historians who stress the ambiguity of the document include Homer Carey Hockett, *The Constitutional History of the United States* (2 vols., New York, 1939), I, 260–62, II, 255–56; and Alfred H. Kelly and Winfred A. Harbison, *The American Constitution: Its Origins and Development* (New York, 1963), 143–46, 212–13. "In summary," Alfred H. Kelly and Winfred A. Harbison conclude, "it is clear that the Convention did not make a decisive disposition of the locus of sovereignty in the new union." *Ibid.*, 143. For the more common view that the Constitution clearly establishes a perpetual union, see Edward S. Corwin, "National Power and State Interposition, 1787–1861," *Michigan Law Review*, X (May 1912), 535–51; Andrew C. McLaughlin, *A Constitutional History of the United States* (New York, 1935), 214–19, 438–39; Bernard Schwartz, *A Commentary on the Constitution of the United States: The Powers of Government* (New York, 1963), 30–37; Edward Dumbauld, *The Constitution of the United States* (Norman, Okla., 1964), 59–60; and Clinton Rossiter, *1787: The Grand Convention* (New York, 1966). According to Clinton Rossiter, "The Constitution . . . put the stamp of irrevocable legitimacy on the three great legacies of 1776: independence, republicanism, and union. From these three commitments there could now be no turning back. . . ." *Ibid.*, 261–62. Historically, of course, this statement is accurate, but I am unable to find such clarity in either the Constitution or the debates over ratification.

conceded that the language of the document is not conclusive. "Perpetuity," he said, "is *implied*, if not expressed, in the fundamental law of all national governments. It is safe to assert that no government proper, ever had a provision in its organic law for its own termination." Lincoln then tried to place the burden of proof on the secessionists, claiming that they could not destroy the Union "except by some action not provided for in the instrument itself."[26] Unfortunately, the secessionists could argue with equal plausibility that Lincoln could not preserve the Union except by some action whose constitutionality would also be in doubt.

Because of the ambiguities of the Constitution, those who built the case for perpetuity eventually turned to the debates at the Philadelphia convention for explanations and amplification. Instead, they found baffling inconsistencies and obscurities. The delgates never engaged in a discussion that produced a clear consensus that the Union formed by the Constitution was to have perpetual life; nor did they arrive at an understanding about the related matter of federal options if one or more states should attempt secession. To be sure, Madison later recalled that "It appeared to be the sincere and unanimous wish of the Convention to cherish and preserve the Union of the States."[27] But that was merely a pious wish shared by federalists and antifederalists alike, not an interpretation of agreements reached in formal debates. Some delegates did hint at the idea of a perpetual union circuitously—for example, when they agreed that the government was to operate on the people directly rather than through the states, and when they decided to circumvent the state legislatures and secure ratification "by the supreme authority of the people themselves."[28] Occasionally a delegate expressed a general purpose, unrelated to any specific clause in the Constitution, that might give comfort to future nationalists. Thus, Gerry of Massachusetts asserted that "we never were independent States, were not such now, and never could be. . . . The States and the advocates for them were intoxicated with the idea of their *sovereignty*."[29] George Read of Delaware called for a national government that would be strong enough to obliterate the states, one that would "soon of necessity swallow them all up."[30]

However, sentiments such as these usually were expressed in support of proposals that were rejected and therefore do not elucidate the

487

[26] Basler, Pratt, and Dunlap, *Collected Works of Abraham Lincoln*, IV, 264–65. Italics added.
[27] *Letters and Other Writings of James Madison* (4 vols., Philadelphia, 1867), I, 344.
[28] Farrand, *Records of the Federal Convention of 1787*, I, 122–23.
[29] *Ibid.*, 467.
[30] *Ibid.*, 136.

Constitution as adopted. For example, Madison favored a congressional veto of state legislation in order to ''controul the centrifugal tendency of the States; which, without it, will continually fly out of their proper orbits. . . .'' He also urged strong federal authority over the state militias, because ''the greatest danger is that of disunion of the States.''[31] Neither power was granted. At another time, Madison spoke eloquently against the coercion of a state by federal military power lest it ''be considered by the party attacked as a dissolution of all previous compacts by which it might be bound.''[32] This was not the only occasion when Madison seemed to give comfort to both perpetualists and secessionists.

During the Philadelphia debates, several delegates viewed the prospect of secession quite philosophically, offering neither a federal remedy nor a doctrine of perpetuity. Rufus King, speculating about circumstances that might cause the southern states to secede, concluded that they would always be in a position to say, ''do us justice or we will separate.''[33] Because the country was so large, Nathaniel Gorham of Massachusetts doubted that it would ''150 years hence remain one nation.''[34] William Blount of North Carolina predicted privately that in ''not many Years'' the states would be ''distinct Governments perfectly independent of each other.''[35]

Most arresting is the contribution that George Mason made to the mechanics of secession, should it ever be attempted. Mason opposed referring the Constitution to state legislatures for ratification, ''because succeeding Legislatures having equal authority could undo the acts of their predecessors; and the National Govt. would stand in each State on the weak and tottering foundation of an Act of Assembly.''[36] For this reason, he favored ratification by the people through state conventions. Of course, the logic of this argument leads to the conclusion that succeeding state conventions, having equal authority, could undo the work of their predecessors—precisely what the secessionists of 1860–1861 believed. Thus, delegates to the Philadelphia convention, in effect, explained both what proved to be the principal justification for

[31] *Ibid.*, 165, II, 388.
[32] *Ibid.*, I, 54. James Madison explained that his purpose in urging federal control of state militias and federal power to veto acts of state legislatures was to avoid the necessity of military coercion of a state. But after the Constitution failed to grant these powers, Madison's warning remained on the record: that the alternative, coercion, might cause a state to dissolve its connection with the Union.
[33] *Ibid.*, 596.
[34] *Ibid.*, II, 221.
[35] *Ibid.*, IV, 71.
[36] *Ibid.*, II, 88.

secession (violations of the compact) and the method by which it might be accomplished (through a state convention).

The debates over ratification in the state conventions and in the press merely heightened the uncertainty about whether secession was a reserved right of the states. In a general evaluation of the debates, Alpheus T. Mason observes that "strategic considerations drove the contestants on both sides to minimize and exaggerate. To quiet the fears of opponents, advocates of ratification said things which, in later years, proved embarrassing to themselves and misleading to scholars."[37] Some Federalists stated clearly and openly their belief that the Union was to be perpetual and that the federal government would have sufficient power to prevent secession. George Washington, in his letter transmitting the Constitution to Congress, declared that the goal that the convention had "kept steadily in . . . view" was "the consolidation of our Union."[38] Jay, in *The Federalist*, affirmed that "the great object" of the convention was to "preserve and perpetuate" the Union.[39] In the Massachusetts convention, several delegates maintained that the federal government would be able to protect the Union from the acts of "designing and refractory states."[40] In South Carolina, Federalist Charles Cotesworth Pinckney urged his countrymen to "consider all attempts to weaken this Union, by maintaining that each state is separately and individually independent, as a species of political heresy. . . ."[41]

489

However, most Federalists cautiously confined such opinions to their private correspondence or evaded the issue altogether. Blunt assertions that ratification was a perpetual commitment were hardly calculated to convert the doubtful and might even lose some supporters; hence, the Federalists were decidedly more intent on giving assurances that the states would retain their sovereignty. The declaration by John Dickinson of Delaware that the Union would be "a confederacy of republics . . . . in which, the sovereignty of each state was equally represented," was by no means uncommon.[42] In their formal resolutions of ratification, the state conventions merely agreed to "assent to, and ratify" the Constitution; none acknowledged that it was entering a perpetual Union. Seven states demanded a constitutional amendment explicitly declaring,

[37] Alpheus Thomas Mason, "The Federalist—A Split Personality," *American Historical Review*, LVII (April 1952), 627. See also Mason, "The Nature of Our Federal Union Reconsidered," 502–21.
[38] Tansill, *Documents Illustrative of the Formation of the Union*, 1003.
[39] Cooke, *Federalist*, 12.
[40] Elliot, *Debates in the Several State Conventions*, II, 35. See also *ibid.*, IV, 59–60, 187–88.
[41] *Ibid.*, IV, 301.
[42] Ford, *Pamphlets on the Constitution*, 205.

in the words of the Massachusetts resolution, "that all Powers not expressly delegated . . . are reserved to the several States, to be by them exercised." Virginia's convention affirmed "that the powers granted under the Constitution being derived from the People of the United States may be resumed by them whensoever the same shall be perverted to their injury or oppression. . . ."[43] The New York and Rhode Island conventions, attempting to reassure those with lingering doubts, adopted a similar resolution.

Several prominent Federalists made substantial contributions to *both* sides of the debate between nationalists and advocates of state sovereignty. At the Pennsylvania ratifying convention, even so rugged a nationalist as James Wilson, having one day affirmed that "the bonds of our Union ought . . . to be indissolubly strong," could another day assure the timid that "those who can ordain and establish may certainly repeal or annul the work of the government. . . ."[44]

Madison urged the delegates to the Philadelphia Convention to give the federal government sufficient power to prevent a dissolution of the Union. When he learned that the New York convention might reserve the right to withdraw from the Union if certain constitutional amendments were not adopted, his private advice to Hamilton was unequivocal: "My opinion is that a reservation of a right to withdraw . . . is a *conditional* ratification, that it does not make N. York a member of the New Union. . . . The Constitution requires an adoption *in toto*, and *for ever*. . . . In short any *condition* whatever must viciate [sic] the ratification."[45]

In contrast, Madison's contributions to *The Federalist* sound no such warning of a perpetual commitment; rather, they dwell on the theme that the states will retain much of their sovereignty. Ratification, he explains, "is to be given by the people, not as individuals composing one entire nation; but as composing the distinct and independent States to which they respectively belong. . . . Each State . . . is considered as a sovereign body independent of all others, and only to be bound by its own voluntary act. In this relation then the new Constitution will . . . be

[43] Tansill, *Documents Illustrative of the Formation of the Union*, 1009–59, 1018, 1027. The North Carolina convention proposed an additional amendment: "That Congress shall not declare any state to be in rebellion without the consent of at least two-thirds of all the members present of both houses." *Ibid.*, 1049.

[44] Jensen, *Documentary History of the Ratification*, II, 383, 478.

[45] Harold C. Syrett and Jacob E. Cooke, eds., *The Papers of Alexander Hamilton* (24 vols., New York, 1961–   ), V, 147, 184–85. In his reply Madison added: "This idea of reserving [the] right to withdraw was started at Richmd. and considered as a conditional ratification which was itself considered as worse than a rejection." See also Irving Brant, *James Madison, Father of the Constitution, 1787–1800* (Indianapolis, 1950), 225–27, 229–30.

a *federal* and not a *national* Constitution.'' The powers delegated to the
federal government, Madison adds, ''are few and defined. Those which
are to remain to the State Government are numerous and indefinite.''[46]
At the Virginia ratifying convention he asked: ''Who are the parties to
. . . [the Constitution]? The people—but not the people as composing
one great body; but the people as composing thirteen sovereignties.''[47]
The contest in Virginia was close, and Madison's comforting description
of the new political order was important in carrying the day for the
Federalists.

Hamilton's course during the debates over ratification indicated a
readiness to say almost anything that would assure Federalist success. At
the Philadelphia Convention, no proposal to curb the power of the states
had been too drastic for him—even federally appointed state governors
with power to veto acts of the legislatures. The federal government, he
said, must have full sovereignty, for ''the states will be dangerous . . .
and ought to be extinguished . . . or reduced to a smaller scale.''[48] The
finished Constitution disappointed Hamilton, and he feared that a
dissolution of the Union would be ''the most likely result.'' His only
hope was that a ''good administration'' might ''triumph altogether over
the state governments and reduce them to intire [sic] subordination,
dividing the larger states into smaller districts.''[49]

491

However, while there was danger that New York might not ratify,
Hamilton suppressed his true feelings and courted those who were waver-
ing with beguiling expressions of respect for the states. To be sure, in *The
Federalist*, he hints at an ''indissoluble'' union, but in an ambiguous
context which leaves it unclear whether he is merely expressing a hope
or stating what he considers to be a fact. He also observes that the
federal government would have power to enforce its laws without state
assistance, but he says nothing about federal authority over states that
try to secede.[50] Beyond these ambiguities, which were characteristic of
Federalist rhetoric, Hamilton makes two rather astonishing comments.
First, in *Federalist* 33, he declares with sweet innocence that the
Constitution's ''necessary and proper'' clause, which he would use with
great effect as secretary of the treasury, ''may be chargeable with

[46] Cooke, *Federalist*, 254, 313. Alpheus Thomas Mason stresses this aspect of Madison's
contributions but, in my opinion, places too much responsibility on him alone for the ambiguity of
The Federalist. Mason, ''The Nature of Our Federal Union Reconsidered,'' 512–19.
[47] Elliot, *Debates in the Several State Conventions*, III, 94.
[48] Tansill, *Documents Illustrative of the Formation of the Union*, 979–88; Farrand, *Records
of the Federal Convention of 1787*, I, 328.
[49] Syrett and Cooke, *Papers of Alexander Hamilton*, IV, 276–77.
[50] Cooke, *Federalist*, 73, 103.

tautology or redundancy, [but it] is at least perfectly harmless."[51] Second, in *Federalist* 28, he suggests forms of protective state action against a threat of federal tyranny:

It may safely be received as an axiom in our political system, that the state governments will in all possible contingencies afford complete security against invasions of the public liberty by the national authority. . . . The Legislatures . . . can discover the danger at a distance; and possessing all the organs of civil power and the confidence of the people, they can at once adopt a regular plan of opposition, in which they can combine all the resources of the community. They can readily communicate with each other in the different states; and unite their common forces for the protection of their common liberty.

Thus, Hamilton concludes, the people would be able, "through the medium of their state governments, to take measures for their own defence with all the celerity, regularity and system of independent nations. . . ."[52] This, I think, is a fair description of both the justification and the method of nullification and secession when they were attempted in later years.

While the Federalists quieted the fears of the doubtful with equivocations and comforting promises that state sovereignty would survive ratification, the Antifederalists, ironically, warned that the Constitution would in fact create a perpetual union. Latter-day nationalists might have taken much comfort from descriptions of the new Union provided by the opponents of ratification. Only occasionally did Antifederalists agree with John Smilie of Pennsylvania that if the people changed their minds, "they will still have a right to assemble another body . . . to abrogate this Federal work so ratified."[53] More commonly, they spoke of ratification as a binding commitment that could not be annulled. Luther Martin cautioned that if a Bill of Rights were not adopted later, "you cannot free yourselves from the yoke you will have placed on your necks."[54] A Pennsylvania Antifederalist asserted that the question of ratification "involves in it not only your fate, but that of your posterity for ages to come. . . . Consider then duly before you leap, for after the Rubicon is once passed, there will be no

[51] *Ibid.*, 205. Thus, observes Mason, "Hamilton undercut the basis of [John] Marshall's jurisprudence" and enabled John Taylor to assert that the principles of state sovereignty "are forcibly sustained" in *The Federalist*. Mason, *States Rights Debate*, 196. At the New York ratifying convention, Hamilton apparently did read Madison's letter against conditional ratification, without identifying the author. Syrett and Cooke, *Papers of Alexander Hamilton*, V, 193.

[52] Cooke, *Federalist*, 179–80.

[53] Jensen, *Documentary History of the Ratification*, II, 376.

[54] Paul Leicester Ford, ed., *Essays on the Constitution of the United States, Published during Its Discussion by the People, 1787–1788* (New York, 1892), 376.

retreat.''[55] No nationalist ever stated the essence of his case more succinctly than the New York Antifederalist, Robert Yates. The proposed Constitution, he said, ''will not be a compact entered into by states, in their corporate capacities, but an agreement of the people of the United States, as one great body politic. . . .''[56]

The key word in the Antifederalist attack was ''consolidation,'' which in its application meant the reduction of the states to impotence in a perpetual union. According to Richard Henry Lee, ''The plan of government now proposed is evidently calculated totally to change, in time, our condition as a people. Instead of being thirteen republics, under a federal head, it is clearly designed to make us one consolidated government.''[57] Whitehill of Pennsylvania complained that the phrase ''We the People of the United States'' meant that ''the old foundation of the Union is destroyed, the principle of confederation excluded, and a new and unwieldly system of consolidated empire is set up upon the ruins of the present compact between the States.''[58]

The Antifederalists, not the Federalists, occasionally declared bluntly that the remedy of secession would not be available to a state whose citizens found the new Union despotic. Smilie, on further reflection, decided that the federal government ''must be too formidable for any single State, or even for a combination of the States, should an attempt be made to break and destroy the yoke of domination and tyranny. . . .''[59] Martin foresaw a time when a state might be driven to resist federal oppression. But, he noted, the proposed Constitution provides that a citizen who supports his state would be ''guilty of a direct act of treason; reducing, by this provision, the different states to this alternative,—that they must tamely and passively yield to despotism, or their citizens must oppose it at the hazard of the halter, if unsuccessful. . . .''[60] Thus, a few Antifederalists, to advance their cause, tried to force a clarification of federal-state relations; but the Federalists, appreciating the value of ambiguity, were usually too cautious to respond.

The consequence was that, in 1789, when the present Union came into existence, the question whether a member state could secede at will remained unresolved. In spite of the occasional oblique hints of the

493

[55] John Bach McMaster and Frederick D. Stone, eds., *Pennsylvania and the Federal Constitution, 1787–1788* (Lancaster, Pa., 1888), 593.
[56] Edward S. Corwin, *Court Over Constitution: A Study of Judicial Review as an Instrument of Popular Government* (Princeton, 1938), 247.
[57] Ford, *Pamphlets on the Constitution*, 282. See also James Curtis Ballagh, ed., *The Letters of Richard Henry Lee* (3 vols., New York, 1914), II, 472.
[58] Jensen, *Documentary History of the Ratification*, II, 393.
[59] McMaster and Stone, *Pennsylvania and the Federal Constitution*, 269.
[60] Elliot, *Debates in the Several State Conventions*, I, 382.

Federalists and warnings of the Antifederalists, the debates over ratification had been remarkably unenlightening. No state convention made the right of secession the subject of extended inquiry; not one of *The Federalist* papers is devoted to the matter; nor was it aired in the press or in the flood of pamphlets written by the friends and foes of the Constitution. In short, the Founding Fathers, hoping for the best, left the question of perpetuity to posterity.

Perhaps it was inevitable that in the young republic a decisive resolution of this crucial matter should have been long delayed. What is surprising is that even a theoretical argument for a perpetual union—at least for one that can be described as systematic and comprehensive— failed to materialize for many years. Such an argument is not to be found in the writings of Hamilton or, as far as I have seen, in the writings of any other early nationalist. The Supreme Court, as we know, did not confront the issue directly until after the Civil War. Indeed, though threats of secession were common and were soon supported by an elaborate case for state sovereignty, some forty years elapsed before a comparable counterargument for perpetuity bolstered the Union cause.

Meanwhile, the most common perception of the Union was as an experiment whose future was uncertain at best. The Union was valued less for its own sake than as a means to certain desirable ends, especially the protection of the people's liberties and the defense of the country from enemies abroad. Not many were inclined to challenge John Randolph when he declared in 1814 that the Union was "the *means* of securing the safety, liberty, and welfare of the confederacy and not itself an end to which these should be sacrificed."[61] Apparently almost everyone, even the most ardent believers in state sovereignty, thought of disunion as a calamity. "Among the upright and intelligent," wrote Edmund Randolph, "few can read without emotion the future fate of the States, if severed from each other."[62] But there were few signs of the kind of American national identity from which might grow a concept of a perpetual union as an essential end in itself. As William T. Hutchinson observes, "The weakness of [the people's] nationalism is not surprising. If their loyalty to Great Britain, centuries-old in the background of many of them, could not outlast a decade of discontent charged against their mother country, it could hardly be transformed overnight into a heartfelt allegiance to a newly-born United States of America."[63]

[61] Nagel, *One Nation Indivisible*, 13–31, provides a good analysis of the concept of the Union as an experiment. The quote from John Randolph is on page 19.

[62] Ford, *Pamphlets on the Constitution*, 269.

[63] William T. Hutchinson, "Unite to Divide; Divide to Unite: The Shaping of American Federalism," *Mississippi Valley Historical Review*, XLVI (June 1959), 6–7.

Almost from the start, anxiety about the future of the Union centered on the prospect of a separation along sectional lines. In 1792, both Thomas Jefferson and Hamilton warned President Washington of this danger. According to Jefferson, disunion was possible because "the division and interest happens unfortunately to be so geographical." Hamilton reported that, in both North and South, "there are respectable men who talk of separation, as a thing dictated by the different geniusses [sic] and different prejudices of the parts."[64] A few years later, a Boston writer also perceived the potential of disunion in the "coincidence which happens to exist between the *political differences*, and the *geographical divisions* of the United States."[65] Hamilton's own fiscal policies contributed significantly to the earliest stirrings of sectional unrest. In 1790, the Virginia General Assembly denounced federal assumption of state debts as repugnant to the Constitution and proclaimed its members "the guardians . . . of the rights and interests" of the people, the "sentinels placed by them over the ministers of the federal government."[66] Hamilton, after countenancing in *The Federalist* the very role that Virginia was playing, now wrote in alarm that her action was "the first symptom of a spirit which must either be killed or kill the constitution of the United States."[67]

Distressed by the signs of sectional tension, Washington devoted much of his Farewell Address to stressing the value of the Union. He urged his countrymen to reject "whatever may suggest even a suspicion that it can in any event be abandoned" and to rebuke "every attempt to alienate any portion of our country from the rest." Above all, he resorted to what was at that time the most persuasive appeal: "Is there doubt whether a common government can embrace so large a sphere? Let experience solve it. . . . It is well worth a fair and full experiment."[68] Thus, Washington rested his case on the prevalent idea of a political experiment, not on a concept of a perpetual union.

Soon after Washington's appeal, Madison and Jefferson formulated an ingenious doctrine of state sovereignty that stood for many years as a formidable challenge to any notion that the Union's permanence was underwritten by the Constitution itself. Their Virginia and Kentucky Resolutions of 1798–1799 held that the Constitution is a compact to

[64] Paul Leicester Ford, ed., *The Writings of Thomas Jefferson* (10 vols., New York, 1892–1899), VI, 492; Syrett and Cooke, *Papers of Alexander Hamilton*, XII, 254.

[65] Boston *Independent Chronicle and the Universal Advertiser*, Aug. 20–23, 1798.

[66] W. W. Henning, ed., *Statutes at Large of Virginia* (Philadelphia, 1823), XIII, 237–38.

[67] Syrett and Cooke, *Papers of Alexander Hamilton*, VII, 149.

[68] James D. Richardson, ed., *A Compilation of the Messages and Papers of the Presidents* (10 vols., Washington, 1899), I, 213–24.

which "each State acceded as a State"; that the states had reserved the
right to judge when the federal government exceeds its powers; that
such measures are "unauthoritative, void, and of no force"; that states
can "interpose" their authority to arrest the evil of unconstitutional
federal acts; and that nullification is a "rightful remedy" in such cases.
These resolutions, especially Jefferson's, adopted only a decade after the
ratification of the Constitution, contained the essential ingredients of the
case not only for nullification but for secession as well.

Yet even their passage evoked no detailed unionist rebuttal. Nine
states, all controlled by the Federalists, responded with assertions that
the federal judiciary was the proper judge of the constitutionality of acts
of Congress. Several of them denounced Madison's and Jefferson's
resolutions as "inflammatory and pernicious" or "dangerous in their
tendency." The Massachusetts legislature affirmed that the states were
united "by a common interest, which ought to render their Union
indissoluble." The most forceful reaction came from the New Hampshire legislature, which resolved to defend the Union "against every
aggression, either foreign or domestic" and to "support the government of the United States in all measures warranted by the [Con-
stitution]."[69] Though these hostile responses to the Virginia and
Kentucky Resolutions indicated the need for a well-reasoned counterargument, the Federalist legislatures, like the Federalist press, left the
need unfilled.

496

However, the public reaction did include one early, fragmentary
statement of the case for a perpetual union—not from a political body or
public meeting but, ironically, in a pamphlet by another Virginian, the
staunch Federalist Henry Lee. "In point of right," Lee argued, "no state
can withdraw itself from the Union. In point of policy, no state ought to
be permitted to do so." The burden of his case rested on the premise
that the federal government "was created by, and is entirely dependent
on, the people." The state governments "are not parties to the . . .
[Constitution], they did not form or adopt it, nor did they create or
regulate its powers. . . . The people, and the people only, were competent to those important objects." The Constitution, he concluded,
"was proposed not to the different state governments, but to the people
for their consideration and adoption. The language of the instrument is
no longer the language of the states. . . . It was sanctioned by the people

---

[69] Elliot, *Debates in the Several State Conventions*, IV, 537, 539; Frank Maloy Anderson,
"Contemporary Opinion of the Virginia and Kentucky Resolutions," *American Historical Review*,
V (Oct., Dec. 1899), 45–63, 225–52.

themselves, assembled in their different states in convention.''[70] This
single, relatively brief, formulation of a case against state sovereignty
and the right of secession is the only one that I have discovered in the
Federalist period. If there were others, they were rare, for even the
Virginia and Kentucky Resolutions more commonly elicited sentimental
unionist appeals, doleful descriptions of the tragic effects of disunion, and
admonishments to give the "experiment" a chance to prove itself.

During the Republican era, the Louisiana Purchase, the embargo, and
the War of 1812 provoked northeastern Federalists to take a turn at
calculating the value of the Union. An address prepared by the minority
in the House of Representatives who had voted against war in June
1812 claimed that the Union was based on "a form of government in
no small degree experimental, composed of *powerful* and independent
sovereignties. . . .''[71] Timothy Pickering of Massachusetts found "no
magic in the sound of Union. If the great objects of union are utterly
abandoned . . . let the Union be severed. Such a severance presents no
Terrors for me.''[72] Threats of this kind usually educed the same mild
responses as those evoked in the Federalist era. Jefferson loved the
Union, but to him it was always a means rather than an end in itself; and
in his mind the question of secession centered on its wisdom, not its
constitutionality. He had toyed with a threat of secession when he wrote
the Kentucky Resolutions, and he had discussed it with John Taylor
purely in terms of its expediency. During his presidency, Jefferson
viewed with equanimity the prospect of an eventual separation of the
eastern and western states: "God bless them both and keep them in the
union if it be for their good, but separate them if it be better.''[73] Even
young John Quincy Adams could see no alternative to acquiescing in
secession if it were attempted. "I love the Union as I love my wife," he
wrote. "But if my wife should ask for and insist upon a separation, she
should have it, though it broke my heart.''[74]

The consensus in all sections still seemed to be that the future of the
Union was uncertain and largely dependent on the practical value of its
survival. In 1815, Joseph Story urged that useful public works be

497

[70] [Henry Lee] *Plain Truth: Addressed to the People of Virginia* (Richmond. 1799). 13. 22.
19–20.
[71] Washington *National Intelligencer*, July 18, 1812.
[72] Quoted in Nagel, *One Nation Indivisible*, 19.
[73] Merrill D. Peterson, *Thomas Jefferson and the New Nation: A Biography* (New York, 1970),
610, 623–24, 772, 1003.
[74] Worthington Chauncey Ford, ed., *Writings of John Quincy Adams* (7 vols., New York,
1913), II, 525–26.

undertaken in order that "the United States will be endeared to the people. . . . Let us prevent the possibility of a division, by creating great national interests which shall bind us in an indissoluble chain."[75] Samuel H. Smith, in a Fourth of July oration, pinned his hopes for perpetuity not on the wording of the Constitution but on a mystical belief that the Union was "the emanation of Divine Beneficence" and therefore "stamped with the seal of Heaven."[76] Occasionally, especially during the War of 1812, these by now traditional appeals were punctuated with sharp denials that the states were completely sovereign. "There is no inherent power left in any state, without the consent of congress, to recede," asserted one nationalist. "Massachusetts cannot prevent [its] agents from being *hanged by the neck* for the *first* overt act they commit against the confederation of the Union," warned another.[77] But neither advanced an argument to offset the well-developed case for the sovereignty of the states.

Once again, as during the Federalist period, the only impressive, though still fragmentary, presentation of a case for a perpetual union that I have found came from a Virginian—Thomas Ritchie, editor of the Richmond *Enquirer*. During the War of 1812, in a series of editorials, Ritchie denounced the allegedly disloyal elements in New England who wished "to dash to pieces the holy ark of the Union of our country."[78] These editorials culminated in one that accused the delegates to the Hartford Convention of plotting secession and warned that "the first act of resistance to the law is *treason* to the U.S." The editorial concluded thus:

No man, no association of men, no state or set of states *has a right* to withdraw itself from this Union, of its own accord. The same power which knit us together, can only unknit. The same formality which forged the links of the Union, is necessary to dissolve it. The *majority of States* which form the Union must consent to the withdrawal of *any one* branch of it. Until *that* consent has been obtained, any attempt to dissolve the *Union*, or obstruct the efficacy of its constitutional laws, is Treason—Treason to all intents and purposes. . . . This illustrious Union, which has been cemented by the blood of our forefathers, the pride of America and the wonder of the world must not be tamely sacrificed to the heated brains or the aspiring hearts of a few malcontents. The Union must be saved, when any one shall dare to assail it.[79]

[75] Quoted in Albert J. Beveridge, *The Life of John Marshall* (4 vols., Boston, 1919), IV, 145n. For a similar view, see the letter of "Publius" in Richmond *Enquirer*, April 26, 1815.

[76] Washington *National Intelligencer*, Aug. 4, 1813.

[77] *Ibid.*, April 28, 1814 (letter of "Hortensius"), Dec. 2, 1814 (letter of "Aurora").

[78] Richmond *Enquirer*, July 3, Nov. 27, 1812, Aug. 27, 1813, Jan. 22, 1814.

[79] *Ibid.*, Nov. 1, 1814.

Ritchie's rhetoric, to be sure, was more passionate assertion than reasoned argument, but it was as far as the case for a perpetual union had developed even at the end of the War of 1812.

For more than another decade, the idea of the states irrevocably united by unbreakable constitutional commitments and, to the extent necessary, by federal force, was seldom voiced. Thus, in 1815, a long oration entitled "Permanency of the American Union," delivered by an unidentified speaker before the Literary and Philosophical Society of Charleston, still described a voluntary union bound by tradition, affection, and practical interests. The thought that the Union is temporary, he said, "would chill the hope of every patriot." However, "we think we see by the lights of history, that the American union is permanent," because "time is preparing new cords to encircle and bind us more closely and more firmly." Commerce unites the nation in mutual dependence; the press helps to "effect uniformity of opinion and of conduct"; and the "anticipation of the future grandeur of united America . . . will never allow the sentiment of Union to be cold." Hence, he concluded, from the adoption of the Constitution, "wealth and happiness, the fruit of union, have confirmed our determination to remain forever one people. . . . [The] union is the result of *reason*, sympathy and general interest, not (like the nations of Europe) of compulsion. In the retrospect we see every thing to revive and animate *affection*, nothing that can irritate the pride or provoke the anger of *any one* of its members."[80] In short, the experiment was a success, and, because the Union had proved its value, love for it had grown apace. But, until then, love for the Union had not generated a compelling case for perpetuity.

The debate over Missouri's application for admission as a slave state provoked an unprecedented outburst of secession threats. According to Daniel P. Cook, an Illinois congressman, "The sound of disunion . . . has been uttered so often . . . and has become so familiar, that it is high time . . . to express our solemn disapprobation. . . ." Secession, wrote an editor, "has been spoken of publicly and privately—on the floor of congress and in private coteries . . . and [is] regarded as an event likely to happen."[81] The threats did not emanate from Southerners alone. Senator Walter Lowrie of Pennsylvania warned that if the choice were

---

[80] "Permanency of the American Union. Being Part of an Essay Delivered Before the Literary and Philosophical Society of Charleston, in 1815," *Niles' Weekly Register*, XII (June 7, 1817), 228–30.

[81] *Annals of Congress*, 16 Cong., 1 Sess., 1106 (Feb. 4, 1820); Lexington *Kentucky Reporter*, March 22, 1820.

between a dissolution of the Union and the extension of slavery, "I, for one, will choose the former." John Quincy Adams wrote in his diary, "If the Union must be dissolved, slavery is precisely the question upon which it ought to break."[82] Both Jefferson and John Adams feared that the Union would not survive, and even the young nationalist, Henry Clay, told John Quincy Adams that "he had not a doubt that within five years from this time the Union would be divided. . . ."[83]

The Missouri crisis did produce a number of brief, dogmatic assertions of federal supremacy. For example, Representative Joshua Cushman of Massachusetts declared that "sovereignty resides, not in minute portions or States, but in the whole people whose will, expressed in their Constitutional organs, is the law, and must be obeyed." The people of the United States gave the federal government "ample powers, competent not only to ordinary, but to extraordinary exigencies. Hence we may hope for the durability and perpetuity of our Republic." Cushman urged that "the proud and aspiring States . . . be taught to know their distance, to lower their lofty crests, to revolve in their humble orbs around the National Government. . . ."[84] But this outburst, and others like it, did not supply the still missing articulation of a concept of a perpetual union. As in the past, the characteristic response to secession talk was an appeal to both sentimental and practical motives for keeping the country united. William Plumer, Jr., of New Hampshire, reminded the malcontents that "our Confederacy is not so easily destroyed; it is cemented by the mutual interests of all its members; and the understandings, the affections, and the hearts, of the people are knit together in one common bond of indissoluble union."[85] Thus, even Republican nationalists, in the heat of the Missouri controversy, failed to challenge the firmly established and much-used case for state sovereignty with a full-blown unionist case of their own.

During the years of uncertainty about the nature and future of the Union, the United States Supreme Court delivered some of the most impressive challenges to the state sovereignty school. Although the Court under Chief Justice John Marshall never gave an explicit opinion on the right of secession—and was never asked to—it repeatedly emphasized the supremacy of the federal government in the exercise of its

[82] *Annals of Congress*, 16 Cong., 1 Sess., 209 (Jan. 20, 1820); Charles Francis Adams, ed., *Memoirs of John Quincy Adams, Comprising Portions of His Diary from 1795 to 1848* (12 vols., Philadelphia, 1874–1876), V, 12.
[83] *Ibid.*, IV, 525–26.
[84] *Annals of Congress*, 16 Cong., 1 Sess., 1294–98 (Feb. 14, 1820).
[85] *Ibid.*, 1436 (Feb. 21, 1820).

constitutional powers.[86] In *Fletcher* v. *Peck*, Marshall ruled that a state "is part of a large empire; . . . a member of the American union; and that union has a constitution the supremacy of which all acknowledge, and which imposes limits to the legislatures of the several states. . . ."[87] In *McCulloch* v. *Maryland*, he stressed the "supreme law of the land" clause and affirmed that the federal government, "on those subjects on which it can act, must necessarily bind its component parts."[88] In *Gibbons* v. *Ogden*, Marshall reiterated this point, adding that in 1787, when the sovereign states "converted their league into a government, . . . the whole character in which the States appear, underwent a change. . . ."[89]

By far the sharpest of Marshall's decisions relevant to the nature of the Union—that in the case of *Cohens* v. *Virginia*—appears to have been shaped in part by the Missouri crisis that immediately preceded it. In the most forceful language he ever used on the question of state sovereignty, Marshall wrote:

501

That the United States form, for many, and for most important purposes, a single nation, has not yet been denied. In war, we are one people. In making peace, we are one people. In all commercial regulations, we are one and the same people. . . . America has chosen to be, in many respects, and to many purposes, a nation; and for all these purposes, her government is complete; to all these objects, it is competent. The people have declared, that in the exercise of all the powers given for these objects, it is supreme. . . . The constitution and laws of a State, so far as they are repugnant to the constitution and laws of the United States, are absolutely void. These States are constituent parts of the United States. They are members of one great empire—for some purposes sovereign, for some purposes subordinate.

Marshall concluded that the people who had made the Constitution can unmake it, but this supreme power "resides only in the whole body of the people; not in any sub-division of them. The attempt of any of the parts to exercise it is usurpation, and ought to be repelled by those to whom the people have delegated their power of repelling it."[90] Thus, Marshall clearly affirmed the power of the federal government to resist an attempt by a state or "a section of the nation" to unmake, or overthrow, the Constitution of the United States. What he still left

[86] As early as 1793, the Court under Chief Justice John Jay, in the case of *Chisholm* v. *Georgia*, traced the Union back to the Declaration of Independence and affirmed that as to the purposes of the Union, the states are not sovereign. *Chisholm* v. *Georgia*, 2 Dallas 419 (1793).

[87] *Fletcher* v. *Peck*, 6 Cranch 87 (1810) at 136.

[88] *McCulloch* v. *Maryland*, 4 Wheaton 316 (1819) at 405.

[89] *Gibbons* v. *Ogden*, 9 Wheaton 1 (1824) at 187.

[90] *Cohens* v. *Virginia*, 6 Wheaton 264 (1821) at 413–14, 389.

unsettled was whether a state had the right not to unmake the Constitution but peacefully to separate from the Union it had created. That, of course, was the crucial question of 1861–1865.

By the end of the 1820s, after the government under the federal Constitution had been in operation for forty years, the prevailing view of the Union in the political rhetoric of the time still remained that of an experiment, albeit one that had already shown much promise of success. Though secession had been threatened repeatedly and the idea of secession as a constitutional right of the sovereign states was fully developed, the secessionist argument still lacked a comprehensive and effective rebuttal. More than that, the language of state sovereignty had become deeply embedded in the American vocabulary. Almost everyone spoke of the Union as "our confederacy," of the Constitution as a "compact." The term "sovereign" was associated with the states far more than with the federal government; and state legislatures took for granted their right to "instruct" their United States senators on how to vote on important legislation. Meanwhile, formulations of the idea of a perpetual union remained rare, brief, and incomplete.

Of course, this does not mean that, during the four decades following ratification of the Constitution, the state of the Union had not changed. It had, after all, survived, and with each passsing year an attempt to dissolve it was bound to become an increasingly serious and formidable undertaking. Love for the Union had become well-nigh universal, secession a disaster dreaded by all—even by those who believed it to be a constitutional remedy for unbearable grievances. Forty years had afforded time for the emergence of numerous interest groups possessing practical reasons for wishing to preserve the Union, especially those involved directly or indirectly in interstate commerce. Indeed, hardly any group existed that would not be in some degree adversely affected by disunion. These interests, together with the sense of nationhood and pride in American citizenship that had developed during and immediately after the War of 1812, made almost inevitable the eventual construction of a case for a perpetual union.[91] The western world was entering an era of romantic nationalism, and the United States was much affected by its impelling force.

The spark that finally set off what can only be described as an explosion of unionist rhetoric was the nullification controversy in South Carolina. Between 1830 and 1833, all of the ideas that formed the core

[91] For the gradual evolution of the idea of the Union as an absolute good, see Nagel, *One Nation Indivisible*, 104–44.

of the case for a perpetual union were embodied in the speeches or writings of at least a half dozen major politicians and constitutional scholars. Among these, Daniel Webster's reply to Robert Y. Hayne, while the most famous and certainly the most eloquent, is by no means the most penetrating or comprehensive. Webster presented much of what became the classic unionist argument and denied that a state can protect secessionists from the penalties for treason, but the heart of his response was a traditional, sentimental appeal for the Union as a blessing to mankind. He rejoiced ''in whatever tends to strengthen the bond that unites us, and encourages the hope that our Union may be perpetual.''[92]

Soon after Webster had finished, Senator Edward Livingston of Louisiana delivered a less glittering but far more trenchant speech against nullification and the alleged constitutional right of secession. His key assertion was that in all the ''attributes of sovereignty, which, by the federal compact, were transferred to the General Government, that government is sovereign and supreme; the States have abandoned, and can never reclaim them.'' They had, by the Constitution, ''unequivocally surrendered every constitutional right of impeding or resisting the execution of any decree or judgment of the Supreme Court. . . .'' A state, he agreed, might elect in an extreme case to attempt secession, but such action ''is not a right derived from the constitution.'' Rather, it is an extralegal right, and ''whenever resorted to, it must be at the risk of all the penalties attached to an unsuccessful resistance to establish authority.''[93]

503

In 1831, in a Fourth of July oration, John Quincy Adams presented a case for perpetuity that was notable for its emphasis on the Union's historical origins. The states, he claimed, were the offspring of the Union, whose existence was announced in the Declaration of Independence. By that Declaration, the people of the united colonies ''had bound themselves, before God, to a primitive social compact of union, freedom and independence.'' Thereafter, ''no one of the States whose people were parties to it, could, without violation of that primitive compact, secede or separate from the rest.'' Nullification, he said, was a virtual attempt to dissolve the Union, ''to organize an insurrection against the laws of the United States; to interpose the arm of State sovereignty between rebellion and the halter, and to rescue the traitor from the gibbet.'' In short, nullification ''would, however colored, and

[92] *Works of Daniel Webster* (6 vols., Boston, 1851), III, 248–347, 258.
[93] *Register of Debates in Congress*, 21 Cong., 1 Sess., 266, 270 (March 15, 1830).

however varnished, be neither more nor less than treason, skulking under the shelter of despotism.''[94]

Story, in his *Commentaries on the Constitution*, published in 1833, amplified the historical argument and culled passages from *The Federalist* and the ratification debates that bolstered the case against state sovereignty. From his rather selective reading of this literature, he concluded that the Federalists had always emphasized the Constitution's ''character as a permanent form of government, as a fundamental law, as a supreme rule, which no State was at liberty to disregard, suspend, or annul. . . .'' In an exhaustive examination of the nature of compacts, Story found no basis for the contention that the Constitution was a mere compact between sovereign states. He thought it significant that at the ratifying conventions no state reserved the right ''to dissolve its connection, . . . or to suspend the operation of the Constitution, as to itself.'' Therefore, he concluded, the Constitution was ''framed for the general good and designed for perpetuity.''[95]

Of the many writers who joined the attack on the South Carolina nullifiers, James Madison was no doubt the most prolific. Until his death in 1836, he devoted much of his time to refuting those who claimed that his Virginia Resolutions and Jefferson's Kentucky Resolutions of 1798–1799 justified nullification or secession. Numerous efforts, he often complained, ''are made to stamp my political career with discrediting inconsistencies.''[96] He responded with a flood of letters, essays, and memoranda asserting that what South Carolina now claimed the right to do was not what he and Jefferson had had in mind thirty years earlier. The Virginia Resolutions, Madison insisted, gave ''not a shadow of countenance to the doctrine of nullification.''[97] His defense was not altogether convincing, but in developing it he made a significant contribution to the emerging nationalist case for a perpetual union. There is a great difference, he wrote, between ''the claim to secede at will'' and the right to secede ''from intolerable oppression.'' The first is ''a violation, without cause, of a faith solemnly pledged. The latter is

[94] John Quincy Adams, *An Oration to the Citizens of the Town of Quincy, on the Fourth of July, 1831* (Boston, 1831), 7, 17–18, 35–36.
[95] Joseph Story, *Commentaries on the Constitution of the United States* (2 vols., Boston, 1833), I, 146–270.
[96] Gaillard P. Hunt, ed., *The Writings of James Madison* (9 vols., New York, 1900–1910), IX, 471. The letter cited is one of Madison's most elaborate defenses against charges of inconsistency. For an account of Madison's role during the nullification crisis, see Irving Brant, *James Madison, Commander in Chief, 1812–1836* (Indianapolis, 1961), 468–500.
[97] Hunt, *Writings of James Madison*, IX, 587. Irving Brant believes that Madison did not intend to justify nullification, but he is unsure what Madison did have in mind and admits that he ''used language whose gravity suggested such a power. . . .'' Brant, *James Madison, Father of the Constitution*, 463.

another name only for revolution, about which there is no theoretic controversy."[98] For ordinary disputes over the powers and jurisdiction of the federal government, the Constitution recognizes the Supreme Court, not the individual states, as the final arbiter. Madison branded state nullification as a "preposterous and anarchical pretension" to which the Constitution gives not the slightest support.[99] Collectively, these writings of his last years constitute something approaching a revised version of his contributions to *The Federalist*, with the new emphasis decidedly more on the national features of the Constitution and less on the surviving aspects of state sovereignty. Most important, he was now open and explicit in denying the constitutional right of secession by individual states.[100]

Among the numerous formulations of the concept of a perpetual union that appeared during the nullification crisis, one stands above the rest for its incisiveness, coherence, and comprehensiveness: President Andrew Jackson's Proclamation on Nullification of December 10, 1832. This document, prepared for Jackson by Secretary of State Edward Livingston, comes close to being the definitive statement of the case for perpetuity.[101] It is so complete that even the Supreme Court, in *Texas* v. *White*, could find no additional argument of any significance. The proclamation embraces the crucial nationalist assumption that the Union is older than the states: "Under the royal Government we had no separate character; our opposition to its oppressions began as *united Colonies*. We were the United States under the Confederation, and the name was perpetuated and the Union rendered more perfect by the Federal Constitution." How was it possible, then, "that the most perfect of these several modes of union should now be considered as a mere league that may be dissolved at pleasure?"[102]

The notion of a right of secession, Jackson claimed, grew out of the mistaken belief that the Constitution is only a compact between states whose sovereignty was not diminished by the act of ratification. Yet the Constitution was not framed by the states but by the people, "acting

505

---

[98] *Letters and Other Writings of James Madison*, IV, 293.

[99] Hunt, *Writings of James Madison*, IX, 472.

[100] *Ibid.*, 383–403. This letter was published in the *North American Review*, XXXI (Oct. 1830), 537–46. See also Hunt, *Writings of James Madison*, IX, 573–607.

[101] Richardson, *Messages and Papers of the Presidents*, II, 640–56. The proclamation was not notable for its originality, because the ideas in it had been stated by others, including Edward Livingston, during the nullification crisis. As early as 1824, Livingston had advanced nationalist arguments in support of federal aid for internal improvements, but he offered no argument for a perpetual union until his speech in the Senate in 1830, cited above. See William B. Hatcher, *Edward Livingston: Jeffersonian Republican and Jacksonian Democrat* (Baton Rouge, 1940), 305–06, 348–51, 382–86.

[102] Richardson, *Messages and Papers of the Presidents*, II, 650.

through state legislatures when they made the compact . . . and acting in separate conventions when they ratified those provisions.'' Thus, they formed ''a *government*, not a league. . . . It is a Government in which all the people are represented, which operates directly on the people individually, not upon the States.''[103] The individual states did not retain all their sovereignty, for their citizens transferred their allegiance to the government of the United States and became American citizens. ''How, then, can that State be said to be sovereign and independent whose citizens owe obedience to laws not made by it . . .?''[104] Showing a respect for the Supreme Court that had been less evident in the past, Jackson proclaimed it, rather than the states, the proper authority to settle disputes arising under the Constitution and laws of the United States. He denied that the right to secede was a constitutional remedy reserved to the states, for such action ''does not break a league, but destroys the unity of a nation.'' Secession is an act of revolution, which ''may be morally justified by the extremity of oppression; but to call it a constitutional right is confounding the meaning of terms. . . .''[105]

506

Jackson's conclusion appears to be the model from which Lincoln drew inspiration for some critical statements in his first inaugural address. Jackson warned the people of South Carolina that he would fulfill the obligation imposed on him by the Constitution ''to take care that the laws be faithfully executed.'' In this he had no discretionary power, for ''my duty is emphatically pronounced in the Constitution.'' Therefore, if an attempt at disunion should lead to ''the shedding of brother's blood,'' that result could not be attributed to ''any offensive act on the part of the United States.''[106] Having urged South Carolinians to consider the dangers they risked, Jackson closed on a softer note with an appeal to their love for the Union.

Before the enactment of the tariff compromise of 1833, the concept of a perpetual union had achieved its full development, and a President of the United States had pledged himself to use all the power of the federal government to uphold it. Yet, even after the nullification controversy, when the theoretical justification for the use of force stood ready to be invoked in a national crisis, most Americans still dreaded such a remedy, as did Jackson himself. During the sectional conflicts of the 1840s and 1850s, they continued to cherish the hope that love for the Union, together with the Union's obvious benefits, would suffice to hold

[103] *Ibid.*, 648.
[104] *Ibid.*, 650.
[105] *Ibid.*, 648–49.
[106] *Ibid.*, 654–56.

it together. Even so, by 1833, to the nationalists the Union had become an absolute, an end in itself; and, in retrospect, it seems clear that by then the time had passed when the people of a state might resort to the remedy of secession without confronting the coercive authority of the federal government. The arguments for perpetuity of Webster, Livingston, John Quincy Adams, Story, Madison, and Jackson, among others, had brought the days of our political innocence to an end.

Nevertheless, an adequate explanation of the events of 1861 must take into account the fact that the case for state sovereignty and the constitutional right of secession had flourished for forty years before a comparable case for a perpetual union had been devised. Because that case came so late, because the logic behind it was far from perfect, because the Constitution and the debates over ratification were fraught with ambiguity, the pessimistic premonition of John Quincy Adams, expressed in a letter of 1831, was tragically fulfilled. "It is the odious nature of the question," he wrote, "that it can be settled only at the cannon's mouth."[107]

507

[107] Calvin Colton, ed., *The Private Correspondence of Henry Clay* (Cincinnati, 1856), 313.

FEDERALISM AND LABOR REGULATION IN THE UNITED STATES AND AUSTRALIA

THE field of labor regulation provides an interesting comparative study of the two federal states, the United States and the Commonwealth of Australia. The broad outline of the constitutional structure of Australian federalism was drawn from the United States Constitution, yet the insertion of a special reference to labor disputes in the Commonwealth Constitution, as a result of political conditions at the time of Australian federation, has not resulted in greater power accruing to the Commonwealth government than to its American counterpart. The overwhelming importance of the commerce power in the United States and its negligible importance in Australia indicate the widely differing effects of constitutional interpretation. Yet this is itself reversed, in the case of labor regulation at any rate, by a different social philosophy, a different political attitude to the question of equality of standards. It is instructive to trace the constitutional and political forces which have shaped the present structure of labor regulation in these two countries and to see the way in which a unique pattern of government activity develops within a framework borrowed from a country similar in many respects, yet differing also in fundamental ways.

The objects of this article, therefore, are:

1. To describe the differing constitutional positions concerning the regulation of labor in the United States and Australia.

2. To describe the standards of regulation instituted by federal and state governments in each country within these constitutional frameworks in sufficient detail to draw out the salient features, especially as regards uniformity or the lack of it.

3. To indicate the political attitudes in each country which are responsible for these differing patterns of regulation.

Let us look first of all at the American structure of labor regulation, its constitutional basis and its achievements.

I.   *The United States Federal Legislation*

In the United States, of course, no specific mention of labor regulatory powers is made in the Constitution. The authority for the major federal laws in this field is drawn from the federal power over interstate commerce. These laws are the National Labor Relations Act (the Wagner Act) of 1935 as amended by the Labor-Management Relations Act (Taft-Hartley Act) of 1947, and the Fair Labor Standards Act of 1938. These Acts regulate the processes of collective bargaining and set up minimum wage standards and maximum working hours, and control the use of child labor.

First let us examine the constitutional position as far as the Labor Relations Acts are concerned, for, with certain statutory exemptions, the potential coverage of these Acts is as wide as the commerce power itself.[1] They provide us, therefore, with an opportunity of discovering to what extent federal power over labor could be exercised if the federal government desired to push it to its limits under present constitutional interpretation.

509

It is significant that the history of the Labor Relations Acts falls into three distinct periods. The period 1935 to 1944 saw the delineation of the limits of the jurisdiction of the National Labor Relations Board by the Supreme Court. During that time all the jurisdiction cases that came before the Court were settled in favor of the N.L.R.B. From 1944 to 1950 no cases on the jurisdiction of the Board were decided by the Court, and the Board itself was left to decide, case by case, the coverage of the Acts. The third period commenced in 1951 when three cases were decided by the Court on the jurisdiction of the Board under the Taft-Hartley Act as applied to certain trade unions. The Court upheld the federal power in these cases also.[2] It seems, therefore, that the Court has passed the effective power of deciding the coverage of the Acts on to the Congress and the Board. Thus Mr. Justice Frankfurter has said:

[1] Russell A. Smith, *Labor Law—Cases and Materials* (Indianapolis, 1950), p. 117.

[2] N.L.R.B. *v.* Denver Building and Construction Trades Council, 341 U. S. 675 (1951); International Brotherhood of E.W. *v.* N.L.R.B., 341 U. S. 694 (1951); United Brotherhood of C. and J. *v.* N.L.R.B., 341 U. S. 707 (1951).

When the conduct of an enterprise affects commerce among the states is a matter of practical judgment, not to be determined by abstract notions. The exercise of this practical judgment the Constitution entrusts primarily . . . to the Congress, subject to the latter's control by the electorate.[3]

After the war, therefore, the N.L.R.B. found itself in a position in which it could virtually delimit its own jurisdiction. The important fact about the post-war decisions of the N. L. R.B., however, is that the Board has preferred *not* to push its jurisdiction to its ultimate constitutional limits. In many cases the Board has refused to take jurisdiction because to do so would be unlikely "to effectuate the policies of the Act".[4] Thus states have taken jurisdiction over areas which the N.L.R.B. has declined to process, either by agreement between the state and federal boards, or merely by the adoption of jurisdiction by state boards until ousted by the federal authority. In the 1948 dispute between Robert N. Denham, the general counsel to the N.L.R.B., and the Board itself, while not denying Mr. Denham's assertion that he could "conceive of very few businesses over which there is not at least technical jurisdiction,"[5] Mr. Hertzog, the chairman of the N.L.R.B., asserted that the Board did not wish to push its jurisdiction to the limits. The Board, therefore, in October 1950 set out definite rules on the limits within which it intended to exert its jurisdiction in the prevailing circumstances.[6]

It is true that the Supreme Court has at times suggested that there *are* limits to the federal power over commerce. For example, the Court has said that regulation cannot be carried to the point where control would be exerted over "effects upon

[3] Polish National Alliance of the U. S. *v.* N.L.R.B., 322 U. S. 643 (1944), at p. 650.

[4] Duke Power Co. case, 77 N.L.R.B. No. 103 (1948).

[5] *Hearings before Subcommittees of the Committee on Education and Labor and the Committee on Expenditures in Executive Departments,* House of Representatives, "Investigation of interpretation of the term 'affecting commerce' as used in the Labor-Management Relations Act, 1947", 1948, p. 18.

[6] See *Annual Report of the National Labor Relations Board, 1950,* p. 7, and revised standards declared in 1954, *Annual Report of the N.L.R.B., 1954,* pp. 2–5.

interstate commerce so indirect and remote that to embrace them . . . would effectually obliterate the distinction between what is national and what is local and create a completely centralized government."[7] However, interpretation of the Commerce Clause by 1939 had gone so far as to make Mr. Justice McReynolds complain that "so construed the power to regulate interstate commerce brings within the ambit of Federal control most if not all activities of the nation."[8] And, indeed, federal courts have upheld the jurisdiction of the N.L.R.B. over a local dairy, a retail lumberyard, and a local bakery. In each of these cases certiorari was denied by the Supreme Court.[9]

From this history it is clear that the potential scope of federal power is very great. To what extent has this power been exercised? An estimate has been made by R. J. Rosenthal both of the total present coverage of the Acts, and of the numbers of workers exempted by statute or for other reasons.[10] These figures suggest that there are 10,301,722 "employees in businesses not 'affecting commerce' and/or over which the board does not wish to exert jurisdiction."

We conclude, therefore, that the federal power in this field is very wide, and that though there may well be a limit to federal power, short of complete coverage of all workers, that limit has not yet been reached. It seems quite certain that wide extension of the scope of federal regulation would be accepted by the Supreme Court. In fact, in the past, the Court has been prepared to go at least as far as the federal government in this

511

[7] N.L.R.B. *v.* Jones and Laughlin Steel Corporation, 301 U. S. 1 (1937), at p. 37.

[8] Dissenting opinion in N.L.R.B. *v.* Fainblatt, 306 U. S. 601 (1939), at p. 610.

[9] See cases cited in evidence of general counsel to the N.L.R.B. *Hearings before the Joint Committee on Labor-Management Relations on the operation of the Labor-Management-Relations Act, 1947–June 1948*, p. 1157. It should be noted that in certain cases lower courts have found against the jurisdiction of the N.L.R.B.; see cases cited United States Supreme Court Reports (Annotated), 83 L.ed. 696–8.

[10] R. J. Rosenthal, "Exclusions of Employees under the Taft-Hartley Act", in *The Industrial and Labor Relations Review*, July 1951, pp. 556–570. The figures he gives are:

Annual average civilian labor force	61,442,000	100.0%
Employees covered by Wagner Act	34,343,363	55.9%
Employees covered by Taft-Hartley Act	30,905,167	50.3%

sphere. Both Congress and the National Labor Relations
Board have gone out of their way to limit the extent to which
their powers have been applied.

II. *American State Labor Legislation*

We have seen in the previous pages that federal legislation
on labor relations and conditions has only a limited coverage.
This is particularly true of the wages and hours and child labor
laws. In 1954 the Fair Labor Standards Act covered some 24
million wage and salary earners out of a total civilian labor
force of over 61 millions.[11] Thus there was great need, in the
absence of adequate federal legislation, for the states to pass
their own laws if uniform standards were to be set up throughout
the nation. Let us examine, therefore, the condition of state
legislation in the post-war period.

In the middle of 1954 only five states had minimum wage
laws which covered men as well as women and minors, while
twenty-one more states had minimum wage laws for women and
minors only.[12] At the same date all forty-eight states had
enacted some legislation on maximum working hours, although
in Delaware, Tennessee, Vermont and Virginia no men were
covered, while in some other states the coverage of male workers
was restricted to those employed on public works or in very
small areas of industry or transport.[13] Every state has adopted
a child labor law applying to the employment of minors up to
sixteen, eighteen, and in some cases twenty-one years of age.
These state child labor laws "follow a well-defined pattern.
Even so, they still vary widely in the standards or conditions
they set up. They are also extremely uneven in the occupations
to which they apply."[14]

The coverage of the federal Labor Relations Acts is much

512

[11] *The Annual Report of the Secretary of Labor, 1954*, p. 22.

[12] "Labor Laws and Their Administration: Proceedings of the 37th Convention
of the International Association of Government Labor Officials", September 8–10,
1954, *Labor Standards Bulletin*, No. 179, 1955, U. S. Dept. of Labor.

[13] See "State and Federal Hours Limitations—A Summary", *Labor Standards
Bulletin*, No. 116, 1950, and *Annual Digest of State and Federal Labor Legislation*,
Labor Standards Bureau, Dept. of Labor, 1950 to 1954.

[14] "State Child Labor Standards", *Labor Standards Bulletin*, No. 98, 1949, p. v.

wider than in the case of the Fair Labor Standards Act, yet because of the refusal by the National Labor Relations Board to assert jurisdiction over many fields of industry and commerce, there is a large area which does not come under federal regulation. However, only eleven states have passed comprehensive labor relations acts; four of these are of the nature of the Wagner Act, while the remaining seven incorporate both protective provisions and provisions restrictive of labor which were in the nature of precursors of the federal Taft-Hartley Act.[15] The wide coverage of the federal legislation in this field may account for the relatively small number of states with labor relations laws, but it should be noted that those states which have enacted such legislation contain nearly 40 per cent of the nonagricultural labor force of the country. The coverage of both federal and state acts together is therefore very great.

III. Labor Regulation in Australia

In Australia the history of industrial regulation is a long one, and one with its own peculiarities. The inclusion of the provision for federal regulation of labor disputes in the Constitution of the Commonwealth is an indication of the nature of Australian thought on the place of government action in this field. Our concern here is to see how far the constitutional structure of Australia has affected the development of its system of labor regulation. We shall, therefore, examine the labor legislation of Commonwealth and states before passing on to a comparison of the political forces underlying the American and Australian patterns of regulation.

The constitutional position in Australia concerning the regulation of labor is very stable. Recent High Court decisions, in this field, have been largely confirmatory of earlier well-established principles,[16] and there is on this topic an extensive literature.[17] We intend to do little more here, therefore, than

---

[15] See C. C. Killingsworth, *State Labor Relations Acts* (Chicago, 1948), pp. 1-3.

[16] E.g., Rex *v.* Kelly (1950), 81 C.L.R. 64, which affirmed the principle that the Arbitration Court, or a Conciliation Commissioner, might not make a "common rule".

[17] O. de R. Foenander has written much on the Australian industrial law. Most useful, perhaps, are his *Studies in Australian Labour Law and Relations* (Melbourne,

to recite the more important points of constitutional law on this subject.

(1) The legislative power of the Commonwealth in this field is limited to "conciliation and arbitration for the prevention and settlement of industrial disputes extending beyond the limits of any one state". The Parliament may not legislate generally in the field of industrial regulation but only for the settlement or prevention of disputes.

(2) A dispute in which the Commonwealth can be possessed of jurisdiction must be a real and genuine dispute.

(3) "Industry" connotes a situation in which labor and capital coöperate. This covers "white-collar" and "black-coat" workers.

514

(4) State employees are covered by Commonwealth awards where the state carries on industrial or commercial undertakings, but where state activities are "regal" in nature, they are not covered.

(5) An industrial dispute "extends beyond the limits of any one state" when either the disputants or the subject matter of the dispute is located in, or relates to employment in, two or more states of the Commonwealth.

(6) The law of any state must cease to operate if it is inconsistent with a valid award of the Commonwealth Arbitration Court.

It is essential, therefore, that we acknowledge and emphasize the fact that the scope and power of the Commonwealth government are severely limited as to both the manner in which the Commonwealth may legislate on industrial matters and the number of workers who come under its jurisdiction. The numerous referenda which have been designed to alter this state of affairs have all resulted in a refusal to extend the power of the Commonwealth over industrial matters. Accepting this as a situation which is unlikely to be altered in the near future, we must examine the conditions of Australian workers in 1954

1952), and *Industrial Regulation in Australia* (Melbourne, 1947). General descriptions can also be found in H. S. Nicholas, *The Australian Constitution* (Sydney, 1952), chap. xviii; and G. W. Paton, ed. *The Commonwealth of Australia: The Development of Its Laws and Constitution* (London, 1952), chap. 12, "Individual Law", by Geoffrey Sawer.

in order to see what effect this restriction of Commonwealth power has had upon labor standards.

In Australia, as in the United States, large numbers of workers come solely under state regulation as far as their labor conditions are concerned. The jurisdiction of the Commonwealth Court of Conciliation and Arbitration is restricted to the prevention or settlement of industrial disputes extending beyond the borders of any one state, and thus it is difficult at any one moment to say how many workers are subject to its awards. But those workers who are organized in unions of more than one hundred members[18] are potentially under federal regulation as they can quite easily ensure that an interstate dispute covering them can be engineered.[19] The actual coverage of federal awards is, however, wider than the union membership; for, although the Court is precluded from making a "common rule" for an industry,[20] it can nevertheless make awards covering nonunionists employed, or to be employed in the future, by employers who are party to a dispute.[21] We can, therefore, get some idea of the present coverage of Commonwealth awards from the figures of trade unionists in 1953. In that year the total number of wage and salary workers in civilian employment (excluding employees in rural industry and female private domestics) was 2,560,500 of whom 1,679,758 were members of trade unions.[22] Of these, 99.8 per cent belonged to unions of one hundred or more members, but unions actually registered with the Commonwealth Court had a membership of only 1,378,200 representing 82 per cent of the total membership of all trade unions. The membership of unions and the unions registered with the Commonwealth Court have both grown tremendously over the years, but the

515

[18] Commonwealth Conciliation and Arbitration Act, 1904, sec. 55 (1) (b).

[19] *Essays on the Australian Constitution*, R. Else-Mitchell, ed. (Sydney, 1952), p. 208.

[20] Australian Boot Trade Employees Federation *v.* Whybrow and Co. (1910), 11 C.L.R. 311 (Whybrow's Case).

[21] Metal Trades Employers' Association and Others *v.* Amalgamated Engineering Union and Others (1935), 54 C.L.R. 387.

[22] Figures of union members etc. are taken from the 1953 *Labour Report*, Bureau of Census and Statistics, Canberra.

fact that large numbers belong to unions which are still not registered with the Commonwealth Court is some indication of the extent to which state regulation has satisfied these workers when compared with Commonwealth awards.

These figures indicate that many workers depend upon the states for the maintenance of their working standards. Each of the six states has legislation setting up Industrial Courts or Wages Boards with power to fix wages, hours of work and other conditions. As far as the basic wage is concerned, a close uniformity is achieved throughout Australia. In three states, New South Wales, Victoria and South Australia, legislative provision is made for the state tribunals to follow the awards of the Federal Court in the declaration of the basic wage,[23] while in the other states the Commonwealth awards are closely followed. This is illustrated by the following table which sets out the Commonwealth and state weekly basic wage awards for the six capital cities applicable in November 1954.[24]

	Commonwealth Award	State Award
New South Wales	243/-	243/-
Victoria	235/-	234/-
Queensland	218/-	225/-
South Australia	231/-	231/-
Western Australia	236/-	246/6
Tasmania[25]	242/-	242/-

These figures clearly show that a high degree of uniformity exists as regards the basic wage. Western Australia has had in operation a higher basic wage award than the Commonwealth award for Perth, at least since 1929. Queensland also has frequently had a higher rate than the Commonwealth award. The degree of uniformity achieved at the present time is perhaps

[23] New South Wales, Industrial Arbitration (Amendment) Act (No. 9 of 1937); Victoria, Factories and Shops Acts, 1934 and 1936; South Australia, Industrial Code Amendment Act (No. 65 of 1949, and No. 20 of 1950).

[24] Source: *Labour Report, 1953*, pp. 57 and 80.

[25] No state award is declared in Tasmania but Commonwealth awards are generally followed.

not as great as these figures suggest, for the quarterly adjustment of basic wage rates by the states has not always conformed to dates of Commonwealth adjustments, but in the past this has been no more than a detail.[26] What is important is that state tribunals have assured a generally uniform basic wage throughout Australia.[27] This then ensures the satisfaction of those whose social philosophy demands equal treatment throughout the land.[28]

Turning now to the question of maximum working hours, the most important facts are the decisions of the Commonwealth Court of Conciliation and Arbitration to fix a 44-hour week (in 1927) and then a 40-hour week (in 1947). Legislation introducing a 44-hour week in state-regulated industries had been passed prior to the Commonwealth Court's decision, by New South Wales in 1926 and by Queensland in 1924. In other states, however, the achievement of this standard was left to state tribunals and it was not completed until 1941.[29] It was a very different story with the change to the 40-hour week. Once again New South Wales established the new standard before the Commonwealth Court made its award, and although the decision of the Court was not given until 8 Septem-

517

[26] The decision to suspend quarterly adjustments of the basic wage announced by the Commonwealth Court of Conciliation and Arbitration in September 1953, in view of the prevailing inflation, resulted in similar suspension of quarterly adjustments in New South Wales, South Australia, Western Australia and Tasmania, and also in Queensland, but in the last-named state only in February 1954, thereby resulting in the development of a sizable gap between Commonwealth and Queensland rates. Victoria initially suspended quarterly adjustments but resumed them by legislation in November 1953. (See *Labour Report, 1953*, pp. 72–80.) The general uniformity between Commonwealth and states rates thus survived, initially at least, a considerable shock. It is too early to conjecture what might happen should the Commonwealth Court maintain its ban on quarterly adjustments over a long period of rising prices. The New South Wales government recently announced its decision to resume quarterly adjustments in the state basic wage. *The Times* (London), August 10, 1955, p. 7.

[27] It should be noted that state legislation may not apply to all groups of workers in the state. Some, such as market gardeners and other rural workers, may be excluded.

[28] Such uniformity is not so noticeable in the field of the basic wage rates for adult females. In Queensland and in Western Australia in 1954 these tended to be well below Commonwealth rates. *Labour Report, 1953*, pp. 57 and 80.

[29] *Labour Report, 1950*, p. 72.

ber 1947, by the beginning of 1948 the other five states by legislation or by decisions of industrial tribunals had all adopted the new working week.[30]

This uniformity is not universal throughout Australian labor legislation. The legislative provision for workmen's compensation, as in the United States, is largely in the hands of the state governments.[31] There is great variation between state laws in this field, and in the benefits which they provide. In the opinion of one expert, "in this as in other fields the time for some approach to uniformity is long past."[32]

IV. *Politics and Labor Legislation*

In the two previous sections of this article we have described the way in which the regulation of labor conditions and labor relations has responded to the constitutional and administrative aspects of the federal structure in the United States and Australia. In a sense what we have been discussing might be called the "mechanics" of federalism: the way in which these countries operate the machinery of government in the special circumstances of a federal constitution, and the results which have been achieved. However, there is a great deal more to be learned from the experience of these countries by looking at the "dynamics" of labor regulation—labor politics—without an understanding of which the real significance of these patterns of regulation is lost. By looking at the political realities which have formed the patterns of labor regulation in the United States and Australia we may form an opinion upon the real importance and significance of constitutional forms.

Briefly what we have learned from previous pages is this. In the United States the constitutional limitations upon federal regulation of labor have not operated to restrict such regulation since the middle of the nineteen-thirties; at the same time, while many state governments have passed protective legislation, many have failed to do so and others have actually passed

[30] *Ibid.*, p. 73.

[31] The Commonwealth has legislated for workmen's compensation for federal territories and for seamen engaged in interstate commerce.

[32] Sawer, *loc. cit.*, p. 290.

legislation restrictive of labor.   In Australia, on the other hand, we have a very different picture.   The Commonwealth government has clearly found itself limited by constitutional factors, and the limits of possible future extension of such legislation (without constitutional amendment or without a somewhat radical change in judicial interpretation) are very real.   But the state governments of Australia have, either by legislation or by administrative practice, instituted labor protective standards generally as high as or even higher than Commonwealth standards.   We may say then that in the country where constitutional limitations are more significant a more complete coverage of labor legislation has been achieved and a very much higher degree of uniformity has been established throughout the nation.

519

The state of labor legislation in the United States in 1950 can be explained only in terms of the political forces which were at work on both Congress and the state legislatures during the preceding twenty years.   There were, and still are, important factors which have produced the rather extraordinary patterns of coverage and standards in the American legislation:

(1) The catastrophic depression of the early nineteen-thirties raised a storm of indignant protest from labor and its supporters, which was not to be denied.   The swift passage of the National Industrial Recovery Act and the relative ease with which the later National Labor Relations Act was passed are suitable indications of this feeling and its impact on Washington.   However, almost as soon as the feeling was aroused it began to abate.   And this abatement of the sympathetic attitude toward labor has continued to the present date.   The increase of the pressure on Congress, even by 1937, for the limitation of the benefits to be bestowed upon labor is seen in the smaller general coverage of the Fair Labor Standards Act of 1938 and the insertion of a number of exemptions to that Act which were not incorporated in the National Labor Relations Act.   The force of this anti-labor sentiment was clearly expressed in the Taft-Hartley Act of 1947.   In 1949 the question of the coverage of the Fair Labor Standards Act was raised by the introduction of bills into Congress designed to made the Act applicable to enter-

prises "affecting commerce" on the same basis as the National
Labor Relations Act;[33] the House Committee on the bill rejected
this proposal while the Senate Committee on Labor and Public
Welfare refused even to consider the topic in its report.[34]

(2) Parallel with this growth of anti-labor sentiment was
the decline in the militancy of the labor organizations themselves. They tended to concentrate upon consolidation of
earlier gains, rather than on attempting to widen the scope of
their activities. As Samuel Lubell has expressed it, "The labor
dynamo has slowed down."[35] He has also pointed to the fact
that the American labor unions in the past have been by no
means united in their approach to questions such as labor regulation or government controls generally. The unions have
geographical, sectional and craft interests which determine
their attitude toward government, rather than any single doc-
trinaire approach.[36]

(3) The Congressional attitude during the past twenty years
toward labor legislation is mirrored by the activities of state
governments. A good example comes from state labor relations
acts. Spurred on by the example of the Wagner Act five states
passed "Little Wagner Acts" in 1937. These Acts were "labor
protective" in character, but by 1939 the climate of opinion
had altered sufficiently for two of these state Acts, those of
Wisconsin and Pennsylvania, to be amended to include provisions restrictive of labor unions.[37] In the same year other
laws of the restrictive type were passed in Minnesota and Michigan, and while two states—Rhode Island and Connecticut—
have since passed "protective" legislation, in 1941 and 1945,
respectively, restrictive laws have been passed by Kansas (1943),
Utah (1947) and Colorado (1947). Perhaps more significant

[33] H.R. 2033.

[34] Report of House Committee on Education and Labor, Fair Labor Standards
Act Amendments of 1949, *Report* No. 267, 81st Congress; Report of Senate Committee on Labor and Public Welfare, Fair Labor Standards Act Amendments of
1949, *Senate Report* No. 640, 81st Congress.

[35] *The Future of American Politics* (New York, 1952), p. 180.

[36] *Ibid.*, pp. 186–187.

[37] Killingsworth, *op. cit.*, pp. 1–3.

is the large volume of legislation restrictive of unions, but not of a comprehensive nature, passed by state governments in post-war years,[38] including the passage of seventeen state "right-to-work" acts by mid-1954. There has been a certain amount of state legislation in recent years on the subject of fair employment practices, but this was due not so much to a movement in favor of labor as such, but was simply part of the developing campaign against race discrimination in general.

(4) The Democratic party has tended to be the party of Small Business and the Republican party the party of Big Business. This has meant that since 1933 there has been a great deal of pressure exerted by small business men's organizations for exemption from labor protective legislation. While the large businesses were unable to avoid regulation, the farmer was able even in 1935, on account of his depressed condition and his influence with the legislators, to get exemption for farm labor from the National Labor Relations Act. By 1937 the other small business interests were sufficiently strong to obtain a crop of statutory exemptions from the Fair Labor Standards Act.

521

(5) Business generally has been active in its efforts to keep subjects of government regulation under state, rather than federal, jurisdiction. As V. O. Key has pointed out,[39] this desire springs from the realization that the influence which can be exerted by business groups is generally much greater in the state legislatures than in Congress. However, as we have seen, constitutional limitations have not prevented Congress from ousting the states completely from the field of labor regulation; Congress has not tried to oust them.

These are, therefore, strong forces which have operated to limit the scope and content of federal labor legislation in the United States. These factors have very little to do with the federal structure of constitutional law, but they are the very stuff of "federalism" in the United States. That is to say, these are some of the real political impulses that underlie both

[38] *Ibid.*, Appendix, pp. 267–298.

[39] *Politics, Parties, and Pressure Groups* (New York, 1952), pp. 115–118.

the federal structure of government in the United States and the lack of uniformity of regulatory legislation.

In Australia we found a pattern of labor regulation very different from that in the United States, and, as we should expect, the political factors involved are very different also. The most obvious and the most significant factor in the Australian scene is the importance of the Labor party. Both in the states and in the Commonwealth the Labor party was early in a position to affect very deeply the political life of Australia either by actually holding the reins of power, or by holding the balance of power by virtue of its early status as a strong third party. The Australian Labor party has always been deeply concerned with social legislation and not unnaturally the question of labor regulation has been an object of continuing interest to the party. We are concerned here, however, with an explanation of the reasons for the levels of labor conditions which have been achieved in the Australian states, and the fact that the Australian federal structure has not prevented the achievement of a high degree of uniformity in labor regulation throughout the continent.

522

It is significant that, although early state legislation setting up industrial arbitration systems was passed by both Labor and anti-labor governments, in the three states which have legislation requiring state tribunals to follow Commonwealth awards on the basic wage this legislation has been passed in the periods of power of non-labor governments. The motives which have brought about such legislation are various. They are:

(1) Political reasons in the narrowest sense. In New South Wales in 1937 the United Australia Party-Country Party coalition introduced the bill to bring about conformity of the N.S.W. basic wage to the Commonwealth basic wage in its last few months in office after five years during which the state basic wage awards had at times lagged behind Commonwealth awards In the view of Mr. John T. Lang, leader of the Labor opposition, the government was "on the eve of an election . . . anxious to throw a sop to the workers whom it has been exploiting the

whole of the time it has been in office."[40]   The Commonwealth
Court had just declared a new basic wage making the gap between
state and Commonwealth awards quite large, but, whatever
the truth of the N.S.W. government's motives in this matter,
it illustrates the importance of industrial legislation as a political
factor in the Australian states, where labor is highly organized
both industrially and politically.

(2) The desire for uniformity.   Both employers and employees
have at times favored uniformity between state and federal
basic wage awards.   Employers have found that higher Commonwealth awards put some of them at a competitive disadvantage.
The employers in Victoria were particularly strong in their
demands for a uniform law.[41]

(3) Fear of industrial unrest due to lower state awards.
The Liberal-Country League Premier of South Australia was
conscious of this fear in 1946 when the Commonwealth basic
wage seemed likely to outstrip the state award.[42]

(4) A desire to retain state courts and tribunals, that is to
say an expression of "states' rights" and a belief in the value
of the existing federal, decentralized organization of labor
regulation.   Long and serious deficiencies between state awards
and Commonwealth awards would ensure that unions would
take the necessary steps to come under the higher awards of the
Commonwealth Court, and would eventually leave state tribunals without anyone to regulate.

(5) The growth of a general belief in the need for, and the
desirability of, uniformity in awards throughout Australia.
As a Liberal member of the New South Wales Legislative Council
said in 1950, in the debate on a bill[43] to keep the state basic
wage in line with the Commonwealth wage following a new

523

[40] New South Wales, *Parliamentary Debates* (1937), p. 1077.

[41] See statement of Colonel Harry Cohen, Honorary Minister, Victorian *Parliamentary Debates*, 25 September, 1934, vol. CXCV, p. 2201.

[42] "In the event of the Arbitration Court granting a wage substantially higher
than the state living wage, a chain of circumstances which would be highly undesirable are likely to arise.   Workers under the state living wage would feel that
they were being frustrated and the difference in wages would lead to industrial
disputes and disruption." Hon. T. Playford, South Australia, *Parliamentary
Debates*, 3 December, 1946, p. 1335.

[43] Industrial Arbitration (Basic Wage) Act, 1950 (N.S.W.).

determination of the basic wage by the Arbitration Court in October 1950: "This bill emphasizes more than anything else that in this type of legislation we have to follow largely the footsteps of the Federal jurisdiction. . . . The court has given its judgment and, following upon that, *it becomes obvious* that the judgment must apply throughout Australia."[44]

The gradual growth of this belief and its increasing force and importance are indicated by the increased tempo of state action to bring state awards into line with changing Commonwealth awards. This has already been noted in the example of the speed with which the new 40-hour week was instituted in state jurisdictions compared with the institution earlier of the 44-hour week. As far as the basic wage is concerned it is admirably illustrated by the way in which the South Australian government has introduced legislation, *in anticipation* of changes in the federal award.

These factors have ensured that the wages and hours standards of state-regulated workers should not fall below those of workers under the jurisdiction of the Commonwealth Court. In the three states where there is no statutory requirement that state tribunals should follow Commonwealth awards there is, as we have seen, a close relation between federal and state awards. The Courts and Wages Boards of these states have been no less blind to the necessities of the situation than have the legislatures of the other states. Following the decision of the Commonwealth Arbitration Court in October 1950, the Court of Arbitration of Western Australia on December 7 declared the basic wage for the state. The President of the Court stated:

> We cannot pretend to ignore the effect of the Commonwealth Court's decision. We know that in practice that decision will be adopted not only throughout Federal awards but also in state awards and determinations in Victoria, New South Wales, Tasmania, and probably also in South Australia. . . . I do not believe it to be a practicable proposal in present times that Western Australia alone should be out of step with Australia as a whole.[45]

[44] The Hon. A. D. Bridges, New South Wales, *Parliamentary Debates*, 15 November, 1950, pp. 1523–1524. My italics.

[45] Justice Jackson, *The Western Australian Industrial Gazette*, vol. XXX, Nos. 3–4, p. 339.

The employers' representative on the Court also expressed his belief in the desirability of bringing Western Australian awards up to the level of Commonwealth awards.[46]

This means that, as far as the standards of wages and hours are concerned, the forms of state control are retained, but in reality the Federal Court makes the effective decisions. The state courts are not wholly rubber stamps for Commonwealth decisions, however. Other conditions of work and other causes of dispute are dealt with on their initiative: such matters as the fixing of areas for the application of differential rates in town and country, the fixing of margins for skills and the regulation of other conditions of labor, all of which may have a peculiarly local flavor—all these are dealt with by state tribunals for those workers under their jurisdiction.

525

* * * * *

This comparison of American and Australian provisions for labor laws indicates an interesting interrelationship between law and politics in this sphere. It is quite clear that constitutional law, both written and judge-made, has played a large part in the shaping of the present systems of labor regulation in these two countries. This is particularly true of Australia, where, in spite of liberal interpretation by the High Court of constitutional provisions, the bounds to federal expansion have been maintained. It is, however, just as clear that constitutional provisions have not prevented the development of labor conditions which are *politically* essential; they have merely channeled the political forces along a certain route to the achievement of these standards. Where constitutional provisions threatened the development of uniform standards in Australia the tide of political activity swept round and past the constitutional issue to bring about the desired end.

In the United States, after the problems of the thirties were passed, the determination of the complex and irregular structure of labor regulation is to be traced to political attitudes and administrative convenience rather than to the decisions of the courts. To put it at its simplest, in the field of labor regulation

[46] E. B. McKenna, *ibid.*, p. 341.

the significant difference between the American and Australian scenes is not the difference of constitutional form or interpretation, but the fact that in the United States labor is a pressure group, or rather a series of pressure groups, while in Australia labor is a party. This is, of course, a gross oversimplification and it ignores the undoubted drawbacks and anomalies of both systems of labor regulation, but it points the truth that, in this field at any rate, political forces are the real determinants of the patterns of regulation and the constitutional structure is an important though secondary factor in the situation.

M. J. C. VILE

UNIVERSITY OF EXETER
  ENGLAND

526

Federalism in the Foundation
and Preservation of the
American Republic

Jean Yarbrough*
University of Connecticut, Groton
for Peter

For students of the republic, it usually comes as a surprise to learn that federalism, the uniquely American contribution to the theory and practice of free government, was considered by many of the Framers to be one of its most serious defects. Far from praising this novel arrangement of power—which resulted in neither a consolidation nor a confederation, but in the creation of two constitutionally protected governments, each sovereign in its own sphere, many of the Framers viewed the powers reserved to the states with suspicion and hostility. As far as they were concerned, the safety and happiness of the American people required not a balance between the federal and state governments, but a preponderance of power in the national government. Seen in this light, the relevance of the Framers' views of federalism is obvious: they anticipated and approved the steady expansion of the national government into state and local affairs as essential to the preservation of liberty. Then as now, federalism appears to some to be antithetical to the rights of the citizens and to the common good.

The purpose of this paper is to examine the role of federalism in the political thought of two leading founders, James Madison and Alexander Hamilton, and to challenge the assumptions upon which it rests. I will try to show that their rejection of federalism is based upon too narrow a view of the problems of preserving republican government. The preservation of the republic requires additional checks to safeguard liberty from abuse by the national government,

527

*The author gratefully acknowledges the generous support of the University of Connecticut Research Foundation and the cheerful assistance of Mrs. Helen Petty, research librarian, University of Connecticut, Groton.

© PUBLIUS, The Journal of Federalism, The Center for The Study of Federalism, Summer 1976

and more importantly, the promotion of civic virtue. The *principle* of federalism contributes to this end and, hence, is vital to the maintenance of the republic. Seen in this light, the relevance of the Framers' view of federalism is more complicated: an understanding of why they failed to appreciate the federal principle may shed some light on certain contemporary problems whose roots lie in the defects of the foundation.

I

The Constitution of the extended republic was chiefly a response to the problem of liberty. The presumed failure of the states to guard against the evils of faction led Madison and other supporters of free government to urge that the confederation of sovereign states be replaced by a vigorous national government in which the states would be retained, but in a clearly subordinate role. This is not, however, the origin of modern federalism. For Madison's initial hostility to the states, based on his belief that as independent political associations they endangered liberty, caused him to propose a government which was not only national—by which he meant empowered to act directly upon the citizens[1] —but far more consolidated than the principle of federalism allows.

Not only were the states to lose their representation as political bodies, but they were to be deprived of the bulk of their powers as well. The principal justification for these proposals was that the people are the source of all political power, and their happiness and safety are the sole objects of government. Since the states' contribution to these ends was minimal, they should be stripped of their power and independence. Accordingly, Madison proposed that the national government be equipped with an absolute veto over all state acts.[2] Nothing short of this "defensive" power would protect the citizens against encroachments by the state governments.

Had Madison's original proposals succeeded, the Constitution would have established a basically consolidated, rather than federal, republic. For the principal characteristic of American federalism is the recognition that within their limited but proper sphere the states

---

[1] James Madison to N. P. Trist, December 1831, in *The Records of the Federal Convention*, ed. Max Farrand, 4 vols. (New Haven and London: Yale University Press, 1937), III:517.

[2] James Madison to George Washington, 16 April 1787, in *The Forging of American Federalism*, ed. Saul K. Padover (New York: Harper and Row Publishers, 1953), p. 185; and *Federal Convention*, I:27, 165.

are free to govern themselves, subject only to constitutional restraints.[3] What Madison and the other radical nationalists at the
federal convention sought, then, was not a federal system, but the
reduction of the states to something resembling administrative agencies. As such, their existence would have depended upon the will of
the general government and that government's estimation of their
ability to be "subordinately useful." This is the relation which the
towns bear to the states, and Madison recommends it as the model
for relations between the states and the national government. As
"corporations dependent upon the General Legislature,"[4] the states
could continue to perform "beneficial" tasks, but they would lack
the power to act unjustly.

The difference between these two positions is profound, for it
stems from opposing views of how liberty and the general good are
best secured. Federalism rests on the assumption that a large consolidated government is itself a danger to liberty, since it must necessarily degenerate into monarchy—if not in name, at least in principle.
Dividing power between the state and federal governments lessens
this danger, but even then, abuses are likely since power is of an
encroaching nature. Federalism further assumes that such invasions
of rights may be carried out by the national government as well as
the states;[5] consequently, it provides constitutional protection to the
states as political bodies so that both governments may act as barriers
against the undue accumulation and abuse of power by the other.

Administrative decentralization, on the other hand, assumes that
the states as political associations are the primary threat to liberty.
Consequently, it seeks to reduce them to local corporations, whose
purpose is merely to administer those objects to which the general
government cannot conveniently extend. So unnecessary are the
states as political bodies to the protection of liberty that, were it
possible for the general government to "extend its care to all the
minute objects which fall under the cognizance of local jurisdiction,"[6] there would be no need to retain the states at all. Their
function is purely administrative.

---

[3]Although the states also retain their constituent power, the new federalism depends
much less upon the participation of the states in the national government, especially since
there is no recall or bloc voting in the Senate.

[4]*Federal Convention*, 1:357-358; also Hamilton, 1:287.

[5]See, for example, George Mason's speeches of 7 June and 20 June in *Federal Convention*, 1:115-116 and 340.

[6]*Federal Convention*, 1:357-358.

529

According to this view, liberty is secured not by a balance of power between the state and federal governments, but by a preponderance of power in the national government whose powers are properly distributed and whose officers are duly dependent upon the people. This was the view of Madison and Hamilton at the federal convention. Consequently, they opposed the compromises which resulted in the modern federal republic; their support for the Constitution was given in spite of its federal aspects.

II

However surprising it is to discover the antipathy of many of the leading Framers toward the federal principle at the secret debates of the convention, it is even more surprising to discover that these views are subtly reiterated in the *Federalist Papers*. For not only does the title seem to support this principle, but the papers themselves appear to be sympathetic to the states. Yet beneath the apparent praise of the states as bulwarks of liberty, there is the constant reminder that one reason why a vigorous national government is necessary is because the states have failed to protect public and private rights.

These views are not openly stated, however, because one of the tasks of the *Federalist* was to persuade citizens that the Constitution establishes a republic which is sufficiently "federal" in the older meaning of the word, i.e. confederal. Accordingly, they addressed themselves to the objection that the national government possessed too many powers and the states too few to preserve liberty. The main tack of the *Federalist* was to emphasize the present power and authority of the states, while at the same time implying that in the future the national government would be supreme. The argument for national supremacy the *Federalist* wisely leaves to experience.

Against the objection that the Constitution gives too many powers to the national government, Madison argues that the specific powers vested in the general government are consistent with the objects of government and, hence, are both necessary and proper. The *Federalist* then turns to the more difficult issue of implied powers. For even more than enumerated powers, critics feared that these provisions and rules of constitutional interpretation—by which the general government could exercise any power consistent with the great aims for which the Constitution was established, even if that power was not expressly granted—would serve as the "pernicious engines by which

... local governments ... (would) be destroyed and ... liberties exterminated."[7]

Against the abuse of these powers in particular, and the totality of powers vested in the national government in general, the *Federalist* offers three safeguards. The first is psychological. The national government will have no incentive to absorb the objects of the states because these ends are so puny. Men in high office are ambitious: "the regulation of the mere domestic police of a state appears to men to hold out slender allurements to ambition." Thus, the states are safe from encroachments "because the attempt to exercise those powers would be as troublesome as it would be nugatory."[8] This, however, is a curious defense.

The second check is institutional. Should the national legislature overleap its bounds, the executive and judiciary will restrain it because they possess the "constitutional means and personal motives" to do so. If this fails, the people can in the last resort elect new representatives. Here, Madison, recurring to the federal principle, suggests that the states may play a part. Sensitive to national encroachments, they will sound the alarm and awaken the citizens to the necessity of changing the federal representatives. Even then, Madison manages to turn this federal argument to national advantage. The great benefit of vesting power in the national government is that there are states to restrain it.

531

> There being no such intermediary body between the state legislatures and the people, interested in watching the former, violations of the state constitutions are likely to remain unnoticed and unredressed.[9]

Nevertheless, Madison does not believe that resort to the state governments will be necessary to preserve liberty; the proper distribution of power among the three branches of the national government and a due dependence of these officers upon the people will be sufficient in most cases to restrain national encroachments.

The third check against abuse by the national government is constitutional. Implied powers extend only to those objects which the Constitution entrusts to the national government. In these areas, it is true, the power of the national government is subject only to the limitations which the Constitution imposes. But the Constitution does not give the national government power over all objects.

[7] *Federalist* No. 33, in *The Federalist*, ed. Jacob E. Cooke (Middletown, Conn.: Wesleyan University Press, 1961), p. 204.

[8] *Federalist* No. 17, pp. 105-106.

[9] *Federlaist* No. 44, p. 305.

It was not, however, sufficient to show that the Constitution vested in the general government only those powers which were necessary and proper, that these powers were adequately checked, and that all other powers remained with the states. The *Federalist* had also to satisfy its critics that the powers reserved to the states were adequate to protect their rights, and the rights of their citizens. This meant that the authors had to persuade their opponents that the states did retain sufficient power to predominate, since they believed that it was only by the states remaining supreme that liberty would be secured. Although Madison and Hamilton had fought to prevent just this, and supported the Constitution precisely because it promised to reverse this tendency of "confederations," they could (putting their own opinion of such measures aside) nevertheless point out the considerable powers reserved to the states, and their probable effects.

532

Not only did the states participate in the conduct of national affairs, but their powers were "numerous and indefinite." It is true that Hamilton had termed these powers "tedious" and "uninteresting," but this is only from the perspective of men with great ambition. Matters of local legislation might not attract men who aspired to national fame and glory; but as far as the citizens were concerned, they were matters of the highest importance, for they touched on "all those objects which, in the ordinary course of affairs, concerned the lives, liberties, and properties of the people." [10] Consequently, it seemed likely that the citizens would be more attached to the states. Their confidence and loyalty—together with the powers remaining in the states—made it probable that these local governments would not only check national encroachments, but that they would actually predominate.

This then is the surface argument of the *Federalist*—an argument which Madison and Hamilton could make in part *in spite of* their private opinions and in part *because* of their genuine fear that the states were still too powerful. For the *Federalist* does not doubt the combined power of the states to act, or for that matter, even a single great state; what it doubts is that the states will act in the interests of the general good. More likely the states would continue to protect their own privileges and powers by executing the wishes of a factious majority.

In spite of those dangerous centrifugal tendencies, Madison and Hamilton supported the Constitution because they expected these

[10] *Federalist* No. 45, p. 313.

tendencies to subside in the future. The *Federalist* suggests that, as the people became more familiar with the general government and experienced the benefits of its superior administration, they would welcome its extention "to what are called matters of internal concern." [11] For they would recognize that their rights are better protected by the national government than by the states. Consequently, the people would overcome their natural tendency to love best what is near, and would think of themselves as citizens of the United States. The decline of the states, therefore, seemed inevitable—not because of usurpation, but ironically because "in republics strength is on the side of the people." [12] And in the future the people were more likely to support the national government because it provided greater security for their rights.

Still, Madison sought to assure the states that even if the citizens do grow more attached to the national government, the states need not fear annihilation: there are limits to how far the federal powers can be advantageously administered. [13] Thus, Madison returned to his arguments at the federal convention. As the national government established itself at the center of American life, the proper role of the states would be to administer those objects to which it was inconvenient for the national government to extend.

533

Thus, in spite of its seeming defense of the states as a barrier against encroachments by the national government, the *Federalist* suggests that the proper relationship between the states and the federal government should be administrative rather than political because it believes that the states endanger liberty. Accordingly, liberty will be better secured in the future when the national government is supreme: the states will be less able to meddle in national affairs and the federal government will be restrained from abuses by the internal arrangement of its powers [14] and the dependence of its officers on the people. [15] For the *Federalist*, representation and the proper distribution of power provide the keys to republican liberty. To Madison and Hamilton federalism was important in the foundation of the American republic only in a negative way: it allowed for the removal of matters concerning the general good from the states to the national government and, in so doing, insured greater dignity and justice for the rights and interests of all.

[11] *Federalist* No. 27, p. 174; and *Federalist* No. 46, p. 317.
[12] *Federalist* No. 31, p. 198.
[13] *Federalist* No. 46, p. 317.
[14] *Federalist* No. 31, p. 197; and *Federalist* No. 44, p. 305.
[15] *Federalist* No. 28, p. 178; and *Federalist* No. 46, p. 322.

III

Still the question remains: what role does federalism play in the preservation of the American republic? [16] To be precise, were Madison and Hamilton correct in assuming that the principal danger to republican liberty was the failure of the states to control the effects of majority faction? In the following pages I will suggest that this understanding of the problems of preserving republican government was inadequate. First, because as Madison shortly discovered, liberty can also be endangered by the national government. And second, because even when the national government is able to resolve domestic disputes more impartially than the states, republican government requires more than superior administration. Enlightened and public spirited citizens are essential, and this requirement clashes with the removal of public affairs to a distant and disinterested national government. To the extent that the federal principle satisfies these requirements, it is necessary for the preservation of the republic.

534

In his defense of the necessary and proper clause in *Federalist* No. 44, Madison sought to assure the citizens that if the national legislature overstepped its bounds, it would be restrained by the executive and judicial branches. Although Madison acknowledged that the states might also play a role, it was only in the last resort. In general, the proper distribution of power among the three branches of the national government, each of which represents the people, would secure liberty.

It was not long, however, before this thesis was tested and found wanting. The failure of the federal and federalist courts to strike down the Alien and Sedition Acts as unconstitutional usurpations of power by the national government changed Madison from an ardent nationalist to a supporter of the federal principle. The Virginia Resolutions reflect this change in Madison's political thought: for here the states are cast as defenders of the constitutional system against encroachments by the national government.

The point of the Virginia Resolutions is that the Constitution creates a government of specific and enumerated powers. When the national government overleaps these bounds by construing its powers too broadly, it is the proper function of the states to restrain it. In such cases, the states

[16] For a somewhat different interpretation, see Martin Diamond, "The *Federalist's* View of Federalism," in *Essays in Federalism*, ed. George C. S. Benson (Claremont, California: Institute for Studies on Federalism, 1962), pp. 21-64.

have the right and are in duty bound to interpose for arresting the progress of the evil, and for maintaining in their respective limits the authorities, rights and liberties appertaining to them. [17]

The failure to resist these encroachments will result in a "speedy consolidation," because as the states grow weaker, they will lose the affections of the citizens and become objects of contempt. [18] Whereas Madison saw nothing objectionable in such a development in 1787 when the general government seemed in need of all the help it could get against the centrifugal tendency of the states, the rapid success of the national government in establishing itself, due in part to the early triumphs of the Federalist Party, made Madison see consolidation in an altogether different light. The man who once defended a veto over all state acts, and who announced that if the national government could conveniently administer all local objects, "no fatal consequence" could result from the abolition of the states, now recognizes that there are dangers in consolidation. Consolidation would increase the power and patronage of the executive—it being impossible for the deliberative branch to extend its care to the ever increasing objects of legislation. This strengthening of the executive branch at the expense of the legislature would obviously and inevitably "transform the present republican system of the United States into an absolute, or, at best, a mixed monarchy." [19]

535

Thus, it was Madison's recognition that, despite internal checks, the national government was also capable of encroaching upon the rights of the citizens and dangerously consolidating political power, which led him to defend the legitimate power and authority of the states. This revised view of the dangers to republican liberty was what caused Madison to change his earlier opinion of the states as useful administrative agencies of the national government and to defend them as political bodies necessary for the preservation of liberty. It was precisely because the Constitution recognized the states as political associations that they were able to safeguard the rights of the citizens and to resist the tendency toward consolidation.

That Madison later supported the federal principle does not, however, mean that he became an advocate of states' rights. States' rights insists that the Constitution is a compact among the sovereign states and, consequently, that in all disputes arising under the Constitution,

---

[17] James Madison, *The Writings of James Madison*, ed. Gaillard Hunt, 9 vols. (New York and London: G. P. Putnam's Sons, 1906), VI:326.

[18] Ibid., p. 333.

[19] Ibid., p. 327.

the states, as parties to the compact, must judge the issue for themselves. Federalism, on the other hand, acknowledges the constitutional division of power between the national and state governments, but it recognizes the supremacy of the Constitution over the governments, and the people over the Constitution. Accordingly, it is not the states as political units which are supreme, but the people in those states, for whose happiness both the state and national governments exist. Under the federal principle, then, the states contribute to the defense of the constitutional system by maintaining the distribution of power essential to the happiness of the people.

Taking the Resolutions by themselves, it is easy to see why Madison has been accused of advocating states' rights. For the Resolutions maintain that the powers of the federal government result from a "compact to which the states are parties," and that "in case of a deliberate, palpable, and dangerous exercise of other powers not granted by the compact," the states have a right and duty to interpose. Appeal was then made to the other states to concur with Virginia in declaring the Alien and Sedition Acts unconstitutional and to take the necessary and proper measures for cooperating to maintain their rights and authorities.

But when we consider the Report of 1800, written to clarify his position in the Resolutions, it is clear that Madison was supporting federalism and not states' rights. For the Report removed the ambiguity surrounding the word "states" and defended the necessity and propriety of the measures proposed in a manner consistent with the principles of the Constitution. Although Madison conceded that the term "states" is vague and ambiguous, he maintained that in the Resolutions it meant "the people composing those political societies in their highest sovereign capacity." This is the sense in which the Constitution was submitted to the "states," in which it was ratified by the "states," and consequently, in which the "states" are parties to the compact under which the federal powers arise.[20] Accordingly, whenever the federal government exceeds its rightful limits by exercising powers not granted to it, it is the right and duty of the *people* in the states to interpose to restrain these violations. Madison rejected the authority of the state governments to judge in these cases because it was the people in the states who were the parties to the compact.

This means, however, that the judiciary is also not competent to resolve such disputes since it too has only delegated authority. In

[20] Ibid., p. 348.

these "great and extraordinary cases" only the parties to the compact, that is the people in the states, can determine when the Constitution has been breached. [21] Still, there is nothing improper in these measures. Although the people are the final judges of the constitutionality of the laws, their decisions, as embodied in the declarations of their state legislatures, are only "expressions of opinion." [22] They were not intended to substitute for the judgment of the courts, but rather to arouse the citizens to "promote a remedy according to the rules of the Constitution." As such, the Virginia Resolutions are not only consistent with the Constitution, but they tend to preserve it by returning to first principles in speech. As a "declaratory recurrence to the principles of the Revolution," [23] the Resolutions alert the citizens to dangerous encroachments upon their rights in time to avoid an actual return to first principles.

What the Virginia Resolutions signify, then, is Madison's recognition that the states can play a positive role in maintaining liberty. As constitutionally protected political societies, they can resist the tendency toward consolidation and check invasions upon the rights of the people. Although ultimately it is the people in the states who are supreme, the states contribute to their safety and happiness by preserving the constitutional balance necessary for republican liberty.

537

IV

However important federalism is to the protection of liberty, its first function, according to the republican tradition, was to foster civic virtue, for no republic could be preserved without virtuous citizens. According to the tradition, civic virtue meant a willingness to put aside private interest for the sake of the common good. This personal sacrifice was achieved, in part, by the citizens sharing in public affairs; participation taught them to care for what they held in common. Federalism made participation possible by allowing the republic to remain small enough for the citizens to enter the public realm. Consequently, federalism was essential to the preservation of the republic since it provided a way to promote civic virtue without sacrificing protection against external dangers.

This aspect of the tradition the Framers emphatically rejected. Direct participation by all the citizens would require the subdivision of the states into city-sized republics. Not only was such a proposal

[21] Ibid., p. 349.
[22] Ibid., p. 402.
[23] Ibid., p. 352.

incompatible with the greatness of America, but it was incompatible with the protection of liberty. In general, the mass of people are incompetent to conduct public affairs in person. A small territory compounds this difficulty, since it provides no protection against majority faction. Moreover, the Framers gradually came to realize that the requirements of disinterested virtue clashed with their commitment to civil liberty. For civic virtue, as the tradition understood it, not only required participation, but depended upon harsh laws which suppress individual interest and opinions.

That the Framers of the American republic sought primarily to safeguard civil liberty does not, however, mean that they abandoned the traditional concern with virtue. For they did not believe that republican government could be sustained without regard to the character of the citizens. As Madison remarked at the Virginia Ratifying Convention:

> if there be ... (no virtue among us), we are in a wretched situation. No theoretical checks, no form of government, can render us secure. To suppose that any form of government will secure liberty or happiness without any virtue in the people is a chimerical idea. [24]

Nevertheless, because their paramount commitment was to individual liberty, the virtue required to sustain the republic could not be of "heroic" [25] proportions. In other words, civic virtue cannot rest upon either the government's compelling a homogeneity of interests, passions, and opinions, or upon the participation of the citizens in public affairs via the federal principle. Both these methods are incompatible with liberty.

Instead, the Framers sought to encourage virtue primarily through social means. Although lacking the power and right to legally suppress individual differences, these institutions—the chief of which were education and religion—could instruct the citizens in their public duties by appealing to social mores and individual conscience. Thus, one way in which the Framers sought to circumvent the dilemma of the liberal republic—a dilemma which rested on the fact that the government was prevented by its commitment to private rights from entering into those concerns which were necessary to its preservation—was by relying upon the institutions of society to do what it could not.

[24] Jonathon Eliot, ed., *Debates on the Adoption of the Federal Constitution,* 5 vols. (Philadelphia: J. B. Lippincott Company, 1901), III:536-537. For a different view, see Paul Eidelberg, *A Discourse on Statesmanship* (Urbana: University of Illinois Press, 1974).

[25] Perhaps nowhere is this shift away from "heroic" virtue more obvious than in the political thought of John Adams, though the term itself is taken from *Cato's Letters,* by John Trenchard and Thomas Gordon.

Nevertheless, the Framers also recognized that moral and religious motives are not sufficient to direct the citizens toward the public good. Consequently, additional safeguards were necessary. The solution they proposed was to multiply the interests and sects in society by the extension of the republic, and to arrange the internal structure of government so that interest checks interest, and power checks power, thereby preventing the triumph of faction.

There is, however, a difference between these two mechanisms. Social pluralism discourages the formation of majority faction, but it does little to improve the political character of the people as citizens. Indeed, the largely economic nature of this diversity tends to strengthen the habits and attitudes which undermine civic virtue.

The proper distribution of political power, on the other hand, does more than discourage the formation of faction in the absence of "wise and virtuous rulers." For it seeks to instill a certain amount of civic virtue in those who do not already possess it. By designing offices in which the interest of the man coincides with his duty, and which are further restrained by the interests and powers of the representatives in other branches, the Framers sought to compel lesser men to moderate their interests in the direction of the public good. The point here is that even if a man's motives are selfish, the gradual moderation of interest toward duty will eventually teach him to care for the common good. The Framers' reliance upon institutional devices was not a substitute for civic virtue, but another means of promoting it among men who are not virtuous. It is true that this virtue never reaches the level of pure disinterestedness, but it does improve the character of public men to some extent, and in a manner which is consistent with the Framers' commitment to civil liberty.

Moreover, the proper distribution of political power seeks to encourage the best men to enter public office. For it provides them with the opportunity to fulfill their own interests, interests which in this case coincide with the good of the republic. [26] Even with the best men, then, virtue is not heroic, but depends upon the mutual fulfillment of interest and duty, which public responsiblity can provide.

Thus, the difference between the Framers' solution to the problem of virtue in the citizens and in their representatives was that for the citizens, the solution takes place almost entirely outside the public

539

---

[26] *Federalist* No. 72, p. 488; and Gerald Stourzh, *Alexander Hamilton and the Idea of Republican Government* (Stanford: Stanford University Press, 1970), pp. 101-106.

realm. The citizens were to be educated in political and moral principles, but for the most part, the only public activity in which the
citizens would "participate" would be in the selection of their representatives. The Framers of the Constitution made no provision for
institutions in which ordinary citizens could publicly appear to have
their various interests and passions moderated or their opinions refined by deliberation with their fellow citizens. Yet since civic virtue
requires participation, the virtue that the Framers tried to foster was
insufficient for the preservation of the republic. Upon reflection, it
appears to be concerned more with private morality than with public
virtue.

540 What makes this absence of public virtue dangerous to the preservation of the republic is that, even though the citizens no longer
participate in public affairs, they remain the fountain of all political
power. For it is inevitable that when citizens retain political power
but are deprived of any opportunity to exercise it, except for the
solitary act of electing their representatives every few years, they will
misuse or abuse their power. [27] Without experience in political affairs, they will not recognize that the public realm is governed by
standards which are independent of, and sometimes in conflict with,
the requirements of the private domain. [28] Thus, the failure to provide institutions in which the citizens can participate creates an entirely novel problem for the preservation: it corrupts the republic at
the grass roots, for it reserves power to the people without teaching
them how to use it.

V

Since civic virtue requires participation in political affairs and not
simply "closeness" to government, federalism, as we know it, cannot
meet the requirements of civic virtue. For federalism refers to the
constitutional distribution of power between the general government
and the states; it does not include constitutional guarantees for the
municipalities, the one place where, indeed, because of their small-
ness, citizens would have the greatest opportunity to participate.

[27] Alexis de Tocqueville, *Democracy in America*, ed. Phillips Bradley, 2 vols. (New York: Alfred A. Knopf, 1966), II:320-321.
[28] Hans Morgenthau, *The Purpose of American Politics* (New York: Vintage Books, 1964), pp. 197-215; and Hannah Arendt, *On Revolution* (London: Faber and Faber, 1963), pp. 279-285.

These local units are actually creatures of the states;[29] as such, they lack the constitutional powers to defend themselves against state encroachments. Yet if civic virtue is essential to the preservation of the republic, and if local units are the most likely area where citizens can participate, the question arises: why didn't the Framers try to promote civic virtue by extending protection to these local governments?

One answer is the federal system itself, for it is precisely the constitutional recognition of the autonomy of the states over their domestic affairs which precludes intervention in local affairs. Thus, the irony of the federal solution is that the measures required to preserve the political independence of the states, i.e. the non-interference in the relations between the states and their local governments, leaves the Constitution powerless to prevent the state governments—which governments, to add to the irony, the Framers so heartily mistrusted when it came to the protection of private rights—from sapping the foundation of the republic by depriving the citizens of their public rights.

541

Yet I do not mean to imply that the Framers would have incorporated these self-governing communities into the structure of the federal republic had they not been caught in this dilemma. This seems unlikely for several reasons. First, the Framers did not maintain that it was participation simply which fosters a concern for the common good, but participation in a particular set of institutions designed to promote such care. Yet the factors which compelled this concern for the common good depended upon conditions of largeness; hence, they were necessarily absent in local governments, and to some extent, even in the states. Thus, the first reason why the Framers were unenthusiastic about local self-government was because they feared that without a multiplicity of interests, the proper distribution of powers and nobility of purpose, political activity would degenerate into faction.[30]

Second, the Framers generally assumed that what most men want is a secure and comfortable life. This being the case, not only was participation in political affairs unnecessary for men to be happy, but by taking them away from the pursuit of gain and the enjoyment

[29]I wish to thank Professor Daniel J. Elazar for having pointed out to me that during the revolutionary period the question of the relationship of local governments to the states had not yet been definitively resolved. Especially in the North, and more particularly in New England, there was considerable support for the doctrine of the inherent right to local self-government. This doctrine existed side by side with the opposite interpretation that the local governments are the creatures of the states. Only later was the dispute resolved in favor of the latter interpretation, which came to be known as Dillon's Rule.

[30]Madison, in *Adoption of the Federal Constitution*, III:256.

of the fruits of their labor, it may actually make them unhappy. As for the few who are motivated by political ambition and the love of fame, the objects of local government are too puny. Thus, the implication is that the Constitution of the extended republic satisfies the desires of most men: it provides political men with a space in which to win honor and glory and it frees ordinary citizens from politics so that they may pursue their private happiness without interference.

Yet, since prior to the foundation of the republic, Americans did to some extent associate freedom and happiness with the citizen's right to participate in political affairs, even if the public realm extended no further than the town hall. Why, then, did the Framers understand happiness and freedom almost exclusively in terms of the protection of private rights and the promotion of moral virtue? Ironically, it was precisely the participation of the citizens in public affairs during and after the war for independence which accounts for the third reason why the Framers were unsympathetic to local self-government. For the activities of independence unleashed a destructiveness which the Framers properly recognized could not continue once the republic was established. Thus, the problem of the foundation was not how to preserve the power and spirit of the towns and voluntary associations but, on the contrary, how to defuse them.

It is true that during the revolutionary era widespread participation by the people had all too frequently ended in violent majority faction and mob rule;[31] indeed, the Constitution is largely a response to this problem. But, although the Framers correctly recognized that once the republic was founded it could not continue to tolerate acts of violence by the citizens, they did not recognize to what extent this violence was characteristic of the foundation, rather than of political activity in general. Nor can the glory of the foundation— understood as the opportunity to lay the foundation for freedom— counteract this view. Although the Framers considered constitution-making one of the highest human activities, it nevertheless remains unique to the foundation. It cannot, as Madison properly recognized in *Federalist* No. 49, provide a model for the politics of the preservation.

This means, however, that the Framers' solution is flawed, for their failure to recognize that not all political activity by the citizens is either destructive or unique to the foundation (such as the delib-

---

[31] Gordon Wood, *The Creation of the American Republic 1776-1787* (Chapel Hill: University of North Carolina Press, 1969), pp. 319-328.

eration and debate surrounding the framing and ratification of the Constitution), leads them to channel the entire energy of the revolution into private enterprises, rather than seek to direct some of this energy toward activities which promote civic virtue and, hence, contribute to the preservation of the republic. [32]

In other words, because they mistakenly assumed that the foundation provided a model for all political activity, they necessarily failed to understand what the preservation of the republic required. Their emphasis upon violence, and if not violence, their belief that once the republic is established there will be nothing for the citizens to do, makes the larger question of the preservation appear to be the same as stability. Yet since the Framers promoted stability by encouraging the citizens to devote themselves to the pursuit of wealth, the requirements of stability actually ·undermine the political virtues necessary to the preservation of the republic. [33] Ironically, then, the defect of the Framers' solution is that it succeeds too well, for not only does it discourage later generations of citizens from acting violently but it discourages them from acting at all. [34]

543

VI

The Framers' failure to protect the local institutions, which allow the citizens to participate in public affairs, cannot be understood as a repudiation of the need for civic virtue to sustain the republic. Rather, it is a failure to understand what civic virtue requires. Given the tremendous activity of the citizens during the revolution, they thought it was sufficient to speak of civic virtue in terms of moral and political education. It is a testimony to the vitality of the towns that they did not believe it was necessary to provide constitutional protection for these local units. Indeed, they feared that these political associations would encourage too much spirit.

The towns were—and to some extent, continue to be—schools for civic virtue. By providing ordinary citizens with the opportunity to share in the activities of the republic according to their competence, they mitigate the worst effects of materialism and individualism. Moreover, these self-governing communities put teeth into the claim that the people are the source of all political power, for alone among the institutions of the republic, these governments provide the citi-

[32] Hannah Arendt, *On Revolution*, pp. 234-242.
[33] George Anastoplo, *The Constitutionalist: Notes on the First Amendment* (Dallas: Southern Methodist University Press, 1971), pp. 214-216.
[34] Wilson Carey McWilliams, *The Idea of Fraternity in America* (Berkeley: University of California Press, 1973), p. 173.

zens with a space in which to exercise their political power jointly
with their fellow citizens. Consequently, it is these elementary republics which make citizenship in the extended republic meaningful—and
in a manner consistent with liberal democracy—for these local institutions are all that the citizens in our heterogeneous society have in
common politically.

Despite their role in promoting civic virtue, the Framers did not
seek to incorporate these local institutions into the Constitution by
extending the federal principle to include them because they feared
that too much participation would endanger liberty. According to
the Framers, the purpose of federalism is to protect civil liberty, not
civic virtue; consequently, it applies only to the relations between
the states and the general government.

It is true that increasing the opportunities for political activities
involves certain risks: the people may act unjustly; they may seek
political power for their own ends; they may be incompetent. But
without political activity, there is lethargy, and lethargy also endan-
gers the republic. The problem of republican government, then, is
that it requires more than stable and wise administration; it requires
active and alert citizens who understand the meaning and enjoy the
exercise of their liberty. This means that the preservation of the
republic is precarious, since it requires balancing the conflicting
claims of civil liberty and civic virtue.[35] Although there can never be
a perfect solution to this problem, I have tried to suggest that the
Framers' efforts are flawed because they place too much emphasis
upon protecting civil liberty against faction, with the result that they
then endanger it by lethargy.

Ironically, the way out of this dilemma lies, in part, in the expanded use of the principle they so much distrusted at the foundation:
federalism. The principle of federalism, understood as the constitutional recognition and protection of independent spheres of political
activity—and hence capable not only of expansion as Madison suggested, but of division—serves the needs of both civil liberty and civic
virtue. By preventing the consolidation of political power and by
creating centers of power capable of checking each other, it protects
liberty. By bringing the republic within reach of the citizens on
matters within their competence, it promotes virtue. Seen from this
perspective, the principle of federalism is both conservative and revolutionary: it provides a means of conserving the spirit of the revolution in a manner consistent with the Framers' commitment to civil
liberty and, hence, is vital to the preservation of the republic.

[35]Michael Walzer, "Civility and Civic Virtue in Contemporary America," *Social Research* 41, no. 4 (Winter 1974):593-611.